EMMELINE PANKHURST

WOMEN'S AND GENDER HISTORY
Edited by June Purvis

CHILD SEXUAL ABUSE IN VICTORIAN ENGLAND
Louise A. Jackson

CRIMES OF OUTRAGE
Sex, violence and Victorian working women
Shani D'Cruze

EMMELINE PANKHURST
A biography
June Purvis

FEMINISM, FEMININITY AND THE POLITICS OF WORKING WOMEN
The Women's Co-operative Guild, 1880s to the Second World War
Gillian Scott

GENDER AND CRIME IN MODERN EUROPE
Edited by Margaret L. Arnot and Cornelie Usborne

GENDER RELATIONS IN GERMAN HISTORY
Power, agency and experience from the sixteenth to the twentieth century
Edited by Lynn Abrams and Elizabeth Harvey

IMAGING HOME
Gender, 'race' and national identity, 1945–64
Wendy Webster

MIDWIVES OF THE REVOLUTION
Female Bolsheviks and women workers in 1917
Jane McDermid and Anna Hillyar

NO DISTINCTION OF SEX?
Women in British universities 1870–1939
Carol Dyhouse

POLICING GENDER, CLASS AND FAMILY
Britain, 1850–1945
Linda Mahood

PROSTITUTION
Prevention and reform in England, 1860–1914
Paula Bartley

SYLVIA PANKHURST
Sexual politics and political activism
Barbara Winslow

VOTES FOR WOMEN
Edited by June Purvis and Sandra Holton

WOMEN'S HISTORY: BRITAIN 1850–1945
Edited by June Purvis

THE WOMEN'S SUFFRAGE MOVEMENT
A reference guide, 1866–1928
Elizabeth Crawford

WOMEN AND TEACHER TRAINING COLLEGES 1900–1960
A culture of femininity
Elizabeth Edwards

WOMEN, WORK AND SEXUAL POLITICS IN EIGHTEENTH-
CENTURY ENGLAND
Bridget Hill

WOMEN WORKERS AND GENDER IDENTITIES, 1835–1913
The cotton and metal industries in England
Carol E. Morgan

EMMELINE PANKHURST

A biography

June Purvis

London and New York

First published 2002
by Routledge
11 New Fetter Lane, London EC4P 4EE

Simultaneously published in the USA and Canada
by Routledge
29 West 35th Street, New York, NY 10001

Routledge is an imprint of the Taylor & Francis Group

Typeset in Goudy by Taylor & Francis Books Ltd
Printed and bound in Great Britain by TJ International Ltd, Padstow, Cornwall

British Library Cataloguing in Publication Data
A catalogue record for this book is available from the British Library

Library of Congress Cataloging in Publication Data
Purvis, June.
Emmeline Pankhurst: a biography/June Purvis.
Includes bibliographical references and index.
1. Pankhurst, Emmeline, 1858–1928. 2. Suffragists–Great Britain–Biography.
3. Suffragists–Great Britain–Political activity. I. Title.

JN979.P28 P87   2002
324.6'23'092–dc21   2002024911

ISBN 0–415–23978–8

TO ALL THOSE FEMINISTS, PAST,
PRESENT AND FUTURE, AND THEIR
STRUGGLE FOR EQUALITY FOR WOMEN

CONTENTS

List of illustrations   xi
Acknowledgements   xiii
List of abbreviations   xv

Introduction   1

1 Childhood and young womanhood (1858–1879)   9

2 Marriage and entry into political life (1880–March 1887)   18

3 Political hostess (June 1887–1892)   25

4 Socialist and public representative (1893–1897)   39

5 Widowhood and employment (1898–February 1903)   51

6 Foundation and early years of the WSPU
  (March 1903–January 1906)   65

7 To London (February 1906–June 1907)   79

8 Autocrat of the WSPU? (July 1907–September 1908)   96

9 Emmeline and Christabel (October 1908–January 1909)   113

10 'A new and more heroic plane' (January–September 1909)   122

11 Personal sorrow and fortitude
   (September 1909–early January 1911)   135

CONTENTS

12 The truce renewed (January–November 1911)   155

13 The women's revolution (November 1911–June 1912)   173

14 Break with the Pethick Lawrences (July–October 1912)   190

15 Honorary treasurer of the WSPU and agitator
   (October 1912–April 1913)   200

16 Prisoner of the Cat and Mouse Act (April–August 1913)   217

17 Ousting of Sylvia and a fresh start for Adela
   (August 1913–January 1914)   232

18 Fugitive (January–August 1914)   250

19 War work and a second family (September 1914–June 1917)   268

20 War emissary to Russia: Emmeline versus the Bolsheviks
   (June–October 1917)   292

21 Leader of the Women's Party (November 1917–June 1919)   300

22 Lecturer in North America and defender of the British Empire
   (September 1919–December 1925)   318

23 Last years: Conservative parliamentary candidate
   (1926–June 1928)   339

24 Niche in history   354

   Notes   364
   Select bibliography   418
   Index   430

ILLUSTRATIONS

Plate section 1

1   Richard Marsden Pankhurst, 1879, Institute of Social History, The
    Sylvia Pankhurst Archive, Amsterdam
2   Sylvia, Adela and Christabel Pankhurst, c. 1890, Institute of Social
    History, The Sylvia Pankhurst Archive, Amsterdam
3   Emmeline Pankhurst with Harry, 1890, Institute of Social History, The
    Sylvia Pankhurst Archive, Amsterdam
4   Emmeline Pankhurst, 1906, Museum of London
5   Emmeline Pankhurst arrested February 1908, as she led a deputation to
    parliament armed only with a rolled resolution for women's suffrage and
    a few lilies of the valley, Museum of London
6   Nellie Martel, Emmeline Pankhurst, Mary Gawthorpe, Una Stratford-
    Dugdale and Mary Leigh, Mid Devon by-election, January 1908, Herbert
    Morris, Newton Abbot, June Purvis
7   Emmeline Pankhurst at her stall, NUWSPU Exhibition, July 1908,
    Museum of London
8   Emmeline and Christabel Pankhurst in prison uniform, October 1908,
    Museum of London
9   Christabel Pankhurst, Emmeline Pankhurst, Emmeline Pethick
    Lawrence and Sylvia Pankhurst, c. 1909, Museum of London
10 Emmeline Pankhurst campaigning in March 1909, Museum of London

Plate section 2

11 Emmeline Pankhurst, in mourning for her son, Harry, January 1910,
    Museum of London
12 Emmeline Pankhurst, Boston, October 1910, Museum of London
13 Emmeline Pankhurst recuperating after a hunger strike, 1913, a
    photograph of Sylvia by her bedside, Museum of London
14 Emmeline Pankhurst, Chicago 1913, Museum of London

15 Annie Kenney and Emmeline Pankhurst in Women's War Work
    Procession, July 1915, Museum of London
16 Emmeline Pankhurst and her four adopted daughters, Kathleen King on
    her knee, Catherine Pine next to Elizabeth Tudor, Joan Pembridge on
    the rocking horse, and Flora Mary Gordon (Mary) next to the Nursery
    Assistant, c. 1919, Museum of London
17 Emmeline Pankhurst, Victoria 1920, June Purvis
18 Emmeline Pankhurst with Commander Maria Botchkareva and a soldier
    of the Women's Battalion of Death, Petrograd 1917, Warwick Kenney-
    Taylor
19 Emmeline Pankhurst, Whitechapel and St. George's election
    campaigning, 1927, June Purvis
20 Emmeline Pankhurst's statue in Victoria Tower Gardens, Westminster,
    1930. It was moved to another site in the Gardens, closer to the Houses
    of Parliament, in 1956.

ACKNOWLEDGEMENTS

I would like to express my grateful thanks to all those who, over the ten years that I have been collecting research for this book, have made it possible including Gail Cameron (formerly at the Museum of London) and David Doughan, retired from the Fawcett Library now renamed the Women's Library. My research assistant, Michelle Myall, undertook many mundane tasks with meticulous care and good humour. I owe an especial debt to Sandra Holton and Elizabeth Crawford, for many interesting discussions, and to Heather Laughton for the many finds we have acquired together. The late Jill Craigie was exceptionally kind to me in allowing me access to her suffrage collection and I can never repay the debt I owe her husband, Michael Foot, for granting me exclusive access to her archive. During the course of my work, I made contact with one of Emmeline Pankhurst's adopted daughters, Kathleen King. Now aged and nearly blind, her friendship is something that I greatly value as well as that of Warwick Kenney-Taylor, son of Annie who was most generous with the reminiscences of his mother. Elizabeth Hodgson, daughter of Mary Hodgson (née Gordon), another of Emmeline's adopted girls, spent many hours trying to find her mother's birth certificate, without success. Nyra Goode and her late husband, Phillip, kindly photocopied letters for me in their private collection.

I am indebted for financial support for the research for this book to The British Academy's Small Grants Scheme, and the University of Portsmouth Research Funds. Emotional and culinary support has especially come from Michael and Catherine who have endured my endless discussions about 'Mrs. P'. Friends and colleagues on the conference circuit have offered advice and critical comments from which I have learnt much, although any errors remain my own. I am grateful to the Master and Fellows of St. John's College, Oxford, for awarding me a scholarship in 1996, which gave me time to undertake research in the Bodleian Library.

I am also grateful for the assistance given me by staff at the following numerous libraries and institutions over the years, including the staff of the National Library of Scotland in Edinburgh, the Fryer Library, University of Queensland, the British Library in London, the Women's Library in London, the National Trust (Dyrham Park), the Museum of London, the Sydney Jones

Library, University of Liverpool, the House of Lords Record Office in London, the Public Record Office in Kew, the Bodleian Library in Oxford, the Archive Collections, University of East Anglia, Manchester Central Library, the Schlesinger Library, Radcliffe College, Massachusetts, Princeton University Libraries, the Library of Congress, Washington DC, the Smithsonian Libraries, National Museum of American History, Washington DC, the Institute of Social History, Amsterdam, Trinity College, University of Cambridge, Aberdeen Art Gallery and Museum, the Harry Ransom Humanities Research Center, University of Texas at Austin, the Fales Library at the Elmer Holmes Bobst Library of New York University, the John Rylands University Library, University of Manchester, the Mitchell Library, State Library of New South Wales, the National Library of Ireland in Dublin, Smith College, Northampton, Massachusetts, the Lilly Library, Indiana University, the Walter Clinton Jackson Library, University of North California, the National Library of Australia in Canberra, Nottinghamshire County Record Office in Nottingham, the Special Collections at the Northwestern University, Illinois, and Girton Library at the University of Cambridge.

Grateful thanks must also be expressed to the Museum of London and the International Institute for Social History in Amsterdam for permission to reproduce some photographs. Every attempt has been made to contact copyright holders. The author and publisher would like to apologise in advance for any inadvertent use of copyright material and thank all those libraries and individuals, and especially Richard Pankhurst, grandson of Emmeline, who have kindly given their permission to make quotations. Indeed, Richard Pankhurst has been most helpful and interested in this book. Although he may not agree with some of the views expressed here, he has been generous enough to exchange information with me. I hope that nothing I state in this book causes him pain.

Last, but not least, I would like to thank all the staff at Routledge, especially Vicky Peters, Áine Duffy, Lauren Dallinger and Sünje Redies for their support, encouragement, patience and professionalism. It is a privilege to work with them.

ABBREVIATIONS

BL	British Library
CNCCVD	Canadian National Council for Combating Venereal Diseases
CP	Christabel Pankhurst
DMC	David Mitchell Collection
DORA	Defence of the Realm Act
ELFS	East London Federation of the Suffragettes
EP	Emmeline Pankhurst
ESPA	E. Sylvia Pankhurst Archive
EWEP	Elizabeth Wolstenholme Elmy Papers
HHP	Henry Harben Papers
HLRO	House of Lords Record Office
HRHRC	Harry Ransom Humanities Research Center
ILP	Independent Labour Party
ITGWU	Irish Transport and General Worker's Union
IWSA	International Woman Suffrage Alliance
LEAs	local education authorities
LG Papers	Lloyd George Papers
LL	*Labour Leader*
LRC	Labour Representation Committee
MASC	Maud Arncliffe Sennett Collection
MNSWS	Manchester National Society for Women's Suffrage
NAC	National Administrative Council
NAWSA	National American Woman Suffrage Association
NUWSS	National Union of Women's Suffrage Societies
NWPP	National Woman's Party Papers
P-L Papers	Pethick-Lawrence Papers
PRO	Public Record Office
SFC	Suffragette Fellowship Collection
SSC	Sophia Smith Collection
TBG Papers	Teresa Billington-Greig Papers
US	United Suffragists
VfW	*Votes for Women*

ABBREVIATIONS

WCJL	Walter Clinton Jackson Library
WFL	Women's Freedom League
WFLMB	Women's Franchise League Minute Book
WGE	Women's Guild of Empire
WL	Women's Library, London Guildhall University
WPU	Women's Political Union
WSF	Workers' Suffrage Federation
WSPU	Women's Social and Political Union

INTRODUCTION

Emmeline Pankhurst is remembered today, at least in popular memory, as the heroine of the votes for women campaign that was waged in Edwardian Britain, the feminist leader of the Women's Social and Political Union (WSPU or Union), the most notorious of the groupings campaigning for the parliamentary vote for women on equal terms with men.[1] Emmeline founded the WSPU as a women-only organisation and under her leadership the spectacular and heroic deeds of her followers 'hijacked the movement's image as they hijacked the action at the time'.[2] The popularisation of such a version of events was captured in Midge Mackenzie's BBC TV series, *Shoulder to shoulder*, watched by millions in 1974 and by her book on the series, published the following year.[3] Some twenty-five years later, Emmeline Pankhurst topped the polls amongst *Observer* and *Daily Mirror* readers as the woman of the twentieth century, and even came second in the *Daily Mirror's* top ten women of the Millennium.[4] However, despite the hold of Emmeline Pankhurst on the popular imagination, no modern full-length biography has been written about her to complement the earlier accounts of her life.[5]

Emmeline Pankhurst had five children but her two sons died and it was her three daughters – Christabel, Sylvia and Adela – who became associated with their widowed mother in the suffrage campaign. After her death, her eldest daughter, Christabel, began writing a memoir of her mother but although the manuscript was completed by the mid 1930s, the book was published posthumously, in 1959, one year after Christabel herself had passed away.[6] Upon its publication, *Unshackled: the story of how we won the vote* proved to be less a biography of the WSPU leader than a more general account of the WSPU's campaign. The first full-length biography of Emmeline Pankhurst, *The life of Emmeline Pankhurst*, was published many years earlier, in 1935, and was written by Sylvia Pankhurst, the only one of Emmeline's three daughters from whom she remained estranged at the time of her death.[7] Sylvia was a socialist feminist whose world-view was often at odds with the women-centred perspective of her mother and Christabel, generally acknowledged as Emmeline's favourite child.[8] As Chief Organiser of the WSPU, Christabel worked closely with Emmeline during the suffrage campaign, forming and directing policies with which Sylvia

1

disagreed, especially in regard to the breaking of any association, at least at central level, with the Labour movement. Eventually Sylvia, seeking to fuse her socialism and feminism, formed a grouping amongst the working classes in the East End of London called the East London Federation of the Suffragettes which, although formally linked to the WSPU, followed its own independent line in that it would not attack the Labour Party nor Labour parliamentary candidates unsympathetic to women's suffrage, advocated mass rather than individual protest and included men as well as women members. The differences in tactics and policy led Emmeline and Christabel to expel Sylvia and her Federation from the WSPU in early 1914. The bitterness Sylvia felt towards her mother deepened during the First World War when she found Emmeline's patriotism a betrayal of the ideals in which the family had been reared, an affront to the memory of her father, Dr. Richard Pankhurst, a radical lawyer who had died in 1898; the screw turned further when, towards the end of her life, Emmeline stood as a Conservative parliamentary candidate. Such differences of view influenced the way Sylvia portrayed her mother in *The life of Emmeline Pankhurst*. Emmeline, whose politics are seen as suspect, is presented as a weak leader, 'a follower in many things', especially of Christabel's policy.[9] A woman whose 'impressionable nature' was influenced by 'a narrowly exclusive feminist school' which refused 'to admit that the welfare of the working woman, either as mother or wage-earner, was in any degree involved in raising the status of the working class as a whole'. Emmeline is also portrayed as a leader of a single-issue campaign, the winning of the parliamentary vote for women, rather than a radical pressing for a wider range of reforms.[10] Yet Sylvia cannot quite come to terms with such a damning analysis and towards the end of her book attempts to reconcile the differing political allegiances of herself and her mother by placing Emmeline in a more favourable light, by reclaiming her for socialism – '[I]t is certain that, however she may have termed it to herself, some sort of Socialism was always at the back of her mind.'[11]

However, *The life of Emmeline Pankhurst* was not widely read and it was Sylvia's earlier autobiographical account of the votes for women campaign, *The suffragette movement*, published in 1931, with its more hostile, unflattering picture of the WSPU leader, that became influential.[12] In the preface to her book, Sylvia states that it is largely made up of memories. Memories of her disagreements with her mother and Christabel float throughout the text, shaping her interpretation of historical events from a socialist feminist perspective that draws upon, according to Kathryn Dodd, a well-established ethical political vocabulary of 'popular struggle', akin to religious evangelism.[13] It is fair to say that *The suffragette movement*, as a history of a *women's* movement, is in many ways a curious read. The two key heroines, Emmeline and Christabel Pankhurst, are continually criticised while two heroes, namely Sylvia's father, Richard Pankhurst, and her former lover, the socialist Keir Hardie, are brought to the fore, as well as Sylvia herself. As Jane Marcus perceptively observes, in Sylvia's version of the women's suffrage movement she is 'the heroine' who keeps the socialist faith of her father, the Cinderella daughter liberated by a fairy godmother in the form of the socialist giant, Keir Hardie, while her mother and Christabel are the 'wicked' people, the 'separatist feminists', 'isolated man-haters', and celibate 'unsexed viragoes' who caused split after split within the movement. Sylvia claims that her arrangement to get the anti-suffrage Prime Minister, Asquith, to receive her East End delegation in June 1914 was the key to winning the vote. Thus weak from hunger striking, she is driven to the House of Commons where she is surrounded by socialist men – George Lansbury, Henry Nevinson, Joseph Wedgwood and Keir Hardie. Sylvia Pankhurst, Marcus continues, thus claims victory in the name of socialist feminism, a victory less over the government as over 'her real enemies, her mother and sister ... who have become increasingly more aristocratic and concerned with personal power ... She and her united charwomen have won the vote.'[14]

What Marcus particularly misses in her informative reading of *The suffragette movement* is Sylvia's bitter portrayal of her hated sister, Christabel, as an evil force upon their easily swayed mother, called 'Mrs. Pankhurst' throughout the book. Christabel, the apple of their mother's eye, becomes demonised as the betrayer of socialist feminism, the sister who marginalises class and socialism by recruiting into the WSPU middle-class women of all political persuasions and who, in the later stages of the WSPU campaign, initiates a separatist feminist sex war.[15] And, as a separatist feminist, Christabel is labelled a Tory – 'I detested her incipient Toryism.'[16] Not just an angry socialist but also a 'rejected daughter', Sylvia takes her vengeance upon her mother by presenting her as both a failed leader and a failed mother who neglected her less favoured children, Sylvia, Adela and especially Harry.[17] What historians have rarely commented upon in reiterating all too frequently this scenario is that in drawing such a picture in *The suffragette movement*, Sylvia often contradicts earlier claims made in her 1911 book, *The suffragette*, and in her biography of her mother. For example, in *The suffragette movement* she accuses her mother of callousness when leaving the sick Harry for her planned USA trip but in her biography of Emmeline she points out that her mother 'steeled herself to persevere with her journey'.[18] Such contradictory statements led Jill Craigie to suggest that Sylvia Pankhurst was an 'inveterate liar'.[19] Such a judgment is, perhaps, too harsh. All of us write different versions of events at differing times in our lives. Nevertheless, we cannot ignore the fact that Sylvia's differing versions of events often make her unreliable in print, especially since she cites no footnotes whereby we could check the accuracy of her statements. The researcher using the three main texts that Sylvia wrote on the suffrage movement therefore faces a number of problems, especially if there are none or few other accounts with which they may be compared.

Despite these inconsistencies, Sylvia Pankhurst's *The suffragette movement* became the authoritative reading of Emmeline Pankhurst, especially after George Dangerfield, writing from a masculinist perspective, adopted and adapted this script in *The strange death of Liberal England*, first published in 1935 and reprinted at least up to 1972. As the first male historian to treat the women's suffrage movement seriously, his plot had the power of a 'first' history from which few subsequent historians could escape.[20] Dangerfield belittles the suffragette movement, labelling it as a 'brutal comedy', a 'puppet show' where the strings are carefully manipulated by Emmeline and Christabel Pankhurst. Both women are seen as opportunists, seeking to rise above their impecunious middle-class background in provincial Manchester, and as despots who 'dictated every move, and swayed every heart, of a growing army of intoxicated women'. He continues, 'They had only to say the word and castles and churches went up in flames, pictures were slashed, windows shattered, the majesty of parliaments and kings affronted.' And there, above the lurid picture, 'the forms of Emmeline and Christabel Pankhurst scour the furious scene like a pair of risen but infernal queens'.[21] Drawing upon the comparatively new field of psychoanalysis, Dangerfield sought for the cause of militancy in some 'irrational and unconscious element' of 'the human soul', an element that came particularly to the fore when women entered political life. The 'outrageous Suffragette Movement', he claims, was a rejection of the respectable, smothering security offered to women, a movement in which woman became 'suddenly aware of her long-neglected masculinity'. Thus militancy is linked with the 'homosexual movement', and is a form of 'pre-war lesbianism' which is 'more sensitive than sensual', a form of behaviour where woman leaves the company of man and goes 'out in the wilderness, there to be alone with herself and her sisters'.[22] As Holton persuasively suggests, for Dangerfield the suffrage campaigns of the early twentieth century appeared as a symptom of both social and individual pathology.[23]

More recent group biographies of the Pankhurst women have not deviated largely from this path. David Mitchell's 1967 text *The fighting Pankhursts* attempts to assess the careers and achievements before and after suffrage of not only Emmeline, Christabel and Sylvia but also of Adela, the least-known daughter in this remarkable political family. But his story is written from a masculinist perspective that is riddled with demeaning comments and sexist jibes that belittle the lives of the 'posse of Pankhursts', as he terms them, who circled 'the great, recalcitrant herd with their little lassoes of hope and conviction'.[24] Martin Pugh in his book *The Pankhursts* also colludes in presenting the all-too-familiar scenario. Emmeline Pankhurst is an opportunist who seeks to marry 'an important man' so that she can be upwardly mobile.[25] She is a bad mother as well as a misguided and weak leader of the WSPU since she constantly defers to Christabel.[26] Further, she became the 'target of one of the most frank lesbians in the suffrage movement', the composer Ethel Smyth, who 'often shared Emmeline's room at the Inns of Court hotel and entertained her at her home in Surrey'.[27] The hints about Emmeline's lesbianism, which is never defined but assumed to involve genital contact, is particularly prurient in a newspaper article where Pugh claims that the suffragette leaders, including Christabel, engaged regularly in 'lesbian love trysts'.[28] Pugh does not discuss

Sylvia's close relationship with an American woman, Zelie Emerson, which Barbara Winslow has described as 'very intense, possibly even sexual' but assumes that Sylvia, who has an affair with Keir Hardie, the founder of the fledgling Labour Party, is heterosexual.[29] For Pugh it is Sylvia, the feminine socialist feminist who cries easily, who is the heroine of the Pankhurst family, just as she represented herself in *The suffragette movement*. Consequently, he makes at least fifty-eight references to the latter and only thirteen to Christabel's *Unshackled*.

In 1977, *The suffragette movement* was reprinted in a cheap and widely read paperback edition by Virago Press. Its narrative about the women's suffrage campaigns was eagerly devoured by a new generation of feminist historians – including myself – keen to find out about our foremothers. Strongly influenced by Second Wave Feminism, it was socialist feminist voices, like Sylvia's, that became the dominant approaches within the new feminist history that sought to record 'history from below', to find out about the lives of 'ordinary' women rather than their more well-known sisters. And it was Sylvia's portrayal of her mother in *The suffragette movement* that became the dominant representation.[30] The middle-class Emmeline Pankhurst who had deserted socialism, supported the war effort during the Great War and turned to the Conservative Party during the last years of her life, became an unfashionable figure, often dismissed as bourgeois, right wing, autocratic, ruthless, divisive and patriotic; in particular, the suffrage organisation that she founded and led, the WSPU, was portrayed as middle class, reactionary and narrow in its aims, a group that failed to mobilise the working classes and address their economic, political and social needs.[31]

Socialist feminist historians were not alone in drawing such a picture. A number of male historians, admiring the liberal feminist approach of Millicent Garrett Fawcett, leader of the National Union of Women's Suffrage Societies (NUWSS), who encouraged feminists to work closely with men, also presented a negative portrayal of the WSPU leader. This view is epitomised in an essay by Brian Harrison where he contrasts the law-breaking, 'militant' tactics that Emmeline Pankhurst advocated with the reasonable and sensible law-abiding, 'constitutional' approach that Millicent Fawcett upheld.[32] Millicent Garrett Fawcett and her peaceful campaigning 'suffragists', as NUWSS members and women suffrage supporters generally became known, were usually credited with winning the parliamentary vote for women while Emmeline Pankhurst and her unruly band of 'suffragettes' or 'militants', as WSPU members were commonly termed, were seen as hindering the women's cause, especially from 1912 when more extreme forms of militancy were adopted, such as destroying letters in post boxes, setting fire to empty buildings, large-scale window-smashing in London's West End and the slashing of paintings in public art galleries.[33]

Sympathetic accounts of the WSPU's militant campaign are to be found only amongst a minority of writers.[34] But these texts offer a general overview of suffragette activity rather than a biography of the WSPU leader. There are a few friendly biographies of Emmeline Pankhurst, written by Josephine Kamm,

Harold Champion and Rupert Butler, but these are slim, 'great figures in history' texts, aimed at a young readership – as are three picture books, written for children, where her life is presented as exemplary.[35] There are also a few sympathetic portrayals that focus in depth on Emmeline Pankhurst but these are only of essay length and concentrate only on her suffrage life.[36] Emmeline Pankhurst led an active political life both before and after her suffrage days, which has largely been ignored by present-day researchers. An assessment of her life and work in a modern full-length biography is long overdue.

In recent years the process of writing biography has been subjected to critical scrutiny.[37] Concerns have been raised about the complexities of interpreting written, visual and oral sources as well as about the ways in which biographers relate to their subjects, shaping accounts in particular ways. For some critics, biography is a fiction, a creation of the biographer who weaves a seamless narrative, creating coherence and causal connections that bear little relation to the lived experience of the person being studied. The self, it is sometimes argued, is not unitary and coherent but shifting and fragmented. Furthermore, the spotlight approach on a 'key figure' as an agent of change in history may represent what Susan Grogan has termed the last gasp of modernism in the uncertainties of our 'postmodern' age which refuses to accept master narratives that purport to explain the movement of history in this way.[38] While such debates alert the biographer to the fallacy of believing that one can construct the 'real' person rather than an interpretation of that subject, it is also important to remember that the postmodern critique itself is the product of a particular historical moment in time and does not invalidate the necessity for biography. Individuals respond in different ways to differing historical situations, and a study of any particular life can help both to illuminate these situations as well as aid our understanding of the person being studied.

All biographical interpretations are selective, and my interpretation of Emmeline Pankhurst's life is no exception; my own life story is written into this account in complex ways. In particular, I write as a white, heterosexual, middle-class feminist who admires the leader of the WSPU. Further, as Olive Banks and Elizabeth Sarah argue, we cannot understand Emmeline and Christabel Pankhurst unless we see them as feminists who, some decades earlier, pioneered a number of concerns that were central to radical feminists in Second Wave Feminism in the 1970s – the power of men over women in a male-defined world, the recognition that while men retained a monopoly of power socialism could be just as disadvantageous to women as capitalism, the importance of a women-only movement as a way for women to articulate their demands and raise their consciousness, the commonalities that all women share despite their differences, and the primacy of putting women rather than considerations of say, social class, political affiliation or socialism, first.[39] To make this connection is not unproblematic since some of the WSPU militants, living in the 1970s, distanced themselves from the 'Women's Libbers' of the day, arguing that the suffragette campaign had been spiritual while Women's Liberation was primarily materialistic.[40] Nevertheless, I contend that in regard to a feminist world-view, the ideas expressed by Emmeline Pankhurst were more akin to those expressed by radical rather than socialist feminists in Second Wave Feminism.

My interpretation of Emmeline Pankhurst's life then will differ in many aspects from that offered in the dominant narratives that we have considered so far and continues the questioning about the ways in which we socially construct and culturally produce stories about feminists in the past. And since I am a professional historian, it is an interpretation that is grounded in the extant sources, especially the primary sources, rather than being a purely literary fiction. Where, as indicated earlier, I have found contradictory statements about Emmeline Pankhurst, I have consulted a range of other sources, so that accounts can be compared, and have often indicated this in the footnotes. But ultimately, as with all biographers, my interpretation of Emmeline Pankhurst's life will be based on my 'feeling' about her, after a decade or more in the sources. While most biographers of women favour a chronological, narrative form, which is the form I adopt, I also draw upon other popular approaches which place the individual in a web of friendships or offer a thematic focus that present the shifting identities of their subject.[41] Overall, it may be useful, as Liz Stanley suggests, to see the production of biography as a 'kaleidoscope' where each time you look you see something rather different, composed of the same elements but in a new configuration, rather than as a 'microscope' effect where the more information you collect about your subject, the closer one is to 'the truth'.[42]

These considerations are particularly pertinent when considering the writing of the life story of Emmeline Pankhurst. Emmeline Pankhurst was a woman of extraordinary beauty, a fighter for the women's cause in which she passionately believed, a charismatic leader and speaker who inspired the fiercest devotion and charmed most of those who heard her. Yet many who knew her commented on her contrasts and contradictions. She could be gentle and fiery, idealistic and realistic, creative and destructive, kind and ruthless, democratic and autocratic, invincible and vulnerable, courageous and afraid.

While the views of her contemporaries will be important sources to consider, we also need to find the voice of Emmeline herself, her own subjectivity, her own sense of her experiences, her own self-representation. However, since she was very much a woman of action, a doer who considered herself incompetent with a pen, she left few articles, papers or personal letters, and those that are extant are scattered in various collections. She had no desire to write her auto-biography but was eventually persuaded to tell her story when she was recuperating, in 1913, from one of her many imprisonments; an American femi-nist journalist, Rheta Childe Dorr, compiled the life story from interviews with Emmeline and from suffragette literature. *My own story*, published late in 1914, was written in haste, mainly for propaganda purposes; it contains some factual errors, indicating that Emmeline had neither the time nor the inclination to check the proofs.[43] Consequently, some historians have dismissed it as a source for the serious scholar.[44] Indeed, Pugh refers to Emmeline's My own story just twice in his group biography of the Pankhurst women, and in one instance even cites the title incorrectly.[45] Such haughty condemnation cannot be sustained. All sources, whether a personal text such as an autobiography, or an official document such as a government report or the more general category of published commentary and reporting, have their characteristic strengths and weaknesses.[46] In My own story, Emmeline's voice speaks to us loud and clear as she presents her moving apologia for the increasing use of violence that she sanctioned in the women's suffrage campaign.

I hope that in the following pages I capture something of the magic and complexity of her personality as well as the double burden that she faced as a political leader and mother, and that in the process, I do full justice to this feminine feminist who was both of her time and before her time. This book is aimed at the general reader as well as an academic audience.

1

CHILDHOOD AND YOUNG
WOMANHOOD (1858–1879)

It is commonly stated that Emmeline Goulden was born on 14 July 1858,[1] but her birth certificate records the following day as the date of birth, at Sloan Street, Moss Side, Manchester. Perhaps she was born around midnight and her parents, Robert Goulden, a cashier, and his Manx-born wife, Sophie Jane (née Craine), decided after the birth was registered some four months later, that the 14th was the appropriate date. Perhaps Emmeline herself created the myth many years later; as a young woman she developed a passion for all things French and 14 July was the anniversary of the storming of the Bastille in Paris in 1789, an event that marked the beginning of the French Revolution. Perhaps Emmeline's birth certificate became lost and she had not seen the recorded date; after all, during the years when she was the leader of the WSPU, she lived like a nomad, without a permanent home, and it would have been difficult to keep family papers under such circumstances. But one thing is certain: Emmeline *believed* she was born on the auspicious 14th and it is highly likely that her parents told her so. As she said in 1908, 'I have always thought that the fact that I was born on that day had some kind of influence over my life … it was women who gave the signal to spur on the crowd, and led to the final taking of that monument of tyranny, the Bastille, in Paris.'[2]

The eldest girl in a family of ten children, Emmeline was a lively and precocious child, the rebellious streak in her nature being enhanced by stories about how her parental grandfather had narrowly escaped death at the Peterloo franchise demonstration in Manchester in 1819 and, with his wife, had taken part in demonstrations in the 1840s against the Corn Laws which imposed duties on imported foodstuffs. Emmeline could read by the incredibly early age of three. The young child also learnt, with a similar ease, how to play the piano at sight but would never practise and it was reading that was her favourite pastime, tales of a romantic and idealistic nature, such as John Bunyan's *The pilgrim's progress* and *The holy war*, being especially popular.[3]

The rich, industrial city of Manchester, at the heart of the manufacturing North, was a city of contrasts, with the poor living in overcrowded, insanitary tenements and the more affluent in spacious detached and semi-detached houses. Manchester was also at the forefront of dissenting politics during this period, a time of 'heart-stirring struggles for constitutional liberty and the freedom of the human mind and personality'.[4] Robert Goulden, being on the side of liberation in these matters, was an ardent supporter of the abolitionists in the American Civil War and prominent enough to be appointed to a committee which welcomed to Manchester the anti-slavery campaigner, Henry Ward Beecher, visiting England on a lecture tour. Sophie Goulden was an abolitionist too and frequently explained the evils of slavery to her growing family by reading to them Harriet Beecher Stowe's novel, *Uncle Tom's cabin*. Almost fifty years later, Emmeline could still vividly recall the thrill of listening, at bedtime, to her mother telling the story of the beautiful Eliza who fled for freedom over the broken ice of the Ohio River. She also recollected how one of her earliest memories was of the time she accompanied her mother to a large bazaar, held to raise money to relieve the poverty of the emancipated black slaves and, entrusted with a lucky bag, she collected pennies from willing supporters of the cause. 'Young as I was – I could not have been older than five years – I knew perfectly well the meaning of the words slavery and emancipation.'[5] Such fundraising events, together with the stories of oppression and liberation, made a permanent impression, Emmeline believed, on her character, awakening in her 'the two sets of sensations to which all my life I have most readily responded: first, admiration for that spirit of fighting and heroic sacrifice by which alone the soul of civilisation is saved; and next after that, appreciation of the gentler spirit which is moved to mend and repair the ravages of war.' Such sentiments were further fired by her admiration for Thomas Carlyle's *History of the French Revolution*, a book she discovered when about nine years old and which she insisted 'remained all my life a source of inspiration'.[6] As Holton has elaborated, Carlyle's view of history as an unpredictable process, where individuals were confronted with a choice of ensuring a better world in the future, or of allowing society to degenerate into chaos, a view where revolt could be glorified, not simply justified, was of the greatest importance for understanding Emmeline's future role in the campaign for women's enfranchisement and what may be termed her 'romantic outlook'.[7]

Robert Goulden prospered in his employment and became a partner and manager of a new cotton printing and bleach works at Seedley, on the outskirts of Salford. His growing family moved to a big white house, Seedley Cottage, surrounded by large gardens and meadows that separated it from the factory nearby. Although Emmeline enjoyed the delights of the countryside, she lived close enough to the poor to gain an insight into the appalling social conditions and hardships under which they laboured. Neither were holidays spent on the Isle of Man, where her parents owned a house in Douglas Bay, entirely carefree for Emmeline. While she joined in the swimming and rowing, country walks and visits to her grandmother and uncle, as the eldest girl in a large family, maturity was forced upon her early as she helped to look after her four younger sisters and five brothers.[8] Such a situation was not unusual, even in comfortable middle-class homes where a nursemaid was employed, as Carol Dyhouse has revealed. Looking after younger siblings was considered the most natural duty of the elder middle-class daughters, an early lesson in femininity.[9]

Despite these early responsibilities, Emmeline remembered her childhood with affection, as a time when she was protected with love and comfort, rather than the deprivations, bitterness and sorrow which brought so many men and women in later life to a realisation of the social injustices of Victorian society. Nevertheless, while still very young she began 'instinctively to feel that there was something lacking, even in my own home, some false conception of family relations, some incomplete ideal'. This vague feeling took a more definite shape when her parents discussed the issue of her brothers' education 'as a matter of real importance' while the education of Emmeline and her sister Mary, about two and a half years Emmeline's junior, was 'scarcely discussed at all'.[10] Robert and Sophie Goulden, although more liberal than many other Victorian parents, held traditional views about the expected future role of their daughters, mainly that they should be prepared for lives as ladylike wives and mothers rather than as paid employees.[11] Thus despite the fact that Emmeline was a gifted child whom her brothers nicknamed 'the dictionary'[12] for her command of language and accurate spelling, she followed the typical path of most middle-class girls of her day by attending, when she was about nine years old, a small, select, girls' boarding school, run by a gentlewoman. The main aim of such family-like institutions was not academic but the cultivation of those social skills that would make their pupils attractive to potential suitors.[13] Although Emmeline was taught reading, writing, arithmetic, grammar, French, history and geography, undoubtedly in an unsystematic way, the prime purpose was to inculcate in the pupils 'womanly' virtues, such as making a home comfortable for men, a situation she found difficult to understand. 'It used to puzzle me … why I was under such a particular obligation to make home attractive to my brothers. We were on excellent terms of friendship, but it was never suggested to them as a duty that they make home attractive to me. Why not? Nobody seemed to know.' An answer came to her question one evening when, feigning sleep in her bed, she heard her father say, 'What a pity she wasn't born a lad.' Emmeline's first impulse was to sit up in bed and protest that she did not want to be a boy but, instead, she lay still, listening to her parents' footsteps pass towards the next child's bed. For many days afterwards, she pondered on her father's remark but decided she did not regret being a girl. 'However, it was made quite clear', she recollected, 'that men considered themselves superior to women, and that women apparently acquiesced in that belief.'[14]

Such a view Emmeline found difficult to reconcile with the fact that both her parents were advocates of equal suffrage for women and men, another frequent topic of debate in the Goulden household. Her devoted father, to whom his eldest daughter was his favourite child, used to set Emmeline the task of reading the daily newspaper to him, as he breakfasted, an activity that helped to sharpen an interest in politics. Still young when the Reform Act of 1867 was passed, which extended the parliamentary franchise to all male householders and to men paying more than £10 annual rent in the boroughs, she did not understand fully the implications of the changes that were introduced but remembered well some of the controversy that it provoked. A chance to show her support for the Liberal Party, of which her father was a member, came in the first election after the bill when the daring Emmeline persuaded the willing Mary to follow her in the mile-long walk to the nearest polling booth, in a rough factory district. Since both girls were wearing new winter green frocks with red flannel petticoats, the colours of the Liberal Party, she had suddenly decided that they should parade before the queues of waiting voters, daintily lifting the edge of their skirts, in order to encourage the Liberal vote. When the nursery maid caught up with the children, she angrily stopped such a display of impropriety.[15] The incident showed, perhaps, an early liking for performance that may have been related to her father's main hobby. Robert Goulden was a well-known amateur actor in the Manchester area, especially of Shakespeare's plays, which he knew by heart, and the young Emmeline probably watched him, admiring his skills.[16]

When she was fourteen years old, the future leader of the WSPU attended her first suffrage meeting. Coming home from school one day she met her mother setting out to hear Lydia Becker who was Secretary of the influential Manchester National Society for Women's Suffrage and also a key figure in the Victorian women's rights movement. An enthusiastic Emmeline begged to be taken too since she had long admired Miss Becker as the editor of the *Women's Suffrage Journal* which came to her mother every month. A plain, bespectacled woman with her hair pulled back tightly into a bun at the back of her head, Lydia Becker's appearance and rather stern countenance was frequently the butt of gibes in a sexist press.[17] But she was much in demand as a suffrage speaker. Her talk this day enthralled and excited the schoolgirl so much that she left the meeting 'a conscious and confirmed' suffragist. 'I suppose I had always been an unconscious suffragist. With my temperament and my surroundings I could scarcely have been otherwise.'[18] Manchester was then the centre of the women's enfranchisement campaign and other important activists who lived in the city or surrounding areas included Elizabeth Wolstenholme, Ursula Bright and her husband, Jacob, and Dr. Richard Pankhurst, a radical barrister who was a member of the far left of the Liberal Party and an advocate not just of women's rights but also other advanced causes of the day.[19]

Emmeline, who had not yet met Richard Pankhurst, the man destined to become her husband, was preoccupied with her forthcoming stay in France. Her parents wanted their eldest daughter to be an accomplished young lady and so sent her to Paris where she became a pupil at the Ecole Normale de Neuilly, a pioneer institution in Europe for the higher education of girls. The Paris of her schooldays was a city still bearing the scars of the recently ended Franco-German war in which France had been defeated; even Emmeline's school, which had served as an infirmary for the sick and wounded, had walls riddled with shell and the marks of bullet shots.[20] But worse was the suffering of the

Parisians under the indemnity that had been imposed upon them. From this time onwards, Emmeline developed a lifelong prejudice against all things German and a lifelong love for all things French, including Paris itself, 'the city of her desire'.[21] The headteacher of her new school, Mademoiselle Marchef-Girard, believing that girls' education should be as thorough and as practical as that of boys', included in the curriculum subjects such as chemistry, book-keeping and the sciences, as well as the ladylike skill of embroidery. But since the lessons were conducted in French, in which Emmeline was not fluent, she was unable to participate fully. The change of circumstances and the climate upset her disposition so the visiting doctor advised she be excused classes and be allowed to run around and amuse herself. Taking full advantage of the freedom granted to her, Emmeline explored Paris with another solitary pupil, the beautiful Noémie Rochefort who had been placed in the school for refuge rather than instruction. The two young women became close friends and roommates, Emmeline listening intently to the anxious Noémie's constant talk about her father, Henri Rochefort, a well-known Republican, communist and swordsman who had been imprisoned in New Caledonia for the part he had played in the disastrous Paris commune. The stories about his duels, imprisonment and daring escape in an open boat fired the imagination of the impressionable pupil from Manchester who quickly acquired fluency in the French language.

Emmeline spoke highly of the liberal curriculum taught to the pupils, which she supplemented by reading a large number of French novels. The founder of the school and editor of *Nouvelle Revue*, Madame Adam, took an interest in her English pupil and was 'exceedingly kind', inviting Emmeline not only to her house but also to her soirées where many famous men of the day were present.[22] Such socialisation into the appropriate form of conduct considered suitable for young middle-class women worked its magic. Emmeline, now eighteen years old, returned home to Manchester:

> having learnt to wear her hair and her clothes like a Parisian, a graceful, elegant young lady … with a slender, svelt figure, raven black hair, an olive skin with a slight flush of red in the cheeks, delicately pencilled black eyebrows, beautiful expressive eyes of an usually deep violet blue, above all a magnificent carriage and a voice of remarkable melody. More than ever she was the foremost among her brothers and sisters.[23]

Despite Emmeline's sophistication, however, she was still expected to take her place as the eldest daughter in a large family, doing various feminine tasks such as helping to dress her sisters, redecorating the drawing-room, and looking after the youngest girl. In any crisis, she never seemed to be at a loss. When a lamp, which was lit, became detached from the ceiling at a school event, she had the presence of mind to rush forward and catch it in her hands; when some window curtains caught fire in the house, she hastily pulled them down to put out the blaze. Yet, despite such decisiveness and confidence in these respects,

Emmeline could be painfully shy of any sort of artistic or emotional expressiveness. She was once overcome by nervousness at a school concert, unable to play a few bars alone on the piano; the embarrassing situation was saved by a quick thinking teacher who leant across the young woman's shoulders and played the necessary notes.[24]

As a middle-class daughter at home, involved in her family's domestic routine, Emmeline missed the variety and excitement of her Paris schooldays and longed to return to the city she had taken to her heart. An opportunity came the following year when Mary, in her turn, was sent to the Ecole Normale de Neuilly and Robert Goulden allowed Emmeline to accompany her. As what was termed a 'parlour boarder',[25] Emmeline had plenty of free time to renew her friendship with Noémie, now the wife of the Swiss painter, Frederic Dufaux, and the mother of a baby girl. Noémie was keen for her dear friend to marry and live near her in Paris, where they could both be mistresses of their own households and cultured hostesses, entertaining well-known literary and political figures. Emmeline shared the dream and, as was typical of the later Victorian age, saw a husband as 'her door of opportunity'.[26] Noémie approached a suitable man of literary distinction who declared himself willing to marry the charming young Englishwoman, provided she brought to the marriage a dowry. Emmeline readily agreed. She had felt embarrassed by the breakfast table scenes at home when her mother had presented to her father the outstanding household bills and was determined that, if ever she married, she must have an income of her own; in a society where wives were not paid, but financially dependent upon their husbands, a dowry could bring 'self-respecting security'.[27] However, when she approached her father on the matter, he was outraged. He stormed that he would not sell his daughter for money, did not approve of a foreigner for a husband nor of living abroad and promptly demanded that Emmeline return home immediately, to act as his housekeeper, since her mother and all her brothers and sisters were on holiday and the housekeeper was ill.[28] Without a dowry, her suitor now withdrew his offer of marriage. An indignant Emmeline, furious at being abandoned so casually, despite the fact that her heart had not been engaged, was angry with her father who, she believed, had deprived her of a happy and fulfilling life in Paris.

It was the summer of 1879 when Mary and a dejected Emmeline returned home to Manchester. The house and garden were quiet without the chatter of the younger children and the two sisters wondered about their future. Robert Goulden now took a firm line with Mary and stubbornly refused to yield to her plea to become an actress, an occupation considered not respectable, especially for the daughter of a prosperous factory owner.[29] Mary concentrated on her painting and displayed some of her work for sale in a local shop which caused another row with her father. People would think he was short of money, he pointed out, to allow his daughter to demean herself in this way, and such a rumour could ruin his business. When Sophie Goulden returned home with the other children, there were further scenes as the two eldest daughters complained that they were expected to stay at home, dusting the drawing-room or arranging the flowers, while their brothers were being prepared for useful occupations, including the family business. Their mother confided that she feared her tall, upstanding sons might marry imprudently and urged her daughters to make the home attractive for them. On one occasion, when Mrs. Goulden ordered Emmeline and Mary to fetch their brothers' slippers, the spirited young women defiantly remarked that if she was in favour of women's rights she did not show it at home.[30] Emmeline found such scenes particularly rankling since, as she later explained:

> I was always anxious to have outside work; as a girl I felt strongly the necessity of women being trained to some profession or business which should enable them to be self-supporting. It is important that they should avoid the degradation of forced dependence upon husbands and male relatives, not only for subsistence, but for every little private call. Women are the better and happier for occupation; it raises them socially and intellectually.[31]

Eager to be doing something useful in the world, Emmeline went with her parents to an important political meeting addressed by Richard Pankhurst. There had been much debate as to whether Britain should join forces with Turkey in its war with Russia, a position that Dr. Pankhurst, a pacifist leading the peace group in Manchester, had strongly opposed. Standing with her parents on the outside steps awaiting Richard's arrival, the first Emmeline saw of him was his 'beautiful hand' opening the door of his cab as the vehicle pulled up.[32] When he stepped out to be greeted by the waves and cheers of the crowd, her heart leapt. Richard Pankhurst, now forty-four years old, had resolved to stay single all his life, in order to devote himself to public life. But he noticed the strikingly beautiful and elegant young woman, at least half his age, and decided to woo her. The second son of Henry Francis Pankhurst, an auctioneer, and Margaret Marsden, he had been brought up as a Baptist dissenter and evangelical liberal. Richard had attended Manchester Grammar School and Owens College (later Manchester University) and although a brilliant scholar, had been barred from Oxford University because of his ·Nonconformity. Nevertheless, he greatly distinguished himself at the University of London from which he graduated in 1858, the year of Emmeline's birth, with a Bachelor of Arts, a Bachelor of Law in 1859, and a Doctor of Law, with the gold medal, in 1863. After practising as a solicitor, he had been called to the Bar at Lincoln's Inn in 1867 and then returned to Manchester to join the northern circuit.[33] Regarded as a political extremist, he was affectionately known in Manchester as 'our learned Doctor' or 'the Red Doctor'.[34]

On 8 September 1879 Richard Pankhurst wrote formally to Emmeline, 'Dear Miss Goulden, There is, as you know, now in action an important movement for the higher education of women. As one of the party of progress, you must be interested in this ... '.[35] Emmeline was astonished and flattered that this learned man with twenty years of public service should pay attention to her, a young, inexperienced woman of twenty-one years old. They fell in love. It was, as Rebecca West put it many years later, 'an astounding match'.[36] It mattered little to Emmeline that Richard was not dashingly physically attractive. He was below medium in height, for a man of his time, with a gold-red beard covering the greater part of his face, a broad, lofty forehead crowned with a mane of ruddy hair, blue-grey, bright eyes, and a shrill, high-pitched voice. But he had a wonderful smile, and, above all else, was an idealist.[37] Here was her hero, a man with an intense hatred of injustice who struggled to make the world a better place by fighting for unpopular causes, such as education for the working classes, and women's rights, a man who had been an ardent sympathiser with the North in the American Civil War. Republican and anti-imperialist, Dr. Pankhurst was also an advocate of the abolition of the House of Lords and of nationalisation of the land. His involvement in the early women's suffrage movement had included, amongst other activities, acting as counsel in the 1869 case of Chorlton v. Lings, a law suit which based women's claim to the parliamentary vote on the authority of ancient precedents; he had also drafted the first bill aimed at giving women the vote, introduced unsuccessfully into parliament by Jacob Bright in 1870.[38]

The courtship of the 'Red Doctor' and the lively Emmeline Goulden was short and intense, with the ever watchful Sophie Goulden accusing her daughter of not keeping a 'proper maidenly reserve' and of ' "throwing herself at him" '.[39] By 23 September Richard was writing to Emmeline as his 'Dearest Treasure' although, predictably, he also conversed on wider social issues, in particular their common interests in reform. 'In all my happiness with you', he wrote, 'I feel most deeply the responsibilities that are gathering round us. ... Every struggling cause shall be ours.' Stressing the useful work they could jointly undertake, he pleaded, 'Help me in this in the future, unceasingly. Herein is the strength – with bliss added – of two lives made one by that love which seeks more the other than self. How I long and yearn to have all this shared to the full between us in equal measure !'[40]

The appeal to Emmeline, whose 'ardent nature' had moved her to desire to do 'some great thing' was intoxicating.[41] Richard was still a member of the Manchester Married Women's Property Committee which had been formed in 1868 to campaign against the property disabilities of wives who, once married, gave their property (as well as their legal identity) over to their husbands. In the autumn of 1879, the agitation for reform was in full swing, with campaigners pressing for married women to enjoy the same rights as single women and for wives as well as husbands to have separate property interests.[42] Perhaps it was an awareness of these debates that prompted Emmeline to suggest to her intended that they dispense with a legal church ceremony and form a free union – 'Wouldn't you have liked to try first how we should get on?'[43] The wise Richard loved Emmeline too much even to contemplate such an idea. He knew from his long involvement in the women's movement that middle-class women who lived in non-legal unions were the subject of vicious gossip and hampered in their public work. One of his co-workers, Elizabeth Wolstenholme, had been six months pregnant in a free union with Ben Elmy, a situation that caused 'much fluttering in the suffrage dovecotes' before she was persuaded that it was in the interests of the cause she served to formalise her marriage, which she had done in October 1874.[44] One year later, Millicent Garrett Fawcett, a key figure in the nineteenth-century women's suffrage campaigns, had insisted that Elizabeth resign as secretary of the Married Women's Property Committee on the grounds 'that what happened before you were married has been and is a great injury to the cause of women'.[45] Richard had no wish for the woman who had captured his heart to face a similar fate. Emmeline's shocked parents considered any form of marriage other than a legal union in a church ceremony out of the question for their headstrong eldest daughter or any daughter.

Unexpectedly, Richard's mother fell ill and died. The recent death of his father, and now his mother, was a heavy blow at such a time, especially since Richard had lived for most of his adult life with his parents. A dutiful son, he was bowed with grief, living alone in what was now an empty, silent house. His sadness was so heavy that Emmeline feared he would break under the strain of coping with the emotional distress while also trying to fulfil his demanding work activities. The wedding was hastened since 'the lonely one could not be kept waiting'.[46] On the eve of their wedding, as they parted in happy anticipation of the next day, Richard told Emmeline yet again how unendingly he loved her when she asked 'Are you sure you will always love me and want me for ever?'[47] Later that night, an anxious Sophie Goulden came to Emmeline's room. Conscious that she had not explained to her daughter about the sexual aspects of marriage, she announced, 'I want to talk to you.' The bride to be, not wanting anything to cast a shadow over the beauty of her courtship, hastily replied, 'I do not want to listen.'[48] Since Richard was in mourning for his dead parents, a white wedding, with full orange blossom for the bride, and Emmeline's four younger sisters as bridesmaids, had not been considered appropriate. Instead, a brown velvet bridal dress had been made at a local department store, Kendal and Milne. When the dress was delivered at the last moment the following day, Emmeline wept to find an unwanted row of brass buttons stitched down the front, protesting it made her look 'like a little page-boy'.[49] Only a few people were invited to the Church of England service, which took place, by licence, on 18 December 1879, at St. Luke's, Weaste, in the parish of Eccles in the county of Lancaster. Six persons were signatories to the marriage, including Emmeline's father and her sister, Mary.

2

MARRIAGE AND ENTRY INTO POLITICAL LIFE (1880–MARCH 1887)

The newly married Emmeline, settling into her new home at 1 Drayton Terrace, Old Trafford, Manchester, was soon pregnant. Anxious to be a good wife and companion, she confided to Richard how conscious she felt about the gap between his erudition and her own limited knowledge, asking for his help and advice. Eager to please, Richard earnestly drew up a list of serious books for Emmeline to study, but the young lively wife found the course of instruction dull. She soon abandoned her plan for self-education and returned to reading fiction. All her life she was to remain a copious novel reader, cleverly and quickly skimming the pages to select what interested her, dealing with newspapers in the same manner.[1] But it was an active rather than sedentary life that Emmeline's ardent nature desired, and marriage to Richard soon enabled her to develop her powers in those causes in which she was already interested.

By March 1880 she is listed as a member of the Executive Committee of the Manchester National Society for Women's Suffrage which included not only her husband and Lydia Becker but also Alice Cliff Scatcherd, wife of a textile factory owner in the Leeds area and a radical suffragist.[2] Like Elizabeth Wolstenholme Elmy, Alice Scatcherd was critical of many aspects of the existing forms of marriage and refused to wear a wedding ring or to attend a wedding service in the established church where brides had to pledge a vow of obedience to their husbands.[3] In addition to meeting and working with such non-conventional, strong-minded women, Emmeline also became part of the network around the Manchester Married Women's Property Committee to which she was co-opted, as 'a compliment to her husband', and on which she found herself 'the youngest and least informed' of its members.[4] Through such work, the idealist Emmeline wanted to prove herself a worthy partner to her husband in his great reforming mission.[5] More ambitious for him than for herself, she hoped he would become a Member of Parliament and 'do great things for the working masses' such as rescuing them from poverty, bad housing and overwork. She was determined that his wings, 'as reformer and champion of great causes', should not be clipped or weighed down by his marriage and was hopeful that her father would settle property on her now that she was a wife and expecting a baby; such a gesture would give her some economic independence as well as help in her cherished project of enabling Richard to give up his legal practice and concentrate on public work.[6] When Robert Goulden informed his eldest daughter that a property settlement was not imminent, Emmeline was bitterly disappointed.

The baby, a girl named Christabel Harriette, was born at home on 22 September 1880. The young mother herself nursed the contented Christabel who slept much and cried little.[7] Over the next few years, Emmeline did not escape the fate of the majority of women in the nineteenth century, whatever their material and social circumstances, namely frequent childbirth.[8] She selected the name Estelle for a second girl, born in the same house on 5 May 1882, with Richard adding Sylvia, the latter being the only name to which the new addition to the family would later respond.[9] With a growing young family and not too healthy bank balance, a decision was now made to leave urban Manchester and return to the big Goulden family home in the leafy outskirts of Salford. A servant, Susannah, was employed to nurse Sylvia and to help generally, thus enabling Emmeline to continue with her political work. Being a mother was never Emmeline's primary identity. As she later explained, 'I was never so absorbed with home and children ... that I lost interest in community affairs. Dr. Pankhurst did not desire that I should turn myself into a household machine. It was his firm belief that society as well as the family stands in need of women's services.'[10] Creating such a space for herself was important to Emmeline, a fact which Richard wisely encouraged and understood; he wanted a wife who would share his enthusiasm for struggling causes, including his battles within the Liberal Party over the war controversy. When the Rev. Paxton Hood was hounded from the pulpit for preaching in his Manchester constituency three sermons against imperialist expansion and the war, Richard and his father-in-law, Robert Goulden, supported the beleaguered man. The wealthy pro-war faction in the Manchester Liberal Association, however, then succeeded in ousting the well-known local citizen, Abel Heywood, a pacifist in the present crisis, as the Liberal candidate to stand in the next general election in favour of their own man; the manoeuvre caused further dissension since Heywood was well respected and had previously stood twice as the representative of Liberal interests in parliamentary elections. Richard, tired of all the in-fighting, bided his time and then, in July 1883, resigned from the Liberal Party and announced his intention of standing as an Independent at the next general election. Within two months, a by-election was called in Manchester and since the Liberals refused to contest the seat the fight was between Richard and the Tory candidate.[11]

Emmeline, who adored her husband, was ardent for his success, as were both her parents, her father acting as Richard's agent. Pregnant with their third child, she helped as best she could, supporting Richard's radical election address which advocated, amongst other things, the abolition of the House of Lords, the disestablishment of the Church of England, nationalisation of the land, adult suffrage for men and women, free compulsory secular education, and Home Rule for Ireland, an issue on which no other contender had yet made a stand. The Manchester Liberal Association, furious at Richard's defection, instructed its members not to vote for him while most of the press condemned his defence of the Irish cause, suggesting that it was the strongest reason not to support him at the poll. While fighting against such odds, Richard also made his candidacy a much harder task by announcing his intention of abiding by the new Corrupt Practices Act, not yet in force, which forbade the use of paid canvassers and the taking of voters by cab to the election poll and also set a limit on election expenses. His opponent, who had fewer scruples about such matters, spent £5,559 on his expenses while Richard's amounted to a mere £541.[12]

An anxious Emmeline, resentful against those whom Richard had once supported and who now refused to support him, rushed impulsively to Lydia Becker, asking her to make an official declaration in Richard's favour, in the name of the Manchester Women's Suffrage Society. Much to Emmeline's astonishment, Miss Becker coldly refused, telling the young wife that her husband was a 'fire-brand'. With anger in her heart, Emmeline wept when she told Richard the news.[13] Emmeline may not have known about the past disagreements between Lydia Becker and her husband, otherwise she may not have sought Miss Becker's help so eagerly. In 1874, one of the bitterest disputes between the two had erupted over Lydia's support for a women's suffrage bill sponsored by William Forsyth, a Conservative MP, which explicitly excluded married women; she reluctantly advocated a pragmatic acceptance of a franchise limited only to single women since it would enfranchise at least 800,000 widows and spinsters. Lydia had expected Richard Pankhurst to support her in this controversial move but he refused to do so, standing firm with Jacob and Ursula Bright, and Elizabeth Wolstenholme, in vehemently opposing any measure that excluded married women.[14] In addition to this history of past disagreements, there may have been also another more personal reason for Lydia's reluctance to support Richard Pankhurst's candidature as an Independent in 1883. There were persistent rumours that she had once been 'sweet' on the learned doctor and greatly disappointed when he married someone else.[15] If the rumours were true, then the sight of the visibly pregnant Emmeline pleading for support for her husband to the woman he had slighted, may have stiffened Lydia's resolve. Later, she seemed to relent a little in her stand when she wrote about Dr. Pankhurst's candidature, praising the way in the past he had given 'active and valuable help to the advancement of the position of women'; but the impact of such kind words on the earnest Emmeline was destroyed by the calm observation that since the 'extreme Radical' Dr. Pankhurst and the 'staunch Conservative' Mr. Houldsworth both expressed adherence to women's suffrage, the women's cause would be supported, whoever was the victor.[16]

The scale of Richard's defeat, just 6,216 votes cast for him against 18,188 for Mr. Houldsworth, shocked Emmeline. She felt keenly her husband's disappointment and must have been delighted when their third baby, a boy named Henry

Francis Robert ('Frank'), was born on 27 February 1884. Frank became an especial favourite with Richard, 'his heart's core'.[17] By now, however, Emmeline had found that politics could be an expensive business. Richard had to pay his own election costs but, more seriously, the controversy he had created had lost him many well-to-do clients. Shortly after his election defeat, he had successfully defended a court case against Manchester City Corporation in favour of small market traders upon whom an extra tax was being levied in addition to the regular charge. While this success endeared Dr. Pankhurst to the working classes and to his wife, it further antagonised rich businessmen. Nor was Emmeline's father unaffected by these developments. Part of the boycott against Richard became directed at him; financial problems arose in Robert Goulden's business, from which he never recovered, and the stress caused his health to fail. The difficult situation was not helped by unresolvable differences in political outlook between the once thriving industrialist and his son-in-law. Richard, since his resignation from the Liberal Party, had been espousing socialist views with which his father-in-law passionately disagreed. Emmeline sided with her husband and thus found herself again in conflict with her father.[18]

The tensions became so unpleasant at Seedley Cottage over the following year, that Richard and Emmeline decided they had to leave the Goulden home. Emmeline was expecting another baby and not keeping well during this pregnancy, suffering acutely from neuralgia and dyspepsia; often she was incapacitated by migraine attacks, from which she suffered all her life.[19] Mary decided to leave with her sister and Richard, to make her home with them; that way she could escape hearing the constant stream of criticism that her parents were directing against their eldest daughter and her socialist husband – who had become an agnostic – and also help Emmeline in the running of the home. On 19 June 1885, another daughter, Adela Constantia Mary, was born at the new house at 66 Carter Street, Chorlton upon Medlock, near Greenheys.

In the new Pankhurst home a rather traditional pattern was soon established. Each morning Emmeline would brush her husband's coat before he left for work, complaining about his pockets bulging with the smallest editions of his favourite books and little black note-pads that he kept regularly on his person for various jottings that came to his mind. The watching children would often hear her protesting, 'Some surgeon will stop you in the street one of these days and ask you to leave him your body for dissection – you make such a sight of yourself!'[20] Then the children would rush to the high, narrow window in the nursery to wave father goodbye as he went to work, his red hair now turned grey. When he returned home in the evenings, the excited offspring would hurry to find out what new book he had bought for them and anxiously wait to be read or told a story. He would often proudly say, 'My children are the four pillars of my house!' and insist that 'Life is nothing without enthusiasms!' as he encouraged them to work for others. 'If you do not grow up to help other people you will not have been worth the upbringing!' 'Drudge and drill!' and 'To do, to be, and to suffer!' were other frequent exhortations as the middle-aged father tried to instil in his children a sense of duty to society. When he appeared in evening dress, they would watch with admiration as Emmeline put in the diamond studs that had belonged to Richard's own father, 'preparing him lovingly' for some important function where he had to speak.[21]

Emmeline had remedied her earlier unsuccessful attempts at managing the weekly housekeeping allowance by asking the faithful Susannah to take control of the budget since the servant could stretch the money further than the mistress.[22] But she longed to have some means of economic independence of her own so that she would not have to worry over such matters but be a financial support to her husband. Again, she approached her father about the property he had promised her, on her marriage. Still bearing the scars of the recent differences of opinion between them, Robert Goulden promptly informed his eldest daughter that no such promise had been made. Emmeline never saw her father again. She longed to fulfil her childhood dream of moving to London; there, she believed, Richard would stand a better chance of being elected to parliament.[23] The opportunity came sooner than she expected when a few months later the Liberal government, with Gladstone as Prime Minister, resigned.

Richard was invited by the Rotherhithe Liberal and Radical Association to stand as their parliamentary candidate in the November general election of that year, 1885. He gladly accepted but insisted on standing as a Radical, with a similar socialist election address as before: 'This is the hour of the people and of the poor. ... There must be for every man a man's share of life, through education, free and universal, training for work through technical teaching; full citizenship.'[24] Eager to help her husband in this important mission, Emmeline wrote in August to Caroline Biggs asking her if she and other London women working for the suffrage cause would assist Richard's candidature. In September, she also wrote to Florence Balgarnie of the Manchester National Society for Women's Suffrage, thanking her for bringing Richard's candidature before the committee.[25] Then, despite the fact that she still had not fully recovered from the birth of the last child, Emmeline accompanied Richard to London.[26]

Emmeline wanted no controversies to wreck Richard's chances during this campaign but had not reckoned with the tactics of his Conservative opponent, Colonel Hamilton, and of Charles Parnell, leader of the Irish Nationalists. Colonel Hamilton was determined to present Dr. Pankhurst as a man of dubious character and printed a handbill accusing him of atheism, a view that held a certain notoriety in mid-Victorian Britain. Although Richard denied the libel, it was known that he was not a Christian but an agnostic. Emmeline, sensing the onset of defeat, became indignant at the uproar that broke out and begged Richard to find some way to silence his critics. When he retorted that he had publicly denied the libel, she protested that it was not enough; they must attend church together to show he was not disrespectful of Christian beliefs, even if he did not share them. 'I understand these people', she insisted, 'I know what to do; you have always got your head in the clouds!'[27] But going to church did nothing to still the controversy. Even more disastrous for Richard, a fervent advocate of the Irish cause, was the fact that Charles Parnell instructed his followers to vote against all government candidates, irrespective of whether they supported Home Rule or not; Parnell believed that such a strategy would destroy the majority enjoyed by Gladstone and force him to grant Home Rule which he carefully had not excluded from his election manifesto. On polling day the Colonel received 3,327 votes, Richard 2,800. Crushed by a second defeat, Emmeline was particularly upset by the way her husband had been treated by the leader of the Irish Nationalists, but Richard defended Parnell's policy pointing out that tactics of constant obstruction could eventually wring from a hostile Liberal government surrender on the Home Rule issue. 'That was a valuable political lesson', Emmeline recalled, 'one that years later I was destined to put into practice.'[28]

Richard decided to take a court action against the authors of the libel, the case being tried in May 1886 by Justice Grantham who gave a verdict for the defendant. Since Grantham himself had stood as a Conservative candidate in the November general election and only recently been appointed to the Bench by the short-lived Conservative government, his ruling was called into question, especially by influential radical newspapers, such as the *Pall Mall Gazette*, edited by William Stead, with whom Richard corresponded.[29] Emmeline was enraged. Fiercely protective of her husband, she revealed her courage by writing a forthright and contemptuous letter to Justice Grantham:

May 14th, 1886

My Lord, – Your judgement of Wednesday, and your summing up to the jury to-day, are the concluding acts of a conspiracy to crush the public life of an honourable public man. It is to be regretted that there should be found on the English Bench a judge who will lend his aid to a disreputable section of the Tory Party in doing their dirty work; but for what other reason were you ever placed where you are?
I have, my Lord, the honour to be
Your obedient servant,
Emmeline Pankhurst.[30]

'Let him send me to prison! I want to go to prison for contempt of Court!' she protested to those who would listen.[31] But the judge did not respond to the accusations and did not reply to her letter.

Richard decided to appeal against the rulings of Justice Grantham, and in March 1887 a jury found in his favour, awarding him £60 damages of which he agreed to accept just forty shillings. Financial burdens from the cost of the election and the libel actions were now pressing. But Richard would not abandon his radical politics in order to make a comfortable living from his legal practice, and neither did Emmeline want him to do so. As close partners in the causes they espoused, they agreed, as Christabel later commented, to forgo the wealth that her father could have made in his legal work.[32] But there may also have been another reason why Emmeline supported Richard in the course he adopted, a course that meant an inevitable conflict 'between purse and pocket'.[33] According to Adela, her father 'hated' his profession, his heart being in politics.[34]

3

POLITICAL HOSTESS
(JUNE 1887–1892)

Richard's legal and political work was taking him increasingly to London, where Emmeline now longed to live; the metropolis, the centre of the English political system, would offer Richard a better chance of fulfilling his dream of becoming a Member of Parliament. Determined to help him financially in his political efforts by earning an income of her own, she decided that the opening of a shop could be a solution to their problems and settled on 165 Hampstead Road which comprised a shop with living accommodation above. The children were brought from Manchester and stayed with Susannah in lodgings until the new home was ready, while Emmeline, bubbling with enthusiasm, had the exciting task of choosing, within her limited means, stock for the new venture. She bought an array of fancy goods, such as milking stools and photo frames, which she enamelled in pale colours and Mary decorated with painted flowers.[1] When 'Emerson and Co.', as the shop was called, was opened, Emmeline moved 'in a radiant daydream'.[2]

Her hopes of earning large profits, however, were soon to be dashed. Although the estate agent had told her that the shop premises were located in a rising area, the goods stocked in Emerson's were too elegant for the neighbourhood where market stalls selling cheap goods were pitched in the streets. The family budget had to be managed carefully with no extra spending on what Emmeline saw as unnecessary items, even at Christmas time.[3] Then there was also the cost of Richard's frequent trips to Manchester where he still had a number of legal cases. During these separations from her husband, Emmeline always looked forward to his loving letters which inevitably included some reference to their present political life and hopes for the future. 'We ought to feel that we are going through a preparing trial. So much is going on, in which we ought to be a part.' After nine years of marriage, he still spoke of his strong feelings for her as though it was the eve of their wedding. 'You know how I love you and want to cherish your life. How splendid you were on Saturday – in all that unconscious loveliness! Dear heart, I hold you to mine!'[4]

The late 1880s, recollected Emmeline, was a time 'of tremendous unrest, of labour agitations, of strikes and lockouts. It was a time also when a most stupid reactionary spirit seem to take possession of the Government and the authorities.'[5] Despite the fact that she and Richard were often together only at weekends, they participated in a number of protests, such as the free speech gathering held in Trafalgar Square on Sunday 13 November 1887 at which well-known socialists, such as John Burns, William Morris and Annie Besant, spoke. William Morris, an upper middle-class artist, poet and craftsman, and Annie Besant, who had achieved notoriety in 1877 when she had republished with Charles Bradlaugh an old birth control pamphlet, were soon to become frequent visitors to the Pankhurst household. On 'Bloody Sunday', as it became known, the mounted police prevented the meeting taking place by attacking the crowd with truncheons, some 150 being injured and about 300 arrested. One man, Alfred Linnell, died as a result of injuries sustained when a police horse trampled him to death. Emmeline and Richard, riding in a coach with Linnell's family, were amongst the 100,000 mourners at the funeral.[6] The following year Emmeline enthusiastically supported the strike of women in Bryant and May factories who were protesting about the sacking of some of their colleagues for giving information about pay and working conditions to Annie Besant. The women not only made matches by hand, dipping them into the dangerous chemical phosphorous, but also ate their food in the work-rooms, thus developing 'phossy jaw', a disease that rotted teeth and jaw bones; their scandalously low wages, in conditions that Annie condemned as 'White Slavery in London', were even subject to fines for lateness and various mistakes.[7] Shocked by these revelations, Emmeline worked with the strikers and with Annie who, together with Herbert Burrows, another prominent socialist, and the Women's Trade Union League, helped the women to form a Match-Makers Union that demanded better working conditions from their employers. Public support for the strike was so successful that a large amount was raised for strike pay, enabling the women to press successfully for some changes.[8]

In addition to participating in such protests, Emmeline sometimes accompanied Richard on his trips to Manchester, Mary managing the household in her absence. It was on one such occasion, on a September day in 1888, that four-year-old Frank fell ill. In the morning, Susannah had taken the children out for a walk, pushing the three-year-old Adela, with her weak legs in splints, in a pram. Frank, in his new reins, ran happily beside, pretending to be a horse. When the children returned home, he suddenly developed a cold, flushed cheeks and a persistent coarse cough. An anxious Emmeline rushed back from Manchester to find her son in a critical condition. Frank had not been visited by their own doctor, who was away, but by two unknown doctors who had mistakenly treated him for croup only to discover too late that he was suffering from diphtheria. He died in the middle of the night on 11 September. Emmeline's unearthly cries and weeping for her dead boy woke up the two eldest girls to whom Susannah explained, in hushed whispers, what had happened.[9] Mary, who was present at the death, had the sad task of informing the registrar.

Distraught in her grief, Emmeline did not know how to break the news to Richard. Fearing that a telegram would be too much of a shock, she contacted instead her eldest brother, Walter, who hastened to London and then travelled back to Manchester, to break the news to his brother-in-law.[10] Richard was devastated; the sudden early death of his favourite child was a deep sorrow that remained with him always, claimed Christabel, and seemed to give him new tenderness for his surviving children.[11] Emmeline ordered two portraits of little Frank, with his dark hair and long black eyelashes, but then found she could not bear to gaze at them; she hid them away, in a bedroom cupboard, out of sight.[12] Neither could she bear to hear his name mentioned. When defective drainage at the back of the house was found to be the cause for Frank's diphtheria it aroused in her 'a bitter revolt' against the deprivations of poverty. Had she not chosen that 'dismal neighbourhood', she told herself, her boy would still be alive; the doctors would have treated him very differently had she gone to them, 'not as a little shopkeeper, but as the wife of a distinguished lawyer'.[13] The issue of the effect of deprived living conditions upon the health and moral welfare of the working classes in London had, of course, been much discussed after the sordid revelations in Andrew Mearns' much publicised pamphlet *The bitter cry of outcast London*, first published in 1883 and then excerpted in the *Pall Mall Gazette*.[14] It must have been particularly difficult for Emmeline and Richard to know that their little son was the victim of those insanitary conditions that also plagued the poor.

The surviving children were hurried away to the relative safety of Richmond, Emerson's was closed and the premises advertised to let. With a heavy heart, Emmeline feverishly sought forgetfulness by channelling her energies into a whirl of activity. Undaunted by the failure of her first shop, she was determined to open another, and, more importantly, to make her home a meeting place for people involved in the advanced causes of the day that she and Richard supported. With this end in view, Emmeline rented a large house in a respectable middle-class area, at 8 Russell Square. She took great delight in furnishing it in the fashionable style of the time, especially with the brilliant colours of the East. As Sylvia vividly tells us, her mother put up 'Japanese blinds of reeds and coloured beads, and covered the lamps with scarlet shades; their ruddy glow shone a cheerful welcome to us when we came home on dark winter afternoons'.[15] The first floor, comprising two large inter-connecting rooms that would make an ideal place for meetings and conferences, was decorated in yellow, Emmeline's favourite colour, with a frieze of irises painted by Mary; since Emmeline hated gas, the large space was lit by tall oil lamps, with yellow shades.[16] Some of the stock of the new Emerson's that she opened initially in Berners Street, off fashionable Oxford Street, was put in the new home – old Persian plates, Chinese tea pots, oriental brasses, rugs from Turkey and cretonnes in the style of William Morris. Attempting to make a comfortable, stylish home, at a moderate cost, the practical, energetic Emmeline did as much of the work herself that she could – laying carpets, hanging pictures, making curtains and even upholstering furniture. Richard kept apart from all the hustle and bustle, burying himself in his own work. An idealist who was hopeless at any kind of manual task, he wandered around his new surroundings, admiring his wife's efforts with the frequent comment, 'I am a helpless creature!'; even the carving of the Sunday joint he handed over to her.[17] When guests came to dinner, Emmeline dressed the table with pretty arrangements of gauze and flowers. Her skill at sewing was evident in the feminine clothes she made for herself and for the children. She never liked the 'rational' dress that some radical women advocated, such as the short skirts and short hair that Annie Besant sported or the trousers worn by Helen Taylor, step-daughter of the great Liberal MP John Stuart Mill who, during the parliamentary discussion of the 1867 Reform Act, had supported the women's cause by moving, unsuccessfully, that the word 'man' should be replaced by the word 'person'.[18] For Emmeline, who never went outdoors without her veil, feminine dress was regarded as indispensable for public work, an aspect of her character that in Sylvia's view made her mother 'a woman of her class and period'.[19]

But Richard was enchanted. 'Not the bitterest critic of Mrs. Pankhurst ever suggested', noted that perceptive observer Rebecca West, 'that her husband did not find her, from beginning to end of the nineteen years of their marriage, a perfect wife.'[20]

Their house at 8 Russell Square soon became a centre for political gatherings of a wide array of social reformers – socialists, Fabians, anarchists, suffragists, free thinkers, agnostics and radicals. In order to draw an audience, such At Homes invariably included some form of entertainment, such as a recitation, but above all it was the elegant and beautiful Emmeline Pankhurst, in a trained velvet dress, the hostess who made her guests welcome and occasionally sang in her moving contralto voice, who impressed the visitors. One remembered her as 'a living flame. As active as a bit of quicksilver, as glistening, as enticing. ... She looked like the model of Burne-Jones' pictures – slender, willowy, with the exquisite features of one of the saints of the great impressionists.'[21] In addition to William Morris and Annie Besant, visitors to these gatherings included Florence Fenwick Miller, journalist, lecturer and popular educator; Tom Mann, a socialist and trade union activist; the Russian refugees Kropotkin, Stepniak and Chaykovsky; American suffragists and abolitionists, such as Elizabeth Cady Stanton and William Lloyd Garrison; R. B. Haldane and Jacob Bright, both Members of Parliament and supporters of women's suffrage; James Bryce, British Ambassador in the United States; Alice Scatcherd; Mr. Hodgson Pratt, a worker for international peace, and Emmeline's hero from her Paris schooldays, Henri de Rochefort, living in exile in London.[22] The regular visits of Rochefort, who had refused to learn English on the grounds that it would ruin his native tongue, revived in Emmeline her old passion for all things French. She declared that Richard, who spoke French 'with punctilious exactitude, his love of the precise word causing a frequent recourse to the dictionary', must have some French blood in his family background; he was so unlike the typically stolid

Englishmen. The visit of Rochefort's daughter, her old schoolfriend, Noémie, with her three children, brought back happy memories of times in Paris.[23]

Emmeline's interest in women's suffrage was not lost in all this activity but still a key concern. The tensions in the women's suffrage movement, of which she was only too aware, took another direction that autumn of 1888 when the Central Committee of the National Society for Women's Suffrage, which represented all the suffrage societies, called for a special general meeting to be held on 12 December, for the purpose of revising its rules so that the Executive could approve the affiliation of any women's organisation which had aims other than women's suffrage. The move was opposed by, amongst others, Lydia Becker, its secretary, Millicent Garrett Fawcett and Lilias Ashworth Hallett who feared that such a change would bring the affiliation of party political women's organisations and thus destroy the non-party character of the National Society which, it was believed, had enabled it to gain a majority of members of the House of Commons in favour of women's suffrage; the presence of such organisations too might even advance the campaigns of male parliamentary candidates who opposed the women's cause or would vote against it.[24] On the morning of the 12 December Emmeline, whose membership was still with the Manchester Society, paid a five shilling membership subscription to the National Society so that she could attend the meeting scheduled for noon. Florence Balgarnie, in a hastily written note to her, expressed the views of the Society's Executive when she pointed out that although Emmeline was technically qualified to attend, it was hoped that women who had only recently joined would not press their entitlement.[25] Emmeline, a determined woman, presumably insisted on her right to be present since she is listed amongst the delegates at the stormy meeting which raged for three and a half hours. When the majority voted for the change, the dissident minority, headed by Lydia Becker and Millicent Garrett Fawcett walked out of the hall, thus bringing about a damaging split in the main women's suffrage society.[26] Although Sylvia Pankhurst claims that her mother intended to vote against the proposed revision of the rules, it is fair to assume that the opposite is true since Emmeline became a subscriber to the 'new rules' organisation, now called the Central National Society for Women's Suffrage, based in Parliament Street, and usually referred to as the 'Parliament Street Society'.[27] Those who had opposed the change established an alternative 'old rules' organisation retaining the 'old' name of the Central Committee of the National Society for Women's Suffrage, based at Great College Street, commonly known as the 'Great College Street Society'. Once again it would appear that Emmeline had disagreed with the views of Lydia Becker who now branded the members of the Parliament Street Society as the 'left-wing' and 'extreme left' sections of the women's suffrage movement.[28] The exclusion of married women from the demand for the vote had been an issue dividing the two groups. However, although the Parliament Street Society broadly supported the married women's claim, it was not united on the matter, as Emmeline and Richard soon found out. At its first annual meeting, the 'ultra-Radicals', as

Holton terms them, led by Richard, tried unsuccessfully to persuade those present that the Society should at least withdraw support for bills which explicitly excluded married women.[29]

By the time of the Special Meeting on 12 December, Emmeline and Richard had some private news to celebrate; Emmeline was pregnant again. Over the coming months she became convinced that the child she was carrying was a boy, 'Frank coming again'.[30] Amid much rejoicing, their last child, a son, was born on 7 July 1889. Harry, as the new baby became known, was a strong, healthy child and since mother and baby seemed to be doing well Richard went off to a legal case in Manchester. Soon after his departure, Emmeline suddenly haemorrhaged severely. Panic and fear descended in the household when her own doctor was not available since both Mary and Susannah thought Emmeline was dying. The children were sent hastily to the basement, out of hearing of all the fretful talk, and besieged an ashen-faced Aunt Mary with questions about a sick pet while Susannah, clad in cap and apron, ran through the streets, seeking a doctor. Her plaintive cry, 'My mistress is dying', eventually brought one to Russell Square who saved Emmeline's life.[31] Richard was telegraphed and returned home in great distress to find that the crisis had passed.

Emmeline had now borne five children over a span of nearly nine years, a common experience for middle-class women in Victorian Britain. Where she was unusual, however, was in her insistence on reworking middle-class Victorian social conventions so that she combined her duties as a wife and mother with running a shop, organising political meetings in her home, campaigning for her husband's political career, and carving out time for her own political interests. Her advanced views were typical of a new stereotype of middle-class femininity that was much discussed in novels, in plays and in the press in the late 1880s and 1890s, the 'new woman'.[32] The 'new woman' challenged custom in many ways by engaging in a wide range of activities outside the private sphere of the home; she could be found in employment, seeking higher education, fighting for women's legal and political rights and challenging the traditional view that women were inferior to men. Emmeline had the energy and determination to break free from the expected mould for a Victorian, middle-class wife and mother of her day, and had the support of her husband in her desire to do so. It is no surprise, therefore, that she recovered fairly quickly from the near fatal circumstances after the birth of Harry and focused her energies, once again, on the two reformist issues which she and Richard cherished most, namely women's suffrage and the removal of the disabilities of married women. Although she retained her subscription to the Parliament Street Society until 1893, she and Richard were closely associated in 1889 with the formation of an organisation to champion the cause of married women, the Women's Franchise League.

Holton claims that the Women's Franchise League, which has left few records, was founded by three women who, like Emmeline and Richard, were located within radical-liberal suffragist circles.[33] Its treasurer, Alice Scatcherd, and its first secretary, Elizabeth Wolstenholme Elmy, were old acquaintances of the Pankhursts. Harriet McIlquham, the first chair of its Executive Committee, had established the right of married women to be elected Poor Law Guardians, and to vote at parish meetings, thus proving 'in her own person, that marriage is no legal bar to the enjoyment and exercise of electorate and elective rights, at any rate in matters parochial'.[34] Emmeline also claimed that she was 'one of the [League's] founders'[35] and was probably present at a League meeting held at her house on 23 July 1889, just two weeks after Harry was born. However, she was not present at the League's inaugural meeting held two days later although her name does appear as a member of the first provisional committee. Amongst the early recruits to membership, which probably never numbered more than a couple of hundred, were Florence Fenwick Miller, Josephine and George Butler and Harriot Stanton Blatch, daughter of the American suffragist Elizabeth Cady Stanton. Harriot, living in England since her marriage to an Englishman, was soon to become a friend of Emmeline's, inviting Sylvia and Christabel to stay at her home in Basingstoke, a provincial market town in Hampshire.[36] In these early years, the League drew upon the transatlantic network formed by Harriot's mother who became a corresponding member. It also had links with the earlier abolitionist movement in the States since William Lloyd Garrison, the younger, spoke at the inaugural meeting, warning that the key obstacle that the abolitionists had faced was support from those who urged moderation and gradualism. His emphasis upon a firm approach that rejected 'compromise and the pragmatic manoeuvring of parliamentary and party politics'[37] would appeal to Emmeline, as would the links, advocated by some of the League's leadership, to the emerging socialist and labour movements. In particular, it is within the League that Emmeline served her political apprenticeship as a future women's suffrage leader.

The League often disparagingly referred to its rivals as 'the Spinster Suffrage party' while the more moderate groups, in their turn, argued 'Half a loaf is better than no bread!' against what they saw as the League's wild and impractical proposals.[38] But overall, the League saw itself, in Holton's phrase, as 'the voice of Radical suffragism', the group that put forward an advanced programme for all women – unmarried, married or widowed – that aimed to obtain not just the vote but eradicate women's civil disabilities.[39] Alice Scatcherd, speaking at the inaugural meeting, proudly proclaimed that the League wanted to obtain 'full and equal justice for women with men' and elaborated on how women were in revolt against that most Victorian of feminine virtues the 'complete self-effacement … the complete abnegation of self'.[40] Such a broad programme of social reform, dear to Emmeline's heart, must have been frequently discussed at League gatherings, often held in her home.

During these years, Emmeline and Richard were friendly with other radical liberals such as Sir Charles and Lady Dilke but they were especially close to Jacob and Ursula Bright. When the Brights were suddenly recruited to the League's leadership in early 1890, Elizabeth Wolstenholme Elmy feared that

Emmeline and Richard had deliberately 'engineered' the move as part of a plan to re-establish the political career of Sir Charles whose reputation had been ruined when he was cited as a co-respondent in a much publicised divorce case four years earlier.[41] His supporters, she believed, hoped that he could rebuild his parliamentary career by sponsoring measures on both women's suffrage and the need for independent parliamentary representation from within the labour movement, a dual focus which she thought could lead to divided loyalties. Whether the Pankhursts had 'engineered' the recruitment of the Brights to the League inner circle for such purposes is difficult to determine. But there was a tie of 'strong affection' between the two couples, Emmeline being particularly close to the older Ursula Bright who held an 'almost maternal love' for the charming hostess of 8 Russell Square.[42] At the request of Ursula Bright, Emmeline later joined the Women's Liberal Federation.[43]

The League held resolutely to the principle of championing the cause of married women and, unlike the other suffrage societies, refused in 1889 to support two private members' measures on women's suffrage brought before parliament since one bill included a proviso to exclude women under coverture (the doctrine whereby women upon marriage lost their own separate legal identity which was subsumed under that of their husbands) while the other bill would not enfranchise wives either. That married women lost the civil standing they had once held as single women, a status that could only be regained if widowed, was deeply offensive to League members. Coverture was seen as a doctrine that epitomised the subordinate and slave-like status of wives, robbing them not only of their property but also of ownership of their own bodies. The League challenged attempts to exclude married women from suffrage measures by adopting and adapting for its own use Richard Pankhurst's Women's Disabilities Removal Bill, first introduced to the Commons in 1870 by Jacob Bright. The three clauses of the League bill stated that in all legislation relating to the right to vote at parliamentary, municipal, local and other elections, 'words importing the masculine gender shall be deemed to include women'; that no woman 'shall be subject to legal incapacity from voting at such elections by reason of coverture', and that no person 'shall be disqualified from being elected or appointed to, or from filling or holding, any office or position, merely by reason that such person is a woman, or, being a woman, is under coverture.'[44] With such provisions, this bill became the 'first' women's suffrage bill to expressly include married women.[45]

Richard Haldane, a young, radical, Liberal MP who was a frequent speaker at 8 Russell Square, brought the bill before the Commons in 1889 and 1890, but, much to Emmeline's disappointment, did not advance it. With a few other women League members, Emmeline interviewed Dilke in the Lobby of the House of Commons, urging him to take the bill to a vote. She smouldered with indignation when he replied that the measure was simply a declaration of principle which could not possibly become law for fifty years.[46] Equal divorce and inheritance rights for women were also advocated by the League, which even published Richard's pamphlet arguing for the abolition of the House of Lords.[47] Some League members found it all too much. Alice Scatcherd wrote in despair in late October 1890 to Harriet McIlquham who had resigned her membership. 'I had no idea that you dissented from any one of the League's principles. ... The Colbys retire because of Home Rulers & Socialists being on our Committee. The Mallesons because of Divorce. ... What next? Who next?'[48]

Emmeline would have had little sympathy with those who complained about the radical views of the League's leadership and its expanding links to the socialist and labour movements since she and Richard had shown their commitment to socialism by joining the Fabian Society, one month earlier. Although her husband's legal knowledge and varied talents were useful to the League, it was Emmeline rather than Richard who was assuming a more prominent role within the organisation. When Elizabeth Wolstenholme Elmy resigned as paid secretary in May 1890, Emmeline took over for a short time, but in an unpaid, honorary capacity.[49] She dealt, amongst other things, with correspondence. On 11 July 1890 she wrote an apologetic letter to a Mrs. Wood who had complained that she had not received information about forthcoming meetings, explaining that there were 'incomplete lists' in regard to future events and membership. 'We feel very much at how great a disadvantage Mrs. Elmy's action has placed us. Meetings were settled & then suddenly she discontinued acting with us & we had to go on as best we could.' Ending on a positive note, she hoped that Mrs. Wood and her husband 'will be able to come to me on the 19th. I think you have had a card already but to guard against any mistake I enclose another.'[50] At the Executive Committee meeting of the League held later that month, Emmeline announced her resignation as honorary secretary and proposed that Ursula Bright and Countess Schack be appointed, jointly, to the post, which was accepted.[51] Most probably she had found the work too tedious and time consuming, especially since she was also acting that month as honorary secretary to the International Congress on questions relating to women, where her knowledge of French was particularly useful.[52] Within the League, Emmeline was quickly learning a range of skills that related not only to public speaking but also to committee procedures, radical agitation, and promotion and representation of the League's policy. At the Executive Committee meetings she regularly proposed and seconded resolutions, occasionally acted as chair, made a number of suggestions for promotion of policy, participated in numerous discussions about effective political tactics and was often put forward as a candidate for various forms of civic work.[53] One must, therefore, question Sylvia's assertion that, within the Women's Franchise League, Emmeline found it an ordeal, 'evaded as far as possible', to introduce a lecturer, to read out a list of announcements, or to rise from her seat stating, ' "I second the resolution." ' Within the League, Sylvia continues, Emmeline regarded herself 'as the helper and understudy of her husband, and of that able woman, Ursula Bright'.[54] Although Ursula Bright often offered advice about political tactics to the younger woman, she also acknowledged the initiatives that Emmeline took and the importance of her work. 'I am glad you are so confidant', she confided in one letter marked 'Private' to Emmeline, 'I shall leave the Manchester Committee with joy in your hands & under your direction.'[55] But it is Sylvia's claim that, within the League, her mother regarded herself 'as the helper and understudy of her husband' that is especially problematic, since it is a view that does not accord with Emmeline's own representation of herself at this time.

The Woman's Herald considered Emmeline Pankhurst prominent enough to be interviewed for its issue of 7 February 1891, introducing her as an 'earnest speaker' who 'for a long time has been known as an active and successful worker in the cause of women, which she has so much at heart'. When the interviewer asked Emmeline if she found her political work and the running of her business, where she superintended her shop assistants for about eight hours a day, a bar to her domestic duties, she replied decisively:

> In no way; I enjoy to the full the happiness of home. I have four little children, who, I might say, are quite as happy, quite as well looked after, as any children. They are devoted to me; indeed, I think they appreciate me all the more because they do not see too much of me. I have an excellent nurse and governess to whom I can confidently entrust my children. I do not think the mother is the best instructress of her own offspring in any way; she is often too indulgent; the constant intercourse may, in my opinion, be the reverse of beneficial. My children look forward to my return as a treat; I have two days a week I can devote entirely to them.[56]

Praising her husband as being one of the first to promote the extension of the franchise to women, she spoke warmly of the support and encouragement he gave her. 'In all women's questions I have his earnest help and sympathy', she boasted. When asked about her views on politics, she replied, 'I am a Radical, devoted to the politics of the people, and to progress, especially where the education, emancipation, and industrial interests of women are concerned.'

Far from being 'the helper and understudy of her husband', Emmeline appears as the more ambitious and active of the partnership in regard to women's suffrage. 'I feel deeply', she continued to the interviewer, 'how much the Suffrage and active work will do for the independence and happiness of women.' Then in words that were to echo in future years, when she would be the most notorious of the women suffrage leaders, advocating that her followers should rise up and demand their rights from a repressive Liberal government, she said:

> I recently wrote a letter to the *Star* ... [appealing] to the Liberal leaders to take up Women Suffrage, as a practical measure in the Liberal policy. It will be a great loss to that party, and a gain to the forces of reaction, if the Liberals neglect this call upon their principles and allow the Conservative party to grant justice to women in giving them

the Parliamentary vote, as I believe they will. I venture to assert that the *women of the land mean to have the vote*, and that at an early date. Agitation to educate and to organise is going on rapidly. ... Women will insist on being heard at the Bar [Door] of the House [of Commons] to assert their claim to vote – a claim that is supported by constitutional right and ancient practice. It is a crying injustice that women cannot exercise their right to vote. Here I am a householder, an employer of labour, and heavily taxed, yet I am refused the vote which my porter may enjoy. I often feel inclined to refuse to pay these unjust taxations, and let the bailiffs seize every stick and sliver of my furniture until I get my vote. When once we have the vote, the right to work, the due preparation for work, will be placed for women, I believe, on larger lines, and will be followed by great and beneficial results, in giving to all women a wider outlook and a more varied field of activity and influence.

When the interview ended, and Richard entered the room and saw his 'lady',[57] as he usually called Emmeline, with their children now around her, he felt blessed. 'Does not this prove conclusively that neither business nor politics can in any way take from all that we desire and look for in the wife and mother?' he commented.[58] Undoubtedly he glowed with pride when, in December of that year, Emmeline acted as hostess to a Conference on the Programme of the League, held in their home over three evenings so that working people could attend; although League members had offered to pay the cost of the refreshments and arrangements, Emmeline generously refused such kindness.[59]

Emmeline and Richard's advanced views on the role of women in society were typical of the 'new woman' stereotype of middle-class femininity discussed earlier although there were many aspects of this image that Emmeline did not embrace. This blending of traditional and modern is, perhaps, especially evident in the way the children were brought up. Their children's lives had to be organised to fit into her busy schedule, and, in typically Victorian manner, she was a stickler for discipline although often softer than her harsh words. The tempestuous Emmeline, often tired from the juggling of her political interests, domestic responsibilities and financial constraints, could move swiftly 'from crossness to kisses.'[60] As Adela recollected, her mother could speak impulsively and say 'very hard things in her anger, but cooled down quickly'.[61] Usually it was the servants who enforced Emmeline's orders, the discipline growing in severity by its delegation to others. Sylvia, recalling that her mother would tolerate 'no likes and dislikes', remembered how the children would be scolded for not eating their often lumpy and cold porridge or dawdling when out walking when their boots were tight.[62] Emmeline was also traditional in feeling too embarrassed to talk to Christabel and Sylvia about 'the facts of life'. When some big boys in the Square garden asked Adela some 'strange questions', Emmeline scolded the elder girls for leaving their younger sister alone and then, later, haltingly said, 'Father says I ought to talk to you.' But the girls were told nothing and the subject was never raised again.[63] Emmeline also held conventional middle-class views about the education of her daughters, arguing against sending them to school, where she feared that they would 'lose all originality'; in particular, she strongly disagreed with Richard's idealistic suggestions that they should be sent to an international Marxist school for child refugees and destitute children from all over the world or to the state-supported local Board School that largely drew upon a working-class clientele.[64] Instead, Christabel, Sylvia and Adela had a home-based, unsystematic education where they had access to their father's book-lined study, often gave each other lessons or were tutored by a governess. But in other ways, Emmeline and Richard were very unconventional parents.

Their joint interest in politics was the central issue around which family life revolved so that their children were not segregated from adult life but 'bobbed like corks' on its tide, rarely playing games but more commonly participating in the political gatherings held in their home.[65] They joined in the serious talk of political discussions and generally helped by giving out leaflets, collecting money in small brocade bags and printing notices, such as 'To the Tea Room'.[66] The two eldest daughters, Christabel and Sylvia, were treated from an early age as if they were grown up so that they became confident young people who could argue with their mother and impress their views upon her.[67] The two younger children, Adela and Harry, fared less well. 'We lived too much together and within ourselves to be healthy-minded', Adela recollected, 'and brooded over troubles that other children in more healthy surroundings would have forgotten in five minutes.'[68] While Adela viewed her mother with a mixture of both love and fear, her father was a more distant figure of authority; both Adela and Harry were terrified of him, unable to comprehend his lectures on socialism, capitalism, religion and suffrage.[69]

Firm in her desire to see married women explicitly included in any new women's suffrage measure, Emmeline, with Richard, was rumoured to be involved in a plan, in April 1892, to break up a meeting organised to support a bill introduced by Sir Albert Rollit, a Conservative MP. This bill proposed to give the parliamentary vote only to those propertied widowed and single women who were eligible to vote in local elections. Although all the other suffrage societies, including the Women's Emancipation Union led by Elizabeth Wolstenholme Elmy, supported Rollit's bill, the Women's Franchise League vehemently opposed it. Without the authority of the League's Executive Committee, some of the League's leadership – including Emmeline and Richard, Ursula Bright, Alice Scatcherd, Helen Taylor, the socialist George Lansbury, and two members of the Marxist Social Democratic Federation, Herbert Burrows and H. M. Hyndman – signed and circulated a leaflet urging working men and women to attend a meeting that was being held in support of the bill, on 26 April 1892 in St. James's Hall, London. The leaflet claimed that the bill was 'class legislation' which aimed to enfranchise 'middle-class women and spinsters' and exclude the 'married women of the country' and 'women lodgers' (who lacked property).[70] On the day, Elizabeth Wolstenholme Elmy and her husband arrived early at the hall and found that League supporters had not only leafleted the seats but were about to take over the platform – which Mr. Elmy tried to prevent happening. During the scuffle, Emmeline presented her platform ticket which Mr. Elmy tore up, claiming that it was forged.[71] When the meeting began, further interruptions occurred. Richard Pankhurst 'and a lady' sent up an amendment urging that no measure for women's suffrage was worthy of support which did not embody the principle of full legal enfranchisement for all women, a proposition that was vigorously supported by George Bernard Shaw, the author and playwright, who then entered into a fiery exchange of views with Herbert Burrows who was sitting at the back of the hall.[72] As the noise grew louder and louder, Burrows rapidly made his way towards the platform amidst threats from the chair of the meeting that he would be removed from the hall. League friends, thinking Burrows was being ejected from the meeting, followed him in a rush. The reporters' table on the platform collapsed under the onslaught, coats, hats and notebooks being trampled under foot. During the hand-to-hand fight that ensued, massive brass railings in front of the platform were torn down. League members and their supporters, estimated to be about 200, gained control of the platform where they cheered and denounced Rollit's bill.[73]

The League's response to the Rollit bill caused four resignations from its Executive Committee, including that of Harriot Stanton Blatch. 'She is not a strong soul like dear old Mrs. Cady Stanton', Ursula Bright later confided to Emmeline.[74] The furore was widely reported in the press and Richard Pankhurst felt obliged to state, in the columns of the *Personal Rights Journal*, that there had been no plan to break up the meeting.[75] Emmeline retold the story to the League Executive Committee meeting held on 2 May 1892, where approval was given, with one exception, for the £20 that had been spent on printing, distributing and posting the leaflet.[76]

Emmeline would have had family matters on her mind at this time since her father, to whom she had not spoken for a number of years, had died unexpectedly in late April, when on a visit with his wife to the Isle of Man. Memories of happier times probably entered her thoughts as she wrote of his 'sad & dreadfully sudden death' to Mr. Nodal, a Stockport newspaper proprietor, asking him to commemorate her father's memory. 'I, his eldest daughter, can remember the earnest part he took in the great struggle against slavery in the United States of America, in the Free Trade movement & in all good causes', she reminisced. 'When a boy of, I think, 14 he became a member of the Anti-Corn Law League. In later years he, as you know, did & suffered much to throw light into dark places in Municipal affairs.' Emmeline continued:

> It would be a great comfort & solace to his family to see some public recognition in the press of his native city, of the services rendered by

him to the cause of man. ... My father was always very modest as to the value of the political work he did. He preferred to be a simple soldier in the army of progress. Had he been more self seeking he might, with his undoubted ability & political insights & sagacity, have take[n] a foremost part.[77]

Within just over six years, Emmeline would face another bereavement, that of her husband, but in the intervening years she and Richard faced a range of problems. Already they had had the expense of replacing the old brick drains of Russell Square with a new, approved system and now, during the winter of 1892–3, the five-year tenancy of the ninety-nine year lease came to an end with an unexpected heavy bill for delapidations. Although Richard was a lawyer, he had not checked the details of the lease of which Emmeline too had been unaware. All wear and tear had to be made good, the house redecorated, and the balcony strengthened.[78] After the bill had been paid, they learnt that the money had been wasted since the building was to be demolished.[79] Stunned by such depressing news, Emmeline and Richard reflected on their lifestyle and decided that the time had come to move back to Manchester. They were tired of their frequent separations and the financial burden that Emerson's had become; although the shop had been moved from Berners Street to a site with high overcharges in more fashionable Regent Street, it had never been a commercial success, despite frequent advertisements as an 'Art Furnishers and Decorators' in journals such as the Penny Paper.[80] The painful task of closing the shop she had started so hopefully made Emmeline ill and it was decided to move first to the more relaxing atmosphere of the northern seaside resort of Southport in Lancashire, some forty miles from Manchester.

4

SOCIALIST AND PUBLIC REPRESENTATIVE (1893–1897)

The months spent at the sleepy seaside resort of Southport, in a rented furnished apartment, were 'the most reposeful time' of Emmeline's life, claimed Christabel, with the exception of a year spent long afterwards in Bermuda.[1] Emmeline had no more worries about the lack of customers in her shop nor about how to organise political gatherings in her home on a limited income; she became what she never wanted to be, a full-time wife and mother. Emmeline and Richard, like many middle-class parents of their time, now decided that their two eldest daughters were of the age when they should have formal schooling. And as 'progressive' radicals, they decided to send the twelve-year-old Christabel and ten-year-old Sylvia not to a select, finishing school where they might be schooled in those accomplishments that would attract a suitor, but to the local high school, one of the more academic institutions for middle-class girls that were established during the late Victorian era.[2] When Adela heard that her sisters were to attend Southport High School for Girls, she begged to be allowed to be a pupil there too. Eventually Emmeline gave way, despite her misgivings that her eight-year-old daughter was too young for such formal instruction.[3] Now a housewife at home with her young son Harry and the loyal servant Susannah, without her shop and political meetings, and without the company of her sister, Mary, who had left to marry, Emmeline became 'utterly languid and depressed'.[4] Full-time motherhood had never fitted easily on her shoulders and more so now that it was thrust upon her in a quiet seaside town. Desiring a change of scene, the family moved for the summer of 1893 to rooms in a farmhouse in the pretty village of Disley, in Cheshire, some sixteen miles from Manchester. Here Emmeline seemed to regain some of her old vitality as she took the children on picnics, drove them around the countryside in a trap pulled by a temperamental donkey, named Jack, and helped with the haymaking. 'She seemed as young as ourselves', Sylvia recollected, urging the youngsters to collect the big berries almost out of reach, 'reckless of torn stockings and scratched arms.'[5]

The hunt for a new home in Manchester ended when Emmeline found 4 Buckingham Crescent, Daisy Bank Road, Victoria Park, a big, two-storey house in a block of four, facing fields. While the house was being made ready, the family stayed temporarily at 173 High Street, Oxford Road, Manchester where an Executive Committee meeting of the Women's Franchise League was held on 17 November 1893. At the small gathering, Emmeline, Richard, Alice Scatcherd and Ursula Bright eagerly endorsed the congratulations that had been sent to Walter McLaren and Charles Dilke, amongst others, who had helped to secure the passing of instructions to the Committee on Local Government that it had the power to insert provision for the enfranchisement of married women with appropriate qualifications, on the same basis as that for single women, for the purposes of the forthcoming Local Government Bill of 1894.[6] Ursula Bright had travelled up from London to attend this celebratory meeting, staying with the Pankhursts in their home. Although she and the other League members were jubilant at what they saw as 'their' victory for married women, she was soon expressing doubts to Emmeline that all their efforts might be in vain.[7] Such anxieties were later laid to rest; the Local Government Act, passed the following year, admitted married women to the local franchises on the same terms as single women.

Within the cosmopolitan life of the thriving city of Manchester, Emmeline found plenty of outlets for her renewed enthusiasm for political life. She became a member of the Executive Committee of the Manchester National Society for Women's Suffrage[8] which, since the death of Lydia Becker in 1890, no longer opposed the inclusion of married women in suffrage measures and was reinvigorated with the appointment of Esther Roper as the new secretary. In June 1894, as a leading member of this Society and also of the Women's Franchise League, she helped to organise a demonstration in the Manchester Free Trade Hall to support the women textile workers of Cheshire and Lancashire who were campaigning on behalf of the 'Special Appeal', a statement supported by a range of women who, despite their differing opinions on other political issues, were 'of one mind that the continued denial of the franchise to women, while it is at the same time being gradually extended amongst men, is at once unjust and expedient'.[9] During June, Emmeline also spoke for the Manchester Society at both open-air and indoor meetings alongside her husband and other enthusiasts.[10] And undoubtedly, although she lived in faraway Manchester, she responded to Ursula Bright's request to help all she could in mobilising support for a major suffrage meeting held in early June in the Queen's Hall, Langham Place, London.[11] 'Don't you come unless other business brings you', advised the older woman, affectionately. 'Save your poor strength as much as you can.' Ursula Bright also chided Emmeline for being fearful about financial losses she could face for a League meeting she was organising herself. '*Courage dear little woman* – & don't kill yourself – and don't hesitate to use my cheque if required.'[12]

Emmeline's work with the Manchester Society and the Women's Franchise League were not her only political outlets however. Both Emmeline and her husband were being increasingly drawn into socialist politics, especially through the warm, close friendship they had developed with Keir Hardie, a Scot of working-class origin. The Pankhursts had first met Hardie in 1888, at the International Labour Conference held in London where the confident, elegant and assured Emmeline probably 'dazzled' the man known for his outspoken support for trade unionism and socialism – and for his cloth cap.[13] The acquaintance was renewed the following year at the Paris International Socialist Congress. Emmeline and Richard were delighted when, three years later, Hardie was elected to parliament as a 'Labour' candidate for the constituency of West Ham South; his success was one of many influences that led to the creation of the Independent Labour Party (ILP) in Bradford in January 1893. When the ILP fought, and lost, its maiden parliamentary by-election at Attercliffe in July 1894, with Frank Smith as the candidate, Emmeline and Richard were amongst the campaigners alongside Keir Hardie, Tom Mann, Enid Stacey, Tom Taylor and James Murray of the Yorkshire Miners' Association.[14] 'I am afraid you are attempting far too much for your health', warned Ursula Bright.[15] Although tired from the campaigning, the idealist Emmeline was caught up in the enthusiasm of the developing socialist movement, seeing it as a means for 'righting every political and social wrong'.[16] She decided to join the ILP hoping that it would be a vehicle for improving the many disadvantages suffered by poor women and, in particular, that it would advocate the parliamentary vote for her sex.[17] Much to the disappointment of Ursula Bright, president of the Lancashire and Cheshire Union of the Women's Liberal Association, Emmeline thought about resigning from this organisation, of which she was an executive member. 'Must you leave the L. and C. U.?', Ursula Bright pleaded in early July 1894. 'These continual splits among women weaken us & you all seemed to be working so beautifully together for the meeting [at the Free Trade Hall].' She continued, 'You see how badly the L.P. were beaten at Attercliffe. They have not the sympathy of their own class. There *must* be something wrong in their modes of working. They are *too* violent and contemptuous of other people's methods.'[18] Ignoring the warnings of her older friend, Emmeline joined the ILP but waited a while before resigning from the Women's Liberal Association, probably out of affection for her. In the meantime, Emmeline's local ILP branch unanimously selected her as their candidate to stand for election to the Manchester School Board.[19] Immediately on hearing the news, Harriot Stanton Blatch could not restrain herself from offering a stream of practical advice. If she were standing for the School Board elections, she wrote on 25 July from her home in Basingstoke, she would cut the time devoted to sewing for girls in state elementary schools to the smallest amount. 'Working mothers will rise to the idea if you show how it is a mere case of class legislation.' Advocate drawing, geography and science for both sexes, she urged, as well as the raising of the school leaving age. 'Canvass, canvass … it brings surer success than public meetings.'[20] Whether Emmeline followed such advice we do not know, but she was unsuccessful in the ensuing November election although she topped the poll amongst the three ILP candidates, receiving 26,644 votes compared to 20,939 for J. Harker and 20,939 for J. Stewart.[21] Two months previously, she had finally resigned from the Lancashire and Cheshire Union of the Women's Liberal Association.[22] Emmeline had never forgiven the Liberal statesman William Ewart Gladstone for his opposition to women's suffrage and was only too glad to sever her links with the Liberal Party which she saw as a men's party that used the talents of Liberal women for its own ends. The members of the Women's Liberal Federation, she later recollected, had been given the promise that if they worked with Liberal men in party politics, they would soon earn the right to vote. 'The avidity with which the women swallowed this promise, left off working for themselves, and threw themselves into the men's work was amazing.'[23]

Richard, who had also left the Liberal Party, now followed Emmeline's lead in joining the ILP.[24] He had been hesitant to do so, worried about the effect it might have upon his legal practice.[25] When he formally announced in the press, in September 1894, that he had decided to join the South Manchester Branch of the ILP,[26] his fears were confirmed. Clients began to take their work elsewhere and Manchester City Council no longer required his services. The forthright Emmeline told an interviewer of a local socialist newspaper that since they had both allied themselves to the ILP they no longer received invitations to functions at the town hall.[27] Richard still gave unsparingly free legal advice to trade unions and other socialist groupings, but clearly this did not bring in any income. Furthermore, his health was now giving Emmeline increasing cause for concern. The previous year he had suffered digestive troubles and attained some relief by attending Smedley Hydro in Southport, a hydropathic establishment where water was applied externally to the body of the patient, but he had not been cured and the stomach pains had increased in intensity. A stickler for hard work and duty, Richard none the less continued his exhausting schedule of work and political life, often speaking at open-air ILP meetings with his pretty wife from whom he hid the extent of his suffering.[28]

Emmeline and Richard's home became a place well known for socialist sympathies and ILP speakers who came to Manchester, such as Keir Hardie, Bruce Glasier and his wife, Katherine St. John Conway, invariably stayed at 4 Buckingham Crescent. Although Christabel, Sylvia and Adela now attended Manchester High School for Girls where, as at their Southport school, their father insisted that they were excused from lessons in scripture, Emmeline set little store by the teaching. As she later told one interviewer, '[M]y daughters never went to school until they were about twelve, and then I'm not sure it did them much good. Of course they had some elementary teaching, but I want to develop their individuality above all things.'[29] Developing individuality in her daughters meant, above all else, encouraging them to participate in political life and to read, think and talk about big social issues. The children regularly read the socialist literature that came to the house and accompanied their parents when they spoke on the socialist cause in the deprived working-class districts of Manchester.[30] Emmeline's hopes for the future were now placed in the fledgling ILP and so in the autumn of 1894 she offered to stand for election as an ILP candidate for the Chorlton Board of Guardians in the poor district of

Openshaw. The Manchester Executive of the ILP readily endorsed her candidature and accurately predicted that Emmeline would 'do much good if returned, to humanise the administration of the Poor Law'.[31]

That winter there was a particularly high unemployment rate in Manchester causing immense distress among the working classes since there was no unemployment benefit nor relief for the 'able-bodied poor' from the Boards of Guardians, apart from entry to the dreaded workhouse; such a move was unacceptable to the majority of the unemployed and also impossible to implement since there were insufficient places to house the large number of needy men, women and children. While Keir Hardie, in the House of Commons, denounced the government for offering no help in such times, Emmeline and Richard took the lead in setting up a Committee for the Relief of the Unemployed with Richard acting as honorary secretary and Dr. Martin, who was also standing for election as a Poor Law Guardian, as honorary treasurer. A central office was opened in Deansgate and volunteers raised money through street collections, advertisements and subscriptions. Emmeline formed a women's sub-committee to focus on the needs of mothers and children and was particularly active in soliciting donations of food. Each morning she would drive to Shudehill Market to collect from the stallholders and city merchants free gifts of food which would then be made up into soup in large cooking pots. Later each day, in the bitter cold, from noon till two, she took her place on the lorry, handing out half pint mugs of the hot liquid and pieces of bread. At first about a thousand people were fed daily in Manchester's Stevenson Square, as well as large numbers in the districts of Ancoats, Gorton and Openshaw, but the numbers soon doubled. Meanwhile, Richard Pankhurst and Leonard Hall, a doctor's son, led deputations to Manchester City Council and the Boards of Guardians and sent resolutions to the government, demanding that local authorities should be empowered to acquire the necessary land and machinery that would enable them to provide work for the unemployed, at trade union rates, and that the powers and funds of Boards of Guardians should be extended so that they could give adequate relief.[32] At the height of this unrest, the popular Emmeline was returned as a Poor Law Guardian on 17 December 1894 for the distressed area of Openshaw. She headed the poll with 1,276 votes.[33] This was the first election for a post as a socialist and public representative that Emmeline had won and it was to prove a formative influence on her life.

At her first meeting at the Chorlton Board of Guardians, Emmeline immediately made her mark by presenting a resolution condemning the limited powers granted to such Boards by the local authorities and arguing that decisions in regard to relief should be placed instead with a special committee of the House of Commons. Her resolution had scarcely been defeated when a deputation of the unemployed, led by her husband and Leonard Hall, banged at the door of the Poor Law Offices. Some representatives were admitted and heated exchanges took place during which Emmeline, 'by turns passionate and persuasive', helped to calm and resolve the situation so that the Guardians hastily reversed their decision.[34] They now sent some of their own members to the City Council, pleading that work should be found for the unemployed and that joint action should be taken to prevent such crises occurring again. Emmeline's success in bringing about such unprecedented action revealed the extent of her political skills and her powers as a speaker. It also gave her an esteemed position on the Board of Guardians which she never lost.

As a Poor Law Guardian, Emmeline's compassion for the poor was stirred to its very depths. She was horrified at the conditions she found in the Chorlton Workhouse and could still vividly recollect the detail some twenty years later in her autobiography. Old men and women who were to end their days there sat huddled on backless benches that made their bodies ache. 'They had no privacy, no possession, not even a locker. The old women were without pockets in their gowns, so they were obliged to keep any poor little treasures they had in their bosoms.'[35] Little girls of seven and eight years old, clad summer and winter in thin cotton frocks with low necks and short sleeves, shivered as they scrubbed the cold stones of the long draughty corridors and frequently caught bronchitis. 'At night they wore nothing at all, night dresses being considered too good for paupers.'[36] Pregnant women, most of them very young, unmarried, poor servants did the hardest kind of work, including scrubbing, until their babies were born. After staying for a short confinement of two weeks in hospital, they faced the inevitable choice 'of staying in the workhouse and earning their living by scrubbing and other work, in which case they were separated from their babies; or … they could leave – leave with a two-weeks-old baby in their arms, without hope, without home, without money, without anywhere to go'.[37] Inefficiency and waste was rife in regard to the management of the hospital, insane asylum, school, farm, workshops and food. Each inmate was given daily a poor diet mainly consisting of a certain weight of bread, a large portion of which was left and fed to the pigs who did not thrive on stale bread and, therefore, fetched less when sold.

Emmeline, 'with sorrowful wrath and persuasive plea', did not ask for social reform but demanded it.[38] Always a practical woman, she suggested a number of solutions and, learning from her past political activities, formed alliances with other Guardians sympathetic to her cause. Fierce exchanges took place between Emmeline and the diehards, chief amongst whom was a boot merchant named Mainwaring; when he realised that his outbursts of rudeness were helping 'the charming Mrs. Pankhurst' to win supporters to her side, he tried to control himself by writing 'Keep your temper!' on the blotting paper before him.[39] But Emmeline and her reformers won the day. Within six months of her appointment as a Poor Law Guardian comfortable Windsor chairs with high backs were introduced for the elderly to sit on in the workhouse, and diet and dress changed. The bread was cut into slices and buttered with margarine, each person being allowed to eat as much as they desired, the surplus being made into puddings with milk and currants. Emmeline herself chose new material for dresses and bonnets for the girls and women and was also successful in persuading the Guardians to allow the inmates to go for outings in their own clothes rather than the degrading workhouse uniforms.[40] Reorganisation of the management of the hospital also took place. But it was especially the subsequent changes in regard to workhouse children, against whom Emmeline wished 'no stigma of pauperism' to apply, which warmed her heart.[41] Within five years land in the country had been bought for them and cottage homes built with a modern school, trained teachers, a gymnasium and a swimming bath. Looking back on this time in her life, Emmeline observed that it was her contact with the degraded and despised workhouse girls and women that were 'potent factors in my education as a militant'. She reflected, 'I thought I had been a suffragist before I became a Poor Law Guardian, but now I began to think about the vote in women's hands not only as a right but as a desperate necessity.'[42]

Emmeline's daily contact with the hardships of the destitute and the 'bitter humiliations and inadequacies' of both public and private charity made her acutely aware of the wider social changes that were needed to bring about a fairer and more equal society; knowing that her husband shared her world-view, she became even more determined to help him become an MP so that, along-side Keir Hardie, he could serve the common people.[43] She was, therefore, in high spirits when, in May 1895, Richard accepted the invitation by the ILP to stand as their parliamentary candidate for the district of Gorton, of which Openshaw was a part, in the general election to be held in July of that year. Gorton had been a Liberal seat and the retiring Liberal Member, Sir William Mather, urged his supporters to vote for Dr. Pankhurst as did the president of the local Liberal Association who withdrew from the contest in his favour. As in the Rotherhithe campaign some ten years earlier, the Manchester press reopened old debates about whether Liberal supporters should vote for the 'Red Doctor'. The local Liberal Association then attempted a compromise by suggesting that they would instruct their members to vote for Dr. Pankhurst if the ILP withdrew their candidate in a neighbouring constituency. The ILP refused to do so.

Fearing that her husband would be beaten again by a Tory candidate, Emmeline travelled in vain to see T. P. O'Connor in Liverpool to ask him for the Irish vote. 'We have nothing but admiration for your husband', he replied, 'but we cannot support the people he is mixed up with!' Richard's persistent plea to the voters – 'When Keir Hardie stood up in the House of Commons for the people, with a faithful, earnest, manly appeal, he stood alone ... are you not going to send other men to support him?' – made it quite clear who he was 'mixed up with'.[44] The average voter was highly suspicious of the unknown ILP, especially since it was led by an unconventional man who deliberately flouted tradition in the House of Commons.[45] That Emmeline did not attempt to persuade Richard to distance himself from Hardie says much about the strength of her commitment to socialism and to her friendship with the working-class MP; she merely 'knit her brows fiercely' in silence when voters caustically commented that 'the man with the cap' was her husband's 'leader'.[46]

Emmeline canvassed daily in Gorton, usually accompanied by Christabel and Sylvia, all three taking their meals in the humble, working-class homes of ILP supporters. At one open-air meeting in Openshaw she stood on a soap-box, almost in tears as she pleaded, 'You put me at the top of the poll; will you not vote for the man who has taught me all I know?'[47] But it was all to no avail. The news that Keir Hardie had lost his seat at West Ham, which polled before Gorton, was a severe blow and a warning to Emmeline of the ups and downs of political life.[48] On the evening of the Gorton poll, she did not give up the fight but bravely visited public houses imploring the drinking men to vote.[49] Richard polled 4,261 votes against 5,865 for Hatch, his Conservative opponent. Since he had made known that he could not afford to pay his election expenses, these had been borne by the ILP to the tune of £342; those of the successful candidate were £1,375. After the count, a despondent Emmeline and the children accompanied Richard to an ILP meeting where he gave a short speech. Much to Emmeline's embarrassment, Sylvia wept and could not stop, even when her father joked that, 'There was life in the old bird yet!' On returning home, she chided their daughter, although not in anger, for her outburst of emotion, saying that she had 'disgraced the family'.[50] Emmeline coped with her own bitter disappointment not with tears but with fighting back. The next day she hired a pony and trap and drove alone to Colne Valley to help another ILP candidate, Tom Mann. He too was defeated.[51] When she drove back through Gorton, late at night, some drunken Conservative supporters who had been celebrating the election victory recognised her and, in disgust, threw stones at her. The incident did nothing to lessen Emmeline's resolve to fight for the socialist cause.[52]

For some years, the ILP in the Manchester area had been holding summer open-air meetings in Boggart Hole Clough, an uncultivated space of some sixty-three acres recently acquire by Manchester City Corporation. The chair of the corporation's Parks Committee, Mr. Needham, who had previously stood in past council elections against John Harker, a prominent member of the Trades Council and a well-known ILP speaker, now decided to prohibit further ILP meetings in the Clough. The prohibition was ignored, and on Sunday, 17 May 1896, Harker was given a summons for holding a meeting on the grounds that he was guilty of occasioning an annoyance. Immediately, Richard Pankhurst took on the case but despite his plea that there was no by-law to limit the right of public meetings, Harker was found guilty and fined ten shillings, a judgment which Richard gave notice to appeal. Emmeline and other ILP members faithfully kept up the protest, organising meetings and insisting on the right of free speech in the parks as further prosecutions were issued. Although collections of money were not allowed to be made at such meetings, on 7 June, when a crowd of about 4,000 gathered to hear Leonard Hall, Emmeline defied the ruling by sticking the ferrule of her open umbrella into the ground in order for sympathetic listeners to donate their pennies. Summoned to appear before the Manchester Police Court along with Hall and seven others believed to be associated with the meeting, she appeared on 12 June looking assured and composed, her long slender fingers clad in black gloves resting on the rail of the dock before her, an elegant pink straw bonnet on her head.[53] Her fellow 'conspirators' were all men and included, besides Harker and Hall, George Vomers, labourer; Charles Brierley, brass moulder; Samuel Smalley, insurance agent; William Tweedale, farmer; Charles Moss, furniture broker and John Hempshall, traveller.[54] Speaking in her own defence, the defiant Emmeline announced that she would pay no fine and would continue to speak at the Clough as long as she was permitted to be at large. Two of the men who also refused to pay their fines, namely Harker and Hall, were sent to prison for one month but the case against Emmeline was continually adjourned. Remaining free, Emmeline took over the leadership role of chair for the meetings that continued to take place Sunday after Sunday. She spoke enthusiastically to the crowds, which might number 15,000, her pink bonnet visible from a distance; since it rapidly faded in the summer sun, she made it anew time and time again.[55] On one such occasion, 21 June 1896, Bruce Glasier noted in this diary that the scene at the Clough was 'a magnificent sight ... Mrs. Pankhurst's ... words rang clearly thro the dell ... she passed out of Park gates with an enthusiastic crowd in her train.' When she had her name taken by the authorities, Emmeline expressed her determination to go to prison rather than pay any fine.[56] But although the fine remained unpaid, she was never sent to prison probably because the magistrate feared the indignation of the public if he treated a middle-class woman in such a manner.[57] When interviewed for *The Labour Leader*, the ILP weekly edited by Hardie, the question of whether she was prepared to go to prison was pursued again. 'Oh, yes, quite', replied Emmeline emphatically. 'It wouldn't be so very dreadful, you know, and it would be a valuable experience.' She explained how she was able to go to prison without the hardships of most of the other women she knew. 'I have had quite a number of offers of help in the housekeeping, and so on, from relatives, and though they are not at all Socialists they are quite indignant at this persecution.'[58]

At another Sunday meeting held on a sunny day in early July, Emmeline and Richard, accompanied by their children, drove up to the gates of the Clough in an open barouche, Keir Hardie and Mary Goulden occupying seats in the same conveyance. On arriving at the gates, Emmeline and Hardie walked together to the meeting place, smiling and acknowledging the cheers of the crowd of about 50,000 that echoed around the ravine. Emmeline flourished on the experience, enjoying the rapport with the good-natured listeners. 'Stipendiary Headlam adjourned the cases for a week to see what would happen to-day', she told her sympathetic audience. 'What happens is that I and the other women who were before him on Friday are here doing that same thing as we were accused of doing before.' More cheering broke out. Emmeline waited for the noise to subside before she continued. 'Councillor Needham's friends say he is being boycotted. We as Socialists can sympathise with anyone who is boycotted. We know from painful experience what it means.' After another great cheer, someone shouted 'Dr. Pankhurst', and Emmeline explained how her husband, who had been in the vanguard of the democratic movement for twenty-five years, knew what it was to be boycotted. After she had finished her address, Keir Hardie then spoke, amid much cheering too.[59] Emmeline was present again at the evening welcome meeting, held on 11 July, to celebrate the release of Leonard Hall, earlier that day. She sat next to Hall in a wagonette as a brass band led the way to Manchester's Stevenson Square. When Fred Brocklehurst, president of the Manchester ILP, was released one week later, all her family were among the guests invited to the ceremonial breakfast.[60] As we shall later see, brass bands and welcome breakfasts would become important aspects of the ceremonial pageantry of the WSPU.

As the protests over the right of free speech showed no sign of abating, Manchester City Council attempted to gain control of the situation by passing in August a new law prohibiting all meetings in the parks except by the special authorisation of its Parks Committee – which meant that permission would be denied to the ILP. The new ruling was yet again ignored and the situation only resolved when the Home Secretary put pressure on the City Council to adopt another new by-law and to give an undertaking that no reasonable application for the use of parks for public meetings be denied. Emmeline and other ILPers rejoiced in the news while the Manchester Law Students' Society in their annual mock trial at the Assize Courts parodied the events by presenting a 'Mrs. Chorlton Board' and a 'Dr. Blank Hurst' who supported a 'Swear Hardie' in his claims for £100,000 damages for an assault in 'Winterhill Clough'.[61] But despite such good-natured humour, nothing could detract from Emmeline's role as the heroine of the socialist struggle for the right of free speech in Boggart Hole Clough. She never forgot the political lessons she learnt in the struggle, of drawing upon popular support and standing firm, as ways to secure a victory when one was sure that the cause was just.

But fame in the Clough and devotion to a cause could also have a downside, especially for a wife and mother with four children. While the confident Christabel remembered these Manchester years as the best of all in their private family life,[62] Harry and Adela often felt neglected and unloved by their frequently absent parents. 'I have often see my brother Harry, with little white face ... as though turned to stone', Sylvia wrote. A solitary child, he was slow at learning, something that must have worried his parents.[63] The plump Adela, feeling that she was ignored by her parents, decided to run away from school. Brought back home by the kindly headmistress, she refused to speak. According to her biographer, the unhappy Adela was in the throes of a nervous breakdown and spent a year away from school, followed by a holiday with her aunt Bess in Aberdeen. Emmeline and Richard were as kind and understanding as they could be, the elderly father reading poetry to his distressed child, the anxious mother playing the piano. Soothed by these and other attentions, Adela slowly recovered and returned to school a much more contented child. But her breakdown, insists Coleman, was an index of her 'emotional fragility'.[64]

In addition to these family worries, Emmeline also had to face increasing financial difficulties. Richard's prominent role as defence lawyer in the Boggart Hole Clough agitation plus that fact that he had been elected earlier in 1896 as a member of the National Administrative Council (NAC) of the ILP caused, yet again, a fall in demand for his legal services. Financial worries meant, of course, that money would be spared only for what was considered important, namely political activities rather than holidays and recreation or expensive clothes. Thus at the beginning of autumn that year, Emmeline travelled to Bradford for its municipal and parliamentary elections, speaking alongside Keir Hardie. On Saturday, 24 October, she dined with other ILP members at the home of Margaret McMillan, a socialist stalwart in the Bradford area, and was described by one of the guests as 'lively as a cricket, full of clever comment, criticism and scandal'.[65] Similarly she and Richard did not hesitate when asked by Tom Mann to travel to Antwerp to protest against the imprisonment by the Belgian government of Ben Tillett for trade union activities. Open-air protests, held with James Sexton, were dispersed by the police who also arrived soon after an indoor meeting had been held. Although Sexton was subsequently arrested and deported, the same fate did not befall Emmeline and Richard.[66] The excitement of such political life must have contrasted sharply with the more mundane family activities that Emmeline engaged in that year, including attending the christening of her goddaughter, Nell Hall Humpherson's sister.[67]

The New Year of 1897 saw Emmeline continuing her usual range of social and political activities, including the 'unique feat for I.L.Pers' of being returned unopposed to the Chorlton Board of Guardians, an honour she shared with Dr. Martin.[68] Emmeline's happiness at her success was marred, however, by worries about Richard's health; the severe pains in his stomach were becoming more frequent. Deciding that the country air might help to restore him to full health, she searched for a suitable residence and eventually found Vale Wood Farm in Mobberley, Cheshire. Here the family, uprooted once more, stayed from the spring to the autumn of 1897. Richard travelled by train to Manchester each day where his legal practice was based and Christabel, who was studying logic, French and dressmaking, accompanied him several times a week. The younger children no longer attended school.[69] Yet even in the peace and quiet of the country, Emmeline and Richard could not desert their deep commitment to the socialist cause nor to those financially worse off than themselves. In particular, the imprisonment of Leonard Hall, one of the Clough protesters, had left his pregnant wife and their family destitute. Although the ILP eventually offered some financial help, it was inadequate. On his release, Hall became seriously ill, largely as a result of the anxieties he had suffered, and a fund was set up for his family. Emmeline and Richard decided to help by offering the proceeds of one hundred picnic teas, at a charge of one shilling each, to members of the ILP and of the highly popular cycling clubs associated with the socialist newspaper The Clarion, edited by Robert Blatchford; the day fixed for the great event at Vale Wood Farm was Whit Sunday, 12 June 1897.[70]

Although Emmeline continued with the Poor Law work, even giving a joint paper with another woman Guardian, Mrs. Sale, at the September 1897 Northern Poor Law Conference,[71] Richard and his troubles were increasingly occupying her time. She gave her full support to her husband when attempts were made by some Manchester City Councillors to buy off his opposition to a costly and unnecessary culvert scheme to dispose of sewage. Richard's fight had been going on for about one year; he had written a number of letters to the press, condemning the scheme, and also led a deputation to the town hall to protest against misleading propaganda. In September 1897 some City Councillors intimated to him that if he accepted the culvert scheme, he would be retained as Counsel for the Corporation in the private bill necessary to get the scheme through parliament, whereby he would be paid a fee of about £10,000. That such a consideration 'weighed with him not a straw',[72] despite his financial worries, was a view that Emmeline ardently shared. She admired her husband's integrity and idealism and had no patience with the humbug and seedy side of local politics. When the Lord Mayor of Manchester demanded that a poll of the ratepayers be taken on the issue, the result was 20,528 for the culvert and 49,069 against.[73] It was a great victory for Richard about which Emmeline and the children felt justly proud, despite their financial difficulties. But out of the hearing of his children, Richard shared with Emmeline his regrets that he could not do more to realise his ideals nor to eliminate those 'social evils' which people from all strata of society were 'openly condemning and attacking'.[74]

5

WIDOWHOOD AND
EMPLOYMENT
(1898–FEBRUARY 1903)

Richard's health seemed to improve with the country air on the farm in Mobberley and so the whole family returned to their Manchester home during the autumn of 1897. Emmeline continued with her Poor Law and ILP work, and was soon back into her energetic routine again. Since the Boggart Hole Clough protest, her standing within socialist circles had been high and an indication of her popularity became apparent the following Easter when she was elected a member of the National Administrative Council (NAC) of the ILP, the only 'lady', as the *Labour Leader* termed it, to be so honoured.[1] But politics aside, Emmeline and Richard now had to make a number of decisions about their children, especially about the future for their two eldest daughters.

The artistic Sylvia was given every encouragement to develop her talent and so Emmeline and Richard arranged that by the following summer she should study with Elias Bancroft, a well-known Manchester artist, who lived down the other end of Buckingham Crescent. The bookish Christabel, on the other hand, was undecided as to her future career. Some years previously she had decided against becoming a professional ballet dancer, much to her mother's disappointment, and nothing else had replaced this early enthusiasm.[2] As no firm decision had been made about Christabel's future direction, the matter had been left in abeyance. Now that she was seventeen years old, however, approaching eighteen, it seemed a good idea to honour an agreement that Emmeline and Noémie Rochefort had made many years ago, that if they ever married and had daughters, they should exchange them for a year so that each child could learn the French or English language and the different ways, as the case might be. It was agreed that in June 1898 Emmeline would take Christabel to Geneva, where Noémie now lived, and bring Lillie back to Manchester. The weeks of preparation before the trip were a happy time for Emmeline; she busied herself with dressmaking, anxious that her graceful daughter should appear in elegant clothes of which she could be proud.[3] On the day of their departure, Richard said his tender goodbyes before leaving for the office. Emmeline suddenly panicked. Knowing of Richard's poor state of health she threw her arms around him, crying terms of endearment, 'gripped by a sudden fear'. Then she composed herself and brushed her fears away. Later, when it was time for mother and daughter to leave, Emmeline pleaded to Sylvia, 'Look after Father!', a charge that the sixteen-year-old took very seriously since she idolised the man.[4]

Once the train journey had begun, Emmeline began to relax and take an interest in the places they passed through, especially Paris; she had long wanted to show Christabel the city where she had studied and which she loved. But the daughter was less enchanted with Paris than the mother. 'Christabel takes it all with her usual calm', Emmeline wrote back to Richard.[5] Once in Switzerland, Emmeline and Christabel travelled to Corsier where Noémie was holidaying. Here they spent sunny days relaxing by the lake, rowing, motoring and enjoying the scenery. One day, when Christabel sat writing to Sylvia, Emmeline asked her to include a message – 'Mother says will you make a parcel of "Studios" & put some drawings of your own in – some of your charcoal things etc. Also you must not ride too much on your bicycle.'[6] Emmeline, like any mother, was keen for others to see the work of her talented, artistic daughter, and also anxious that Sylvia, a less accomplished cyclist than Christabel, should not run the risk of another accident.[7] A letter from Richard to his wife, the last she was ever to receive from him, spoke loving words. 'When you return, we will have a new honeymoon and reconsecrate each to the other in unity of heart.'[8]

One day soon afterwards, at tea-time in the garden at Corsier, a telegram addressed to Emmeline arrived. It was from Richard. 'I am not well. Please come home.'[9] In an agitated state of mind, Emmeline left immediately leaving Christabel behind. On the train from London to Manchester, on 5 July 1898, someone entered Emmeline's compartment and opened an evening newspaper. She saw a black border and read of the death of her own husband. In deep shock, Emmeline cried out as the passengers tried to comfort her.

Arriving home well after midnight, Emmeline found in the house not only the children and Ellen, the nursemaid, but also her brother, Herbert, her sister, Mary, and Susannah, both of the latter now married. The visitors had come to comfort the children and help, generally. The thirteen-year-old Adela and eight-year-old Harry were in bed but Sylvia, who had just turned sixteen, was still up. And it was especially the ashen-faced Sylvia, who had waited for her mother to arrive, that the grief-stricken Emmeline held closest to her. Sylvia had longed for Emmeline to return yet dreaded it. 'Mother, I did not send for you; I did not get a doctor till Sunday.'[10] Emmeline murmured no reproach since she was anxious for her daughter, the responsibility she had borne and the shock she had endured. Although Adela and Harry had been brought to see their sick father, they had left for school before he passed away. It was Sylvia who had been in the room when Richard had died, holding the oxygen tube that he needed to make his breathing easier.[11] Later that day, Emmeline registered the death of her fifty-eight-year-old husband from a gastric ulcer which had perforated his stomach. Under the category of description of informant she wrote 'Widow of deceased'. She was forty years old.

Emmeline was heartbroken. She and Richard had been comrades in struggling causes for nineteen years, and devoted to each other. Now all was gone.

Overwhelmed in her grief, Emmeline felt an indescribable loneliness. The tragic look that overcast her face at this sad time never quite left her through all the ensuing years, observed Christabel.[12] In the *Labour Leader*, Keir Hardie offered comforting words, speaking of the warm sympathy thousands of men and women felt towards Mrs. Pankhurst and her children. They have the consolation of knowing, he pointed out, that he whom they mourn 'has left behind a memory for integrity and courage which is priceless. ... A scholar, a gentleman, a brilliant conversationalist, a faithful friend, an affectionate father, Dr. Pankhurst has gone from our midst, and our movement and the world are the poorer for his loss.'[13] On Saturday 9 July, Emmeline and her children headed the funeral cortège which left Victoria Park accompanied by a large deputation from the ILP and a contingent of the Clarion Cycling Club, all wearing white rosettes. The deputation left the procession at Old Trafford, proceeding by train to Brooklands Cemetery which the rest of the procession reached at half past three. After the coffin was lowered into the ground, a number of addresses were given. Fred Bocklehurst began by saying that, in the absence of a religious service, he had been asked to say a few words. In his tribute he observed that Richard Pankhurst had been a student of social questions and an exponent of the problems they raised, long before it was fashionable to live in the slums and labour politics became the serious thought of learned men. Alice Cliff Scatcherd then spoke, emphasising that it would not be fitting that no woman's voice should be heard on this occasion. There was no aspect of the women's movement in which Dr. Pankhurst had not taken a noble part, she commented, and the progress that women had made towards freedom was very largely due to his influence. He had said to her, over and over again that 'if women did not protest now they would regret it hereafter, because they would never succeed'. Women had protested, she insisted, although it appeared hopeless. 'To those women who mourn him ... he would always be an inspiring memory', she concluded. Leonard Hall and the Rev. T. Horne, a personal friend of the Pankhursts and chaplain to the Chorlton Workhouse, also gave addresses, as did Bruce Glasier who had been asked to do so by Emmeline – although Glasier later privately recorded that he thought the graveside speeches 'very unsuitable', with the exception of his own few 'simple words'! After the funeral, he called on Emmeline who expressed anxiety about her future.[14] Keir Hardie was not there for Emmeline to talk to. He had desperately wanted to attend the funeral but had to travel to Scotland to console his wife over the recent death of her mother.[15] Emmeline had the words 'Faithful and true and my loving comrade' engraved on Richard's tombstone; they were words from the poet Walt Whitman that Richard had frequently read to his family.[16]

Emmeline now faced the sad task of issuing through the press warm thanks to all who had sent her and the children letters of sympathy,[17] as well as writing to personal friends, such as the Glasiers. On 12 July she wrote on black-bordered paper to Katherine Glasier, thanking her for her loving words and also expressing gratitude to her husband. She continued:

I cannot write about my loss. You can understand can you not? Will you come & see me soon both of you & the baby dear. He loved you both.

There is much I should like to talk over with you. What to do with books & papers & co. Can you help me? I am struggling with them for I will have no strange hand touch them. You shared his tastes & he would like you here. Am I asking too much. If so do tell me? I shall not mind.[18]

The Glasiers and their baby visited Emmeline a week later and on 23 July Bruce Glasier kindly accompanied her to a meeting in Manchester of the NAC of the ILP.[19]

Christabel, who remained in Switzerland, as her mother wished, communicated with home by letter; as the eldest daughter in the family she expected that her role would be to help her mother and waited to hear what Emmeline thought she should do.[20] With her favourite daughter so far away, Emmeline clung to Sylvia, who now became her mother's closest confidante.[21] Since she could not bear to sleep alone, Sylvia shared her bed; they spent many sleepless nights together, talking about their sorrows into the small hours.[22] Above all what worried Emmeline was how she could support herself and her four financially dependent children, and give her daughters, who were much older than Harry, those opportunities whereby they could earn a living in a job of their choice. Richard had left no will; he had little to leave anyway. A few share certificates, of a face value of under £1,000, must have been worth very little since they were not sold.[23] What he did leave his widow were the debts which he had been struggling for years to liquidate and which Emmeline, with her 'strong, self-reliant nature',[24] was determined to settle. Rejecting a proposal from her solicitor which would lighten her burden at the expense of the creditors, she decided that the only way for the outstanding bills to be settled was by moving to a smaller house, selling the furniture, paintings and books, and economising generally. Her financial plight did not go unnoticed. Robert Blatchford issued in the *Clarion* an appeal to his largely working-class readers for donations to a special fund, a suggestion that Emmeline hastily rejected pointing out that she did not wish working people to subscribe to the education of her children when they could not afford to pay for their own. Instead she urged that any money raised should go towards the cost of building a hall for socialist meetings, in her husband's name.[25] Suggestions by some wealthier people for a 'Dr. Pankhurst Fund' that would perpetuate his memory by raising 'a substantial sum of money and presenting it to Mrs. Pankhurst as a mark of the high regard in which her worthy husband was held' were more successful; a committee was established for this sole purpose with W. H. Dixon and John J. Graham as Honorary Treasurer and Honorary Secretary, respectively.[26] By 17 August, nearly £935 had been collected, including £50 subscribed by Jacob and Ursula Bright, £25 each by Alice Cliff Scatcherd and Mrs. Rose Hyland, ten guineas by well-known local figures, such as Alderman Robert Gibson, the Lord Mayor of Manchester, and £1 from Sir Charles Dilke.[27] Although this fund offered some supplementary help to Emmeline, its administration over the coming years caused her to feel very bitter, as though she and her children were objects of charity.

Emmeline knew that, despite the existence of the fund, she would now have to find employment and so resigned on 30 August from her unpaid, time-consuming work as a Poor Law Guardian.[28] Like so many middle-class women of the Victorian age, she had not been trained for any occupational work and so could think of no other way to earn a living than setting up in business again, despite her earlier failures. Christabel thought her mother's talents wasted in such a project. 'You are so clever', she wrote, 'that it seems strange that there is not something more suited to you.'[29] Initially, Emmeline hoped to establish a dressmaking business but finally decided on opening another shop, like Emerson's, that would sell silks, cushions and artistic wares.

Eager to keep herself busy, Emmeline and her sister, Mary, now Mrs. Clarke, made about two dozen cushion covers, ready for the new shop. They had barely finished the task when the Chorlton Board of Guardians offered Emmeline the salaried post of Registrar of Births and Deaths which had become vacant in a working-class district. Gratefully, she accepted the offer; now she would have both a steady income and a pension on retirement. A humbler house had to be found which would include a suitable room for the registry and eventually Emmeline rented 62 Nelson Street, off Oxford Road, which was filled with cheap, American furniture.[30] She did not abandon, however, the idea of opening a shop and acquired premises for this in the centre of Manchester, in King Street; in addition to the extra income the shop would bring, Emmeline hoped it could be a means of employment for Christabel when she returned from Switzerland.[31] In contrast to Christabel, both Sylvia and Adela now seemed to have their future means of earning a living settled, without too much cost to Emmeline's pocket. Emmeline had recently invited Charles Rowley into her home, to value some paintings she needed to sell; he saw, at the same time, some still life groups that Sylvia had drawn and realising her potential, sent the drawings to the Manchester Municipal School of Art which offered the talented young woman a free studentship.[32] Adela, who wanted to be a teacher, was still at the Manchester High School for Girls, the fees for which Emmeline could no longer afford. It was a relief to Emmeline when a friend advised that her daughter could train free at the lower status, state-aided Ducie Avenue Higher Grade Board School, a chance at which Adela 'jumped'.[33]

By the time of the late November meeting of the NAC of the ILP, which Emmeline attended accompanied by Keir Hardie and Bruce Glasier, the family were settled in their new home, but it was a home of 'distressful atmosphere'.[34] Emmeline, in her deep grief, was taking on more than she could cope with while feeling that her happiness had been destroyed. She was frequently laid low with attacks of migraine during which the kind-hearted Ellen looked after her. Her heart was no longer in public affairs and politics and she had no interest any more in music or in singing.[35] Mary, who had left her unhappy marriage and now lived at 62 Nelson Street, tried to console Emmeline as did Herbert Goulden, Emmeline's brother, who also now lived with the bereaved family, sharing household expenses. Sylvia too was not in good health since she suffered with nervous depression and neuralgia in the head and arms as a result of the traumatic circumstances surrounding her father's death; consequently, she was frequently absent from the first year of her college course. Feeling guilty about holding a free studentship under such circumstances, she persuaded her financially stricken mother to pay her part-time fees for the second year of study although she was awarded another scholarship for the final year.[36] But the sorrow in the household seemed particularly to affect the two youngest children. Harry, a sensitive child, developed acute and permanent astigmatism after catching chicken-pox and then measles. His Uncle Herbert, suspecting that the unhappy boy was playing truant from school, followed him one day and discovered that his nephew was slinking off to railway stations to watch the trains. Deeply worried about what to do for her son, Emmeline consulted a doctor who advised that nothing was wrong apart from the boy's nervousness and lack of self-control.[37] She decided that it was best to remove Harry to another school and then, later, to the Higher Grade Board School.

Adela was also a worry for the heart-broken Emmeline. When she left the High School for the dirty and noisy Ducie Avenue Board School, she became cut off from her friends. 'My health and nerves could not stand it', Adela later wrote, 'and I soon began to be unhappy at home, where gloom descended upon us.' To make matters worse, her head became infected with lice. Emmeline was firmly told by her sister, Ada, by whom she hated to be criticised, that the school was 'unsuitable' for her niece. Eventually Adela went back to the academic High School where the new headmistress, Sara Burstall, encouraged her interest in history.[38]

By now Christabel had returned from Geneva and regained her place as Emmeline's closest confidante, a situation that must have been difficult for the displaced Sylvia to cope with. Emmeline enjoyed the comfort of having her eldest daughter by her side each day in the shop; while Christabel had been away, she had employed shop assistants to cover the hours she could not be at Emerson's, due to her work as a Registrar.[39] The working-class women who came to register births and deaths were glad, wrote Emmeline in her autobiography, to have a woman registrar to talk to. But the dreadful stories she was told, with patient and uncomplaining pathos, were tales she would never forget:

> Even after my experience on the Board of Guardians, I was shocked to be reminded over and over again of the little respect there was in the world for women and children. I have had little girls of thirteen come to my office to register the births of their babies, illegitimate, of course. In many of these cases I found that the child's own father or some near

56

male relative was responsible for her state. There was nothing that could be done in most cases. The age of consent in England is sixteen years, but a man can always claim that he thought the girl was over sixteen.[40]

Such stories confirmed for Emmeline what she already knew, that social reform and the parliamentary vote for women were urgently needed in order for women to have a fairer deal in society.

Since Richard's death, Emmeline had always kept alive a spark of her interest in political activities, especially through her membership of the ILP, and now, in the autumn of 1899, her old fire began to rekindle on the outbreak of the Boer War in South Africa. She saw Britain as an imperialist aggressor, bullying a small community of Dutch settler farmers who were defending their homes and land. The Fabian Society's refusal to oppose the war made her so angry that, with a group of fifteen others, she resigned her membership in March 1900. Her brother, Harold, an actor, was touring South Africa when the war broke out, and when he returned home, his tales of the atrocities further aroused Emmeline's ire. Her opposition to the war, reiterated by her children, brought some reprisals. Harry was fiercely attacked outside the school gates by some of his fellow pupils for arguing for peace; his schoolmaster found him unconscious on the roadside and carried his limp form home. Adela, for a similar stand, was struck in the face by a book thrown at her by a girl in her class at the High School; although a teacher saw the incident, no reprimand was given. Sylvia, in a report for the School of Art magazine on a lecture given by Walter Crane, innocently included his comments on Britannia's trident, 'Let her be as careful to respect the liberties of others as she is in safeguarding her own!' Another student not only demanded that the objectionable essay be deleted but also threatened to break the windows of 62 Nelson Street.[41]

Despite such unpleasant incidences, Emmeline would not relent in her stand. Her gradual return to political life became further noticeable during the general election of 1900. One October afternoon, the elderly Mrs. Rose Hyland came into the shop and told her, 'Keir Hardie is elected for Merthyr Tydfil.' Elated by such news, Emmeline hugged and kissed the astonished woman, crying out, 'That is for bringing the news! He is a good man.' Later she wrote to the newly elected MP, 'Parliament will be more interesting to us now.'[42] Emmeline was pleased when, as part of his victory tour, Hardie came to Manchester's Free Trade Hall in late October and spoke on the Boer War. With other members of the NAC, including Bruce Glasier and Ramsay MacDonald, they all dined together at the Wheatsheaf Hotel.[43] Earlier, Emmeline had been asked to stand again as an ILP candidate in the November elections for the Manchester School Board, and had agreed. This time she was successful.

Emmeline's experiences as an educational representative strengthened her feminist convictions. She was indignant when she discovered, as a member of the Manchester School Board, that male teachers in comparison with their female counterparts had 'all the advantage'.[44] The men had higher salaries than the women, many of whom, in addition to their regular class work, had to teach sewing and domestic subjects, without extra pay. She remained a member of the Board until 31 March 1903 when school boards were abolished by the 1902 Education Act. Emmeline felt it was an insult to women representatives, such as herself, that women were not eligible for election to the local education authorities (LEAs), the new bodies that replaced the school boards. That women should be barred from such representation in local government, despite the struggles for such entry over the last twenty years, was galling to her and yet another indication of women's secondary status when they lacked the parliamentary vote. Under pressure from the Women's Local Government Society and the National Union of Women Workers, the government gave way and agreed to require LEAs to co-opt women members. By such a process, Emmeline, who was strongly recommended by the ILP, became a co-opted member of the education committee on 1 April 1903, a post she held for just over four years. Appointed to the Committee on Technical Instruction, she learnt, yet again, of the disadvantages that women experienced in comparison with men. Thus the Manchester Technical College, considered the second best in Europe, spent thousands of pounds annually on technical training for men with practically no provision for women. Even classes in which women might easily have been admitted, such as bakery and confectionery, excluded them because the men's trade unions objected to their being educated for such skilled work.[45] 'It was rapidly becoming clear in my mind', Emmeline wrote of this time in her life, 'that men regarded women as a servant class in the community, and that women were going to remain in the servant class until they lifted themselves out of it.'[46]

By the time of the 1902 ILP Annual Conference, Emmeline was determined to bring forward a motion that linked the demand for women's voting rights to the necessity for social reform. Thus after the much cheered Keir Hardie had given his report on his parliamentary work, she moved a resolution that 'in order to improve the economic and social condition of women it is necessary to take immediate steps to secure the granting of the suffrage to women on the same terms on which it is or may be granted to men'. The resolution was seconded by Mr. Jowett of Bradford and carried unanimously.[47] Emmeline's success, on this occasion, and involvement in ILP politics at the local level,[48] must have been somewhat dampened in what was becoming an increasing source of irritation to her – the administration of the fund, set up after Richard's death for the welfare of her children.

On 18 July 1902 she wrote a short, brisk note to Mr. Nodal, a Stockport newspaper proprietor and one of the administrators of the fund, complaining about the way she was being treated. 'I enclose a cheque [for] £10 for rent of furniture. I wish to again point out that the arrears are due to no fault of mine. No demand has ever been made either for rent or insurance receipts.' Indignantly, Emmeline then refuted a claim that she had lied. 'My daughter tells me that a statement has been made that I did not send receipts for monthly payments. This is not true. I should prefer in future to pay the rent for furniture quarterly.'[49] Emmeline felt particularly upset about the manner in which members of the committee, especially the Honorary Secretary and Honorary Treasurer, had asked for information about the ages of her children and what they were doing, and had refused to communicate with them; instead she included the necessary information in her letter to Mr. Nodal. Two days later, she wrote again to Mr. Nodal, thanking him for his reply and suggesting it would be fine if she received the cheque before the end of the month. 'All I want', she stated wearily, 'is that the children's money shall be regularly paid & the original arrangement carried out.'[50]

Such matters, although of utmost importance for the welfare of her children, paled into insignificance in regard to the larger social reforms for which Emmeline had campaigned in the past. And now it was Christabel who spurred her mother on again. Christabel, a studious young woman, hated working at Emerson's; her able mind was not stretched by the monotonous tasks she had to do.[51] Seeing her unhappiness, Emmeline had suggested that she attended some classes at Owens College, part of Victoria (later Manchester) University. It was after one lecture there that she met Esther Roper, secretary of the North of England Society for Women's Suffrage and also a committee member of the NUWSS. Christabel had soon developed a friendship with Esther Roper and her companion Eva Gore-Booth, secretary of the Manchester Women's Trade Council, and was drawn into their campaigns to win the vote for working women. The latter cause held a particular appeal for Emmeline. Since Richard's death she had been a working woman herself and a single parent, struggling financially to bring up a family; she also knew, only too well, through her work as a Poor Law Guardian and as a Registrar, about the wretchedness of life for poor working-class women, eking out a miserable existence on wages that were much lower than those paid to their menfolk. By late November 1901, Emmeline, like Christabel, was a subscriber to the North of England Society for Women's Suffrage and by the summer of 1902 she was speaking alongside Eva Gore-Booth, Esther Roper and Christabel at meetings in Lancashire, organised under its auspices.[52] This was part of a successful campaign, sponsored by the Labour Representation Committee, to get David Shackleton elected to parliament in the hope that he would continue the fight for women's suffrage in the House of Commons. Shackleton was returned as the MP for the Clitheroe division in early August.[53]

Following on from this success, Emmeline was soon involved in family matters again, a pattern that had characterised her life in the past and would continue to do so, in the future. She had felt 'triumphant' when, earlier in the year, Sylvia had won a National Silver Medal for designs for mosaic, a Primrose Medal, and the highest prize open to students at her college, namely the Proctor Travelling Studentship, a vacation scholarship that enabled its holder to make a short trip abroad.[54] After some deliberation, Sylvia decided to study mosaics in Venice and frescoes in Florence, and Emmeline accompanied her that August as far as Geneva where the two would spend a month with Noémie Dufaux. En route via Bruges, Emmeline was like a young woman again, delighting in the smell of the ground coffee, the fresh bread rolls, the beautiful paintings and the wonderful architecture, as though it was her first time abroad. 'We were so happy together', recollected Sylvia. In Brussels Emmeline indulged in one of her favourite pastimes, shopping, and bought a hat for each member of the family. When some small mischievous German boys woke up a Swiss governess who was gently dozing, she declared them typical of their race. As memories of her Paris schooldays flooded back into her mind, she commiserated with the governess, telling her about how badly the Germans had treated the French after the Franco-German war.[55]

After a stay with the Dufaux family, Emmeline and Noémie accompanied Sylvia to Venice where they took great delight in buying large quantities of glass for selling in Emerson's. Leaving her daughter behind in an unknown city was not an easy task for Emmeline since the emotional Sylvia could not stop weeping, but Emmeline was comforted by the knowledge that Sylvia was staying with a sensible, middle-aged woman from Manchester who was herself studying in Venice, and lived as the guest of a Polish Countess.[56]

Back home in Manchester, Emmeline soon became embroiled again in another dispute with the male administrators of the Dr. Pankhurst Fund who had passed a resolution that from the 31 December 1902 the allowance to herself for the maintenance and education of her children should be reduced to £50 per annum (payable monthly) until further notice. Emmeline was outraged since she was dependent upon the money for her children's prospects. In late November, she wrote to Nodal again, stating that she assumed he was not present at the meeting since the resolution had been passed unanimously. 'I feel too indignant for expression at this action', she complained bitterly. She pointed out that the subscribers would have handed over the whole amount collected had she not desired that it should be dealt with as they had finally arranged. In a scathing attack, she went on:

> My whole expenses are based on the annual payment as first arranged.
>
> I am sending 15/- per week to my daughter who is studying Art in Venice & who will remain there and afterwards at Florence for some time.
>
> I must insist that I must have at least the regular £8-6-8 per month in order that she may remain there & my third daughter continue at the High School preparatory to going to the College. ... I should have thought (had I been a man) there was something to be encouraged if I saw a woman trying to do the work of a man as well as what is usually thought a woman's & striving to give her children the same opportunities that their father would have done.
>
> It seems however that my crime is that of being too independent.
>
> I feel now that I cannot let this matter go on any further. Either I shall decline to take any more money from the Committee & state

my case to the subscribers or the balance must be paid over to me to deal with.

After all the money is the children's & surely I & they know best how to deal with it.

It is now when none of them, but one is earning that the money is needed.

I shall most certainly much as I hate the whole humiliating business not allow the money to remain at the disposal of persons who can behave as those responsible have done.[57]

A somewhat humbled Nodal replied immediately on receipt of Emmeline's letter, stating that he had been at the Committee meeting when the resolution was passed and had proposed the handing over of the balance of the fund at the end of the year, but that his views and that of two other Committee members were in the minority. In justice to the others, he continued, they were chiefly influenced by the consideration that the balance of the fund 'should now be husbanded for the boy [Harry], to give him the best possible start in life; that it is more difficult and expensive to do this for a youth than for a girl.' The remaining sum was £270 and would be exhausted in less that three years when Harry would be fifteen. 'He ought to go to College longer – unless he should happen to be placed in a good business or profession, where a premium would probably be required. No money to provide this would then be in the hands of the Committee.' In an attempt to act as an intermediary, Nodal emphasised that he had sent 'a condensed memorandum' of Emmeline's letter to the Honorary Secretary and suggested to him the desirability of having another meeting the following week. 'If you have any views or suggestions, after reading my letter, perhaps you will write me', he carefully opined.[58]

Emmeline promptly responded to these suggestions in not one but two letters, both dated the same day, 29 November 1902. In the first she emphasised that she would have no further dealings with Mr. Dixon, the Honorary Treasurer. 'If you will see me I will in confidence tell you all', she confided.[59] The contents of her letter must then have preyed upon her mind and she discussed the situation with her children. Later that day she wrote to Nodal again, saying that since sending her 'hurried reply' that morning, she had thought the matter over 'more fully'. She appreciated what he had said about Harry's education and future and if she had been consulted on that point beforehand or even had the resolution passed by the Committee been sent to her, she should not have felt about the matter as she did now. While she agreed that the majority of the Committee were activated by the best motives and kind feeling towards her, this did not apply to the Treasurer, Mr. Dixon, and the Secretary, Mr. Graham. 'Had Mr. Dixon possessed any delicacy of feeling he would have resigned his office when our differences occurred at the time he acted as my legal adviser [in regard to Richard's estate] & I took my affairs out of his hands. Since that time I have declined to have any dealings with him.'

Why Mr. Graham acted as he did, Emmeline was unsure but he had wounded her with remarks made at their first meeting. 'He certainly insulted me deeply the only time I have seen him since the fund has been in existence by telling me I and my children were objects of charity.'

In a calm manner, Emmeline then outlined the achievements of her daughters. Christabel was still a student 'but at no cost to me'. Sylvia, who was studying art in Italy, was considered by all those who knew her work 'very talented & industrious & no doubt she will make a position for herself after next year as a designer & decorative artist', while Adela had a 'distinct literary gift' and would go from the High School to Owens College. Then the feminist sting came about the way in which the male administrators wanted to give priority to the education of her son at the neglect of her daughters. 'I believe & my husband thought it too that it is quite as important to give opportunity of education to gifted girls as to boys. I am carrying out his wishes in what I am doing.' Arguing her case, clearly and passionately, Emmeline explained about Harry and why the decision of the Committee to withhold the money from her now was against her present needs:

> Harry who although 13 is still in an elementary stage (he was delicate as a little one & went to school late indeed he has only just left kindergarten) will later on follow the same course. He wishes to be an Engineer & I feel for him the Technical School will be the best. However it is too early to decide as to this until he is more advanced. When he is old enough to go to College or to be apprenticed his sisters will be independent & with me will see that their only brother & my only son will have every opportunity. ... If my income from other sources is reduced now at what I maintain is the most expensive stage in the children's lives I shall be obliged to take more money out of the business [Emerson's] instead of as now letting profits go to increase the very small capital with which I started a venture which has been entirely justified by results. I am building up a source of independence for the future there. Even if the worst happened & I died before Harry's Education is complete my life is insured for £1500 & I pay the premiums amounting to over £40 per ann [annum] so that is amply provided for. I have told you all this in order that you may see how right I am in saying that it is for the next 2 or 3 years that the money is of use to us.

Despite this long explanation, Emmeline could not compromise over the original terms agreed for payment of the money:

> I must repeat what I wrote to you this morning. I cannot without a sacrifice of self respect accept any reduced sum. Rather will I try to do without it altogether. I have had a big struggle & so far have succeeded

& will continue to do so. ... For the children's sake I have borne what I would not submit to for my own.[60]

Explaining that the children agreed with what she had written, Emmeline then ended her long letter expressing renewed thanks to Mr. Nodal and regretting that he should be troubled with her private affairs.

The matter was not soon settled, but dragged on. Emmeline's iron resolve would not bend. She was determined that she would not be treated like some child-like woman who had decisions made for her. 'If I had been a recipient of outrelief from a Board of Guardians I should have had more considerate treatment for *they* are allowed to state their case before changes are made', she told Mr. Nodal in early December. An independent minded modern woman, who expected to be given respect in her own right for the public work she had done, she insisted, 'That Fund was intended to be a testimonial to my husband's public work not a relief fund & I who in my small way worked with him am entitled to at least courteous treatment & I *will have it.*'[61] When Nodal did not reply, Emmeline wrote again, shortly after Christmas stating that she was anxious to know what further steps, if any, had been taken. To add to her anxiety, she lamented, a great misfortune had happened in the family:

My youngest daughter has fallen ill with diphtheria & scarlet fever. I have been compelled to isolate her by sending the other members of the family away and as I cannot nurse her myself because of my official work as Registrar I have had to engage a trained nurse.

This is of course a great trial & anxiety to me & also a source of great expense. I have to pay a nurse for an inspection case £2. 2. 0 per week.

There is also rent of rooms for other members of the family & the expenses of doctor etc which accompany an illness.

In spite of all this whatever happens I would not take the reduced sum if sent. I will not be so humiliated.[62]

Emmeline's ultimatum fell on deaf ears. Early in the New Year she was sent a cheque for a reduced amount of just over £4 which she promptly returned to another of the administrators, Sir William Bailey, telling him that she could not accept it.[63] Bailey tried to bring an end to the controversy, telling Nodal that he thought that more money was wanted now than ever would be, in the future. 'It is very unpleasant for you and all of us who have been actuated by a noble motive', he opined, 'to have our feelings assaulted with the knowledge that we are unfortunately not promoting the happiness of those we are intending to benefit.'[64] But the matter was still not resolved.

Emmeline continued her correspondence with Nodal, telling him how the health of Harry had been a great concern since he had been ill away from home and she feared he had caught Adela's fever. To her relief, he was well again and

Adela was convalescing, although she would have to be sent away for a short time while the house was disinfected. 'All this is a great worry', she wrote, 'as I have so much other work to do (as the man as well as the mother of the family) & I feel rather run down & fretful about things especially as, however careful I am, I cannot help spending money freely at a time like this.'[65] If the Committee did not agree to the proposals to resume the level of payments originally agreed, then the balance should be used to found a municipal scholarship bearing her husband's name. She had always intended to do this, when she could afford to do so, and if the children approved. 'If we cannot have the money for their immediate needs without humiliation we had better do without it altogether', Emmeline insisted. 'I shall have to work harder & we must learn to do without some things but better that than lose our sense of independence.'[66]

Emmeline's stubbornness and refusal to compromise paid off. By the end of January 1903 the matter was settled according to her wishes; the old level of payments was to be resumed. 'I shudder to think what would be our plight had I not had sufficient energy & courage to work & earn money independently', she confided in gratitude to Nodal, who had worked on her behalf. 'I am very hard worked just now & what I want most of all is quiet & peace of mind.' She also told him the good news about Adela. 'You will I am sure be pleased to know that my girl is nearly well again. She goes to her Grandmother on the Isle of Man at the end of next week.'[67] By early February, when the cheque from the fund had still not arrived, Emmeline was sick with anxiety. 'I have counted on the money for January & February to pay some of the expenses incident to my daughter's illness & I really need it for apart from illness this is a time of the year when I have heavy charges to meet insurance premiums etc. What must I do?' While afraid that Nodal would think her 'an intolerable nuisance', Emmeline ended her letter by pointing out that 'this wholly unnecessary worry added to my usual hard work & my anxiety during my girl's serious illness is really making me ill.'[68]

As no further letters to and from Emmeline to Nodal are extant about payment from the Dr. Pankhurst Fund we may, perhaps, assume that the contentious matter was finally settled. The struggle to be paid the monies from the Fund on terms that Emmeline wanted was a formative experience in her life. That the personal is political became painfully obvious to her as she disagreed with the male administrators of the monies and firmly stood her ground. No longer the 'wife' of a public man, but an impoverished 'widow', who had to earn a living, she resisted the attempt to force her into such a low status position and insisted on her right to be heard with dignity. The struggle sharpened her sense of her own identity as an individual and as a feminist. In particular, the preference that the male administrators wanted to give to the education of her son, Harry, in comparison with that of her daughters, confirmed her feminist world-view that men saw women as a subordinate class.

6

FOUNDATION AND EARLY
YEARS OF THE WSPU
(MARCH 1903–JANUARY 1906)

Emmeline continued to manage her household with the most stringent economy. It all seemed worthwhile, especially when one day in the spring of 1903, Esther Roper suggested that the clever Christabel should become a lawyer. Despite the fact that women were not then admitted to the legal profession, Emmeline was delighted with the idea. Her eldest daughter had an able mind and would be following in her father's footsteps; furthermore, a knowledge of law might be useful in women's suffrage work. It was decided that Christabel would be coached for her matriculation at Owens College in order to gain the qualifications necessary to read for a law degree and, hopefully, subsequent training as a barrister. Since Sylvia had stayed in Venice long after her scholarship had expired, Emmeline now had to call her back home, partly because of finance and partly because her help was needed in the shop. That Easter, Emmeline and Adela travelled to Paris to accompany the reluctant Sylvia back to Manchester where Emmeline had gone to the expense of hiring for her the attic over Emerson's as a studio. Here Sylvia did her painting and designing, sold some of her work, made window tickets for Emerson's, and assisted in the shop. Like Christabel and Adela before her, she did not like shop work either.[1]

Women's suffrage, once again, had become a constant topic of conversation in the Pankhurst home, but it was a home now without a male head of household; Emmeline was the main breadwinner and she and her eldest daughters were the decision-makers. In particular, the charming twenty-two-year-old Christabel regularly discussed with her mother the way women's issues were being eclipsed in the growing labour movement, and also aired such views in the press. In a letter to the *Labour Leader* in March 1903, Christabel pointed out that at a recent conference, the Labour Representation Committee (LRC) had made no condemnation of the injustice whereby thousands of workers were disfranchised, 'merely because they happen to be women', nor expressed any determination to work for the removal of that injustice. The interests of women, she warned, would not necessarily be safe 'in the hands of the men's Labour Party'.[2] Christabel's fears were echoed by Isabella Ford, recently elected to the NAC of the ILP, who privately told the Pankhurst women that the leadership was 'no more than lukewarm on the subject of votes for women'. Keir

Hardie was the only NAC member strongly in support of women's suffrage, Philip Snowden and Bruce Glasier being actively hostile.[3] Emmeline had always had a close friendship with the Glasiers, writing warm congratulations to Katherine in June 1903 on the birth of a son:

> I am sure you are delighted to have a dear little boy & we are all thankful you have had a good time. Take care of yourself, & don't try to be too clever about getting up. It is better to be over careful at first. You know I am an old hand & can give good advice when you are about again.[4]

That friendship now became strained as Emmeline became acutely aware of Bruce Glasier's opposition to women's enfranchisement.

Like other ILP speakers, Glasier often came to stay at Nelson Street where Christabel fiercely challenged his view that women did not need the vote since they could be represented by men; in particular, she resented his insistence that there was no distinction of sex, only of class. She expounded her views further in the public forum of the *I.L.P. News*. 'Why are women expected to have such confidence in the men of the Labour party? Working-men are as unjust to women as are those of other classes.'[5] Christabel, among the third generation of women campaigning for the vote, had made up her mind that the demand for women's suffrage must be hastened, that it was undignified to keep on pleading helplessly. In particular, she regarded the tactics of the main suffrage society, the NUWSS, which had been formed in 1897 from an amalgamation of smaller groupings, as ineffective. Although the NUWSS claimed to be non-party, it considered the granting of the parliamentary vote to women as a 'natural extension' of Liberal principles and believed that it would be a Liberal government that would enfranchise women.[6] Led by Millicent Garrett Fawcett, the NUWSS had engaged in peaceful, constitutional campaigning, including an annual lobbying of parliament, but no women's franchise bill had been introduced for some six years; furthermore, it admitted men to its ranks.[7] 'It is unendurable', Christabel declared to her mother, 'to think of another generation of women wasting their lives begging for the vote. We must not lose any more time. We must act.'[8] Pondering on the question of how to breathe new life into the movement, Emmeline suggested that progress might be made if the older suffrage workers worked together with the younger, unwearied suffragists. 'After that', she recollected, 'I and my daughters together sought a way to bring about that union of young and old which would find new methods, blaze new trails.'[9]

Sylvia had been working for some months on the mural decorations for Pankhurst Hall, built in memory of her father. Shortly before it was due to be officially opened, on 2 October, she was astonished to hear that the branch of the ILP that used the hall would not allow women to join. Deep indignation was felt in the Pankhurst family, especially by Emmeline, about the discrimination against women taking place in a hall named after a beloved husband and father who had fought valiantly for women's rights. Declaring that she had wasted her time in the ILP, Emmeline agreed bitterly with Christabel's reproaches that she had allowed the cause of women to become effaced and that the time had come to form a women's organisation which ran parallel to it but was not – as some historians have assumed – formally affiliated to the ILP.[10] On 9 October 1903, she said to a small group of women socialist suffragists, 'Women, we must do the work ourselves. We must have an independent women's movement. Come to my house tomorrow and we will arrange it!'[11] The women who gathered at her home the following day voted to call the new organisation the 'Women's Social and Political Union' (WSPU), a name that Emmeline had chosen 'partly to emphasise its democracy, and partly to define its object as political rather than propagandist'.[12] It was decided that the WSPU (like the NUWSS) would campaign for the parliamentary vote for women on the same terms as it is, or shall be, granted to men, and also keep itself free from party affiliation. But unlike the NUWSS, the WSPU was to be a single-sex organisation. 'We resolved', recollected Emmeline, 'to limit our membership exclusively to women … and to be satisfied with nothing but action on our question. Deeds, not words, was to be our permanent motto.'[13] As was characteristic of Emmeline, now she had re-entered the franchise struggle, it became for her the only cause in the world.[14] Her single-mindedness about votes for women, fuelled by her passion to end the unjust and oppressed conditions of her sex, was to be severely tested in the years to come.

In these early days, neither Emmeline not any of her daughters held any office since they did not want the Union to be dismissed as 'just' a family party.[15] Mrs. Rachel Scott was the first honorary secretary but her work was primarily clerical. Weekly meetings were often held in Emmeline's house – described as 'a home of love and unity and confusion'[16] – but sometimes in a small room on the top floor of 116 Portland Street. Although members gave what pennies they could afford, supplemented by the proceeds from jumble sales, the largest financial burden was borne by Emmeline herself who also received donations from sympathisers.[17] During the week, letters would be written from Nelson Street asking for speakers at such events as ILP functions, trade union gatherings, debating societies, Labour Churches and Clarion Clubs, and then Emmeline or Adela would come to the weekly meeting with a list of replies and invitations; volunteers were also sought to draw a crowd at a street corner, park or fairground.[18] There were only five WSPU speakers – Emmeline, her three daughters and a new recruit, Teresa Billington. All were members of the ILP. Teresa Billington, a schoolteacher and an agnostic, had first met Emmeline when she had been sent to see her, as a member of the Manchester Education Authority Committee, in regard to her wish to seek exemption from teaching religion on the basis of conscience. Soon a WSPU member, Teresa remembered how in these early days Emmeline Pankhurst was 'very gracious, very persuasive. To work alongside of her day by day was to run the risk of losing yourself. She was ruthless in an utterly unaggressive way ... by using the followers she gathered around her as she was ruthless to herself. ... She suffered with you & for you.'[19] But, perhaps, what impressed Teresa most was what she called Emmeline's 'assumption of success'.[20] Indeed, Adela and Harry prophesied that their mother would become Prime Minister and Christabel Chancellor of the Exchequer, a suggestion that older WSPU members did not find incredulous, despite their laughter.[21] In high hopes, in December 1904, the small group of WSPU members, feeling that in the past women had been 'too apologetic for their existence, and too submissive', boldly asserted their claim to votes on equal terms with men in a bright yellow pamphlet.[22]

Early in the New Year of 1904, Emmeline was disappointed but not surprised when Christabel's application for admittance to Lincoln's Inn to train as a barrister was refused. Such discrimination against women would be swept away, she believed, once women had the parliamentary vote. She travelled to London to be a member of the gathering of suffragists, mainly from the NUWSS, who waited patiently in a committee room of the Commons on 3 February, the day after the opening of parliament, to lobby for the inclusion of a women's suffrage measure, as a private member's bill, in the coming session. Such annual ceremonies were of 'a most conventional, not to say farcical character', recollected Emmeline. The women would make their speeches, the MPs theirs, the women would thank the friendly members for their support, then the members would renew their assurances that they believed in women's suffrage and would vote for it when they had an opportunity to do so. Then the deputation, 'a trifle sad but entirely tranquil', took its departure, and the MPs 'resumed the real business of life, which was support of their party's policies'.[23] The deputation to friendly MPs on that 3 February followed the same pattern. Sir Charles McLaren presided over the meeting and he and other friendly MPs, including Keir Hardie, expressed their sincere regret that women were still unenfranchised. Emmeline had not been asked to speak but was determined that the occasion should not end with the usual civilities. 'Sir Charles McLaren has told us', she suddenly announced, 'that numbers of his colleagues desire the success of the women's suffrage cause ... [but will he] tell us if any member is preparing to introduce a bill for women's suffrage? Will he tell us what he and the other members will pledge themselves to *do* for the reform they so warmly endorse?'[24] The embarrassed Sir Charles could not reply. The other suffragists departed in anger, telling Emmeline she was 'an interloper, an impertinent intruder'. Who asked her to say something? What right did she have to ruin the good impression they had made? No one could tell how many friendly MPs she had alienated by her 'unfortunate remarks'. Unrepentant, Emmeline returned to Manchester with 'renewed energy', to 'blaze' those new methods that she and her daughters had thought about.[25]

Emmeline continued trying to convert ILPers to the women's cause by touring local branches and appealing for support for a women's franchise bill. Some hope came in early April when she successfully moved the resolution on women's suffrage at the ILP Conference at Cardiff. The socialist women in the country looked to their own socialist party, she began, for a lead on women's suffrage. There were 100,000 women operatives in Lancashire for whom she wanted the vote as she did for women schoolteachers, struggling widows and deserted wives. 'No man was excluded', she insisted, 'because he was a man, but every women was precluded because she was a woman.'[26] A decision was then made to instruct Labour members to introduce a women's suffrage measure in parliament, as well as the promotion of legislation for adult suffrage. Amid the enthusiasm, Emmeline was elected again to the NAC of the ILP, a move that did not please everyone present, especially those such as Snowden who favoured adult suffrage rather than the enfranchisement of women on the same property qualification that applied to men. Glasier commented in his diary, 'I have to urge Snowden to display some grace towards Mrs. Pankhurst.'[27]

Whether such grace was extended is debatable since Snowden now became involved in a bitter exchange in the *Labour Leader* with Christabel which high-lighted not only different approaches to tactics but also different world-views in regard to class and gender politics. Christabel held to her view that sex inequality in the existing franchise arrangements was the key inequality, over-riding inequalities of class. Snowden continually challenged her on this point, reiterating that extending the existing franchise to women would not serve the interests of the working class since a disproportionate number of the enfranchised would be wealthy and propertied women who would not support Labour candidates; he also asserted that the ILP could not promote both an adult suffrage bill and a women's enfranchisement bill at the same time.[28] An angry Christabel, questioning Snowden's assumption of the shared class interests of working women and men, replied that while the basis of the parliamentary fran-chise was not satisfactory, 'by far the most serious defect … is that according to which a person, simply because she is a woman, is for ever deprived of political existence'. While the extension of the franchise on the present basis to women will leave many women without votes, it will 'put an end to the rule of one sex by the other; it will strike the death-blow of the aristocracy of sex'.[29] Acutely aware of these issues that were frequently discussed in her household, Emmeline continued to place her hopes in the ILP, pointing out that the recent decision to instruct Labour MPs to introduce a women's suffrage measure in parliament was a firm indication that 'the Labour Party is also the Woman's Party'.[30] Nevertheless, she also warned, in a joint statement written with Isabella Ford, that an adult suffrage measure would not necessarily include women. The ILP supporters of a women's suffrage measure 'raise this clear issue, namely that sex must not be a disqualification for political rights, because they know that if this is not done the claims of women to the vote will in the near future be again set aside, as they always have been in the past, when extensions of the franchise were being given to men'.[31]

Wary of the growing support for adult suffrage in the ILP, Emmeline greeted the New Year of 1905 by doing something that was quite rare for her, writing an article in which she warned that workers in the Labour Party must make it impossible to betray women again, as they had been betrayed in the past. 'If we obtain the enactment of the Women's Enfranchisement Bill it will ensure that an Adult Suffrage Bill, which we all desire and strive for, must apply to women.'[32] At the LRC Conference in Liverpool, towards the end of January, Emmeline again argued her case, claiming this time that 90 per cent of the women who would be enfranchised under a women's suffrage measure would be 'working women'. But her words failed to persuade her listeners, 483,000 voting in favour of adult suffrage with 270,000 against.[33] A disappointed Emmeline wrote to Selina Jane Cooper, an ILP working-class delegate, commiserating with her and offering practical advice and help:

> I hope you feel more cheerful than when we parted at Liverpool & ready to renew the fight. ... Can you not work to get women on the executive of the [Textile] Union & begin to agitate to get women sent as delegates to next year's Conference. ... If I can be of any use to you in getting the textile women to assert themselves let me know & I will do all I can.[34]

Emmeline was consoled by Keir Hardie who told her that he would intro-duce in parliament the Women's Enfranchisement Bill as a private member's bill. The ballot for private members' bills did not take place until 21 February and so eight days beforehand Emmeline travelled to London in order to plead with MPs to give a place for the measure. She stayed with Sylvia who had taken rooms at 45 Park Walk, Chelsea, in order to take up her national scholar-ship at the Royal College of Art. Crawford observes that although Sylvia, in *The suffragette movement*, gives the impression that she and her mother worked alone in this task, a few other women also lobbied MPs on behalf of the WSPU, including Isabella Ford, Harriet McIlquham, with whom Emmeline had been associated in the early days of the Women's Franchise League, and Mrs. J. G. Grenfell, who had been a member of the Women's Emancipation Union. The aged Elizabeth Wolstenholme Elmy, another WSPU supporter and a friend of the Pankhursts, was also active in writing to MPs from her home in Congleton.[35] Each day Emmeline and Sylvia stood in the lobby of the House of Commons, interviewing MPs who had pledged themselves to support a women's suffrage bill but not one member agreed to give his chance in the ballot, if he drew such a chance, to such a measure. Returning home each evening, often after midnight, a dispirited Emmeline spelt out her anxieties. Her life's work, her husband's long struggle, the efforts of all those who had fought for women's suffrage for so long would be wasted unless votes for women came now. The Liberals would be returned in the next election and introduce manhood suffrage, and then all would be lost. Once all men had the vote, men would not agree to bring in womanhood suffrage. 'Far into the night', Sylvia recollected, 'she railed against the treachery of men and bemoaned the impotence of women! "Poor women!" The overburdened mothers, the sweated workers, the outcasts of the streets, the orphan of the Workhouse.'[36] When Hardie drew no place in the ballot on 21 February, Emmeline despaired. Hardie reassured her that there was hope if they could find an MP who had drawn one of the first fourteen places. One such member, Dr. Shipman, had pledged to another ILP member, Mrs. J. R. MacDonald, that he would sponsor a bill quali-fying women for election to local government bodies. Emmeline's plea to them both to give preference to the more important measure for women's parliamen-tary voting rights was all to no avail. The only member who had not said 'no' was the Liberal MP Bamford Slack, who had drawn fourteenth place in the ballot, and was not in the Commons that day. Hardie immediately telephoned to ascertain Bamford Slack's whereabouts while Emmeline and Isabella set off in a hansom to search for him. When found, Bamford Slack was persuaded to introduce the measure. Writing to the London-based suffragist Dora Montefiore on 19 February 1905, Emmeline recounted the event, expressing her disgust with the lack of support from members of the NUWSS as well as her concern over Adela's health:

> I got home last night very tired, to find my younger girl in bed with a slight attack of pleurisy. Fortunately, she is getting better.
>
> Would you believe it, that with the exception of Miss Ford, none of the W.S. women came to help either on Wednesday night or on Thursday. ... The official Suffragists never made a sign. ... All this makes me feel that years have been lost. If women had worked in the House as the trade unionists do, we should have had Members battling for us session after session. This time we owe it all to Keir Hardie, but we have no right to expect M.P.'s to do more for us than they do for others. The people who secured good places for their measures have done so because they have lobbied incessantly for years.
>
> Of course, it is horrid work, but it has to be done. ... Now we must get to work to get pressure brought to bear on Members by petitions, deputations, lobbying etc., in support of the Bill. Is it possible to form a Women's Parliamentary Committee in London to do this lobbying work? The old-fashioned and official gang will never do it. I have no confidence in them.[37]

The Women's Enfranchisement Bill was set down for 12 May but only as Second Order of the day which meant that anti-suffragists could, if they so desired, talk it out by prolonging discussion of a First Order measure, a bill to compel carts travelling along public roads at night to carry a light at the rear. Those promoting the latter refused to yield to Hardie's plea to withdraw it so that Emmeline became 'almost frenzied' at the foolishness of men who could hold this ' "trumpery little measure" ', as she termed it, against the citizenship claims of women.[38] Despite this drawback, Emmeline recalled that a 'thrill of excitement' ran through WSPU ranks and the older suffrage societies at the news about the bill, the first women's suffrage bill in eight years.[39] Now meetings were held and petitions organised, as new life sprung back into the movement.[40] When Sylvia attended a London meeting organised by the NUWSS in support of the bill, she found it all 'very polite and very tame', very different to the socialist meetings in the North. Fifty MPs, all in evening dress, sat on the platform, one by one giving their support, 'in a few trite words'. Millicent Garrett Fawcett, a 'trim, prim little figure' spoke in a clear, pleasant tone while a number of women gave brief utterances in 'nervous, high-pitched voices'.[41] In the North, Emmeline, Christabel, Teresa Billington and other WSPU members travelled around Lancashire and Cheshire, speaking in the more rousing socialist style; they also wrote letters to the socialist press.[42] The ILP annual conference that year was held in late April in Manchester and Emmeline was determined to make the most of the occasion by hosting a reception for delegates, in her home. The Conference passed a resolution supporting the bill and Emmeline, once again, was elected to the NAC.[43]

On the fateful 12 May Emmeline, accompanied by Elizabeth Wolstenholme Elmy, Isabella Ford and Dora Montefiore, was one of about 300 women who thronged the Strangers' Lobby and surrounding areas, waiting to hear the result. Also amongst the crowd were constitutional suffragists and a large number from the Women's Co-operative Guild, brought there by Nellie Alma Martel from Australia, who had been active in winning votes for women in New South Wales and then stood as a candidate for the Commonwealth Parliament.[44] The debate on the Lighting of Vehicles Bill was spun out from noon till four o'clock by the anti-suffragists who told silly stories and foolish jokes which were greeted with much laughter. As news of what was happening filtered through to the Lobby, an irate but confident Emmeline hastily scribbled a note to Arthur Balfour, the Conservative Prime Minister, informing him that unless he granted full facilities for the bill, her Union would work against his government at the general election. 'The threat was comic', opined Rebecca West many years later; Emmeline Pankhurst was 'a little woman in her late forties, without a penny, without a powerful friend'.[45] And she had been an opponent of the Conservatives for all her political life. In the House of Commons, Bamford Slack rose at four o'clock to move the second reading of the Women's Enfranchisement Bill, and then Mr. Labouchere moved to reject the bill. Keeping an eye steadfastly on the clock, he talked and talked until it was too late for a division to be taken. 'It was the same speech as before that he has made so often before', explained a scornful Emmeline later to the readers of the *Labour Leader*. 'It contained the same jokes, the same coarse references to women, and it was received, as some women saw and heard, by the House with laughter and cheers. ... In this wise our Bill, for which we have worked so long and ardently, was talked out.'[46]

The waiting women outside the Commons grew dismayed and then angry when they heard the news. A number of NUWSS members withdrew. Emmeline, drawing upon her long years of experience of political agitation, decided that the moment had come for a demonstration 'such as no old-fashioned suffragist had ever attempted. I called upon the women to follow me outside for a meeting of protest against the government.'[47] Elizabeth Wolstenholme Elmy began to speak but the police rushed into the crowd of women and jostled them down the steps. The well-dressed, feminine Emmeline, with her air of authority, demanded to know where women could meet to voice their indignation. After some argument, the police inspector took them to Broad Sanctuary, near to the gates of Westminster Abbey, where Keir Hardie joined them. Here the small group demanded government intervention to save the talked-out bill while the police took the names of offenders. This protest, which Emmeline defined as 'the first militant act' of the WSPU, displayed some of the qualities that were to mark her future leadership, in particular, the fact that she could be 'superb in moments of crisis', initiating action and taking command.[48] As we see in this particular instance, 'militancy' for Emmeline Pankhurst meant engaging in forms of behaviour that challenged conventional expectations about women being submissive and accepting of their subordinate status, and especially about middle-class women being genteel and ladylike.[49] Christabel put it in a nutshell when she defined militancy as 'the putting off of the slave *spirit*'.[50]

That summer of 1905, Emmeline, Christabel and the small band of WSPU women departed again from the 'old' way of campaigning for women's suffrage in that they organised a number of outdoor meetings in Lancashire and Yorkshire. Some of these were held on Sunday evenings in Tib Street, Manchester, in association with the Manchester Central Branch of the ILP, and often included a brass band or choir, while others were organised by the Union itself. In mid June, Elizabeth Wolstenholme Elmy told Harriet McIlquham how the NUWSS was 'objecting' to these open-air gatherings which, she insisted, would not be given up 'to please their high respectability'.[51] In addition to now attracting money from sympathisers, the WSPU had a valuable new recruit in Annie Kenney, a young working-class factory operative from Oldham who had been converted to the cause that spring, when she heard Christabel speak. Annie's mother had died early in 1905 and the kind and hospitable Emmeline often invited the slightly built young woman with the thin elfin face, large luminous eyes and powerful voice to her home; that factory machinery had torn off one finger from one of Annie's 'restless, knotted hands' was a frequent reminder to Emmeline of the hazards that working-class women faced in the workplace.[52] Keen to become an effective WSPU speaker, Annie suggested that the Union members should follow the annual fairs or wakes, held during the summer in Lancashire villages, since there they would find a ready-made audience. The young women visited such places as Royton, Stalybridge, Hyde, Mossley, Lees and Oldham, speaking alongside travelling showmen and the sellers of quack medicine; often they relied upon the local ILP to form a 'sort of bodyguard', to keep rowdy elements in order so that they had a fair hearing.[53] Emmeline, on the other hand, focused much more on ILP platforms where she was always in demand. Although extremely busy in the women's cause, Emmeline did not lose touch with other social reforms demanded that summer, also taking part with Christabel and Eva Gore-Booth in the demonstrations to press on the government the necessity of carrying through the Unemployed Workmen Relief Bill. She spoke in early July at the Heaton Park demonstration organised by the Manchester and Salford Trades and Labour Council, the ILP, the Social Democratic Federation, the Manchester, Salford and District Women's Trades and Labour Council, and the Gorton United Trades and Labour Council. She also attended the address on the bill given by Keir Hardie at the Ardwick Empire where she seconded the vote of thanks to her old friend.[54] On 31 July, a demonstration of unemployed, ragged men marched through Manchester; a scuffle broke out with the police, who used their batons, and four men were arrested. Within two weeks the government had found time to pass the bill. That protests, demonstrations and arrests had forced the government to concede was carefully noted by Emmeline, and especially Christabel.

After the failure of the Women's Enfranchisement Bill, Emmeline issued an exaggerated warning which was, nevertheless, a rallying cry. 'Women all over the country are burning with indignation, and the result of that indignation will be felt at the General Election. A fire has been lighted in the country which will burn fiercely until women are free.'[55] The autumn of 1905 brought her fresh hope since a general election was to be held in which it was assumed that the Liberals, who were promising a number of reforms, would be returned rather than the Conservative Party that had held office for twenty years. Christabel felt keenly that the WSPU was 'making no headway, our meetings were not reported … our work was not counting'.[56] In particular, she believed that the old method pursued by the NUWSS of private members' suffrage bills was futile; the only worthwhile course was to seek pledges from those who would become members of the new government which would then make women's suffrage government policy. In discussions with her mother and some other trusted WSPU members, Christabel decided on a more confrontational policy which drew upon a much older male radical tradition of political protest, which she had seen in action, in the socialist movement, and on pre-existing radical currents within the women's movement.[57] What was new was that Christabel wanted women to protest in such a way that they would court imprisonment and thus bring publicity to the *women's cause*. The original plan was for Christabel, Annie Kenney and Teresa Billington to persist in asking a question about votes for women at the Liberal Party meeting to be held in the Free Trade Hall on the evening of 13 October, when Sir Edward Grey, the main speaker, would outline future policy; Emmeline would not participate in the disturbance since to do so might jeopardise her employment as a Registrar, the main source of her income. But the day before the fateful meeting, Emmeline thought it wiser if only Christabel and Annie went to the Free Trade Hall, leaving Teresa free to help organise protest meetings after the event and to write letters to the press.[58] On the evening of the 13th, Christabel bade her anxious mother farewell with the words, 'We shall sleep in prison tonight.' Tucked inside her blouse was a small calico banner that Emmeline had made on which was printed, in black polish, 'Votes for women'. After Sir Edward Grey had concluded his speech, in which there was no mention of women's suffrage, Annie asked the question, phrased in advance by Christabel, 'Will the Liberal government give women the vote?' As expected, no answer was given, and Christabel, unfurling the banner, repeated the question, setting the meeting 'aflame with excitement'.[59] Once the angry cries from the audience had died down, the Chief Constable of Manchester invited the two women to put their question in writing so that it could be handed to the speaker. Christabel and Annie waited again patiently, and found that Sir Edward Grey responded to the vote of thanks, without an answer to their question. Immediately, Annie stood on her chair and asked the question again. The audience howled and shouted as the two women were roughly handled and dragged outside by stewards where Christabel deliberately committed the technical offence of spitting at a policeman in order to be arrested. In the police court the following day, Emmeline heard Christabel and Annie refusing to pay the fines imposed on them and choosing instead one week and three days imprisonment, respectively. She hurried to the room into which the two women were ushered and, with motherly concern, pleaded with Christabel, 'You have done everything you could be expected to do in this matter, I think you should let me pay your fines and take you home.' But her daughter was resolute. 'Mother, if you pay my fine I will never go home.'[60] Emmeline did not disagree. Believing that her first-born had the finest political instinct, she 'identified herself' with the new tactics 'promptly and unreservedly' claimed Evelyn Sharp, evidence not only of her 'perception' but also of her 'perfect understanding' with Christabel. Emmeline Pankhurst had many qualities that made her an exceptional woman, continued Sharp, 'and not the least of them was the vision that primarily enabled her to detect where the younger woman excelled in political acumen and freshness of outlook'.[61] The following evening, Emmeline addressed a crowd of nearly a thousand men and women, who, despite a cold, drizzling rain, assembled in Stevenson Square to protest against the harsh treatment meted out to the two WSPU members. Although she knew she was risking her livelihood, Emmeline stood firmly behind the militant action, saying how she was 'proud to be the mother of one of the two noble girls who had gone to prison in the endeavour to advocate the enfranchisement of women'.[62] When Annie was released on 16 October, Emmeline greeted her at the prison gates with the words that she now regarded her as one of her family. 'Annie, as long as I have a home you must look upon it as yours. You will never have to return to factory life.'[63]

Emmeline attended the large welcome for the ex-prisoners, held at the Free Trade Hall on 20 October, the day of Christabel's release. Organised by Teresa Billington and Sam Robinson, chair of the Manchester Central Branch of the

ILP, the gathering was filled to overflowing. Emmeline glowed with pride as Christabel and Annie were presented with bouquets; then songs of liberty were sung and ILP men vowed support for women's suffrage. Both young women gave stirring speeches while Keir Hardie condemned the 'brutal and unjustifiable' treatment the two had received and lamented the fact that police constables in plain clothes had been at the meeting.[64]

Emmeline's faith in Christabel's new tactics was justified since the defiant stand of the two protesters had become headline news. Most of the press reporting was hostile since 'interruption' of male political discourse in order to support the women's cause, as Jane Marcus terms it, was regarded as unprecedented. Further photographs of 'well-dressed women being thrown out of meetings by burly male stewards' were seen as shocking to a public accustomed to Victorian forms of chivalry.[65] Yet many people wrote letters expressing sympathy with the women, and new recruits flocked to join. As Emmeline joyfully acknowledged, 'the question of women's suffrage became at once a live topic of comment from one end of Great Britain to the other'.[66] From now on, heckling by Union members of politicians and a willingness to go to prison became key tactics of the campaign to force the government to give women the parliamentary vote.

After her imprisonment, Christabel was threatened with expulsion from Owen's College unless she gave a pledge, in writing, not to participate in any further disturbances. Christabel wrote the necessary letter, an action that did nothing to undermine Emmeline's admiration for her clever, cool-headed, eldest daughter. Emmeline often said to Sylvia, 'Christabel is not like other women; not like you and me; she will never be led away by her affections!'[67] But Sylvia's assertion that from the day of Christabel's first imprisonment, their mother proudly and openly proclaimed her eldest daughter to be 'her leader', must be treated with caution.[68] Christabel herself always repudiated such a claim and deferred to her mother whom she saw as the 'Queen of the WSPU' with herself in the role of 'Prime Minister'.[69] Although the relationship between the two was very close, with Emmeline often relying upon Christabel's political instincts, Christabel in her autobiography speaks of her mother with awe, reverence and admiration. In Unshackled, Christabel presents herself very much in the role of 'daughter' to a powerful mother who had to make hard choices throughout the campaign for the benefit not of herself, but the cause she served. 'In 1905 she chose, for the sake of womanhood, the ruin and ostracism and all the suffering implicit for her in her eldest daughter's act, which was also her own act and but the first link in a chain of future acts.'[70] Emmeline is portrayed by Christabel as immensely strong in spirit, a heroine. 'How small we all look in comparison.'[71] She is represented as a spiritual leader who is likened to Giuseppe Garibaldi, the Italian soldier and patriot who created a united Italy. Adapting his words, Christabel claims that her mother 'offered to herself and to her followers insult and abuse and pain and loneliness and loss of friends and the anger of politicians'.[72] During the following years of militancy, there can never be any doubt that Emmeline was regarded as the inspirational leader of the WSPU and Christabel its strategist, especially in regard to short-term aims.[73] Although it is often difficult to untangle who made policy decisions at the leadership level, the trust between Emmeline and Christabel, between leader and strategist, mother and daughter, was absolute and never broken.[74] As Emmeline often said, she and Christabel were 'different sides of the same medal'.[75]

On 4 December 1905, Balfour's Conservative government resigned amid excitement that the long, weary years of reaction were ending and a new dawn of reform beginning. A general election was called for January 1906 and, in the meantime, Sir Henry Campbell-Bannerman, leader of the Liberal Party in opposition, was asked to form an interim government. WSPU members appeared in town after town at meetings addressed by Liberal Cabinet Ministers, heckling and displaying banners on which were printed 'Votes for women'. Keir Hardie was standing in Merthyr Tydfil, South Wales, and when Frank Field, who was running the campaign, feared that the seat was in danger, telegrams were sent to those who might help. Emmeline responded immediately; not only was Hardie a personal friend, he was also the only potential MP upon whom she could rely to introduce a women suffrage measure in parliament. Soon after her arrival in South Wales, Emmeline decided that Annie, with her working-class background, would be a useful worker at pit-brow and trade union gatherings; therefore, as agreed beforehand, she sent a telegram to Manchester, 'Send Annie at once.'[76] Emmeline had a busy and tiring schedule. On 2 November, she spoke to Swansea Socialist Society and the following day to Cwmavon ILP, highlighting the fact that the ILP was the only political party championing women's rights. Women and socialism was the theme of her talk to a large gathering at Bethel Chapel on the 4th while on Sunday, the 5th, she spoke to children at the opening of the Socialist Sunday School in Cardiff and then, in the evening, took the subject of 'Why two women went to prison for the vote' as the theme for her address to Cardiff ILP.[77] Hardie, for his part, supported Emmeline later in the year when, at a large ILP gathering at the Free Trade Hall, Manchester, she moved a resolution that the meeting should re-iterate its belief that it was only by the formation of 'a strong and independent Labour group in the House of Commons' that social legislation could be obtained, and pledge itself 'to do all in its power to secure the return of the Socialist and Labour candidates now standing for election'.[78] The high visibility of the leader of the WSPU during the socialist campaign prompted Mary Gawthorpe from Bramley, Leeds, an ILP member who was sympathetic towards the WSPU, although not yet a member, to ask why women such as Katherine Glasier, Isabella Ford and Emmeline Pankhurst, amongst others, should not be considered as parliamentary candidates.[79] The ILP did not sponsor the issue.

As the general election results came rolling in during late January 1906, the Liberal Party was swept to power with a majority of nearly 100 in the House of Commons; twenty-nine Labour candidates were also returned, including Hardie.[80] Christabel suggested to her mother that their policy of wresting a women's suffrage measure from the 'unwilling grasp' of the new government would be more successful if they worked in London, the home of parliamentary democracy. 'Then only, never before and never after, did I see her flinch', recollected the daughter. 'We can't afford it', Emmeline replied sharply, repeating the statement as Christabel pleaded.[81] Emmeline who, in most cases, paid her own travelling expenses as well as those of some other WSPU members, knew that her limited income would not stretch to covering the cost of intensive campaigning far from her Manchester base; the previous month, she had had to raffle one of Sylvia's painting in order to raise money for fares for London. Nor could she afford to give up her job as a Registrar which she was in constant danger of losing. Christabel, with 'the daring faith of youth', was determined that money should not defeat their aims and since she herself was unable to leave Manchester until she had taken her final degree exams, asked Annie Kenney if she would go to London.[82] Annie agreed. Emmeline advanced £2 to the inexperienced twenty-six-year-old to 'rouse' London and warned her not to speak to any man in the street other than a policeman.[83]

7

TO LONDON
(FEBRUARY 1906–JUNE 1907)

Annie Kenney took up residence with Sylvia, at 45 Park Walk and, with the help of Dora Montefiore and Minnie Baldock, the wife of a fitter in Canning Town, was soon involved in contacting groups of poor women in the East End as well as helping in the planning of a meeting and a procession to take place on 19 February 1906, the day of the opening of parliament.[1] Hardie advised Sylvia and Annie to book Caxton Hall, which could hold 700 people; various newspaper editors promised to give publicity to the events organised by the 'suffragettes', as they had now been christened by the *Daily Mail*. When Emmeline arrived in London in mid February and was told of the ambitious plans, she was aghast. How could they organise such an 'impossible programme'? She would be made to look 'ridiculous by a procession of half a dozen people and an empty hall'.[2] Money was also needed for such a big venture, especially for fares for the East End women and for refreshments in Caxton Hall. Since Emmeline had no money to spare she sought sponsorship from two friends, William Stead and Isabella Ford, who generously donated £25 each.[3] On the afternoon of the meeting, the hall was filled to overflowing with hundreds outside. Emmeline was standing on the platform when news filtered through that there was no mention in the King's Speech of any to reference to women's suffrage. 'We must take a more militant attitude', Emmeline declared. 'The vote is our only weapon to bring about the social legislation we want.'[4] She then led a procession of about 3,000 women, including 300 East End women, many of them carrying babies in arms, to the Commons. In the cold rain, the women waited outside the Strangers' Entrance since only twenty at a time were allowed in to petition MPs. Although no MP could be persuaded to support the women's cause, the experience convinced Emmeline that women were 'awake at last. They were prepared to do something that women had never done before – fight for themselves ... for their own human rights. Our militant movement was established.'[5] The widespread press publicity given to the procession brought fresh recruits to the rank and file membership of the WSPU, as well as to its inner council.

While Emmeline and her followers had been waiting in the Commons Lobby, Keir Hardie, as leader of the new Labour Party, had been replying to the

King's Speech, condemning the way women's suffrage had been ignored. His desire to include women's enfranchisement as a Labour measure was not supported by his colleagues who decided that the five places they drew for private members' bills should be devoted to issues that were foremost in the Party programme, such as the feeding of necessitous schoolchildren, old age pensions and the right of the unemployed to work. When there was some doubt about which measure should take up one of the places, Emmeline demanded that it be reserved for votes for women; instead, the Labour MPs decided for a checkweighing bill, designed to protect the wages of workmen. The insult was hard to bear. Emmeline felt betrayed. Was it for this that she had joined the ILP? Was it for this that she and her husband had suffered boycott? Discussions she now had with her old friend Keir Hardie, at his rooms at 14 Nevill's Court, were painful. Surely he could persuade his colleagues to sponsor a women's bill? Hardie's promise that if he won place for a bill or resolution he would devote it to a women's suffrage measure cut no ice; it must be the Labour Party that sponsored women's enfranchisement. The success of the Labour Party with the bills that it did sponsor that first session of parliament 'only embittered' Emmeline's disappointment.[6]

Later that month of February 1906, Hardie, who had raised £300 to help the WSPU get started in London, gave to Emmeline a letter of introduction to Emmeline Pethick Lawrence, a wealthy, radical social worker who lived in a large apartment in Clement's Inn, close to his own rooms. Hardie had a high regard for Emmeline Pethick Lawrence's executive capabilities and thought she could be a useful colleague to develop the WSPU in the metropolis. After her first visit to Mrs. Lawrence's flat, Emmeline returned to Sylvia disappointed. 'She will not help', she said, 'she has so many interests.'[7] However, a luncheon invitation soon afterwards was more productive, especially when Annie Kenney joined the small group after they had eaten their meal. 'There was something about Annie that touched my heart', remembered Emmeline Pethick Lawrence. 'She was very simple and she seemed to have a whole-hearted faith in the goodness of everybody that she met.'[8] Before her return to England in January 1906 with her husband, Frederick, a lawyer, Emmeline Pethick Lawrence had been visiting South Africa where she had read of the furore over the arrest of Christabel and Annie in Manchester. Now, when Annie told the story in her own words, she no longer held back and agreed to become Honorary Treasurer of the WSPU. She welcomed the new militant approach since she believed that the NUWSS had made the suffrage movement like 'a beetle on its back that cannot turn itself over and get on its legs to pursue its path'.[9] Emmeline Pethick Lawrence brought necessary administrative skills to the growing organisation, as well as considerable wealth and social contacts. In addition to her skills at fund raising, she helped to develop the use of spectacle in WSPU campaigns. The Central London Committee of the WSPU was now formed with Sylvia, who had been Acting Secretary of the smaller initial group, as Honorary Secretary, and Annie as a paid organiser at £2 weekly. The other members included

1 Richard Marsden Pankhurst, 1879

2 Sylvia, Adela and Christabel Pankhurst, c. 1890

3 Emmeline Pankhurst with Harry, 1890

4 Emmeline Pankhurst, 1906

5 Emmeline Pankhurst arrested February 1908, as she led a deputation to parliament armed only with a rolled resolution for women's suffrage and a few lilies of the valley

6 Nellie Martel, Emmeline Pankhurst, Mary Gawthorpe, Una Stratford-Dugdale and Mary Leigh, Mid Devon by-election, January 1908

7 Emmeline Pankhurst at her stall, NUWSPU Exhibition, July 1908

8 Emmeline and Christabel Pankhurst in prison uniform, October 1908

9 Christabel Pankhurst, Emmeline Pankhurst, Emmeline Pethick Lawrence and Sylvia Pankhurst, c. 1909

10 Emmeline Pankhurst campaigning in March 1909

Emmeline, Flora Drummond, Mary Clarke (Emmeline's sister), Lucy Roe (Sylvia's landlady), Nellie Martel, Mary Neal (a life-long friend and colleague of Emmeline Pethick Lawrence), and Irene Fenwick Miller, whose mother had been a member with Emmeline on the Executive Committee of the Women's Franchise League. Within a week of her appointment, the Honorary Treasurer had put the Central Committee on a sound financial and business-like basis; Alfred Sayers, a chartered accountant and old friend, was appointed auditor of the accounts, a stipulation that Emmeline Pethick Lawrence insisted on, before she took up office.[10] By March, Sylvia and Emmeline Pethick Lawrence had only their names on a new WSPU manifesto which claimed that, 'The New Movement for the political enfranchisement of women, initiated by the Women's Social and Political Union, is a people's movement, and is not confined to any section of the community.'[11]

Back home in Manchester, Emmeline continued the WSPU campaign there and had to content herself with reading about the exploits of the militants in London. On 2 March 1906, a small group of women seated themselves on the doorstep of 10 Downing Street when the Prime Minister, Campbell-Bannerman, refused to receive a deputation. One week later, about thirty women went to the same address, requesting an audience, but after waiting about an hour, they were asked to leave. Irene Fenwick Miller then knocked on the door which Flora Drummond managed to open, rushing inside. Both women were promptly arrested. Annie Kenney jumped onto the Prime Minister's car, and began to speak to the crowd, and then she too was arrested. At the police station, the three women were released on the orders of Campbell-Bannerman who promised to receive a deputation of all the women's societies on 19 May. When Annie returned to 62 Nelson Street after these events, Emmeline found her run-down and overstrained and so persuaded William Stead to lend the young woman his cottage in Hayling Island where she rested for a week.[12] Emmeline travelled back down to London for the dinner organised by the Labour Party and held in the House of Commons, on 4 April, to celebrate its formation.[13] Two days later, in a long letter to the *Labour Leader*, she reaffirmed that members of the separate WSPU were committed to the socialist movement but stressed that the enfranchisement of women was the key issue which had to take precedence:

> To secure votes for women is our first object, but all our members take part in the general work of the Socialist movement. ... We do not wish women to relax their efforts for Socialism, for we realise that Socialism is even more necessary for women than it is for men.
>
> What we do maintain is, that the immediate enfranchisement of women must take precedence for us of all other questions. We must, equally with men, vote for the makers of the Co-operative Commonwealth. We also must choose our law-makers. ... It is only by the joint efforts of men and women working together on equal terms

that the social problem can be justly settled. … May the time soon arrive when we shall have secured the emancipation of our sex, and so end the need for a separate women's movement.[14]

At the ILP Easter Conference at Stockton-on-Tees, just over a week later, Emmeline was chosen as a delegate (as was Isabella Ford) for the Labour Party's Conference to be held in Belfast the following year. But the difficulty for Emmeline of remaining within the ILP was to become more accentuated over the coming year as her identity as a feminist conflicted with her loyalty to the Labour movement.

Keir Hardie had won a place to present in the Commons, on 25 April, a Resolution expressing the view 'That, in the opinion of this House, it is desirable that sex should cease to be a bar to the exercise of the Parliamentary franchise.' Convinced that the Resolution would be talked out, Emmeline travelled down to London, determined not to let the moment pass without creating a disturbance. She sat with her supporters in the Ladies' Gallery, behind the heavy brass grille that screened them from the debating chamber. When Samuel Evans, an anti-suffragist MP, began to talk out the Resolution, Emmeline gave a signal to the small group of women who shouted out 'We will not have this talk any longer', 'Divide! divide!' and 'We refuse to have our Bill [sic] talked out', as they pushed flags bearing the words 'Vote for justice to women' through the grille.[15] MPs, including Hardie, were angered by the breach in decorum as the police hastily cleared the gallery. Outside in the Lobby, WSPU members met a hostile reception from ILP supporters, such as Ethel Snowden, who believed they had wrecked all chance of ever winning the support of MPs; Isabella Ford later wrote that it was over this incident that she and Emmeline Pankhurst 'parted company in the ILP'.[16] Despite such disapproval, the militants continued to press their case throwing away, noted Emmeline, 'all our conventional notions of what was "ladylike" and "good form"'.[17] Determined to make the deputation planned for the 19th 'as public as possible', plans were soon underway for a WSPU procession and demonstration.[18] On the appointed day, the women marched from the statue of Boadicea, the warrior queen, at the entrance to Westminster Bridge, to the Foreign Office. Here the Prime Minister met Emmeline Pankhurst and Keir Hardie, as spokespersons for the WSPU and a group of suffragist MPs, as well as representatives from groups of suffragists, co-operators, temperance workers and trade unionists. With passion and dignity, Emmeline pleaded that the WSPU members felt the question of votes for women so keenly that they were prepared to sacrifice for it 'life itself, or what is perhaps even harder, the means by which we live'.[19] This note of personal sacrifice for the women's cause, which the non-militants regarded as bad form, was spoken from the heart. Emmeline relied upon her sister, Mary, to act as her deputy when she was away campaigning and thus unable to fulfil her duties as Registrar for Births and Deaths. The government had written to her on a number of occasions, complaining about her frequent visits to London in order to engage in high profile political work. Emmeline was in a dilemma. She knew that if she could hold onto the post for a couple of years, she would be eligible for a pension; on the other hand, she also believed, as she told Helen Fraser, 'If I go on, we can get the vote in that time.'[20] The shop in King's Street brought no financial security since it was running at a loss and was soon to be closed. Harry was still at school, in Hampstead, while Christabel and Sylvia were not yet in employment. Adela, now an elementary schoolteacher, was the only other family member earning a living; although Emmeline had considered schoolteaching 'rather a come down', she had come to accept the situation.[21] Her old friend, Noémie, wrote a sharp rebuke, telling Emmeline to give up politics and to concentrate her efforts upon placing her daughters in the professions. But the idealistic and determined Emmeline could not do that. She saw her quest for the vote as 'the fulfilment of her destiny, ready to die for it as the tigress for her young'.[22]

When Campbell-Bannerman met the leaders of the suffrage societies on 19 May, he reassured them of his sympathy with their cause but could only preach 'the virtue of patience', explaining that he could do nothing because of the opposition of some of his Cabinet.[23] A meeting of protest was held in Trafalgar Square at which the speakers included not only Emmeline and Keir Hardie but also Eva Gore-Booth, Annie Kenney (dressed as a mill worker, in her shawl and clogs), Dora Montefiore, Selina Cooper, Emmeline and Frederick Pethick Lawrence and Teresa Billington. This was the first large open-air women's suffrage gathering ever to take place in London, although the audience of 7,000 was predominantly male.[24] Now that it was clear that the Liberal government was resolved not to bring in a women's suffrage bill, there was nothing for WSPU women to do, declared Emmeline, but 'to continue our policy of waking up the country, not only by public speeches and demonstrations, but by a constant heckling of Cabinet Ministers'.[25] A particular target was Herbert Asquith, the Chancellor of the Exchequer, known to be the most vehement anti-suffragist of all the Liberal ministers. In mid June 1906, Emmeline and some of her followers, preceded him to Northampton where he was due to speak on forthcoming government education bills. The president of the local Women's Liberal Association indignantly reassured Emmeline that the violence towards suffragettes that had occurred in other towns would not happen in Northampton where women had done so much for the Liberal Party. Emmeline slipped into the hall where Asquith was speaking and sat down in the front row which had been set aside for wives and women friends of the Liberal leaders. She sat in silence, hearing men interrupt the speaker and get answers to their question. At the close of Asquith's speech, she stood up and said she would like to ask a question. She reminded Asquith that he had spoken about the right of parents to be consulted in the matter of their children's education, especially in regard to religious instruction and then said, 'Women are parents. Does Mr. Asquith think that women should have the right to control their children's education, as men do, through the vote?' Immediately Emmeline had finished speaking, she was violently ejected from the meeting, an action that so shocked the president of the local Women's Liberal Association that she resigned her office and joined the WSPU.[26] A little later, when Asquith was speaking in Aberdeen, Emmeline was implored to hold her militants back, on the pledge that Asquith would give an answer on women's enfranchisement to a question put to him quietly by the president of the local Women's Liberal Association there, Mrs. Black. When Mrs. Black rose to speak, however, she was howled down and declared out of order by the Chair of the meeting. When Emmeline rose to protest, she was once again roughly thrown out of the meeting.[27]

Later that month, Emmeline sat in Marylebone Police Court when Annie Kenney, Adelaide Knight and Jane Sparboro were charged with conduct likely to create a breach of the peace before the residence of Mr. Asquith in Cavendish Square, namely attempting to ring his doorbell! After the case was adjourned, she led a procession of several hundred suffragettes to Hyde Park where she moved a resolution calling upon the government to insert in the proposed Plural Voting Bill a clause conferring the franchise on women. She had barely begun to launch her attack on Asquith when Dora Montefiore was arrested; despite a police warning, she had continued to distribute handbills, contrary to the regulations governing Hyde Park.[28] Such arrests for infringing the law and for heckling were now common. Indeed, Emmeline felt particular concern for Adela, a frail child, who was serving a one-week imprisonment in Manchester after being charged with 'disturbance, assault and endeavouring to rescue a prisoner' when heckling a meeting addressed by Churchill and Lloyd George in Belle Vue Gardens. Elaborate arrangements had been taken to keep the suffragettes out, and Adela, who was known in the area, had avoided detection by dressing in her mother's best broad-brimmed hat and silk coat.[29] Emmeline was already back in Manchester the day Adela was released and made sure that she was the first person to greet the heroine who was welcomed by a crowd outside Strangeways Prison. She listened in horror as Adela recounted stories about how she had slept on a plank bed under a dirty blanket, used dirty lavatories, eaten stale bread and coarse porridge, and sewed mail bags.[30]

Such tales of the hardships endured by women, fighting for their citizenship, fired Emmeline's enthusiasm. She demanded the immediate enfranchisement of women and the release of all WSPU prisoners from Holloway Jail, London, at a number of meetings held in the Manchester area over the next month, including the evening demonstrations held in Stevenson Square to welcome the released prisoners. A meeting of 15,000 people in Boggart Hole Clough on Sunday, 15 July, at which both Emmeline and Keir Hardie spoke, was interrupted by rowdy youths; in the confusion, Emmeline Pethwick Lawrence and Elizabeth Wolstenholme Elmy were hustled and Adela nearly trampled under foot. Realising the dangers, Emmeline did her utmost to preserve order. Undeterred by the break-up of the main meeting she then succeeded in holding a smaller meeting close by where she addressed some 1,500 people and in the evening, a further gathering of 1,000. At another great rally of 20,000 people the following Sunday, this time in Stevenson Square, Emmeline and Keir Hardie were warmly received, once again.[31] But Hardie's support for women's suffrage was leading many in the Labour Party to become dissatisfied. Snowden was not alone in complaining that, as a leader, Hardie was 'a hopeless failure. ... He seems completely absorbed with the suffragettes.'[32]

Before Emmeline had returned to Manchester, Sylvia had resigned her Honorary Secretaryship of the London central office, contrary to her mother's wishes. Sylvia's two-year scholarship was drawing towards an end and she wanted to spend more time building up a portfolio so that she could earn a living when her college course ended. She found this impossible to do when WSPU work took up much of her spare time and WSPU members monopolised her workroom during weekday evenings and at the weekends.[33] Emmeline wanted Sylvia to retain the post until Christabel was free to come to London to take up the office of Chief Organiser and preside over the choice of Sylvia's successor; she did not want Sylvia to become a paid organiser, thinking it not fit for too many members of her family to be on the WSPU payroll and neither did Sylvia herself want such a position. When Charlotte Despard and Edith How Martyn, two ILP members, were appointed joint Honorary Secretaries, Emmeline feared there would be 'divided counsels', a prophecy that came to pass.[34] Emmeline's anger at Sylvia's stand had not subsided when she returned home to Manchester. When Sylvia wrote to tell her mother that her college teachers had encouraged her to apply for a free studentship to complete her five-year course, Emmeline did not reply; she was busily preoccupied with other matters including moving house to cheaper accommodation at 60 Upper Brook Street. The brass Registrar's plate was removed from 62 Nelson Street and put up at the new address, the dwindling Emerson's closed down. Amidst these changes, Emmeline rejoiced in the news that the clever Christabel had passed her law degree with First Class Honours, an achievement that would have particularly delighted Richard. On 30 June, a hot summer's day, the proud mother attended the degree ceremony at the university and, as Christabel's degree was being conferred, heard a member of the congregation shout out 'Why have you not brought your banner?' Overwhelming cheering soon drowned out the interruption, a response that must have made Emmeline glow with satisfaction.[35] Sylvia, in the meanwhile, was bitterly hurt that her mother had not answered her letter. 'We were no longer a family', she wrote some twenty-five years after the incident, still remembering the pain, 'the movement was overshadowing all personal affections. I had written to her regularly every second day in all the years of my absences. Now, my last letter unanswered, I ceased to write at all, except on matters of importance.'[36] Christabel's immediate removal to London, where she took up the important post of Chief Organiser for the WSPU, on a salary of £2 10s. per week, must have intensified Sylvia's resentment of her sister, a resentment that was to grow as the political differences between the sisters widened. Christabel took up residence not with Sylvia, who was moving her lodgings to 120 Cheyne

Walk, Chelsea, but with the Pethick Lawrences, at Clement's Inn. She continued to live with them for the next six years.

Emmeline was still living in Manchester, but active in by-election campaigns throughout the year. She does not appear to have been present at the campaign in Cockermouth, in Cumberland, due to poll on 3 August, where Christabel first put into effect the WSPU policy of independence from all political parties, including the Labour Party, by opposing all parliamentary candidates of any political persuasion. The move may have been motivated by the growing support within the ILP and socialist movement for adult rather than women's suffrage,[37] and especially by the reluctance of the Labour candidate, Robert Smillie, 'to push the cause of women to the front'.[38] Christabel believed that Labour parliamentary candidates all too readily dropped the claims of women in order to be elected; further, a pledge to women's suffrage by successful candidates, whether Labour, Conservative or Liberal, was useless since MPs would always give priority to their own party line. Christabel was determined that the WSPU should not become 'a frill on the sleeve of any political party' but that it should 'rally women of all three parties and women of no party, and unite them as one independent force'.[39] Her reaffirmation of the WSPU's 'independent' stance, supported by fellow campaigner, Teresa Billington, nevertheless created uncomfortable political choices for some socialist feminists. Mary Gawthorpe, who represented the Women's Labour League and was there to speak for Smillie, although very sympathetic to the WSPU, turned down their invitation to join them.[40] When the Conservative candidate was returned with 4,595 votes, Smillie polling only 1,436, the defeat was blamed on the WSPU.

Emmeline was quick to defend the new policy while also reasserting her commitment to socialism, a socialism that was based on equality between men and women and broader than formal Labour politics:

> I am a Socialist ... but I am also a democrat: I believe that human freedom should precede social organisation, that no social state deserves to succeed unless it is established with the consent of all sections of the community.
>
> For any form of Socialism to be worthy of the name, it must be established by men and women working together.
>
> I go further, I say that men have *no right* to make laws affecting women until women are free and have power to voice their opinions.[41]

Emmeline also made sure that she attended, with Christabel, a meeting of the Manchester Central Branch of the ILP, held on 4 September 1906, when a motion proposed by the Manchester and Salford ILP Branch to expel Christabel and Teresa from the party was debated. Christabel defended the new policy so successfully that a resolution was passed, by 18 votes to 8, not to expel the women on the ground that they 'have simply endeavoured to carry out the immediate extension of the Franchise to Women which is included in the official program of the party as one of its objects'.[42]

The publicity given to these events brought more recruits to the WSPU as well as interest in the women's cause from well-known people such as Elizabeth Robins, an author and ex-actress, especially renowned for her portrayal of Ibsen heroines. Although born in the USA, Elizabeth now worked mainly in Britain and was keen to write a suffrage play; she contacted Emmeline and the two met in mid September to discuss the idea.[43] Then the energetic Emmeline was rushing off to by-election campaigning in South Wales. On 6 October she wrote to Elizabeth:

> You ought to have been with us in S. Wales last week among the miners. I heard them calling out 'We'll vote for the women'. They are like great children & tears rolled down their big faces as I told them stories of poor Welsh girls stranded in our English cities. I had a perfectly lovely time. 15 meetings in 4 days. I am still as hoarse as a crow.[44]

With little respite, Emmeline then travelled to Glasgow for a demonstration on the 15th; while in that city, she defended the WSPU policy at Cockermouth, emphasising that if women's suffrage had been a 'prominent plank' of the Labour Party campaign, they would have supported the Labour candidate.[45]

In her 1911 book *The suffragette*, Sylvia too writes sympathetically of the Cockermouth policy, pointing out how MPs of all political persuasions would willingly break the pledges on suffrage that they made to women at the bidding of their party leaders. In particular, she praises Christabel for initiating the strategy, the wisdom of which many of the WSPU Committee doubted, and sees it as evidence 'of that keen political insight and that indomitable courage and determination which are so essential to real leadership'. However, in Sylvia's *The suffragette movement*, published twenty years later, a different account is offered in that the independent policy is now interpreted not as anti-party but as anti-socialist, a move to the right. Emmeline Pankhurst is condemned as a weak leader who upholds Christabel 'as an oracle', while Christabel is 'detested for [her] incipient Toryism'.[46] It is a narrative with which Emmeline would not have agreed and is not supported by her contemporary statements at the time. Yet the influential *The suffragette movement* has held a formidable sway with many historians.[47]

When parliament reassembled on 23 October 1906, Emmeline was back in London, leading another deputation to parliament. The Chief Liberal Whip was sent for and asked to obtain a promise from the Prime Minister that a woman's suffrage measure would be considered that session. When a negative reply was received, a demonstration of protest took place in the Lobby as woman after woman sprang up on a settee, began to address the crowd and was dragged down by the police. In the confusion, Emmeline was thrown to the floor; her followers, thinking her seriously injured, crowded around her protectively and refused to move until she was able to regain herself. Ten women were arrested, including Adela, Annie Kenney, Teresa Billington, Emmeline Pethick Lawrence, Minnie Baldock, and Annie Cobden-Sanderson, daughter of Richard Cobden, the well-known agitator for the repeal of the Corn Laws. The following day they were ordered to agree to keep the peace for six months or be sentenced to two months' imprisonment, in the Second Division, the place for common offenders. All chose prison. When Sylvia attempted a speech of protest, on the court steps, she was sentenced to a fortnight in the lowest section, the Third Division. Although Emmeline now had two daughters in prison, it did not deflect her from chairing a meeting at Caxton Hall, immediately after the trial, at which money was readily given to boost WSPU funds. Lady Cook, Mrs. Cobden-Unwin and Mr. Cobden-Sanderson each donated £100 while Frederick Pethick Lawrence promised to give £10 a day for each day his wife was in prison. A wave of public sympathy was felt for the militants at the disgraceful way they had been treated. 'By what means, but by screaming, knocking, and rioting, did men themselves ever gain what they were pleased to call their rights?' asked the *Daily Mirror*. At a NUWSS meeting of over 2,000 women, held on 24 October, the 'noisy methods' of the suffragettes were not condemned but applauded.[48] For the first time, Millicent Garrett Fawcett, president of the NUWSS, publicly supported the suffragettes and their militant deeds:

> Every kind of insult and abuse is hurled at the women who have adopted these methods. ... But I hope the more old-fashioned suffragists will stand by them ... in my opinion, far from having injured the movement, they have done more during the last 12 months to bring it within the region of practical politics than we have been able to accomplish in the same number of years.[49]

Florence Fenwick Miller, whose daughter Irene was one of the imprisoned women, poignantly wrote of how she and Emmeline Pankhurst, who had both been workers for women's suffrage since their teens, were 'proud and thankful' that their daughters are 'willing to give their youth, their rare talents, their prospects, without reserve' to the cause to which their mothers were devoted.[50] Pressure was put on the government by Keir Hardie and others to treat the women prisoners as political offenders and place them in the more comfortable First Division where they could wear their own clothes and have access to writing materials. On 31 October, the Home Secretary, Herbert Gladstone, announced in the Commons that the women would be transferred to the First Division. A jubilant Emmeline Pankhurst told the press how the 'most powerful Government of the time' had been forced to climb down in the face of growing public opinion. 'We are at last recognised as a political party; we are now in the swim of politics, and are a political force.'[51]

Emmeline had reason to be pleased. Now that well-known middle-class women such as Annie Cobden-Sanderson were prepared to go to prison for the women's cause and aristocratic women such as Lady Cook were willing to donate large sums of money to WSPU funds, the way was open for the Union to attract women members from all social groupings and political persuasions, rather than to rely upon those from working-class backgrounds with socialist sympathies. Emmeline was less impressed, however, with the conduct of Fred Pethick Lawrence. His imprisoned wife found her confinement so oppressive that she was heading for a nervous breakdown. Fred, who had taken over his wife's duties as Honorary Treasurer of the WSPU during her absence, wanted to get his spouse out of prison immediately and realised it could only be done if she agreed to keep the peace for six months. When he told Emmeline Pankhurst what he was going to do, she passed 'some scornful remark about the attitude of husbands' but softened her attitude when Fred pleaded, 'Do not make it harder for me than it must be.'[52] After her early release on 28 October, Emmeline Pethick Lawrence went to Italy to convalesce while Fred continued to stand in as Honorary Treasurer until her return, a situation that must have made the leader of the WSPU feel uneasy. Only women could be members of the Union and hold official office yet an exception had been made for the husband of a leading member. But, more importantly, Emmeline Pankhurst never liked Fred Pethick Lawrence. They 'never got on', there was always 'an "atmosphere" between them' recollected Jessie Kenney, one of Annie Kenney's sisters and Emmeline Pethick Lawrence's private secretary.[53] And Emmeline had another niggling concern on her mind at this time, in particular the name Elizabeth Robins was giving to the heroine of her play *Votes for women*, a heroine who, in her past, had become pregnant while unmarried and had then lost her child. 'I have been thinking a great deal about the play & hope you will forgive me if I put two points of view', Emmeline tactfully wrote on 19 November. The heroine's name Christian, suggested Christabel's. 'Now Christabel has no past still many people might connect the imaginary with the real & say that Christian's story is Christabel's. We should not like this to happen should we?' Emmeline's second suggestion was that the heroine should not be an actual member of the WSPU but a sympathiser, drawn to it by 'the insurgent work' of its members. 'Don't think me squeamish but our work is so difficult as it is without paragraphs in the papers when the play appears suggesting that this person or that is the original of the heroine.'[54] Elizabeth agreed with the suggestions and changed the name of the heroine to 'Vida Levering'.

Later that November, after the other prisoners were released early, Emmeline Pankhurst took a small group with her to the by-election at Huddersfield. Their prison stories were told with such effect, she claimed, that the Liberal majority was substantially reduced.[55] The Labour vote also fell, much to the dismay of the Labour Party organisers who, once again, blamed the WSPU women. The resentment was expressed at the Labour Party Conference at Belfast in January 1907 when a motion to support a Women's Enfranchisement Bill, strongly backed by Hardie, was overwhelmingly defeated by 605,000 votes to 268,000, in favour of an adult suffrage measure. In dejected spirit, an emotional Hardie announced that if the resolution that had been carried was intended to bind the action of the Labour Party in the House of Commons, he would have to seriously consider whether he could continue his membership. 'The party is largely my own child, and I would not sever myself lightly from what has been my life's work', he explained. 'But I cannot be untrue to my principles, and I would have to do so were I not to do my utmost to remove the stigma resting upon our wives, mothers, and sisters of being accounted unfit for political citizenship.'[56] Emmeline sat silent amongst the stunned delegates, knowing that she could not advise her old friend to resign from the Labour Party since it would leave him politically isolated. Faced with the threat of Hardie's resignation, the party executive gave its members freedom to choose between women's enfranchisement on existing terms or adult suffrage, a decision which meant that the Labour Party itself would take no action at all.[57]

With these events still ringing in her ears, Emmeline travelled to the by-election campaign in Aberdeen early the following month. She was finding herself in an increasingly difficult position, torn between competing loyalties of gender and class. As the feminist leader of the women-only WSPU she put women first, stressing the need to end sex discrimination in the existing franchise laws which meant campaigning for women's suffrage on the same property terms that applied to men; as a socialist and an ILP member, she was aware of the necessity for raising both working-class men and women through the demand for an adult suffrage measure. At one of Emmeline's Aberdeen meetings, the two local WSPU organisers added to the confusion by seconding a women's suffrage resolution not along official WSPU lines; instead, one organiser referred to adult suffrage and the other to women taxpayers. When the chair of the meeting, Isabella Mayo, attempted to clarify the situation by putting the resolution that WSPU members demanded votes for women in terms of the existing qualifications for men, Emmeline promptly interrupted her. The resolution should be allowed to stand as a demand for complete adult female suffrage, she insisted, an argument that caused some angry exchanges between the women on the platform. Eventually the meeting was closed, the chair 'accepting Mrs. Pankhurst's dictum under protest'.[58] This exchange of views reveals how Emmeline could swing 'between the poles', supporting on some occasions the ILP rather than WSPU position.[59] But the arguments Emmeline advanced at Aberdeen were rarely to be voiced by her again. The time was fast approaching when she would have to leave the ILP.

In the meantime, Emmeline presided over the first 'Women's Parliament', held at Caxton Hall at three o'clock in the afternoon of 13 February, to mark the opening the previous day of the new session of the 'Men's Parliament', so called because women had no share in its election. The plans had been well laid by Christabel, a brilliant strategist, who had encouraged WSPU organisers to find women who were willing to go to prison. Tickets were sold out well in advance and the Exeter Hall was hired to take the overflow. At the meeting, marked with an unprecedented 'fervency and a determination of spirit', a resolution was carried expressing indignation that the King's Speech the previous day had contained nothing about votes for women and demanding immediate facilities for such a measure.[60] The charismatic Emmeline rallied her followers by proposing that a deputation should immediately take the resolution to the Prime Minister. 'We are ready', was the cry of women, amid much cheering.[61] A deputation of about 400 women sallied forth under the leadership of the elderly Charlotte Despard, meeting fierce resistance as it neared Westminster Abbey; foot police punched the women between the shoulders and bumped them in the back with their knees while mounted police reared their horses over them. Hour after hour, further contingents of women tried to reach the Commons and received the same treatment. A group of fifteen women who did manage to reach the Lobby were promptly arrested when they attempted to hold a meeting. By 10 p.m., when the mêlée had ended, sixty women had been arrested, including Charlotte Despard and Christabel and Sylvia. Emmeline endeavoured to prevent her two daughters from being arrested but was unsuccessful and was herself taken to the police station where no charges were brought against her. Fred Pethick Lawrence arranged bail for all those arrested, something that he was regularly to do over the next six years. After the court hearing the next day, vanloads of women were sent to Holloway since all but three of the defendants had elected to go to prison rather than pay fines, the majority being given fourteen-day sentences. Newspaper headlines, such as those in the *Daily News*, 'Raid by 700 Suffragettes, March on the Commons – 60 Arrests, Charge by Mounted Police, Women Trampled Upon and Injured, Free Fight in Palace Yard', highlighted the brutality unarmed women had endured and brought further sympathisers and funds into the WSPU.[62]

Despite the violence, Emmeline's resolve did not weaken. Early in March 1907 she wrote to Sam Robinson, the secretary of the Manchester Central Branch of the ILP of which she was still a member. 'We are doing very well all over the country & demand for meetings & speakers greatly exceeds power to comply.'[63] She had renewed hope that the campaign might soon be over since, for the first time ever, the MP who had drawn first place in the private members' ballot, W. H. Dickinson, a Liberal, said he would introduce a women's suffrage bill. Some weeks earlier, Emmeline had already warned that if the government did not give facilities for the bill, Union members would not 'shrink from death if necessary for the success of the movement. We are not playing at politics in this agitation. If the Government brings out the Horse Guards, and fires on us, we shall not flinch.'[64] But hopes were dashed again as a number of professed suffragists in the Commons complained that the bill was not democratic enough since it would only enfranchise women of the upper classes. The bill was talked out on 8 March.

In response, the WSPU organised another procession to the Commons from a second Women's Parliament, presided over by Emmeline on the afternoon of

20 March. This time Emmeline asked Lady Haberton to lead the hundreds of marchers amongst whom were about forty mill women, recruited by Annie Kenney and Adela; all the mill women and Annie were dressed, as requested, in clogs and shawls. When the women reached the Commons, they were repelled by over 500 police; brute force was used as they rushed repeatedly at police lines. By the end of the evening, seventy-four women had been arrested.[65] The government, Emmeline complained bitterly, was sending to prison women whose 'militancy' consisted merely of trying to carry a resolution to the Prime Minister. 'Our crime was called obstructing the police. It will be seen that it was the police who did the obstructing.'[66] That same evening, while the women were still struggling in the streets, Emmeline left London for a by-election campaign at Hexham in Northumberland.

Emmeline had not led either of the processions from the two Women's Parliaments to the Commons since she was trying to confine herself exclusively to constitutional action that would not result in arrest and imprisonment. She knew that this approach was necessary if she wished to keep her post as Registrar, her sole source of income for herself and her youngest child Harry, still a schoolboy. Emmeline would go to the most extraordinary lengths to get back home in time to undertake her official hours of duty, often travelling alone by night trains; when this was impossible, her sister Mary, as noted earlier, acted as her deputy.[67] For some time now the Pethick Lawrences had begged Emmeline to resign her post so that she could devote herself full time to the leadership of the WSPU; the funds were now sufficient to give her, its key speaker, a guaranteed income of £200–300 per annum. Emmeline, who valued fiercely her financial independence, was reluctant to give up her employment, with the promise of a state pension, for the insecurities of a political campaign, and yet the failure of the Dickinson Bill indicated that she had to do so. She knew that the work of the WSPU was growing in importance; the Clement's Inn headquarters now comprised seven rooms, forty-seven branches had been established, eight paid organisers were employed and the income for the fiscal year from 1 March 1906 to 28 February 1907 was £2,959 4s.[68] As Emmeline prevaricated on the issue, a decision to relinquish her post was 'practically forced upon her' when the Registrar General told her that she had to choose between her political activity and her official position, a situation which Emmeline believed had been engineered by a clique of Manchester Liberals who strongly resented her determined opposition to the Liberal government.[69] On 21 March 1907, she resigned her post knowing that her fees as a speaker would not replace the amount of her government salary and pension.[70] She also decided to give up her Manchester home and provide for Harry's future by apprenticing him to a builder in Glasgow; Mary agreed to become an organiser for the Union. Emmeline barely had time to reflect on these matters when she had to face criticisms about WSPU tactics from suffragists within and outside her own organisation as earlier disagreements surfaced again at the ILP Conference held in Derby at the beginning of April.

Having being warned that the stance of the WSPU at Cockermouth would be discussed, Emmeline had agreed to attend the Conference as the sole representative of the Manchester Central Branch and to defend the policy. She had urged Sam Robinson not to press Christabel nor Teresa Billington to accompany her since she thought neither would agree to do so. 'I will if sent', she argued, 'speak for all. I have greater claims in the forbearance & regard of the Party than they have & am I believe more disposed to make allowances than the younger women.' If after her case was heard, the ILP decided that 'we must go out then we can part good friends. ... I should like to go to the Conference this time so as to clear up everything in a friendly spirit.'[71] At the Conference, ILP member Margaret McMillan read out a message on behalf of Charlotte Despard and Annie Cobden-Sanderson, both WSPU members, and Ethel Snowden and Isabella Ford, who were not, condemning the independent stand at Cockermouth and reaffirming a pledge never to go down to any constituency or take any part in elections unless it was to help the Labour Party. With trembling emotion in her voice, Emmeline disclaimed all connection with the declaration, pointing out that it was only by putting pressure on the present government, by opposing all government nominees, that votes for women could be won; in this policy they were following the tactics of the Irish Party, under Charles Parnell. 'Women could not afford to wait till a Labour Party was in power', she pleaded. Were she a man she admitted her action would be disloyal, but as a women with no political rights she pleaded for special consideration. On every other point she had been loyal to socialism and to the ILP. 'If you think my conduct inconsistent with my membership I will resign', she concluded in a broken voice. 'And if I am to go I will go alone.'[72]

Emmeline's plea caused a stir amongst the delegates which she described in a letter written immediately after the event to Helen Fraser, WSPU Organiser for Scotland:

> I was quite overcome by the response on the part of the men at the Conference to my declaration of independence. It was received with deafening cheers. I was able to make them understand our position as women. It was all a genuine tribute to the righteousness of our fighting policy. ... Men & women cried & protested that we must not leave the Party. Now the ground is cleared our enemies are defeated & we have only to go on with our work.[73]

Despite Emmeline's stand, she was popular enough with the Conference members to be elected as a delegate for the next Labour Party Conference. But that was a long time away and now Emmeline enjoyed the more immediate pleasure, on 9 April, of seeing the first performance of Elizabeth Robins' awaited play, *Votes for women*, at the Court Theatre, London.[74] She went back up to Manchester, where she was soon busily immersed in packing up her belongings at 66 Upper Brook Street. 'I am giving up housekeeping & am in the midst of packing & disposing of books, papers etc the accumulation of many years', she wrote in mid April to Caroline Phillips, a journalist and Honorary Secretary of the Union branch in Aberdeen. 'You will understand that it is not a light task.'[75] Emmeline made sure that all Richard's correspondence and documents, the family birth certificates and other personal papers were not thrown away. In particular, the personal letters from Richard to herself were cherished carefully all through the subsequent years of imprisonment and release, travel, war and residence abroad so that they passed to Christabel on her death; all the other papers Emmeline eventually gave to Sylvia, possibly in 1912, with a request that she would write a biography of her father.[76]

Towards the end of that April 1907, Emmeline met up again with Keir Hardie. Hardie was not well, having noticed just after the ILP Conference a strange numbness all down his left side, probably caused by a small stroke. Sylvia feared he was dying and wrote to her mother who immediately rushed to London. Ramsay MacDonald, a future Labour Prime Minister, saw a frail Hardie walking with Emmeline on one arm and Annie Cobden-Sanderson on the other, a situation which concerned Hardie so much that he wrote to MacDonald the following day explaining that 'Mrs Pankhurst and he had not made a tryst.' When MacDonald saw the two together again, on board a train at St. Pancras station, Hardie was even more troubled and asked Frank Smith to write to explain that the meeting was purely a coincidence, 'he had not the remotest ideas she was anywhere near. It seems she has a Scotch Tour arranged. ... For various reasons he would like you to know this.'[77] But what were the reasons? For some years there had been gossip in Labour Party circles that Hardie, a married man whose wife lived in faraway Scotland, was having an affair with the beautiful Emmeline, a captivating widow who had become, as Glasier was later to phrase it, 'the Delila [sic] that has cut our Samson's locks'.[78] It is possible, of course, that there was some substance to the gossip and that Hardie wished to avoid any hint of sexual scandal. But it was Emmeline's daughter, Sylvia, with whom Hardie – known as 'a great one for the girls'[79] – was emotionally involved, not Emmeline. When or where Hardie and Sylvia first became lovers is impossible to say although her biographer claims that their love affair began soon after Sylvia moved to London, and continued into 1912.[80] In one undated letter to Hardie, written while she was in prison, Sylvia writes of longing to 'feel your dear length pressing on me until my breath comes short'; although Romero suggests the letter was written about 1906, it could easily date to Sylvia's imprisonment in Holloway in February 1907 or a later time.[81] The most likely reason for Hardie's concern about being seen with Emmeline was his fear that it might be interpreted as a sign that he had deserted the Labour Party, won over by the charm of a powerful feminist leader who put women's suffrage before the party's interests.[82] After all both Hardie and Emmeline had written chapters for a recently published volume in which Emmeline had argued that the women's suffrage campaign must be above party politics and based in sex solidarity. '[T]o the women of all parties one appeals that they will, until they have won the vote, forget Party politics and unite in an independent campaign, having for its object the removal of the political disability of sex.'[83] A few months later, both Emmeline and Christabel put the principle into practice when they resigned quietly from the ILP.

8

AUTOCRAT OF THE WSPU? (JULY 1907–SEPTEMBER 1908)

The tensions that had arisen for Emmeline during the ILP 1907 April Conference continued to simmer during the following months when she faced the first and only challenge to her leadership from a group of socialist WSPU members who, in addition to the recent move to disassociate the Union from the ILP, were unhappy with its lack of democratic structures. The WSPU leadership was self-appointed rather than elected, and the Central Committee and the paid organisers (who now included Adela) were appointed by the leaders. Although Teresa Billington had drawn up in 1906 a hastily drafted constitution which recognised members as enfranchised voters and which declared the annual conference to be the ultimate governing power, it was felt that these aspects of organisation were ignored so that the rank-and-file membership did not participate in national policy decisions but was merely informed of them. In particular, it would appear that Teresa Billington-Greig (she had married some months earlier and added her husband's name to her own) felt deep resentment when, with the arrival of Christabel in London, she was transferred to the provinces to establish new branches. In favour of greater branch autonomy and democracy, it was rumoured that she, Charlotte Despard and Edith How Martyn, the Honorary Secretaries of the Central Committee, intended a coup against the leadership, a move that would be made at the annual conference planned for 12 October.[1] Emmeline, campaigning in the Jarrow by-election, wrote to Sam Robinson on 22 June 1907 asking him to let her have the letter he had shown her in Manchester, which she would use 'discreetly', since the 'same disloyalty' was at work again and she wanted the Central Committee to understand what was going on. 'I don't mind open opposition of a fair & straightforward kind but these whisperings & suggestions are not fair fighting. … I am tired with fighting the enemy. That makes it harder to face foes in one's own household.' The same day, in a letter to Sylvia whom Emmeline addressed affectionately as 'dear child', the identity of one of her foes is made clear. 'As for the TBG affair we have just to face her & put her in her place. She has gone too far this time.'[2]

After working in the Colne Valley, West Yorkshire, by-election where Adela and Annie Kenney, amongst others, joined her, Emmeline returned to Clement's

Inn. In between attending various fund-raising functions for the £20,000 appeal, she informed Sam Robinson on 15 August that she had 'to use' the letter he had sent. 'It has been a sad business & has given me a good deal of pain.'[3] Emmeline Pethick Lawrence spoke bluntly to Emmeline and Christabel about the internal tensions, pointing out that she had come into the movement because she had confidence in their policy and did not want to see their leadership 'watered down or diminished or even thwarted by some system of committee control enabling others, without the same vision, to share the leadership'; unless they continued to lead, she would have to reconsider her position.[4] At a meeting held on 10 September, Emmeline reasserted her authority as leader by declaring the constitution of the WSPU relating to organisation annulled, the annual conference cancelled, and the election of a new committee by those present.[5] She then called upon all members at the meeting to give her their loyalty, the majority agreeing to do so. Unable to accept the authority of Emmeline Pankhurst to introduce such changes, Charlotte Despard, Edith How Martyn, Teresa Billington-Greig, Caroline Hodgson and other disaffected members left and formed another grouping which two months later was termed the Women's Freedom League (WFL). Charlotte Despard was elected its President.[6] The WFL was also a militant organisation, with a policy similar to that of the WSPU, to which, of course, militancy was not exclusive. Since the dissenters had originally claimed that their organisation was *the* WSPU, Emmeline's society was initially distinguished from its rival by being called the 'National Women's Social and Political Union' (NWSPU), a nomenclature that was soon dropped in favour of the more popular WSPU. Emmeline and Mabel Tuke now became joint Honorary Secretaries of the Union, Emmeline Pethick Lawrence and Christabel continued as Honorary Treasurer and Organising Secretary, respectively, and Elizabeth Robins, Mary Gawthorpe, Nellie Martel and Mary Neal became members of the Central Committee.

On 13 September, a relieved Emmeline wrote to Elizabeth Robins, welcoming her to the committee and pointing out how they had said as little as possible to the newspaper reporters. 'All our best workers are with us. They are most enthusiastic about future work free from intrigue & wire pulling.' Emmeline also suggested that if Elizabeth was going to send her the advance proofs of the suffrage novel she was writing, *The convert*, then she could devote Sunday to it.[7] When the proofs arrived, Emmeline, who was in Bradford, spent all night reading them, despite the fact that she was feeling 'rather worn out' after rushing about all day and having two meetings. She took the time to make suggestions for change, revealing how she could be thoughtful and caring for women she knew and with whom she worked:

> I like it all immensely. ... The only thing that jars is Mrs. Martel. She is such a good soul really & I fear she will recognise the portrait. I would not have her hurt for worlds. She is horribly sensitive under that surface that repels you. Is it too late either to cut her out or alter her

beyond recognition? I'd rather see her cut out. She is a good fighter & came to our side when we had so few friends. In spite of her little ways which sometimes make me squirm, I am very fond of her & I don't like to think of her being wounded.[8]

However, Emmeline did not write to or visit another WSPU worker whom she had known in Manchester, working-class Hannah Mitchell who was suffering a nervous breakdown at this time. The deeply hurt, class-conscious Hannah felt she had been snubbed and, resolving not to work with the Pankhursts again, joined the WFL. 'I did not realize', she later reflected, 'that in a great battle the individual does not count and stopping to pick up the wounded delays the fight.'[9]

Elizabeth Wolstenholme Elmy was one of many WSPU members delighted with the way Emmeline had dealt with the tensions. 'Mrs. Pankhurst's so-called autocratic action', she confided to Harriet McIlquham, was a necessary 'desperate remedy' to meet a desperate situation. 'The whole intrigue is to make Mrs. Despard the despot of the movement, to put Mrs. Pankhurst & the rest of us under her rule – It is London intrigue of the worst kind all over.' She could remember how she had 'so often *seen & heard* Mrs Pankhurst cleverly & pleasantly tide over difficult situations, keeping her own temper & soothing other people's ruffled tempers', that she could not possibly accept the representations of her conduct and Christabel's give by Mrs. Rowe.[10] For the embittered Teresa Billington-Greig, on the other hand, Emmeline had proclaimed herself a 'dictator' who had 'elected herself and a few personal friends as an autocratic permanent committee answerable to no one in the world, and to sit at her pleasure'.[11] Rather than meet open criticism and discussion, Emmeline and her conspirators had deflected the key issues by cloaking themselves 'in the mantles of saviours who had boldly nipped an insidious conspiracy in the bud and had saved the Union at the price of their most cherished principles', while the dissenters came to be regarded 'as renegades who had plotted to sell the movement to the Labour Party'. This story was seized upon, insisted Teresa, not because of its truth but because 'Mrs. Pankhurst with that quick instinct for effect and that political unscrupulousness which mark her out', knew that it was the kind of excuse 'that would confuse the issue and leave the burden of justification … upon the new rebel group that had refused to submit to her authority'.[12] Emmeline, for her part, offered no apology for the autocratic organisational structure of the Union since she believed it to be the most effective structure for her charismatic style of leadership and the kind of campaigning in which the Union engaged. As she later emphasised:

The W.S.P.U. is not hampered by a complexity of rules. We have no constitution and by-laws; nothing to be amended or tinkered with or quarrelled over at an annual meeting. In fact, we have no annual meeting, no business sessions, no election of officers. The W.S.P.U. is simply a suffrage army in the field. It is purely a volunteer army, and no one is obliged to remain in it.[13]

As Rebecca West was to later comment sympathetically, in the midst of her battle for democracy, Emmeline Pankhurst was obliged, lest that battle should be lost, to become a dictator.[14]

However, it was the Teresa Billington-Greig reading of events, rather than West's, that has become dominant since it was in agreement with the socialist-feminist views of Emmeline's daughter, Sylvia, and elaborated in her influential *The suffragette movement* – 'Mrs. Pankhurst had called upon the members to support her as the dictator of the Union. ... Under the autocracy members and officials could be dismissed as readily as an employer discharges her cook. ... It was made a point of honour to give unquestioning assent to the decisions of the leaders.'[15] Although Sylvia also claimed, in a contradictory manner, that her mother was only 'nominally the ruler of the Union', the main work and policy being directed by Christabel and the Pethick Lawrences, it is the representation of Emmeline Pankhurst as a dictator and autocrat, which has consistently been upheld by later historians.[16] But how accurate is it?

Emmeline's autocratic rule was in theory only since during the years immediately following the 1907 split she did not choose to exercise any direct personal control over the WSPU. Although she was consulted on major policy matters, the daily executive control of the Union was undertaken by Christabel and the Pethick Lawrences, the three being known as the 'triumvirate'.[17] By now Emmeline was constantly travelling around the country, speaking in endless meetings and leading the by-election campaigning. Like a nomadic evangelist, she had no settled home but travelled with her belongings packed in a few suitcases, staying in hotels, rented flats or the homes of friends and supporters. Even when in London, she lived in the Inns of Court Hotel since she did not have a room at Clement's Inn. Although she often stayed as a weekend guest of the Pethick Lawrences in their home *The mascot* at Holmwood, Surrey, the spare room at their Clement's Inn flat was occupied not by Emmeline, but Christabel. When Emmeline appeared briefly at WSPU headquarters, she often felt like an outsider. As Jessie Kenney recalled:

> When Mrs Pankhurst came up from the provinces, she must have naturally felt a little bit out of things ... when so many secretaries were flying around and perhaps scarcely knew her. She was always 'the great lady' and liked people to know it. ... A desk was placed for her in Mrs.Tuke's room so that she would have the company of Mrs. Tuke, and the feeling that she was also the head of all departments.[18]

But it was in the by-election campaigning that Emmeline's personal charisma shone, not in the boring minutiae of day-to-day administration.

When asked some fifty years later to sum up Mrs. Pankhurst in one word, Jessie Kenney replied, 'Dignity'.[19] A small, slender woman who wore delicate kid shoes of size three and a half, Emmeline would stand on the platform looking poised and elegant in a dress of dark purple or black. The impact of her physical persona was immediate. She had an air of authority and although no longer young was still beautiful. Her pale face, with its delicate square jaw and rounded temples, 'recalled the pansy by its shape and a kind of velvety bloom on its expression'.[20] She captivated her audience by her apparent contradictions. Her fragile appearance belied a forcefulness, a driving energy, not usually associated with women described, as she was, as 'so feminine'.[21] Her radical words contrasted with her appearance as a middle-class, law-abiding widow and mother. The power of her oratory was well known and commented upon by friend and foe, alike. She was vibrant, asserted Rebecca West; one felt, as she lifted up her hoarse, sweet voice that she was 'trembling like a reed' but the reed was 'of steel and it was tremendous'.[22] Emmeline could sway great crowds, holding her audience in the palm of her hand as Ethel Smyth, the composer and Emmeline's one-time close friend, describes:

> the fiercest opposition would melt away before she had been five minutes on the platform. She used little gesture beyond the rare outstretching of both hands. ... It was all done by the expression of her face, and a voice that, like a stringed instrument in the hand of a great artist, put us in possession of every movement of her spirit – also of the great underlying passion from which sprang all the scorn, all the wrath, all the tenderness in the world. Notes bothered her and I don't think she ever used them, but no amount of preparation could have bettered the words in which her thought spontaneously clothed itself. I never heard her make a mediocre speech, let alone one that failed to hit the centre of the target.[23]

Mary Stocks, a member of the NUWSS, summed it up when she claimed that Emmeline Pankhurst was a 'spellbinder'.[24]

Yet, while Emmeline might be applauded on a public stage as she travelled tirelessly, she was often lonely. A 'bird of passage in some hotel', she missed the company of her family and friends, especially Christabel; when the spur of the cause flagged, her life seemed 'harsh and joyless'.[25] In spare moments, she would try to keep herself busy with an occasional visit to the theatre, reading or sewing, her favourite pastime.[26] Above all Emmeline, who believed she had an historic role to play, wanted to inspire and encourage her followers. Often this necessitated writing supportive letters or offering comforting words of advice. Earlier in the year, while on a train journey to Scotland, she had written to Jennie Baines in Yorkshire, 'I asked Miss Milne to send you £2 today also literature. ... I have also asked Miss Gawthorpe to try to make time to look you up. If you decide to hold more meetings you could no doubt get her to help and also the Halifax women … Good luck to you. Get a good Branch started.'[27] Sometimes her letters to Union members convey an anxiety about whether a planned visit has been efficiently arranged. In 10 December 1907, she wrote to Caroline Phillips, 'I expect to be in Aberdeen on Thursday the 12th. I leave Kings X at 10am arriving Aberdeen 10.5pm. … I don't know whether you can make arrangements for me to stay with friends. If not perhaps you will take a room for me at the hotel.'[28]

With so much travelling, preparation and encouragement to be given, Emmeline must have looked forward to spending Christmas that year with Christabel, Sylvia and Mary Gawthorpe in Teignmouth, mid Devon, in the vicinity of a pending by-election. Initially, Sylvia had refused when her mother asked her to come since she had recently received a letter which aroused in her 'a sudden storm of misery'; it was probably from Hardie, who was abroad, possibly suggesting that they should no longer see each other. Not wanting to be alone, the sensitive Sylvia decided to join her family, arriving on Christmas Eve when a furious gale was blowing. But the merriment of the three women who greeted her was not suited to Sylvia's melancholy. On the day after Christmas she insisted on returning to London.[29] It is highly probable that Emmeline did not know that her old friend, Keir Hardie, now fifty-one years old, and her daughter, just half his age, were lovers although she must have become aware of the relationship at some time during the subsequent years. In 1913, Ethel Smyth told Emmeline, 'Sylvia will never be a amazon. If it isn't J. K. H. it will be someone else.'[30] But, at Christmas 1907, these matters were not spoken about and Sylvia merely felt her 'mother's disgust' when she left Teignmouth early.[31] Such behaviour, plus Sylvia's continual allegiance to the ILP, undoubtedly helped Emmeline to form an impression of her second daughter as difficult. She could be a possessive mother, brooking no dissent from her views, perhaps a particularly Victorian trait.[32]

The turbulent Newton Abbot by-election that Emmeline fought early in 1908 was made worse by severe frost and an infrequent train service. The hostility shown towards her and her co-worker, Nellie Martel, erupted into violence on 18 January when the result was announced in favour of the Conservative candidate. Both women were attacked by a group of young male clay-cutters who had supported the ousted Liberal candidate whom the two had opposed. Pelted with clay, rotten eggs and snowballs packed with stones, Emmeline and Nellie ran to the haven of a grocer's shop and then out through the back door only to find the hooligans waiting for them. While Emmeline and the grocer's wife managed to wrestle the half-fainting Nellie from the man who was beating her and push her back into the safety of the shop, Emmeline was not so fortunate. As she stood on the threshold of the door, a staggering blow fell on the back of her head, throwing her to the muddy ground. Momentarily stunned, and with her ankle badly bruised, she regained consciousness and found a silent ring of men around her. Afraid that she might be placed in an empty barrel nearby, Emmeline courageously asked, 'Are none of you *men*?'

Although the mob fled when the police arrived, it was two hours before it was considered safe to leave.[33]

On her return to London, Emmeline found Harry staying at Sylvia's lodgings, the builder to whom he had been apprenticed in Glasgow having gone bankrupt. She was both disappointed and concerned that her son was not settled in an occupation. Realising that an outdoor life in the harsh Clydeside winters had been unsuited to Harry's delicate health, Christabel came up with the idea that he would fare better in an office job as a secretary. Emmeline enthusiastically embraced the suggestion, offering to pay for classes in shorthand and typing and to give her son a weekly allowance of £1 per week. She also insisted that Harry should get a reader's ticket for the British Museum, to further his general education. With the matter settled, Emmeline went off to the provinces again, to Leeds, despite the fact that her bruised ankle had not healed. With their mother out of the way, Christabel and Sylvia arranged an eye test for Harry and the purchasing of the spectacles that Emmeline had discouraged. But Harry had less interest in studying than in the suffrage and socialist movements, which drew him 'like a magnet'. Soon he was heckling politicians, chalking pavements, speaking at street corners and doing a range of useful political work.[34]

Once in Leeds, the intense pain in Emmeline's ankle forced her to lie down between meetings and then hobble in and out of motor cars as she rushed from one gathering to the next, expectant that the vote could be won that year. A Liberal MP friendly to the women's cause, Mr. Stanger, had drawn a place in the private members' ballot and 28 February was the day fixed for the second reading of a women's franchise bill. Emmeline's fervour communicated itself to her audiences, especially in the final torchlight procession to Hunslet Moor where an enthusiastic crowd of 100,000 people waited to greet her, Mary Gawthorpe, Rosamund Massy and Rachel Barrett.[35] The police had refused protection for the speakers but the vast crowd kept order and parted to let the speakers through as local women in their broad Yorkshire accents kept up a chorus 'Shall us win? Shall us have the vote? We shall!'[36] Emmeline was succeeding in her aim of rousing women to claim their citizenship rights. As Frances Rowe confided to Harriet McIlquham, 'Mrs. Pankhurst works such appeals and how quickly women respond! A Miss Naylor who a few weeks ago began to take part in the protests at meetings & said she could never *speak*, could not put two words together, is down ... for meetings all over the country.'[37]

Still lame from the injury to her ankle, an elated Emmeline returned to London for the last day of another Women's Parliament, 13 February. 'I have come back to London feeling as I have never felt before, that we are near the end of the struggle', she told her audience at the Caxton Hall. 'I feel that the time has come when I must act.'[38] She proposed to form a deputation to parliament to challenge the Tumultuous Petitions Act, dating from the reign of Charles II, which stated that no person should repair to the King or parliament with the intention of presenting or delivering any petition accompanied by above ten persons. The penalty for breaking the law was a fine of £100 or three months' imprisonment. The day previously, at Westminster Police Court, Mr. Muskett, prosecuting for the Crown, had sentenced suffragettes standing in the dock to the usual two months' imprisonment or a fine of £5 warning them that if they ever offended again, he would revive the Tumultuous Petitions Act. Christabel immediately announced that if the government wanted twelve women or even more to be tried under that Act, they could be found. At the Caxton Hall meeting the next day, Emmeline put the plan into action knowing that, since she was no longer a government employee, she could risk imprisonment. She stated that she would carry a resolution to parliament, demanding the immediate enfranchisement of women, and twelve women – including Annie Kenney, Gladice Keevil and Minnie Baldock – volunteered to accompany her.[39]

As Emmeline limped out with her group of twelve, Flora Drummond hailed a man passing by driving a dog-cart, asking him if he would take Mrs. Pankhurst to the House of Commons – to which he readily agreed. Emmeline was helped up to the seat behind him while the other women formed a line behind the cart. They had not gone far when the police ordered her to dismount. Emmeline limped along with her companions, who would have supported her, but the police insisted that they walk single-file. She grew so faint from the pain of her ankle that she called to two of the women for support. A large, swaying crowd watched the women who were surrounded on all sides by foot and mounted police. 'You might have supposed', commented Emmeline sarcastically, 'that instead of thirteen women, one of them lame, walking quietly along, the town was in the hands of an armed mob.'[40] When the small procession reached Parliament Square, two policemen suddenly grasped Emmeline's arms on either side and told her she was under arrest. Still holding the rolled petition in one hand, and a small bunch of lilies of the valley in the other, she retained a dignified manner as she was taken to Cannon Row Police Station. Released on bail, Emmeline and her band burst in on the evening meeting of the Women's Parliament to a thunder of applause. 'We shall never rest or falter', she rallied her audience, 'till the long weary struggle for enfranchisement is won.'[41]

Emmeline listened with incredulity at the perjuries put forward by the prosecution at the trial who accused the women of 'riotous and vulgar behaviour, knocking off policemen's helmets, assaulting the officers'.[42] Nothing further was said about the Tumultuous Petitions Act; instead, when she tried to speak in her own defence, she was cut short. Christabel, Sylvia and the Pethick Lawrences had managed to gain admission to the crowded police court but not Harry who was waiting outside, in the hall, when Mary Blathwayt arrived. She persuaded a friendly policeman to allow her to go and buy food for the hungry young man and other waiting relatives and friends, and shortly returned with buns, rock cakes, bananas and chocolate.[43] Inside the court, Emmeline had refused to be bound over and so she and eight of her companions were sentenced to six weeks in the Second Division.

This was Emmeline's first imprisonment, the harshness and indignity of which she never forgot. She was ordered to strip – although the authorities did allow her to take off her underclothes in a bath-room – and shivered herself into patched and stained underclothes, coarse, brown woollen stockings with red stripes, a shapeless prison dress stamped with broad arrows, and mismatched old shoes. Despite her prison garb, to the other imprisoned suffragettes Emmeline still retained 'a certain "chic" which none of us ever hoped to acquire'.[44] Once in her prison cell, the hard narrow bed seemed almost welcoming to Emmeline's exhausted body, but the feeling soon passed. The enclosed cell space, like 'a tomb', pressed heavily upon her, causing another attack of migraine.[45] After two days of solitary confinement she was sent to the hospital where, about midnight, she was awoken by the moaning of a woman in labour in the cell next to her own. 'I shall never forget that night, nor what I suffered with the birth-pangs of that woman, who, I found later, was simply waiting trial on a charge which was found to be baseless.'[46] Being in hospital, she was deprived of chapel and of work. Desperate to keep herself occupied, Emmeline asked her wardress for some sewing and knitting. She also translated a French book, brought by the chaplain from the prison library, on a slate that was given her instead of a pencil and paper, and tried to remember the content of some of her school lessons. Finding the cold hard to bear, she asked for her fur coat to keep her warm, but was refused the request.[47]

While Emmeline was in prison, Stanger's Women's Enfranchisement Bill passed its second reading on 28 February by 271 votes to 92; however, the bill was blocked from progressing further since the Speaker had ruled that a vote was only permitted on condition that the bill did not pass to one of the standing committees set up to deal with such measures but to a committee of the whole House – which meant that the government would not provide facilities. On the 28th, Herbert Gladstone, the Home Secretary, made a statement that greatly interested Emmeline and other WSPU members when he suggested that experience revealed that argument alone 'is not enough' to win women's suffrage:

> There comes a time when political dynamics are far more important than political argument. ... Men have learned this lesson, and know the necessity for demonstrating the greatness of their movements, and for establishing that *force majeure* which actuates and arms a Government for effective work. ... Looking back at the great political crises in the 'thirties, the 'sixties and the 'eighties it will be found that people ... assembled in their tens of thousands all over the country. ... Of course it cannot be expected that women can assemble in such masses, but power belongs to the masses, and through this power a Government can be influenced into more effective action than a Government will be likely to take under present conditions.[48]

Such words were honey to the ears of Christabel and the Pethick Lawrences who were soon planning large demonstrations in the provinces and in London.

Emmeline was released from prison on 19 March, one day earlier than expected. The WSPU were holding a meeting at the Albert Hall that evening to mark the end of a Self-Denial Week during which women had stood in the gutter with collecting boxes, sold papers, flowers and toys, swept crossings, sung in the street, abstained from butter, sugar, meat and sweets, held drawing-room meetings and tea parties – all with the aim of contributing towards the £20,000 appeal. Emmeline could have rested quietly at home, surrounded by her loving friends, but ever restless, and with a flair for the dramatic, she made an unexpected entrance at the packed Albert Hall meeting. There was always a sense of performance, of the theatre, in Emmeline's keen use of timing, oratory and costume, and she used it to great effect that evening. Like an actress in the wings, she waited till all the others were seated and then walked quietly onto the stage, to an outburst of ecstatic applause, waving arms and fluttering handkerchiefs. She removed the placard saying 'Mrs. Pankhurst's Chair' and sat down, deeply moved by the warmth of her reception. 'It was some time before I could see them for my tears, or speak to them for the emotion that shook me like a storm.'[49] Waiting till order was restored, Emmeline urged the women to do 'ten times more in the future' than they had ever done. She continued:

> I for one, friends, looking round on the muddles that men have made, looking round on the sweated and decrepit members of my sex, I say men have had the control of these things long enough, and no woman with any spark of womanliness in her will consent to let this state of things go on any longer. We are tired of it. ... They said, 'You will never rouse women.' Well, we have done what they thought and what they hoped to be impossible. We women are roused![50]

By the end of the meeting Emmeline Pethick Lawrence proudly announced that the total sum collected for Self-Denial Week, including the pledges made that evening, was £7,000.[51] The sum would help towards the organisation of a great demonstration planned for 21 June in Hyde Park.

The next morning, Emmeline and the other released prisoners were entertained to a welcome breakfast at the Great Central Hotel, some 300 women being present. When Emmeline rose to speak, the audience stood up and clapped and cheered. With emotion in her voice, she spoke of her prison experiences and then, in a common theme that was to recur in her speeches, enjoined the rich women who were present and whose lives had been sheltered, to go to prison to see the depths of bitterness and hardship there. 'Give us not only your money, but your lives', she pleaded. 'Come and fight with us to win freedom for women.'[52] Soon after Emmeline and the released prisoners were off to the by-election at Peckham Rye, London. In open brakes the women paraded through the streets dressed in their prison clothes, or exact reproductions of them, attracting enormous crowds.

On the evening of the poll, 24 March, Emmeline delivered a lecture at the Portman Rooms on 'The importance of the vote', an address that, unlike many of her other speeches, was published in a one penny pamphlet and sold throughout the subsequent years of campaigning. The lecture offered a feminist analysis of the gender divisions between the sexes which disadvantaged all women while also highlighting the plight of poor women and arguing the case for social reform. Emmeline outlined a number of instances where the laws made by men had ignored the women's side of the issue, as in the case of a widow left with small children who had no claim to any property of her deceased husband if, in his will, he had left it to someone else. Similarly, the divorce laws upheld a double standard. If a man wanted to get rid of his wife, he only had to prove one act of infidelity, but if a woman wanted to get rid of her husband she had to prove either bigamy, desertion or gross cruelty in addition to immorality. The Liberal government's programme for social reform, she continued, did not include bringing an end to such injustices but even included proposals by John Burns, a Cabinet Minister, to introduce legislation to limit the employment of married women on the grounds that it would stop 'infantile mortality and put an end to race degeneracy'. 'Could you have a greater example of the ignorance of the real facts?' she asked. 'I can tell you this, that infantile mortality and physical degeneration are not found in the home of the well-paid factory operatives, but they are found in the home of the slum-dweller, the home of the casual labourer, where the mother does not go out to work, but where there is never sufficient income to provide proper food for the child after it is born.'[53]

Emmeline expounded on the plight of women in the sweated industries, earning a pittance for long hours spent doing a range of backbreaking jobs, such as sewing men's shirts or making boxes. Even professional women, who had faced a long and weary struggle to enter the professions, found that their male colleagues earned higher pay and enjoyed enhanced career prospects. 'There is no department of life that you can think of in which the possession of the Parliamentary vote will not make things easier for women than they are to-day.' In arguing for women's right to equal citizenship with men, however, Emmeline emphasised that the demand for the vote did not mean that women wanted to 'imitate men or to be like men'. Women demanding the vote did not need to give up 'a single one of woman's duties in the home. She learns to feel that she is attaching a larger meaning to those duties.'[54] In stressing women's traditional role in the home, Emmeline was emphasising the differences between men and women and also advancing an argument that had a pragmatic significance. In a society where the suffragettes challenged the separation between the private and the public, between the deep identification of women with the 'social' rather than the 'political', issues of self-representation were critical.[55] Those opposing women's suffrage frequently claimed that its campaigners were

106

mannish and de-sexed. By insisting that suffragettes were womanly, Emmeline was not only showing that women did not have to become like men in order to be worthy of the vote but also developing a strategy whereby feminine women could undertake militant acts.[56] When the Peckham poll was declared, Emmeline heard that the Liberal majority of 2,339 had been wiped out and converted into a Conservative majority of 2,494, a change of nearly 5,000 votes. All the newspapers attributed the Liberal defeat to the 'Lady Suffragists', as the *Pall Mall Gazette* called them. The WSPU regarded the Peckham campaign as 'one of the most inspiring' in its history.[57]

Emmeline and her militants were now an effective force in exposing the Liberal government as an anti-women's suffrage government and could no longer, as Mary Phillips put it, be compared 'to the chirping of sparrows'.[58] The anti-government strategy came into full force after Easter 1908 when the ailing Campbell-Bannerman resigned and Henry Asquith, a well-known opponent of women's enfranchisement, became Prime Minister. Asquith's succession brought about a number of changes in the Cabinet necessitating a crop of by-elections in which, Emmeline proudly recalled, the WSPU succeeded in pulling down the Liberal vote by 6,663.[59] As expected, Asquith refused to give the required facilities for the Stanger Bill but did say that the government intended to bring in a reform bill that would be worded in such a way as to admit a woman suffrage amendment, if any member of the Commons chose to move one, provided the amendment was on democratic lines and had the support of the women of the country, as well as the electorate. Although Liberal suffragists were joyous about Asquith's 'promise', the WSPU denounced it as a 'trick', seeing it as a way to neutralise their by-election work.[60] Nevertheless, the WSPU now eagerly took up the challenge of Gladstone and Asquith to show the extent of support for women's suffrage by advertising the demonstration to be held on Sunday, 21 June. They chalked pavements, distributed handbills, canvassed from house to house, advertised by posters and sandwich boards carried through the streets, and even hired and decorated a boat to sail up the Thames to the Houses of Parliament when MPs were having tea on the terrace.

On 21 June 1908, Emmeline, accompanied by the aged Elizabeth Wolstenholme Elmy, led the seven colourful processions that converged in Hyde Park, attracting crowds of probably half a million.[61] There were several bands and 700 banners fluttering in the breeze on this brilliantly sunny day, including a banner with a picture of the WSPU leader declaring her to be a 'Champion of Womanhood Famed Far For Deeds of Daring Rectitude'. Although the Pethick Lawrences had been in charge of the arrangements, it was Flora Drummond who had organised the march with military precision, each of the processions being under the direction of a Chief Marshal who was aided by a Group Marshal, a Banner Marshal, and a Group Captain. Aware of the impact of spectacle and pageantry, Emmeline Pethick Lawrence had devised the WSPU colours of white (for purity), green (for hope) and purple (for dignity) and had asked women from all over the country to wear white dresses with favours in purple and green. About 40,000 demonstrators marched in the golden sunshine, including Keir Hardie, who walked with his brother amongst the ILP contingent, his wife and daughter following in a brougham. Although Emmeline, on one of the twenty platforms, was surrounded by a group of rowdy young men who drowned her words, most of the disturbance – including that also around the platforms of Christabel and Nellie Martel – was good-humoured. 'Never had I imagined that so many people could be gathered together to share in a political demonstration', she recollected.[62] Indeed, the gathering was the largest that had ever been held in the country on the issue of women's suffrage and attracted widespread coverage in the press. 'Woman's Sunday' ran the front page headline in the *Daily Chronicle*. 'If the demonstration proved nothing else', commented *The Times* reporter, 'it would prove incontestably that the suffragists have acquired great skill in the art of popular agitation.'[63] But Asquith was unmoved. A copy of the resolution passed at the closing of the events, calling upon the government to grant votes to women without delay, was hastily despatched to him by special messenger. On 23 June the Prime Minister curtly replied that he had nothing more to add to his previous statement.[64]

Asquith's response was to prove a critical turning point in the form of action that the WSPU adopted. As Emmeline noted, the WSPU had now 'exhausted argument' and had to choose between two alternatives. '[E]ither we had to give up our agitation altogether ... or else we must act, and go on acting, until the selfishness and obstinacy of the Government was broken down, or the Government themselves destroyed. Until forced to do so, the Government, we perceived, would never give women the vote.'[65] Some two weeks previous to the great demonstration, Christabel had warned that if the government still refused to act after such a public display of support, then the WSPU would be 'obliged to rely more than ever on militant methods'.[66] Asquith's provocation on this and subsequent occasions meant that militancy became a *'reactive phenomenon'*, each shift in militant tactics being a reasoned response to an obdurate government.[67] From now on militancy, which had largely involved heckling of MPs, civil disobedience, and peaceful demonstrations was gradually broadened to include more violent deeds, initially in the form of 'undirected and uncoordinated individual acts', such as window-breaking.[68]

Emmeline called another Women's Parliament, to be held in Caxton Hall on the afternoon of 30 June, and wrote a letter to Asquith, telling him that a deputation would wait upon him at half-past four that afternoon. Also, in defiance of regulations, she sought mass support by inviting the public to join the militants in a huge demonstration to be held that evening in the hallowed ground of Parliament Square. The Commissioner of Police immediately issued a proclamation warning the public not to assemble, although he insisted that the approaches to the Houses of Parliament must be kept open. Carrying a women's suffrage resolution in her hand, Emmeline set forth at the appointed time with twelve other women, including Emmeline Pethick Lawrence. When they reached the House they were informed that Asquith would not receive them. The women returned to Caxton Hall. At eight o'clock that evening, suffragettes ventured forth in twos and threes into the dense crowd gathered in Parliament Square which was cordoned by 2,000 foot and mounted police. Those who had volunteered for prison, attempted to make speeches as they clung precariously to the iron railings of Palace Yard until the police pulled them down, flinging them into the moving, swaying and excited crowd which included a number of roughs who had come to amuse themselves.[69] Enraged by the violence shown to their comrades, Edith New and Mary Leigh took a taxi to Downing Street and threw stones at two of the windows of Asquith's official residence. They were amongst the twenty-nine arrested, which also included Jessie Kenney and Mary Clarke, Emmeline's sister.[70] Since this was the first wilful damage ever undertaken in the Union's history, Edith New and Mary Leigh sent word to the WSPU leader that, having acted without orders, they would not resent her repudiation. Far from repudiating them, Emmeline promptly visited them in their police cells, and 'assured them' of her approval, an act which caused some WSPU members, such as Helen Fraser, to resign their membership.[71] The magistrate, when sentencing the two window-breakers to two months in the Third Division warned them that 'it would be far better … to adopt gentle methods. They would not attain their object by trying to terrify men.'[72] Emmeline pertly noted that window-breaking when Englishmen do it is regarded as an 'honest expression of political opinion'; when undertaken by Englishwomen, however, it is 'treated as a crime'.[73]

The action of Edith New and Mary Leigh throws further light on the issue of Emmeline Pankhurst's 'autocratic' rule. The popular representation of rank-and-file members as cultural dupes who mindlessly followed the orders of their dictatorial leaders is troubling since it denies feminist women agency for their own actions. As Vicinus highlights, 'autocracy' contained a strange paradox: any suffragette who accepted militancy to the full was following the policies of the leaders although, at the same time, she was making her own independent judgment about which acts she should engage in. Furthermore, as Stanley and Morley make clear, one cannot maintain a case for the Pankhurst leadership manipulating their followers like puppets on a string; the WSPU, they point out, was a loose coalition of women whose opinions, analyses and actions differed enormously and who might try out new tactics (as Edith New and Mary Leigh did) without discussion or the approval of Emmeline Pankhurst.[74] These important insights into the nature of militancy are supported by more recent studies of the regional branches of the WSPU which reveal a more complicated picture than that commonly assumed, suggesting that such branches enjoyed a considerable degree of autonomy that often reflected local circumstances.[75] This is not to deny, however, that in the higher echelons of the WSPU the structures were undemocratic and that close control was kept on the purse strings.

During the oppressively hot summer of 1908, the energy of the fifty-year-old Emmeline seemed to know no bounds. She regularly spoke, with Christabel and

Emmeline Pethick Lawrence, at 'At Homes' held every Monday afternoon at the large Queen's Hall, Langham Place, raising £500 at one such gathering when she appealed for financial assistance for the Union's work.[76] In between these London talks, she joined the by-election campaigning in Pudsey in Yorkshire and Pembroke in Wales where she met up with friends, made some new acquaintances and found time to engage in some relaxation.[77] While staying at the Mariner's Hotel, Haverfordwest, Pembrokeshire, Emmeline and Miss Douglas Smith were joined by Annie Kenney and Mary Blathwayt whom they met at the station. The following day, Sunday, 5 July, Emmeline had lunch with the young women and other workers and then, in the evening, joined some of them for a stroll.[78] But all did not run smoothly. Emmeline found the tram service in the area 'very inadequate' and hoped, via the offices of Professor Ayrton, the distinguished scientist, that a Mrs. Gregory would lend her motor car.[79] A car was duly supplied but, on the following day, it broke down for two hours on the way to St. David's. An anxious Emmeline was glad to relax that afternoon in the company of Annie and Mary, the three visiting the ruined palace and the cathedral in the town, where they all signed the visitors' book. After her talk in St. David's that evening, which Annie chaired, Emmeline was cheered as she drove away.[80]

Emmeline had announced, after the Hyde Park demonstration, that similar events would be held in the provinces and so she spoke at Nottingham on 18 July, Manchester the following day and Leeds on the 26th where a crowd of 100,000 gathered.[81] It was especially the warm reception that she received at Heaton Park, in her home town of Manchester, that Emmeline enjoyed. Accompanied by Adela, Christabel, Annie and Mary Gawthorpe, a Yorkshire woman known as a witty speaker, some 150,000 people were drawn to the thirteen platforms, one of which bore the words 'Manchester first in the fight'.[82] Although Emmeline had planned to chair the celebratory breakfast party for the release of Mary Leigh and Edith New on 22 August, she was persuaded 'with difficulty' to lengthen her holiday with Flora Drummond in Scotland. Christabel took her mother's place and read out a telegram from the Union leader, 'Heartiest greetings and congratulations to our dear released prisoners. Courage like theirs must win freedom for women.'[83]

Refreshed from the change of scene, Emmeline then travelled in September to campaign in the Newcastle by-election where some of the local socialist women were critical of her style and influence. 'How very theatrical they are', commented one member of the Women's Labour League, Lisbeth Simms, of the WSPU speakers generally. She was appalled at the amount of money the WSPU raised in distressed areas of Newcastle and when she attended Emmeline's meeting on 14 September, 'wished she'd had her shilling back'. Although most ILP members had complimentary tickets, others had to pay an entrance fee of 6d., 1s. and 2s. At the meeting, a further £30 was raised, perhaps two years wages for a local working woman.[84] Similarly, Nellie Best from Middlesbrough complained that there were 'ladies of wealth and position' leading the suffrage movement who wore 'evening dresses' at the London At Homes. 'Is this intended to debar servants, laundresses, &c.? Unless all women workers force themselves into the Suffragist movement before the vote is won, and throw their weight of their influence on the side of the workers, we may find ourselves eventually dominated and exploited.'[85]

Emmeline was not immune to these issues. Despite her resignation from the ILP, she never lost her deep compassion for the plight of poor women and of the necessity for social reform. Neither did she lose her links with the socialist movement, although the ties inevitably became less close. The claims of socialist historians Garner and Pugh that the 1907 split reflected the growing conservatism of Emmeline and Christabel, 'a straightforward left and right split', as Garner terms it, a claim that is probably based on Sylvia Pankhurst's representation of her mother, must be challenged.[86] Many of the reforms that Emmeline wanted were those that socialists advocated too and many of the rank-and-file suffragettes with whom she worked retained, at the local level, membership of both the ILP and the WSPU.[87] As Leneman has pointed out, in Scotland, where Emmeline Pankhurst was known, there were socialist women such as Bessie Stewart, Agnes Husband and Anna Munro in the WFL, but many of the 'keenest socialists', such as Mary Phillips, Janie Allan and later, Jessie Stephen and Helen Crawfurd, were in the WSPU.[88] Similar patterns were undoubtedly repeated elsewhere, as Cowman found in Liverpool where the WSPU branch was founded by Mrs. Morissey, a socialist.[89] For Emmeline Pankhurst, as for many of these women, votes for women was a women's question, not a class question. The first issue of *Votes for Women* had broadcast this message loud and clear – 'Come and join us, whatever your age, whatever your class, whatever your political inclination … if you have any class feeling you must leave that behind when you come into this movement. For the women who are in our ranks know no barriers of class distinction.'[90] Nevertheless, the comments of women like Lisbeth Simms and Nellie Best reveal that how different social classes related to each other was often a problematic issue, especially for some working-class women. While middle-class women could exercise and enjoy the economic and cultural capital of their class background, working-class women often struggled to realise their power.

After her campaign in the North East had ended, Emmeline travelled back down to London in order to greet at the prison gates of Holloway on 16 September the four women – Vera Wentworth, Maud Joachim, Elsie Howey and Florence Haig – who had served the longest and most severe sentences yet inflicted upon any of the suffragettes, three months. She considered it important to be there since she had missed the novel breakfast party for Edith New and Mary Leigh, a spectacular event that the leaders of the WSPU now regarded as very significant for making converts to their cause. As Emmeline Pethick Lawrence emphasised, 'The sight of the women who have suffered so bravely, and their words of greeting to the world as they come back to it, must go straight to the heart of everyone present, whether previously friend or foe to the woman's movement.'[91] On 16 September, the colourful breakfast party celebrations were re-enacted as the released prisoners were conducted to a carriage decorated with heather and purple and white flowers while fifty suffragettes, in full uniform, harnessed themselves to the traces. Flora Drummond then mounted the box, and at her command of 'Go!' the women drew the carriage, preceded by a band playing the 'Marseillaise'. Emmeline was amongst the WSPU members who walked behind the carriage and the general public, which grew as the procession reached the Queen's Hall where the breakfast was to be held, fell in at the rear. Presiding at the breakfast party, she was greeted with a 'storm of applause' as she rose to speak. Pocket handker-chiefs and table-napkins were waved, and 'For she's a jolly good fellow' sung again and again as the leaders and the four released prisoners rose to address the large audience.[92] Such webs of love and friendship offered Emmeline a supportive framework which she, in her turn, helped to sustain and inspire. The feeling of collectivity that such events fostered, the belief in the common bond that united all women, the emphasis upon sex solidarity rather than class interests, formed the backbone of the suffragette movement.

9

EMMELINE AND CHRISTABEL (OCTOBER 1908–JANUARY 1909)

After the long, hot summer of 1908, the cooler days of autumn were a welcome relief to Emmeline as she resolved to form another deputation to the House of Commons on 13 October, the day after the reopening of parliament. She was awaiting a reply to a polite letter she had sent to Asquith some time ago, asking if his government intended to carry that autumn session Stanger's Women's Enfranchisement Bill which was still before the Commons. On 9 October a negative reply was received. Emmeline had already warned that women would enter the House, 'and, if possible, the Chamber itself. ... Women have a consti-tutional right, being voteless, to plead their cause in person.'[1] The plans were now put into action.

Emmeline wanted to mobilise mass support for the WSPU demand for constitutional representation in a so-called 'democracy' and so decided to call upon the general public to aid the women. On Sunday, 11 October, when together with Christabel and Flora Drummond she addressed large crowds from the plinth of Nelson's monument in Trafalgar Square, thousands of handbills were distributed stating 'Men & Women, Help the Suffragettes to Rush the House of Commons on Tuesday Evening, 13th October, 1908 at 7.30'. 'The police were there', recollected Emmeline, 'taking ample notes of our speeches. We had not failed to notice that they were watching us daily, dogging our foot-steps, and showing in numerous ways that they were under orders to keep track of all our movements.'[2] Soon a summons was issued to all three women to appear at Bow Street police station on the 12th, on a charge of inciting to riot. Ignoring the order, the three women appeared instead at a crowded At Home at Queen's Hall where Emmeline defiantly announced, 'We are here, and we shall not go to Bow-street until they come and take us.'[3] The agitated audience expected arrests to be made, but instead the magistrate, Henry Curtis Bennett, adjourned the hearing until the next day. On the morning of the 13th, Christabel sent a note to Inspector Jarvis appointing their own time and place for arrest. 'We shall not be at the office, 4, Clements Inn, until six o'clock to-day, but at that hour we shall all three be entirely at your disposal.'[4] Incensed at this disregard for his authority, Curtis Bennett ordered their immediate arrest but despite an extensive search of WSPU headquarters, the women could not be found. Emmeline and Christabel had retreated to the roof garden of the Pethick Lawrences' private flat where, under a blue autumn sky, they were making preparations for their long absence. At six o'clock prompt, they walked calmly down to the WSPU offices where they were joined by Flora Drummond. The journalists who had been hovering in the corridors all day, got their story and flash photographs were taken as the waiting police read out the warrants for arrest. The three were then taken to Bow Street police station where the late hour meant that their request for bail could not be made, thus necessitating a night in the police cells.

Emmeline, who wanted to be in good form for the pleading of her case in court the following day, became anxious since there were no beds in the cells, only wooden benches. Earlier that day, Lady Constance Lytton, not yet a WSPU member, had visited Clement's Inn and, offering to help, been given the task of approaching the Home Secretary with a view to securing First Division treatment for the prisoners as political offenders. Unsuccessful in this task, she then went to the police station where she met Emmeline for the first time. Awed by Emmeline's presence, Constance willingly accepted the Union leader's plea to try to get them released so that they could have a comfortable night's rest. When Constance eventually found Curtis Bennett, he told her he could do nothing on behalf of the prisoners, although he did point out that the taking in of food and bedding to the cells was a matter for the police to decide.[5] Meanwhile, Emmeline had telegraphed James Murray, the Liberal MP for East Aberdeen and father-in-law of one of the younger WSPU members, explaining their plight. Immediately he arranged for beds from the Savoy Hotel to be erected in the cells, supervising the task himself, and for a delicious meal to be served from a table set with damask tablecloth, silver, candlesticks, brightly coloured fruit and flowers. When a breathless Constance and Emmeline Pethick Lawrence, whose helped had been enlisted, arrived with bedding and rugs, they found that everything had been provided to make the stay as pleasant as possible.[6] Yet, despite the relative comfort of her cell, Emmeline spent a restless night.[7]

The defendants had decided that Christabel, with her legal training, should act as their lawyer. It was with a proud mother's heart that Emmeline sat in the packed police court watching her eldest daughter conduct skilfully her first case at law. Emmeline had resolved to lift the political activity of her followers out of the 'squalid atmosphere' of the police court, where cases could be summarily dealt with, into the full arena of trial by jury, and so Christabel asked the magistrate at the outset that their case be sent for trial, a request which was refused.[8] In a brilliant move, she subpoenaed two members of the government, Herbert Gladstone, Home Secretary, and Lloyd George, Chancellor of the Exchequer, since both had been present at the WSPU demonstrations on 11 and 13 October. The case was adjourned for a week so that the defence could gather evidence and procure witnesses.

Emmeline's admiration for her eldest daughter rose to new heights when, in the crowded court room, the clever, articulate Christabel with her quick, legally trained mind, stated their case, teased out the meaning of the term 'rush' and cross-examined the two Cabinet Ministers. The two men were ridiculed and embarrassed, especially when Christabel quoted militant phrases from past speeches given by Lloyd George and pointed out that Herbert Gladstone had said, in a House of Commons debate, that women fighting for the vote should take action on their question. The humiliation went further when she quoted the historic words of Herbert Gladstone's father, the illustrious Liberal statesman, William Ewart Gladstone. 'I am sorry to say that if no instructions have even been addressed in political crises to the people of this country, except to remember to hate violence and love order and exercise patience, the liberties of this country would never have been attained.'[9] Although Emmeline and Flora Drummond also questioned the two men, it was the young, charming Christabel's audacious advocacy that captured the headlines, a fascinated press calling her 'Suffragette Portia'.[10] The event attracted widespread publicity so that the trial was like 'a suffrage meeting attended by millions'.[11]

As the trial proceeded, Emmeline's concerns about the effectiveness of the WSPU campaign if its two key leaders were imprisoned, which seemed likely, did not lessen. Realising the strategic importance to the women's movement of the well-known ex-actress Elizabeth Robins, with her dramatic skills and powers of persuasion, Emmeline wrote to her on 23 October, unashamedly asking her to use her influence with important people during the time the leaders would be absent and to devote her considerable talents to the women's cause:

I may not see you again for six months for I have a feeling that the magistrate means to give us as long an imprisonment as the law allows him. Facing this withdrawal from human society as I do may I without vexing you speak faithfully to you what is in my mind?

I believe that you could do more for the woman's movement if you could let yourself go a little more than you do. You have influence with many people which could be made useful if you made those people who admire you & believe in you feel what people who know Christabel & me feel about us. ... You have the gift of personal magnetism in a far greater degree than I have by nature. Naturally I am a very ordinary matter of fact person. It is very difficult for me to express feeling of any kind. All this natural reticence & diffidence has been overcome by my strong impulse to devote myself to the work.

It would be a great comfort to me during these months if I knew that you with your great gifts were giving yourself heart & soul to the Cause. ... Of the women who are left at the helm Mrs Lawrence will be the one to bear the heaviest burden. My daughter Sylvia will do her best to help her but she will need much more than Sylvia can give to replace Christabel & myself. May I hope that you also will be at her side?[12]

The following day, the final day of the trial, the three defendants gave their summing-up speeches. Christabel spoke first, claiming that the police court was like a 'Star Chamber' since there was no trial by jury. The authorities knew perfectly well, she told the presiding magistrate, that if the case were heard before a jury they would be acquitted.[13] When Emmeline rose to address the court, she assumed an appearance of calm that she did not feel. Beginning quietly and courteously, addressing Curtis Bennett as 'Sir', she endorsed all that Christabel had said about the unfairness of their trial in a common police court. Then, in her 'irresistible voice, as rich in minor as in major tones',[14] she made a poignant speech, relating her life experiences as a wife associated with the political work of her husband, and as a Poor Law Guardian and School Board member where she had learnt about the unjust marriage, divorce and illegitimacy laws that inflicted great suffering on women who had no right of legal redress. As a widow, she had performed 'the duties which ordinary men have had to perform, by earning a living for her children, and educating them'. She had held an official post for ten years, as a public officer, under the Registrar. 'Well, sir, I stand before you, having resigned that office when I was told that I must either do that or give up working for this movement.' The positioning of herself, in such a public forum, in women's traditional roles as wife, mother and hard-working widow, enabled Emmeline to present herself as 'feminine', a public self that facilitated her political activism – and revealed the depth of her commitment to the women's cause.[15] Because of the legal injustices to women that she learnt about, 'I have tried, with other women', she pleaded, 'to get some reform of these laws.' Yet although they had tried to be patient and 'womanly', using constitutional methods, presenting larger petitions than were ever presented for any other reform, holding greater public meetings than men have ever held for any reform, the vote was denied them.[16] Assuming the full responsibilities of leadership, Emmeline stated, 'I am here to take upon myself now, sir, as I wish the prosecution had put upon me, the full responsibility for this agitation', a theme that was to be reiterated throughout the years of WSPU campaigning. Then she closed her speech with characteristically determined but inspiring words:

> [I]f you decide against us to-day, to prison we must go, because we feel that we should be going back to the hopeless condition this movement was in three years ago if we consented to be bound over to keep the peace we have never broken. ... Although the Government admitted that we are political offenders, and, therefore, ought to be treated as political offenders are invariably treated, we shall be treated as pickpockets and drunkards; we shall be searched. I want you, if you can, as a man, to realise what it means to women like us. We are driven to do this, we are determined to go on with this agitation, because we feel in honour bound. Just as it was the duty of your fore-fathers, it is our duty to make this world a better place for women than it is to-day. ... If you had the power to send us to prison, not for six months, but for six

years, for 16 years, or for the whole of our lives, the Government must not think that they can stop this agitation. It will go on. ... We are here not because we are law-breakers; we are here in our efforts to become law-makers.[17]

Emmeline's pleading moved her listeners to tears; even the face of Curtis Bennett quivered. However, no mercy was shown. The magistrate found the defendants guilty and, denying them political status, ordered they be bound over to keep the peace for twelve months, in default of which Emmeline and Flora Drummond would serve three months, and Christabel ten weeks, in the Second Division. All three chose imprisonment. To an entranced public Emmeline Pankhurst now became the 'embodiment of the nation's motherhood, striving magnificently for citizenship, churlishly thwarted and betrayed'.[18]

Emmeline's first act on reaching Holloway was to demand that the Governor be sent for. When he arrived, she told him that suffragettes would no longer submit to be treated as ordinary law-breakers and therefore would refuse to be searched and to undress in the presence of the wardresses. For herself, Emmeline claimed the right as a political offender to speak to her fellow political prisoners during exercise or whenever she came in contact with them. While the Governor agreed to waive the search and to allow the changing of clothes in the privacy of one's own cell, he informed Emmeline that he would have to refer her third demand to the Home Secretary. Immediately, Emmeline sent a petition to Herbert Gladstone asking to be treated as a political prisoner with the right to have books and newspapers of her own selection; to be allowed to do literary work and needlework of her own choosing; to see her secretary and deal with correspondence relative to her public work; to associate, to a reasonable degree, with Christabel, Flora Drummond and the other imprisoned suffragettes; to wear her own clothing, and to provide her own food.[19]

Then a severe attack of migraine, which necessitated removal to a hospital cell, laid Emmeline low; she was barely able to struggle to her feet when the Governor visited her with the news that the Home Secretary had refused all her demands. In the cell next door was Flora Drummond; she was in the early stages of pregnancy and having fainted, had been removed to the hospital wing. When Flora was told she would be released early, on grounds of ill health, she cried out loudly to the Union leader, 'The Home Secretary has ordered me out!' 'I am glad', Emmeline replied, as the wardress scolded her for breaking prison rules, 'because now you will be able to carry on the work.'[20]

As Emmeline slowly regained her health, her wrath about the silence rule grew stronger. On Sunday, 1 November, at the afternoon outdoor exercise in the cold and cheerless autumn weather, she called out to Christabel to stand still till she came to her. Christabel halted. A trembling Emmeline walked to her, linking arms and speaking in low tones. 'I shall listen to everything you say', cried a wardress running towards Emmeline who tersely replied, 'You are welcome to do that, but I shall insist on my right to speak to my daughter.' Another wardress who had left the yard, now returned with a large number of officers. Emmeline was hastily rushed to her cell while the other suffrage prisoners cheered her. For their 'mutiny', they were given three days' solitary confinement while Emmeline, unrepentant, told the Governor that she would never submit to the silence rule again: 'To forbid a mother to speak to her daughter was infamous.' For such a remark she was labelled a 'dangerous criminal' and sent into solitary confinement, without exercise or chapel, a wardress being stationed outside her cell to see that she communicated with no one.[21]

Emmeline now heard, mistakenly, that Christabel was ill. In desperation, she made an application to the Board of Visiting Magistrates to be allowed to see her daughter, which was refused, with the crushing comment that she could reapply in a month when the answer would depend on her conduct. 'A month! My girl might be dead by that time', was her anguished comment. The anxiety caused another migraine attack. As she lay on her bed in the early evening of Saturday, 7 November, she could hear faintly the singing of the Women's Marseillaise and also cheering which helped to lighten the burden of her 'pain and loneliness'.[22] A demonstration of encouragement for imprisoned comrades and of protest against the petty and inhuman regulations of Holloway had been arranged. Brass bands played and Sylvia, Flora Drummond and other released prisoners sat in wagonettes, some in home-made prison dresses identical with the Holloway uniform, while the rank-and-file and general public fell in behind. By the time the procession reached Holloway, where they circled the prison twice, cheering Emmeline enthusiastically as they passed the hospital wing, it was about half a mile in length and thousands strong.[23] Contrary to the assumption of most historians, in these early years of the militant campaign, Emmeline was a popular leader, as she challenged the terms of women's political subordination.

Before Emmeline's solitary confinement, Adela – who had succeeded Helen Archdale as WSPU Organiser in Yorkshire – had visited her mother in prison and now a number of people, including Sylvia, Keir Hardie and Annie Cobden Sanderson, applied for visiting permission – and were refused.[24] Another large WSPU demonstration was held but since the roads to the prison were blocked by 1,000 police, the women demonstrators, led by Mrs. May, shouted into a megaphone, with all the strength of their lungs, 'Mrs. Pankhurst!' The crowd then took up the name which echoed back and forth. The exercise was repeated with the shout of 'Christabel!' 'They *must* have heard', the protesters told each other.[25] Continual pressure on the government, including the asking of questions in the Commons, eventually led Gladstone to concede that Emmeline and Christabel could be allowed to spend one hour of each day together. When Emmeline was also granted the right, after one month's imprisonment, to write one letter, her identity as a leader took precedence over that as a mother. She wrote not a personal letter to any of her children but a public letter for her followers, to be published in *Votes for Women*:

I am glad after weeks of absence and silence to be able to write to you. … I have been very ill, but I am better, in good spirits, and quite determined, as I am sure you know, to remain here to the end of the term imposed. … It is a great joy and support to me to know that although I am withdrawn from active work for a time you are working harder than ever. … In all you are doing my heart is with you.[26]

To militants within the prison also, especially those young women in prison for the first time, Emmeline offered encouragement whenever possible. 'Mrs Pankhurst was absolutely lovely to me in Holloway', wrote Kathleen Brown to Una Dugdale, 'whenever she could she spoke to me – or pressed my hand.'[27] Gradually, a few more meagre concessions were granted by the authorities to the Union leader and her daughter, including the delivery of two newspapers daily, permission for which was obtained through the efforts of Keir Hardie.[28] 'Mother & Christabel were in good spirits when I saw them on Tuesday last', Sylvia informed Elizabeth Robins on 26 November 1908.[29] Such fortitude brought forth admiration from many, including Emmeline's old friend and mentor, Ursula Bright, now confined to a wheelchair. The action of the militants seems to have rekindled her interest in the women's movement, from which she had withdrawn following her husband's death.[30]

Preparations were well in hand for the celebrations to mark the release of Christabel and Emmeline on 22 December and 9 January, respectively, when unexpectedly, the government released both women, and Mary Leigh, on Saturday, 19 December. A grateful Constance Lytton, who had now joined the WSPU, immediately wrote to Gladstone thanking him for this 'delightful Xmas box'; Clement's Inn 'was alive with joy' at the unexpected news.[31] The welcome breakfast held on the 22nd at the Inns of Court Hotel, decorated with evergreens and the banners and flags of the Union, was a rapturous occasion. When Emmeline rose to speak to the 500 women and men present, there were loud cheers followed by the singing of 'Rule Britannia'.[32] After breakfast, a colourful procession of about 200 Union members marched through the West End, passing through crowds of sightseers who were unusually silent. In front walked Charlotte Marsh, carrying a tricolour, after which Emmeline Pethick Lawrence, Flora Drummond, the Kenney sisters and the Union organisers led the way in front of a band. A number of WSPU members, wearing the Union colours, followed, marching four abreast, together with five members mounted on white steeds led by cockaded grooms. Then came the flower-decked wagonette, drawn by four white horses, with a banner inscribed 'To Victory', bearing Emmeline, Christabel and Mary Leigh. Closing the spectacle was a decorated motor car. When the procession travelled through Holborn and along Oxford Street the bands struck up the Marseillaise and 'See the conquering hero comes'. [33]

That evening, at an enthusiastic meeting attended by thousands in the Queen's Hall, the Union's colours were again evident not only in the decorations, but also in the clothes worn by those seated on the platform; while the chair and officials wore white dresses, Emmeline wore purple, and Christabel, pale green silk. Since the day was known as 'Christabel Pankhurst's Day', Emmeline took a less prominent role, allowing her daughter to speak first. She glowed with motherly pride when Christabel, the 'heroine' of the evening, was greeted with frantic cheering and shouting from the gallery and the stalls.[34] When Emmeline rose to address the meeting, she too was greeted by a great outburst of cheering; then someone stepped forward and presented to her a replica of a medal struck to commemorate the winning of the Bastille in the French Revolution. With grateful thanks, she remarked, 'I was born on July 14, the anniversary of the destruction of the Bastille. I shall treasure and wear this medal because I have always thought that the fact that I was born on that day has had some kind of influence over my life.'[35] Weakened by her imprisonment, she made a brief speech, gladly acknowledging the freshness of approach that the energetic Christabel brought to the campaign:

> I am glad that this is not my night, because I have not any longer that physical vigour of youth, which has just filled me with so much maternal pride. But I am thankful to say that though I have not the physical vigour of youth I have come out of prison with as much youthful spirit as the youngest girl in this hall ... after all, what have we, my daughter and I, done more than the other women who have been to prison this year?[36]

Despite her tiredness, Emmeline made a firm pledge, that in future they were going to demand the treatment given to men political offenders in this and in other civilised countries. She drew to a close by stressing the importance of women working together for the vote, rather than individually, helped by the best men.[37]

Early in the New Year, on Thursday 14 January 1909, the WSPU held a special meeting to honour the release of Emmeline and Mary Leigh. Mary Leigh was unable to attend and so an inscribed clock was formally presented to her, in her absence. But the evening belonged to Emmeline, a feminist icon, who was received by the whole audience standing and cheering. The Union leader was presented with a gold chain and pendant of amethysts, pearls and emeralds – the colours of the WSPU – as a symbol of the dignity, purity and hope she had brought into her followers' lives 'by her great passion for humanity'. A book bound in purple morocco, listed in purple and green ink on its white vellum pages the names of the subscribers, and spoke of 'the deep devotion of our hearts ... our gratitude and love'.[38] With controlled emotion, Emmeline addressed her audience, emphasising that if the Prime Minister did not include a votes for women measure in the King's Speech before parliament then they would demonstrate again, as they did before. Then she made an appeal for more women to join the suffrage agitation, particularly asking the younger women to volunteer to serve prison sentences. Directly and simply, Emmeline clearly told those women who could not help in any way, even by holding drawing-room meetings or assisting at public meetings in halls, that they 'must pay a fine. They must give money to Mrs. Pethick Lawrence, in order that the work which other people will perform can be done effectively.'[39] When the collection was taken, £300 was received in promises which, together with the money collected and the sale of tickets made a total of over £400.

'Thursday's meeting was very wonderful', Emmeline later wrote to Elizabeth Robins from the comfort of her room at the Inns of Court Hotel. 'I am very British I fear & feel very dumb & stupid when called upon to show my personal feelings in public. Still all the same the feelings are there!'[40] Emmeline's gift of inspiring service and devotion was by now legendary. 'While we admired Christabel', recalled one Union member, 'we loved Mrs. Pankhurst.'[41] Mary Phillips, a Scottish suffragette, expressed the thoughts of many Union members that January when she enthused that their leader's splendid courage in fighting with her sister women and for them, together with the complete trust she placed in them, gave her 'a place in the hearts of those who know her best'.[42] It was a devotion that enabled Emmeline to become one of the most powerful feminist leaders of a women's movement for all time.

10

'A NEW AND MORE HEROIC PLANE' (JANUARY–SEPTEMBER 1909)[1]

During 1909 Emmeline's life continued in a similar pattern to that of previous years, namely touring the country to win converts for the cause, speaking at by-elections, and short stays in London to lead deputations to parliament. Yet, looking back on her life, she saw 1909 as an important point in the suffrage struggle, partly because of the WSPU decision never again to submit to being classed as ordinary criminals and partly because it was the year when the Liberal government was forced to go on record, publicly, in regard to the oldest of popular rights, the constitutional right of petition. 'We had long contemplated this step, and now the time seemed ripe for taking it.'[2]

In the closing days of 1908, Asquith, speaking on the government policy to be carried out in the New Year, commented on the number of deputations which came to him, all asking for different things to be included in the King's Speech. 'I am disposed myself to agree with them all', he commented 'for, as each group in their turn come to me, I recognise in them some of our most loyal and fervent supporters.'[3] Emmeline felt deeply indignant that Asquith should listen favourably to the deputations by men and ignore the women's demands. Hastily, she wrote him a letter asking that a small deputation laying out the case for the immediate enfranchisement of women should be received. Asquith refused the request. On 25 January 1909, the day of the first meeting of the Cabinet Council, a small deputation from the WSPU went to 10 Downing Street and asked to see the Prime Minister. When the women, one of whom was Mary Clarke, Emmeline's sister, refused to go away, they were arrested on the charge of obstruction and four of them later sentenced at Bow Street Police Court to one month's imprisonment in the Second Division. At the trial, Mary Clarke voiced the views of all militants and many women and men throughout the country when she asked, 'Is it not time that some other method were found of dealing with this question than by sending the women taking part in it to prison?'[4]

Emmeline had not been in London on the 25th since she had been speaking in Leicester and then, in early February, shortly after the trial, in Torquay, Plymouth, Brighton and Eastbourne.[5] She felt deep anger at the way the deputation had been treated and was especially worried about Mary whom she visited in prison. The two had been close from childhood, and the thought that Mary, who was unhappily married and lived apart from her husband, was now in solitary confinement in Holloway, experiencing what she herself had recently been through, filled Emmeline with foreboding. Remembering how, during her last imprisonment, C. P. Scott, the powerful liberal editor of the *Manchester Guardian*, had taken an interest in the plight of the women political prisoners, Emmeline wrote to him on 7 February, seeking his help:

> I visited my sister Mrs. Clarke yesterday and found that she had just been removed to hospital.
>
> She is very weak & depressed & I fear that although in hospital she will have better food and more comfortable surroundings these will do her little good because she is in absolute solitude both in her cell & during exercise. Her companions remain in the ordinary prison.
>
> As you are aware she has no writing materials nor does she see newspapers.
>
> Will you use your influence with the Home Secretary to get her permission to exercise with her companions & to see newspapers?
>
> I am exceedingly anxious about her & Miss Douglas Smith who is very nervous & this is my excuse for troubling you in the matter.[6]

Scott duly contacted Gladstone who was not sympathetic. 'It is the old story', Gladstone insisted; 'these ladies make a great fuss about going to prison, and as soon as they get there they wish to be relieved of its main inconvenience.' He also mentioned how Mr. Clarke had written to him. 'He seems singularly hostile to the views of Mrs. Pankhurst (and his wife) on Women's Franchise! but he asked that special attention should be paid to Mrs. Clark's [*sic*] health. I had a report three days ago which was quite satisfactory.'[7] Scott seems to have persisted in his endeavours to wring some concessions since on 12 February Emmeline wrote to him from Bristol, where she was to speak at the Colston Hall that night, stating that what he proposed to do was excellent. She explained that she would be unable to see him in London the following Monday since she would be in Glasgow. 'My daughter Christabel however will be there ... & I am sure would much like to see you if you can make an appointment to meet her either at your office or ours. Mr Asquith as you know is still obdurate so the fight goes on.'[8] The crowded Colston Hall meeting, which Annie Kenney chaired, was another great success for Emmeline. After the tremendous greeting of welcome had quietened, she began in humorous fashion, saying that she would have visited Bristol some time ago, but had fallen 'into the hands of the officers of His Majesty's Government, and her visit was delayed'. Laughter and applause rang around the hall as she held her audience in the palm of her hand.[9]

Soon Emmeline was back on the by-election trail, campaigning vigorously in Scotland where she was joined, for some of the time, by a number of other

WSPU members, including Christabel, Adela, Flora Drummond, Mary Leigh, Nellie Crocker, Hertha Ayrton, Elsa Gye, Ada Flatman and Gertrude Conolan.[10] Adela had been sent to Aberdeen earlier that winter, to organise a six-month campaign, and Helen Fraser was horrified when she greeted her at the railway station since she had difficulty with breathing. 'Did your mother see you when you left last night?' she enquired. She thought Adela replied, 'Yes'.[11] But Emmeline, who could be firm in the way she organised her family, had not realised the extent of her youngest daughter's illness; furthermore, the 24-year-old Adela loved her mother dearly and did not like to upset her plans. Nevertheless, the woman doctor who successfully treated Adela was scornful about the way she had been allowed to travel when suffering from pneumonia.

It was while she was in another city of Scotland, Glasgow, that Emmeline wrote to Scott again, thanking him for all he was doing for the Holloway prisoners and for the news that her sister was better. 'She is not strong but can "endure" better than anyone I have ever known', she explained. Then she pressed home the point that 'friends' of the WSPU ought to impress upon the Liberal government that it should remove the grievances which have led women who were naturally law abiding to commit the offences for which they are put in prison. 'Please don't think I am ungrateful to you', she ended, 'I am indeed but forgive me for urging you to treat our women's question politically for until it is so treated we must go on with the sacrifice we are making of health possibly even of life.'[12] Scott's intervention was not successful; Gladstone decided that Mary Clarke could not be allowed newspapers since, unlike Emmeline Pankhurst, she was in prison for only one month and was not in a condition of 'nervous excitability'.[13]

No mention had been made of women's suffrage in the King's Speech and so Emmeline held another Women's Parliament in Caxton Hall, on 24 February, from which another deputation of women went forth, led by Emmeline Pethick Lawrence. The women, who included Lady Constance Lytton, Daisy Solomon and Helen Watts, the deaf daughter of a Nottingham clergyman, were soon arrested and taken to Cannon Row police station. Emmeline, Mabel Tuke, Jessie Kenney and Isabel Seymour, amongst others, visited them much to the delight of Helen who wrote to her parents that the visitors 'have been beaming at us all through the hole in the door, & making us all feel puffed up'.[14] Emmeline was in court the following day, with Christabel and Lady Betty Balfour, sister of Constance Lytton, by her side, where she heard the women's refusal to be bound over and sentences passed of from one to two months' imprisonment.[15] Then she was back in Scotland again, campaigning. This time she took her recently released sister with her.[16] Emmeline was comfortable with Mary; there seems to have been no sisterly rivalry between them, as had developed between two of her own daughters, Christabel and Sylvia. Mary had long ago accepted that her elder sister could be an influential force in the women's campaign for the parliamentary vote, and had been supportive in helping Emmeline to become a well-known political figure.

From Scotland, Emmeline then campaigned in Lancashire and the Midlands, with the occasional flying visit to London to speak at the Monday afternoon At Homes in the Queen's Hall. She also pleaded in *Votes for Women* for WSPU members to show how much they valued the work of the imprisoned Emmeline Pethick Lawrence by contributing towards the cost of buying what 'our devoted Treasurer' had always wanted for Union work – a motor car decorated with the Union's colours.[17] In private, Emmeline had confided to Scott that although she feared for Emmeline Pethick Lawrence's health, since she was not strong, they did not wish to get Mrs. Lawrence released 'on the ground of illness. She would very much object to this being done.' Instead, Emmeline had asked Scott if he could help in any way to get the sentence reduced from two months to one, in parity with that served on Charlotte Despard, leader of the WFL.[18] Emmeline also warned the government that the WSPU could not remain quiet in the face of their refusal to deal with women's suffrage this parliamentary session. 'Militant action is again forced upon us, and so strong is the indignation of our women that, in addition to our London members, others are coming from Lancashire ... to join yet another deputation.'[19] After the eighth Women's Parliament, held on 30 March, the deputation, led by the elderly Georgiana Soloman, widow of the Governor General of South Africa, with Dora Marsden, a graduate of Manchester University as the standard bearer, sallied forth to the Commons. Twelve arrests were made, including one man, a journalist, who objected to the way the women were being treated. At Bow Street Police Court the next day, Patricia Woodlock, who already had three previous convictions, was sentenced to three months in the Second Division and the rest to one month.[20] 'The time was rapidly approaching', noted Emmeline, 'when the legality of these arrests would have to be tested.'[21] She therefore planned for a yet more spectacular Women's Parliament to be held on 29 June, when the WSPU would insist on the ancient right of petition. But private matters impinged on Emmeline's public life again when, to her acute distress, her son, Harry, was unexpectedly taken ill.

Harry, who was back at Joseph Fels' farm in Essex, had suddenly developed serious inflammation of the bladder and was brought to the nursing home of two members of the WSPU, Nursing Sisters Gertrude Townend and Catherine Pine, at 3 Pembridge Gardens. Emmeline was deeply shocked when she was told that Harry needed an examination, under chloroform, fearing that it was 'the precursor of a fatal result'.[22] Her fears subsided, however, when her son came round safely from the anaesthetic and some of the symptoms of his illness appeared to recede. In a more optimistic, but nevertheless cautious, mood she wrote to Dr. Mills asking if it would be possible to alter Harry's next appointment with him from Saturday, 3 April to Monday, the 5th:

> Mr Pethick Lawrence has very kindly invited Christabel, Harry & myself to go with him to Margate for the weekend and on my telling him the position of affairs he suggested that I should write & ask you if

we can put off our appointment with you until Monday morning in order that Harry may have the change of air until then. He thinks that if Harry has to undergo treatment he will be braced up by the change. Of course we are entirely in your hands in the matter. ... I shall feel very obliged if you will let me know as soon as possible this evening your decision so that Mr Lawrence may either retain or cancel the rooms.[23]

As Harry was showing some improvement, Dr. Mills probably did not object to the change of plan.

Soon Emmeline was back in the provinces, campaigning in Sheffield. The busyness of her life left her little time to be with her children. Christabel and Adela she saw regularly while the skills of the artistic Sylvia, who was not an accomplished platform speaker and had neither 'the beauty nor the poise of her mother & elder sister',[24] were put to good use in creating designs and decorations for the women's cause. But Harry lived at a distance and was always a worry to his mother; his health was delicate and he was unsettled. Furthermore, in the days before a National Health Service, the not wealthy Emmeline had to pay Harry's medical bills as, in this instance, when she later sent Dr. Mills a cheque for £4 4s.[25] Realising that she needed to earn more money in order to care for her son, Emmeline wrote to an old American friend from her Women's Franchise League days, enquiring about the possibilities of a lucrative paid lecture tour in the USA in the autumn. '[Y]our Mother ... spoke of her desire to earn some money so as to be able to secure for Harry the best of medical care and asked if I could put her in touch with some reliable lecture bureau', recollected Harriot Stanton Blatch in a letter to Christabel.[26] Meanwhile, Emmeline made sure that she spent some brief spells in London during April and May when she could see Harry and also participate in a range of activities where she felt her presence to be necessary. One such event was the release of the Union's Treasurer.

Recognising the importance of comradeship for the success of the WSPU, and also for the effectiveness of its leaders, Emmeline urged all members to be present at the Holloway gates at eight in the morning on 16 April when Emmeline Pethick Lawrence was due to be released. 'She must feel that not only is she a leader of a great women's movement, she is the friend and comrade of every woman in the Union, and we are there each and all of us as members of our great and united family of women', Emmeline pleaded.[27] At the appointed hour, Emmeline, Christabel and Annie Kenney were amongst the 1,000 people gathered at the gates who gave hearty cheers as the Treasurer of the WSPU was released. Emmeline spoke of the breakfast welcome at the Criterion Restaurant, attended by between 400 and 500, as 'our private family welcome' to someone whom they all loved, valued and had missed. But it was the imposing procession that marched in the sparkling sunshine the following day from Hyde Park to the packed Aldwych Theatre, where Emmeline gave a welcome to the Union's

Treasurer, that captured the public imagination. The parade was led by Elsie Howey, dressed in armour as a suffragist Joan of Arc flying her purple, white and green oriflamme and riding on a large white horse.[28] Joan of Arc, the saintly French warrior, who was imprisoned and burned at the stake, was to become the patron saint of the WSPU, upheld as the embodiment of both female militancy and its persecution. A woman who transgressed gender roles by dressing in a male suit of armour, Joan of Arc held a deep symbolic importance for the suffragettes; as Marina Warner points out, she defied the limitations of her sex from a position of unorthodox femininity.[29] This was a theme that Emmeline understood as she sought to arouse and inspire women to assert their citizenship rights in the domain of the public sphere of the 'political', usually regarded as the preserve of men. Although her discourse, as we have seen, often emphasised the 'womanliness' of her militants, she also employed a traditionally male, military language to describe the WSPU and its membership – the Union was a 'suffrage army', and its members 'soldiers' who fought in 'wars' or 'battles'.[30]

Towards the end of April, Emmeline was in London for another aspect of the WSPU's work, namely its international links. We are so bound up with the struggle here, *Votes for Women* told its readers, that we are 'apt to lose sight of the world-wide significance of the movement. It is not the women of Great Britain we are fighting for, it is the womankind of the world.'[31] The fifth Congress of the International Woman Suffrage Alliance (IWSA) was to open in London on 26 April and Emmeline was anxious that no opportunity should be lost to explain militant methods to its delegates. This was considered particularly necessary since the WSPU had applied in 1906 to become a member of the IWSA, a move that was vigorously opposed by Millicent Garrett Fawcett, leader of the NUWSS. Since the IWSA had a policy of allowing only one national organisation per country to play a direct part in its proceedings, members of the WSPU could only be admitted as 'fraternal delegates'.[32] That April, it was Millicent Fawcett and not Emmeline who represented England at the Congress.

Emmeline was now an international figure, the deeds of the suffragettes attracting world-wide press coverage in countries such as the USA, Europe and Australia, but notoriety was usually attached to her name as the leader of a militant rabble. Just like British women, observes Rupp, IWSA members were divided on the appropriateness and wisdom of militant tactics.[33] A decision was made therefore at Clement's Inn to try to win the support of IWSA delegates by inviting them to share in the celebrations for the release of WSPU prisoners and, in particular, to participate in a meeting to be held at the Albert Hall on 29 April. On the appointed evening some 200 delegates attended the crowded gathering, including women from Australasia, Finland and Norway who already had the parliamentary vote. Emmeline and Christabel both gave stirring speeches, explaining why militancy was necessary. The self-sacrifice of the suffragettes who had suffered imprisonment for the cause was then acknowledged as, one by one, they were presented with a 'Holloway' brooch and an illuminated scroll signed by Emmeline, both of these artefacts having been designed by Sylvia.[34]

Emmeline's assessment of the success of the evening is not recorded but Rosa Manus, page to the President of the IWSA, spoke of her dislike and ambivalence. All the women seated on the platform, who had been to prison, held big banners and flags in their hands, she wrote to Catharine Waugh McCulloch, an active member of the National American Woman Suffrage Association (NAWSA), and when Emmeline or Christabel Pankhurst spoke a word they approved of 'they *all* called out together – here here!! [hear hear!!] or if they disapproved – shame – shame. It is a ridiculous way ... Everybody who at first thought they like the work of the suffragettes changed their opinion after that evening ... they do no end of harm by the way they act and go about in their noisy ways.'[35] Although Emmeline would have been disappointed with such a response, she had faith in the 'noisy' methods that caught the public's attention. Women had to stand 'shoulder to shoulder', fighting with the suffragettes until the final victory was won.[36]

By now, Harry's health had improved sufficiently that he was able to accompany his mother to the WSPU grand bazaar or 'Exhibition', as it was called, held in the Prince's Skating Rink, Knightsbridge, from 13 to 26 May, to raise money for the cause. Sylvia and seven ex-students from her art college had worked day and night for some three months to complete the twenty-foot high beautiful murals, painted on wood, that were used to decorate the walls of the hall and then used again at another event.[37] Nearer the time of opening, the exhibition was advertised by demonstrations and by the newly formed WSPU drum and fife band, in smart military uniforms, lead by drum major, Mary Leigh, as well as by placards attached to the Treasurer's new 15 horse power Austin motor car, painted and upholstered in the WSPU's colours.[38] Emmeline chaired the opening ceremony at which Dr. Elizabeth Garrett Anderson, the only woman mayor in England, gave the address. The colourful bazaar included two replica prison cells, a refreshment department with an ice cream soda fountain sponsored by a wealthy American supporter, Mrs. Baille Guthrie, and stalls of flowers, farm produce, dolls, books, needlework, china, jewellery, curios and millinery – as well as entertainment offered by the Aeolian Ladies' Orchestra, the Actresses' Franchise League and Edith Garrud, an expert in ju-jitsu.[39] Emmeline's own stall was devoted to millinery, 'the epitome of womanliness'.[40] By her side stood her tall, slender son – whom Teresa Billington-Greig once disparagingly called 'the only girl in the family'.[41] Emmeline's mother's heart swelled with happiness as people commented – 'What a charming boy. ... I did not know you had a son.'[42] The nineteen-year-old, eager-to-please Harry, so like his father in his support for the women's cause, was proud of all his mother had achieved and anxious, as the only man in the family, for her comfort. He personally knew the hostility that campaigning for the women's cause could arouse since a hostile crowd had once attempted to overturn his barrow full of 'Votes for Women' literature.[43] Like all helpers at the exhibition, Harry must have been delighted when he heard that £5,664 had been raised and 250 new members recruited to the WSPU.[44] As he now seemed fit, Emmeline thought it would be best if he went back to the farm since she believed, mistakenly, that an active, outdoor life would help him to become stronger. Perhaps also, at the back of her mind, was the thought that her gentle, shy boy needed to mix more in the company of men rather than with his sisters and all the other women in the WSPU.[45]

Emmeline was in London in mid June for the welcome breakfast party for Patricia Woodlock, a member of the Liverpool WSPU, who was released after three months' imprisonment in Holloway. She spoke of how over and over again Patricia Woodlock had 'taken a front place in the fighting line ... being five times arrested and four times imprisoned'. Her own resolve, she confided to her audience, to lead the deputation on 29 June was largely due to the way in which Patricia Woodlock had endured her solitary prison confinement. Amid great applause, Emmeline then pinned on the breast of 'this brave pioneer' in the suffrage army a special medal 'For Valour', as well as presenting her with an illuminated address and Holloway brooch. During that evening's grand procession, Emmeline sat next to Patricia Woodlock in an open carriage and then travelled with her, and the WSPU drum and fife band, to the public welcomes in Lancashire.[46]

On 23 June, six days before the important 'Right of Petition' deputation that she had called for late June, when Emmeline would run the risk of imprisonment again, the indomitable leader of the WSPU wrote to Elizabeth Robins, 'I wish I could get the breathing space in the country on the eve of the battle but it cannot be. I am resting as much as possible this week.'[47] But despite her preparation, Emmeline could neither predict nor control the direction the movement might take. She attached no particular importance to the action, the following day, of WSPU member Marion Wallace Dunlop, a sculptor and illustrator, who was arrested for printing on the wall of St. Stephen's Hall in the House of Commons an extract from the 1689 Bill of Rights, 'It is the right of the subject to petition the King, and all commitments and prosecutions for such petitioning are illegal.'[48] Yet Wallace Dunlop's subsequent behaviour, when later imprisoned, was to shape the future direction of WSPU policy.

Obviously, Emmeline could not be aware of these future developments when on 29 June she led a small deputation of eight women through the crowded streets to the House of Commons. The leader of the WSPU, commented the journalist Henry Nevinson, walked alone, in front, 'pale, but proud and perfectly calm, with that look of courage and persistency on her face which I should not like my enemies to wear'.[49] Emmeline, who had already written to Asquith, stating that a deputation would wait on him at eight o'clock on the evening of the 29th, knew that there was a strong feeling in the Commons that this time the women should be received; Keir Hardie, also asked questions in the House about the matter, much to the delight of the recently formed Men's Committee for Justice to Women.[50] Yet when the women reached the entrance to St. Stephen's at the appointed hour, Chief Inspector Scantlebury, in charge of the Commons police, passed Emmeline a note from the Prime Minister saying he was unable to receive them. The small group, which included the aged Georgiana Soloman and seventy-six-year-old Dorinda Neligan, who had been headteacher for some thirty years at Croydon Girls' High School, refused to move as Emmeline insisted, 'I and the ladies who are with me are subjects of the King, and we have come here in the assertion of a right.'[51] Afraid that the frail elderly women could not endure the inevitable jostling of being forced back and returning again and again until arrested, Emmeline quickly decided to secure immediate arrest by committing the technical assault of striking Inspector Jarvis lightly on the cheek: 'I understand why you did that', he said quietly. The other policemen, however, did not grasp the situation and began pushing the women. 'Shall I have to do it again?' asked Emmeline softly, to which the Inspector replied, 'Yes'. So Emmeline struck him a second time, and then he ordered the arrests.[52] Soon other small groups of suffragettes, in twos and threes, surrounded by mounted police, made desperate dashes from Caxton Hall towards the Commons, encountering on the way a 'maelstrom of shouting and swaying humanity'.[53] Lady Frances Balfour, although not a WSPU member, was amongst the crowd with her sister, Lady Betty, also a non-militant. She described to Millicent Garrett Fawcett, leader of the NUWSS, how at one point they had both been knocked over but were picked up by the police and of seeing 'one tall girl driven like a leaf up and down Whitehall' and others like her.[54] In protest against the way their fellow militants were being brutally treated, a small group of suffragettes broke windows in the Home Office, the Privy Council Office, the Treasury Offices as well as in the official residence of the First Lord of the Admiralty. In order to avoid harm to any persons inside the buildings, the stones were wrapped in brown paper and attached to a string. One of the stone-throwers, Mrs. Bouvier, later pointed out that stone-throwing had been lately engaged in by miners in Staffordshire in order 'to show their displeasure', while men who had thrown stones in the recent Winchester riots had not been punished for it but 'their grievances righted'.[55] It would appear that none of the WSPU leadership knew of the action beforehand, but approved of it retrospectively the following day when Christabel spoke of the window-breaking as 'essentially right, appropriate, and fitting'.[56]

Emmeline was amongst the 108 women and 14 men arrested and it was decided that her case, together with that of the Hon. Evelina Haverfield, daughter of Lord Abinger, should be treated as the test cases for the right to petition. At Bow Street Police Court the next morning, Emmeline and Evelina Haverfield were charged with obstructing the police in the execution of their duties. While Mr. Henle defended Evelina Haverfield and Emmeline presented her own case, both women pleaded that by the Bill of Rights and the terms of the Tumultuous Petitions Act, they were legally entitled to petition the Prime Minister as the representative of the King. Since the magistrate was uncertain about this particular point, the case was adjourned until 9 July when Lord

Robert Cecil appeared on behalf of Evelina while Emmeline, again, presented her own case. The magistrate, Sir Albert de Rutzen, ruled that although he recognised the right of petition, he considered that a Member of Parliament could not be compelled to receive those who wished to petition him. In delivering this judgment, he also expressed himself willing to state a case, if it were desired, for a higher court, as he felt that the issue that had been raised involved an exceedingly important point of constitutional law. He agreed to do this on the undertaking that Emmeline would make no further attempt to send a deputation to parliament until the case was decided, to which she agreed, until the end of the year. All the eight members of the deputation were released in the interim. An appeal heard in December 1909 by the Lord Chief Justice, decided against the two women; in giving judgment, he acknowledged the right of women to petition the Prime Minister but did not recognise the right of deputation to him. There was no inherent right to enter the House of Commons, and the women should have desisted when they received word that Mr. Asquith was unwilling to receive them.[57] The leadership of the WSPU regarded the judgment as a legal tangle which was bad 'in the fundamentals of constitutional liberty'. If Asquith, by a technicality of law could keep the letter of the Constitution, 'he is none the less guilty of breaking the spirit of it by his action'.[58] The determined Emmeline, appalled that the ancient constitutional right of petition had been destroyed, refused to accept the judgment as final. 'Far from discouraging or disheartening us, it simply spurred us on to new and more aggressive forms of militancy.'[59]

In between the arrest of Marion Wallace Dunlop in June and the December ruling, important developments took place in the militant movement that lifted it, Emmeline claimed, onto 'a new and more heroic plane'.[60] On 5 July the imprisoned Marion Wallace Dunlop, on her own initiative, began a hunger strike in an effort to be granted political offender status and placed in the First Division; after ninety-one hours of fasting, she was released.[61] The fourteen women convicted of stone throwing on 12 July were determined to follow her example. When their request to the Home Secretary to be transferred to the First Division was turned down, they refused to wear prison clothes or to clean up their cells; since the weather was unbearably hot, they then broke their cell windows in order to get some fresh, cool air. Thrust into damp, verminous, ground floor punishment cells for disobedience, they went on hunger strike, and were released.[62] Much to the embarrassment of the government, the hunger strikers recounted their experiences in great detail.

Emmeline was campaigning in Derbyshire while the women were in prison and fully endorsed Christabel's support, on behalf of the WSPU leadership, for their protest. While staying at the Devonshire Hotel, Buxton, before they were released, she wrote an angry letter to C. P. Scott about a report of the suffrage prisoners that had appeared in the *Manchester Guardian*. 'If you won't use your influence to end this unequal struggle at least you might refuse to allow your paper to be used to misrepresent women who are unable to defend themselves

& who are making a fight for decent treatment of political prisoners in an English prison.' Scott's reply, which Emmeline hastily sent to Christabel, did nothing to appease Emmeline's anger. On 21 July she mockingly told him that he and other men 'who profess to support our claim' are making it quite clear that they prefer the smallest party advantage to freedom for women:

> Had these heroic women who have come to the door of death in their fast in Holloway been bomb throwing Russians you would have been full of indignant horror but as they are women of your own race who have exercised the greatest self restraint & done the very minimum of violence ... you & other men take it all quite calmly. ...
>
> Can you wonder that we are driven to think that men do not yet recognise women as human beings suffering from intolerable grievances largely due to unjust laws imposed upon them by men [?]
>
> It is this apathy & indifference on the part of men who profess to believe in our Cause that is responsible for all that has happened in the past & that may happen in the future.[63]

Emmeline's critique of her supposed male supporters, however, seemed to do little to dent her popular appeal to both sexes. The very same day that she wrote to Scott she was campaigning with Mrs. Massey in the High Peak district where the audience was very receptive. 'It is quite surprising', commented Bruce Glasier in his diary, 'to see *young* men *and* women evidently sincerely touched by their appeal. Everyone credits them with great ability and earnestness.'[64]

Despite Gladstone's accusation that the fourteen hunger strikers had intentionally engaged in kicking and biting some of the wardresses, a claim strongly denied by the WSPU, there was general optimism amongst the Union leaders that the hunger strike was an effective strategy for quick release since their legal advisers had suggested that any resort to forcible feeding by the prison authorities would be illegal.[65] Christabel and Emmeline were soon to be proved sadly wrong in their faith in the government's response to the new tactic which had moved far beyond the civil disobedience of the early days of militancy.

Attempts were now made to either exclude or restrict women from attending Liberal public meetings. With great ingenuity and courage, suffragettes up and down the country hid in bushes and under platforms, scaled roofs, let themselves down through skylights in order to interrupt meetings with the dreaded calls, 'Votes for women!', 'Why do you not treat women as political prisoners?', 'When are you going to give justice to women?', 'Will you not put your Liberal principles into practice?'[66] Since heckling at public meetings was now difficult to engage in, some militants made their protest by breaking windows with bricks and stones as on 20 August when Asquith was speaking at the Sun Hall, Liverpool.[67] Emmeline was in Glasgow on this day, having been driven to Scotland a week earlier by Vera Holme, the WSPU's newly appointed chauffeur, when Adela was arrested together with Margaret Smith and two young

American WSPU members, Alice Paul and Lucy Burns; the four had tried to force their way past the police into a hall where a Liberal Party meeting was being held. With motherly concern, Emmeline accompanied the women to the police court the next day only to find that they had arrived five minutes after their case had been called. Refusing to wait for the women, despite the fact that they were on the premises, the magistrate had closed the court and forfeited the bail. Angry at such high-handed action, Emmeline and the other bailee, Thomas Kerr, made a vigorous protest, even visiting the Chief Constable, but all to no avail. The four offenders decided not to appear again, when summoned, and to Emmeline's relief, the authorities took no further action.[68] She now continued her Highlands tour, sometimes with Adela and Lady Constance Lytton by her side, and in late August, while sailing on a steamer from Oban to Fort William, wrote a cheerful letter to Elizabeth Robins:

> I am having a very good time here in the north although I have managed to catch a rather bad cold. Very silly of me!
>
> This part of Scotland is all new to me. I had no idea the country was so lovely.
>
> We had a W.S. meeting at Oban last night – very good & sympathetic. It was one of many in which I verily believe we have converted many antis.
>
> · One meeting does more good than endless arguments with stupid people.
>
> They have to sit & listen.[69]

Emmeline's peace was soon to be shattered.

On 17 September, Asquith spoke at Bingley Hall in Birmingham. Since women were barred from the meeting, a small group of twelve suffragettes were determined to make their presence felt. In particular, Mary Leigh and Charlotte Marsh, WSPU Regional Organiser for Yorkshire, climbed onto the roof of a nearby house early in the day, axes in their hand. They loosened slates on the roof and when the Prime Minister's car drew up, flung them onto the vehicle, breaking the windows and the lamp – while taking care not to hit Asquith or his chauffeur. The women shouted, 'No surrender' as a hose pipe was turned on them and stones hurled, in an attempt to force them down. Eventually the two were led away wet, wounded and in their stockinged feet, their shoes having been lost in the struggle on the roof. Mary Leigh and Charlotte Marsh were sentenced to three months' and two months' hard labour, respectively, in Winson Green Gaol while the other militants who had broken windows received shorter sentences.[70] Although the WSPU leadership had not advocated these spontaneous attacks on private property by the rank-and-file membership, which could undermine their authority to determine the direction of the militant policy, Emmeline, Christabel and Emmeline Pethick Lawrence had little choice but to endorse it. Emmeline, in reply to criticisms from the

Daily News that she should censure such disgraceful developments, replied calmly:

> It is very good of the editor ... to credit me with so much power, but I want to say that the women in this movement are in it not at my behest or at my request, but because they feel a burning desire to promote this cause of votes for women ... and if I were so false to this movement as to turn coward now and ask them to stop, I believe and I hope that they would refuse to stop because of my appeal. But I cannot make any such appeal with a full sense of my responsibility. As one of the foremost movers in this agitation, I say I have more hope of success now than I ever had during nearly thirty years of patient agitation.[71]

Christabel, in a letter to *The Times*, pointed out that they had been driven by the government to the use of stones since women were now banned from attending public political meetings while Emmeline Pethick Lawrence reiterated a similar point in *Votes for Women*.[72]

In Winson Green Gaol, the women went on hunger strike and within a week, the authorities had responded with artificial feeding; food was poured down a rubber tube that had been forced either up the nostril (the most common method) and into the stomach or, after a steel gag had been used to prise a mouth open, down the throat (the more painful operation) and into the stomach.[73] Although the word 'rape' was not used by the women who were subjected to forcible feeding, the instrumental invasion of the body, accompanied by overpowering physical force, great suffering and humiliation, was akin to it.[74] With disbelief, shock and deep anger, Emmeline, Christabel and Emmeline Pethick Lawrence condemned the government for inflicting upon the exhausted and starved bodies of women, who had been driven to 'the last extremity' of passive resistance, 'the horrible outrage of the gag and feeding tube'.[75] At a protest meeting in the Temperance Hall, Birmingham, Emmeline emphasised that the leaders of the WSPU 'took upon themselves full responsibility for the actions of the brave women ... in Winson Gaol'.[76] Thus began that vicious circle of hunger striking and forcible feeding that was to dominate WSPU policy over the next five years.

11

PERSONAL SORROW AND FORTITUDE (SEPTEMBER 1909–EARLY JANUARY 1911)

Emmeline implored Keir Hardie to help the women's cause by asking questions about the forcible feeding of the Winson Green prisoners at question time in the House of Commons, a request he willingly undertook at the first available opportunity, on Monday, 27 September, when Philip Snowden, Labour MP for Blackburn, also persisted in demanding information from the government. Emmeline's anger deepened when she heard that Mr. Masterman, speaking for the Home Secretary, justified the practice as the 'ordinary hospital treatment' that was applied in cases where prisoners refused food, and that his replies had been punctuated by 'laughter' from other members of the House.[1] The impassioned and compassionate WSPU leader, who claimed that she was hopeless at writing, took up her pen and wrote an article for *Votes for Women*, accusing 'a Liberal Government in Free England' of torturing women in an attempt to crush the women's struggle for their citizenship rights.[2]

Emmeline and her militants were not alone in their condemnation. In addition to a storm of indignant letters to the press, the Prime Minister was sent a memorial of protest signed by 116 doctors, including well-known names such as Victor Horsley, C. Mansell Moullin and W. Hugh Fenton. Henry W. Nevinson and H. N. Brailsford, leader-writers for the *Daily News* and supporters of the women's cause, resigned from that newspaper in protest against their editor's support for the government's action pointing out, 'We cannot denounce torture in Russia and support it in England'.[3] Emmeline knew about their resignation the day before their letter appeared in *The Times* and, reflecting on her own past life, immediately wrote to Nevinson, on 4 October 1908, expressing her concern:

I am sorry Mr. Brailsford & you have been driven to resign. Your absence from the paper will in so many ways be a loss.

I know you don't want me to say anything about the material consequences to you yet I can't help telling you that I am thinking a good deal about them.

Through all our married life my husband and I had to contend with the little worries which for most of us must always be the accompaniment of doing one's public duty and although small things count for nothing when making momentous decisions they make themselves unpleasantly felt later on. I hope therefore that there may not be too much personal loss added to the severance of party ties which your resignation must mean.[4]

Mary Leigh had been one of the first militant prisoners to be artificially fed and now, using her case as a test case, the leaders of the WSPU began legal proceedings against the Home Secretary and the prison authorities at Winson Green on the grounds that an assault had been committed, a charge that came to court some two months later and was not upheld, on the grounds that forcible feeding was necessary to preserve her life and that minimum force had been used.[5] That forcible feeding by the government could now be the expected response to hunger striking by suffragettes added to Emmeline's heavy responsibilities as the WSPU leader.[6] But, in addition, private anxieties about the health of the delicate Harry were also pressing.

As noted in the last chapter, for some months now Emmeline had been in contact with Harriot Stanton Blatch about planning an autumn lecturing tour of the USA, primarily as a means of earning extra income for Harry's medical fees. In 1907, Harriot Stanton Blatch had founded the New York Equality League of Self-Supporting Women, an organisation that was open to 'any woman who earns her own living, from a cook to a mining engineer'.[7] This suffrage society of working women, with an emphasis upon the common bond between the industrial and professional woman worker, must have greatly appealed to Emmeline who, as a penniless widow, had had to earn enough to support herself and four children and was now financially responsible for her only son. That the Equality League had brought into the American suffrage movement a 'new and aggressive style of activism',[8] added to its attraction. Once Harriot Stanton Blatch had elicited from the immigration authorities that Emmeline's prison convictions would be classified as political rather than criminal offences, and thus serve as no bar to her entry to the USA, the arrangements for her to speak under the auspices of the Equality League were placed on a firmer footing.[9] By mid August, Emmeline was joyfully telling Elizabeth Robins that her American tour was finally settled. 'I am having a whole cabin to myself in fact travelling quite "en prince". ... I don't think the authorities will care to make a martyr of me.'[10] The White Star Line generously allocated Emmeline the best cabin, for the ordinary fare, on the steamer *Oceanic*, due to sail on 13 October. Some months earlier, Miss Birnstingl had offered to accompany Emmeline on the trip and warmly, Emmeline had turned her down. 'Do not fear that I shall be lonely for I have many friends who will go with me, if I need them, who are not yet sufficiently keen to take up active work as you have done. ... I greatly appreciate the affection which led you to write to me.'[11] It was decided that Dorothy Pethick, sister of the Treasurer of the WSPU, would accompany Emmeline on her tour, her first visit to the USA.[12]

Emmeline was extremely busy in the early days of October, speaking at important meetings in London, on 7 October, at Edinburgh on the 9th, and at Liverpool two days later. Then unexpectedly, a few days before she was due to sail, she was confronted with devastating news: Harry had been struck down with inflammation of the spinal cord and was paralysed from the waist down. The sick young man was taken from the farm to the Pembridge Gardens nursing home in London where the sight of her boy unable to use his legs, and in great pain, tore at Emmeline's heart. Knowing that she needed money for Harry's care, especially if he were to become an invalid, and advised by Dr. Mills that her son would have the very best attention, Emmeline felt she had no choice but to undertake her lucrative lecturing trip although she confided to Miss Birnstingl 'I don't like going at all.'[13] She left her son under the skilled care of Dr. Mills, Nurses Pine and Townend, and under the overall charge of her sister, Mary, and her daughters. However, since Mary was a WSPU Organiser in Brighton, Adela was campaigning in Scotland and Christabel was the Organising Secretary of the WSPU, it seems to have been Sylvia who bore the brunt of the responsibility – and who failed to tell Adela, who was particularly close to Harry, about their brother's illness.[14] For Christabel, her mother's decision to leave her sick son was based on 'necessity'.[15] A resentful and embittered Sylvia, on the other hand, writing of the incident over twenty years later in *The suffragette movement*, portrays her mother as heartless, implying that she was responsible for Harry's eventual death. 'So ruthless was the inner call to action, that … she persevered with her intention … there was never a moment of doubt as to where she should be substituted – on the platform or by the bedside of her son. The movement was paramount.'[16] When Adela read Sylvia's account of these events in 1931, she was upset. Harry, she commented 'would surely be hurt to know that Sylvia used the opportunity which his dependence on her in the last few months of his life gave her to make money by trying to blast his mother's reputation'.[17] Yet, in her later biography of her mother, Sylvia changes her story. This time she claims that Emmeline 'steeled herself to persevere with her journey, declaring that he [Harry] would recover as before'.[18] Such contradictory statements have been missed by historians who have taken the account in the influential *The suffragette movement* as the standard reading of events.

Christabel, Sylvia and Emmeline Pethick Lawrence were amongst those who bade Emmeline goodbye when she caught the boat train from Waterloo on the 13th. The voyage, with its bracing sea air, gave Emmeline a chance to rest and to look forward to her lecturing tour, the only kind of 'holiday', as Christabel knew too well, her mother would take.[19] 'Welcome to the first political leader among women in the history of the world', cabled Harriot Stanton Blatch in a wireless message to Emmeline, shortly before she docked.[20] But news of the impending arrival of an internationally known militant feminist had already caused controversy in the USA and continued to do so. While many welcomed the opportunity to hear 'The World-famed Leader of the English Suffragettes', as she was described by the J. B. Pond Lyceum Bureau that had exclusive management of her tour, some questioned the wisdom of the visit.[21] Carrie Chapman Catt, the leader of moderate suffragism in New York, feared that Emmeline's charisma and advocacy of militancy might produce a 'deluge of suffrage anarchy' while another well-known suffragist, Anna Garlin Spencer, refused to endorse the visit.[22] But nothing could dampen Emmeline's enthusiasm for this tour, her first visit to the USA. 'I shall never forget the excitement of my landing', she recollected five years later, 'the first meeting with the American "reporter", an experience dreaded by all Europeans.'[23]

Harriot Stanton Blatch was amongst the small number of Equality League members, complete with 'Votes for women' banners, allowed by the American authorities to greet Emmeline on her arrival at New York on 20 October. The *New York Times* opined that the stylish Emmeline, 'a small gentle-looking woman in a gray checked travelling wrap, wearing a gray fur hat encircled with a mauve veil, looks younger than the pictures which have reached America … more like a nice, home-keeping mother than a political leader'.[24] But the 'nice, home-keeping mother' had a large trunk of suffrage literature on which she and Dorothy Pethick had to pay $7 duty. Not missing an opportunity for fun and publicity, Emmeline and Dorothy recuperated part of the extra outlay by selling leaflets to the customs officers, who raised their hats and cheered them as they left the dock.[25] The incident set the tone for the rest of the tightly packed tour as, wherever Emmeline went, enthusiastic crowds came to hear her.

Dubois makes the point that in planning Emmeline's American visit, Harriot Stanton Blatch struggled to keep the social class extremes of women together as well as the range of suffrage organisations. Thus, on the evening of the 22 October, just two days after her arrival, Emmeline spoke to 2,500 people at Tremont Temple, in conservative Boston, as a guest of the Massachusetts Woman Suffrage Association and the Boston Equal Suffrage Association for Good Government. 'The enthusiasm was unusual from an audience expected to be reserved', commented the *Boston Herald*. 'She was continually interrupted by bursts of applause, sometimes by hurrahs, as she reached a climax in her description of the stages in the struggle to put the Suffragette question in the forefront of practical politics.'[26] Emmeline's speech, however, was not just about the suffrage campaign; she also spoke about her sick son. 'As the youngest of her family, he has always been "her baby", and though the doctor assured her it would be all right for her to go, she was in acute anxiety till she got the good news that he was better.'[27] Despite her popularity in Boston, it was Emmeline's lecture at Carnegie Hall, New York, given under the auspices of the Equality League, that grabbed the headlines.

The 'little Englishwoman', as she was termed by the *New York Times*, captured the heart of the 3,000 strong audience, nearly all women, on the evening of 25 October. Four hundred members of the Equality League, representing 'all shades and grades of professional and industrial work – lawyers, doctors, nurses, artists etc.', sat on the platform. In the boxes sat a number of wealthy suffragists, as well as representatives from the Women's Trade Union League, the National American Women's Suffrage Association, the Medical Women's Society, the Collegiate Equal Suffrage League, the Women's Progression Suffrage Union, and the William Lloyd Garrison League. In order that poorer working women could attend the meeting, Harriot Stanton Blatch also made sure that hundreds of free tickets were distributed.[28] As the dignified Emmeline rose to speak, a deep hush fell. Standing on the platform in a mauve velvet dress with large, loose sleeves lined in dull green, over a skirt of the same shade of green and white close-fitting lacy blouse, she looked 'as if she were ready to pour a cup of tea in an English vicarage'.[29] But at her first words – 'I am what you call a hooligan' – a great wave of warm, sympathetic laughter erupted.[30] And this was part of the secret of Emmeline's charismatic power as a speaker. Her dignity and ladylike femininity made it impossible for people in her presence to believe the 'scurrilous things' the press wrote about her.[31] Was the 'cultured gentlewoman', as F. L. Bullard described her, really a hooligan?[32] The New York Post had no doubts. Those expecting the leader of the '"screaming sisterhood"' to be a 'bold, coarse, aggressive, unfeminine woman' found themselves listening to a speaker of 'attractive voice, of refinement, and of rare ability'.[33]

For two hours, wrote the admiring Arthur Ruhl, Emmeline Pankhurst spoke without notes, without repetition or fatigue, without even pausing for a drink of water, absolutely confident of her cause, and absolutely in control of her audience. When the long address explaining the necessity for militancy in the WSPU had ended, she then dealt with half an hour of heckling.[34] Two days later, Emmeline wrote to Elizabeth Robins, explaining how she had met her sister-in-law, Margaret Drier Robins, President of the Trade Union League, at the Carnegie Hall. 'The orthodox suffrage movement here is just where ours was a few years ago', she observed, '& it needs women of your sister's stamp to get it out of the rut & bring it into real life. ... I am having a really wonderful time.'[35]

After visits to Rochester, Pittsburg and Buffalo, and then to Toronto, in Canada, where at one meeting an estimated 5,000 people were turned away, Emmeline came back to the States for a farewell meeting; the big gathering, held in Cooper Union Institute, New York, on 30 November, was sponsored by the Collegiate Equal Suffrage League and the Collegiate Institute.[36] 'I had never heard mortal speech so appealing, so uplifting', commented Helen Garrison Villard. 'There were men in that audience who cried, and I know that it was with difficulty that I kept my own tears back.'[37] Before Emmeline began to tell, once more, the story of the women's fight for freedom in Great Britain, she expressed her gratitude to the American people for the kindness and sympathy they had shown her. Then, in a speech that was replete with references to the women's army, campaigns, battles and final victory, she took time to explain the term 'militant' since she knew that the woman militant was regarded as a female deviant, especially when engaged in the violence of stone throwing.

Suffragettes were members of a 'militant' movement, 'inasmuch as the women in it stand up and protest, with all the strength of their being, against the injustices of women'. Emmeline justified the new stone throwing policy, pointing out that it was 'a time-honoured argument in my country, just as I have been told the revolver is in yours'. However, suffragettes who threw stones were classified not as political offenders but as 'the very lowest criminals', and once in prison, working-class militants were treated more harshly than those from higher social class backgrounds, a situation that could not be tolerated. 'Lady Constance Lytton was released: she was not forcibly fed; but Mary Leigh, the workingman's wife, was forcibly fed for five weeks, to the point of death, before they opened the prison doors and let her out.'

A recurring theme in Emmeline's speeches, that of the common bond between all women as they fought for the right to enfranchisement, a bond that transcended social class differences, was reiterated once again. 'We have broken down class distinction between women', she cried, to great applause, and continued:

> We are all women, we are all born under a ban, and whether the wife or daughter of the rich man or the poorest man in the land, we are all outclassed because we are women. We have got a common cause … if there is any distinction of class at all, it is because the privileged women, the honored women, are doing the hardest and most unpleasant parts of the work. They think it is their duty to relieve their sisters from that. If you see a woman selling papers in the streets, or practising the hunger strike, in most cases it is the woman who has never had to face the struggle for existence.[38]

Dubois, writing from a socialist feminist perspective, interprets Emmeline's speech as advocating an expanded field of action for upper-class women, who would take the lead in the militant army, 'displacing working women'.[39] My reading offers a different analysis. Emmeline Pankhurst was always a practical politician, seeking practical solutions to complex issues. She knew that single and married working-class militants faced more constraints on their time and pocket than their more fortunate middle-class sisters, so it was practical that more middle-class women endured imprisonment and other hardships, in the name of the comradeship of all women. Whereas socialist feminists, such as Dubois, emphasise class conflict as the central dynamic in society, a conflict that divided women, for feminists such as Emmeline and Christabel Pankhurst, the central concern was ending the sex discrimination against women in parliamentary voting, a cause that united women. In holding such a world-view, Emmeline never lost sight of the wretched conditions of life for most working-class Edwardian women; neither was she reluctant to speak out on their behalf, as in this speech, when she condemned the harsher treatment that working-class militants might experience in prison.

With the wild applause of the previous night's meeting still ringing in her ears, Emmeline set sail on 1 December 1909, the day her 'right of petition' case was heard in London. As we saw in the last chapter, her case, along with that of Evelina Haverfield, was dismissed, with costs. Both women had already instructed their solicitor that they would refuse to pay costs, and so Emmeline knew that a prison sentence awaited her. Perhaps this weighty matter, together with her worries about Harry, accounted for her change of moods on her voyage home. Alice Morgan Wright, a young American sculptor, travelling on the same liner as Emmeline and Dorothy Pethick, confessed to a friend:

> You should have seen her [Mrs Pankhurst] at one moment huddled up in her deck chair with the sorrows of the universe marked out all over her face, and the next ... the four of us hoppity skipping up and down the ... deck at top speed! Needless to say these little episodes occurred at night when the decks were otherwise deserted and only Orion & co to bear witness.[40]

However, when Emmeline arrived in England on 8 December, on the *Mauretania*, she learnt that some unknown friend had paid her fine of £5, rather than see her sent to prison.[41] She did not question this kind gesture since she now heard the bitter truth from which both Sylvia and Christabel had tried to protect her, namely that Harry would never walk again and that his future was bleak.

Christabel, as the eldest and favourite daughter, felt a special responsibility about the conveyance of such news, explaining to Dr. Mills, 'As to Mother, I want things to be made as easy as possible. At the very best it will be very terrible I am afraid.'[42] Emmeline was stunned when she was told that her only son would be permanently an invalid. 'He would be better dead!' was her despairing cry.[43] It was decided that Sylvia, who was less active in the suffrage movement than her sisters, would stay with Harry until he was stronger, and then resume her artistic career. The following evening, on 9 December, Emmeline spoke at a welcome home meeting at the Albert Hall.[44] Earlier that day, Charlotte Marsh had been released from Winson Green Gaol, after serving a three months' sentence; she had been forcibly fed by tube 139 times.[45]

The Pankhurst family, determined to do all they could for Harry's welfare, were grateful when some suffragist friends, who were going to stay in India for a year, placed at their disposal their house and servants. The convalescent Harry was to be moved there the following day when his old bladder illness returned. A worried Dr. Mills called in consultants who confirmed that there could be no hope of recovery; Harry might live, at the most, for three weeks. Emmeline could not believe that her only son was dying; neither could she bring herself to tell him the diagnosis of the doctors.[46] All the excitement of the women's movement that fired Emmeline was drained from her; she hovered by her boy's bedside, 'dull as spent ashes'.[47] She attended some WSPU functions, as was necessary, and published jointly, with Emmeline Pethick Lawrence, a statement about WSPU policy for the forthcoming general election, but the Christmas message to all WSPU members was left to Emmeline Pethick Lawrence to write.[48]

While sitting by Harry's bedside during some of the long nights, Sylvia listened to his remembrances of his childhood, and of his hard life on the farm. It wrenched her heart. One night he confided that he had fallen in love with a young woman of his own age, Helen Craggs, whom he had met when by-election campaigning in Manchester the previous year. Harry longed to see her again. Next morning, Sylvia contacted a Mrs. May, asking her if she could find the young woman. Soon Helen was at the nursing home. 'Think of him as your young brother', begged Sylvia. 'Tell him you love him; he has only three weeks to live.' To Sylvia, who watched the young couple, with 'anxious absorption', Helen's tenderness was very real.[49] And it was. Many years later, Helen confided to Grace Roe that Harry was her first and only love.[50] But for Emmeline, a possessive mother, the sight of the growing tenderness between the two young people was too much to bear. She chided Sylvia for acting on her own initiative, without consulting her first. This young woman was taking from her 'the last of her son'.[51]

Emmeline, her daughters and Helen were at the nursing home for Christmas, the last they would ever spend with Harry. On New Year's Eve a mournful Emmeline wrote to Elizabeth Robins, 'I came back from my American visit hoping to find my boy on the way to recovery but alas he is still very very ill & I am here with him now.'[52] She was at Harry's bedside on 5 January 1910 when he died and she undertook the painful task of registering his death the next day. Emmeline was inconsolable, broken, remembered Sylvia; 'huddled together without a care for her appearance, she seemed an old, plain, cheerless woman. Her utter dejection moved me more than her vanished charm.'[53] Emmeline had lost all the men in her immediate family – little Frank, her beloved husband, and now her twenty-year-old son. Four days later, she wrote to Mary Phillips, the WSPU Organiser in Bradford, where she was due to speak, 'If you can arrange it I would be grateful if Bradford friends would just behave to me as if no great sorrow had come just now. It breaks me down to talk about it although I am very grateful for sympathy. I want to get through my work and know that you will help me to do it.'[54]

Emmeline's elder brother, Herbert Goulden, kindly stepped in once again to help his sister by buying Harry's cemetery plot and paying the funeral expenses.[55] As the family drove to Harry's burial on 10 January, Emmeline was bowed as Sylvia had never seen her. Emmeline and Richard had been unable to face the sad task of arranging a headstone for their first little son, and neither could she contemplate it now. She asked Sylvia if she would see to everything, choosing something she liked. 'Sylvia, remember, when my time comes, I want to be put with my two boys!'[56] Emmeline was due to speak in Manchester that evening, at the Free Trade Hall, and the organisers were wondering whether she would come. But her power of detachment, her ability to subordinate her private grief to the wider claims of the women's movement, 'always a distin-guishing mark of her character', came to the fore again.[57] She caught the train from London to Manchester where over 5,000 people were waiting, including a strong force of Liberals who wanted to interrupt the meetings. Una Dugdale recollected that Emmeline's speech was electrifying. The audience was amazed that she had travelled to speak to them; those who came to create a disturbance were silenced by the pathos of her words. 'Surely every mother here knows that I would rather be quiet to-night, by my own fireside with my sad thoughts, and it is only a sense of my great responsibility and duty in this campaign that has urged me to appear.'[58]

With a heavy heart, Emmeline now threw herself into the by-election work that was part of the general election campaigning. To what extent the heavy losses sustained by the Liberals in the January 1910 general election were due to WSPU policy is debatable, but they were returned with no overall majority in the Commons polling only 275 seats while the Conservatives held 273, the Irish Nationalists 82 and Labour 40.[59] Realising that the new political situation might be useful to the women's cause, Henry Brailsford set about forming a Conciliation Committee for Women's Suffrage which eventually consisted of fifty-four MPs across the political spectrum. Although initially doubtful about this new venture, the WSPU leaders offered their support, Christabel explaining that the Conciliation Committee might avert the need for 'stronger militancy' since mild militancy was more or less 'played out'.[60] On 31 January, Emmeline declared that there would be a truce on militancy, only peaceful and constitutional methods being used.

Undoubtedly the increasing severity of the treatment being meted out to imprisoned suffragettes, widely publicised in the press, put additional responsi-bilities on Emmeline's shoulders and contributed to the making of such a decision. Just before Christmas, Selina Martin, a working-class prisoner, had been forcibly fed in Walton Gaol, Liverpool, despite the fact that it was contrary to the law for remand prisoners to be treated in this way. She had been kept in chains at night and roughly frog-marched up the stairs to a cell, her head bumping on each step.[61] Then, on 11 January, Lady Constance Lytton, in the guise of a working-class seamstress, 'Jane Warton', had been arrested in a protest outside Walton Gaol. Constance had felt ashamed that she had received preferential treatment when on hunger strike in October 1909; rather than being forcibly fed, she had been released after only two days. Determined to test whether the prison authorities would recognise her need for exceptional favours without her aristocratic name, she had assumed a new persona. In prison, 'Jane Warton' went on hunger strike and was forcibly fed eight times before her true identity was discovered. Her release on 23 January, and subsequent newspaper accounts about the brutality of her treatment, created a storm of protest.[62]

Such matters had weighed heavily on Emmeline as she discussed with Christabel and Emmeline Pethick Lawrence whether or not the WSPU should call a truce. By trying to focus her thoughts on the women's cause, Emmeline could hold her composure in public as she struggled privately to control the overwhelming heartbreak about Harry's death that threatened to submerge her. On 3 February 1910 she wrote to Elizabeth Robins:

> Forgive me for not writing to you sooner & believe that the delay does not mean that I do not value your dear letter of sympathy.
>
> In the time of self reproach for things left undone & bitter regret for what might have been perhaps prevented had I rightly understood your letter has given me comfort.
>
> I am sticking to my work as best I can. I dare not give myself up to grief it would be selfish & hurtful in every way.[63]

Three days later, Emmeline confessed to Elizabeth, 'Work is the only cure for the thoughts I find so uncontrollable just now.' She was busy planning 'missions to women', which would be held all over the country to rouse women to demand the vote. Emmeline explained that she had returned recently from Liverpool where she had spent a morning with the newly released Selina Martin and Elsie Howey. 'Selina Martin's story is a dreadful one. They are both much shaken by the horrible experience.'[64] When speaking at a large meeting at Liverpool's Sun Hall, Emmeline had expressed the hope that the early release of the two women indicated an 'amnesty' on the part of the government. While warning that the by-election anti-government policy would continue unless there was a promise of a women's enfranchisement measure in the King's Speech, she hoped the time had come when prison would be unnecessary and the methods 'which women themselves held so obnoxious' had done their work.[65]

The Conciliation Committee, with Henry Brailsford as its secretary and Lord Lytton, brother of Constance, as its chair, drew up a Women's Franchise Bill that was deliberately drafted along narrow lines in order to win the support of the Conservatives. Thus it did not seek to give the parliamentary vote to women on equal terms with men, but to extend it to women possessed of a household qualification or of a £10 occupation qualification; however, a wife could not be qualified in respect of the same property as her husband.[66] All the women's suffrage societies decided to support the bill, at least in public. However, since widows and spinsters would be favoured under these terms, women lodgers excluded and relatively few wives and working-class women given the vote, not all suffragists were wildly supportive. While speaking in the West of England, Emmeline, wisely, voiced her reservations in private to Henry Nevinson; she also explained that she had told Brailsford of her objections, but that he had 'overborne' her.[67]

This trip to the West of England, one among many that included 'women's missions' as well as WSPU gatherings, brought Emmeline some comfort since she met up again with the WSPU Organiser for the region, Annie Kenney. Emmeline's own mother had died that spring and her death, coming so soon after Harry's, added to her deep sorrow. Although Mrs. Goulden had had a stroke some years ago, she had recovered enough to lead an active life and to continue following, with the greatest pride, the exploits of her eldest daughter and granddaughters in the suffrage movement.[68] Now that another link with her past life had been severed, Emmeline was only too glad to see Annie whom she loved 'as her own child'.[69] Annie was very friendly with the Blathwayt family who lived at Batheaston, and on 15 April she accompanied the WSPU leader to Eagle House, the Blathwayt home, where they had supper and stayed overnight. The following day, Emmeline was asked to follow the customary practice for WSPU visitors to Eagle House, namely to plant a tree in that part of the garden known as the 'suffragette field'. Once the deed was completed, a photograph was taken of the Union leader, spade in her hand, standing by her cedrus deodara, with Mary Blathwayt and Annie Kenney to her right. Although Mary Blathwayt's mother, Emily, had resigned her membership of the WSPU in September 1909, since she disapproved of the stone throwing violence, she still admired Emmeline and welcomed her; and her home continued to be a well-known centre of hospitality for suffragettes for some years to come. 'Mrs. Pankhurst is still very thin', Emily recorded in her diary, 'but she gained about a stone weight in a week by (as she says) eating less, but she took rusks instead of bread and only very thin toast.'[70]

Martin Pugh claims that Mary Blathwayt's diaries reveal that Eagle House became a centre for suffragette lesbians indulging in 'short-lived sexual couplings', 'one-night stands'. 'In the diary', he asserts, 'Kenney appears frequently and with different women. Almost day by day Mary says she is sleeping with someone else.'[71] This theme is especially elaborated upon in his book where the problematic term 'lesbianism' is never defined.[72] Although, as Alison Oram and Annmarie Turnbull point out, the idea of 'lesbianism' in the 1980s and 1990s encompassed a range of identities, from the 'feminist woman-identified-woman (emphasising community and politics) to a specifically sexual definition (emphasising powerful eroticism and transgression)', Pugh associates lesbianism with the latter aspect.[73] '[T]he physical nature of Annie Kenney's relationships seems clear from the evidence of the private diaries', he asserts; 'she slept so frequently with her female friends and colleagues that it would be surprising if her feelings were not those of a lesbian.'[74] Yet his evidence to support such a claim is slim, based upon five entries in Mary's diaries! More importantly, Pugh gives a twenty-first century interpretation to the phrase 'sleeping with', seeing it as involving sexual intercourse. It was common for suffragettes campaigning in the early twentieth century to share beds when they were put up in other people's houses and this does not necessarily mean that they were lesbians – although some undoubtedly were, whether they shared beds or not. Pugh's eagerness to speculate about the sexuality of suffragettes is not confined to Annie Kenney. The determination of another WSPU member, Grace Roe, he continues, 'to protect the reputation of Christabel and Emmeline in the context of the suffrage campaign led her to obscure what she knew about their private lives'.[75] Such innuendo, without any firm evidence to support such claims, trivialises and belittles the contribution of the WSPU leaders to the women's cause. For Pugh, writing from a masculinist perspective, the political commitment of suffragettes became a 'substitute for love affairs [i.e. with men], and hero-worship [of women] an alternative to physical passion [i.e. with men]'.[76] Although he does not suggest that Annie Kenney 'slept with' Emmeline Pankhurst during her visit to Eagle House in April 1910, the implication is there. Emmeline looked upon Annie as a daughter, not a lover. And she had other things on her mind at the time than sexual couplings.

Plans were now well under way for the procession of 28 May which Emmeline regarded as a last chance for a peaceful demonstration to reveal the strength of demand for women's enfranchisement. Although the procession was organised by the WSPU, it would include representatives of over 130 militant and non-militant suffrage groupings, demonstrating to the world, Emmeline insisted, 'the essential unity which underlies any differences of method and of policy'.[77] When King Edward VII died unexpectedly, on 6 May, the WSPU leaders, as a mark of respect, postponed the scheduled franchise demonstration until 18 June. Emmeline, who attached particular importance to the prisoners' contingent in the forthcoming process, pleaded for volunteers to stand in for those ex-prisoners who were unable to take part on the day. 'I believe that the sacrifice of personal liberty that others may be free, the willing endurance of suffering in order to gain the power to help the helpless, always has been, and always will be, the most powerful appeal to the sympathy and imagination of the great mass of human beings.'[78] The two-mile-long procession that marched from the Embankment to the Albert Hall on that sunny day of 18 June was in high spirits since four days earlier Mr. D. J. Shackleton, MP, had successfully introduced the Women's Franchise Bill as a private member's bill to the Commons. The 10,000 marchers with 700 banners and accompanied by forty bands, included all ages, ranks and occupations of women, aristocrats as well as box makers and shirt makers; detachments from the Colonies, France, America, Germany, Sweden, Denmark, Holland, Norway and Italy also took part, illustrating international support for the women's cause in Britain. However, it was the 617 strong Prisoners' Pageant, all carrying wands to which was affixed a silver broad arrow, and the contingent of women graduates in caps and gowns, that seemed to attract the special attention of the press. 'It was a thing of sheer beauty', opined the *Morning Leader*, 'a multitude of fine women, wearing beautiful dresses, carrying beautiful flowers, and holding beautiful banners … the applause of a vast concourse of onlookers followed it right along its nearly three miles route.'[79] When the procession arrived at the Albert Hall, Lord Lytton, as chair of the Conciliation Committee, was the chief speaker, but Emmeline preceded him with a short speech that opened with the phrase, 'One word: Victory!' She then read a resolution calling upon the government to grant facilities for the Women's Suffrage Bill that session. £5,000 was collected for the WSPU campaign fund.[80]

Asquith, however, was determined that no such facilities should be granted, although he was content for the bill to be granted a second reading. When his decision was announced in the Commons, five days after the great procession, the WSPU leaders were bitterly disappointed but not entirely despondent since he also made the ambiguous statement that 'the Government recognises that the House ought to have opportunities, if that is their deliberate desire, for effectively dealing with the whole question'.[81] Emmeline clung to the last shreds of optimism, writing to Elizabeth Robins on 6 July that there seems 'good hope that the Conciliation Bill will really weather the storm & get into harbour'.[82] On 12 July, the bill passed its second reading with a majority of 109; however, both Asquith and his Chancellor of the Exchequer, now Lloyd George, voted against it. The Commons then voted to follow the 'mischievous course', as Emmeline denounced it, of sending the bill to a committee of the whole House which meant that it could not be brought up for its committee stage unless given special facilities. 'Could women be blamed if, realising that they were tricked again, they reverted to those clumsy methods of forcing the question that they had been compelled to adopt in the past?'[83]

On 23 July, the anniversary of the 1867 Hyde Park demonstration when working men had agitated for the vote, the WSPU organised another great peaceful procession to that Park with meticulous care and new spectacular themes in order to attract a large crowd for the second time that month. A number of other suffrage groupings also participated, including the Actresses' Franchise League, the Irish Suffragists, the Women's Freedom League, the Men's Committee for Justice to Women, the New Union for Men and Women, the Men's League for Women's Suffrage, the Women's Tax Resistance League, the Fabian Society, the New Constitutional Suffrage Society, the Men's Political Union for Women's Enfranchisement, the International Women's Franchise Club, and a contingent of women representing New Zealand and Australia also joined in.[84] But the NUWSS refused to join the procession since the WSPU leaders had given no guarantee that they would refrain from a resumption of militant tactics before the 23rd.[85] Since the number of people involved was so large, the police suggested two processions rather than a single one. Emmeline, wearing a long white cloak, walked side by side with the joint honorary secretary, Mabel Tuke, in the West Procession which formed at Shepherd's Bush; immediately in front of her were the WSPU's popular drum and fife band while three horsewomen, Maud Joachim, the Hon. Evelina Haverfield, and Vera Holme headed the gathering, followed by the colour bearers. When the colourful West and East processions reached Hyde Park, Emmeline presided over one of the forty platforms as did her three daughters, Christabel, Adela and Sylvia, and her sister, Mary Clarke. In addition to this kinship network, the chairs of the other WSPU platforms were women that the Union leader knew well, including Emmeline Pethick Lawrence, Dorothy Pethick, Charlotte Marsh, Flora Drummond, Annie Kenney, Dora Marsden, Lady Constance Lytton, Mary Leigh, Georgina and Marie Brackenbury, and Ada Flatman.[86]

It was estimated that about a quarter of a million people, all friendly, assembled in the blazing sunshine that day, demonstrating to Asquith, Emmeline hoped, mass support for women's enfranchisement.[87] Despite her misgivings about the eventual success of the Conciliation Bill, those who stood by her platform would have heard her give a stirring message of hope, that the large number of women gathered there was a 'sure sign that they would gain their cause'.[88] For Henry Nevinson, the organisation of the day was 'perfection'. The laurel wreaths at the top of the long white staves, the oblong entablatures inscribed with the word 'Justice', the host of brilliant banners in the WSPU's colours, 'all gave the effect of a Roman army on the march'. Eric Northwood, on the other hand, writing for the left-wing *Clarion*, saw the Hyde Park procession as 'a most lady-like demonstration', with 'no opposition' and 'no noisy enthusiasm'.[89] Emmeline's fear of treachery by the government was confirmed later on that day when Asquith informed Lord Lytton that the Conciliation Bill would be granted no further time that session.[90]

Despite their bitter disappointment, the WSPU leaders decided to wait until parliament reconvened in the autumn, after the summer recess, to see if the government would grant facilities for the bill, although some of the more ardent rank-and-file members disagreed with that decision. Annie Kenney recollected:

> It was at big crises like these that Mrs. Pankhurst's influence was felt. The truce would never have been kept by the more fiery Militants had it not been for her extraordinary powers of gentle persuasion. The most rebellious spirits grew calm in her presence, the most obstinate grew amenable. They adored her. There is no other word for it.[91]

Nevertheless, Emmeline warned that the patience of women had its limits. If facilities for the bill were not granted, there would be another demonstration to the Commons.[92] Christabel began to lay plans for such an event.

August was holiday time for the WSPU and gave Emmeline an opportunity to slow down her pace of life, but there were always Union matters to attend to. On 19 August she wrote again to C. P. Scott, asking this time for his help in advertising in the *Manchester Guardian* for donations for a public testimonial for the aged Elizabeth Wolstenholme Elmy, one of her oldest suffrage friends. 'She will not live much longer', Emmeline observed, 'indeed I fear that she will be soon numbered with those who have died heartbroken & despairing of ever obtaining justice at the hands of hypocritical politicians. Well some of us mean to make a good fight for it before we are old & helpless as she is.' Emmeline also commented bitterly in her letter on the dishonesty of Lloyd George, who pretended to be a friend of women's suffrage while opposing and misrepresenting the one bill which had the greatest chance of becoming law that year. 'Can you & other Liberals wonder that we have come to the conclusion that we must take up again the weapons we laid down after the General Election?'[93]

After speaking in Wales, Emmeline, accompanied by Una Dugdale, then travelled to the Scottish Highlands for 'a month's combination of business and pleasure', as she termed it.[94] In the isolated rural communities, Emmeline was dependent upon the generosity of that network of WSPU members and sympathisers who answered Una's appeal for help with hospitality, the loan of motor cars, and the advertisement and arrangement of meetings.[95] 'Mrs Mansell Moullin is having me the first week end so the Bridge of Allan meeting can be fixed up for the Monday or Tuesday & the North Berwick one to follow', Emmeline informed Una from Duncans Farm, Billinghurst, Sussex, where she was staying prior to her tour. 'I shall have Mrs Cranfield's car for that week.'[96] When her Highland tour had ended, the Union leader then sailed in early October to Ireland where, escorted by the Irish suffragist Gretta Cousins, she toured all the major towns, explaining how important it was for Irish women to support the forthcoming demonstration in support of the Conciliation Bill. The 'most famous woman in England', as Margaret Ward called Emmeline, was enthusiastically received; several members of the militant Irish Women's Franchise League offered to undertake what they described as 'danger service' on the next deputation to parliament.[97]

Back in England, Emmeline could not resist the temptation to join the by-election campaigning in South Shields and Walthamstow, but encouraging volunteers for the demonstration planned originally for 22 November was her main preoccupation now. 'Our power as women is invincible, if we are united and determined. ... I know that you will not willingly stand aside at this time. Will you write and tell me whether you can join the deputation?', she pleaded in late October in a general letter sent to the WSPU membership.[98] Evelyn Sharp, a WSPU Organiser for Kensington North, hastily explained that she was unable to participate, to which an understanding Emmeline replied:

> Don't worry! After all it would never do for our best speakers to get shut up for they will be needed to keep up popular indignation while the rest of us are in prison. Names are coming in well.
>
> Do what you can between now & the Albert Hall meeting to get people to go there & to persuade women who cannot do your work to volunteer for prison.[99]

At the big Albert Hall meeting held on 10 November 1910 in support of the Conciliation Bill, at which £9,000 was raised, Emmeline spoke alongside Christabel, Emmeline Pethick Lawrence and Israel Zangwill, the novelist and staunch supporter of the women's cause. That Emmeline should be on a platform with a male speaker was not unusual at this stage of the militant campaign; she occasionally shared a platform with Henry Nevinson who, the day before, had noted in his diary that Brailsford had complained to him that he 'had trouble with the Pankhursts; accuses them of having no means but threats and flattery: says they are wrecking all his diplomacy, and refuses to go on the platform. Almost incredible, but both sides are difficult.'[100] Brailsford would not have been happy with Emmeline's address to the enthusiastic audience at the Albert Hall when, after calling for an end to the veto on the Conciliation Bill, she warned, 'If the Bill, in spite of our efforts, is killed by the Government, then ... I have to say there is an end to the truce.'[101] Soon Christabel was informing WSPU members that the date for the large demonstration had been changed to Friday, 18 November, presumably to coincide with the opening of parliament.

When parliament reconvened that day, Asquith announced to the Commons that as the conference with the House of Lords over its power of veto had broken down, he had advised the King to dissolve parliament; in the intervening days before the dissolution was due to take place, on 28 November, precedence would be given to government business. Emmeline was speaking at the Caxton Hall when the news filtered through that Asquith had made no mention of the Conciliation Bill. Immediately she led to the Commons a deputation of over 300 women, which divided into contingents of twelve, on a day that was to become known as 'Black Friday'. Emmeline's group included some well-known and aged suffragists, including Elizabeth Garrett Anderson, the pioneer woman doctor and twice mayor of Aldeburgh, Hertha Ayrton, the distinguished scientist, Annie Cobden Sanderson, the Princess Sophia Dhuleep Singh, Georgiana Soloman, the Hon. Evelina Haverfield, and Dorinda Neligan. Despite some rough hustling and jostling from a few men, the crowd was mainly friendly and made a clear pathway for the distinguished group which reached the door of the Stranger's Entrance about half past one, to the cheers of the multitudes that filled the streets. 'We stood there for hours', Emmeline recollected, 'gazing down on a scene which I hope never to look upon again.'[102] The small detachments of women that appeared every few minutes in Parliament Square trying to join her, including her sister, Mary, were treated with exceptional brutality by burly policemen who, acting under the directions of the Home Secretary, Winston Churchill, attempted to refrain from making arrests and used a variety of means to force the women back. The women were punched in the face and shoulders, their arms and thumbs twisted; thrown from one policeman to another, many in plain clothes, the militants were kicked and cast to the ground. Many of the assaults were sexual in nature as skirts were lifted high and knees thrust between legs. When Henry Brailsford and Dr. Jessie Murray later published a report about the violence on Black Friday (and on 22 and 23 November, when smaller demonstrations were held), based on testimonies of women who took part in the marches and on evidence volunteered by eye-witnesses, the most frequently voiced complaint 'was variously described as twisting round, pinching, screwing, nipping, or wringing the breast ... often done in the most public way so as to inflict the utmost humiliation'. This form of assault also had a more sinister aspect in that, as Jorgensen-Earp points out, it was commonly believed at that time that physical injury to a woman's breast was the primary cause of breast cancer. [103] After two stressful hours of watching the brutal way her followers were being treated, a horrified Emmeline, Elizabeth Garrett Anderson and Hertha Aytron were conducted to the Prime Minister's room, only to be told that he would not see them. Inside parliament, Asquith refused to listen to those MPs such as Keir

Hardie and Sir Alfred Mond who urged him to receive the deputation. When Emmeline heard that Lord Castlereagh had moved as an amendment to the motion to devote the remainder of the session to government business a proposal which, if carried, would have brought immediate provision of facilities for the Conciliation Bill, she cried out, 'Is there not a single *man* in the House of Commons, one who will stand up for us, who will make the House see that the amendment must go forward?' Asquith then resorted to 'his usual crafty device of a promise of future action', Emmeline bitterly recollected, and 'all save fifty-two [MPs] put their party loyalty before their manhood'.[104] She was not amongst the 115 women and four men who, after six hours of struggle, were eventually arrested. The following day all were released, an embarrassed Home Secretary declaring that no public advantage would be gained by proceeding with the prosecution.[105]

Four days later, 22 November, Emmeline was speaking again at Caxton Hall when a message reached her that Asquith had made a statement that after the general election the government would, if still in power, give facilities in the next parliament for a bill that would be so framed as to admit of free amendment; no mention was made of the Conciliation Bill. Christabel rose to explain to the audience the significance of Asquith's blow, saying, 'We will take nothing but next session. The promise for next parliament is an absurd mockery of a pledge. ... They have been talking of declarations of war. We also declare war from this moment.'[106] After a great outburst of indignation and cheering had subsided, Emmeline announced with that decisiveness that was characteristic of her leadership, 'I am going to Downing Street. Come along, all of you.'[107] Taking a new and uncrowded path to the Prime Minister's residence, the police had time only to form a single cordon across the narrow street. When Emmeline reached them she did not pause or slacken her pace, observed an eyewitness, Henry Nevinson, but with that 'look of silent courage and patient, almost pathetic, determination that everyone now knows so well', walked straight into their midst, the deputation following, hesitating no more than she.[108] She had a marvellous way, remarked one of her daughters, 'of remaining, in the midst of crowds and struggles, as calm and proudly dignified as a queen going to her coronation – or perhaps to the scaffold in some unrighteous rebellion against her proper majesty'.[109] This time when violent struggles broke out, Emmeline was amongst those arrested; further arrests took place in the evening when militants broke windows of houses of some of the Cabinet Ministers. Mary, Emmeline's sister, had promised suffrage friends in Brighton that she would not participate in the demonstration that day and risk further manhandling; they feared for her health since Mary had been ill after the Black Friday violence. But Mary was determined to go to London and register her protest in some way on the 22nd. That evening, she went to Cannon Row Police Station to visit Emmeline who was being held pending her trial the next day; when the police authorities refused Mary permission to see her sister, she threw a stone through one of the windows, and was immediately arrested.

The following day, the two sisters appeared amongst the 159 women and three men defendants at Bow Street Police Court. Emmeline was discharged since no evidence was brought against her. Mary fared less well; pleading guilty to breaking a window, judgment was deferred until a few days later when she was one of 75 women sent to prison, in her case for one month.[110] In that week's *Votes for Women*, Emmeline published a special message of thanks to all those who had taken part in the deputations for their 'magnificent courage and self-restraint ... I feel myself deeply honoured to be your leader.' But she also stressed the importance of winning mass support, of educating public opinion as to their point of view, and so asked every WSPU member to secure, during the ensuing week, at least one new permanent subscriber to the newspaper.[111]

The women who suffered physical injuries at the hands of the police during 'Black Friday' later told Emmeline, 'We cannot bear this.' It was preferable to engage in stone throwing, with its hasty arrest, than to participate in a legal march that ended in prolonged struggle with the forces of the law.[112] Such considerations had an important influence upon the future direction of militancy. For the present, Emmeline was concerned to offer some practical help to Mrs. Hawkins, one of the imprisoned working women who had engaged in the recent demonstrations and left her husband to look after their home and children. Since Mr. Hawkins was now in hospital, suffering from a doubly fractured leg after scuffles broke out when he asked Winston Churchill a question about women's suffrage, his wife wanted to be released so that she could go back home to their children in Leicester. On the morning of 28 November, Emmeline went to Holloway and paid her fine.[113]

Later that day, at the Queen's Hall meeting, at which both Emmeline and Christabel gave stirring addresses, Emmeline spoke frequently about the 'joy of battle' that militants experienced as they fought for the freedom of womanhood. Praise was given too to that 'little gallant band of men' who, in their 'new chivalry', were supporting the women's cause. In the future, she hoped there would be not a mere handful of men but 'thousands upon thousands' who would insist on justice for women. 'There have been times', Emmeline reflected sadly, 'when we have felt very inclined to be bitter about the men of this country ... [but] I want as a woman to thank our men friends for having sweetened our hearts about men, for having done something to take the stigma off their sex where this movement is concerned.'[114] Such statements add credence to Holton's claim that the militant standpoint reflected an appeal 'to an essentially chivalrous conception' of male–female relations, that although Mrs. Pankhurst spoke often of the wrongs of women and children at the hands of men, she also relied on men's capacity 'to rise above their lower natures when confronted with the "sorrowful wrath" of women'.[115]

At the same meeting, however, Christabel gave a different emphasis to the role of men in the women's movement. Although she spoke of our 'men friends' and of the 'men who are prepared to fight with us', she also stressed that the all-male Conciliation Committee, with Lytton as its chair and Brailsford as its secretary, should not overstep its supportive role in the women's cause by assuming a leadership role. The Conciliation Committee has been giving us good advice, she said, but when:

> we find ourselves at variance with ... [them] we are bound to prefer our own opinion and our own judgment. One thing we lay down here definitely and finally; this is a woman's movement, led by women, and we are not prepared to surrender the leadership of this movement to men, however well meaning, however earnest, and however devoted.[116]

Such pronouncements by Christabel probably account for Brailsford's disillusion with the Pankhurst leadership since he told Nevinson, the day after the Queen's Hall meeting, that he was 'much distressed at the W.S.P.U. distrust of him & their action agst his advice'.[117] But these Queen's Hall speeches make clear that both Emmeline and Christabel, despite their differing emphases, welcomed men's support for the women's cause. The differing shades on the 'problem of men' in the women's movement, that each addressed, reflected, perhaps, their own individual biographies. The older woman, a widow, had been happily married for eighteen years to a man she adored and with whom she had worked in the women's rights movement. Her impatient, unmarried thirty-year-old daughter, on the other hand, was one of the new generation of university-educated women, trained to think clearly and logically, and yet barred from further training as a lawyer because she was a woman. Where both mother and daughter converged in their thinking was in their insistence that the militant movement was a women's movement where men had a limited role and would always be outsiders.

After the Queen's Hall meeting, Emmeline was soon campaigning hard again, since a general election had been called. At Wisbech the local WSPU Organiser, Grace Roe, recollected that the Union leader spoke 'about five times every night' despite the fact that she was not in a good state of health and living on a liquid diet. 'Simply marvellous ... she was so frail.'[118] Two days before Christmas, Emmeline presided over the welcome luncheon in the Criterion Restaurant for the released Holloway prisoners, including her sister, Mary. 'It was plain to those who knew her best', observed Emmeline, 'that her health had suffered seriously from the dreadful experience of Black Friday and the after experience of prison.'[119] Nevertheless, Mary then hastened that evening to Brighton and returned on Christmas Eve to the London home of her brother, Herbert Goulden, where she joined Emmeline and other family members. At the mid-day meal on Christmas Day, Mary quietly left the table saying she felt tired and wanted to lie down. When Emmeline went upstairs to see her, she found her dying. Mary had burst a blood vessel in her brain.

Emmeline was devastated. Last Christmas, her only son lay dying, in the spring her mother had died, and now this Christmas she had lost her beloved sister who had been a second mother to her children. Early on Boxing Day morning, she went to Sylvia's studio in Linden Gardens with the sad news; Sylvia had spent her Christmas alone there since she had to revise the final chapters of her forthcoming book, *The suffragette*, and also prepare for her American tour which was due to start early in the New Year. Mother and daughter clung to each other, united in their grief as Emmeline remembered her favourite sister and Sylvia her favourite aunt.[120] On 27 December 1910, a grieving and weary Emmeline wrote to C. P. Scott, conveying the sad news and imploring him to use his influence with the government:

> She is the first to die. How many must follow before the men of your Party realise their responsibility?
>
> I write to you not only because you saw her in prison but because I believe you perhaps more than any single man outside the Cabinet have the power to bring this dreadful struggle to an end.
>
> Directly Parliament meets we must begin again unless something is done.
>
> This year has seen the breaking for me of three of my closest bonds to this world my boy, my mother & my dearest sister.
>
> Can you wonder that today I want beyond all other things to end this fight quickly & get rest?[121]

But there was to be no quick end to the suffrage struggle for the weary Emmeline, nor any rest from her family responsibilities. On 1 January 1911, she wrote to Una Dugdale from the Crown Hotel, Lyndhurst, in the New Forest, where she was staying for a few days with Mabel Tuke and Emmeline Pethick Lawrence, asking for any information that Una and her sister, Joan, might have about Mary Clarke's work in Brighton that could be used in the memorial notice that Mrs. Lawrence was writing. Warmly, Emmeline thanked Una and Joan for attending the funeral. 'It was a great help to see your two dear faces on Thursday.'[122] A few days later, she wrote to Elizabeth Robins, explaining that it was 'very hard to see my sister go that awfully sudden way. ... She was always very good & loving to me & the children & I owe her much & now we can never repay except by renewed devotion to the cause she loved.'[123] On 6 January, Emmeline accompanied Sylvia on the boat train to Southampton, staying on board to the last moment, smiling at her 'wistfully from the quay'.[124] She then returned to London to ponder again on the 'problem' of Adela.

12

THE TRUCE RENEWED
(JANUARY–NOVEMBER 1911)

Adela, the WSPU Organiser for Sheffield, had not been happy in the women's movement for some time. Although she had not been as fond of her aunt Mary as Sylvia had been, Mary had been a second mother to the younger Pankhurst children and her death, coming so soon after Harry's, must have 'intensified' Adela's sorrow.[1] Furthermore, distrust had grown up between Adela and Christabel who, Sylvia claimed, regarded their younger sister 'as a very black sheep amongst organisers' because she was a fervent socialist when the WSPU was supposed to be free from party affiliation.[2] Adela felt that the WSPU was losing ground and tried to voice her concerns about the militant policy to Christabel. Some fifty years later, she could still remember clearly Christabel's reaction. '[U]nfortunately she took it amiss – was even persuaded I was about to found a counter-organisation with myself as a leader. This was so far from my intention that the suggestion when it was put to me deprived me of speech!'[3] The years of poor health and hard work, coupled with the suspicions that had now arisen and the grief over the loss of close relatives brought Adela close to breaking point. She tried to resign from the WSPU but Emmeline Pethick Lawrence persuaded her to stay on for what Adela described as 'another miserable year'.[4]

Emmeline was always motherly and kind towards Adela, which is one reason why her youngest daughter loved her so much. And, as a mother, Emmeline tried, not always successfully, to keep the peace between her daughters. But it was Christabel who was 'the darling' of her heart,[5] and it was Christabel's political judgment that she trusted, not Adela's. Emmeline's admiration for Christabel's brilliance as the WSPU's key strategist was her Achilles heel. One early WSPU supporter, said to be Annie Cobden Sanderson, is reported to have said, 'Mrs. Pankhurst would walk over the dead bodies of all her children except Christabel and say, "See what I have given for the cause".'[6]

That New Year of 1911, Emmeline considered Adela's concerns about the policy of the WSPU ill-timed. She was at a low ebb, near despair, her faith in British justice and especially in men having being seriously undermined. C. P. Scott had advised Emmeline to be patient when campaigning for the vote, a suggestion that elicited a scathing and defiant response:

How many more women must die before you say 'the time is now' ...
even now you are not really moved. Still you say 'patience & prepare'.
And you could do so much through your paper. ... Our duty as women
is clear. We must go on no matter what the danger or the cost to
ourselves. We cannot submit to the affairs of the nation of which we
are a part being any longer settled by men who do not hold themselves
responsible to women as well as to men. Do, I beg of you, help us to
retain our belief in human justice & recover our faith in & respect for
men by prompt action.[7]

The ink had barely dried from her pen when a personal and very public attack
was made against her.

On 12 January, the New Age published the first of three articles by Teresa
Billington-Greig which offered what the Anti-Suffrage Review termed a 'bitter,
contemptuous, and stinging denunciation' of WSPU activists. Announcing her
resignation from the post of Secretary of the WFL, a militant organisation
which she had helped to found in the split from the WSPU in 1907 and which
did not approve of attacks on persons or property, Teresa reserved her scorn for
what she saw as the autocratic style of the leaders of the WSPU 'Mrs.
Pankhurst, Miss Pankhurst, and Mrs. Pethick Lawrence'. This dictatorship, she
asserted, which seeks emancipation in a hurry, imposes 'a yoke of emotional
control by which the very virtues of the members are exploited; they produce a
system of mental and spiritual slavery. The women who succumb to it', she
continued, 'exhibit a type of self-subjection not less objectionable than the
more ordinary self-subjection of women to men, to which it bears a close relation.' Furthermore, the WSPU had suppressed free speech, edged out the
working-class element from the ranks and become 'socially exclusive, punctil-
iously correct, gracefully fashionable, ultra-respectable, and narrowly religious'.[8]
The attack was reported in all the main newspapers, the Daily Express even
covering the story on its front page and politely pointing out that although the
WSPU now included women of title among its members, the number of
working-class members had also increased.[9]

Emmeline and the other two WSPU leaders held their tongues about such a
scathing denouncement, at least in public. Despite their discreet silence, there
was no escaping the bad publicity since the three articles were soon incorpo-
rated into a book with the title The militant suffrage movement, emancipation in a
hurry, published in late March.[10] Nevinson's assessment of the treacherous
attack, as he called it, as '[m]ere jealous vanity & hatred', harmful outside the
women's movement rather than within it, was not entirely accurate.[11] There
was a small but growing minority of WSPU members, including Mary
Gawthorpe and Dora Marsden, who were not entirely happy with the style of
leadership and direction of the WSPU. Furthermore, conflicts and tensions
appeared to be developing between the London headquarters and the local
organisers in the regions.[12]

If Emmeline had been ignorant of these developments, the Billington-Greig attack would have opened her eyes and made her more determined, through her personal influence, to hold the WSPU together. In an organisation with no written constitution, her charismatic power as its leader was critical. Her long years of political activism, in both the socialist and women's movements, had taught her that divisions and strife were almost inevitable. It was during this troubled time that Ethel Smyth, a well-known modern composer of a *Mass in D* as well as three operas – *Fantasio*, *Der Wald* and *The wreckers* – entered Emmeline's life.

Ethel had written to Emmeline the previous September, wondering if she could be of any practical use to the militants, whom she greatly admired but from whom she had held aloof for some time; she had subsequently abandoned her musical career, joined the WSPU in order to devote two years to the women's cause, and composed for the Union a tune titled 'The march of the women', to which Cecily Hamilton then fitted the words.[13] 'The march of the women' was first performed on 21 January 1911, at a welcome social evening for released prisoners. Emmeline spoke with emotion in her voice as, before the music was sung, she introduced the composer, a woman who was to become one of her closest friends over the next few years. 'Although others may find better words in which to thank Dr. Smyth, no one could feel as deeply as I do the gratitude for her services to the women's cause that I so feebly express to-night.' The stirring march was then sung by a choir to a rapturous welcome from the audience; from now on this hymn and call to battle became the anthem of the WSPU, replacing the 'Women's Marseillaise'.[14]

During January and February, the WSPU renewed its truce, engaging in no militant action, since there was some uncertainty about the status of a women's suffrage measure in the new parliament, which first met on 6 February. Yet again, the Liberal Party was returned to power, the composition of the new House of Commons being very much the same as before; Asquith was reappointed as prime minister. Although no reference was made to women's suffrage during the King's Speech, three MPs who were members of the Conciliation Committee secured the first three places in the private members' ballot and Sir George Kemp, who drew first place, announced that he would sponsor a woman suffrage bill. The Conciliation Bill was now revised; the £10 qualification, to which Lloyd George amongst others had objected, was dropped and the new bill now related only to women with a household qualification in the hope that it would make amendment possible and also attract more support.[15]

Emmeline, despite her misgivings about any support from Asquith for a woman suffrage measure, continued to campaign vigorously over the coming months for the Second Conciliation Bill which was due to have its second reading on 5 May. She now had a new chauffeur, Aileen Preston, the first woman to qualify for the Automobile Association Certificate in Driving, and also a new car, a large Wolseley, given to her by Mary Dodge, a wealthy American patron of Ethel Smyth who gave the musician £100 a year for life and also bought her a country cottage at Hook Heath, near Woking.[16] Aileen Preston's family were horrified when they heard about her new job with 'that dreadful woman'; they thought she was going 'straight into the dark arms of Hell'.[17] But Aileen loved the work, for which she was paid £1 a week. Since Emmeline was travelling so much in the car, she used it to carry not only her luggage but also WSPU literature and other material that might form the basis for a speech, as her chauffeur explained:

> We were very, very heavily laden with an enormous amount of litera-ture piled on the top which I had to reach by climbing up a little ladder.
> We would start off about half past ten in the morning and then we'd have a puncture. Mrs. Pankhurst never got out of the car, she never moved from her papers, so I used to jack her up with the car. I took that for granted. She was always absolutely absorbed in working out her speech for the next meeting or reading some book on social welfare. In my mind all the time was, 'Mrs. Pankhurst's got to be there.' That's all that mattered. Her meeting was the only thing that mattered, and we always got there in time.[18]

While thus being transported from one by-election to another, Emmeline continued to offer support and advice to WSPU members, especially the organ-isers. 'I think when you go to Gloucester you will find the Sec of the old society there quite friendly & willing to make Mrs Lawrence's meeting a success', she advised Ada Flatman, the WSPU Organiser for the county of Gloucestershire, in mid February. 'I think Lady Maude Percy would if invited take the Chair. ... Congratulations on last night. It was a fine meeting & meant much hard work.'[19] In Wiltshire, where a by-election was being held at Westbury, Emmeline spoke at a number of different meetings, some of them women-only, and met up with Christabel, Emmeline Pethick Lawrence and Annie Kenney. Shortly afterwards, she made a surprise appearance at the Portman Rooms, London, where the Hon. Evelina Haverfield had organised an entertainments evening by the Actresses' Franchise League.[20] Then Emmeline was off campaigning in places as far afield as Portsmouth, Peterborough, Edinburgh, Glasgow and Ayr.[21] In view of her hectic schedule, it is hardly surprising that she did not feel well enough to undertake yet another planned tour; campaigning was taking its toll on her health. The protective and concerned Christabel, who was no longer living with the Pethick Lawrences but had moved into a nearby flat, asked Lady Constance Lytton to take her mother's place, which she gladly agreed to do. 'Thousands of thanks for taking it but it has been a blessing', wrote a grateful Christabel. 'Mother was really not fit to do the meetings & then go through her personal share in the protest. ... The little time of quiet has done her so much good. You must take care of your precious self now.'[22]

With Christabel at her side, Emmeline spoke at a large WSPU gathering held at the Albert Hall on 23 March in support of the Second Conciliation Bill. However, the evening belonged to the Australian suffragist Vida Goldstein, who spoke about enfranchised women in her own country, and to Ethel Smyth. Ethel remembered the wonderful experience of processing up the centre aisle in her beautiful Mus. Doc. robes with Emmeline by her side, and being presented with a baton by the Union leader in recognition of her services for composing 'The march of the women'. She then conducted the choir in a performance of the song, the entire audience joining in.[23]

For some months now, the WSPU had been planning to support the Census boycott organised by the WFL, for the night of 2 April. The 'No vote No Census' campaign appealed to militants and constitutionalists alike, as a form of passive resistance against the government's refusal to grant women full citizenship. All-night events were planned throughout the country so that protesters could leave home during the time the enumerators were taking the Census, a form of protest that aroused, according to Emmeline, 'a chorus of horrified disapproval' from the conservative public, epitomised in a leading article in The Times.[24] Emmeline hastily responded to the editorial, asserting, 'The Census is a numbering of the people. Until women count as people for the purpose of representation in the councils of the nation as well as for the purposes of taxation and of obedience to the laws, we advise women to refuse to be numbered.'[25]

As no pledge on women's suffrage had been secured from Asquith by 1 April, Emmeline, like most protesters, returned her Census form with the words, 'No vote no census' scrawled across it.[26] On Census night, she attended a concert organised by the WSPU at Queen's Hall, walked with about 1,000 other suffragists round and round Trafalgar Square until midnight, and then chaired an all-night entertainment at the Scala Theatre which ended at three in the morning. Then she joined other protesters at the Aldwych Skating Rink which was open from 3 a.m. to 8 a.m. for roller skating. 'Some skated while others looked on', recollected Emmeline, 'and enjoyed the admirable musical and theatrical entertainment that helped to pass the hours. ... An all-night restaurant near at hand did a big business.'[27]

According to Ethel Smyth, she and Emmeline left the Rink early so that they could both watch the dawn rise over the Thames from the window of Emmeline's hotel room where Ethel sometimes occupied the second bed. Ethel recollected the event as an almost mystical experience:

> Our foreheads pressed against the window pane staring silently into the dawn, gradually we realised that her love for down-trodden women ... her hope of better things for them ... my music ... our friendship ... that all this was part of the mystery that was holding our eyes. And suddenly it came to us that all was well; for a second we were standing on the spot in a madly spinning world where nothing stirs, where there is eternal stillness. ... Not a word passed between us, but we looked at

each other, wondering why we had been so troubled. … Neither of us ever forgot that dawn.[28]

Ethel dressed in a mannish style that evoked an androgynous appearance and being by temperament an enthusiast for any cause she espoused, eagerly embraced the colours of the WSPU in her everyday dress, usually with results that only drew attention to her 'ill-conceived deviancy'.[29] As Sylvia Pankhurst observed, Ethel Smyth had 'little about her which was feminine'. Her features, which were clean cut, were 'neither manly nor womanly, her thin hair drawn plainly aside, her speech clear in articulation, and incisive rather than melodious, with a racy wit'. Wearing a small, mannish hat, old and plain-cut country clothes, hard worn by weather and usage, 'she would don a tie of the brightest purple, white and green, or some hideous purple cotton jacket, or other oddity in the W.S.P.U. colours she was so proud of, which shone out from her incongruously, like a new gate to old palings'.[30] Vicinus comments that Ethel Smyth never referred to herself as a 'lesbian' in any of her seven volumes of autobiographical writings, even though she foregrounded her passionate *cultes*, as she termed them, for aristocratic, mothering women.[31] The beautiful, elegant and feminine Emmeline Pankhurst fitted the mould. Ethel fell in love with her, attracted by her 'authority' as 'master'.[32] But her account of their friendship is not just that of a 'soldier's view of her general' but that of a 'failed love affair', as Marcus tellingly puts it.[33]

Although some historians suggest that Ethel and Emmeline were involved in a lesbian relationship, it is highly unlikely that they were lovers in any physical sense; Emmeline was too much the politician to risk the scandal of such an involvement and Ethel often developed passions for women (and men) that were not reciprocated.[34] And, surprisingly, historians have often ignored what Ethel herself notes in her memoir, that she fled to Egypt, after devoting her promised two years to the women's cause, in order to escape the 'combined pull of the suffrage and human affection', namely her feelings for Emmeline.[35] For Emmeline, her close friendship with Ethel Smyth, coming so soon after her sister's death, fulfilled a need in her for human warmth and helped to lift the fog of bereavement. The two women had much in common. Both were fifty-three years old; both were fiery and dramatic in temperament; both were strong willed and determined, and both were fighters and pioneers in a man-made world. Ethel Smyth, one of the few women composers of any note, frequently complained that her music was not treated fairly by the critics since it was regarded as the work of a woman.[36] Flamboyant and theatrical, used to performing on a stage, the spectacle, songs, and ceremonies of the WSPU held a particular appeal for Ethel.[37] Now, in this year of the truce on militancy, she threw herself into teaching as many suffragettes as possible her 'March of the women' and conducting concerts of her own works.

A few days after the Census boycott, Emmeline made a return visit to Ireland, speaking to enthusiastic audiences, although, as Murphy emphasises, there was to be a limit to the amount of 'English zeal' acceptable to the Irish suffragists.[38] Then she returned to London and, after a few days rest, began a speaking tour of North Wales on 11 April. That day, while staying at the Castle Hotel, Ruthin, she wrote to Ada Flatman, the WSPU Organiser for the forth-coming Cheltenham by-election, since she planned to be there shortly, and made it clear the kinds of meetings she wanted organised for her. 'I'm not much use for open air work but can take any number of indoor meetings in halls small or large. You know I attach great importance to women's afternoon meetings for you get after results from them.'[39] Two days later, Emmeline wrote a hurried note to Ada explaining that she could not now come to Cheltenham. 'I have had an urgent call to London for Wednesday & shall be engaged over the week end. Will try to come to you before the end of the election, say the 26th.'[40] Why Emmeline was suddenly to be in London for Wednesday, 19 April, we do not know. But it was the day that Sylvia was due to return from her American tour and it is possible that she wished to greet her daughter on her return.

What Emmeline did not know was that the lonely Sylvia, travelling on her own during her time in the USA, had been writing love letters and poems to Hardie. In one of these letters, Sylvia hoped that she and Hardie could develop extrasensory perception as a way of communicating with each other. '[W]hen people have discovered the full power of thought transference … we shall just sit back and look at each other … as much as I love my Darling's arms about me, sweet as kisses are, I rather think it would tend to make us less dependent on those kinds of things.'[41] Hardie, who was interested in spiritualism and had attended seances, as Emmeline had once done, replied to 'my little sweetheart' that while he agreed with her in some respects, 'without the touch & actual presence there could not be the same satisfaction'. He also informed Sylvia, 'Have not seen your Mother this week. She has got her motor & the weather has been good & I presume the two things have combined to keep her busy.'[42] Emmeline would have been horrified if she had known about the contents of these letters since there was 'a strong puritan streak' in her nature.[43] Furthermore, there must be no sexual scandal for WSPU members, especially for a member of her own family and certainly not now, when the second reading of the Second Conciliation Bill was near.

Emmeline gave a stirring speech in support of the bill at a Queen's Hall meeting on 23 April. She stressed the extreme urgency for women to have the vote now, in order to prevent 'worse mistakes and worse blunders' being made in legislation in the future, as in regard to the new insurance scheme the government was going to introduce. As a feminist who put women's issues first, she asked – what share were women going to have in this scheme? The most pressing need, she suggested, was insurance for maternity:

> It seems to me that if we are to have insurance schemes at all (and I
> have no objection whatever, in fact I think it would be a very desirable
> thing that the working class, who form the bulk of the population,

should have their lives made as secure a possible) ... that we ought to go right to the root of the matter and see that those who have the responsibility of the future, the women of the country, the mothers of the nation, whose employment costs so much risk of human life, should be made absolutely secure.

With prophetic words, she closed her speech crying, 'We believe that this cause of the emancipation of women is not only the greatest cause in the Twentieth Century, but we believe it is also the most urgent and the most necessary.'[44]

Such arguments held some sway. The Second Conciliation Bill had gained wide-spread support throughout the country, resolutions in its favour had been passed by eighty-six city, town and urban district councils; even the ILP, from which Emmeline had resigned four years earlier, had passed a resolution calling for an 'immediate settlement of the question of the enfranchisement of women on the same terms as men'.[45] The bill passed its second reading on Friday, 5 May, by the enormous majority of 167. When Emmeline announced the news at a vast meeting held that evening at Kensington Town Hall, there were prolonged and enthusiastic cheers. 'Let us make up our minds to-night to put all else aside', she pleaded with her audience, 'and to work as we have never worked before' in order to make certain that facilities for the bill were granted this session of parliament.[46]

When Asquith had pledged in the autumn of 1910 that, if a Liberal government were returned to power, facilities would be given for a women's suffrage measure, he was careful to say that this would be in the next parliament, not in the next session. This was an anxious time for Emmeline. She wrote to Elizabeth Robins on 26 May, 'So far nothing but rumours as to the Govt's intentions!!!' Elizabeth had been trying to arrange for the WSPU leader and Ethel Smyth to visit her that weekend, but it was impossible, Emmeline insisted since Ethel was busy while she was not spending the weekend with the Lawrences at Holmwood but had engagements in London. 'Perhaps when you come to London for the 17th we could lunch together. If you will eat with me I'll try to secure her.'[47]

Emmeline, who had been somewhat chilly when she first met Ethel was now involved in what Ethel termed 'the deepest and closest of friendships'.[48] Ethel's country cottage, named *Coign*, was a frequent retreat for the WSPU leader, a place where she could relax and talk over her anxieties with a trusted comrade and share home comforts. The only other inhabitants at the cottage were a large, shaggy, grey, Old English sheep-dog called Pan, and a rather quiet, middle-class housekeeper. Aileen Preston remembered that in the early summer of 1911 she often drove the WSPU leader to *Coign*. 'It was a wonderful trip. Dr. Ethel could improvise, and keep Mrs. Pankhurst perhaps an hour or an hour and a half, perfectly happy just sitting in her drawing-room, playing to her.' Although Ethel was no great singer, she was well known for her versatility when seated at a piano where she could play a variety of orchestral parts and sing the various tunes of a range of voices. The chauffeur, however, did not join in these musical sessions. 'I used to wait outside on a little bench, under an open window and listen, with the nightingales literally within a few yards from me in the woods.'[49]

Sometimes on these occasions Ethel would urge Emmeline, who was always in need of money, to earn large sums through writing newspaper articles that both American and British editors eagerly sought. But Emmeline, who felt uneasy with a pen, would not oblige, despite the fact that some of the money she might earn could be spent on those beautiful clothes she so admired. There was no more 'irresistible magnet to Mrs. Pankhurst than a sale', recollected Ethel, 'no severer trial to people who loathe gazing into shop windows than to walk down Regent Street with her any day'.[50] Emmeline would not be hurried. 'With your perpetual *come* on! *come* on!' she once said sharply to Ethel, 'you are as bad as a husband.' When Ethel pointed out to Emmeline that some of the money she might earn through writing could be legitimately spent on pretty dresses instead of being cast into the WSPU treasure chest she would agree, but then add wistfully, 'Besides which it is my *duty* to look as nice as I can on the platform. I would do it, dear, if I could, only I really *can't!*'

Ethel persevered, especially when she heard that the Union leader had been offered the princely sum of £100 for just one short article. One evening, when Emmeline was at *Coign*, sitting comfortably in an armchair by the fireplace, pince-nez perched crookedly on her nose, hastily scanning the newspapers for items that were of interest to her, Ethel broached the subject. 'I tell you I can't and won't do it. Please leave me alone', was the reply. But the musician found a clever way to manoeuvre the situation; she fired a number of questions at Emmeline who, despite her plea of 'I wish, dear, you would leave me in peace', nevertheless gave enough information to form the basis of an article. Ethel sat up all night, editing and polishing the ghost-written piece which she read to an approving Emmeline the next morning. She then put the article in an envelope in Emmeline's bag for her to address and post when she arrived at the WSPU offices. When Ethel enquired a few days later whether the editor had paid for the article, Emmeline revealed she had forgotten about it. 'The editor? what editor – what are you talking about? … I must have thrown it away with a lot of old papers.'

The visits to *Coign* lightened Emmeline's day but never deflected her from her main purpose of campaigning for the parliamentary vote for women. She was despondent when, on 29 May, Lloyd George reiterated in the Commons Asquith's view that no time could be found for the Second Conciliation Bill that session, without jeopardising government measures; a day would be granted in 1912 for another second reading of the bill with a week set aside for the further stages. Emmeline interpreted his statement as an attempt to deter the WSPU from ending the truce and from holding a procession in connection with the coronation of the King in June.[51] The WSPU did not, however, immediately reintroduce militancy since Christabel was informed privately that Sir Edward Grey would make a statement that would clarify the situation; the awaited statement, made on 1 June, said that the week set aside for the bill would be 'elastic' and that the opportunity offered for its passage through parliament a real one.[52]

Grey's statement seemed to give Emmeline a new upsurge of hope as she poured all her energies into advertising the great demonstration, planned for 17 June, that would show once again the support for a women's suffrage measure. The WSPU-sponsored Women's Coronation Procession, in which twenty-eight other suffrage groupings would take part, was in response to the Royal Processions, planned for 22 and 23 June, which would be overwhelmingly representative of the 'manhood of the Empire', with no place for women, the 'King's loyal subjects'.[53] On 8 June, accompanied by Emmeline Pethick Lawrence, Mabel Tuke and Vida Goldstein, she opened the WSPU Kiosk at the Festival of Empire, held at the Crystal Palace, at which leaflets about the forthcoming procession were given away as well as WSPU merchandise sold.[54] Emmeline sought too the help of Elizabeth Robins. 'Various literary people are writing advance letters or articles about it [the procession] & its significance to the papers & we wonder if you will try to get something into either the Morning Post, Standard or Telegraph.'[55] Emmeline's hope for a settlement of the women's franchise question rose higher when she learnt that Asquith had explained to Lord Lytton, in a letter dated 16 June, that, although the Government was divided on the merits of the bill, they were 'unanimous in their determination to give effect, not only in the letter but in the spirit, to the promise in regard to facilities which I made on their behalf before the last General Election'.[56] In hindsight, she observed bitterly, 'we had something yet to learn of the treachery of the Asquith Ministry and capacity for cold-blooded lying'.[57]

As Tickner points out, the procession of between 40,000 and 50,000 women that marched from the Embankment to the Albert Hall on 17 June, from at least twenty-eight suffrage organisations, was the largest, most spectacular, most triumphant, most harmonious and representative of all the demonstrations in the campaign.[58] On this bright but cool June day, Flora Drummond, on horseback, led the way followed by the colour bearer, Charlotte Marsh. Emmeline and the other WSPU officials – Christabel, Emmeline Pethick Lawrence and Mabel Tuke – walked behind Marjorie Annan Bryce gallantly mounted as Joan of Arc. Walking five abreast, the other participants marched in contingents as banners and pennants fluttered in the breeze and seventy bands played. The Prisoners' Pageant, nearly 700 strong, gave place to the Historical Pageant, illustrating the forms of political power held by British women through the ages. Then came the Empire Pageant and International Contingent, representing countries as far afield as Fiji, Finland and Roumania, followed by a host of other colourful groupings. Elizabeth Wolstenholme Elmy, who had spent forty-six years of her life fighting for the vote, reviewed the seven-mile-long procession from a seat on a balcony in St. James's Street decorated with a banner stating 'England's Oldest Militant Suffragette Greets Her Sisters'; she was saluted by the women who dipped and raised their pennants.[59] The sense of optimism that the Second Conciliation Bill would succeed, together with the 'spirit of harmony' temporarily existing between the militants and constitutionalists, produced a pageant to rival the King's Coronation Procession, as well as to question women's exclusion from it.[60] The leaders of the two main women's suffrage groupings, the NUWSS and the WSPU, were both full of praise for the day. Millicent Garrett Fawcett told Maud Arncliffe Sennett, 'I never was surer of anything in my life than that it was the right policy for the Cause, for the Nat. Union to cooperate in it.'[61] A joyful Emmeline, at a triumphant WSPU meeting held at the Albert Hall immediately after the pageant, told her audience:

> What does this demonstration of ours mean? It means victory! ... We have proved that we can combine; we have proved we can put aside all personal beliefs and all personal objects for a common end; we have proved that women have great powers of organisation; we have proved that women have great artistic capacity ... we know that in proving all these things we have shown that women, alongside with men, are worthy to build up a humanity that men can never make without our help.[62]

Emmeline Pethick Lawrence announced that the WSPU Campaign Fund had now reached £103,400. The WSPU would never organise such a large-scale demonstration again; 'the limit' of public spectacle had been reached, 'not just as a political device, but as a practical possibility'.[63]

Emmeline needed a rest; the hard slog of campaigning, participating in processions, and giving rallying speeches to her followers was taking its toll on her health. Christabel stepped in and took her mother's place at one meeting out of London while Emmeline spent some time in the country relaxing and visiting a sick friend. Immediately she returned to London on Sunday, 25 June, she tried to contact the sculptor Alice Morgan Wright who was visiting England and casting a head of the Union leader. Disappointed to find that Alice had returned to France, Emmeline wrote an affectionate letter to her the next day explaining why she had stayed in her country retreat rather than return to the metropolis for the weekend:

> As for Friday, staying away was a matter of common sense. I found on Wednesday evening that I could not get a cab to the station & had 3 miles to walk in the rain. The trains were uncertain & very crowded & when [I] arrived in London I should have to fight my way on foot, with a bag to carry, through crowds out to view the illuminations, from Waterloo station to the hotel. It seemed a foolish thing to attempt such a task so I gave it up & remained quietly in the country.

I am sorry my dear child for your disappointment & wish I had seen you again before you left.

As for the sculpting make your mind quite easy. Its enough to be a martyr to the photographers. If anyone victimises me (which is doubtful) it shall be you.[64]

Later that week, Emmeline had the pleasure of being accompanied by two of her daughters, Christabel and Sylvia, to a concert in the Queen's Hall where Ethel conducted the London Symphony Orchestra in a repeat performance of some of her works.[65]

Despite attendance at the occasional concert or a short visit to *Coign*, suffrage work was always foremost in Emmeline's mind, and, at this particular moment of time, the passing of the Second Conciliation Bill. Anxious that nothing should hinder its progress, she had written to Elizabeth Robins a few days before the concert, pointing out that the suggested meeting with Sir Edward Grey should not be too long delayed 'because it is important to know what the friends of the Bill mean its final form to be as soon as possible'.[66] One week later the persistent Emmeline wrote to Elizabeth again, advising her on how to organise her planned autumn gathering of influential friends in aristocratic and political circles:

> Christabel & I have talked the matter over & we do not like the idea of your having sole responsibility & expense & think perhaps you could get some friend who has a house in London to collaborate with you (or more than one friend).
>
> Lady Sybil Smith & her mother Lady Antrim are helping in a similar way & neither of them has a house. They make use of some friend for an At Home or a luncheon or dinner. Last week Lady Antrim got the Dowager Duchess of Argyle to give a luncheon party for MPs. Lady A invited the guests. Lady Betty Balfour who also lives in the country borrowed a house for a dinner party recently. Cannot you get Lady Lewis or some of your friends to do as much for you? In sending out invitations you could couple the hostess's name with yours.[67]

Although Elizabeth did not wish to become a pawn in the hands of Emmeline and Christabel, using her influential connections for suffrage ends, she admired them both and often found it hard to resist their demands; in particular, she respected Emmeline whom she described as 'one of the Great People of the time. ... But Lord! What a force behind that frail refined face!'[68]

Up to now the WSPU at by-elections had always opposed the government's candidate on the grounds that his election to parliament would strengthen the opposition of the government to women's enfranchisement. However, since Asquith now promised time the following year for all stages of the Second

Conciliation Bill, Emmeline and the other WSPU leaders decided to suspend the anti-Liberal government policy, provided candidates stated their support for the bill and agreed not to support widening amendments which would make it unacceptable to Conservative supporters; each individual by-election candidate, irrespective of their political allegiance, would now be assessed by the WSPU in regard to these issues. It would appear that only two Liberal candidates were vigorously opposed by the WSPU during the time this policy was in operation.[69] This new direction emphasised both the willingness of the WSPU leadership to bend to changing circumstances as well as its optimism that the votes for women question could finally be settled. The new policy was put into action when Emmeline joined in early July the by-election campaign at Wellington, West Somerset where she accidentally left her purse behind. On 8 July, when staying at the Plume of Feathers Hotel, Minehead, she wrote a grateful note to Ada Flatman, thanking her for sending the lost property. The same day she also wrote to Helen Archdale who had recently informed Emmeline that Adela was ill with a sore throat. 'I think she ought to take her holiday as soon as possible', advised a worried Emmeline, '& not speak more than she can help or even talk which I suppose she would think a very hard saying!' After thanking Helen for looking after Adela, Emmeline closed her letter, 'Love to A & the children'.[70] Then it was back to London for a big meeting at the London Pavilion on 17 July where a jubilant Emmeline was greeted with prolonged cheering as she said that very soon votes for women would be 'an accomplished fact'.[71]

Now that the summer had arrived, Emmeline welcomed the chance to leave dusty London and go campaigning in Wales. On 31 July she wrote from Llandrindod Wells to Miss Birnstingl, thanking her for the pleasant rest she had provided at Colwyn Bay. 'I feel much refreshed & stronger. … We arrived here safely but very late after many adventures on mountainous roads & in thunder storms.'[72] At a particularly successful meeting held in Llandudno, she warned, 'Suffragists did not mind open opponents like Lord Cromer or Mrs. Humphrey Ward. It was opponents who were not so outspoken who were dangerous. They were wolves in sheep's clothing.'[73] Her words had a particular resonance over the coming weeks since behind the scenes, Lloyd George was working against the Second Conciliation Bill. In mid August, while Emmeline was in Scotland, *Votes for Women* reported that Leif Jones, MP, had asked whether the government's promise of facilities for next session applied to any woman suffrage bill or exclusively to the Conciliation Bill, and that Lloyd George, in the absence of the Prime Minister, was reported to have replied that the promise of facilities was given for the Conciliation Bill; but he also added that any bill capable of free discussion and amendment which secured a second reading would be treated by the government as falling within their engagement. If the statement was accurate, opined *Votes for Women*, then the government was breaking faith not only with the Conciliation Committee but also the woman suffrage societies and could expect the WSPU to 'revert to a state of war'.[74]

It would appear that Lloyd George was advocating a wider measure of giving a vote to every wife of an elector by virtue of her husband's qualification, thus enfranchising about six million women in addition to the one and a half million who would benefit under the original terms of the Second Conciliation Bill. The prospect of such a large-scale addition to the electorate, the WSPU leadership believed, would be seen as absurd and only wreck the all-party support for the Conciliation Bill, a situation about which Lord Lytton was gravely concerned.[75] He wrote to Asquith, stating his misgivings and asked for another statement of the government's intention. On 23 August, Asquith replied, 'I have no hesitation in saying that the promises made by, and on behalf of, the Government, in regard to giving facilities for the "Conciliation Bill", will be strictly adhered to, both in letter and in spirit.'[76] Although the WSPU leadership gave a cautious welcome to such reassurances, Lloyd George was privately undermining Asquith's statement. On 5 September, when Emmeline was at Fraserburgh, he wrote to the Master of Elibank, the Liberal Party's Chief Whip, complaining that the Second Conciliation Bill would play into the hands of their enemy since it would add 'hundreds of thousands of votes throughout the country to the strength of the Tory Party', a view upheld by many other Liberal officials. The Liberal Party should make up its mind, he suggested, 'that it will either have an extended franchise which would put the working-men's wives on to the register as well as spinsters and widows, or that it will have no female franchise at all'. It looks to me, he continued, that 'through sheer drifting, vacillation and something which looks like cowardice', the Liberals were likely to find themselves in the position of putting 'this wretched Conciliation Bill' through parliament. 'Say what you will', he concluded, 'that spells disaster to Liberalism; and, unless you take it in hand and take it at once, this catastrophe is inevitable.'[77]

Emmeline was unaware of these private discussions but, like Christabel, already deeply distrustful of Lloyd George. Her tour in Scotland was not running easily. While at Skelmorlie, Ayrshire, she informed Una Dugdale that she had to cancel a meeting in Helensburgh since there was a transport strike. But even more serious was the financial situation. 'No money practically came into the funds last week except of my getting & I find I must make a special effort to raise funds in Scotland. ... The expense of the car is greater naturally than the train & we must provide for this as well as for the Union funds.'[78] Where the meetings were successful, representatives of a range of political opinion usually sat on the platform, as at Lady Cowdray's At Home, held on Saturday 9 September at Dunecht House, near Aberdeen, for which over a thousand invitations had been sent. Lady Betty Balfour, sister of Lady Constance Lytton, and a Tory, travelled especially from Nairn to chair the meeting; her presence was seen as evidence of the non-party spirit amongst suffragists at this time, and as a good omen for the success of the Second Conciliation Bill. In her speech Emmeline explained how the Conciliation Committee came into existence not to conciliate women, but to conciliate

Members of Parliament. 'They had all agreed to support the Conciliation Bill', she stressed, 'although it did not give women all they were entitled to ... because they recognised that ... it did remove the worse grievances women had to complain of ... [that] the fact of their being born women, should make them incapable of having citizen rights.'[79] It was, presumably, at such meetings that Emmeline sold picture postcards of herself, usually obtainable from WSPU shops, since she had asked Miss Birnstingl to arrange for fifty to be sent to her.[80]

While Emmeline was in the Highlands, she wrote again to Helen Archdale, advising that Adela should relinquish her post as WSPU Organiser for Sheffield, and now follow the college course she wanted to do. A worried Emmeline did not favour London, since she thought Adela 'in her present nervous condition' would never settle down to studying there, because of all the excitement of the women's movement. Instead she thought somewhere healthy and quiet by the sea would be best:

> I'm not wedded to Aberystwith [sic] but thought of there because the college is good & within our means. If she preferred St Andrews I'm agreeable. ... She would not be lonely living in a college with other young women of her own age. On the contrary I'm sure she would make friends & become less morbid & introspective. ... I really am anxious about her future. She is very clever in many ways but quite a child in others & physically is not strong. I shall not be happy or comfortable until I feel she is better equipped to make her own way in the world & more self reliant. I'd rather find more money & feel the most is being made of it while I've the strength & power to earn it for I cannot leave her independent. She will always unless she marries have to earn her living.[81]

Emmeline had already planned another lucrative lecture tour to North America that autumn, in order to earn some money for the professional retraining of her twenty-six-year-old daughter, and she now met up with Adela, to finalise the college plans. Adela wanted to go to Aberystwyth, but Emmeline later confided to Helen Archdale that she did not think her daughter was 'well enough just now for a stiff entrance exam ... altho she looks well there were many signs of nerve weakness as she talked to me'. Hoping that Adela had talked matters over with Helen, Emmeline asserted, 'I will agree to any course always stipulating that she must study in a healthy country or seaside place.'[82]

Emmeline was tired when she arrived back in London, but the prospect of her lecturing tour in the USA and Canada, to be undertaken under the auspices, again, of the J. B. Pond Lyceum Bureau, seemed to revitalise her. 'The voyage there and back always rests me', she said, almost the only rest, Christabel commented many years later, that her mother ever got.[83] In cheery mood, Emmeline wrote in mid September to Alice Morgan Wright, now in the USA, who wanted to meet her, on her arrival, explaining that she and Dorothy

Pethick would sail on the *Oceanic* on 4 October. 'I shall be very glad to see your welcoming face when we land.'[84]

Two days before her departure, Emmeline chaired an enthusiastic afternoon meeting at the London Pavilion after which she hurried to Woking where Ethel Smyth chaired her evening address. The meeting closed in a now familiar way, with Lady Sybil Smith leading the audience in a rendering of 'The march of the women'.[85]

Ethel was amongst the small party of friends – which included the Princess Duleep Singh, Lady Constance Lytton, Mabel Tuke, Kitty and Alfred Marshall, Victor Duval, Annie Kenney and Emily Wilding Davison – who greeted Emmeline at Waterloo station on that grey Wednesday morning of 4 October when she arrived with Sylvia and Dorothy Pethick to catch the 9.45 a.m. boat train to Southampton. She was wearing a small felt hat, tied round with a purple and green shot chiffon scarf, and a dark blue serge suit onto which Constance Lytton pinned a sprig of ivy geranium. Photographed by *The Standard* and inter-viewed by one of its reporters, the WSPU leader confidently asserted, 'We mean to have the vote next year.' Then the two travellers, together with Ethel and Sylvia, boarded the train which steamed out of the station floating from the front of its engine a tricolour in purple, white and green. At Southampton docks the small group was met by local WSPU members who presented their Union leader with a bouquet in the colours. As Sylvia and Ethel stood on the quay, waving goodbye, the ship's siren blew loudly. Sylvia later wrote that the 'adored Mrs. Pankhurst, smiling and waving to us from the deck, was forgotten by the musician, who snatched a note-book from her pocket and scribbled eagerly, exclaiming in her ecstasy: "A gorgeous noise!" '[86]

The Pond Lyceum Bureau gave advance notice that anyone who wished to book Mrs. Pankhurst for a lecture engagement were advised to apply early, her subjects being 'The triumph of women's suffrage in England', 'The English woman's fight for the vote' and 'The militant movement'.[87] On the day of her arrival in New York, 13 October, where custom officials allowed onto the quay just four people from the great crowd that had gathered to greet her, Emmeline wrote to Mrs. Page, Vice President of the Boston Equal Suffrage Association, accepting the invitation to say in her home. 'I did not answer your very kind invitation in England because I had very little idea of my engagements until I landed here.' Emmeline was especially delighted to hear that the state of California had just voted to grant women equal suffrage with men. 'Is it not splendid?'[88]

Wherever she went, Emmeline found a newly awakened women's movement in the USA which had been spurred into action partly through the influence of the WSPU. A Women's Political Union (WPU) had been formed with the same colours as those of the WSPU, and purple, white and green decorations adorned the hall in the Brooklyn Academy of Music, New York, when Emmeline gave her inaugural speech on 17 October. As she made her appear-ance, the roof rang with applause that lasted for a full five minutes; then Harriot

Stanton Blatch, President of the WPU, introduced the speaker 'as the woman who in all the world is doing the most for the suffrage'.[89] Wherever she went, Emmeline received warm hospitality and while in New York was the guest of Mrs. and Dr. John Winters Brannan. Since the latter was head of the city hospitals, he was able to take Emmeline on visits to a range of institutions, including a workhouse and penitentiary. For Emmeline, the conditions she found there were 'infinitely superior to the English prisons where women are punished for trying to win their political freedom'. The visit to the Night Court for Women, on the other hand, where she and her friends sat on the bench with the magistrate, was a profoundly shocking experience. 'The whole business was heart-breaking', she later recorded. 'All the women, with one exception – an old drunkard – were charged with solicitation. ... It all seemed so hopeless, and it was clear that they were victims of an evil system.'[90] It was hardly surprising that at her next port of call, Cleveland, Emmeline spoke of the white slave traffic in America. 'Why is there such a thing?' she asked. 'It is because women are cheap. Because they are not paid enough to keep soul and body together. ... Give us the vote and there will be no such thing. ... The women will eradicate it.'[91]

The breathtaking pace of her tour continued as she then took a fourteen-hour train journey from Cleveland to Louisville, Kentucky, where the NAWSA was holding a Convention. Since the train was delayed, Emmeline entered the hall at 10 o'clock in the evening, one hour later than scheduled, and was greeted by a storm of applause as many women forced their way through the crowded aisles in an effort to reach her side and touch her hand. 'She looked as fresh as a daisy', wrote the eager Eleanor Garrison to her mother while the *Louisville Courier* commented that Mrs. Pankhurst's costume was 'in quiet taste. She wore a black picture hat with black plume, and her cheeks were flushed, probably due to her haste in reaching the hall.' The moment she appeared on the platform, claimed another American newspaper, 'one realised by what power of personality she has become the best loved and best hated woman in England. ... We have never seen any personality that instantly impressed itself more than does Mrs. Pankhurst.'[92] At the Convention Emmeline met many of America's well-known suffragists including Dr. Anna Shaw, Jane Addams and Carey Thomas, Principal of Bryn Mawr College for Women.

Emmeline and Dorothy Pethick, by courtesy of Carey Thomas, stayed in Louisville at the Seelbach Hotel where the adoring Eleanor Garrison was also a guest. 'I was amazed to see them so little lionized', wrote an astonished Eleanor to her mother. 'They took themselves about a lot & I found myself walking down to the hall with Mrs. Pankhurst just as if she were anybody.' The night before, Eleanor's friend, Lucy Wills, had invited Emmeline and Dorothy to a meal in the underground restaurant of the hotel, much like the crypt of a church. The band played so loudly and the table was so large, that the four could barely hear each other speak. According to Eleanor, the distinguished guests 'ate quite heartily & consumed large steins of bier! Mrs. P said she didn't object at all.' After the meal, the four joined Anna Shaw's group where some fat women 'asked every kind of ignorant question of Mrs. P., were amazed that she had been to prison, asked what her husband thought of it & caused some chortles from Lucy & Miss Pethick'. On another occasion, the impressionable Eleanor observed how no provision had been made for taking the English visitors back after a reception and so they all squeezed into Mrs. Lewis's car alongside two other passengers. The jolly group were taken for a long ride in the parks and then to tea at the Woman's Club. 'It has just been one round of pleasure every minute', Eleanor confided to her mother, 'no time to breathe between the excitements.'[93] It was a sentiment that Emmeline would have shared.

When she was asked how soon the women of England would get the vote, Emmeline, unhesitatingly replied, 'Next year. ... After five years of civil war we have got a promise of time. In the next session of Parliament a Woman Suffrage Bill will be introduced.'[94] But her confidence was soon to be shattered. Emmeline was in the city of Minneapolis on 7 November when she was cabled the devastating news that Asquith had announced that a Manhood Suffrage Bill would be introduced next session which would allow amendment, if the Commons so desired, for the enfranchisement of women. 'I ... was so staggered', she recollected, 'that I could scarcely command myself sufficiently to fill my immediate engagements.' Her 'first wild thought' was to cancel all engagements and return to England, but knowing how Christabel would react to Asquith's statement, she decided to remain in the USA and cabled back home 'Protest imperative!'[95] 'Can they not see the deep insult of a Manhood Suffrage Bill after all that has happened?', she wrote to Clement's Inn.[96] All the WSPU leaders knew that the policy of seeking a woman suffrage amendment to a bill that would enfranchise every adult man rather than one that integrated such a proposal on equal terms was doomed to failure since it could not be carried without government support; furthermore, the proposal to enfranchise such a large number of women would destroy the all-party suffragist majority that was forthcoming for the Second Conciliation Bill, alienating in particular moderate Liberals and Unionists. Christabel immediately announced that the WSPU would 'at once revert to their anti-Government policy' and began organising a deputation for 21 November.[97] The women's movement in England, observed Emmeline, now entered upon 'a new and more vigorous stage of militancy'.[98]

13

THE WOMEN'S REVOLUTION
(NOVEMBER 1911–JUNE 1912)

As Emmeline continued her North American tour, she was still wondering if she should return home and had been enquiring about the dates and times of voyages from New York. On 11 November 1911, she wrote to Alice Morgan Wright expressing her concerns, as well as giving news of her adventures:

> It has been impossible to answer your letter earlier. The rush of events has been so great. ... I am quite excited at your news that I am to visit Albany for I have heard nothing about it! My only fixture in the United States in January is in New York on the 12th – the day before I return home.
> I am almost afraid I may have to cancel that engagement because of the new move on the part of the English Government. This introduction of a *Manhood* Suffrage Bill means more fighting for us & I may have to hurry back.
> We (Miss Pethick & I) are having a very interesting time.
> Yesterday we motored in a blizzard to see the Minnehaha falls through a park full of Longfellow reminiscences. Ohio meetings are very good & I think suffrage work promises well in the future.
> I hope we shall see you again before you go back to Paris.[1]

Emmeline then travelled to Milwaukee and further north to Duluth before venturing south again, to Omaha in Nebraska, arriving there on 16 November. Since an important WSPU meeting was being held in London that day, she made sure that she sent a cablegram well in advance so that it could be read out to all present. 'I share our indignation at the Government's insult to women, and am ready to renew the fight. Shall return with practical help from America.' Her fighting message was echoed by the other WSPU leaders.[2] The following day, Christabel and Emmeline Pethick Lawrence led the WSPU delegation in the deputation of nine women's suffrage societies that Asquith and Lloyd George had agreed to meet but, as expected, Asquith refused to abandon the Manhood Suffrage Bill. The WSPU issued a statement saying that hostilities would be resumed.

On 21 November, as Emmeline Pethick Lawrence led a deputation from Caxton Hall to Parliament Square, another smaller group of women, armed with bags of stones and hammers smashed the windows of not only government offices but also of the National Liberal Federation, the Guards' Club, the *Daily Mail* and *Daily News*, Swan and Edgar's, Lyon's Tea Shop, Dunn's Hat Shop, two hotels, as well as some small businesses, including a tailor's shop and a bakery.[3] Emmeline Pethick Lawrence was amongst the 223 arrested that day.[4] Christabel, steeped in the history of reform movements, hastily defended the resumption of militant action and its new direction, namely attacks on private as well as public property. Men had got their vote by riot and rebellion, she told her audience at the Savoy Theatre on 23 November, and that was how women must get it. Amidst applause and loud cheers, she said that in view of what men had done in the past to win enfranchisement, they had nothing to be ashamed of for what they did in the window-smashing demonstration.[5] Christabel was engaging in what Jorgensen-Earp terms 'reformist terrorism', whereby it was hoped that a crisis would be created thus pressurising the government to respond to the women's demand.[6]

Emmeline Pankhurst in the USA kept in close touch through cable about the shift in policy and was staying in Cincinnati when she wrote to Alice Morgan Wright about these developments:

> I must return home not later than the 6th January (i.e. sail from New York). Have just had cable to that effect so the proposed Carnegie Hall meeting will have to be postponed or cancelled or advanced. If I can get Albany in between the 1st Dec & time of sailing I will come otherwise the meeting must be abandoned. Very sorry but the 'storm centre' needs me. Mrs Lawrence is in prison & I know not how many more. It is very hard not be there also![7]

The following day, 24 November, Lloyd George, Chancellor of the Exchequer, gave a provocative speech at Bath, claiming that the Second Conciliation Bill had been 'torpedoed' by the announcement of the Manhood Suffrage Bill which would make way for a broad and democratic amendment for women's suffrage and enfranchise, not a limited class of women just to suit the Tory canvasser, but also the working man's wife.[8] Christabel reacted angrily. 'We shall never believe that Mr. Lloyd George is a genuine supporter of a democratic franchise for women until he secures that it be made a Government measure', she thundered in an early December issue of *Votes for Women*. In the same issue, a message from Emmeline was published, encouraging British women to engage in a 'civil war', the outcome of which would be the withdrawal of the unjust Manhood Suffrage Bill. 'I long to be back in the glorious struggle', she continued. 'In a few days I go to Canada to rouse the women of that vast Dominion of ours to unite with the women of the Mother Country in their fight for justice. ... I send deep love and gratitude to the women of our splendid army.'[9] But the announcements by the WSPU leaders were regarded as irrational and insane by an irritated Chancellor, who breakfasted with C. P. Scott. '[T]hey must be mad', opined Lloyd George. 'They are mad', agreed Scott. 'It's just like going to a lunatic asylum and talking to a man who thinks he's God Almighty', retorted Lloyd George, who felt upstaged by the militant leaders' exposure of his supposedly radical views.[10] But there was nothing mad about Emmeline. Nor did the Canadian press see her in that way. When she spoke in Massey Hall, Toronto, on 12 December, she was described as 'eminently womanly and essentially sane. She is logical, witty and graceful, with the convincing force of the woman who knows whereof she speaks. ... Justice is her plea, and, as a pleader she is most effective.' Nevertheless, it was also suggested that she lacked that vitality so evident when she spoke in Toronto some two years earlier.[11]

Keen to be back home, Emmeline wrote again to Alice Morgan Wright, glad that they would be travelling back to England together. 'Will you secure a cabin for me at lowest rate possible for the exclusive use of one to myself', she asked. 'I am feeling rather tired & shall be glad when I get on board the steamer for a good rest.' Emmeline gave her itinerary to Alice. That evening they would make their way to Fort William, and then on to Winnipeg and Victoria. On 21 December they would go to Seattle, in the equal suffrage state of Washington, where they would spend Christmas. Then they would travel back across the States, via Butte in Montana.[12]

On 28 December 1911, en route from Seattle to Chicago, a weary but fascinated Emmeline wrote to Elizabeth Robins, reflecting on her endless journeying and the constant flow of new people she was meeting:

> You will be surprised to get this letter from me knowing what a dreadful correspondent I am. ... This tour of mine is a strange experience. I do not stay long enough in any place to learn very much of either place or people & my mind is full of impressions.
>
> I almost went to Florida but the distance was too great to cover for one meeting.
>
> What a huge country this is. I have lost count of the thousand of miles I have travelled.
>
> Out of all the confused impressions comes clearly the fact that everywhere the woman's movement is growing steadily.
>
> I believe Canada is quite ripe & is only waiting for leaders. Oh to be young again with all this wide world to conquer![13]

In Britain, WSPU militancy had taken a different turn earlier that month. On 15 December, Emily Wilding Davison, a well-known freelance, rank-and-file militant, was arrested for trying to force a piece of linen saturated in paraffin and alight, through the slot of a letter box just outside Parliament Street post office, something which she claimed she had already done to two other post-boxes earlier that day, acting entirely on her 'own responsibility'.[14] When she came before the court, the accused claimed that she had engaged in such action partly as a protest against the vindictive sentence and treatment of 'my comrade, Mary Leigh' (who had been sentenced to two months' imprisonment in contrast to Constance Lytton, whose sentence was only two weeks), and partly because she wished the government to include reference to a woman's suffrage measure in the King's Speech. In the agitation for reform in the past, Emily explained, 'the next step after window-breaking was incendiarism', and so she engaged in such an act 'in order to draw the attention of the private citizen to the fact that this question of reform is their concern as well as that of women'.[15] This was the first incidence of incendiarism in the WSPU campaign and, yet again, such militant action, which was to become common over the next few years, had been initiated not by the leadership but by an ordinary member; furthermore, as Morley and Stanley point out, this militant act arose within the context of feminist friendship and worries about what was happening to one particular comrade.[16] Although Emmeline was in the States at the time, she later praised the protest, in her autobiography, written with hindsight, because of 'its prophetic character'.[17] However, Morley and Stanley suggest that the situation at the time was quite different in that Emily Wilding Davison was not in favour with the WSPU leadership since she was an unpredictable militant who went her own way rather than obeying central directives, and, consequently had had her employment with the WSPU terminated in 1910, although she retained her Union membership; in addition, she was critical of the 'leadership' for its failure to do anything about the heavy sentence passed on her friend, Mary Leigh.[18] While Emily Wilding Davison's relationship with Emmeline Pankhurst may have been uneasy, on more than one occasion, as noted earlier, Emmeline had highlighted in her speeches the unjust disparity in treatment that was meted out to the working-class Mary Leigh and the aristocratic Lady Constance Lytton, daughter of Earl Lytton who had once been British Viceroy in India. When, early in the New Year, the severe sentence of six months' imprisonment was passed on Emily Wilding Davison, Emmeline must have been concerned. It was to this state of affairs that she returned home on 18 January 1912, determined upon a more serious form of militancy, a view that had already been aired in Christabel's defence of the broken windows policy.[19] The words 'Sedition!' and 'The Women's Revolution' were now upon Emmeline's lips.[20]

She had barely arrived at Tilbury Docks when she was almost immediately back into the swing of campaigning and addressing the weekly Monday afternoon meeting. On Saturday 20 January she spoke in Wales, at Carmarthen and Llanelly, and on the 22nd at a welcome home meeting at the London Pavilion where the audience rose to their feet and cheered and cheered as she entered.[21] Speaking of the Prime Minister's 'great betrayal' of his pledge with regard to the Second Conciliation Bill, she then congratulated the women who had taken part in the raid of 21 November, thanking them from the bottom of her heart for what they had done, for their promptitude, their courage, and their devotion in that time of crisis. If they were not to be allowed to go to the House of Commons to plead for themselves, then she herself would be the first stone-thrower.[22] Emmeline then went on to speak about her three months' tour, and how the militancy of the women of England was arousing women in the States and in Canada where a branch of the WSPU had been founded. That very day, Brailsford wrote to Millicent Garrett Fawcett saying that he had seen Mrs. Pankhurst who regretted 'having ever looked at "that abominable Conciliation Bill", and declares that they will never tolerate anything but a Government measure of full sex equality. She is optimistic & even triumphant. If she fails to force the P. M. to take up Adult Suffrage (& for this she still hopes) she is sanguine of destroying this and every succeeding Government.'[23]

There was little time to rest as Emmeline continued her campaigning, yet she was determined not to let physical exhaustion dampen her spirit. On 11 February she wrote an affectionate letter full of news to Alice Morgan Wright:

> Since I saw you last I have been in many places. Last week I was in Wrexham[,] Chester[,] Liverpool[,] Cardiff. This week Leicester[,] Market Harboro'[,] Newcastle on Tyne[,] Sunderland[,] North Shields.
>
> Tomorrow I go to Wolverhampton & hence to Lincoln. Then back of [to] London for a few days. So you see I am kept well at it.
>
> People here told me that I was 15 years younger for my American trip but already the good effect is wearing off. Our beautiful English climate plays havoc with me …
>
> Here all our minds are full of what will be in the King's speech. We are preparing for action so expect to hear of broken windows ere long. … When the time comes for renewed action I shall be quite ready for a rest. This work of rousing the women that I have to do is very exhausting.
>
> Write to me whenever you like to my dear child so long as your work is not interfered with & you do not mind if I do not always reply.[24]

The government in the King's Speech delivered on 14 February announced, as expected, a Reform Bill for men only. Emmeline's anger intensified when it became apparent that the bill, as drafted, might be impossible of amendment to include woman suffrage, a point hinted at by The Times.[25] Although third place in the private members' ballot was won for the Second Conciliation Bill, the WSPU leadership were convinced that the success of such a measure had been destroyed and therefore expressed interest only in a government-backed women's suffrage measure. On 16 February, at a dinner at the Connaught Rooms to welcome those window-breakers who had served sentences of two months – including Helen Archdale, Sarah Benett, Olive Wharry, Francis Rowe and Vera Wentworth – the charismatic Emmeline exercised her authority as leader of the WSPU by drawing up the lines of engagement for the women's revolution. 'It is perhaps one of the strangest things of our civilisation', she pointed out, to think that women in the twentieth century are in a world 'where they are forced to say that an appeal to justice, that an appeal to reason, that evidence of their fitness for citizenship, should be of less value than the breaking of panes of glass.' Praising Emmeline Pethick Lawrence and the deputation that she had lead on 21 November for forcing a Cabinet crisis, she announced that the weapon and argument that they were going to use at the next demonstration on 4 March, which she was going to lead, was the stone. 'If the argument of the stone, that time-honoured official political argument, is sufficient, then we will never use any stronger argument.' Passionately, Emmeline outlined her reasons for the endorsement of the new tactics, pointing out how for years women had submitted patiently to insult and to assault:

> Women had their health injured. Women lost their lives. We should not have minded that if that had succeeded, but that did not succeed, and we have made more progress with less hurt to ourselves by breaking glass than ever we made when we allowed them to break our bodies.

Emmeline then calmly announced her intention of leading her followers to destroy public and private property on a much larger scale than previously. '[W]e are going on the next demonstration in full faith that this plan of campaign, initiated by our friends whom we honour to-night, will on this next occasion prove effective.'[26]

Although Emmeline expected to be arrested for making such a speech, which was widely reported in the press, this was not so. Ironically, at the very moment when she had been stating the political necessity for more serious militant action, Charles Hobhouse, a Cabinet Minister, had been asserting, at an anti-suffrage meeting in Bristol, that in the case of woman suffrage there had not been the kind of popular feeling which accounted for the burning of Nottingham Castle in 1832 or the pulling down of the Hyde Park railings in 1867, prior to the passing of the Reform Bills in these two years. Hobhouse's provocative speech was 'like a match to a fuse'.[27] As Emmeline Pethick Lawrence pointed out, the holding up to women of the example of men in 1832 and 1867 indicated that Mr. Hobhouse took 'the very grave responsibility of inciting them to serious forms of violence in comparison with which Mrs. Pankhurst's exhortation is mildness itself'.[28] Emmeline Pankhurst, who endorsed such views, was not well again so that Lady Constance Lytton was asked to take her place at three scheduled meetings at Bristol, Shrewsbury and Stroud.[29] The poorly WSPU leader retreated to *Coign* where, on a secluded part of Hook Heath, Ethel Smyth taught her how to throw a stone by aiming her missile at the largest fir tree. 'One has heard of people failing to hit a haystack', remembered Ethel, 'what followed was rather on those lines. I imagine Mrs. Pankhurst had not played ball games in her youth, and the first stone flew backwards out of her hand, narrowly missing my dog.' With each failed attempt, Emmeline assumed a more and more ferocious expression until a loud thud proclaimed success and a 'smile of such beatitude' stole across her face that Ethel collapsed in laughter amongst the heather. Emmeline was not amused.[30]

On returning to Clement's Inn, Emmeline hastily wrote to Ethel a letter which was never posted but later found in a police raid on WSPU offices. The WSPU had always announced in advance when their demonstrations would be held and Emmeline had already written to Asquith telling him about the deputation for 4 March. But now Emmeline told Ethel about another plan:

> On Friday [1 March] there will be an unannounced affair, a sort of skirmish, in which some of our bad, bold ones will take part, an unadvertised affair. I shall take part, but not in the way I told you of – that is off. On Monday [4 March] there will be the affair as originally planned. C. and I have talked it over. My cough is troublesome. I must take care, or I shall not be very fit for the fray at the end of the week. There may be a long trial. I will meet your train on Monday.[31]

On 1 March the WSPU struck for the first time without warning. At half past five in the afternoon, Emmeline, Mabel Tuke and Kitty Marshall drove in a taxi to the Prime Minister's residence at 10 Downing Street and broke two of the windows. They were immediately arrested. The following hour, at intervals of fifteen minutes, small relays of harmless looking, well-dressed women armed with hammers hidden in muffs, smashed plate glass windows in fashionable shops and major department stores in London's West End while a smaller number created a fresh disturbance some two hours later. Emmeline, described by *The Times* as 'the notorious agitator for the Parliamentary franchise for women', was amongst the 121 arrested who, it was claimed, had broken nearly four hundred shop windows causing about £5,000 worth of damage.[32] In Bow Street Police Court the following day, she reminded the magistrate that women had failed to get the vote since they had failed to use the methods of agitation used by men. To support her case, Emmeline pointed out that within the last fortnight, a member of the government, Mr. Hobhouse, had said that women had not proved their desire for the vote because they had done nothing akin to that which characterised men's protest in 1832, when they burnt down Nottingham Castle, and in 1867, when they tore down Hyde Park railings. Defiantly but politely, Emmeline told the magistrate that she hoped the demonstration would show the government that the women's agitation would continue:

> If not, if you send me to prison, as soon as I come out of prison I will go further, to show that women who have to pay the salaries of Cabinet

Ministers, and who help to pay your salary too, Sir, are going to have some voice in the making of the laws which they have to obey.[33]

Emmeline was sentenced to two months' imprisonment in the Third Division.

Further unannounced window-smashing on Monday, 4 March, led to another ninety-six arrests amongst whom were Ethel Smyth and Louisa ('Louie') Garrett Anderson, daughter of Elizabeth Garrett Anderson and a doctor, like her mother. A Union meeting planned for the evening, advertised in handbills that bore Emmeline's signature and invited the public to join the protest in Parliament Square, was reduced by a heavy police presence to a series of isolated incidences.[34] Determined to strike at the WSPU leadership, the government ordered Scotland Yard to act. The following day the police swooped on WSPU headquarters with a warrant for the arrest of the Pethick Lawrences and Christabel who, together with Emmeline and Mabel Tuke, were charged with 'conspiring to incite others to commit malicious damage to property'.[35] Only the Pethick Lawrences were found since Christabel now lived in a flat nearby. Jessie Kenney in a note had warned Christabel about what was happening while Fred Pethick Lawrence had hastily sent Evelyn Sharp in person, to tell the tale, as well as to ask Christabel to countersign a cheque enabling the transfer of WSPU funds into Hertha Ayrton's bank account.[36] Christabel spent the night in hiding and, fearful of what would happen to the WSPU if all the leaders were in prison, escaped to Paris where as 'Amy Richards' she attempted single handedly to lead the movement at a distance. Before she left England, she wrote a letter to the trusted Annie Kenney asking her to act as her deputy until her mother and Emmeline Pethick Lawrence were free to assume leadership in England once again. 'My relief, when I learned of her flight', recollected Emmeline, 'was very great, because I knew that whatever happened to the Lawrences and myself, the movement would be wisely directed.'[37] A less welcome aspect of the raid on Clement's Inn for Emmeline was that the police, in a determined effort to find evidence of conspiracy, took away many private keepsakes that she had cherished carefully over the years. 'They went through every desk, file and cabinet, taking away with them two cab loads of books and papers, including all my private papers, photographs of my children in infancy, and letters sent me by my husband long ago. Some of these I never saw again.' The police also 'terrorised' the printer of Votes for Women so that although the paper was printed as usual that week, about a third of its columns were left blank.[38]

These events in early March, especially the scale of the window-smashing and of Emmeline's role as leader of the demonstration, received widespread condemnation in the press. On 2 March, The Times in its editorial referred to 'Mrs. Pankhurst and her maenads' while two days later Mr. Lasenby Liberty, owner of the fashionable West End store, claimed that, as a victim of the recent raid, he wanted to ask Mrs. Pankhurst 'to state the mental process by which they deem the breaking of the very shrines at which they worship 'will advance their cause'.[39] As the gap between the tactics of the militants and constitutionalists irrevocably widened, concerns were expressed by women in both camps, publicly and privately. Millicent Garrett Fawcett, addressing a meeting on 3 March, made it clear that the NUWSS 'stood exactly where it had always stood, in very strong disapprobation of the use of physical force and physical violence as means of political propaganda'.[40] Elizabeth Garrett Anderson, who had once accompanied Emmeline Pankhurst in a demonstration to the House of Commons but had resigned from the WSPU over the use of such violent tactics now wrote to Millicent, her sister, expressing scathing comments about the once admired militant leader. 'Katie Thompson sent me rather a large cheque today for the Cause. I have written to ask if I may hand it to you. I certainly do not mean to give it to Mrs. Pankhurst. I think she & the P Lawrences have shown very little fortitude or dignity.' The arrest and sentencing to six weeks with hard labour of her daughter, Louie, undoubtedly helped to fuel Elizabeth's anger. Indeed, she was of the view that the Government should have handled the matter differently. 'If Mrs. Pankhurst & the other leaders had been fined £3000 each & smaller fry like Louie £1000 & upwards it wd pay for the windows & they wd all dislike it every much.'[41]

Emmeline had her own personal worries at this time. When she entered Holloway she found herself in the anomalous position of being both a convicted offender serving a two months' prison sentence, and also a prisoner on remand, waiting to be charged with a more serious offence. Refusing to give up her watch and writing case, she told the governor that she and her two companions expected more privileges this time, but none were initially given. On 6 March, she was again in Bow Street Court where she was formally charged, together with the Pethick Lawrences and Mabel Tuke, with having 'wantonly conspired and combined together, unlawfully and maliciously, to commit damage and injury to an amount exceeding £5 to plate-glass windows' and also with 'unlawfully aiding, abetting, counselling, and procuring the commission of offences against the Malicious Injuries to Property Act'. Not in the best of health, Emmeline's voice broke as she explained that she was unwell; clinging to the rails of the dock, she asked to whom she should apply for facilities for the preparation of her defence. However, she quickly regained her composure when the warders began to lead the prisoners back to their cell, proudly commanding, 'Don't touch me!'[42] Back in her damp, sunless cell, away from the block where other suffragettes were held, Emmeline's illness soon developed into bronchitis. The sound of imprisoned militants singing the 'March of the women' during the dreary round of exercise, while Ethel Smyth, with hand thrust through the bars of her cell window, conducted proceedings with a toothbrush, did little to raise her spirits. But when her companions threatened a hunger strike unless they were granted the privileges of political offenders, Emmeline rose to the occasion and advised them to desist, on the understanding that such privileges would soon be conferred.[43]

Emmeline's own petition for release on bail so that she could recover her health and prepare her case was refused. She was, however, removed to a more comfortable cell in the hospital wing but found a cockroach in her bed and another on the wall; the officials advised her not to let her bedclothes touch the floor as the insects probably came in through the grating of a disused heating apparatus. Always fastidious about her person, Emmeline was repulsed by such unhygienic conditions. The granting of permission to see her solicitor, Alfred Marshall, and her secretary, was double edged since they could only visit her in the presence of a wardress and a member of the prison clerical staff who made notes on what she said, contrary to the rules governing prisoners on remand who had to prepare a defence against a graver charge. Such conditions made it difficult for Emmeline to prepare her case, despite the fact that she was allowed access to copies of *Votes for Women*, press cuttings and books of political speeches. Such concessions could be granted to Second and Third Division prisoners under Rule 243a, which the Secretary of State had approved in 1910 with the suffragettes in mind; taking advantage of the new rule, Emmeline also ordered in her own food, including a daily half pint of Chateau Lafite.[44]

On 17 March, Emmeline was suddenly released to the block where the other suffragettes were held and placed in a cell adjoining that of Ethel Smyth. A kind-hearted matron often bent the rules, leaving the two friends together in Emmeline's cell at tea-time, locking them in, and then forgetting to come back to conduct Ethel to her own cell. Although glad of such kindnesses, Emmeline would not let such favours soften her attitude to the prison authorities and often said in cold scorn, 'I would throw up any job rather than treat women as you say it is your DUTY to treat us.'[45] Nevertheless, the more relaxed atmosphere in the suffragette wing permitted various amusements which brought some relief from the oppressive atmosphere of Holloway. Ethel recollected, 'How we got the materials – calico, purple, white, and green tissue paper and so on, not to speak of hammer and nails – I cannot remember, but designs and mottoes breathing insult and defiance would embellish the courtyard walls for hours before they were discovered and torn down.' At one idea of Ethel's, however, 'Mrs. Pankhurst drew the line.' Ethel asked the tailoring section in the prison to cut out a large pair of convict half-breeches but in two identical pieces so that one could not tell front from back – and, presumably, neither male from female needs. She sewed the pieces together, in the apple-pie-bed manner, and then hung the garment up in the exercise yard together with the motto, 'A Mus. Doc.'s notion of small clothes.' The prim Emmeline, deeply concerned that a prank in such bad taste might damage the women's cause, especially if leaked to the press, scolded Ethel for her ribald sense of humour and ordered the immediate removal of the offending object.[46]

On 28 March the Second Conciliation Bill was due to have its second reading. That very morning, *The Times* published a letter from Sir Almroth Wright, MD, FRS, in which he claimed that women were unfitted for the vote largely on physiological grounds and, in particular, that there was 'mixed up' with the militant suffragists 'much mental disorder', stemming from the fact that they were recruited from that excess of single women who 'had better long ago have gone out to mate with its complement of men beyond the seas'. If women's suffrage arrives in England, he maintained, 'it will have come as a surrender to a very violent feminist agitation – an agitation which we have traced back to our excess female population and the associated abnormal physiological conditions'.[47] Suffragists of every shade rallied to support the militants but the statement fed a deep undercurrent of prejudice against women. The bill failed by fourteen votes to pass its second reading, a defeat that came as no surprise to Emmeline. That evening, in a show of solidarity with their absent leaders and in defiance of their treatment at the hands of a Liberal government, a record number of members attended the WSPU meeting in the Albert Hall, over £10,000 being promised for the fighting fund. Although a number of MPs claimed to have voted against the bill because of WSPU tactics, the militants pointed out that the bill had been killed in advance. Lloyd George's support for an alternative adult male suffrage measure meant the loss of many Liberal and Labour supporters while the Irish Nationalists opposed the bill in order to avoid the possible resignation of Asquith, and breakup of his Cabinet, at a time when they hoped to win Home Rule for Ireland.[48]

Emmeline's hearing in the police courts, which had dragged on for three weeks, finally ended; Mabel Tuke was acquitted but the WSPU leader and the Pethick Lawrences were committed for trial at the Central Criminal Court, the Old Bailey. On 4 April, the day before Good Friday, Emmeline was released on bail, her prison sentence for window-breaking having been remitted until after the conspiracy trial. Amid widespread public concern for her health and treatment by the prison authorities, the Rev. Hugh Chapman warned, 'We constantly kill our prophets and afterwards erect their sepulchres.'[49]

That Easter, Emmeline retreated to the country to recuperate. On 12 April she felt fit enough to travel to *Coign* where Ethel Smyth was waiting, having also been released on the same day as Emmeline after serving just three weeks of her two-month sentence with hard labour (there had been no hard labour). That day Emmeline wrote a caring reply to the frail Constance Lytton whose own health had been impaired by imprisonment and who was anxious about the WSPU leader:

> When I see you I will tell you how I spent my Easter holiday. I am now feeling ready for the future. I hope you will soon be well again & that you will take better care of yourself in future. I go to Holmwood this afternoon for the week end & am looking forward to long talks with my co-conspirators. Much as I should wish the absent one [Christabel] to be there also I am glad that she is free to direct the ship even from a distance as she is doing in 'V for W'. What a fine article hers is this week.[50]

The fact that Christabel's whereabouts were kept secret, and that the authorities did not know where she was residing, added to Emmeline's pride in the political flair of her eldest daughter. That unsigned articles outlining WSPU policy continued to appear in Christabel's weekly column in *Votes for Women* deepened the mystery – where was the elusive woman? On 12 April, when Emmeline wrote to Mrs. Billinghurst thanking her warmly for her contribution towards the cost of the conspiracy trial, she again expressed her confidence in her eldest daughter. 'Whatever happens to us we "conspirators" know that the movement will go on & that our splendid members will be loyal to my daughter, Annie Kenney & Mrs Tuke who will guide the ship in our absence.'[51] At a farewell reception for the leaders later that month, before their expected imprisonment, Emmeline told her followers to remain steadfast and when it came to political action, not to listen to any friends outside the movement but to trust those whom they had chosen as their leaders. Without naming Christabel and Annie Kenney, she said, 'Read the paper. Take your political instructions from the leading articles. Consult with those who remain at Clement's Inn to be consulted with regard to policy.' Adding a cautionary note, she pleaded, 'If there is one thing that could hurt us in prison, if there is one thing that could break our hearts, it would be the thought that your affection for us should be used to weaken your determination to go on with this movement.'[52]

In the meantime, Sylvia had returned from the USA on 8 April to find suffragettes being mobbed in the London streets as resentment against the 'wild' women became increasingly physical.[53] Sylvia had heard with dismay about the mass window-breaking and strongly disapproved, as did the American suffragists she met.[54] Whether she expressed these views openly to Emmeline is doubtful since she knew that her mother supported the new policy and did not want to force a breach with her. But, as a deeply committed socialist and supporter of the Labour Party, Sylvia still upheld the same view that she held in the summer of 1909 when the WSPU leadership defended small-scale stone-throwing, namely that the movement required 'not more serious militancy by the few, but a stronger appeal to the great masses to join the struggle'.[55] That her mother had consistently tried to marshal the support of the public on the women's question, she conveniently ignored; nor did she comment on the failure of the WFL too in this respect, despite its democratically elected leadership and its close links to the socialist movement. Sylvia particularly welcomed the growing commitment of the Labour Party to women's suffrage, evident at its conference in early 1912 when a women's suffrage resolution had been passed, but was only too well aware that it was Millicent Garrett Fawcett, leader of the NUWSS, and not the WSPU leadership, who was sympathetic to an electoral alliance with that body.[56] The political gulf between Emmeline and Christabel on one side, and Sylvia on the other, was widening.

Sylvia had earned enough in the States to support herself for some time and, as she explains in her book *The suffragette movement*, she was now determined to give all her time to the women's cause since any other project she attempted would pall by its insignificance:

> To prevent the cause from being beaten back for a generation, as had happened to many a cause, a large popular agitation for the vote itself must be maintained at fever heat, and the fate of the prisoners always kept in the public eye. The four most prominent had been seized; others would follow. Every one of us would be needed.[57]

My reading of that passage is that Sylvia saw the new situation – Christabel in France and the impending imprisonment of her mother and Emmeline Pethick Lawrence – as an opportunity to lead the WSPU, to bring it 'back', as she conceived it, to its socialist 'roots'. This is conjecture, of course, but one of her biographers also offers such an analysis.[58] Disguised as a nurse, Sylvia crossed the channel and visited the elder sister (known as 'Miss Amy Richards') who was staying in a flat in the Hotel Cité Bergère (and later in another flat in the Avenue de la Grande Armée). There is only one account of this meeting and it is written by Sylvia, nearly twenty years after the event, in *The suffragette movement*. According to this source, when Sylvia asked how she could best help at this time of crisis, Christabel replied, 'When those who are doing the work are arrested, you may be needed, and can be called on.' Further pressed by Sylvia, Christabel suggested, 'Well, just speak at a few meetings.' The tongue-tied Sylvia, expecting to be asked to lead the WSPU, was hurt by this exchange, feeling that she was being pushed to the sidelines; she was unable even to tell her elder sister about her doubts on the new militant policy, fearing that Christabel would 'thrust aside whoever might differ from her tactics by a hair's breadth'. Sylvia remained silent. 'I made no comment. I had always been scrupulous neither to criticize her nor oppose her, to show no open divergence of opinion in relation to the movement. I was still prepared to uphold her, and for the sake of unity to subordinate my views in many matters to hers.' Her one consolation was that Christabel's 'refusal to ask any service of me would leave me the more free to do what I thought necessary in my own way'.[59]

Sylvia had misread the situation. Contrary to the impression given in *The suffragette movement*, she had not played a major role in WSPU political life, did not hold an official position, opposed the policy of political independence from all men's political parties, including the Labour Party, and was not regarded as an engaging speaker. Her major talents lay in artistic work and in writing, and in these respects she had made a considerable contribution to promoting the WSPU's work; furthermore, she was having an affair with a prominent Labour figure who was a married man, Keir Hardie, an involvement about which both her mother and Christabel now knew. Bearing all these factors in mind, it is highly improbable that Sylvia was even considered by Emmeline and Christabel as a possible leader for the WSPU in a time of crisis. Before she had taken the boat to France, Christabel had written a letter not to Sylvia but to the faithful

Annie Kenney, asking her to act as her deputy. 'I trust you implicitly', she wrote, a sentiment that one feels she could not express to her sister.[60] On 27 April, Sylvia was billed as speaking at a WSPU meeting in Palmer's Green, London.[61]

Emmeline, who probably heard from Sylvia and Christabel different versions of their meeting, had still not fully recovered her health and was worried about preparing her defence. Needing more time, Mr. T. H. Healy, KC, applied on her behalf on 24 April for a postponement of her trial, and was refused. The following day, while resting in the comfort of her room at the Inns of Court Hotel, the fifty-three-year-old Emmeline wrote a despairing letter to Elizabeth Robins:

> Yesterday, as you may have seen, the application was refused! I am making one more effort for I do not feel fit to face the strain involved in conducting my own defence. I wonder how the Home Sec. would like to undertake such a piece of work lasting over several days so soon after coming out of prison added to all the other elements in the situation. The strain of the past 6 years tells on me more & more, my mind does not work as quickly as it used to do & it has not yet recovered from the effect of prison. Even young women tell me that in prison it is impossible to concentrate on anything & that it takes some time after one is liberated for this mental paralysis to wear off. I suppose these people do not realise how brutal they are. All this talk of chivalry forsooth & yet they, with all the power of the nation at their disposal, knowing they mean to have me sent back to prison, won't give me time (at the most 3 weeks) to get back enough strength to make a good fight for my liberty! Well it will recoil on their own heads. Slowly but surely the net of official misrepresentation & repression is breaking & every new act of injustice helps.[62]

The same day Emmeline penned a short note to Una Dugdale, complaining of how the 'enemy' insisted on his 'pound of flesh at the earliest possible moment', irrespective of her state of health.[63] Eventually, a third application for postponement of the trial, until 15 May, met with success.

The Old Bailey conspiracy trial began and ended in a blaze of national publicity as newspapers covered the six-day event in detail. When the charges were read out, the proceedings opened in characteristic form since the proud Emmeline, who disliked references to her age, refused to state how old she was. Acting in her own defence, she cross-examined witnesses and questioned evidence, and produced her own witnesses, including Ethel Smyth, in order to support the argument of the defence, as outlined by Fred Pethick Lawrence, that the conspiracy and incitement in the case were not that of the defendants but of the government which had 'deliberately deceived and thwarted the women's movement'.[64] During the closing days of the trial, when Emmeline addressed the court on 21 May, she poignantly stated, 'I will try to make you understand what it is that has brought a woman no longer young into this dock.' Quietly, she reminded Judge Coleridge, whom she addressed courteously as 'My Lord', that his father forty-three years ago pleaded on behalf of women in a test case that arose out of the Reform Act of 1867 as to the right of women to be placed on the electoral register. One effect of that case decision, which said that women were not persons for the privilege of voting, was that she and Emmeline Pethick Lawrence were persons to be punished but not persons to have any voice in the making of laws which they might break. Movingly, as in previous speeches, she pointed out how her experiences as a Poor Law Guardian had revealed to her the wretched living conditions of poor women and children and how she had sought to change the law to help those less fortunate than herself. She had come to realise, however, that the old constitutional methods she had followed in order to get the vote for women had failed, and so in 1903 she founded the WSPU. The militants in the WSPU, Emmeline reassured the court, were not criminals but political activists, seeking political reform. Furthermore, she insisted:

> I want you to realise that no step we have taken forward has been taken until after some act of repression on the part of our enemy, the Government – because it is the Government which is our enemy – it is not the Members of Parliament, it is not the men in the country; it is the Government in power alone that can give us the vote.

Summing up her case, Emmeline maintained that it was not the defendants who had conspired, but the government who had conspired against the militants as they tried to crush the suffrage agitation.[65] The fight of the militants was a just war, based on moral conviction.

Emmeline's admirers were visibly moved by her one and three-quarter hours' oration. For Nevinson, it was 'one of the noblest speeches I have heard'. For Laurence Housman, a Bohemian suffragist, playwright and illustrator, who was not present at the trial but later read a full account, Emmeline's speech made 'my heart ache more than any other speech I have ever read on the suffrage'.[66] The all-male jury found the defendants guilty although they unanimously expressed the hope that, 'taking into consideration the undoubtedly pure motives' which underlie the suffrage agitation, 'the utmost clemency and leniency' would be exercised. Justice Coleridge coolly ignored the plea and, refusing the appeal by the defendants to be treated as political prisoners, pronounced the severe sentence of nine months in the Second Division. Emmeline Pankhurst and Fred Pethick Lawrence were also ordered to pay the prosecution costs.[67]

Emmeline Pankhurst and Emmeline Pethick Lawrence were soon back in Holloway while Fred was sent to Brixton. The two Emmelines were warmly but respectfully welcomed by the other imprisoned militants who invited them to join in the various activities that they organised. Chairs were placed against the wall of the wardresses' home as the 'dress circle' for the two leaders who watched a performance of a scene from Shakespeare's *The merchant of Venice*. The two Emmelines, in their turn, also entertained their companions by telling stories, and even joined in a game of 'Here we come gathering nuts in May on a cold and frosty morning'.[68] But a pressing family matter was now on Emmeline Pankhurst's mind. An anxious Adela travelled to London to see her mother but was refused a visit. Sometime earlier, she had told her mother that she wanted to train as a gardener, a decision which had disappointed Emmeline but which she nevertheless accepted. Adela now wanted to finalise the financial arrangements with Emmeline, even if she was in prison, since she needed the money that Emmeline had carefully saved from her last lucrative American tour for the £200 enrolment fee at an agricultural college.[69] Emmeline had to delay the matter until a more convenient time. In the meantime, together with the Pethick Lawrences, she threatened to hunger strike unless granted political offender status and placed in the First Division, a plea that was vigorously supported by Keir Hardie and George Lansbury, another Labour MP, in the House of Commons. Other influential figures, both national and international, also added their voice of protest by writing to newspapers and to Asquith. Success was attained on 10 June, when all three prisoners were placed in the First Division. The two Emmelines were given adjoining cells which they furnished with comfortable chairs, tables, their own bedding and towels; they wore their own clothes, ordered in food and were allowed books, newspapers and writing materials.[70] Emmeline Pankhurst was elated, 'We had gained our point that suffrage prisoners were politicals.'[71] Her joy was short-lived since she soon found out that transfer to the First Division was for the leaders only, not for the rank-and-file members. It was decided that if the government refused to grant First Division status also to the other 78 suffragettes imprisoned in Holloway, Winson Green and Aylesbury, then all WSPU prisoners, including the leaders, would go on hunger strike.

On 19 June, the hunger strike started. Three days later, forcible feeding began. Again, Adela, now a student at Studley Agricultural College, travelled to see her mother who had just begun her hunger strike and was refused permission, as was Herbert Goulden.[72] Emmeline, now nearly fifty-four years old, was experiencing hormonal changes of mood and hot flushes since she had been going through the menopause for some time, and had been treated by Dr. Agnes Savill.[73] But her own discomfort was nothing compared to the horror of forcible feeding that she heard all around her. 'Sickening scenes of violence took place almost every hour of the day, as the doctors went from cell to cell performing their hideous office. ... I shall never while I live forget the suffering I experienced during the days when those cries were ringing in my ears.'[74] Emmeline, already physically weakened by fasting for three days, was with Mrs. Pethick Lawrence in her cell on Saturday, 22 June, when doctors and nine wardresses came to feed the latter by force, and joined with her in the attempt to resist. After the two women were separated and Emmeline was back in her own cell, she heard the brutal operation being carried out. 'I sprang out of bed and, shaking with weakness and with anger,' she recollected, 'I set my back against the wall and waited for what might come.' In a few moments, her door was flung open and the doctors and wardresses stood there. 'Mrs. Pankhurst', began the doctor. Instantly Emmeline grabbed a heavy earthenware jug from a table nearby, and with hands that had suddenly regained their strength, held it head high. 'If any of you dares so much as to take one step inside this cell I shall defend myself.' Nobody moved or spoke for a few seconds. Then the doctor muttered something about tomorrow doing as well, and the intruders retreated.[75] Assuming an air of authority, Emmeline demanded to be admitted to Mrs. Pethick Lawrence's cell where she found her companion in a state of collapse. The prison authorities would never attempt to forcibly feed again the leader of the WSPU, but Emmeline did not know this at the time. The following day she was racked with anxiety so that night she woke up, feeling she was suffocating; she began to turn cold and could not see. The hastily summoned doctor tried to persuade her to take some Brand's Essence, but she refused; it was only when he informed her that she was released that she agreed to take some food.[76] The day after her release, George Lansbury, in an historic scene in the Commons, walked up the floor of the House and when he reached the ministerial bench, pointed a finger at Asquith, shouting angrily, 'You will go down to history as the man who tortured innocent women.'[77]

14

BREAK WITH THE PETHICK LAWRENCES (JULY–OCTOBER 1912)

As soon as she had recovered from her imprisonment, Emmeline, using the name 'Mrs. Richards', now took the first of many visits to Christabel in Paris where she would confer about militant policy, take rest and seek cures for her poor health. In early July 1912, mother and daughter travelled to Boulogne, staying at the Hotel de Paris from where Emmeline wrote to Alice Morgan Wright, 'I don't yet know how long I shall remain with Amy [Christabel] but probably for a week or two. As soon as I can face a railway journey in the heat, I shall no doubt come to Paris for a day or two & will let you know beforehand.' Five days later, Emmeline wrote to Alice again, assuring her, 'I am flourishing & eating just like other people although I still get tired very easily & going up stairs is trying to my breathing apparatus.' She also added, 'Mr. & Mrs. L [Lawrence] arrived here yesterday & are staying until Sunday. ... They also are much better although still rather weak & shaky.'[1]

On 13 July, while all the WSPU leaders were in Boulogne, Helen Craggs, Harry Pankhurst's first love, was arrested in Britain having being found at 1 a.m. in the garden of Nuneham House, the country home of Lewis Harcourt, one of the government's leading 'Antis'. Inside bags she had been carrying were found bottles containing nearly three pounds of inflammable oil, four tapers, two boxes of matches, twelve fire-lighters wrapped in tow, nine picklocks, an electric torch, a glass-cutter, thirteen keys, and a note. The note, addressed to 'Sir', stated that she had taken part in every peaceful method of propaganda and petition, and had now been driven to realise 'that it has all been of no avail, so now I have accepted the challenge given by Mr. Hobhouse at Bristol, and I have done something drastic'.[2] This was the first serious arson attempt by a WSPU member, and neither Emmeline nor Christabel knew about it. Later, when Helen was subsequently sentenced to nine months' hard labour (she was released after hunger striking for eleven days), Emmeline announced that Helen had acted 'solely on her own responsibility. I will ... never repudiate or disown any woman who is fighting in this cause.'[3]

Prior to the arrival of the Pethick Lawrences on 10 July, Emmeline and Christabel had decided that the WSPU should adopt more vigorous forms of militancy, in order to force the government to concede. Mild militancy and argument had not won the parliamentary vote for women, and so now they must adopt the more violent methods that had won enfranchisement for men in the past. 'The struggle had been too long drawn out', observed Emmeline. 'We had to seek ways to shorten it.'[4] She had written to the Pethick Lawrences, who were soon to embark on a holiday to Switzerland, asking them to break their journey at Boulogne so that they could discuss the future direction of WSPU policy. Neither Emmeline Pankhurst nor Christabel record details of the meeting in their memoirs, although Fred did, some thirty years later. According to Fred, the four walked together on the cliffs above Boulogne where he and Christabel fell into conversation at some distance from the two Emmelines. Always in the habit of telling Christabel what he thought, Fred pointed out that the window-smashing raid had aroused 'a new popular opposition, because it was for the first time an attack on private property', and therefore, before it was repeated or graver acts of violence committed, there was need for an educational campaign to make the public understand the reasons for such extreme action. Fred took it for granted that Christabel would return to London and resume her leadership of the campaign, a move, he believed, which would place the government in the awkward predicament of having to choose between repeating the conspiracy trial in her case, or of declining to do so. Whichever course they adopted, Fred assured Christabel, her position and that of the WSPU would be enhanced. Christabel disagreed strongly with Fred's analysis and argued that any current popular opposition was not different from that which had been revealed when other new forms of militancy had been introduced, and that the right method of overcoming it was to 'repeat and intensify the attack in the early autumn'. She suggested that because her policy was 'revolutionary', it was necessary for her to remain outside the reach of the government, so that whatever happened to the movement, she would be in a position to continue to 'direct it'. When the two Emmelines, who were some paces away, heard the heated discussion, they came and joined in. 'Mrs. Pankhurst, as a born rebel, was even more emphatic than Christabel that the time had come to take sterner measures', remembered Fred. 'She appeared to resent the fact that I had even ventured to question the wisdom of her daughter's policy.' Emmeline Pethick Lawrence, however, was of the same view as her husband. 'We did not pursue the matter further', commented Fred, as he closed his account of the meeting. 'Next morning, after a friendly talk with Christabel, we departed for Switzerland.'[5]

Christabel and Emmeline talked the matter over, after the departure of the Pethick Lawrences, thinking through the implications of the divided views amongst the WSPU leadership – and Fred's role in it all. That same day, Sunday, 14 July, Emmeline's 'birthday' and Bastille Day, Emmeline wrote to Helen Archdale thanking her for telling her about the arrangements for Adela's holiday, which she thought were fine. 'I should have liked to ask her to come to me here for a time', Emmeline lamented, 'but am just on the point of going to take a cure somewhere for I do not get well as quickly as I should like. The expense too is great & just now I am obliged to spend more money than I feel I can well afford.' She expressed the hope that when she returned to England, she would be able to take a short holiday with Adela. Her concern for Adela did not abate, as she continued:

> Is it necessary that Adela should be up at 6 a.m. during the holidays? If she is paying £2.2s. per week for her board alone it seems to me she should only work if she wishes. Dr. Hamilton must see that she is tired & needs rest. The crossness is evidence of that. I think for the 1st week of her holiday she should be in bed late with a book & just laze about the grounds & country side. Surely this can be arranged.
>
> I sent A a summer dress yesterday addressed to you. I hope it will suit her. It may be too big & long but it can easily be altered. A hat she must get herself in Birmingham.

After speculating about Adela's future, when she finished her agricultural course next March, Emmeline went on to thank Helen for her kindness to the young woman while also expressing her impatience with her youngest daughter and, like most parents, offering excuses for her behaviour:

> I cannot tell you how glad I am that you are with her at Studley. She ought to think herself a very fortunate girl. She has a family life & a College life in one without cares or responsibilities. How many women at her age are overburdened with worries of a terrible kind. Why won't she be happy. Later on she will wonder at herself & be sorry that she is not more appreciative of all your goodness to her. Of course at heart she really is. The crossness is only on the surface & I am sure a little rest will put that all right.[6]

Perhaps Emmeline found it somewhat ironic that as Adela was beginning to withdraw from her WSPU work, another daughter, Sylvia, was increasingly being brought into the WSPU fold, or so it appeared. In London, against a background of forcible feeding of WSPU prisoners, Sylvia and Flora Drummond had been busy organising a large demonstration to take place in Hyde Park on this 14 July, to celebrate Emmeline's 'birthday' and Bastille Day.[7] The local London branches of the WSPU were responsible for this demonstration which included twenty-one platforms of upwards of fifteen different societies including the ILP, the WFL, the New Constitutional Society of Women Suffrage, the Women's Tax Resistance League, the Cymric Suffrage Society, the Irish League for Women Suffrage, the Men's League for Women's Suffrage and Men's Federation, the Actresses Franchise League, the Church League for Women Suffrage, and the Women Writers Suffrage Society. Massed bands were the centre of the meeting and at three o'clock, Ethel Smyth in her academic robes, hatless in the blazing sun, conducted 'The march of the women'. Keir Hardie and George Lansbury were amongst the many men speakers.[8] Four days later, while Emmeline was on a week's motoring tour of Normandy with Mabel Tuke, Gladys Evans attempted to set fire to the Theatre Royal, in Dublin, where Asquith had just seen a performance; later that evening, as the Prime Minister was driving to the Gresham Hotel with his wife and John Redmond, the Irish political leader, Mary Leigh placed a small hatchet, on which was inscribed 'Votes for women', into the carriage. Gladys Evans and Mary Leigh were both subsequently sentenced to five years' imprisonment although these sentences eventually lapsed.[9] Yet again, neither Emmeline nor Christabel knew before-hand about the protest that these two militants engaged in although, once they did, they were 'determined to stand by them'.[10]

After Emmeline had moved to a quieter and cheaper hotel in Boulogne, the Hotel Dervaux, which charged £10 a day and which was paid, like all her expenses, out of WSPU funds, she then made a brief trip to London. The rooms in Clement's Inn that the WSPU were using had been reclaimed by the land-lord and Emmeline was instrumental in finding new headquarters, at Lincoln's Inn House, and in negotiating the lease.[11] She then travelled back to France, and on to Evian les Bains, near Geneva, to take her cure. The incessant rain and the rigours of her treatment made the time seem dull, and she was relieved when Mabel Tuke and Ethel Smyth arrived. Emmeline stayed longer than she intended since the doctor discovered 'a bladder trouble of old standing for which the Evian water is very good'. The extra days also enabled her to see her 'oldest friend', Noémie, who still lived near Geneva, and was due to return home soon.[12] When Mary Leigh and Gladys Evans were sentenced in August to five years' imprisonment, Emmeline wrote for her followers a message of encour-agement that appeared in the 16 August issue of *Votes for Women*:

> This latest outrageous act of reprisal, while it covers the Government with shame, will only strengthen the determination of militant Suffragists to fight for women's freedom to the end, at no matter what cost to themselves.
>
> Mrs. Leigh and Miss Evans ... whom we love and honour for their splendid courage, have brought the agitation to a crisis where the Government must face two alternatives, either they must prepare to send large numbers of women to penal servitude, or give women the vote without further delay.
>
> In a few short weeks the holidays will be over, and the W.S.P.U. will be at work again. My enforced absence during the past critical weeks has been hard to bear, but when Parliament re-opens I shall be with you, ready to fight by your side and prepared to share the penalties which this contemptible Government may think fit to impose in the vain hope of crushing our movement. The end is in sight, and very soon the victory will be ours.[13]

Not everyone, however, was impressed by Emmeline's defence of those who engaged in arson. On 22 August, Millicent Garrett Fawcett claimed that however honest and devoted the militants might be, they were 'the chief obstacles in the way of the success of the suffrage movement in the House of Commons and far more formidable opponents of it than Mr. Asquith or Mr. Harcourt'.[14] For Adela, who strongly disapproved of the new militant tactics and, claimed Helen Fraser, was really at heart 'a constitutional suffragist', the time had come to leave the organisation of which her mother was the leader.[15]

Adela had participated in her last by-election campaign earlier that month, in North West Manchester. Sylvia had been the Organiser for the WSPU contingent and Adela, and later Helen Archdale, were among the group of workers. Shortly after the by-election, according to her biographer, Adela retired from the WSPU 'as tired as a woman twice her age', knowing that she could no longer 'follow blindly' the policy of her mother and Christabel; disliking violence, preferring socialism to feminism, 'grasping at a life of her own ... sticking to her convictions, wayward yet undefeated, Adela Pankhurst left the suffragette battlefield'.[16] Emmeline regarded her youngest daughter's departure from the WSPU as not only inevitable but also necessary, for Adela's health and happiness.

During her brief sojourn in London that summer, Emmeline had found herself in control at WSPU headquarters for the first time, no longer the 'outsider' visiting from the provinces. And she liked it. The Pethick Lawrences had not been there since they had extended their holiday by visiting relatives in Canada. Neither Emmeline Pankhurst nor Fred Pethick Lawrence had paid the costs levied at the conspiracy trial in May; while Emmeline had no assets for the government to seize in default of payment, this was not the case for Fred whose country home was occupied by bailiffs while he was still on the American continent. At a meeting in Boulogne, Emmeline talked the matter over with Christabel, Annie Kenney and Mabel Tuke, and came to the conclusion that the Pethick Lawrences had become a liability to the Union. The government could strip them of their fortune thus putting pressure on the WSPU to curb further militancy; further, sympathetic suffragettes would organise collections on the couple's behalf thus diverting necessary funds from the war chest while increasing the revenue of an oppressive government. On 8 September, Emmeline wrote what she termed 'a business letter' to 'Mrs. Lawrence' regarding 'the situation as it seems to us to affect you and Mr. Lawrence, and your position in the Union as treasurer'. Emmeline explained:

> It is quite evident that the authorities and also the Insurance Companies and property owners mean to take full advantage of the fact that they can attack Mr. Lawrence with profit and through Mr. Lawrence weaken the movement. So long as Mr. Lawrence can be connected with militant acts involving damage to property, they will make him pay. Nothing but the cessation of militancy (which of course

is unthinkable before the vote is assured) or his complete ruin will stop this action on their part. They see in Mr. Lawrence a potent weapon against the militant movement and they mean to use it. This weapon is a powerful one. By its use they can not only ruin Mr. Lawrence, but they also intend, if they can to divert our funds. If suffragists, feeling strongly as they do the injustice of one having to suffer for the acts of others, raised a fund to recoup Mr. Lawrence, it would mean that our members money would go finally into the coffers of the enemy and the fighting fund would be depleted or ended. It would also reduce militancy to a farce for the damage we did with one hand would be repaired with the other. ... I know you will understand me when I say that if to ruin Mr. Lawrence would help the Woman's Cause I should think it worthwhile for what is the individual as compared with the Cause? When however far from helping it is a source of weakness, a positive injury, then the case is different! What is to be done?

This is what we suggest after long and anxious thought. It is a way of retaining your active participation in a great Imperial Movement which is just beginning and at the same time of preventing the Government from striking at the militant movement in England through you. The Union has paved the way by my two visits to Canada, by the establishment of the first W.S.P.U. there, by the presence of scattered members and by the deputation to Borden [the Canadian Premier]. Will you for a time lead the Imperial Suffrage Movement in Canada? It is a great mission and a great role. ...

Please show my letter to Mr. Lawrence and discuss it with him and believe that I have left unwritten many expressions of affection and appreciation which we all feel very deeply.[17]

Emmeline Pethick Lawrence, after talking the issues over with her husband, wrote a polite, cool reply to 'Mrs. Pankhurst'. 'Perhaps you are not aware that the present situation does not take my husband or me by surprise.' Completely ignoring the suggestion that they might live in Canada, she went on, 'Our answer is that we shall continue to be jointly responsible with you in the future as we have been in the past, and that the more we are menaced the harder we will fight until victory is won.'[18] The Pethick Lawrences expected to return home in early October.

Emmeline returned to England some weeks before their arrival, telling *The Standard* on 21 September that she felt better than she had done for a long time, and that she was glad to be back. The day before, she was one of a small group at Euston Station bidding farewell to Barbara Wylie who was departing for Canada in order to bring the Canadian members of the WSPU into closer touch with the WSPU centre in London.[19] Soon afterwards, Emmeline and Mabel Tuke set about superintending the removal into the new WSPU headquarters, a somewhat awesome task that Emmeline lightened by spending a number of pleasurable evenings at the theatre, seeing the renowned French actress Sarah Bernhardt and attending a production of *The winter's tale*. When Alice Morgan Wright wrote to her, worried about what might happen in the future if she continued the militant policy, Emmeline replied on 2 October in a jaunty, optimistic manner:

> It will be time enough to worry when something happens & even then it is superfluous for I always come out at the right end of difficulties & dangers. The prospect of being an old lady I don't find at all alluring & therefore don't mean to become one a minute sooner than is inevitable even if I were quite quite sure that you would then be willing to bear with the humours of a cantankerous old person. No my dear we must all live in the present as pleasantly as we can. So there is my sermon.[20]

That very day, when the Pethick Lawrences arrived at Fishguard, they were met by a friend who warned them that they were to be ousted from the WSPU. 'I don't believe it! Impossible! Incredible! You are dreaming!' exclaimed Emmeline Pethick Lawrence.[21] When she and Fred went to Lincoln's Inn House the following morning, they found that no rooms had been set aside for them; Annie Kenney and Mabel Tuke refused to speak to them, conversations stopped abruptly as they approached. 'Next day', recollected Fred, 'Mrs. Pankhurst invited us to her room. She then told us that she had decided to sever our connection with the W.S.P.U.'[22]

Both the Pethick Lawrences were shattered. They felt that Christabel, who had lived with them for six years and whom they treated as a daughter, could not be party to such a decision, but Emmeline was resolute. She invited the stunned couple to meet her a few days later in a house in the west of London. When they arrived, they found to their surprise Christabel there also. Since Christabel's residence in Paris had been made public that September, Emmeline had thought of a ruse to get her daughter to England secretly, under the noses of the police. She visited France, booking a first class ticket for the home-bound boat while Christabel, in disguise, slipped unobtrusively on to the same steamer as a second class passenger. That Christabel had risked detection in order to speak to them brought little comfort to the Pethick Lawrences since she told them that she and her mother 'were absolutely united in this matter'.[23] The Pethick Lawrences realised that appeal was futile and pondered on the 1907 split when they had begged Emmeline Pankhurst to cancel the constitution and cancel the annual conference. 'Mrs. Pankhurst was the acknowledged autocrat of the Union. We had ourselves supported her in acquiring this position several years previously; we could not dispute it now.'[24] They decided, generously, not to drag the issue out into the public arena, for fear of splitting loyalties in the WSPU and damaging the cause to which they were deeply committed.

A final meeting to determine the terms of the separation was held in Boulogne, in a small hotel facing the quay. Control of *Votes for Women*, which was running at an annual loss of about £2,000, would revert back to the Pethick Lawrences. The memo, signed by the foursome, also stated, 'At the request of Mrs Pankhurst, Mrs Pethick Lawrence resigns all connection with the WSPU & Mr Pethick Lawrence resigns control of the Woman's Press.' In order to release the Pethick Lawrences from all liability, the WSPU, which had assets of about £10,000, would find 'another guarantor', in place of the proposed guarantorship of Mr. Pethick Lawrence, for Lincoln's Inn House, '& also set aside & place in the hands of a trustee a sum of £2,000 to meet any of the liabilities for which Mr & Mrs Pethick Lawrence are at present responsible'. Further, the Pethick Lawrences would devote 'such of the various sums promised by themselves to the funds of the WSPU as are not yet paid', to the working expenses of *Votes for Women*, and they would 'retire from participation' in the Albert Hall meeting planned for 17 October. A statement was prepared for later publication in *Votes for Women*:

> At the first re-union of the leaders after the enforced holiday [,] Mrs. Pankhurst and Miss Christabel Pankhurst outlined a new militant policy which Mr & Mrs Pethick Lawrence found themselves altogether unable to approve.
>
> Mrs. Pankhurst and Miss Christabel Pankhurst indicated that they were not prepared to modify their intentions[,] and recommended that Mr and Mrs Pethick Lawrence should resume absolute control of the paper, Votes for Women [,] & should leave the Women's Social & Political Union.
>
> Rather than make schism in the ranks of the Union [,] Mr & Mrs Pethick Lawrence consented to take this course. In these circumstances [,] Mr & Mrs Pethick Lawrence will not be present at the meeting at the Royal Albert Hall on October 17.[25]
>
> Christabel Pankhurst   E. Pankhurst
> F W Pethick Lawrence   E. Pethick Lawrence

Emmeline felt it was necessary to formalise matters and so asked the Pethick Lawrences to attend the 14 October meeting of the WSPU Central Committee, of which she was chair. The atmosphere was strained. Emmeline began by declaring that where confidence no longer existed, working together was impossible. Since Fred was not an official member of the Committee, she pointed out that he could not state his case, but was politely overruled. Fred then stated his defence, and after the ensuing discussion, Emmeline curtly asked the Pethick Lawrences to leave the WSPU. Elizabeth Robins and Mary Neal in particular protested against such a judgment but Emmeline, with that queenly air of authority that had disarmed many a police officer, calmly put them in their place by pointing out that they had rarely attended meetings and had 'deliberately neglected to inform ourselves'.[26] The Pethick Lawrences then walked out. The following day, Elizabeth Robins wrote to Emmeline, tendering her resignation from the Central Committee.

Although it had been agreed with the Pethick Lawrences that the statement about the leadership split would appear for the first time in print in the 18 October issue of *Votes for Women*, Emmeline sent a brief account of events to all WSPU members in a letter dated 16 October. The tone of her letter was tactful and complimentary to those she had ousted, as she sought the backing of the rank-and-file for her continued leadership. 'History has taught us all', she commented, 'that divided counsel have been the ruin of more good causes than anything else of which we know, and when such a situation arises separation is inevitable.' Although Mr. and Mrs. Pethick Lawrence were no longer working with us as colleagues, 'our hearts are full of gratitude to both ... for all they have done with unsparing generosity and unfailing sacrifice of time, energy and devotion for the Union in the past, and the memory of our association with them will always be cherished as a treasured possession.'[27] She enclosed with the letter a subscription form for the new official journal of the WSPU, *The Suffragette*, to be edited by Christabel from Paris, a move which brought home forcibly to the deeply hurt Pethick Lawrences the extent of the pre-planning. Fred's objection to the news of the split being leaked before the agreed date elicited an icy reply from the leader of the WSPU. 'My instructions were that it [the letter] was to be so posted as *not* to reach the addresses earlier than Votes for Women was published. If a few copies were posted earlier than was intended it must have been by accident. It was certainly without my knowledge.'[28]

Thus ended for the Pethick Lawrences their personal association with Emmeline and Christabel. 'There was something quite ruthless about Mrs. Pankhurst and Christabel where human relationship was concerned', mused Emmeline Pethick Lawrence some twenty-five years later. 'The cleavage was final and complete. From that time forward I never saw or heard from Mrs. Pankhurst again, and Christabel, who had shared our family life, became a complete stranger. The Pankhursts did nothing by halves!'[29] She firmly believed that their dismissal from the WSPU was the work of the impetuous and fiery Emmeline Pankhurst who, she told Nevinson, was known as an 'enfant terrible'.[30] She contended that 'Mrs. Pankhurst' had accepted with 'extreme reluctance' the temporary truce of militancy, and had 'little use' for the exercise of patience. 'Excitement, drama and danger were the conditions in which her temperament found full scope. She had the qualities of a leader on the battlefield.' While Christabel lived with us, she continued, she agreed that we had to advance in militancy by slow degrees, but since she had escaped to Paris, Christabel had gone completely over to her mother's standpoint. Mrs. Pankhurst, the former Honorary Treasurer of the Union pointed out, 'had always regarded Christabel, and to a lesser extent herself, as the main, if not the sole, inspiration of the movement. She had been distressed by the way in which Christabel consulted us about everything and was influenced by our opinion.'[31]

Sylvia Pankhurst too, in her biography of her mother, is of the view that it was Emmeline Pankhurst who took the lead in the expulsion of the Pethick Lawrences. Yet the matter is not clear cut as Sylvia herself must have recognised since four years earlier, in *The suffragette movement*, she claimed that the decision was Christabel's![32]

Neither Christabel nor Emmeline, in their memoirs, cast any light on the matter but deal with the 1912 split in a brief and matter-of-fact way. Annie Kenney, however, had no hesitation in saying that the expulsion of the Pethick Lawrences was Christabel's idea. The faithful Annie was Christabel's closest friend, her loyalty earning her the nickname in WSPU circles of 'Christabel's Blotting Paper'. Annie travelled regularly in disguise to Paris in order to consult about the direction of WSPU policy and recollected that Christabel would not tolerate interference with policy-making, even from the Pethick Lawrences. 'Once people questioned policy her whole feeling changed towards them.'[33] There was also the problem that, before the split, Fred, usually called 'godfather' by the suffragettes, was beginning to push himself to the fore, despite the fact that the WSPU was an organisation which only women could join. 'I think it was a pity that Mr. Lawrence began to insist that he should have more recognition, and that he should be on the platforms with the leaders', noted Jessie Kenney. 'It seemed as though the temperature of the platform and the meeting went down when he spoke at length. Too many facts and figures, too dull, and nothing like the sparkle that Christabel and Mrs. P.L., my sister Annie and Mrs. P would bring to the meeting.'[34] Jessie remembered that on one occasion when bouquets and tributes were being handed to Christabel, Emmeline Pankhurst commented, 'How godfather would like to have these.' Instantly, Jessie thought 'something was up. The split in this sense began months before it happened.'[35]

But there were also other reasons why Emmeline wanted the Pethick Lawrences out of the WSPU. She was 'always jealous' of their closeness to Christabel and had 'never got on' with Fred who had been 'almost infatuated' with her daughter; this latter fact, may, of course, have partly accounted for the atmosphere and antipathy that was always present between herself and Fred.[36] The expulsion of the Pethick Lawrences enabled Emmeline to spiritually regain her beloved daughter. But, just as important, the expulsion also gave Emmeline more power. Emmeline, very much 'the great lady', had shown no gratitude but 'irritation' at the way the administrative machinery of the WSPU had been organised by the Pethick Lawrences and Jessie Kenney.[37] With the Pethick Lawrences out of the way, she could reduce her tiring, itinerant life as the leader of the by-election campaigns in the provinces and be a much more visible and dominant presence in central London. She had founded the WSPU and now, with Christabel, she could bring the organisation back under Pankhurst control.

15

HONORARY TREASURER OF THE WSPU AND AGITATOR (OCTOBER 1912–APRIL 1913)

On 17 October 1912, Emmeline Pankhurst stood alone on the platform at the Albert Hall. There was a tense feeling amongst her audience since the statement about the split had appeared that morning in both *Votes for Women* and *The Suffragette*, circulated one day earlier than their scheduled publication date. The rank-and-file membership had had no say in the expulsion of the Pethick Lawrences and now Emmeline had to draw on all her powers of persuasion to present the *fait accompli* as a favourable move, that was only a small part of a much broader and more important initiative. After emphasising the need for unity of purpose and of policy, Emmeline made a brief reference to the statement and began to outline the new militant policy which would include relentless opposition not only to the party in power, the Liberals, but also the Irish and Labour Parties which supported the anti-suffrage government. With great mastery and emotion, she carried her audience with her as she explained how militant women were the victims rather than perpetrators of violence, including sexual violence ('outrages'), and how they were a fighting force for the progress of all women in a society which upheld a double moral standard:

> Now, why are we militant? ... I tell you, women, in this hall that you who allow yourselves to be tricked by the excuses of politicians, have not yet awakened to a realisation of the situation. The day after the outrages in Wales, I met some of the women who had exposed themselves to the indecent assaults of that mob. ('Shame!') ... one woman ... said she did not feel she could even tell her husband or her son the nature of the assault, and then I said to her – 'How could you bear it?' ... And she said, 'All the time I thought of the women who day by day, and year by year, are suffering through the White Slave Traffic' – ('Shame'). ... In our speeches on Woman Suffrage, we have not dwelt very much on that horrible aspect of women's lives, because some of us felt that to think of those things, to speak very much about them, was apt to cause a state of feeling which would make it impossible for us to carry on our work with cheerful hearts ... until women have the Vote,

the White Slave Traffic will continue all over the world. Until by law we can establish an equal moral code for men and women, women will be fair game for the vicious section of the population inside Parliament as well as outside it.

With pathos in her voice, Emmeline went on to talk about other matters with which voteless women, who had no power, had to contend, namely the sexual exploitation of little girls who could be made pregnant, infected with VD, and used as child prostitutes:

> Even if we tolerated the degradation of the grown women, can we tolerate the degradation of helpless little children? When I began this militant campaign – ('Bravo!') – in the early days of the movement, I was a Poor Law Guardian, and it was my duty to go through the workhouse infirmary, and never shall I forget seeing a little girl of thirteen lying in bed playing with a doll, and when I asked what was her illness I was told she was on the eve of becoming a mother, and she was infected with a loathsome disease, and on the point of bringing, no doubt, a diseased child into the world. Wasn't that enough? (Cries of 'Yes'). A little later, in a by-election campaign against the Government candidate in Leeds I had occasion to visit a Salvation Army hotel in that city, and in the matron's room there was a little child, eleven years of age. She didn't look older than eight, and I said: 'How was it she was there? Why wasn't she playing with other children?' And they said to me: 'We dare not let her play with other children; she has been on the streets for more than a year.' These, women in this meeting, are facts. These are not sensational stories taken from books.

Emmeline argued that the only way to put an end to such horrible evil was to join the women suffragists in their great moral mission of freeing half of the human race by empowering women with the parliamentary vote. 'Go and buy your hammer.' Thus she led to the main point of her talk, encouraging women to engage in a range of militant acts and, in particular, her official endorsement of secret attacks on public and private property:

> Be militant in your own way. Those of you who can express your militancy by going to the House of Commons and refusing to leave without satisfaction, as we did in the early days – do so. Those of you who can express their militancy by facing party mobs at Cabinet Ministers' meetings, and remind them of their unfaithfulness to principle – do so. Those of you who can express your militancy by joining us in the anti-Government by-election policy – do so. Those of you who can break windows – (great applause) – those of you who can still further attack the sacred idol of property so as to make the Government realise that

property is as greatly endangered by women as it was by the Chartists of old days – do so.

And my last word is to the Government. I incite this meeting to rebellion. (Tremendous applause and great enthusiasm). You have not dared to take the leaders of Ulster for their incitement. Take me if you dare! ('Bravo!') But if you dare, I tell you this – that so long as those who incite to armed rebellion and the destruction of human life in Ulster are at liberty you will not keep me in prison. (Great applause).[1]

Emmeline's defiant note, that she would fight alone, if need be, that the cowardly government was employing a double standard in the lenient way it treated the Ulster male leaders in comparison with the harsh punishment inflicted upon herself, that she could not be kept in prison, evoked admiration from her appreciative audience. Even the sisters of the deposed Emmeline Pethick Lawrence, who knew the inside story of the split, fell under her sway.[2] George Lansbury and Mabel Tuke were then called upon to speak, followed by Annie Kenney who announced that at the next election, if a Labour man – with the exception of Mr. Lansbury – stood for parliament at a by-election, the WSPU would oppose him as well as government candidates.[3] Annie was echoing here the words of Christabel who, in that week's *The Suffragette*, outlined in detail the anti-Labour Party policy.[4] It was left to Emmeline to explain to a bewildered *Daily Herald* reporter that this policy did not mean that the WSPU was against socialism:

> We are not going to oppose Socialism. We are not out against Labour and Socialist ideals. It is the party we are going to fight. ... As a party, the Labour men are forming a section of the Coalition Government. It is that Government whom we look upon as the enemy, and we cannot treat one part of that army differently from any other part. ... With the rank and file of the party we have no quarrel. They, we believe, are with us. Our resolution, passed over and over again in the East End campaign and elsewhere, shows that plainly enough. I am receiving letters frequently from working men and women up and down the country in support of the movement, and I am convinced there is a real and profound discontent amongst such Labour people at the inaction of their representative. ... [Labour men] must get the party to pledge itself to make votes for women the foremost thing in their Parliamentary programme.[5]

Despite the enthusiasm at the Albert Hall meeting, most WSPU members were shocked by the news of the split; just £3,600 was taken in the collection and promises of further donations, an indication, perhaps, of divided loyalties amongst the rank-and-file.[6] It would appear that while a number of WSPU members accepted the reasons for the split, agreeing with their leader that it was the cause rather than the individual that was important, the WSPU lost many of its most influential supporters. As Annie Kenney sadly reflected in her memoirs, 'The old days were over ... the fight continued, but the Movement, as a Movement, lost. The two had gone who had been the creative geniuses of the constructive side of a word-famed fight.' Elizabeth Robins was of the opinion that what the Pankhurst leaders failed to recognise, despite their shrewdness, was that the Pethick Lawrences brought 'steadiness' to their 'force and fire'.[7] From now on the WSPU was increasingly driven underground as some militants secretly engaged in terrorist acts of violence, initially targeted at letter-boxes and fire alarms. By early December, the government was claiming that 5,000 letters had been damaged – by red ochre, jam, tar, permanganate of potash, or varnish and various inflammable substances, especially phosphorous – while some 425 false fire-alarm calls had been made; some twenty-seven convictions were secured in regard to the latter but only one for the much larger number of attacks on post boxes.[8] Under such conditions, suffragettes had to decide whether they supported the 'Panks' or the 'Peths', as *Punch* put it. Jessie Kenney recalled that loyalties became 'even fiercer' while Rachel Barrett enthusiastically commented 'the Lawrences are just the Lawrences & this is the movement'.[9]

Emmeline now became Honorary Treasurer of the WSPU, with responsibility for raising finances, an enormous responsibility for her already burdened shoulders. That she chose to take on this role, which had proved taxing to Emmeline Pethick Lawrence, was a grave error of judgment. As leader of the WSPU, she would have been wiser to have chosen a trusted Union member for the post; that she chose, instead to be *both* leader and Honorary Treasurer meant that she concentrated too much power in her own hands, opening herself to accusations about how the money was spent, a grumble that was to rumble on for many years to come. Further, such a concentration of power meant that, at the personal level, Emmeline exposed herself further to accusations of autocracy while at the organisational level, she put the future of the WSPU at risk if she became ill or, as seemed increasingly probable, was arrested and imprisoned. While the financial accounts continued to be kept carefully and audited regularly, she introduced the additional safeguard – since police raids were now a constant fear – of keeping the books in duplicate in different, secret locations.[10] Still restless, but unshaken in her belief that the new form of militancy was the right one to win the parliamentary vote for her own sex, she spoke at the usual London meetings and undertook some meetings in the provinces, often receiving a less than warm welcome. Emily Blathwayt now refused to put up overnight the WSPU leader when she came to speak at Bath that autumn since she was 'going about inciting to violence'; but Emily, nevertheless, showed support in a different way, by paying Emmeline's hotel and taxi bills.[11] But it was Emmeline's work in the East End of London, rather than the provinces, that attracted newspaper headlines at this time.

That October and November, she campaigned in the East End, speaking in solidly working-class areas such as Limehouse, Bow and Bethnal Green, as part of Sylvia's initiative to win mass support for the WSPU. Sylvia had decided to settle in the area since it had a long history of working-class and feminist activism upon which she wanted to build. Despite her disagreement with her mother as to WSPU tactics, she shared Emmeline's deep concern for the lot of working-class women, and wanted to fortify their position when the vote was won as well as rouse them 'to be fighters on their own account'.[12] Emmeline agreed to Sylvia's request for WSPU headquarters to be responsible for the shop she rented in Bow while the Kensington, Chelsea and Paddington branches agreed to act in a similar capacity for the shops opened in Bethnal Green, Limehouse and Poplar. Together with Zelie Emerson, a wealthy young American woman whom Sylvia had recently met in Chicago and who had followed her to London, Sylvia organised open-air meetings. This was not always an easy or pleasant task since although many working-class women attended, young rowdy men might throw stones, fishes' heads and paper soaked in a nearby public urinal at the speakers.[13]

The foundation of the East End campaign took place about the same time that George Lansbury, the MP for Bromley and Bow, a fervent supporter of women's suffrage, began to advocate that his fellow Labour MPs should vote against the government until women were given the vote, a view that had the strong support of Emmeline and Christabel. The Labour Party, however, did not wish to vote against the government on such issues as Irish Home Rule and the Trade Union Bill, and so informed the recalcitrant member that since the party had paid part of his election expenses and he had won his seat under their sponsorship, he must either leave or toe their line. Emmeline urged Lansbury not to leave but to get resolutions of support for his position passed at meetings in his constituency, a suggestion that Lansbury found unacceptable.[14] He resigned from the Labour Party and decided to stand for re-election as an independent socialist, campaigning specifically for women's suffrage. In early November, he travelled to Boulogne to confer with Emmeline and Christabel who gave him their full support. It was the first time that a parliamentary seat was fought primarily on a women's suffrage platform, and the first time that the WSPU sponsored a candidate.[15]

Emmeline, praising Lansbury for his 'self-sacrificing fidelity to principle', immediately called for subscriptions to the election fund.[16] But further tensions arose within her family when a trusted Union member, Grace Roe, rather than Sylvia, was appointed as the organiser of the WSPU's Lansbury campaign. Although the ideological differences between Emmeline and Christabel, on the one hand, and Sylvia, on the other, may have played a part, perhaps major, in the displacement of Sylvia, it is not the whole story.[17] Both Emmeline and Christabel may have thought that any leak of Sylvia's affair with Keir Hardie during the campaign would only bring embarrassment and defeat. Furthermore, it is highly likely that Emmeline, known for her plain speaking, had already told her 'wayward' daughter that she would no longer tolerate the liaison if she was developing a higher profile in the WSPU. This may help to explain why Sylvia's affair with Hardie began to fade after she began her work in the East

End, a possible factor that neither Romero nor Winslow mention.[18] Whatever the 'facts' at the time, a disappointed Sylvia, writing many years later in *The suffragette movement*, spoke disparagingly of how 'Mrs. Pankhurst ... took no part in the organization of the [Lansbury] campaign. She devoted herself purely to speaking at the meetings arranged for her.'[19]

The contemporary records reveal that Emmeline spoke tirelessly on Lansbury's behalf. Although other groupings such as the NUWSS, the WFL and the Men's League for Women's Suffrage also had offices and speakers in the district, it was Emmeline, regarded as 'one of England's finest orators', who grabbed the headlines.[20] The Union leader, who wanted the vote as a tool for social reform, shone particularly when she spoke at one crowded meeting, in a hall packed with very poor women who had brought their little children and fretful babies with them. For Beatrice Harraden, it was an occasion she would never forget. 'It is my belief that one has to see and hear Mrs. Pankhurst with the very poorest class of women in order to have seen and heard her at her very best', she wrote. 'The passionate and yet tender concern for her own sex would seem to be at its finest expression, and her cry for justice at its truest vibration when she stands amongst these women, whose sufferings and disadvantages she knows.'[21] But it was not just compassion that fired Emmeline's oratory. She was a seasoned campaigner, skilled in the handling of an audience. When she was asked, 'Why does Lansbury stand up for the women instead of for the poor?', Emmeline replied with a counter-question, 'Who are the people who are working for a penny and for a halfpenny an hour?' Immediately women in the audience cried out, 'Me! Me!'[22]

But rhetoric could not win the day in an election campaign where the WSPU and the Poplar Labour Representation Committee, which had supported Lansbury, were unable to co-operate and a plethora of voices on his behalf produced 'ideological babel'.[23] On election day, 26 November, Lansbury lost his seat by 751 votes to the Unionist candidate; he had previously held a majority of 863. Emmeline put a brave face on her disappointment. She told the *Daily Herald* that although they would have been pleased to see Mr. Lansbury elected, the fact that over 3,000 men voted directly for women's suffrage was 'very gratifying, and it was perfectly certain that Mr. Lansbury would have been returned by a large majority if it had not been for the action of the Liberal Party, and the unsympathetic spirit of the organised Labour Party'.[24]

The election defeat illustrated again to Emmeline the deep prejudices against women's suffrage within men's political parties and also the futility of using legal and constitutional means to win the vote. From now on, distrust of the Labour Party became more pronounced within the WSPU leadership, a situation that had already caused some socialist militants, such as Mona Taylor in the Newcastle WSPU, to resign her membership.[25] Sylvia Pankhurst too found herself in an uneasy situation since she was now told by WSPU headquarters to close down the East End work. However, she persuaded her mother to change her mind, pointing out that she could organise a deputation of East End working women, preferably to seek an audience with Lloyd George.[26]

At a meeting at the London Opera House on 2 December, held in honour of Lansbury, Emmeline warned that the anti-government policy would be continued at by-elections 'with renewed vigour' while other forms of militancy would develop 'as necessity arises ... the women's civil war is going on and what fresh developments are to come depends upon those who can give us the vote and won't'.[27] By such argument, she placed the responsibility for militancy not on the militants but on an all-male oppressive government that refused to give women justice. One of her audience, Nevinson, commented that although Emmeline spoke well, 'faith in her is much shaken'.[28] Plain-clothes policemen, who were also present, made notes of all that was said in order to send transcriptions to the Home Office. From now on Emmeline was regarded as a dangerous subversive whose movements had to be monitored. Three days later, amidst public condemnation of the letter burning, the woman who had threatened civil war engaged in the feminine task of opening the Christmas Presents Sale at Lincoln's Inn House.[29] Emmeline Pankhurst, leader of the militant suffragettes, was a woman of contrasts.

The concern with sexual morality and especially the double moral standard, which Emmeline had specifically raised in her Albert Hall speech, now became a much more focused issue in statements from the WSPU leadership, primarily as a tactic to arouse women to commit militant deeds on behalf of their sex and defenceless little girls, action intended to bring women's enfranchisement and social reform. Christabel, in one of her important policy statements in an early December issue of *The Suffragette* stated, 'What is the object of the letter-burners? It is to abolish White Slavery. It is to put an end to hideous assaults on little girls. It is to stop the sweating of working women.' On 9 December, when speaking at the London Pavilion, Emmeline referred to the murder of the Woking girl scout, Winnie Baker, and, to loud cheers, emphasised that these attacks upon young children were 'sufficient justification for civil war on the part of the women, in order that they might secure their political rights and obtain stronger legislation'.[30] There was nothing original about such concerns, as historians such as Jeffreys, Jackson and Bland have so ably revealed; from the 1880s onwards, the feminist demand for a single moral standard for men and women alike became central to the women's movement.[31] The day after her stirring Pavilion speech, Emmeline undertook the more mundane task of writing to Alice Morgan Wright, apologising for the delay in sending a receipt for her subscription to *The Suffragette*:

> I am sorry you have had to wait so long but if you only knew how many claims there are upon me just now you would not wonder that I make my friends wait.
>
> I am looking forward with great joy to the holidays so that I can have long lazy days in bed. When I have slept & lazed my full I shall come to Paris for a week & so hope to see you if you are there.

I am as you see still at large for in spite of provocation the enemy will not have me.[32]

As the festive season approached, Emmeline retired to Ethel Smyth's cottage at Hook Heath from where she wrote to Henry Harben, a wealthy barrister who had dramatically resigned as the Liberal Party candidate in the midst of a by-election because of his party's attitude to women's suffrage. Emmeline, with the responsibility of raising funds for the WSPU, expressed the hope that Harben could enlist the support of 'more monied men' since the WSPU by-election campaigns were costly. 'I hear privately', she confessed, 'that there is still a deficit on the Bow & Bromley election.' She ended her letter by inviting Harben and his wife to join her in Paris during the early days of the New Year. 'It would be so useful to talk over future action with my daughter whose ideas are always helpful. I should so much like to see more of Mrs. Harben for one feels attached to the wife of a man who is doing so much as you are.'[33]

On 16 December, Asquith had told the House of Commons that the Manhood Suffrage Bill would have its second reading after Christmas.[34] Millicent Fawcett now swung the weight of the NUWSS behind the proposed women's suffrage amendments to the long-delayed bill, and put strong pressure on the WSPU to suspend militancy in order not to wreck such progress. Emmeline and Christabel refused to budge, believing that the amendments had no hope of being carried. Early in January 1913, Emmeline sent a letter to every WSPU member, explaining the Union position, and emphasising the importance of further militancy, as a moral duty, after the amendments were defeated:

There are degrees of militancy. Some women are able to go further than others in militant action and each woman is the judge of her own duty so far as that is concerned. To be militant in some way or other is, however, a moral obligation. It is a duty which every woman will owe to her own conscience and self-respect, to other women who are less fortunate than she is herself, and to all those who are to come after her.

If any woman refrains from militant protest against the injury done by the Government and the House of Commons to women and to the race, she will share the responsibility for the crime. Submission under such circumstances will be itself a crime.

I know that the defeat of the Amendments will prove to thousands of women that to rely only on peaceful, patient methods, is to court failure, and that militancy is inevitable.

We must ... prepare to meet the crisis before it arises. Will you therefore tell me (by letter, if it is not possible to do so by word of mouth), that you are ready to take your share in manifesting in a practical manner your indignation at the betrayal of our cause.[35]

Despite being marked 'Private and Confidential' a copy of the letter was forwarded anonymously to Scotland Yard in an envelope bearing a Manchester postmark.

On 13 January, when Emmeline addressed a WSPU meeting, plain-clothes detectives were present. Emmeline protested, amongst other matters, against the sentences of nine months' imprisonment recently passed on Louisa Gay and the crippled May Billinghurst, who had been forcibly fed that morning. Then, tactfully, she told her audience there would be no more militancy until the 'foredoomed' amendments had been debated. 'We are not going to give them an excuse to put the blame on our shoulders, and we have got to accept the responsibility.'[36] It was Evelyn Sharp, who had resigned from the Union over the Pethick Lawrences split and was now an editor of *Votes for Women*, who had persuaded Emmeline to suspend the onset of militancy. Emmeline, however, held little hope that the amendments would be passed, nor did she expect the deputation of working women, drawn from all parts of London and the provinces, to result in success; although the Chancellor of the Exchequer, Lloyd George, and the Secretary of State for Foreign Affairs, Sir Edward Grey, met twenty of the demonstrators, who included teachers, laundresses, nurses, pit-brow women, mill hands and fisherwomen, the replies made by the two ministers were considered 'shifty and vague'.[37]

Emmeline's fears of treachery on the part of the government were justified. The Speaker of the House of Commons ruled that the women's suffrage amendments were out of order since they would so change the nature of the Manhood Suffrage Bill that a new bill would need to be introduced. On 27 January Asquith announced in the Commons that he regretted that the bill would be dropped that session. 'Either the Government are so ignorant of parliamentary procedure that they are unfit to occupy any position of responsibility, or else they are scoundrels of the worst kind', thundered an angry Emmeline. Despite Asquith's denials of complicity and deception, the WSPU alleged that the government had used this particular mode of 'torpedoing' the amendments as an 'expedient held in use in the event of a Woman Suffrage amendment being carried'. The only way the Prime Minister could fulfil his pledge to women was by 'introducing a Government measure giving Votes to Women. He refuses to do this. Let no one after this talk of him as a man of honour!'[38] Addressing large and enthusiastic audiences later that day, Emmeline announced, 'It is guerilla [*sic*] warfare that we declare.' Human life they regarded as sacred, but 'if it was necessary to win the vote they were going to do as much damage to property as they could'. When she was asked, she continued, why the militants attacked the property of people who were not responsible for the unenfranchised state of women, she replied, 'They are all responsible unless they put a stop to the way in which women are being treated.' The WSPU had a 'plan of campaign', the details of which they could not make public.[39] The following evening, in heavy rain, Flora Drummond and Sylvia Pankhurst lead a deputation, demanding equal suffrage, to the Commons; windows of government offices in Whitehall and in large West End shops were broken and both women were amongst the forty-nine arrested. The crowds who had once cheered the suffragettes, were now menacing. 'It is a significant sign of the changed temper of the public in their attitude towards Suffragette militancy that ... many of the women had to be protected by the police from hostile crowds', commented the *Pall Mall Gazette*.[40] Nevinson lamented that the old-style deputations, so spectacular in the past, were no more, 'indeed the organising & inspiring spirit has gone, the implicit confidence & faith, ever since the split'.[41]

For Emmeline, however, the new militant policy of attacks on property was now the only way to make the general public angry, so that it would pressurise the government to grant the women's demand. At a WSPU meeting held on 30 January, therefore, she praised her militant followers and reiterated that she took full responsibility for all acts of militancy.[42] Yet she was also very conscious of the hostility that the women's war was arousing and conscious of the need to court the goodwill of sympathisers who would help released prisoners recover from their ordeal. 'Will you let me know how many you can put up so that my secretary can hand the information on to the prison Committee', she wrote to Agnes Harben when thanking her for her kindness in offering to look after some of the women.[43] When Emmeline met Nevinson at Charing Cross on 31 January, she was impatient with him when he advised restraint. 'She also said rather fiercely that it was impossible for Christabel to return: she had the finest political insight & the time for great speeches was gone. Also that no reconciliation or alliance with the Lawrences would ever be possible.'[44]

What Nevinson did not know was that earlier that day, the WSPU had engaged in a new form of militancy in the Birmingham areas when 'Votes for women' had been cut into golf courses and acid poured into the ground. Over the next three weeks, other forms of damage to public and private property, especially arson, took place as an orchid house at Kew Gardens was burned, the refreshment house at Regent's Park was destroyed, pillar boxes set on fire, and a railway carriage set ablaze; in addition, telegraph and telephone wires were cut, a jewel case at the Tower of London smashed, and windows at London clubs broken. Few of the militants committing such secret and sporadic attacks were caught by the police.[45]

At the end of the first week of February, Emmeline quietly returned from a short trip to Paris; rested, and knowing that she was being watched by the police, she felt physically stronger for her next speech on 10 February when she admitted that she was 'the head and front' of those who were offending the public by destroying orchid houses, breaking windows, cutting telegraph wires and injuring golf greens, and that in many instances, she had 'incited people to do these acts'.[46] Now staying in a small furnished flat at 159 Knightsbridge rather than the Inns of Court Hotel, Emmeline wrote a warm letter the following day to Elizabeth Robins, in New York, explaining how she had to write now, on her return from Ipswich and before going to bed, since she was 'uncertain' as to what would happen tomorrow. 'I am daily expecting to be arrested for conspiracy, sedition, etc.' She also confided, 'Although we do not see much of each other I am very fond of you & value your friendship greatly & it warms my heart to know you still care for Christabel & me.'[47] The government were indeed biding their time and waiting to arrest the agitator. On 18 February, at a meeting of the Putney Branch of the WSPU, Emmeline provocatively mused, 'I wonder why I am here to-night. ... I have been breaking the law myself, and not only that I have been instigating and inciting and preparing and urging other people to do the same. Well, how is it that I am still at large?'[48] The following day, after Lloyd George's empty and partly completed house in Walton Heath, Surrey, was wrecked by a bomb, Emmeline said at a WSPU meeting held in Cory Hall, Cardiff:

> We have not yet got all the members of the present Government in prison but we have blown up the Chancellor of the Exchequer's house. ... We have tried blowing him up to wake his conscience. ... Ladies and Gentlemen, we are firmly convinced ... that this is the only way to get women's suffrage. We shall never get this question settled until we make it intolerable for most people in this country, until we make the question such a nuisance you will all want to find a way of getting rid of the nuisance. We have tried everything else. ... I say that for all that has been done in the past, I accept responsibility. That I have advised, I have incited, I have conspired.[49]

Emmeline's speech was transcribed by Edward James, a reporter on the staff of the *Western Mail*, owned by Sir George Riddell, proprietor of the *News of the World*, who was building the house for Lloyd George.[50] A copy of the transcript was immediately sent to the Home Office. The government swung into action. On 24 February, shortly after two o'clock in the afternoon, Emmeline was arrested at her Knightsbridge flat for procuring and inciting women to commit offences contrary to the Malicious Injuries to Property Act, 1861. The *Pall Mall Gazette* estimated that the cost to the public of the last week's outrages by the suffragettes was £6,000 while *The Standard* calculated that the total cost of seven years of militancy was £500,000.[51]

There was some booing mingled by cheers as Emmeline arrived at Epsom Police Court the following day; several of her followers talked with her and she was presented with a bouquet of lilies of the valley and violets, which she held during the proceedings. Bail was granted, James Murray, a former Liberal MP for East Aberdeenshire, and Rosina Mary Pott, of Kensington, being accepted as sureties. When Emmeline returned to court the next day, however, bail was not permitted since she refused to give an undertaking not to attend meetings until the Guildford Assizes met in May. On being told that she would be committed to Holloway, as a remand prisoner awaiting trial, Emmeline declared she would adopt the hunger strike. 'If I am alive to be tried at the Summer Assizes, it will be a dying person they will try', she cried. Emmeline was in a state of 'terrible anxiety' over the fate of Sylvia who was being forcibly fed in prison.[52] After the working women's demonstration on 23 January, the WSPU had closed its offices in the East End but Sylvia had stayed on and, with her supporters, formed a radical, militant organisation called the East London Federation of the Suffragettes (ELFS) which was a part of the WSPU.[53] A community organisation with close ties to the labour movement, the ELFS/WSPU was not solely concerned with women's suffrage, although it was a prime focus; it admitted men but was always led by women. Sylvia was the elected Honorary Secretary and the wealthy Norah Smyth, niece of Ethel, its Financial Secretary. Sylvia hoped that the ELFS/WSPU would broaden the social base of the women's movement and bring in larger numbers of supporters, especially from working-class women. On 17 February, she had led an East London demonstration and thrown a stone into an undertaker's window, an act which others quickly emulated. It was for this offence that she was now serving two months' imprisonment in Holloway, in the solitary confinement of a hospital cell.

Unknown to Sylvia, who received not a whisper of news from the inside or outside world, her mother was committed to the same prison. Emmeline had immediately gone on hunger strike. After twenty-four hours, the government agreed to move her case to the Central Criminal Court at the Old Bailey so that it could be heard in the April assizes. Under these circumstances, Emmeline gave the required undertaking not to incite agitation and was released on bail on 27 February. Cancelling her immediate engagements, she travelled to Paris to consult with Christabel on future action if she should be committed to prison after her forthcoming trial. 'Mother is in the best fighting spirit that I have _ever_ seen her in & that is saying something', wrote Christabel to Elizabeth Robins. 'She will have a nice Easter holiday before the trial.'[54]

On her return to England, Emmeline stayed in her Knightsbridge flat for a few days before travelling to Scotland and then back down to Woking. 'I am using Dr. Ethel Smyth's house while she is away in Vienna as a place of rest & quiet', she wrote to Elizabeth Robins. 'I would so much like to see you between now & the 1st of April (the date of my trial). ... Do try to come & see me.' Elizabeth was staying at her home at Henfield, Sussex, having just completed a voyage from the States; since she still felt unwell, Emmeline helped by making most of the arrangements. 'I have been studying maps & consulting local timetables & it seems to me that you would have to change at Guildford to get to Woking', she told the ex-actress and writer. 'I could meet you there with a car & bring you here by road & so save the fatigue of changing. I have jotted down trains from Horsham to Guildford both before & after lunch & if you let me know which you decide to take I will meet you.' The inveterate traveller listed six train times in her letter.[55]

As the WSPU destruction of property continued, and WSPU prisoners, including Sylvia, were being forcibly fed, Emmeline continued to give her weekly address at the London Pavilion. 'One feels that the persons who are mainly guilty of incitement [to violence]', she uttered coolly on the 17 March, 'are the people who are governing this country.'[56] The following day, when a protest meeting against forcible feeding was held under the auspices of the National Political League, the imprisoned Sylvia wrote her mother (addressed as 'Dearest Mother') an anguished letter which Zelie Emerson, a fellow prisoner, smuggled out of Holloway. The narratives spoken and written by those experiencing this excruciating torture emphasised that one struggled and resisted when the tubes were forced into the body, not simply because of the pain, but also because to remain passive would seem like collusion, or as Mary Richardson later put it, 'give one the feeling of sin; the sin of concurrence'.[57] It is this aspect of resistance that Sylvia emphasises in her heart-rending letter to Emmeline, a letter in which she insists that she is following the 'correct' ideological line. But the statement may also be read as the cry of a daughter who felt neglected by her mother:

> I am fighting, fighting, fighting. I have four, five and six wardresses every day as well as the two doctors. I am fed by stomach-tube twice a day. They prise open my mouth with a steel gag, pressing it in where there is a gap in my teeth. I resist all the time. ... The night before last I vomited the last meal and was ill all night, and was sick after both meals yesterday. ... I am afraid they may be saying we don't resist. Yet my shoulders are bruised with struggling ... whilst they hold the tube into my throat.
>
> I used to feel I should go mad at first, and be pretty near to it, as I think they feared, but I have got over that, and my digestion is the thing that is most likely to suffer now.[58]

Emmeline was distraught and angry at the barbaric practices inflicted on her daughter; whatever the differences of view between them, Sylvia was still her child. She persuaded the socialist *Daily Herald* to publish Sylvia's letter and was greatly relieved when her daughter was released soon after, on Good Friday, 21 March; in addition to the refusal to eat food, Sylvia had added the protests of thirst and sleep strikes and thus been released early, on medical grounds, serving only five weeks of her sentence. The following day, a more cheerful Emmeline wrote from *Coign* to 'My dear friend', her usual address for Elizabeth Robins, 'I know you will rejoice with me that Sylvia is released. The news came by telephone late last night & in a few minutes I am leaving by car to see her.'[59] Arriving at the nursing home at Pembridge Gardens, Emmeline was surprised to find Keir Hardie there, his face 'haggard and seamed with sorrow, his hair long and unkempt'.[60] When in prison, Sylvia had written to Hardie but the letter, smuggled out at the same time as the message to her mother, had not been delivered to him; believing she was acting in her daughter's own interest, Emmeline had kept the letter at Lincoln's Inn House. Now mother and lover were united by Sylvia's bedside, in their concern for her. The physical condition of her daughter deeply shocked Emmeline. In addition to her weight loss, the veins of Sylvia's eyes had been ruptured so that they appeared like two great blobs of blood in her thin drawn face. Geraldine Lennox, observing the bedside scene that Easter Saturday morning, recollected that Emmeline's face 'was as the face of one being crucified'.[61] As Sylvia began to recuperate slowly, Emmeline reported to Elizabeth Robins that her daughter's nerves were 'quieter & stronger' but it would be some time before a full recovery was made. 'She has lost about 2 stones in the 5 weeks. Her eyes which were very bloodshot are getting better. How could they do it? She is going in the car to 'Coign' on Thursday. I think I shall go with her until Saturday & spend week end with C in Boulogne.'[62] The letter that Sylvia had written to Hardie was now returned to her from WSPU headquarters, 'on the pretence that the address was indistinct'.[63] The thirty-year-old daughter would never forgive her mother for this interference in her private life.

Emmeline had barely welcomed Sylvia back when another family matter presented itself. Helen Archdale informed Emmeline that Adela was soon to finish her course. 'I did not realise that Adela's time at Studley came to an end so soon', confessed Emmeline, writing from 159 Knightsbridge. 'Are the examinations over?' With the uncertain date of her trial and its outcome hanging over her head, Emmeline tried to be helpful in regard to Adela's uncertain future plans. 'I don't like the idea of her being a source of expense to you if she goes with you to Italy & even then having no future plans', Emmeline confided to Helen. 'Oh what a pity that she did not get that American post. Sylvia poor child is a wreck for the time but is gaining strength.'[64] Immediately she had finished writing to Helen, Emmeline composed a letter to Adela, expressing concern about the cost of her proposed trip to Europe with the Archdales and about Adela's intention to leave college before she had secured employment:

My dearest Adela

I got Mrs. Archdale's letter last night when I returned here. I gather from it that you are going to Italy with her. I fear this means a very great expense for her & I cannot help beyond giving you some money for personal expenses! I don't like the idea of it at all especially as nothing is settled about a future engagement for you. Have you asked Dr. Hamilton to take you on either with or without salary for a time until you get a permanent post. Surely she would do this as you have been a paying pupil so long. It would be more experience & people would be more ready to take you from there. Do talk to her about it. I am really very anxious about your future & fear that if you leave the College before getting a post it will increase the difficulty of getting one. I shall see you in London next week. You can stay here & so save expense of hotel. I have the flat until April 9th ...

Now do talk to Dr. H or get her to find you something temporary.
Love
Mother
Sylvia is very weak but improving[65]

Despite her heavy responsibilities as the leader of the WSPU, Emmeline did not ignore her private duties as a mother, however inadequately Sylvia and Adela thought she performed them. But, as noted earlier, Emmeline was always very possessive of her daughters, even when they were grown women. This, together with their early socialisation that stressed the importance of fighting enthusiastically for worthy causes, was not a situation likely to create family unity. Emmeline passed onto her daughters a high dose of her own rebellious spirit so that, eventually, they would scatter to different parts of the world. For that Easter of 1913, however, she was pleased when Adela gained her diploma and was then offered employment as head gardener at Road Manor near Bath, the home of Mrs. Batten Pooll, a WSPU supporter.[66]

Such family issues intruded on the time that Emmeline had to prepare her defence for her trial at the Old Bailey, which began on 2 April. The night before, she wrote to Elizabeth Robins who was unwell and unable to travel to London to see the trial, 'I am wonderfully well all things being considered.' She added, reflectively, 'Of course tonight I am full of doubts & fears that I shall not be equal to the part tomorrow but I daresay I shall be "all right on the day".'[67] At her trial, where Emmeline pleaded not guilty to the charges of inciting certain persons unknown to place explosives in the house being built for Lloyd George at Walton Heath, she conducted her own defence, aided by her solicitor, Alfred Marshall. Basing her case not on legal grounds but on moral and political considerations, she outlined the wrongs that women suffered and then delivered a magnificent oration:

Over one thousand women have gone to prison in the course of this agitation, have suffered their imprisonment, have come out of prison injured in health, weakened in body, but not in spirit. I come to stand my trial from the bedside of one of my daughters, who has come out of Holloway Prison, sent there for two months' hard labour for participating with four other people in breaking a small pane of glass. ... She submitted herself for more than five weeks to the horrible ordeal of feeding by force, and she has come out of prison having lost nearly two stone in weight. She is so weak that she cannot get out of her bed. And I say to you, gentlemen, that is the kind of punishment that you are inflicting upon me or any other woman who may be brought before you. I ask you if you are prepared to send an incalculable number of women to prison ... if you are prepared to go on doing that kind of thing indefinitely. ... We are women, rightly or wrongly, convinced that this is the only way in which we can win power to alter what for us

are intolerable conditions. ... Only this morning I have had information brought to me which could be supported by sworn affidavits, that
there is in this country, in this very city of London of ours, a regulated
traffic, not only in women of full age, but in little children ... these are
the things that have made us women determined to go on, determined
to face everything, determined to see this thing out to the end, let it
cost us what it may. And if you convict me, gentlemen, if you find me
guilty, I tell you quite honestly and quite frankly, that whether the
sentence is a long sentence, whether the sentence is a short sentence, I
shall not submit to it ... if I am sent to prison. ... I shall join the
women who are already in Holloway on the hunger strike. ... Have you
the right, as human beings, to condemn anther human being to death
– because that is what it amounts to? ... You have not the right in
human justice, not the right by the Constitution of this country, if
rightly interpreted, to judge me, because you are not my peers. You
know, every one of you, that I should not be standing here, that I
should not break one single law if I had the rights that you possess. ... I
break the law from no selfish motive. I have no personal end to serve,
neither have any of the other women who have gone through this
court during the past few weeks, like sheep to the slaughter. Not one of
these women would, if women were free, be law-breakers. They are
women who seriously believe that this hard path that they are treading
is the only path to their enfranchisement. ... There is only one way to
put a stop to this agitation. ... It is not by deporting us, it is not by
locking us up in gaol; it is by doing us justice. And so I appeal to you
gentlemen in this case of mine, to give a verdict, not only on my case,
but upon the whole of this agitation. I ask you to find me not guilty of
malicious incitement to a breach of the law.[68]

Despite her powerful and moving address, the jury found Emmeline guilty,
with a strong recommendation to mercy. When asked if she had anything to say
before judgment was passed, Emmeline commented, 'I have no sense of guilt. I
feel I have done my duty. I look upon myself as a prisoner of war. I am under no
moral obligation to conform to, or in any way accept, the sentence imposed on
me.'[69] Justice Lush replied that although he found sentencing her 'a very painful
duty', and acknowledged that her motives were not selfish, her crime was both
'serious' and 'wicked'. Paying regard to the recommendation of the jury, the
least sentence he could pass was three years' penal servitude. Emmeline calmly
listened, but her supporters uttered loud cries of 'Shame!' and cheered as she
was conducted out of the dock. An angry Justice Lush restored order by clearing
the courtroom of all women who filed out proudly singing the 'Women's
Marseillaise'.[70]

That evening, Annie Kenney said to a meeting of about 250 people, 'Do
they think that because our leader, Mrs. Pankhurst, is in prison, we are going to

sit down like a flock of sheep? … Militancy will be more furious than before.'
She asked those who sympathised with militancy to join the WSPU and 'to do
one deed within the next 48 hours'.[71] The following day, a fresh wave of secret
militancy began; empty country houses and railway carriages were set on fire, a
bomb exploded in Oxted Station blowing out all the walls and windows, the
glass of famous paintings was smashed with hammers.[72] Through all this guerrilla activity, as with previous and future militancy, orders were given that
human life should not be endangered. As Emmeline reiterated to one audience,
'Human life for us is sacred', a command that was still vividly remembered by
one aged suffragette in the 1960s. 'Mrs Pankhurst gave us strict instructions …
there was not a cat or a canary to be killed; no life.'[73] Consequently, arson and
bombing attacks on empty buildings were usually planned to take place at
night. Nor were suffragettes to be fanatical, committing suicide for their cause.
'[W]e say', continued Emmeline, 'if any life is to be sacrificed it shall be ours; we
won't do it ourselves, but we will put the enemy in the position where they will
have to choose between giving us freedom or giving us death.'[74] Such considerations weighed lightly with the public who condemned bitterly the attacks on
property. *The Standard* echoed the thoughts of many when it noted that the
campaign of reprisal was wearing out the public patience. The WSPU, it was
alleged, was nothing more than 'a little band, of notoriety-seeking and
misguided females … drawn almost exclusively from … an upper class of more
or less well-educated and well-to-do women'. The only solution was for the
militant movement, 'a mischievous imposture', to be broken up.[75]

16

PRISONER OF THE CAT AND MOUSE ACT (APRIL–AUGUST 1913)

Emmeline, in her lonely Holloway prison cell early in April 1913, went on hunger strike for nine terrible days, subsisting only on water. A vigil was kept at the prison gates by relays of her loyal followers. A migraine attack added to her anguish of body and mind as she sadly reflected on how distant, though certain, their goal of women's suffrage seemed to be. The eiderdown, quilt and pillow that had been sent in from outside were now taken away, on orders from the Governor who offered instead to send her a Nonconformist minister. Desperate to appear at the 10 April meeting at the Albert Hall (it was to be the last WSPU meeting to be held there), she threatened to take off her clothes or walk about all night in order to ensure release. Mrs. Pankhurst 'appears to be very nervous about herself' noted a Home Office report.[1] Vulnerable, depressed and in a state of collapse, Emmeline believed she would not survive and wrote some messages on two small cards to Ethel Smyth which she asked Miss Harper, a kind wardress of whom she was fond, to post secretly. 'You will smile to hear that during sleepless nights I sang the "March" and "Laggard Dawn" [another of Ethel's suffrage songs] in such a queer cracked voice', she told Ethel. Acknowledging that she had been through a difficult time, Emmeline nevertheless optimistically noted, 'But that is over, and now that the end is perhaps near I want you to know how happy I am, lifted above these dismal surroundings and feeling certain that if I am to die good will come of my going.'[2]

Keir Hardie regularly asked questions in the House of Commons about Emmeline's health and treatment, thus helping to keep the issue in the public eye.[3] On 11 April, the day after the Albert Hall meeting at which the large sum of £15,000 was raised, the Governor came to her cell and read out a Special Licence under the Penal Servitude Acts which would release her for only fifteen days, provided she informed the police of all her movements. The notorious Prisoners Temporary Discharge for Ill-Health Bill, which had been rapidly passed through its various readings, had been specially drafted to deal with such troublesome suffragettes; but it did not receive the Royal Assent until 25 April. Under the 'Cat and Mouse Act', as it became known, suffragettes or 'mice' in a state of poor health could be released into the community to recover sufficiently to be clawed back by the 'cat' to complete their sentence. When the Governor presented Emmeline with her licence that Friday evening, she summoned up what strength she could and tore it into strips. 'I have no intention of obeying this infamous law. You release me knowing perfectly well that I shall never voluntarily return to any of your prisons.'[4]

The Home Office instructed the Governor to telephone Special Branch at Scotland Yard as soon Emmeline had left and, in particular, to give the address of her destination; it was 9 Pembridge Gardens, the nursing home run by Catherine Pine. One stone lighter in weight, suffering from irregularities in her heartbeat, weakness and prostration, Emmeline should have been conveyed there on a stretcher; the prison authorities sent her away sitting up in a cab. Visiting the nursing home, Ethel Smyth found the sight of Emmeline heart-rending; her skin had turned yellow and was tightly drawn over her face, her eyes were deep sunken, and there was a dark flush on her cheeks. Some twenty years later Ethel was still haunted by 'the strange, pervasive, sweetish odour of corruption' hanging about Emmeline's room, as she was nursed back to health, a smell unlike any other and due, she supposed, to the body feeding on its own tissue. 'I often hoped that Mrs. Pankhurst, the most meticulously dainty of beings, had no idea of this sinister effect of hunger-striking and am glad to believe she hadn't, for she would have minded that almost more than anything.'[5] It was while she was in the nursing home that Emmeline heard that Annie Kenney had been arrested and released on bail, and summonses issued against Flora Drummond and George Lansbury.

Unable to walk or digest solid food, Emmeline was given a liquid diet of raw eggs and lemon.[6] Her slow recovery was not helped by the presence of hordes of detectives who constantly watched the building, night and day. Emmeline worried that their presence, and the crowds of curious onlookers who came to stare, were doing harm to the nursing home, the main source of Nurse Pine's livelihood. Dr. Flora Murray, who was attending to her, arranged for her patient to be transferred to the home of WSPU member Hertha Ayrton, at 41 Norfolk Square. On the day of her departure, probably 23 April, Emmeline was strong enough to write to Agnes Harben thanking her for the gift of a 'pretty "sitting up" jacket'. She explained, 'I had sent all my trunks down in to the country & had not one at hand so that it is most useful. I am wearing it today with very great delight.'[7] That evening, Emmeline was conveyed in an ambulance to 41 Norfolk Square where the waiting Hertha Ayrton was shocked by what she saw:

> It was horrible to see her being carried upstairs in a long white bed, looking as if it were no living thing that was lying there. She had a white silk handkerchief over her head, and was lying quite still, and it was all ghastly. ... There are two or more detectives in front, two at the back, one at least on the roof of the nearest empty house; and a taxi waiting to pursue, if Mrs. P. should get up and run away![8]

On 28 April, the day that Emmeline's licence expired, she was visited by Sylvia and her solicitor, Alfred Marshall, who stated to the press that if Emmeline was moved back to Holloway, it would probably kill her.[9] The following day Emmeline's medical attendant received a letter from the Home Office saying that a warrant had been issued for her rearrest and that it would be presented that day, at noon, by a police officer accompanied by a medical inspector who would ascertain whether she was fit enough to be removed to prison. The news spread quickly. Two large tricolours were hung from the upper storey of the house while small groups of loyal women gathered on the doorstep and at other strategic points so as to evade 'Move on' directions from the police. They loudly booed Dr. Smalley, Medical Inspector of Prisons, when he arrived with the police. Once inside the house, Hertha Ayrton, with Herbert Goulden by her side, firmly announced that Emmeline refused an examination while Emmeline herself gave no reply to the doctor's questions. Dr. Smalley ruled that the patient was too ill to be moved and that her licence would be renewed; he also commented that she 'seemed about to burst into tears'.[10]

If Smalley's assessment of Emmeline's emotional state was accurate, it was a vulnerable side of her nature that Emmeline did not wish her followers to see. She knew that as leader and Honorary Treasurer of the WSPU she had to appear strong and forceful. The forging of her identity, as a charismatic, militant, woman leader, a relatively new type of femininity, could admit of no weakness. Yet the burdens that lay upon her shoulders were enormous. The large WSPU meetings, where substantial donations were made and speakers incited members to engage in attacks on property, had been curtailed; on 15 April, E. R. Henry, the Commissioner of Police of the Metropolis, acting on directions from the government, had informed Lincoln's Inn House that they would no longer be permitted to hold meetings in Hyde Park, Wimbledon Common, and other public open spaces in the metropolitan area.[11] Now, at the end of April, another blow was struck. On 30 April, the police raided WSPU headquarters arresting Harriet Kerr, the office manager, Beatrice Sanders, the financial secretary, Rachel Barrett, an assistant editor on The Suffragette, Geraldine Lennox, its sub-editor, Agnes Lake, its business manager, and Flora Drummond. They were charged with conspiring to cause damage to property. The story was covered in every newspaper, many devoting the front page to pictures of the women.[12] In the police court, Mr. Bodkin, on behalf of the Public Prosecutor, said that the action had been taken with a view to 'putting down what has become a danger to a civilised community'.[13] Annie Kenney's flat was also raided as well as Victoria House Press which was printing The Suffragette for the first time that week, the previous printer having decided that the affair was too risky. Annie was later arrested at Dover, as she returned from France, and further detentions included those of Edwy Clayton, a chemist, who had aided the WSPU, and Sidney Drew, the manager of the Victoria House Press.[14] The raids produced a number of artefacts and documents that would be used in the subsequent trials, including a collection of hammers, 'Crime Record

Books' that listed the convictions and release of WSPU members, as well as expenses incurred on various journeys, and a log that detailed Emmeline's own expenses, including travel and taxi fares.[15] Emmeline took some comfort in the knowledge that raids were expected and that the WSPU was run as an army, with understudies ready to undertake the duties of those arrested. Thus Grace Roe took over Annie Kenney's role as Chief Organiser. Further, *The Suffragette* continued to appear weekly, as different presses printed it, and women were soon allowed to enter WSPU headquarters although two policemen stood on duty outside.[16]

Emmeline, whose priority now was to fully recover her health so that she could still be an effective leader, decided to leave London for the fresh air and peace and quiet of the Surrey countryside. On 2 May, accompanied by Nurse Pine, she travelled in an ambulance to *Coign*; Ethel Smyth was not there but on the continent. Although the police were notified of Emmeline's plan, and raised no objection, detectives in a fast car followed her all the way. Immediately she arrived, they guarded the cottage on all sides amid rumours that she might even try to escape to France by aeroplane.[17] Emmeline was not fit enough to attend any of the gatherings held on Sunday, 4 May, the culmination of weeks of angry protest against the government's action in prohibiting public meetings. But WSPU members, with their flags, were amongst the large crowd of 30,000 that gathered in Trafalgar Square, and in the brief meetings, broken up by the police, held in Hyde Park.[18] These gatherings were an indication that there was anger, at least amongst socialist and suffrage groupings as well as some members of the general public, at the government's oppressive treatment of the militants. The following day, Emmeline felt much better, her spirits lifted, and she wrote a chirpy letter to Ethel:

> To-day I had a glass of champagne, and fish. ... All the old Adam (or, Eve, which is better) is coming back, and I begin to realise the glorious fight ahead of me when the 15 days are up. O kind fate that cast me for this glorious role in the history of women![19]

As Emmeline's correspondence with Ethel reveals vividly, her temperament was one of sunshine and showers, of highs and lows.[20] In buoyant mood, she prepared for her followers a suitably upbeat statement. 'We shall pass in triumph through this new crisis. Be calm, be strong, be faithful to one another and to the Union, and all will be well.'[21]

But triumph seemed to be far away since on 6 May a private member's bill to enfranchise women of twenty-five years and upwards, who were householders or the wives of householders, was defeated by 47 votes on its second reading in the Commons.[22] That same day the arson campaign took a different turn as empty churches, such as St. Catherine's, Hatcham, South London, were destroyed by fire. The public condemnation expressed in all the major newspapers, fuelled by subsequent fears about a bomb in St. Paul's Cathedral,[23] was undoubtedly echoed privately by many WSPU members, such as Mary Blathwayt who resigned her WSPU membership. But, as Hannam observes, both Mary and her mother retained friendships with WSPU members and seemed reluctant to criticise former colleagues.[24]

According to Annie Kenney, Emmeline Pankhurst never felt as comfortable with the 'burning days' of the WSPU campaign as she did with the milder forms of militancy.[25] But Emmeline also prided herself in being part of that older tradition of popular protest for liberty and freedom that had included incendiarism when men had campaigned for franchise reform. And, as she regained her strength, resting at *Coign*, she became increasingly irritated with the police surveillance of her movements. 'I never went to the window, I never took the air in the garden without being conscious of watching eyes', she recollected. When Ethel pondered one very rainy day whether she should take out umbrellas to two detectives who had made a sort of cave amongst the prickly gorse bushes, Emmeline's voice from the spare-room bed hastily settled the matter. 'Nothing of the sort', she sharply retorted. 'Don't make things pleasant for them!'[26] Eventually Emmeline planned to end the intolerable, siege-like situation by announcing that she would attend the WSPU meeting at the London Pavilion on 26 May. On that hot, sunny day, Emmeline, dressed in pale grey, limped out of the cottage, supported by Ethel Smyth and Nurse Pine. She attempted to enter the Union car that she had ordered and from which Dr. Flora Murray had alighted. But detectives kept their hands on the doors of the vehicle, asking where she was going. Protesting at such treatment and overcome by weakness and the heat, Emmeline fell back, fainting onto Ethel's knee. The police called a taxi and she was rearrested, to continue her three years' prison sentence under the 'Cat and Mouse' Act. The vehicle that took her to Holloway was followed by four cars of her supporters, vociferously cheering the prisoner. When the prison was reached, the women alighted quickly, attempting, unsuccessfully, to rush the open gates and invade the precinct. Knowing that she would be arrested, Emmeline had already prepared a letter to be read out to the afternoon meeting at the Pavilion. 'No power no earth can break the spirit of our militant women', she wrote, 'and I warn the Government that all their methods of repression will fail ignominiously. … We are soldiers engaged in a holy war, and we mean to go on until victory is won.'[27] The dramatic pictures of her arrest at *Coign* featured on the front page of many newspapers.[28]

Back in Holloway, Emmeline refused any medical examination and went on hunger strike. Suffering from a severe attack of dyspepsia as well as sleeplessness, her physical condition deteriorated so that she was released on 30 May, on a seven-day licence. *The Standard* commented wryly that at this rate, she could be expected to complete her sentence in about eighteen years hence.[29] But Emmeline, under the Cat and Mouse Act, was to serve just six weeks of her three-year sentence. On this occasion, as so many, she was cared for by Nurse Pine, but at a different address, at 51 Westminster Mansions, the flat of WSPU member, Ada Cecile Wright who had six convictions against her and was travelling to New York.[30] When Sylvia visited her mother she found her 'worn and haggard' but less exhausted than she expected; she listened to stories about her father, how Emmeline had dreamt about him in prison and seen 'his kind face' looking down on her.[31] On 2 June, Emmeline wrote to Henry Harben, reassuring him that although she was physically very weak, 'I can again face the ordeal if they decide to take me back to prison. I shall not ask for any extension of the license of course.' What Emmeline did not know was that the Commissioner of Police of the Metropolis had recommended that if she did not return to prison when her licence expired, she should not be rearrested, provided she stayed quietly at home and refrained from attending WSPU meetings, a constraint with which she would never have agreed.[32]

Fate intervened on 8 June when Emily Wilding Davison, the freelance militant, died as a result of injuries sustained when she ran onto the race course on Derby Day and tried to catch hold of the reins of the King's horse, Anmer. The incident was captured on newsreel and seen by thousands who went to the cinema, including Mary Leigh and Ruth Gollancz.[33] It was widely assumed that Emily had committed suicide, sacrificing her life as a 'petition' to the King as a way to end the suffering of her comrades and to ensure the granting of votes for women, although there is no conclusive evidence that this was the case.[34] Her death, occurring at a time when militants were protesting about Emmeline's own treatment under the Cat and Mouse Act, fearing that she would die, stunned the WSPU rank-and-file and its leader. Although Morley and Stanley rightly point out that Christabel wrote of Emily's death in *The Suffragette* as a '"martyr's death" pure and simple', a plausible explanation that was 'far too good an opportunity to be missed', it is important not to minimise how the tragedy must have affected Emmeline Pankhurst.[35] She must have pondered on whether Emily who, after all, had been a friend of the trusted Grace Roe – now given the task of organising the funeral – had been protesting against her Union leader's treatment. In shock and grief, Emmeline forgot about the troubled relationship that Emily had often had with the WSPU leadership and wrote a warm tribute to 'one of our bravest soldiers' who had 'gladly laid down her life for women's freedom ... in our grief we rejoice that she succeeded by her heroic deed in calling attention to the great struggle for the emancipation of women. We who remain can but honour her memory by continuing our work unceasingly.'[36]

Scarcely able to leave her bed, Emmeline was none the less determined to attend the funeral knowing, as she explained to a journalist, that she expected to be returned to prison and the hunger strike.[37] As she stepped into the street from her flat on 14 June, accompanied by Sylvia and Nurse Pine, Emmeline was rearrested. Five thousand women marched in the solemn funeral procession, clad in black carrying purple irises or in white bearing white lilies. The coffin was draped with a purple pall on which were worked in white two large broad arrows. An empty carriage, drawn by two horses, with groups of hunger strikers marching behind and before it, was a poignant reminder that while the disciple might be honoured in death, the leader was subjected to an infamous act of parliament. Vast, largely silent crowds lined the streets. When the coffin was carried into St. George's Church, Bloomsbury, for a short memorial service, militants dressed in white lined the way on either side, giving a military salute. After the service, the coffin was conveyed to King's Cross station where it was placed on the 5.30 train to Morpeth, Northumberland, Emily's birthplace.[38] Emily's funeral, covered in all the major newspapers, was the last of the great suffragette displays of sisterhood and feminism. Churlishly, the disapproving national leadership of the NUWSS refused to take part or even send a wreath but in view of the feminist friendships that cross-cut formal organisations, many rank-and-file NUWSS members must have attended.[39] It is ironic that Ray Strachey, a NUWSS supporter, claimed fifteen years later in her influential book 'The cause': a short history of the women's movement in Great Britain, that Emily Wilding Davison's death 'startled and indeed roused the country. ... All over the world people read of it'; it was a turning point in public opinion so that people felt that it 'was time the struggle ended'. This view was strongly evident at the time. Laurence Housman was not alone in recollecting how Emily's death changed the views of many thousands who had been 'careless or indifferent' to women's suffrage to see it as 'a serious thing'.[40]

Back in Holloway, an angry Emmeline went on hunger strike and was admitted to hospital. The Governor reported that she refused to undress and was, '[v]ery irritable and more illogical than usual in conversation. Refuses medical examination, all food and medicine. Says that, if she had strength, she would assault me and all officers of the Prison and commit damage.'[41] Two days later, Emmeline was released on a seven-day licence to 51 Westminster Mansions. Many voices condemned the barbarity of her treatment. In a leading article on 18 June, the North Mail asked whether Mrs. Pankhurst should be pardoned since if the 'in-and-out process' continued, she would die. 'Mrs. Pankhurst is not a criminal, though she has been indicted for a criminal offence. It may not be the business of the law to analyse her motives, but there is no man living who does not agree that her motives are mainly political.' The influential playwright and suffragist, George Bernard Shaw, in a letter to The Times opined that the moment chosen for the latest arrest of Emmeline Pankhurst was 'a revolting one', a feeling he believed that was shared by a large body of the paper's readers. '[T]here is nothing to be said for pursuing her, now she is out, with a game of cat-and-mouse that will produce on public feeling all the effect of vindictive assassination if she, like Miss Davison, should seal her testimony with her blood.' Rebecca West, in the Clarion, expressed similar sentiments, fearing that the government was 'going to murder Mrs. Pankhurst'.[42] However, for an embittered Dora Marsden, who had resigned from the WSPU in 1911 and was now editor of The New Freewoman, with its trenchant attacks on the style of leadership of the Pankhursts, it was all too much:

Mrs. Pankhurst *has* given of herself in this agitation. She has literally abandoned her judgment and her original ambition, which was to be an active participant in state politics. ... The wild passion of women's insistence [on the vote] spent; the effective mouthpieces and actionists fallen out from her ranks; herself in the process of rapidly advancing invalidism, alternating between prison and nursing home, her mouth effectually closed; her daughter settled as a quiet pamphleteering suffragist aboard; and the vote? In the dim and speculative future! ... She began to 'lead a Cause', and imperceptibly the Cause became Leader – leading where all causes tend – to self-annihilation. Mrs. Pankhurst may die and great is the Cause. What Cause?[43]

While such matters were debated academically in the press, Emmeline played out the scenario with continual wreckage to her body. Although Sylvia later represented her mother in *The suffragette movement* as being driven by Christabel, whose policies she faithfully followed, a view that Ethel Smyth also echoed when she observed that Emmeline became Christabel's 'willing executant', some caution must be exercised in reading such claims.[44] As noted in the Introduction, Sylvia wrote her book not only from a socialist perspective but also from the viewpoint of a rejected daughter, while Ethel's failed 'love' affair with Emmeline coloured how she subsequently saw events. What both authors failed to acknowledge is the way that Emmeline's increasingly dominant role in WSPU politics also made her an increasingly powerful figure. At the heart of the women's struggle with the British government, she became *the* epitome of female militancy, struggling for justice for her sex. Further, by focusing attention on herself, Emmeline was *protecting* Christabel, who was living out of the firing line, in Paris. Emmeline trusted Christabel's cool logic and her political judgment, a view shared by many other militants. Gerald Lennox, a front-line activist, commented, it was 'the wish of all' that Christabel should be out of the country 'for on her depended everything. Prison was faced cheerfully, knowing that she was "outside" to carry on. And she never let us down. She was the balanced, clear-sighted brain of the Movement.'[45] It was a view that the fiery, emotional Emmeline, with her passionate devotion to the women's cause, would have heartily endorsed. Emmeline knew her own strengths and weaknesses. As Jessie Kenney recollected, 'I have seen Mrs. Pankhurst herself, in the confusion of battle break down and sob, "If only I knew what Christabel would do now!" That's what we all wanted to know, and she never failed us.'[46] But other militants in the WSPU had different views. Mary Leigh thought that the attempt to run the WSPU with Christabel in Paris and Emmeline in and out of prison a ludicrous situation. Several times after Emily Wilding Davison's funeral she travelled to France and on one occasion firmly told Christabel that 'the militants were loyal but sick of taking orders from young office girls' while the leaders were in prison and Christabel resided in Paris.[47] But Christabel remained unmoved.

Emmeline was due to return to Holloway on 23 June, but did not do so. Knowing that she could be rearrested at any time, she tried to calm her nerves by writing to that network of feminist friends and colleagues who helped to sustain her. On 24 June, she expressed concern to Elizabeth Robins about the ex-actress's ill health and low spirits. 'This saddens me for although I am very weak & have various troubles (digestive & otherwise) my spirits are excellent. Let me know when you can come.'[48] The women who had been arrested in the raid of the WSPU offices were now being released, and on 25 June, Emmeline sent warm wishes to the freed Agnes Lake, the business manager, since she felt that her case was a particularly hard one where the 'injustice & wickedness' of the prosecution were glaring. 'I hope you have not suffered very much & that you are regaining strength quickly.'[49] By the end of June, Emmeline was again in contact with Elizabeth Robins. She was feeling very upset since she had been followed by the police in a taxi when she had been out for a drive that afternoon:

> Today the drive has not done me much good because of the nervous agitation caused by not knowing whether or not I should be arrested. Now however that I have won the right to get some outdoor exercise I shall improve. I thought you would be glad to know.
>
> Please send me particulars of the Normandy cure when you can for I am quite eager to know about it. C is at Deauville. A friend who saw her last Saturday gives me an excellent account of her health.[50]

Emmeline's two other daughters were continuing their different paths and giving her cause for concern. Without telling her mother, Adela had given up her gardening job at Road Manor and was with the Archdales in Europe. Not wishing to bother Emmeline, Adela had not told her how hard and exhausting the experience had been. For the sum of 35 shillings per week, Adela had worked from six in the morning to six at night, finishing at four o'clock in the afternoon on Saturdays; often she was so weary by the weekend that she lay in the fields until she had enough strength to stagger home. The cottage where she had boarded in a nearby village had defective drains and the landlady's cooking had been so appalling that Adela could eat nothing but eggs, which made her bilious. Adela told Maud Joachim, a WSPU member who came to visit, about one disastrous day when thirty peacocks invaded the gardens she tended and ate all the cabbages, leaving none for her to deliver to the house; Maud Joachim told the story to Sylvia who then repeated it to Emmeline. 'Sylvia was as hot against me as all the rest', recollected bitterly the youngest Pankhurst daughter some twenty years after the event, 'she repeated the offending words to mother in order to make her angry with me.' Emmeline scolded her youngest daughter for complaining about her lot so that Adela felt she had been disloyal to her mother. For the unhappy young woman it seemed best to escape by following up secretly a possibility she had raised with

Emmeline earlier in the year.[51] Now, in the summer of 1913, Adela found herself in the peaceful Ticino Valley in Switzerland, acting as a governess to the Archdale children, Alec and Betty.[52]

Sylvia, despite her political differences with her mother, was following much more closely in her footsteps. On 3 July she was served with a summons under an old statute passed during the reign of Edward III, which attempted to prevent her from speaking in public, a procedure that was also adopted with George Lansbury. Sylvia ignored the summons and spoke at a public meeting held in the East End on 7 July. A near riot broke out as men and women in the audience tried to prevent her arrest. In court the next, day she was sentenced to three months' imprisonment. Sylvia had encouraged the East End people to protest against the Cat and Mouse Act, and a number of gatherings campaigning for its repeal took place, including a large meeting held in the Queen's Hall on 8 July, under the auspices of the National Political League. In Holloway, Sylvia immediately went on a hunger and thirst strike. After a few days, she also walked about her cell incessantly, until she fainted, the sooner to secure her freedom. On 13 July she was released and taken to 28 Ford Road, Bow, the home of Mr. and Mrs. Payne, who were shoemakers. Here, in this small terraced house, Sylvia was to be nursed back to health, attended by Dr. Flora Murray who had also looked after her mother and many other 'mice'. 28 Ford Road was to be Sylvia's home for the next year. During this period she often wrote unpaid articles for the *Clarion*, the *Merthyr Pioneer* and the *Glasgow Forward*, all socialist newspapers, as well as some paid articles for the American press.[53]

Emmeline came to visit Sylvia, exchanging details of their prison experiences. Henceforth, wrote Sylvia, 'we were chasing each other in and out of prison, as though it had been a race between us, until she had served forty-two days in ten imprisonments, and I, in nine imprisonments, had served sixty-five days'.[54] Emmeline was tired of the waiting game the prison authorities were playing with her. She wanted to assert the right to be a free citizen in the way that Sir Edward Carson, leader of the Ulster Unionists in Northern Ireland, was free; he had incited people to violence if Home Rule was passed and yet not been arrested by the government. On the afternoon of Monday, 14 July, Emmeline unexpectedly appeared at the WSPU meeting at the London Pavilion. Annie Kenney, another 'mouse' out on a licence, had just finished speaking, when Emmeline walked onto the stage. The startled audience gasped and amidst tremendous enthusiasm, gave her a standing ovation on this particular day, Emmeline's 'birthday'. Emmeline had missed speaking on public platforms and was not going to lose this opportunity to exercise her authority as the WSPU's leader:

> Now I wondered as I came along to this meeting if I should find the physical strength to speak to you ... [C]oming as I have off my sick bed which I have kept intermittently during ... three months, I thought to myself, 'At any rate, I must say one thing – that a defiant deed has

greater value than innumerable thousands of words' ... You know there is something worse than apparent failure, and that is to allow yourself to desist from doing something which you are convinced in your conscience is right, and I know that women, once convinced that they are doing what is right, that their rebellion is just, will go on, no matter what the difficulties, no matter what the dangers, so long as there is a woman alive to hold up the flag of rebellion. I would rather be a rebel than a slave. I would rather die than submit; and that is the spirit that animates this movement. ... I mean to be a voter in the land that gave me birth or that they shall kill me, and my challenge to the Government is: Kill me or give me my freedom: I shall force you to make that choice.[55]

Emmeline was outlining here an important aspect of militancy, namely that the struggle in a just cause was a moral issue in itself whereby suffragettes could maintain their integrity against the oppressive power of the government. The struggle against that power gave the suffragettes an inner strength, a moral superiority, whereby they could make their mark collectively, in the wide sweep of history, as a force for reform.

While the meeting was proceeding, Scotland Yard had been informed that two of its most infamous 'mice' were speaking. A strong force of detectives moved in to guard the doors. As Annie emerged from the main exit, a struggle broke out as women and men tried, unsuccessfully, to protect her from arrest. While the fighting was proceeding, Emmeline walked calmly out of the hall, through the crowd and hailed a taxi which took her back to Westminster Mansions. Police soon arrived and walked up and down outside her flat, keeping watch.[56] Five days later, on Saturday 19 July, Emmeline received there a group of bailies and town councillors who had come to London from Scotland to appeal to Asquith to repeal the Cat and Mouse Act and to grant the immediate enfranchisement of women; Asquith refused to meet them.

Later that day, Emmeline successfully outwitted the watching police in a ruse that caused some amusement. Soon after eleven o'clock at night, a number of women and men arrived outside Westminster Mansions. Several women then emerged from the building, one of whom was heavily veiled and of Emmeline's build and appearance. Immediately the detectives tried to arrest her, much to the annoyance of the bystanders who put up a fight and shouted cheers for 'Mrs. Pankhurst'. Further police reinforcements arrived and the woman was eventually driven away with two officers who soon discovered that they had been chasing a decoy. When detectives returned to the scene, they found that their quarry had left in a private car that had been waiting in a side street. Emmeline had slipped away to Hertha Ayrton, at 41 Norfolk Square.

When Emmeline arrived at the London Pavilion the following Monday, she managed to get past the police cordon outside the building but could not escape those waiting inside. As she was making her way to the platform, heavily veiled, a detective roughly seized her arm. 'Women, they are arresting me!' she cried as pandemonium broke out. The militants struggled unsuccessfully with the police for the possession of Emmeline, even using hatpins to disarm the enemy. Emmeline was taken again to Holloway. When the cab reached the prison gates she refused to get out and was forcibly carried inside, to the hospital wing.[57]

Refusing to undress and get into bed, since that would indicate she was staying, Emmeline lay on the bed, covered with blankets. She was worried about Sylvia, another 'mouse' out on a licence, who was due to speak at Bromley Town Hall that evening, and followed her example by going on both a hunger and thirst strike, in order to get a quick release. When the Governor visited her, he commented, 'You are very cheap to keep' and ordered three days' close confinement. Emmeline refused all medical examinations. 'I said to the prison doctor', she related, 'that his desire to examine me was not prompted by intention to help me as a patient, but to ascertain how long it was safe to keep me in prison, and I was not prepared to assist him and the governor in any way, or to relieve them of responsibility.'[58] The medical officer, however, suggested a more vulnerable side to his 'patient', when he reported, on 23 July that she was 'evidently in an emotional state and seemed distressed at her own position and also because she thought her daughter [Sylvia] might be in the same plight as herself'.[59] Emmeline decided to force her release by doing what Sylvia had done, walking up and down her cell until she collapsed. The prison authorities found her gasping and half unconscious and released her on a seven-day licence on 24 July, once again to 51 Westminster Mansions. Emmeline was in a severely weakened state. She was now fifty-five years old and had less recuperative powers than the thirty-one-year-old Sylvia; saline solutions had to be given by transfusion to save her life. She had also contracted jaundice from which she never fully recovered.[60]

Keir Hardie, outraged at her treatment, asked questions that evening in the Commons. If the government was not prepared to adopt the only method of putting an end to this agitation by bringing in a bill for the enfranchisement of women, he thundered, then 'this method of barbarism' of the Cat and Mouse Act should not be continued in its present form.[61] Further requests for a pardon for Emmeline were made, including two drawn up for presentation to the King by the London Graduates' Union for Women's Suffrage; the first had been signed by six prominent London men, including Sir Edward Busk, Sir Victor Horsley, Professor Karl Pearson and Sidney Webb, and the second by 474 teachers and graduates. The Home Office also received petitioning letters that contrasted the treatment of Emmeline with that of a man who had been sentenced for assaulting young girls and then released on grounds of ill health; the Bishop of Lincoln, the Bishop of Kensington, and Albert Dawson, the editor of the *Christian Commonwealth*, were amongst the signatories.[62]

Emmeline's licence did not expire until 31 July. Although she was very ill, she decided, against her doctor's orders, to make the most of the opportunity by attending the London Pavilion meeting on 28 July. She was wheeled in seated in a nursing chair, with a nurse in attendance. The hurricane of cheers subsided as the audience saw how frail and emaciated their leader looked. She tried to rise, but sank back into the cushions in her chair. '[A]fter the first broken efforts [she] recovered that superb & pathetic voice', noted Nevinson. Emmeline told of her recent prison experiences and ended her message on her familiar defiant note. 'I mean to carry on my work as a speaker until the close of the Session, so far as my strength allows, and if rearrested shall resume the hunger and thirst strike. In all seriousness, we say that the Government must give us the vote, or give us death.'[63] Amidst a great outburst of cheering, Annie Kenney ran forward spontaneously and throwing her arms around Emmeline's neck, kissed her several times. After Emmeline had left the platform, her licence was auctioned and sold for £100 to an American who was present, a particularly innovative way for the Government to contribute to WSPU funds!

The day of the Pavilion meeting, a worried C. P. Scott, editor of the *Manchester Guardian*, wrote to Lloyd George complaining that there seemed to be 'no sense' in the way Mrs. Pankhurst was being treated. 'The woman is obviously being killed by inches & the Home Secretary is merely dodging death.'[64] Many clergymen too were now of the view that Emmeline should be pardoned. On 7 August, 160 of them presented a petition to Asquith expressing their abhorrence at the workings of the Cat and Mouse Act, which was not only 'exciting much unrest and widespread indignation' but also 'seriously endangering the moral standard of the nation, as well as the stability of the law and order in the State'. Although the Prime Minister received the petition, he refused to grant an audience.[65] Four days previously, forty militants had inaugurated a new form of protest at St. Paul's Cathedral. During the litany at the morning service, they chanted a special verse:

> Save Emmeline Pankhurst!
> Spare her! Spare her!
> Give her light and set her free!
> Save her! Save her!
> Hear us while we pray to Thee!

At the conclusion of the Lord's Prayer, the women continued to sing and were asked to leave the Cathedral.[66] From now on, such protests frequently took place at services in places of worship. And from September onwards, additional protests were made in theatres and restaurants against forcible feeding.[67]

Emmeline did carry on her work as a speaker that summer, without rearrest. An International Medical Congress was held in London, at which she spoke, and a number of the delegates attended WSPU meetings at the Kingsway Hall on 5 and 11 August since the effects of the Cat and Mouse Act on the physical well-being of suffragettes was a hot topic of debate. On 5 August Emmeline delivered a rousing speech condemning those doctors who administered forcible feeding on women caught under the notorious Act, which was a disgraceful piece of legislation 'to a civilised country like ours in the twentieth century'. Conscious that she could win a number of the audience to her side, she was tactful enough to praise those doctors present who were willing to discuss 'the greatest evil in the civilised world ... prostitution', and went on to explain how it was not until women had the power of the parliamentary vote that such evils – including 'the worse disease of all, the most contagious, the most destructive of mind and soul' (a euphemism for VD) – would be eradicated.[68]

Emmeline did not attend the free speech demonstration held in Trafalgar Square on Sunday, 10 August, but Sylvia, a 'mouse' on a licence, did. The rally of between 20,000 and 30,000 people was held under the auspices of the Free Speech Defence Committee and the socialist *Daily Herald* League to protest against the imprisonment of George Lansbury; its speakers were mainly well-known trade unionists, Labour men, socialists and socialist feminists, such as Keir Hardie, John Scurr, Ben Tillett, Charlotte Despard and Sylvia. Although Emmeline had sympathy for the plight of Lansbury, it was WSPU policy to remain independent of allegiance to any of the major political parties of the day. Before the meeting, Sylvia had refused to comply with a request from Frank Smith that she should not ask the people to march to Downing Street; she feared that the Labour Party was too subservient to the Liberal government, a view that was shared by a number of other socialists. The issue was a particularly sensitive one for her since Christabel had been emphasising this very point in recent issues of *The Suffragette*.[69] And Sylvia knew that her mother took the same line. She told Hardie of her answer to Frank Smith and sensed his dislike; their relationship was cooling and she did not see him again until the following summer, having told him 'it was too painful, too incongruous he should come in the midst of the warfare waged against him and the Labour Party by the orders of my sister'. When Emmeline came to see her daughter, she complained that she would have come earlier but had heard that Hardie would be present and, claimed Sylvia, 'feared to encounter him. She spoke as though he were a person a Suffragette should be ashamed to meet. So far had divergence of opinion on tactics, not on principles, destroyed her old friendship.'[70] At the demonstration on the 10th, the frail Sylvia was upheld by her supporters; she stood by a WSPU flag bearing the inscription, 'Deeds, not words' and said, 'it is the argument of sticks and stones from the East End that is going to win freedom for women. Come to Downing Street.'[71] A fight broke out with the police during which Sylvia was amongst the eighteen people arrested.

With one of her daughters again in Holloway, Emmeline spoke at the last summer meeting of the WSPU on 11 August. She addressed especially the medical men in the audience, asking them to question that popular medical belief that the women's movement 'was a kind of hysterical wave that needed medical investigation'. When suffragettes were imprisoned, she explained, medical specialists visited them 'with a view to finding evidence of mental derangement'. They were, however, 'sane women who were in full revolution'. She believed that both she and Annie Kenney, also speaking at the meeting, had not been rearrested because of the presence of so many men who 'would think that the Government, in treating the women as they had treated them, had over-stepped the bounds of humanity'.[72] Shortly after this event, a decision was made to form a bodyguard that would protect Emmeline and Annie. The WSPU was weary of seeing the brutality with which both women were dragged back to prison 'whilst men who are inciting others to attack both life and property go unmolested'.[73] Gertrude Harding recollected that it was a 'proud moment' when Grace Roe told her that she was to be the person who selected and led the group. 'All volunteers … must be completely trustworthy, in good physical shape and be ready at a moment's notice to do battle with the police in defence of Mrs. Pankhurst.' The bodyguard of about thirty women were given instruction in ju-jitsu and carried small Indian clubs tied around the waist, under their skirts.[74]

17

OUSTING OF SYLVIA AND A FRESH START FOR ADELA (AUGUST 1913–JANUARY 1914)

It was a great relief to the exhausted fifty-five-year-old Emmeline when she was allowed to travel openly to France on 15 August 1913, the day that parliament was prorogued, and spend two months with Christabel; the previous day Sylvia had again been released, good news that brought her mother some cheer. Emmeline was in desperate need of a cure and rest after the struggles of the last five months; her time with Christabel would also give them the opportunity to plan the autumn campaign.

Christabel was staying at the fashionable watering-place of Trouville, as the guest of the wealthy American suffragist Mrs. Belmont, and Emmeline and Annie Kenney joined her there. As international figures, early icons of the twentieth century, Emmeline and Christabel particularly attracted media attention. 'We are here for a holiday and a rest', said Emmeline to persistent interviewers, 'and we wish to be left alone.' One reporter found them there sitting in the casino gardens, prettily dressed, with no outward sign that they were 'the trio that defied a Cabinet and made a Government look foolish'. Christabel had a French look about her in her pink frock with a fetching hat to match and a red jacket, but Emmeline was dressed all in black, relieved only by the trimming of a large white lace collar. 'It was noticeable that Mrs. Pankhurst has picked up wonderfully as the result of her rest', the reporter continued. 'When she arrived here she was gaunt and haggard, the result of the "Cat-and-Mouse" treatment in England. Now she is bright and beaming, and, judging from her smiling face, one would imagine that she had never seen the inside of an English prison.' After some refreshment, the three strolled along the sea front and paid a visit to the gambling saloon where a crowd was standing by a table intent upon a game of 'petits chevaux'. The three women watched the players, Emmeline wanting to know 'what the little horses were for, and how the money was staked'. With a smile, Christabel initiated her mother into the mysteries of the game, and the trio subsequently left 'without having ventured a franc upon the hazard'.[1]

By early September Christabel had returned to Paris while Emmeline was staying at the Hotel des Thermes in Bagnoles de l'Orne. From here Emmeline wrote to Helen Archdale in early September since Adela had not settled in well as a governess and wanted to leave. Emmeline felt embarrassed by what she saw as Adela's irresponsible behaviour and apologised:

> How sorry I am that our naughty child is giving you so much trouble. I have already adopted the course you recommend with her. Just before I left London she wrote about going to Canada. I replied that I would not sanction her giving up her post & would find no money this year. If next year she was still in the same mind I would do so. I quite agree that the best thing for A just now is that she must be made to feel a sense of responsibility. She has taken her post [,] she has the college she wanted [,] money has been spent & expectations raised & she must stick to her bargain like a good girl.
>
> I had a letter in reply that she would do so. Surely nothing further has happened since!
>
> I will write to her from here.

Emmeline wondered if she should have ventured further afield and paid Helen a visit. Helen was having problems of her own; her husband was having an affair,[2] and Emmeline offered consolation. 'I am sorry you have private & personal worries. They are the hardest to bear still with patience & philosophy everything is finally settled.' After explaining that she would soon be joining Christabel in Paris, Emmeline thanked Helen for all her help. 'Dear Mrs. Archdale how much I appreciate all your kindness to me & mine. Recent years would have been more difficult for me but for your goodness.'[3]

Emmeline had decided that she would undertake another paid lecture tour in the USA in the autumn, thus giving herself the benefit of two relaxing voyages, the relative freedom of speaking without the fear of rearrest, and the chance to earn some money for the women's cause.[4] Now that she was Honorary Treasurer of the WSPU she had to thinks of ways to raise money for the 'war chest', as she termed it, especially since the British government restricted her movements. Joan Wickham was appointed as her agent and sailed early to New York, Mrs. Belmont putting at her disposal an office at the headquarters of the Political Equality Association. The American press buzzed with the news; although the *New York Journal* was enthusiastic, most newspapers were more cautious, even hostile. On 14 September the *New York Times* ran a long article headed, 'What will New York do with Mrs. Pankhurst?' If Emmeline Pankhurst is not allowed by the immigration authorities to land in this country, the article began, 'the sighs of relief which will waft her on her homeward way will amount to a respectable gale'. A dilemma was highlighted. Although most of the American suffrage leaders said they honoured Mrs. Pankhurst, they did not approve of her methods. 'Her visit is going to put them in an awkward position. If they don't pay any attention to her they will be accused of a slight to a women who has spent her life working for "the cause". If they do show her attention, their action may be interpreted as an approval of militant methods.'[5] The loyal

Harriot Stanton Blatch had shown her support by inviting Emmeline to a dinner of welcome from the Women's Political Union while Dr. Anna Howard Shaw refused to extend such an honour on behalf of the National Society, even complaining that thousands would pay to hear the English militant who would then take the money back home at a time when every penny that could be raised was necessary for the cause in the States.

William F. Bigelow, editor of the American journal *Good Housekeeping*, had a nose for a good story. He wanted to publish a series of articles, even an autobiography, by the notorious militant and asked Rheta Childe Dorr, a journalist who had met Emmeline and Christabel, for advice on the matter. Rheta, a feminist, replied that he should send her personally to Europe, to persuade Mrs. Pankhurst, a suggestion with which the editor readily agreed. Rheta arrived in Paris to find Emmeline preparing for her voyage, in one week's time. Emmeline declined the offer, but when Rheta suggested that she would undertake most of the drudgery, writing at Emmeline's dictation, she agreed it could be done while pointing out that most of her notes and documents were in London; the journalist crossed the Channel to pick them up. Emmeline liked the younger woman, who was living apart from her husband, and had to earn enough to support herself and her son. Having just completed a financially disastrous assignment in Finland, Rheta was keen to please and to make a success of this venture. Meanwhile, the Home Office decided it should not interfere in the decision as to whether Emmeline should be granted admission to the USA but that it should be a matter left to the immigration authorities in that country; however, if inquiry was made of the British Ambassador in Washington, he could inform the US government that Emmeline had been sentenced to three years' penal servitude and was now illegally at large and liable at any time to be arrested without warrant and returned to prison.[6]

Before Emmeline left for the USA, Ethel Smyth came over to Paris to say goodbye. Ethel's two years of active involvement in the WSPU had come to an end and Emmeline was glad that her friend was trying to pick up the broken threads of her music life. She 'winced a little', however, when Ethel told her that she had decided to spend one year composing in the relative isolation of Helouan, in Egypt, where the post was 'slow and uncertain', but eventually gave the plan 'her blessing'.[7] On Saturday, 11 October 1913, Christabel waved goodbye to Emmeline and Rheta Childe Dorr as the French liner, *La Provence*, left port. Also watching the departure were two Scotland Yard detectives.[8] For the week-long voyage to New York and back, and also during free days on the tour, Emmeline dictated an account of her life and was pleased with the way the journalist put the story together.[9] The oral history was eventually supplemented by information gleaned from the feminist press and published weekly the following year in *Good Housekeeping* and then collectively, in late 1914, as Emmeline's autobiography, *My own story*.

When Emmeline arrived in New York harbour on 18 October she was not allowed to land but detained at Ellis Island where she was taken before a Board of Inquiry which had a dossier of her legal case in England, presumably supplied by the British authorities. At the end of her hearing it was stated that the immigration authorities had ordered her deportation as an undesirable alien, on the grounds that she was guilty of 'moral turpitude'. Emmeline hastily retorted that if she were guilty of moral turpitude so were 'their ancestors and all the ancestors of those American colonists who tossed tea overboard in Boston Harbour'.[10] There was such an outburst of indignation from suffragists and the general public about the deportation order that on 20 October President Wilson reversed the decision. 'I knew I could rely upon American justice and fair play', said Emmeline tactfully, as standing up in a car she addressed an enthusiastic crowd when she landed in New York.[11] The detention order added to her aura as, apart from her first speech the following day, at Madison Square Garden, New York, crowds flocked to hear the infamous and charismatic militant speak.

Since the date of the Madison Square meeting had had to be rearranged, because of the detention order, only 3,000 people paid to hear her address. More noticeable, however, was the absence on the platform, apart from Mrs. Belmont, of prominent American suffrage workers. As Emmeline gave a review of the reasons for militancy in Britain to a half empty hall she emphasised, 'Nothing ever has been got out of the British Parliament without something very nearly approaching a revolution. ... Men got the vote because they were and would be violent. The women did not get it because they were constitutional and law-abiding.'[12] Although she spoke of the joy of battle, tears came to her eyes when, towards the end of her speech, she spoke of the imprisonment and forcible feeding of her daughter, Sylvia. But her request for a cash collection evoked no enthusiasm and, according to the New York Times, increased the streetward movement of the crowd. When Eleanor Garrison went onto the platform, hoping to have a word with the WSPU leader, she found the women around Emmeline so concerned for her safety that they quickly rushed the speaker through the crowds, permitting not even the shaking of hands. The overall verdict of the New York Times was that while Emmeline 'made an impressive figure' as she stood on the platform in her black dress of brocaded crepe with a dark tunic trimmed with gold Chinese embroidery and edged with black bead fringe, her reception was 'courteous'.[13] A tired Emmeline was determined that her lukewarm reception at Madison Square should not set the tone for the rest of her tour. With zest, before she left New York, she joined Harriot Stanton Blatch in making a feature film about political corruption – 80 million women want? – in which both women played themselves. Advance notices for the film, which was released the following month, claimed that 'no more advertised personages can be found to-day' than the two militant leaders.[14]

After the Madison Square Garden fiasco, Emmeline was thrilled when large enthusiastic crowds came to hear her. It was not only her star status that attracted the audiences; interest in women's suffrage was growing as the pace of granting the vote to American women was quickening, some five states granting such rights between 1910 and 1914. Emmeline journeyed on the East coast of America, going inland to places such as Cleveland and Dayton, Ohio, then down to Nashville, Tennessee, then up to Chicago, Minneapolis and St. Paul before travelling back to Washington, DC, Boston and Hartford. At Cleveland, she received a five-minute ovation while elsewhere her speeches were frequently interrupted with applause, especially in Chicago where she spent a busy day addressing a number of different meetings. However, her address to 2,000 black men and women gathered at the Institutional Church on South Dearborn Street, Chicago, aroused 'volatile emotions' amongst the black women when she described the 'good they could accomplish for their race by working for the reforms their white sisters advocated'.[15] Emmeline's world-view was that of a common bond of sisterhood between all women; furthermore, she assumed that she could speak on behalf of all women, black and white, poor and rich. To what extent this encounter with black women modified her views we do not know. The WSPU did include racial oppression in its rhetoric, the dedi-cation on the first and subsequent issues of *Votes for Women* stating, 'to all women all over the world, of whatever race, or creed, or calling, whether they are with us or against us, we dedicate this paper'. But the racial analysis was always subsidiary to that of gender and, like many feminist analyses of that time, much less well developed.[16] It was during this tour that one finds in Emmeline's speeches a more resolute determination not to pander to public opinion about the unpopularity of the arson and bombing campaign. In her address at Hartford, on 13 November, she unashamedly stated, 'I want to say that I am not here to apologize. I do not care very much even whether you really understand.' As Jorgensen-Earp points out, such bluntness and contentiousness was unex-pected in women reformers. Emmeline also expressed on this occasion less patience with men than she had in the past. There was no talk of male chivalry but a damming reference to how the average man in the street could not be moved by ethical considerations but by damage to his property. There is a homely English proverb that is 'literally true', commented Emmeline, '"You cannot rouse the Britisher unless you touch his pocket."'[17]

On 8 November, while on the train between Chicago and Toledo, Emmeline snatched a few minutes to write to Mrs. Belmont enclosing a letter from a Dr. Frederic H. Robinson, President of the Sociological Fund of the *Medical Review of Reviews*; the latter had published Christabel's book *Plain facts about a great evil*, a collection of her articles in *The Suffragette* about the double sexual stan-dard, soon to be published in England under the title *The great scourge and how to end it*.[18] Robinson wanted Emmeline to speak at a performance of a new play and had changed the date to suit her. Emmeline sought Mrs. Belmont's help:

> I have told Mr. Robinson that I am asking you to settle the question of the fee with him. Miss Wickham suggests a percentage re the takings. Will you see what can be done. I have told Mr. Robinson that I am raising money to carry on the fight for the vote & our public health in England & so want as large a fee as he can give. ... Some of the

doctors in Chicago are going to sign a protest against forcible feeding & send it to the English Govt. We had a splendid time there also in Minneapolis & Saint Paul. People who had opposed my coming came round & confessed they were wrong & that I had done great good for suffrage here![19]

For one admirer, a reporter for the Canadian newspaper the Toronto *Sunday World*, Emmeline Pankhurst was 'the most talked of person in the world to-day'. Hated and loved, praised and blamed, misrepresented and appreciated, '[n]o queen ever made such a triumphal march through any country as she is making, through the land of Lincoln and Walt Whitman'.[20] But the triumphal orator, applauded on the public stage, still had private, family matters to attend to. She wrote to the unsettled Adela, who wanted to travel, telling her that some friends had invited her to go with them to Chicago, the following spring.[21]

Emmeline's farewell meeting on 24 November, in the great auditorium of the Carnegie Hall, New York, was so popular that 1,000 people were turned away. She spoke mainly on the white slave traffic and upon the need for an equal code of morals for men and women. 'The English Government is the greatest white slaver there is', she announced. 'It is engaged directly in the white slave traffic in the miserable army of native women it provides for its army and navy in the East.' She went on, 'A broken window is a small thing when one considers the broken lives of women, and it is better to burn a house than to injure little children. This is a holy war.'[22] Everywhere Emmeline had spoken, copies had been sold of *The Suffragette* and of Christabel's book. *Plain facts about a great evil* had caused something of a stir, especially in New York where Anthony Comstock and the Society for the Suppression of Vice tried to ban it.[23]

On 26 November, Emmeline and Rheta Childe Dorr boarded the White Star liner *Majestic*, due to reach Plymouth on 3 December. Emmeline had collected £4,500 for the WSPU war chest, and while she was away a 'Great Collection' was being organised to greet her return, as well as a women's demonstration to be held in the Empress Theatre, Earl's Court, on Sunday, 7 December; the Home Office had already been warned about plans for the latter.[24] The ship was delayed by one day, and Emmeline was uncertain as to the fate that would await her on her arrival. But even more worrying was the news that Christabel had sent her some time earlier, namely about the very public rift she had had with Sylvia over the direction of WSPU policy. Emmeline had spoken in confidence to Rheta about her worries and also written to Ethel Smyth about the matter.

On 1 November 1913, Sylvia had spoken at a large socialist and trade union rally in the Albert Hall, organised by the *Daily Herald* to protest against a mass lock-out in Dublin and to demand the release of Jim Larkin, one of the key leaders. She spoke on a platform with George Lansbury, James Connolly, the Irish socialist and a leader of the Irish Transport and General Worker's Union (ITGWU), Delia Larkin, sister of the imprisoned Jim Larkin and organiser of the women's section of the ITGWU, Charlotte Despard and Fred Pethick

Lawrence. Shortly afterwards, the *Daily Herald* reported that Sylvia's ELFS/WSPU was to form a People's Army, of women and men, to protect its members from police assault; it also noted that 'every day the industrial rebels and the suffrage rebels march nearer together'.[25] Christabel was furious, and wrote to Sylvia saying that she would reply publicly to the statements. 'I shall repudiate any connection between the Herald League & the WSPU & in this & every possible way shall make it clear that we are absolutely independent of this as of all men's parties & movements.'[26] That Sylvia was speaking on a socialist platform with Fred Pethick Lawrence who had been ousted from the WSPU, must have been galling to Christabel and seen as a dangerous challenge to the leadership of the WSPU that she and her mother now held.

Christabel, in daily contact with her mother, decided that Sylvia had to be disciplined; her public clarification of the matter appeared in the 14 November 1913 issue of *The Suffragette*. There is no truth whatever, she claimed, in the suggestion that the WSPU was marching nearer to any other movement. 'Miss Sylvia Pankhurst', whose campaign in the East End of London is run on 'independent lines' was present in her 'personal capacity' and not 'officially representing the W.S.P.U.'.[27]

Sylvia, for her part, had come to the conclusion that she could no longer keep silent, as in the past, about her differences of view with her sister.[28] And it was a convenient time now to force the issue. She knew that membership of the WSPU was falling and that there was a lot of criticism from militants about the leadership, especially of Christabel who had become, in Morley and Stanley's terms 'a removed and almost mythical "leader over the water", seen by only the very few (or, like Mary Leigh, the very pushy)'.[29] And their mother was in the USA. If Sylvia could force the issue now, she could oust Christabel from the leadership. And Emmeline, who had never repudiated socialism but was fervently critical of the ILP and Labour Party, might be persuaded to toe the line. Sylvia tried to rally support amongst sympathetic WSPU supporters by sending a letter to WSPU branches explaining that she had attended the Albert Hall meeting simply to put the question of votes for women before a large audience of 10,000 people. There was a time, she continued, when the WSPU held far more meetings than any other society, but that was no longer the case, despite the importance of holding such meetings for the recruitment of new militants. The *Herald* League as well as the ILP would shortly be holding meetings at which, she believed, 'Miss Annie Kenney, Miss Richardson and others, will, I am sure, be glad to help so far as they can in speaking … just as I am ready to do whenever possible.'[30] Sylvia also wrote a letter to Christabel, along similar lines, for publication in *The Suffragette*.[31]

The public row between the Pankhurst sisters caused many a gasp of horror from Union sympathisers and members alike, who feared another split. Nevinson raised the matter at a Men's Political Union meeting and, not unexpectedly, his colleagues argued that 'the trouble was deeper, arising fr. Christabel's suspicion & hatred of all men. I … offered to see Mrs. Pankhurst but Harben said I was too deeply suspected, apparently as a friend of the Lawrences'.[32] Annie Kenney expressed her disapproval of Sylvia's tactics by sending a circular letter to all the WSPU branches, strongly objecting to the use of her name, without her knowledge, and disputing some of the facts and views Sylvia had espoused. 'Surely, the I.L.P. is scarcely an organisation for us to take our example by! It belongs to the Labour Party, which is one of the political failures of the day. ... It is to Mrs. Pankhurst and Christabel Pankhurst that we look for guidance in the constructive and political work of the W.S.P.U.'[33] Theodora Bonwick, a member of the Hornsey WSPU, wrote to Sylvia that she was 'very cut up about it all'. She cautioned, 'It seems to me that far too much fuss has been made over a small matter', and explained that she had also written to 'Miss Christabel ... for I cannot bear to think of any further division in our ranks, of what our enemies would think & our members feel.' She begged Sylvia not to take any action until Emmeline had returned from the USA but 'to lie low a little while' so that the public could not make anything of 'what must surely be but a passing trifle'.[34] But the matter was not a passing trifle; it involved fundamental differences between the two sisters in regard to political perspectives and to tactics for winning votes for women, fuelled by their sisterly rivalry. On 27 November, Christabel, the elder sister and Chief Organiser of the WSPU, wrote a stern letter to Sylvia, warning, 'There is room for everybody in the world, but conflicting views and divided counsels inside the WSPU there cannot be.'[35]

Emmeline, on the *Majestic*, due to arrive in Plymouth on 4 December, knew that she might be rearrested and thus prevented from speaking to Sylvia; in the event of this happening, she asked Rheta to undertake the task for her, of bringing Sylvia into line. Christabel, isolated in Paris, had a nagging doubt that Sylvia might twist their mother around her finger. As Ethel Smyth, staying at the Tewfik Palace Hotel in Helouan, was later to explain to the anxious Emmeline whom she affectionately addressed as 'My darling Em':

I think C's one preoccupation – only half a one! – was lest Sylvia should get round your maternal heart re their differences of opinion!! While I was in Paris ... I couldn't help reminding C that I had always said that, given S's brain formation or something she would never fall into line & would always be a difficulty, given the fact that C is not on the spot. Sylvia will never be an Amazon. If it isn't J.K.H. [Keir Hardie] it will be someone else.[36]

On the day before the *Majestic* arrived in Plymouth, Emmeline wrote to Mrs. Belmont. She made no mention of her family concerns but expressed her 'affectionate admiration' for all her American hostess had done to make the tour so successful. 'You are doing a unique work in New York for women & I often wished that Christabel could see & appreciate it as I know she would.' After expressing the hope that Mrs. Belmont would find time to come to Europe and see the work of the WSPU, Emmeline closed her letter on a very personal note. 'I came away without paying for the tonic which Mrs. Morgan sent round to be packed in my trunk. Will you ask her kindly to send me the bill so that I may pay it?'[37] That evening, Emmeline received a wireless message from WSPU headquarters warning that the government intended to arrest her on her arrival; her bodyguard would be waiting at the dockyard to defend her.

On 4 December, the *Majestic* anchored in the harbour where the tugboat that usually met her was resting between two large grey battleships. Suddenly, recollected Emmeline, two women, spray drenched and standing up in a power-driven fisherman's dory, dashed swiftly past the steamer calling out, '"The Cats are here, Mrs. Pankhurst! They're close on you – ".' As their voices trailed away into the mist, the police swarmed onto the deck and rearrested Emmeline, for the fifth time under the Cat and Mouse Act. 'They had sent five men from Scotland Yard, two men from Plymouth and a wardress from Holloway, a sufficient number, it will be allowed, to take one woman from a ship anchored two miles out at sea', she recollected wryly.[38] Refusing to co-operate with the enforcement of the Cat and Mouse Act, Emmeline was carried off the ship and taken to Exeter gaol where she went on a hunger strike. She was treated kindly by the prison staff, one of whom confided to her that she was being kept there until after the evening meeting of welcome at the Empress Theatre on Sunday, 7 December. With the £4,500 that Emmeline had raised, the 'Great Collection' now totalled £15,000, a substantial sum that indicated that the WSPU still had a lot of support and was not so unpopular as some historians have assumed.[39] Further, the protests against forcible feeding continued as a large gathering of Anglican bishops and clergy condemned the practice as 'an outrage on humanity' and 'unworthy of a Christian community'.[40] Meanwhile, Rheta Childe Dorr had written to Sylvia, 'Your mother wishes me to see you and to have a talk with you about certain matters which we discussed. I hope we can meet within a few days.'[41]

Emmeline was released from Exeter prison on the Sunday evening, at ten o'clock at night, under a licence to return to the same prison on 15 December. The news was greeted with much cheering by the 5,000 present in the Empress Theatre where Flora Drummond, in the chair, spoke of 'our beloved leader' and declared that 'never, never again will the Government get Mrs. Pankhurst. Our bodyguard will grow stronger daily. Every woman who is worthy of her name, and determined to play her part must send in her name to me, and we shall have a bodyguard that will even face battleships.' She also explained how there were many empty seats in the theatre that night since many letters containing tickets for the meeting had been tampered with in the post by a 'cowardly Government' in a 'dastardly attempt' to stop the meeting being held.[42]

Accompanied by the elderly Dr. Frances Ede and Nurse Pine, Emmeline now travelled openly to Paris to confer with Christabel about the WSPU campaign. Writing to Ethel Smyth on 10 December, from Christabel's flat, 11 Avenue de la Grande Armée, Emmeline recounted her adventures of the last few days, her restless spirit relishing the excitement and mystery:

240

11 Emmeline Pankhurst, in mourning for her son, Harry, January 1910

12 Emmeline Pankhurst, Boston, October 1910

13 Emmeline Pankhurst recuperating after a hunger strike, 1913, a photograph of
Sylvia by her bedside

Chicago.
Oct. 1913.

14 Emmeline Pankhurst, Chicago 1913

15 Annie Kenney and Emmeline Pankhurst in Women's War Work Procession, July 1915

16 Emmeline Pankhurst and her four adopted daughters, Kathleen King on her knee, Catherine Pine next to Elizabeth Tudor, Joan Pembridge on the rocking horse, and Flora Mary Gordon (Mary) next to the Nursery Assistant, c. 1919

17 Emmeline Pankhurst, Victoria 1920

18 Emmeline Pankhurst with Commander Maria Botchkareva and a soldier of the Women's Battalion of Death, Petrograd 1917

19 Emmeline Pankhurst, Whitechapel and St. George's election campaigning, 1927

20 Emmeline Pankhurst's statue in Victoria Tower Gardens, Westminster, 1930. It was moved to another site in the Gardens, closer to the Houses of Parliament, in 1956.

What a time I have had since Thursday morning! All things work out for the best; had I not been taken to Exeter, my first bout with the enemy would not yet be ended. But fortunately the Exeter doctor is a gentleman – the leading doctor of the place – and from the first I realised he would not allow himself to be used by the Government. I therefore went quietly to bed, drank some soda water, and just refused food. I allowed him to feel my pulse. He was much moved and kept saying 'You are a resolute woman' in admiring tones!!! On Sunday morning Dr. Smalley (Home Office) came. I gave him one of my storms and refused to let him touch me.

Some day I must tell you the dramatic story of my arrest, the gunboat, the crowd of police who boarded the streamer, hurried me away on a launch to a fort, and hence in two motors full of police over Dartmoor to Exeter. It must have cost hundreds of pounds. ... I came here via Calais in ambulance and carrying chairs, and return on Saturday. ... Am wonderfully well and shall be ready for the next round on Monday when my licence is up.[43]

Even allowing for the fact that Emmeline may have exaggerated how well she felt, to ease the worries of Ethel, living far away in Egypt, the letter expresses how determined she was to play the authorities at her own 'cat and mouse' game, as best she could. The game was an expression of her contempt for the British government as well as means of keeping her mind active and her spirits high, especially since detectives were watching the flat in Paris.

Emmeline returned to England on 13 December, within the terms of her licence. Inspector Parker, another detective and a wardress boarded her train to London but waited until Dover town to rearrest her, entering her carriage as its occupants were making tea. When Emmeline enquired upon the grounds for the arrest, she was told that she had broken the terms of her licence by not notifying the police of her change of address. 'Judging from her appearance', wrote the sceptical Inspector, 'Mrs. Pankhurst was in good health, and up to the time of her arrest, did not exhibit those symptoms of collapse which she assumed after we had intimated that she was to consider herself in custody.' During the journey to Victoria station, Emmeline called Dr. Ede and Nurse Pine to her side, saying, 'I want these men to hear what I say. There is an unsigned Will in my luggage. As you have deprived me of an opportunity of signing this Will, I want you to witness that it is my Will, in case it is contested at any time.'[44] The drama reached a crescendo when the group arrived at Victoria. Knowing that Emmeline's bodyguard was waiting there, the police had cut off all approaches to the arrival platform. Not a passenger was allowed to leave a carriage until the notorious 'mouse' had been dragged along the platform. Emmeline was treated so roughly that she cried out in pain, all to no avail. She was then thrown into a waiting car, her coat being pulled up from the arms over her head. Surrounding the car were twelve taxis filled with plain-clothes men, four in each vehicle, and three guarding the outside beside the driver; in addition, detectives on motor cycles were nearby.[45]

Back in Holloway again, Emmeline went on a hunger, thirst and sleep strike. She was released after four days, on 17 December, to Lincoln's Inn House where a hospital room had been arranged for her. Two imprisonments in less than ten days had drained her strength and the coldness of her cell had brought on a painful neuralgia. Her licence was until 23 December, two days before Christmas. Fresh outbreaks of militancy occurred in protest against her harsh treatment, the damage from arson attributed to the suffragettes being higher in December – about £54,500 – than in any previous month in 1913. Although only seventy militants were imprisoned in 1913 compared with a peak of 240 in 1912, the scale of the arson damage in 1913 was estimated to be £271,000, a sum that far exceeded any previous estimates for damage caused by earlier forms of militancy, including window-breaking. By December 1913 a distinct change in the pattern of militancy had occurred in that fewer but more serious offences were being committed.[46]

Ethel Smyth was beside herself with worry. On 16 December she wrote to Emmeline an emotional and effusive letter, telling her that the telegram she had recently received had brought such relief that she would not scold her for the expense. 'I really only want to see the one & only person who is in my thoughts. How wise I was to go so far away – Here I shall have, if anywhere, patience and gain power over myself.' Concerned about what the future held for Emmeline, Ethel ended her letter on an affectionate note. 'Thank you again for your wire my darling – Yes – think of me at every crisis – I can never tell you what you are to me – what I think of you.'[47] In her reply to her beloved friend, Emmeline gave a very detailed account of her imprisonment:

> In Holloway I lay on the ground exhausted, but with wit enough to complain, and firmly refused to be examined. I was so worn out that I could not resist when they put me to bed, just as I was. I lay there till next morning through the usual visits of Governor, Matron, and doctor, but again refused to be examined. I had by then recovered enough to make plans. I got off the bed and said I would not lie on it again. For two nights I lay on the concrete floor and also a great part of the day. I never took off my clothes or shoes, only wiped my face and hands; my head was tied up in scarf and I did not do my hair! On Tuesday I said to the Doctor, 'Two nights I have lain there' (pointing to the floor). 'From now on I will not do that but shall walk the floor till I am let go or die.' I kept on till 9 p.m. when the Dr. came to tell me I was to be released next morning.
>
> Over and over again each day he came and said: 'Will you let me examine you?' My answer was always, 'No.' 'Very well', he said each time and marched out. When he told me I was to be let go he said among other things: 'You have achieved your end and I suppose you think me a

tool of the Government.' I felt it was a battle of wills. Well, mine was the strongest, especially as he was responsible for me and had no clue to my condition of health. ... This is just to tell you not to be anxious. I shall weather many storms yet, and O how thankful I am you were away![48]

The struggle by Emmeline against the Liberal government had become very much a personal, feminist struggle against an oppressive male state, yet she knew that it could only be won by women working together, collectively. Appropriately, her Christmas message to her 'friends and fellow-soldiers' stressed the importance of women being united in their fight, so that with the winning of their political enfranchisement in 1914 they could begin 'the great task of national regeneration that lies before the women of the world'.[49]

Emmeline had no intention of returning to Holloway on 23 December, when her licence expired. *The Suffragette* stated quite openly that she would soon be travelling to Switzerland, to recover her health, a tale she also told to Ethel.[50] But it was a red herring, a ruse to set the police on a false trail. Emmeline knew that as a 'mouse' she was not allowed to leave England and would be shadowed by detectives the moment she left her residence. She devised a plan to give the police the slip, so that she, her brother, Herbert, and Nurse Pine, could all spend the Christmas holiday in Paris with Christabel. On 22 December she wrote from Christabel's Paris flat to an astonished Ethel, explaining how the ruse had worked:

Yesterday at 11 a.m. I left the house, ostensibly for a drive in Mrs. Sidney Williams's car, Miss Pine and my brother with me. In seven minutes we had given the detective and his motor bike the slip, doubling in and out of the streets between Pall Mall and Piccadilly, then off as hard as we could go to Dover where we got the Ostend boat at 4 p.m. We had to walk from the town station right along the railway line to the pier. Oh, what a walk! but I did it and we got clean away, I think without being recognised. Got to Ostend at 8 p.m. Left Brussels at midnight and arrived here at 6 a.m. to-day. You can imagine how tired I am and what my back is like. ... I have been given an extra sum to spend on my holiday and mean to do it, building up strength to go on with the fight.[51]

Despite the constant fear of a voice announcing that she was arrested again as a clutching hand suddenly grabbed her shoulder, Emmeline relished the excitement of the chase, especially when she won.

Jessie Kenney pointed out how these short trips to Paris were vital for Emmeline's physical and mental well-being, an escape from the strain of her responsibilities. The very moment Emmeline arrived in the city, which she loved, 'her spirits soared like that of a girl who had never been to Paris before'. The very sparseness of the flat, with its few home comforts, encouraged Emmeline and Christabel to go out a lot, perhaps to the theatre or a café where they sat and drank coffee. Sometimes, when Annie Kenney was also there, Emmeline would take Annie and Jessie to the sales to buy cheaply some smart French clothes. 'She loved doing this for us and at times Annie and I would feel that she enjoyed being "Mother" to us.' If Jessie was busy working with Christabel, Emmeline would keep quietly out of the way, in Jessie's bedroom that she occupied while in the city (Jessie would move out to a small hotel nearby), relaxing and doing sewing. 'She would never dream of interrupting Christabel', wrote Jessie. Berthe, the housemaid who looked after Christabel, was an autocrat in the kitchen, disliking anyone else to step into her domain, a trait that Emmeline respected when the revered Berthe forgot to bring her camomile tea with a little peppermint, as a relief for her gastric troubles. 'Jessie, do you think I might have some camomile tea?' Emmeline would humbly ask. At mealtimes, however, the roles were reversed as Emmeline's dignity and authority were felt by all:

> When ... she sat at the table for lunch and dinner, she became the great lady that she always was, and always in social life, when her mother was present, Christabel seemed to retire into herself. It was the same with Adela and Sylvia. If they were thrown together Mrs. Pankhurst seemed to dominate the scene whatever it was.

Jessie remembered that when Emmeline's kind, genial brother was present, 'Uncle Herbert' as they all called him, there would be no 'shop' talk but many stories told of the times when he and his sister were young. She particularly remembered one such gathering, perhaps Christmas 1913, when they were all seated at the table. 'How happy Mrs. Pankhurst was to see her eldest daughter with a little place of her own, sitting at the head of her own table, doing the honours of the hostess.'[52]

Despite the 'problem' of Sylvia and the uncertainty about Adela's future, Emmeline seems to have enjoyed that Christmas of 1913, an impression that she conveyed vividly to Ethel Smyth when she wrote to her on 26 December:

> This is more like home to me than anything I have known for years. Paris suits me and Berthe cooks food that agrees with me. I can potter about seeing things, shops included – get up and to bed when I like – see whom I like. And I love being with C. in this way and tidying her up etc. ... I am much better but weak; the worst is getting the internal machine to work again after a thirst strike, and this twice repeated strike with so short an interval makes it harder than ever. But it will come right in time. ... Don't, don't worry about me. ... To-morrow I go to see Sarah [Bernhardt] in a new play.[53]

Ethel, for her part, was also writing to her 'darling Em' that same day, lamenting that it took a week for letters to arrive. 'Keep me always near you – specially at the worst times – & the best.'[54]

The two friends, physically far apart but in each other's thoughts, also wrote to each other again on 29 December. Emmeline was still in high spirits as she recounted the latest news:

> The D. Mail credits us with half a million damage during the year, exclusive of golf links, letter boxes etc.! ... C. has gone out with Mrs. Tuke shopping, and the little dog Fay [a Pomeranian] and I are trying to amuse one another with a paper ball. She is painfully trying to learn the exact locality of her legitimate retiring place and when she chooses a wrong one her contrition is most touching. C. is devoted to her and has her to sleep on her bed every night. This morning I looked in at her, fast asleep with the window wide open, the snow almost coming into the room and little Fay curled up almost in her neck, a pretty sight. I am glad she has her. It keeps one human to have the care of a little helpless creature.
>
> C's book [*The great scourge*] is out at last. Is it not strange that none of the doctors who testify in it to the truth of her statements felt moved themselves to agitate in the matter?

While Emmeline was writing thus to Ethel, Ethel was penning a letter to Emmeline, recalling a tale about a barrister in Cairo who had 'raved about you & whatever speech of yours at [the] Old Bailey he heard & said you were, as speaker, in a class by yourself – & as for yr. charm etc. etc.!' The bond of love, friendship and trust between the two women was especially important to Emmeline at this time in her life while Ethel, a professional woman in her own right, enjoyed the fact that she was an emotional support for such an internationally known notorious rebel. Ethel ended this letter in a characteristically loving tone. 'Goodnight my darling. The thought of you is like a great lighthouse, visible through all the thousand miles of fog between us.'[55] On 1 January 1914, she wrote another affectionate note to 'My darling Em ... I long to see you fiercely sometimes – but crush the feeling back.'[56]

Emmeline was relatively contented. She had a warm, loving friendship with Ethel, in whom she could confide, and she was in Paris with her favourite daughter. But the problem of what was best to do for her unsettled daughter, Adela, had still not been decided, nor had the problem of how to bring Sylvia into line. Emmeline had been in correspondence with Helen Archdale again, apologising for the behaviour of Adela. Adela had had difficulty in finding another job and had decided to become a writer, a career move with which her mother had little sympathy, fearing that she would not be able to earn her living. 'Can she not begin to look out for advts of employment in American papers agricultural and educational [?]', Emmeline asked. Impatient with her restless daughter, Emmeline advised Helen that they both must be firm with Adela, for her own sake. 'It is too dreadful that she should waste all the time & money that has been spent on her training at Studley. It was her own choice to go there & she must be made to take advantage of the training.'[57] Emmeline talked the matter over with Christabel and they both decided that things could not stay as they were. She also agreed with Christabel that they had to take a tough line with Sylvia.

In early January 1914, Sylvia was summoned to Paris. She had recently endured her fifth arrest, and release, under the Cat and Mouse Act, and felt miserably ill; but worse was the thought of what she knew was to come. She travelled in disguise, with Norah Smyth as her companion; her kind uncle, Herbert Goulden, who knew about the situation, accompanied both women to the boat. The only account we have of the meeting is that written by Sylvia herself, in *The suffragette movement*, published in 1931, upon which she heavily draws for a brief description of the event in her later *The life of Emmeline Pankhurst*. The relevant passages in *The suffragette movement* reveal that, despite the passing of time, she still felt bitter about her expulsion from the WSPU. According to Sylvia, when she arrived in Paris she found her mother white and emaciated, willing to stand aside as Christabel, nursing her tiny dog, took charge of the proceedings. She experienced the humiliation of being told by her elder sister that her East London Federation of Suffragettes must become separate from the WSPU and that if she did not immediately choose another name for her organisation, a new one would be given. When Sylvia asked Christabel the reasons for her expulsion, she was told it was because, contrary to WSPU policy, she had spoken on a platform with George Lansbury, who was now editor of the left-wing *Daily Herald* and active in the *Herald* League. Furthermore, unlike the WSPU, the Federation was a working women's organisation with a democratic constitution; appeals for funds only increased confusion about its role and could reduce income intended for Lincoln's Inn House. Sylvia claims that her mother was distressed by the conversation and tried to bring about a compromise by interposing, 'Suppose I were to say we would allow you something. Would you –?' Christabel interrupted, 'Oh, no; we can't have that! It must be a clean cut!' After further exchanges, Sylvia finally said, 'As you will then.'[58]

Thus Sylvia represented herself as being expelled from the WSPU against her wishes, the decision forced upon her not by her mother, but by her elder sister, the betrayer of socialist feminism, the autocratic, inflexible leader of what she saw as a narrow form of feminism which marginalised the influence of class. She stresses that whereas Christabel's earlier speeches had dealt with the industrial status of women as a main impetus for militancy, it was now 'the supposed great prevalence of venereal diseases and the sex excesses of men' that were emphasised.[59] Emmeline is represented as a weak woman who, under the spell of her eldest and favourite daughter, meekly agrees with the expulsion of her least favoured daughter, and who shares the man-hating feminist view. Sylvia claims that she was greatly upset by her severance from the WSPU, but her Federation had already enjoyed a high degree of independence, and now that its separate status was formalised, it went its own way. Soon it had its own weekly paper, *The Woman's Dreadnought*, and later, when the Federation became the

Workers' Suffrage Organisation, *The Woman's Dreadnought* became *The Workers' Dreadnought*. News of the split within the WSPU soon reached the national and international press, including the *New York Times*.[60] A formal announcement was made in *The Suffragette* and Christabel, in a letter to the press, announced that WSPU policy and the programme 'are framed and the word or command is given by Mrs. Pankhurst and myself'.[61]

In view of the absence of other evidence about the split, it is difficult to assess whether Emmeline had wanted a compromise with Sylvia, as Sylvia claimed. What compromise could there be? Emmeline was at one with Christabel that the WSPU must be independent of any alliance with any of the main political parties of the day. She had been 'merciless' before in her 'preservation of party discipline'[62] and could have no other view now, especially for a member of her own family. But the severance troubled her. She wrote to Ethel about it, who promptly sent a sympathetic reply:

> I am so very sorry about Sylvia & know how you must feel; strange that you have also to do these private family executions. ... Sylvia is 'misstitched': and yet it makes me sad to think how, the first time I saw her with you, – ah! do you remember our interview in the Hotel! – she spoke so touchingly of C. – how someone had said Campbell Bannerman had no one in his Cabinet to compare with C. for cleverness! – Why should the sister who so frankly & nicely paid that tribute, decline to come to heel now? – I suppose because then the P.L.s were 'Leaders' too. Also J.K.H. not quite off his pedestal. When it is a question of obeying one's sister as sole arbiter (for she knows you would do what C. wants & probably doesn't understand it is because your own judgement would go with C's) I suppose its harder.[63]

Sylvia refused to leave the WSPU quietly. She applied to join the Kensington branch of the Union while also remaining a member of her East End group; the application was unsuccessful.[64] On 29 January, Emmeline wrote a kind letter to 'My dearest Sylvia', as she addressed her daughter, pointing out that while she was glad that they had settled as to the separate organisations, she and Christabel were still unhappy about the title of her organisation, 'The East End Federation of the Suffragettes' since the words 'The WSPU' and 'The Suffragettes' had become interchangeable. 'The use of the word "Suffragette" would prevent the public from realising that your movement in the East End is something distinct & independent', Emmeline pointed out. Neither did she and Christabel like the terms of the announcement of the split that had been drafted by Sylvia for publication. Seeking to placate her deeply hurt daughter, Emmeline suggested that the 'best way to make it impossible for gossip mongers & malicious journalists some of whom are government tools paid to foment that sort of thing is to concentrate each on our own work & make our supporters imitate our example.' That way, she continued, 'the nine days wonder will soon be at an end

& we shall all become more effective than we have hitherto been'. Emmeline closed her letter with warm greetings. 'Christabel joins me in love & hopes that your cold of which Miss Smyth writes is now better. Much love Mother.'[65]

But Sylvia would not be placated. 'The East End Federation of the Suffragettes' was the title of her organisation, a decision, she claimed, in which she took no part but was made by the members. Their colours were to be the old white, purple and green, with the addition of red. Emmeline was furious. Remembering the naughty little girl who would not eat her cold lumpy porridge, she sent her thirty-one-year-old daughter a scolding:

> You are unreasonable, always have been & I fear always will be. I suppose you were made so!
>
> I enclose the statement we mean to insert in 'The Suffragette' and send to the Press. Had you chosen a name which we could approve we could have done much to launch you & advertise your society by name.
>
> Now you must take your own way of doing so. I am sorry but you make your own difficulties by an incapacity to look at situations from other people's point of view as well as your own. Perhaps in time you will learn the lessons that we all have to learn in life.
>
> With love
> Mother[66]

After this angry exchange, Emmeline and Sylvia drifted further apart and seem to have had little contact with each other.

On 26 January, Emmeline wired Adela, asking her to come to Paris in a couple of days time. A short time before, Adela had been in Locarno where Annie Kenney had visited her, bringing a reprimand from Emmeline and Christabel about the way she had handled an incident in Milan when a reporter had assumed that the 'Miss Pankhurst' was Christabel. Annie had already written to Adela, asking her to promise not to speak in England again, and repeated the request; an indignant and angry Adela made no such promise.[67] Neither did Adela accept the invitation from Sylvia to work with her in her East End group, whose connection with the WSPU had just been severed. 'I refused at once', recollected Adela, 'seeing that the E.L.F. was in opposition to mother and Christabel.'[68]

Christabel, however, did not know that the unpredictable Adela felt this way and suspected her younger sister might join forces with Sylvia, and form a rival faction to the WSPU.[69] She shared her concerns with Emmeline who also desperately wanted to solve the 'problem' of her restless, unemployed daughter, and had decided that Adela should have a fresh start in life in Australia, the homeland of suffragist Vida Goldstein. 'I hope A will take the right attitude about all this', wrote an anxious Emmeline to Helen Archdale. 'We must do what we feel is best for her & all concerned. I have written to … Miss

Goldstein announcing her probable arrival so all is in train.'[70] At the interview in Paris, Adela felt that her mother was 'against' her. 'Mother seemed to think I had not tried to get work and wanted to come into the Movement as Christabel's rival. I did not tell her about Sylvia's offer nor my refusal. Had I done so, she and Christabel would probably have thought better about me.' Shattered by the news that her mother, to whom she was devoted, considered her a failure, a dejected Adela decided not to argue against Emmeline's well-meant plan to send her to Melbourne:

> She [Emmeline] was facing three years imprisonment and it appeared to me that the best thing I could do for her was to make myself independent of the Movement and of her. I was very miserable, but down in the bottom of my heart, hope was stirring. I felt that I was not such a fool or a knave as I had been made out and that in another country I should find my feet and, happiness, perhaps. Nothing would have induced me to enter a fight between Sylvia and the rest of the family and my mother's action in getting me out of the way was best for myself and all concerned.[71]

Emmeline gave Adela her fare to Australia, some woollen clothing and all the money she could spare, a mere £20.

Emmeline had exercised iron discipline again, in regard to a member of her family. As with Sylvia, if there was any suspected challenge to Christabel's role in the WSPU and to the policy they had jointly agreed, the price to pay was expulsion. The women's cause was above family relationships. Now that the 'problem' of Adela had been solved, Emmeline sat down to write to Ethel, giving her the news:

> We are busy getting her ready for the journey ... it is somewhat an expensive business for me, but I feel it is high time she settled down to real work if ever she is to do any. Of course now all is settled I have pangs of maternal weakness, but I harden my heart and have been busy with domestic cares all this time, sewing for Adela and Christabel.[72]

Adela left for Australia, on the *Geelong*, on 2 February 1914. Vida Goldstein, whom Adela had met in London three months earlier, invited her to join her in the women's movement in that country. Determined not to accept the invitation unless her mother approved, Adela wrote to Emmeline, asking for her permission. The anxious mother wrote back, giving her blessing, 'with many loving words'.[73] Emmeline was never to see her youngest daughter again.

18

FUGITIVE
(JANUARY–AUGUST 1914)

While she was in Paris early in the New Year of 1914, Emmeline could not escape hearing the mounting criticism, both public and private, of the autocratic style of leadership in the WSPU, especially of her beloved Christabel. On 13 January, Beatrice Harraden wrote to Christabel, accusing her of being responsible for the dwindling band of loyal workers. 'Never a week passes but that some one has been slighted, rebuffed, or dismissed ... your exile prevents you from being in real touch with facts as they are over here.' In particular, Beatrice asked Christabel plainly whether she sanctioned the 'continued and long drawn out sacrifice of your dear mother' which was 'an appalling nightmare' to which there seemed to be no possible end 'except her death'. Christabel sent a sharp reply, defending the present policy. 'Everything the Union does is done with a view to serving the cause.' She also outlined possible alternative courses of action that Emmeline might follow – serve her three years' penal servitude, declare to the government that she will no longer be a militant or incite others to militancy, or remain abroad while she returned to England. 'I have shown this letter to my mother who is here just now and it meets with her entire approval', Christabel added in a postscript. 'On certain points she would have expressed herself even more strongly especially on the idea of her staying abroad.' But Beatrice would not be deflected. She wrote again, on 20 January, speaking of the grim fate of those caught under the Cat and Mouse Act, suggesting that Mrs. Pankhurst's sacrifice, in the present circumstances, 'is a vain and a useless one, for the simple reason that public opinion has been allowed to die down, because the W.S.P.U. now has no speakers to rouse and educate the country'. Beatrice begged Christabel to 'recall' the friends of the Union, and 'restore ... the old spirit ... still devoted, though distressed'. Christabel refused to budge,[1] a view which Emmeline full endorsed.

Early in February, a 'diplomatic' letter, signed by a number of suffragists, was sent to Christabel about a new suffrage organisation, the United Suffragists (US), whose formal establishment was announced on 6 February. The US, which demanded a government measure to enfranchise women on equal terms with men, was open to both men and women and to militants and non-militants, and was explicitly non-party. It attracted a number of socialists

and disaffected WSPU exiles and supporters whom Emmeline had known –
Henry and Agnes Harben, Henry Nevinson, Evelyn Sharp, Hertha Ayrton,
Jane Brailsford, Dr. Louisa Garrett Anderson, Beatrice Harraden, the Hon.
Evelina Haverfield, Laurence Housman, George Lansbury, Mrs. Israel Zangwill
and the Pethick Lawrences.[2] Emmeline had been given shelter at Hertha
Ayrton's house when a 'mouse' on the run; Hertha, Louisa Garrett Anderson
and Evelina Haverfield had also marched with her on Black Friday while the
Pethick Lawrences had once been key figures in the WSPU. Emmeline must
have felt betrayed.

Still subject to her three-year prison sentence, she evaded detectives and
travelled back to England, more determined than ever to continue her present
course of action. Deaf to the criticisms being made, prepared to meet all hardships, the struggle for the vote was becoming her own personal struggle. Many
years later, Emmeline Pethick Lawrence remarked that although Emmeline
Pankhurst's fight for women's enfranchisement began in a spirit of generous
enthusiasm, in the end 'it obsessed her like a passion & she completely identified her own career with it' while Holton, a present-day historian, goes so far as
to suggest that Emmeline's campaign for the vote became of secondary importance to the struggle itself.[3] But these claims miss the point that, through this
struggle, Emmeline never lost sight of the victory of the franchise, nor of the
feminist struggle against an oppressive male state. And, most importantly, she
was leading by example, staying in the limelight – while also protecting
Christabel who lived faraway.

Hunted by the Liberal government, like a fugitive, Emmeline had to stay at
random in the homes of those brave enough to take her in. On 10 February
1914, a notice appeared in the press saying that that evening Emmeline would
address a public open-air meeting from the residence where she was staying, 2
Campden Hill Square, the home of the Brackenburys. Speaking from a second-
floor balcony to a large crowd of about 1,200, Emmeline challenged the
government to rearrest her, accusing them of cowardice in forcibly feeding
women whom she had incited to militancy while not daring to forcibly feed
herself. She threatened that if sent again to prison, 'I shall come out of it alive,
or I shall come out of it dead, but never, never, will they make me serve three
years' penal servitude.' Then addressing her own followers in the crowd, she
entreated the women to continue fighting 'against the vicious conditions into
which the majority of our sex are born'.[4] During the fierce struggle that broke
out between the police and Emmeline's bodyguard, a heavily veiled woman
dressed in black, presumed to be the Union leader, was struck on the head by a
plain-clothes policeman, roughly handled and arrested. At the police station,
however, it was soon discovered that the woman who had been arrested was
Florence Evelyn Smith, a decoy. The triumphant escapee had to keep her
whereabouts secret, even from Ethel Smyth to whom she wrote of her hide-and-
seek adventures which included 'twelve hours in a tiny pill-box of a landaulette
(three of us!). I had raging toothache all the time, pouring rain, punctured tyres.

... O dear what a time. However it all ended happily at 4 a.m. and I slept until midday after it was all over.'[5]

On the morning of 21 February it was announced that Emmeline would make an address that evening, this time from the balcony of a private house in Glebe Place, Chelsea, the home of a young married couple, Dr. and Gladys Schütze. Writing to Ethel before the meeting, Emmeline enthused about the hospitality of her hosts, 'How wonderful, the way new people are always turning up just when you want them! Doctor Schulze [sic] examined my heart this morning so that we might be prepared with a report if needed, for I am challenging McKenna [Secretary of State] to forcibly feed me.'[6] As noted earlier, Emmeline would never willingly allow the prison doctors to examine her in order to assess her fitness for forcible feeding and, as a way of saving face, they always pronounced that her heart was too delicate to stand the operation, which she knew to be a lie. She wanted a medical certificate stating that her heart was sound, so that she could wave it, if need be, in the face of the prison officials as yet another means of humiliating the government.

From the balcony of the Schütze's home, Emmeline addressed another large crowd of about 1,000 people and then went inside the house, waiting for a convenient moment to evade arrest from the detectives sitting on the doorstep. At 1.45 a.m, she and about twelve others crept quietly down the stairs and stood waiting silently, for about two hours, for a signal outside saying all was safe. The signal never came. 'Oh, how exhausted I felt when at 4 a.m. I crept into bed stone cold', Emmeline lamented to Ethel. 'I got one hot water bottle, but before a second one arrived I was fast asleep. Is it not a mercy to be able to sleep like that after strain or excitement?' The following night, she managed to escape, but only after a fight had broken out with the police. 'I have strong hope that I shall get through all my engagements up to Easter unarrested', Emmeline continued cheerfully to Ethel, as she tried to comfort her worried friend:

> Put your mind at rest about me and my health for I am compelled to take rest between these skirmishes and so keep well. I need not tell you how I am looked after and cared for, indeed absolutely spoiled by the kind good women I am with now, and who put me in cotton wool.[7]

Ever since Emmeline's return from her American lecture tour the Irish question had become increasingly serious. Sir Edward Carson and his followers in the Ulster Unionist Party had declared that if Home Rule were granted to Ireland, with a parliament in Dublin, they would establish a rival, independent government in Ulster. Arms and ammunition had already been shipped to Ulster, men were being drilled, and it seemed as if civil war would break out. The WSPU approached Carson and asked him if the proposed rebel government would give equal voting rights to women; Carson declared that would be so. Asquith, however, concerned about the potential scale of Ulster militancy and the setting up of an alternative government, sought a peaceful solution to the crisis rather than to arrest and imprison the ringleaders. In early March, Carson suddenly announced that he could not commit the Unionists to women suffrage, since his colleagues were not united upon the matter and he did not wish to cause dissent by introducing the issue; further, the proposed provisional government was only a larger extension of local government and, as such, the only possible basis for voting was the municipal register.[8] Dorothy Evans, Organiser for the Ulster WSPU, declared war on Carson and on the Ulster Unionist Parliamentary Committee, and soon after the WSPU began an arson campaign in Northern Ireland which included damage amounting to £20,000 to Abbeylands, a large mansion on the grounds of which the Ulster Unionists held military drills.[9] The lessons of the successful way in which the militancy of Ulster men had influenced the Liberal government were not lost upon Emmeline or Christabel. As *The Suffragette* later commented, the government dare coerce only women, whom they would arrest and forcibly feed. 'Of men – especially of armed men – they are afraid.'[10]

On the very day that Carson had announced his turnabout, 9 March, Emmeline courted arrest again when she was advertised as the main speaker at a public meeting to be held in St. Andrew's Hall, Glasgow, at 8 p.m. The night before she had written to Ethel giving details of her eventful journey to Scotland, revealing how perilous travelling could be:

Here I am writing to you in bed in a Scotch Manse sheltered by a parson of the Church of Scotland! I got here last night after an adventurous journey from the South of England. One entire night was spent in a car. Our motor lights failed, and we could not find the house where we were to sleep in the dark. After trying vainly from 1 a.m. until 3.30 I decided I must sleep, so curled up in the bottom of the car and slept peacefully until six o'clock, to be roused by an inquisitive farm labourer who saw an apparently deserted car and found two women asleep inside and a chauffeur ditto on the box seat. Then in the morning light we found the house. I had breakfast and went to bed until lunch. We had a hired car which did all the dreadful things possible, brakes getting out of order, burst tyres in places where nothing could be done, etc. Still here I am, in time for the Glasgow meeting tomorrow. I hope to get through the Scotch meetings untaken and to get to Ireland. If all goes well I will write to you again from there.

There is now a Scotch bodyguard and they are eager for the fray. Whatever happens will hit the Government. If I get away they will be laughed at, if I am taken people will be roused. The fools hurt themselves every time. Everybody is very kind to me, and I am waited on and coddled far too much. Bless you, don't worry! Try to rejoice in the sportingness of it all![11]

The following night, 9 March, at St. Andrew's Hall, the bodyguard – who included Flora Drummond, Olive Bartels, Mrs. Williams and Lillian Dove-Willcox – were on the platform which had been fortified by barbed wire covered with flags in the Union's colours, tissue paper and flower pots. Police had been swarming about the building all day, looking out for Emmeline, who managed to slip into the hall, walk quietly past detectives, give up her ticket like a member of the public, and walk round the gallery and down on to the platform at 8.15. p.m. According to one eye witness, she looked 'pale and fragile as a snowdrop, with luminous eyes, whose light twelve months of slow torture have not quenched though they have turned her hair to silvery whiteness'.[12] 'Today in the House of Commons has been witnessed the triumph of militancy – men's militancy', Emmeline explained to the packed audience of about 5,000–6,000 persons, 'and to-night I hope to make it clear to the people in this meeting that if there is any distinction to be drawn at all between militancy in Ulster and the militancy of women it is all to the advantage of the women.' Her text for the evening, she explained, was 'Equal justice for men and women, equal political justice, equal legal justice, equal industrial justice, and equal social justice'.[13] All of a sudden, the police burst into the hall and onto the platform where the bodyguard were waiting with their batons, Indian clubs, and hammers. During the fierce fight that ensued, Janie Allan fired blank shots from a revolver. However, the bodyguard were unable to prevent the arrest of Emmeline who was hit over the head by a big constable and knocked to the ground. Badly shaken, she was then dragged into a taxi where she was made to crouch on the floor while a matron and detectives occupied the seats; punched in the back, her ankles and legs bruised and swollen, a dishevelled Emmeline in her torn velvet dress, without her hat or fur coat, was taken to the police station. Here she suffered the further indignity of being placed in a dirty cell with an open sanitary convenience nearby. Demonstrators outside, protesting against her treatment, were dispersed by mounted police.

Emmeline was taken by train back to London the following day, accompanied by two metropolitan police officers, four detectives and a matron. Despite elaborate attempts to prevent any suffragettes following her, when the train reached Carlisle, Mrs. Williams and Lillian Dove-Willcox came running along the platform shouting, 'Are you there Mrs. Pankhurst?' 'Yes, I am here', replied Emmeline from a carriage with its blind drawn. 'Are you all right?' 'Yes.' As the two women boarded the train they cried out, 'We are with you.' Several other suffragettes also climbed on board. At every stop, some of the women went to Emmeline's window and spoke to her, pushing papers and flowers through the small opening at the top. The driver was instructed to stop at Loudoun Road, a small station just north of Euston, placing the front portion of the long train, in which the suffragettes were sitting, in a tunnel while the rear end, which contained the prisoner, was close to the exit. Emmeline, who refused to co-operate in any way, was carried from the train and taken to Holloway without their followers being able to attempt a rescue. Before she arrived at the gaol, she defiantly told Inspector Edward Parker, 'I wish you to inform Mr McKenna that when he attempts to arrest me again he will require a regiment of soldiers; I am a prisoner of war.'[14]

Storms of protest arose, especially in Glasgow, over the brutality of Emmeline's treatment. A few days later, deputations demanding an inquiry were led to magistrates there and to Scottish MPs in London. WSPU members interrupted church services all over Britain, protests were made in restaurants and theatres while a small band of guerrilla activists engaged in terrorist acts that outraged the public. On 10 March, Mary Richardson slashed with a meat chopper the famous Rokeby Venus painting in the National Gallery. 'I have tried to destroy the picture of the most beautiful woman in mythological history as a protest against the government for destroying Mrs. Pankhurst, who is the most beautiful character in modern history', she explained. 'Justice is an element of beauty as much as colour and outline on canvas. Mrs. Pankhurst seeks to procure justice for womanhood, and for this she is being slowly murdered by a Government of Iscariot politicians.'[15] Houses, hayricks, a timber yard and a pavilion were found in flames in different parts of the country while eighteen windows in the house of Mr. McKenna, the Home Secretary, were smashed.[16]

Back in prison, Emmeline immediately went on a hunger and thirst strike. Refusing to be examined or to use her bed, she lay on the floor in her torn velvet dress. At 11.10 a.m. on 12 March the medical officer noted that she complained of pre-cordial pain and although she still refused to be examined, agreed to have a mustard leaf placed over her heart. On the day of her release, Saturday 14 March, on a seven-day licence, he reported that she had spent a restless night and seemed weaker. 'Begged last night not to be left alone. Cell door kept open, and a special officer was detailed to watch her.'[17]

This was Emmeline's seventh release from prison since her sentence at the Old Bailey in April of last year to three years penal servitude. Ethel, in Egypt, was distraught with worry and wired to find out how Emmeline was. 'You can't prepay reply here which made me hesitate – but deferred rate is 6d a word, & I know my dearest you won't grudge a few shillings to give me peace of mind', she later explained.[18] But Ethel was in Emmeline's thoughts and a telegram had been despatched. As soon as she was back in the care of Nurse Pine, at Campden Hill Square, she wrote a long letter to her dearest friend:

> Just a word now that I am out. I found three of your letters waiting for me. If you only could know what a support you are. I have to be something near what you think of me. ...
>
> Well, it is over once more for a time, and I am not as bad as one would think. Dr. Murray was surprised to find me so well. ... Oh, my dear, I fear that all this has broken into your work sadly, but you will have to feel as people do whose sons are at a war, and just go on having faith in my star and a certain way I have of smoothing my path in

prison. All the women officers from the matron down are now devoted to me and were perfect angels; but Oh, it is good to be in a nice bed, with Lady Pine in attendance.[19]

Three days later, 17 March, Emmeline wrote again to an anxious Ethel, reassuring her that she was getting around, eating well and thriving generally. She recounted how Flora Drummond had just been to visit her and that she was hoping to see as many influential people as possible during her convalescence, including the Archbishop. 'I think the authorities got a fright about me this time but they will find there is still a lot of life in me.'[20] Emmeline sent Ethel a photograph of herself. 'So like you', wrote the delighted musician, in reply. 'I have it fixed to my studio wall.' The news about Emmeline's rough treatment, however, was painful for Ethel to read. 'My darling I can't write about you being knocked about – only clench my teeth & try to forget it. Oh how passionately I long for news of you – my dear treasure – Oh heaven help me to stay here & finish my task.'[21]

As the two women continued their correspondence, often writing to each other on the same day, Emmeline slowly regained her health while preparing for an address she was to give at Lowestoft on 15 April, during the annual conference of the National Union of Teachers. However, Asquith suddenly announced that he would take the post of War Minister and offered himself for re-election in his constituency of East Fife, a seat he had contested against a Unionist candidate in 1910. Although there was some uncertainty about whether a Unionist candidate would stand in the election, the lure of leading a WSPU by-election campaign in the constituency of the arch enemy of women's suffrage was too great for Emmeline to resist, despite the fact that she was still physically weak. With her velvet dress cleaned and repaired, she travelled to East Fife, only to find that Asquith was to be returned unopposed. Immediately she returned to Campden Hill Square, from where on 8 April she wrote to Ethel:

> Oh my dear I am so glad to be back safely in this house, for I never felt so like shirking as I did over this last Scotland expedition. I really tried it too soon after the hunger strike. Providence does watch over me, for I don't think I could have stood being dragged back, as I was before, all that distance. The police are thick round this house to prevent my going to Lowestoft as advertised. Rather a sell for them, as I have decided my heart is not strong enough after the rush to and from E. Fife.[22]

The devoted Ethel, who had feared that Emmeline would take the trip to Fife, had already written to her friend, fearful about the effects upon her health. 'I lie awake at night sometimes & see you like Atlas, bearing up the world of women on your dear head', Ethel wrote affectionately. 'I can't tell you what I think of you. ... If you were to come in now all I could do would be to hold you in my arms and ... still be silent. But you would know.'[23] Supportive and open about her feelings, the emotional Ethel tried to analyse the character of the leader of the WSPU, drawing a picture of her as someone who was aloof from the expressions of human feeling, a being destined to lead great causes whose heart she had won:

> [B]y no sort of possibility however much I might have given myself up to it could I ever have swept up crowds & groups as you do. ... But you are the unreadable person because of a particular blend in you which there is in no one else – a sort of humanity that the egoism of the musical (or other artistic) specialist puts out of reach. How ever clever a 'generale' you may be, you cannot re-cast your nature. It is a thing like short & long sight. Your ordinary vision embraces the mass – that's why you have always shrunk from personal relations. ... I am the glorious exception for you – & I think it is the crowning achievement of my life to have made you love me. And proof of your cleverness to have found me – & found a new gift in yourself – the friendship you give.
>
> Yes – I also am getting more & more 'off' men. They are so extraordinarily impossible to respect. Sometimes I wonder if it is because they have always considered themselves 'easy first' – ever since they started that preposterous theory about the rib! [24]

The news that Emmeline was not fit to speak at Lowestoft that Easter was kept a secret; Annie Kenney, also a 'mouse' staying at Campden Hill Square, or 'Mouse Castle' as the suffragettes termed it, offered to take her place. Emmeline spent the time resting, and occasionally writing to friends, such as Helen Archdale, giving her the latest news about Adela who had arrived in bustling Melbourne on 27 March:

> I have had a cable from Adela since she landed & 2 p cs [postcards] sent en route. I am now anxiously waiting for a letter. I hope all will go well with her & that she will settle down happily.
>
> After she had really gone I felt very sad & yet I know it is the only way for her to realise that she is really grown up. We have all treated her like a little girl.
>
> Life for women is so free & stimulating in Australia that I am sure she will like it & derive energy from it ... When I hear from Adela I will let you know. If you get a letter first I know you will do as much for me.[25]

For some months now, it had been announced that Emmeline would lead a deputation to the King, on 21 May. 'We finally resolved on the policy of direct petition to the king', she explained, 'because we had been forced to abandon all hope of successfully petitioning to his Ministers. Tricked and betrayed at every turn by the Liberal Government ... [w]e would carry our demand for justice to the throne of the Monarch.'[26] On 25 February, Emmeline had written to

George V, asking for an audience; the unusual request had been refused, on the advice of the Home Secretary, McKenna, who argued that it was his duty to so advise since the request had come from a person under sentence of penal servitude who was openly defying the judgment of the court. A demonstration to gain entrance to Buckingham Palace now seemed the only alternative to Emmeline who was determined to recover her health in time for the event.

On 21 April she wrote to Ethel again, hoping she would be fit for the day. 'I have been up twice. ... This wretched anaemic heart is all the trouble.' Poor heart or not, Emmeline still had to do some of her WSPU duties while convalescing. 'Suffragette Week' was soon to begin, a time when WSPU members were urged to increase the circulation of their newspaper, and Emmeline had been busy composing her message. 'Oh dear, why do I always feel as if I were in the dentist's chair when I try to write?' she commented to Ethel. 'Pity the sorrows of a poor agitator! I can't speak my mind for they won't let me speak, and I can't write it!! It is indeed a case of being driven to "deeds not words"!'[27] The anguished Ethel had protested to Christabel about her mother's trip to East Fife, knowing that it was too much, too soon, and had received a scolding reply from Emmeline. Ethel promised Emmeline that she would not remonstrate to Christabel again, but pointed out that 'to court a break down seems to me simply stupid – & I still can't understand why *you* did it – as I do so trust your common sense as a rule'. Ethel continued, '*You know*, Em, you need not explain to me that you must fight. ... And of course I shan't write to C. about it again ... being only glad I did, *all the same*.' Despite being emphatic about not apologising for what she had done, Ethel could not bear the pain of upsetting Emmeline, especially since she knew her friend was likely to face yet another imprisonment. She ended her letter with a loving apology. 'Darling I'm so sorry you should be so put out about my writing to C. – But it's over now.'[28] Emmeline, for her part, entreated Ethel not to worry so much and to remember that she was 'always all right, warranted to come out on top of every thing; in fact a cork'.[29]

Still a 'mouse' on the run, who had not returned to prison on 21 March as her licence stipulated, the fugitive Emmeline sought haven where she could find it. In early May she moved to a county retreat 'so remote', she informed Ethel, 'that it seems made on purpose for my purpose. ... It is furnished hardly at all, but has the essentials, bath, with hot and cold water, and good fireplaces.' Here, she explained, under the watchful eye of a female attendant and a bodyguard of one, she and Annie Kenney rested 'on two camp beds, taking an open air cure' on an upstairs porch. 'Already I feel a different being', Emmeline confided. 'Soon I shall be able to write to you about my next resting place, but will not do so till I am safely installed there.'[30] But Ethel remained uneasy. She wrote again on 6 May saying that she understood and accepted Emmeline's insistence that she had to go on fighting her three-year sentence, but her main concern was for her health and for the hard, calculating way in which Christabel was using her mother to bear the brunt of the militant policy:

Your letter did touch me so! about C. & I being your Heel of Achilles bless you! You need never fear any misunderstanding really between us because I admire C. too frightfully to mind very much if she does occasionally what the muses call 'do me an injustice' – such as imagining I wanted you to shirk ... Bismarck rather reminds me of C. in some ways – I mean if any one opposed him he <u>quite rightly</u> hated them. ... [O]ften I say to people what I most passionately admire in C. is her quietly accepting that you have to bear the brunt of the fight – & thinking out how best to use you. I often have said she goes one better than God who sacrificed his son – a young person!! – It is the same <u>hard</u> element that made me kick at the Scotch tour – the calculating element.

Although Ethel was outspoken on the matter, she also feared she might be offending her 'darling Em' by saying such things about her favourite daughter. She thus closed her letter in a typically supportive and loving manner. 'Bless you my dear one & don't ever let one cloud of fear about me & C. come across your sky. ... I love you far too well not to have your one tender spot in view. Always.'[31]

Emmeline, recovering slowly, then moved to a refuge closer to London, ready for the deputation of 21 May, the last national militant event. Although she was aware that many voices were saying that militancy had made the women's movement unpopular with the general public, she was not deterred. Instead, posters advertising the demonstration invited the help of the public by asking them to come and see that the violent and brutal attacks upon women by the police on Black Friday were not repeated. The advertisements also listed the three key aims of the demonstration, namely to demand the parliamentary vote for women, to protest against the torture of forcible feeding, and to claim equal treatment for militant Ulster men and militant suffragists. As Crawford observes, Emmeline had seen that an appeal to the monarch by militant Irishmen, together with a call to arms, had resulted in the convening by the King of a conference on the Irish question and had hoped that a similar concession would be granted to her followers.[32]

Just before the demonstration began at 4 p.m., Emmeline issued a rallying call to the demonstrators. Although she urged the one hundred women not to turn back, whatever happened, their imitation truncheons and eggshells full of red, yellow and green paint were no threat for the 2,000 strong foot and mounted police who were ordered to deal with the deputation in any way save that of arrest. As the women marched from Grosvenor Square to Wellington Arch, they were kicked and beaten while young male hooligans in the crowd treated them roughly. Emmeline, looking ill and exhausted, was amongst the two men and sixty-six women arrested. She had slipped almost unrecognised to the gates of Buckingham Palace when a large burly policeman, Chief Inspector Rolfe, lifted her off the ground in his arms, crushing her ribs. 'That's right!

Arrest me at the gates of the Palace. Tell the King!', shouted a defiant Emmeline as she was carried to a car waiting behind police lines, ready to take her to Holloway.[33] The photograph of the frail-looking Emmeline Pankhurst, lifted off the ground, her face writhing in pain, has become the most reproduced of all images of the suffragette movement. Outraged about the brutal way their leader had been treated and the peaceful demonstration crushed, the militants launched a war of reprisal that included damaging paintings at the National Gallery and the Royal Academy, planting bombs in empty churches and in water mains, protesting in theatres and churches, and smashing mummy cases in the British Museum. The comparison between the treatment of her mother and Bonar Law, the leader of the Conservatives, who strongly backed the militancy of the Ulster Unionists, was not lost on Christabel. 'Why is Mrs. Pankhurst sent to prison, while Mr Bonar Law is left at liberty?', she asked in a leading article in The Suffragette.[34]

Meanwhile, after her eighth hunger and thirst strike, Emmeline was released after five days, on 27 May, to 34 Grosvenor Place, London SW, due to return to Holloway in a week's time. Two days later she wrote to Ethel who was now en route for Vienna, telling her all the news:

> I was released on Wednesday and Pine wired you the moment she knew herself. On Sunday it was reported that I was dead and I don't think McKenna would have been sorry if that had been the result of the horrible bear's hug that huge policeman gave me when he seized me. Fortunately for me I have 'young bones' or my ribs would have been fractured. After it I suffered from a form of nausea just like very bad sea-sickness; however it's all over now and I am getting back my strength slowly but surely. There has been less waste of tissue than on previous occasions and the blood poisoning was not quite so bad either ...
>
> Lying here my heart swells within me at the thought of our women. I shall never forget how, when we saw the Wellington Gates closing on us as we marched towards the park, they dashed forward, flinging themselves against them to prevent their being shut, returning again and again to the charge, their tender bodies bruised and bleeding. 'She urged us not to turn back', said one poor little thing when urged to go away and rest. Bless them! ...
>
> Many of the prisoners were novices, militant for the first time, and almost all adopted hunger-and thirst-strike. Think what it means for a first experience of prison to do the whole thing, *and be ready to do it again!* O my splendid ones![35]

Emmeline returned to the community to find a desperate state of affairs. On the morning of the deputation to the King, the police had raided a flat in Maida Vale where they had found a suffragette arsenal – bags of flint stones, hammers, two handsaws, a quantity of suffragist memoranda, and a plan showing the situation of a country house and the approaches to it. Five women, including Marion Hall and her two daughters, Emmeline and Nellie, were arrested. The Hall family were old friends of the Pankhursts, Leonard Hall having been imprisoned during the Boggart Hole Clough free speech struggle; Nellie was now a WSPU Organiser while her sister had been named after the much admired Emmeline Pankhurst. Two days after the Maida Vale arrests, in a further attempt to crush the women's movement and the printing and sale of *The Suffragette*, Grace Roe, the WSPU's General Secretary, was also arrested in a raid on WSPU headquarters. Although Emmeline knew that Grace's important work would continue under the direction of Olive Bartels, her understudy, the issue of the drugging of prisoners in order to lower resistance against forcible feeding and to destroy morale suddenly now surfaced. 'Grace Roe is being *drugged* and forcibly fed', a shocked and outraged Emmeline told Ethel. 'How can one stay on in a country so horrible?' When the clerk of Alfred Marshall, the WSPU's solicitor, was caught trying to smuggle a powerful emetic to Grace during a professional visit, so that she could be sick and secure an early release, the authorities claimed that the prisoners were drugging themselves, a charge that the WSPU refuted. Libel actions were later issued on behalf of the Holloway medical officers against Dr. Flora Murray and Dr. Frank Moxon who claimed that sedative or hypnotic drugs had been given to the prisoners, and against Emmeline and other WSPU officials.[36]

Emmeline now stayed at the home of Ida and Barbara Wylie, 6 Blenheim Road, which was known as 'Mouse Hole' since suffragettes who recuperated there could, once they were well enough, escape the watching eyes of detectives by scrambling over six garden walls into the home of a secret sympathiser.[37] While recovering at 'Mouse Hole', Emmeline could not escape her responsibilities as Honorary Treasurer of the WSPU and wrote to a number of wealthy supporters encouraging further subscriptions to the self-denial fund, as on 8 June when she penned a letter to Mrs. Badley, wife of the founder of Bedales, a progressive, co-educational boarding school. '[T]he Government ... are attempting as they have previously done, to terrorise our subscribers by threats of legal action. ... I do hope dear Mrs. Badley that you will do all in your power to help me to raise a large sum of money with which to carry on our work to the end of the year.' She asked for the reply to be sent to her under cover as 'Miss Howard c/o Miss Wylie' and for her address to be kept private.[38] The following day the police raided the temporary WSPU offices in Tothill Street, Westminster, and banned its operations.[39]

Emmeline was outraged at McKenna's comments made in the Commons just two days later, 11 June, when the gravity of the situation created by the WSPU militants was debated. In a long speech, McKenna discussed the four alternatives of dealing with the militant women which had been laid before him – allowing them to die in prison, deportation, commitment to a lunatic` asylum, and granting the franchise. The last he would not discuss while the others were rejected as offering no solution to the problem. Instead, he defended the working of the Cat and Mouse Act as adequate to deal with the situation and proposed to proceed against WSPU subscribers by criminal and civil actions to make them personally responsible for damage done so that insurance companies would seek to recover their losses. 'We have only been able to obtain this evidence [about subscribers] by our now not infrequent raids upon the offices', he proudly boasted. 'If the action is successful in the total destruction of the means of revenue of the Women's Social and Political Union', he continued, 'I think we shall see the last of the power of Mrs. Pankhurst and her friends.'[40] 'Mrs. Pankhurst' was not amused. 'McKenna's speech!!' she wrote to Ethel. 'He will not let us die, you see, humane man, but will bring us to death's door as often as he can, and so hopes to make us permanent invalids. Well, we shall see!'[41]

In the midst of these crises, the 'problem' of Sylvia appeared again for Emmeline. Sylvia had decided that a new initiative should be launched to break the deadlock with Asquith who insisted that the WSPU demand for a limited franchise for women, based on a property qualification, was undemocratic, and that the women's movement had not attracted the masses. Sylvia's suggestion to her East London Federation that the members of a deputation to the Prime Minister should be elected at large rallies, open to the public, which should also decide upon the terms of the suffrage demand, was warmly welcomed. At huge public meetings, an almost unanimous decision was made to demand a vote for every woman over twenty-one years of age. When Sylvia wrote to Asquith, asking him to receive the six working women representatives on the evening of 10 June or an earlier date, he refused. She then informed him that she would repeat her hunger and thirst strike, in and out of prison, until he agreed to do so, a move that her followers feared would cost her life. Too weak after her imprisonment to walk in the procession, Sylvia was carried on a stretcher and soon arrested as police dashed in, using their truncheons freely in the ensuing struggle. The march continued on its way and the working women representatives gained admittance to the Commons, although Asquith refused to meet them. They did, however, put their case to the Liberal Chief Whip and to other MPs.[42]

After the failure of the procession, the East London Federation worked tirelessly to rally more support for their initiative, enlisting the help of the United Suffragists whose members included well-known ex-WSPU supporters, such as Henry Nevinson and Evelyn Sharp. Norah Smyth, acting in good faith, wrote to Emmeline, imploring her to bring the WSPU into the campaign. Emmeline was both angry and grieved. She sharply replied to Norah that the East London Federation's actions were not in conformity with WSPU policy and also suggested that the imprisoned Sylvia should not risk her health by continuing with her threatened hunger and thirst strike when released. 'Tell her I advise her when she comes out of prison to go home and let her friends take care of her.' Norah was shocked by the reply while Sylvia scolded her for sending a letter to her mother. 'Did you not understand in Paris that no family or other considerations are permitted to intervene?'[43] The bitter Sylvia did not know that her mother was plagued with pangs of maternal guilt, at least for a short time. 'O how hard it is to have children and friends in a movement like ours', Emmeline confessed to Ethel. 'One's heartstrings are torn so often ... what a price is being paid for the vote!'[44]

When Sylvia was released on the 18 June, in a severely weakened state, she was immediately taken to the House of Commons where she lay on the steps, threatening to starve herself to death in order to force Asquith's hand to receive the working women's deputation. She did not have to wait long. The besieged Prime Minister did not want a martyr on his hands, especially with a general election scheduled for the following year; nor did he want her People's Army, a trained corps of women and men, marching on parliament. As the police were about to move Sylvia, Keir Hardie knelt beside his former lover, telling her quietly that Asquith had agreed to receive the six working women representatives on Saturday morning, 20 June. When Asquith, in his reply to the working women, emphasised that if change in the franchise had to come, 'we must face it boldly and make it thoroughgoing and democratic in its basis', Sylvia believed that the government was paving the way for 'a change of front' on the women's issue.[45] But no immediate change of heart was evident. Asquith had given similar assurances to the NUWSS deputation which had met him in August, the previous year.

Romero speculates about the reasons for Sylvia's motivation at this particular time in her life in subjecting herself to such psychological and physical torture and suggests that she may have been wanting to compete with her mother for publicity on a larger stage or hoping to rekindle her mother's sympathies. Although there may be an element of truth in these suggestions, it is much more likely that Sylvia's deeply held socialist beliefs were the spring for her actions as well as the cause of the increasing divide between herself and her mother.[46] Indeed, as pointed out in the Introduction, Marcus claims that Sylvia's description of these events in The suffragette movement represents a victory for socialist feminism, a victory less over the government than over 'her real enemies, her mother and sister, the separatist feminists' who refused to co-operate with the socialist movement. It is Sylvia 'and her united charwomen' who are presented as making the breakthrough with Asquith, not Emmeline and Christabel.[47]

Such a reading is highly plausible since in The suffragette movement, Sylvia blames Christabel, and by association, also her mother, for the failure to win the vote in 1914. She tells the story of how, after her deputation had met Asquith, she asked George Lansbury if he would arrange for her an interview with Lloyd George, which he did, also being present himself. However, their respective accounts of the interview differ. According to Lansbury, Lloyd George said that he and other leading Liberals were willing to make a public pledge that they would decline to serve as members of any Liberal government cabinet after the next general election which did not make women's suffrage 'the first plank' in its legislative programme. Sylvia went further, claiming that Lloyd George offered to introduce a private member's bill on women suffrage, drawn on broad lines, that he would give 'written guarantees' of this, and that he would 'stake' his 'political reputation' on it. In the meantime, he insisted that militancy was suspended.[48] As Romero points out, Sylvia either incorrectly recalled the event, or changed it to suit her own story line since Lloyd George, as a cabinet minister, was unable to introduce a private member's bill and was unlikely to make such an offer.[49] A private member's bill, however, was the antithesis of all that Emmeline and Christabel had argued for, as well as the suspension of militancy. Here is also further confusion in Sylvia's account since it is unclear as to which suffrage organisation she is representing. Although she was no longer a member of the WSPU, she apparently said to Lloyd George, 'I do not know whether Christabel would consent to a truce to militancy for anything short of a Government measure', to which, she claimed, he answered tartly, 'I shall be quite prepared to debate it with Miss Christabel.'[50]

To Sylvia's annoyance, the news of Lloyd George's supposed change of heart was told by a jubilant Lansbury to Henry Harben who immediately informed Christabel. Once Sylvia knew of this leak, she wrote to her sister, saying that she hoped to engage in negotiations that would resolve the suffrage issue and that she would travel to Paris to see her. A furious Christabel deeply resented Sylvia's plan and interference in WSPU policy. 'Tell your friend not to come' was the sharp message in her telegram to Norah Smyth. In later issues of *The Suffragette* the unbending Christabel thundered that there could be 'no private communications from the Government or from any of its members' on women suffrage since there was nothing over which to compromise. 'There is no room for negotiation as to the *terms* upon which women demand the Vote', she insisted as she stuck to the principle of ending the sex discrimination that women endured. 'Those terms are clearly understood. They are – that women shall vote on the same terms as men.'[51]

Meanwhile, Emmeline, a fugitive on the run, remained totally loyal to Christabel and the policies they had jointly agreed. On 18 June she wrote to Eleanor Garrison in the USA asking if she would collect as much money as she could from sympathisers in Boston for the WSPU cause. 'Our struggle grows more & more intense as we near the inevitable end', Emmeline told her young friend. 'Pharaoh has indeed hardened his heart especially since we added the moral crusade to the suffrage work. Indeed I think the opponents of W.S. hate that more than the vote & now realise that votes for women means less moral license for men.' Emmeline had put just 'London' as her address on the top of her letter, and Eleanor was asked to send any money collected to Christabel in Paris. 'My movements are very uncertain', observed Emmeline, '& as you can understand there are postal difficulties.'[52]

The continued forcible feeding of militants, under horrendous conditions, deeply troubled her; Frances Gordon in Perth was now even being fed through the rectum.[53] When *The Times* on 6 July published a letter by the Bishop of London that offered more condemnation of militancy than of forcible feeding, Emmeline was astounded. She penned a letter to that newspaper protesting against forcible feeding and exposing the double standard that the government was operating; WSPU prisoners, including untried prisoners charged with the crimes of incitement and conspiracy which Sir Edward Carson and his Unionist associates were openly committing daily, without arrest, and for which she had been sentenced to three years' penal servitude, were being tortured by a barbaric practice. 'I ask you to publish this letter', the defiant rebel said, 'because I desire to inform the Home Secretary and his colleagues that to-morrow I shall openly resume my work for the enfranchisement of women, and that when they have effected my re-arrest with its usual accompaniment of brutality and insult I shall resume the strike.'[54]

On 8 July, the day her letter was published, Emmeline was rearrested as she entered the old WSPU headquarters at Lincoln's Inn. Late that night, Frances Parker and Ethel Moorhead attempted to blow up Robert Burns' cottage at Alloway, near Ayr. Back in the Reception Wing in Holloway, Emmeline was stripped and thoroughly searched, the new rule having been introduced since the attempt to smuggle an emetic to Grace Roe. Deeply offended by this new procedure and determined to resist, she was charged with being abusive and using offensive language towards the matron and wardresses who searched her, and with striking one of them. After being subjected to the degrading procedure, during which only indigestion tablets were found, Emmeline lay on the floor, refusing to be helped on with her clothes. As Crawford aptly comments, the image of Mrs Pankhurst, usually so fastidious and personally reticent, lying naked on the floor, under the gaze of prison officials, is not one conjured up by history books. The private view, however, became public, when notes about the strip search were written up for the Home Office, and stored in an archive, now open for all to consult. For Crawford, 'This humiliation more than her commanding oratory and platform presence represents Emmeline Pankhurst's apotheosis and perfectly demonstrates what Teresa Billington-Greig identified as her willingness to be ruthless with herself.'[55]

Brought before a three-man Visiting Committee on 10 July, to be tried for her offences, Emmeline had regained some of her composure. 'I put it to you, gentlemen ... that the Matron has admitted that it was an unpleasant duty. ... Is it not an indignity to subject a woman like me to a forcible search?' Her plea fell on deaf ears. She was sentenced to seven days' close confinement and the forfeit of 168 remission marks.[56] Continuing her hunger and thirst strike, during which she lost nearly a stone in weight and suffered greatly from nausea and gastric disturbances, she was released in an emaciated condition the following day, due to return on 15 July.[57] Cared for by Nurse Pine at Pembridge Gardens, Emmeline was determined not to return to Holloway but to attend a great WSPU meeting to be held at Holland Park Hall on the 16th. On the evening of the meeting, she set out, on a stretcher, accompanied by a number of doctors and clergymen who were to conduct her to the waiting ambulance. Hundreds of people watched as, during a short struggle with the police, she was rearrested and taken back to Holloway.[58] Anticipating such a move, Emmeline had prepared a defiant message to be read at the Holland Park Hall meeting. 'There is talk of negotiation and compromise. No negotiations for us. A Government measure giving equal voting rights to women with men is our demand, and we demand it **Now!** … Let us fight on, loyal to one another and to our great cause.'[59] After the applause from her message had died down, it was announced that the 'Protest Fund' had reached £15,350. This sum, together with an income of £36,896 that the WSPU had attracted during the last year, an increase of £8,000 upon the previous year, are firm indications that Emmeline and the policies she upheld for her militants had not cost the Union all public support,[60] a fact rarely commented upon by the majority of historians. The day following Emmeline's rearrest, a young woman of refined appearance attacked with a butcher's cleaver Millais' unfinished portrait of Thomas Carlyle hanging in the National Gallery. Ironically, Miss Payne did not know that the great historian was one of Emmeline's romantic heroes, his *French Revolution* having been a source of inspiration since childhood.[61] Severely weakened by two arrests in one week, Emmeline was released after a couple of days, due to return on 22 July.

Protests about her treatment continued to be made to the Liberal government, both on a national and international scale. Some time earlier, in July, in far away Sydney, Adela had drawn a packed house when she pleaded emotionally for her mother's release from prison.[62] Despite her now very frail body, Emmeline's passionate concern to end the injustices against her sex did not desert her. She penned a letter to the King, requesting an audience, pointing out that while militant women were imprisoned and tortured, Ulster militant men had been invited to a conference on the Irish question to be held at Buckingham Palace. On 23 July, Lady Isabel Hampden Margesson and Mrs. Corbett were turned away from the Palace as they tried to deliver the letter. The following day, while the conference was meeting in an effort to avert Irish civil war, Lady Barclay and the Hon. Edith Fitzgerald made another unsuccessful attempt to present the petition; since they refused to go away, they were arrested for obstruction although later discharged.[63] The government tried to crush *The Suffragette*, yet again, by arresting its printers and issuing proceedings against all persons involved in its publication or distribution.

Emmeline did not return to Holloway on 22 July but slipped quietly away to France, where she had arranged to met Ethel. Nurse Pine had informed the volatile musician that the leader of the WSPU was 'lower than ever before', but nothing prepared Ethel for the shock when, supported by two of her militants, 'the ghost of what had been Mrs. Pankhurst' tottered onto the quay at St. Malo.[64] Soon afterwards, Christabel joined them. With the two women by her side who were closest to her heart, Emmeline began to rebuild slowly her strength, splashing in the sea for the first time in twenty-five years and discovering that she could still swim. She even taught Ethel a trick or so, such as floating on her back and swimming with her mouth above the water.[65] But the clouds of the Great War of 1914–18 were approaching fast. Emmeline followed the crowds on 1 August who gathered in St. Malo to hear the Mayor read

Germany's declaration of war against France. She listened to the cries of the elderly folk who recollected the Franco-Prussian war of 1870 and remembered her own schooldays in Paris. Her prejudice against all things German and her enthusiasm for France resurfaced in stronger measure in her emotional temperament as she reflected that she had always argued, as leader of the militant women's campaign, that human life was sacred.[66] WSPU headquarters was instructed to inform the membership that all activity was to stop until the present crisis was over.[67] Emmeline's resolve to suspend the militant struggle stiffened when the small country of Belgium was invaded and Britain then declared war on Germany, on 4 August.

The Home Secretary, McKenna, responded half-heartedly to the announcement of the WSPU truce, stating on 7 August that the government would only release those suffrage prisoners who would undertake not to commit further crimes or outrages. On 10 August, a begrudging McKenna, undoubtedly responding to political pressure, reversed that decision, announcing that within a few days, all suffrage prisoners would be released unconditionally.[68] Two days later Emmeline sent a letter to all WSPU members, explaining the situation and announcing a temporary suspension of militant action.[69] The militant campaign had ended.

19

WAR WORK AND
A SECOND FAMILY
(SEPTEMBER 1914–JUNE 1917)

Even though suffrage militancy had been suspended with the outbreak of war, Emmeline knew that it was inevitable that, sometime in the future, women would be granted their citizenship rights. As she wrote the closing paragraphs of her autobiography later that summer of 1914, she forecast, 'Our battles are practically over. ... No future Government will repeat the mistakes and the brutality of the Asquith Ministry.'[1] Although the 14 August issue of *The Suffragette* had been printed, it was not published, and publication ceased until eight months later.

Emmeline was free to return to England without fear of arrest and did so in early September, together with Christabel who had been in exile for two and a half years. As Caine notes, the crisis posed by the First World War brought into prominence questions about the relationship of feminism to nationalism and militarism on the one hand, and to internationalism and pacifism on the other.[2] Such issues were now confronted by the WSPU leadership. Emmeline and Christabel were firmly of the view that, as Christabel put it, they could not be 'pacifists at any price'; their country was at war, and they had to support the national cause.[3] Thus, as Tickner observes, Emmeline guided the WSPU to realign alongside the men of the nation who, at a time when military conscription was voluntary not compulsory, had an opportunity to 'redeem' themselves by offering to engage in battle; militant rhetoric and the image of the 'just cause' remained, but the object of attack shifted to that of German hostility.[4] Just how many WSPU members welcomed the shift in policy is difficult to ascertain. Kitty Marion was of the view that that there was 'much dissatisfaction and withdrawal' of membership.[5]

Although historians have generally portrayed Emmeline's patriotic support for the British government during the First World War as an abrupt about-turn from her suffragette days,[6] they have not explored the ways in which this support was not given uncritically or how she pressurised the government to encourage women to undertake war work, believing that the eventual reward would be the parliamentary vote. In short, little attention has been given to her 'patriotic feminism'. As Joan Beaumont points out, recent feminist writers have projected their own alignment with anti-imperialism and anti-militarism onto the past, seeing imperialism and militarism as incompatible with feminism when this was not so for many women in the First World War.[7] Neither have historians given sufficient weight to Emmeline's passion for France, a country invaded by a German aggressor. Not only was Emmeline a Francophile, she saw France as 'the Mother of European Democracy'; the Allied defence of France, therefore, would preserve that democracy which France had given to the world and which would perish, if France were destroyed.[8] Further, as de Vries points out, a more nuanced reading of the Pankhurst war position reveals a consistency of thought.[9] Emmeline had always emphasised that the struggle for the vote, based on the principles of self-sacrifice, was part of a wider movement for national reform and regeneration. During the war years she insisted, 'I am a patriot when my country is attacked. I believe in working through Nationalism to Internationalism.'[10] Nations, it was now argued, would continue to degenerate until women were granted the vote, and the power that accompanied it, to influence national and international policies. That such a merging of 'feminist' and 'British' viewpoints was possible should come as no surprise. Antoinette Burton has argued powerfully that when researching feminists in the past, we must examine the historical circumstances in which they thought, lived and worked for change. Adapting her analysis, it can be argued that Emmeline and Christabel were embedded in a 'British' culture which was now under threat and were not 'feminists first and British second and bourgeois third' but at the 'crossroads of several interlocking identities'.[11] Mother and daughter skilfully presented themselves as British patriotic feminists as they wove into their speeches themes about the nation, patriotism, imperialism, democracy, internationalism, men's and women's contribution to the war, the benefits of women's war service, and women's enfranchisement. In so doing, they were still challenging well-established definitions of femininity, but in a context that was no longer subversive.[12] In particular, Emmeline, through her emphasis upon the importance of women's right to war service, helped to bring about a blurring of traditional gender roles as women entered the jobs men at the war front had vacated. Yet, at the same time, she also helped to reinforce the traditional differences between the sexes since she spoke at a number of rallies to encourage men to sign up for soldiering at the war front. In this emphasis upon soldiering as men's work, Emmeline was echoing the common view of the time. It was not necessary for women to go to 'the trenches', she insisted, since it was women who brought children into the world and thus perpetuated the race; it was the 'highest duty of woman as the mother' to build up the race 'physically, mentally and morally'.[13] In Emmeline's war discourse, therefore, women were to be both paid workers and mothers, although the emphasis was decidedly on the former.

The first of the WSPU rallies around such themes was held on 8 September at the London Opera House. In the large auditorium, decorated with flags of the Allies, Christabel addressed a crowded meeting on the subject of the 'German Peril'. A proud Emmeline sat as a spectator in one of the boxes as Christabel, standing alone on the vast stage in a dress of pale green, received a tremendous welcome home from the mainly female audience who sang 'For she's a jolly good fellow' and handed up bouquets of roses and lilies.[14] Then, as the applause subsided, the returned exile announced, 'We women are determined that the British citizenship for which we have fought in the past ... shall be preserved from destruction at the hand of Germany.' One thing is certain, she continued. 'You are not now utilising to the full the activities of women. In France, from which country I have just come, the women, while all the able-bodied men are at the front, are able to keep the country going, to get in the harvest, to carry on the industries. It is the women who prevent the collapse of the nation while the men are fighting the enemy.' When the war ended in victory, then women who were paying their share of the price would insist upon being brought into 'equal partnership as enfranchised citizens of this country'. Since full conscription was not yet introduced, Christabel appealed to men to join the comparatively few British soldiers at the war front.[15]

Sylvia was also sitting in the audience, apart from her mother. She listened not with rapture but with grief; a deeply committed pacifist, she resolved to write and speak more urgently for peace. Further, as a socialist, she believed that the war was created by greedy capitalists who would exploit the working classes in every way possible. When she went backstage to speak to Christabel and Emmeline, the meeting was icy; she exchanged only a 'brief greeting' with her mother, 'distant as through a veil'.[16] As Sylvia left the hall, some cheers were raised for her from members of her East London Federation in opposition to the cries for Christabel and Emmeline. The rift between the Pankhurst women, now so public, was to deepen during the coming month as Emmeline and Christabel, shortly after their return to Paris, announced that they would come back to Britain to mount a platform campaign to recruit men for the services. Sylvia wept when she read the news. She never forgave her mother for what she saw as a betrayal of all the ideals for which Richard Pankhurst had stood. She thought of the peace crusade, in the 1870s, when he had courted his young bride-to-be and of Emmeline's support for her husband during the long years he had advocated peace and internationalism. She also recollected her widowed mother's stand, with her children, against the Boer War. On impulse, she later wrote to Emmeline only to receive a condemnation, 'I am ashamed to know where you and Adela stand.'[17] Adela, also an ardent pacifist and now a leading speaker for the militant Women's Political Association in Melbourne, was making inflammatory anti-war speeches in Australia and opposing conscription.[18] It is possible, of course, that the response of the two pacifist Pankhurst daughters was not fired solely by the political differences that divided them from their mother but partly by a desire to hit back at her 'heartlessness' in 'abandoning' her children. Perhaps, too, the response partly embodied an element of defiance and independence against Emmeline's possessiveness and favouritism for their elder sister who had led 'their' mother 'astray', a statement to the world that the dissident daughters had grown up and were no longer tied to her apron strings.

The pacifist view was a minority view during the 1914–18 war, and over the next four years it was Emmeline rather than Sylvia who occupied the limelight in Britain as, together with Flora Drummond, Annie Kenney, Grace Roe and Norah Dacre Fox, she campaigned up and down the country for the war effort, arguing against trade union opposition to women's war work, encouraging men to sign up for the war front, and urging workers in industrial areas not to be tricked by socialism and Bolshevism into strike action. Such thinking does not indicate an abandonment of feminism, the common interpretation of most historians.[19] Emmeline kept a feminist analysis firmly in view during these war years, but it was not socialist feminism nor pacifist feminism; it was a patriotic feminism which emphasised women's contribution to the war effort and to militarism. She had a deep distrust of the male-dominated Labour Party and trade unions, knowing that women's interests took second place to those of men. Further, she believed that strike action by workers could lead to military defeat and the establishment of a society where women would have no equality, but be confined to the home and kitchen. All the political work of the WSPU in advancing the cause of women was useless, she insisted, unless there was industrial peace. '[I]f we do not calm industrial unrest and restore harmony between the workers and those who direct them, if we do not keep up the supply of munitions at the front, all the other work might just as well never have been done.'[20] I have found no evidence whatsoever to support the claim that Emmeline personally handed out white feathers to young men still in civilian dress.[21]

Emmeline's campaign, organised by Grace Roe, began in earnest on 21 September 1914, when she made a speech under the auspices of the WSPU at the Brighton Dome explaining that although she had believed in peace from her childhood, and still did, she had no doubt about the righteousness of this war. The neutrality of Belgium had to be maintained, and it was 'our duty' to stand by the great nation of France. The status of women in Germany was the lowest in the civilised world, and if Germany conquered Britain, all that women had been struggling for would cease to be. Appealing to young men who had not made up their minds, to join soldiers at the war front, she emphasised that in taking part in the war 'we are fighting for our existence as a nation and all the ideals for which our forefathers have fought and sacrificed in the past'.[22] Challenging dominant definitions of femininity, which defined women's work in wartime as voluntary caring work, she insisted that women should enter the jobs of men so that men could be free to go to the war front. The WSPU, she pointed out, held that 'it is not our duty to form relief committees, or open workrooms, or do work of that kind. This duty falls upon the Government of this country.'[23] That she had lost none of the power of her oratory, as she travelled up and down the country with such messages, was borne out in an account of a speech she gave in Plymouth in mid November 1914, a city, she reminded her audience, she had first visited many years ago, when she came with her husband to address a meeting:

The next time I came to Plymouth, or tried to come to Plymouth – (laughter) – I was a militant Suffragette, I was a convict – (laughter) – as I still am. Life is a queer, topsy-turvy thing, isn't it? Here you have a convict, whose license has expired, and not amnestified, actually asking people to enlist and fight for the country (laughter). ... If you go to this war and give your life, you could not end your life in a better way, – for to give one's life for one's country, for a great cause, is a splendid thing – (prolonged applause).[24]

Such ideas were far removed from what Sylvia believed, and also the kind of relief work she was organising through her East London Federation – the setting up of mother-and-child welfare centres, the running of cost-price restaurants, the establishing of toy and shoe-making factories run on co-operative lines, and the founding of a day nursery.[25] Yet, despite her differences with her mother, Sylvia still craved her approval. Accompanied by Norah Smyth, she decided to go to Paris that Christmas and see Emmeline who was staying with Nurse Pine in Christabel's flat, Christabel being away on a lecture tour of the USA. According to Sylvia, her mother would speak of nothing but the war – despite 'perceiving the opposition in our hearts' – and in her vigorous defence of it, seemed 'a very Maenad ... with her flashing eyes'. The pacifist daughter was relieved when the meeting ended. 'We were distant from each other as though a thousand leagues had intervened.'[26] Sylvia was one of the 100 British women pacifists who had signed an open Christmas letter, published in *Jus Suffragii*, to the women of Germany and Austria. 'Do not let us forget our very anguish unites us. ... We must all urge that peace be made. ... We are yours in this sisterhood of sorrow.'[27] The sorrow that Emmeline and Sylvia felt about their opposing views, however, would never unite them.

Emmeline, like so many other people, had expected the war to be over soon. By the New Year of 1915, however, when it was apparent that this was not to be, she voiced more loudly her concerns about the way in which the government was handling the war effort. Her intense dislike and distrust of Asquith, still Prime Minister until his resignation in December 1916, had never lessened and she did not lose the opportunity to criticise his failure to mobilise women to enter men's jobs so that men would be free to go to the war front and replenish the heavy losses that had been sustained. Emmeline told Edith Shackleton, when interviewed by her in late January 1915, 'I'm not nursing soldiers. There are so many others to do that ... it is no more to be expected that our organisers should now necessarily take to knitting and nursing than that Mr. Asquith should set his Ministers to making Army boots or uniforms.' Emmeline's insistence that women should not be expected just to perform traditional womanly tasks was consistent with WSPU policy which had always worked along 'national lines'. She illustrated the point by comparing unfavourably the situation of women in Britain with that of women in France. In Paris, women worked as conductors on the trams, a condition of their employment being that their husbands should be serving in the army. 'It seems to me that the scheme would be practical on the London tramways, too – and, of course, we don't want it to stop at tramways.' Women could become lift operators, clerks or cashiers, indeed, serve as a reserve source of labour. 'Sex has nothing to do with patriotism or with the spirit of service. Women are just as eager to work for the nation as men are', she explained. 'Why should all their splendid energy go to waste or turn to bitterness because they are expected merely to look on in the national struggle and to soothe their feelings by petting the soldiers instead of doing the really hard work of which they are quite capable?'[28]

As Butler comments, this was not the language of the platform agitator and certainly not that of the woman who, only a few years earlier, had responded to a government rebuff by throwing stones through the windows of the official residence of the prime minister.[29] But Emmeline knew that the battle for women's suffrage could not be indefinitely delayed; and she was conscious of the anti-suffragist argument that women could not be given full citizenship since they did not fulfil some of the crucial duties of citizens, including defence of the nation. She wanted to make sure that women, through their war effort, won the respect of the nation, a view that was supported by news conveyed to her by Ethel Smyth. 'By the way', confided the musician, writing from her Woking cottage on Christmas Day, 'did I tell you that Mr. Asquith informed Lady Cunard that we shd. have the vote in 3 years – that he much regretted it because he thought it a mistake but … it had to be!'[30] Confident that victory was assured sometime in the future, Emmeline became during these war years, 'something of an elder stateswoman … regarded with no little respect and even with something like affection'.[31] Both the national and international press commented on this. With the headline 'England cheers Pankhurst; once despised, now loved as most gracious woman', the *Minneapolis Daily News* reported in March 1915:

> Every night Mrs. Pankhurst speaks at the Pavilion, the identical theater from which, every Monday afternoon two years ago, she was spirited away to prevent her from being mobbed. … She appears in various gowns, mostly black, all of exquisite cut. She invariably wears a lace shawl and from her neck hangs a lorgnet [*sic*], which she is never seen to use. There is elegance, poise and restraint in her appearance and in her speech. She is a changed Mrs. Pankhurst. And the England that once hooted her now greets her with cheers of welcome.[32]

Emmeline's demand for women's right to engage in war work, however, did not endear her to industrialists and trade unionists who opposed the entry of unskilled women into jobs traditionally held by men; in particular, since women usually earned less that half the wages of men, trade unionists feared that women employees would undermine their own wages which were predicated on the notion of the male breadwinner. Despite these problems, her efforts and those of others pressing for women's war work came to fruition when, on 18 March 1915, the Board of Trade issued a circular calling upon women able and willing to work to enter their names in a new Register of Women for War Service with a view to meeting both the present and future needs of national industry during the conflict.[33] A week later, when she was in Paris to greet Christabel who had just returned from America, Emmeline told Nancy Astor that the government's decision to mobilise women widened the scope of the WSPU which would hold special women's meetings to get them to enlist. 'As we are engaging halls now I shall be glad if Mr. Astor can let us have his promised cheque to meet these expenses', she stated tactfully. Emmeline also explained how *The Suffragette* would be relaunched to give a clear lead to women. 'Their natural love of peace is causing some suffragists to take action greatly to be deprecated. They are being made use of by very dreadful people without knowing it. This must be counteracted & the "Suffragette" will be useful for the purpose.'[34]

The theme of women suffragists and peace was very much in Emmeline's mind at this time since the well-known English pacifist, Emily Hobhouse, and some Dutch suffragists were organising an International Congress of Women to be held in The Hague from 28 until 30 April, in the hope of bringing peace. The decision split in two the women's movement world-wide. In Britain, Millicent Garrett Fawcett of the NUWSS promptly condemned the move, as did Emmeline. '[I]f you take part in any of these peace movements, you are playing the German game and helping Germany. ... It is for us to show a strong and determined front', she pronounced to loud applause at a speech delivered in Liverpool.[35] For Emmeline, further salt was rubbed into her wounds since Sylvia announced her intention of attending the conference while Adela also adhered to its aims. Emmeline had already been outspoken about what she termed 'the peace-at-any-price crowd' and emphasised that suffragettes supported the war so that 'for generations to come we may be spared war'.[36] She now lost no time in making her views public again to the press which applauded the stand she took. When interviewed by the *Sunday Pictorial* about the peace conference, she forcefully replied, 'It is unthinkable that English-women should meet German women to discuss terms of peace while the husbands, sons and brothers of those women are the men who are murdering our men on the seas and who have committed the awful horrors of the war in Belgium and elsewhere.' The reporter firmly endorsed Emmeline's views, including her public disapproval of Sylvia's intention to be present. 'It is the act of a true citizen, of a mother who deserves well of the State.'[37]

The Home Secretary, McKenna, once Emmeline's old enemy, now found himself in agreement with her views and so contrived to prevent British women travelling to the International Congress. Before the war, British travellers could travel abroad without a passport but fears about spying and other undesirable wartime activity led to the introduction of passports. When Sylvia applied for a passport to attend the conference, her application was refused while permission was withheld from the other British women delegates to board a ship to take them to The Hague. The few British women who did attend included those already in Holland and also Emmeline Pethick Lawrence, one-time Honorary Treasurer of the WSPU and one-time close friend of the WSPU leader. Mrs. Pethick Lawrence had been on a speaking tour of America and, with her husband, had joined the American delegation.[38]

Emmeline issued another call to national unity in *The Suffragette* which was relaunched on 16 April 1915 with the slogan that it was 'a thousand times more the duty of the militant Suffragettes to fight the Kaiser for the sake of liberty than it was to fight anti-Suffrage Governments'. In its pages was soon published a long list of the jobs, hitherto occupied by men, which women now held – railway clerk, railway porter, ticket collector, stationmaster, tram conductor, grocers' assistant, packer, messenger, night telephone operator, motor-van driver, lift attendant, butcher's assistant, railway carriage cleaner, post-girl, news-girl, munitions and armament worker, sheep-dipper, bank clerk, van-guard, clerk in government offices, signaller, cigar and wine department assistant in some of the big stores, and motor agents.[39] *The Suffragette* soon endorsed the war views of prominent politicians that the WSPU had once opposed, such as Lloyd George and Sir Edward Carson; like Emmeline and Christabel, these two men were critical of Asquith's leadership, especially from May 1915 when he decided to form a coalition government with the Conservative and Labour parties. When friends protested to Emmeline about Christabel's editorial line, she replied, 'I don't want her different or liable to her mother's human weaknesses. ... Thank God for her! She is the best bit of work I have done, *and I did not do her by myself.*'[40]

As Emmeline continued her campaigning, her oratory about nation states was often gendered, France being the feminine state threatened by 'the over-sexed, that is to say over-masculine, country of Germany'. Germany denied women the right to speak, or even think, as independent beings. '[T]he Kaiser has already assigned woman's place to the three K's, "Kinder, Kirche, Küche" (children, church and kitchen). This is woman's sphere. The affairs of the nation are no affair of hers.'[41] As Thebaud suggests, such rhetoric can be interpreted as expressing the hope that women might win the battle for the right to vote,[42] and indeed this was so. Emmeline would elaborate on this, as in a speech delivered at the London Polytechnic in June:

> Votes for Women and all that Votes for Women means ... is at stake in this country ... what we asking for and working for and longing for is to preserve these institutions which would admit of women having the Vote. If we lose this war then – and don't make any mistake about it – not only is the possibility of women voting going to disappear, but votes for men will be a thing of the past. There will be no such thing in this country.[43]

That June of 1915 was an especially significant and busy month for Emmeline as she spoke at a number of WSPU 'At Homes' as well as rallies attracting large crowds, as at Plymouth where she addressed a reported ten thousand people.[44] The government, she believed, was still too slow to enlist the skills of millions of capable women who were ready to serve their country. She again demanded universal war service for women and appropriate training, so that women could enter jobs traditionally held by men, especially in munitions factories. She regarded the latter as particularly important since Lloyd George, recently appointed Minister of Munitions, had introduced the Munitions Bill in parliament and issued a call only to men to enrol for such work.[45] An article by Christabel on this theme which appeared in *The Observer* on 27 June 1915 attracted the eye of the King whose secretary wrote the following day to Lloyd George, 'His Majesty feels strongly that we ought to do more to enlist women-workers. ... The King was wondering whether it would be possible or advisable for you to make use of Mrs. Pankhurst.'[46] Lloyd George asked Sir James Murray, MP, a friend of his and of the WSPU, to act as an emissary. When Emmeline received the invitation, asking her to meet Lloyd George, she was astounded; this was the man who was partly responsible for bringing her near to death's door and for the still poor state of her health, and now he was asking for her help. It was hard for her to give an acceptance, although she did. Accompanied by Annie Kenney, Emmeline heard about the grave situation at the war front where men were being sacrificed for want of munitions while the munitions factories were short of labour, due to strong industrial and trade union opposition to the employment of women. Lloyd George asked Emmeline if she would help by organising a great procession of women to demonstrate both their readiness and their wish to engage in war work, especially munitions work.[47] £3,000 would be provided to cover costs. Always a practical politician, Emmeline felt she could do business with the man that she had once so distrusted. 'I pointed out that no demonstration of the sort is needed to rouse women', she explained to Nancy Astor. 'They are ready to respond without it but he wishes us to do it for the effect it will have on "public opinion" meaning of course men.'[48]

As Tickner comments, it was convenient for Lloyd George to exploit the Pankhursts' organisational skills and their claim to speak for women while it also suited the WSPU to carve out a place for itself in the limelight, deliberately courting the support of those 'not actively concerned with the question of "women's rights" in ordinary circumstances'; the 'right to serve' march, she continues, might *almost* be described as the first suffrage procession since the NUWSS pilgrimage of 1913.[49] The significance of Emmeline's stand on women's war work was not lost on the anti-suffragists. Mrs. Humphry Ward confessed to Lord Cromer, another arch anti, that Mrs. Pankhurst and Christabel 'have been extra-ordinarily clever! – and I *know* that the line they have taken in actively supporting the war, and trouncing Mrs. Fawcett's pacifists, have won over a number of people'. She believed that it would not be so easy to fight the WSPU, after the war was over, since all their militancy could be forgotten – 'I sometimes wonder in my secret thoughts', Mrs Ward confided, 'whether we are not already beaten!'[50]

With just a fortnight to plan the procession and deputation to Lloyd George, to be held on 17 July, the staff in the WSPU office swung into action under the direction of Grace Roe. Lord Northcliffe, the newspaper proprietor and also a fierce critic of Asquith, was approached for his support, which he gladly gave; he also promised that when the issue of women's enfranchisement was raised again, his newspapers would support the campaign. On notepaper headed 'Women's War Service', with the address as Lincoln's Inn House, Emmeline sent out an appeal for volunteers, 're-casting' the procession as the WSPU's rather than the government's initiative.[51] She had lost none of her old touch as in direct, simple language she noted that, if women were allowed to help the war effort, it could make the difference between defeat and victory. 'So grave is our national danger, and so terrible is the loss of precious lives at the front due to shortage of munitions, that Mr. Lloyd George, as Minister of Munitions, has been asked to receive a deputation and hear women's demand for the right to make munitions and render other War Service. ... Will you help?'[52] *The Suffragette* printed a call for 700 banner bearers, 300 marshals, 300 paper sellers and 400 young women dressed in white and announced that it was 'every woman's duty' to march in the War Service Procession.[53]

Emmeline was determined that this rally, which would include some ninety bands playing hymns of the Allies and patriotic airs, would attract the maximum publicity; she was not disappointed. Despite the high wind and driving rain, the press coverage of the event was widespread and ecstatic, beyond the 'wildest dreams' of the efficient WSPU Organisers.[54] 'There has never been a procession like it', enthused *The Observer*. 'The line of women, four abreast, stretched along the Embankment from Westminster to Blackfriars. They were women of all classes – ladies of title, working women, and in the majority women and girls of the middle classes.' It was a 'perfect triumph of organisation', claimed the *Daily Telegraph*, 'and demonstrated once more in a particularly striking manner the capacity of women to plan big undertakings on successful lines'. All of the 20,000 marchers, clad in macintoshes or cloaks, were divided into 125 contingents, each woman carrying a flag of the patriotic colours of the Union Jack – red, white or blue – rather than the more familiar purple, white and green; sometimes the colours were massed together, sometimes mingled. Some carried banners with texts that declared, 'Russian women are serving their country, why cannot we?', 'For men must fight and women must work', 'Shells made by a wife may save her husband's life', and 'What women are doing in France we can do'. In the pageant of the Allies, one of the most striking figures was the Madonna-like woman draped in dark purple, bare footed in the mud, carrying a torn flag, who typified Belgium at war, mourning over her children. Emmeline walked immediately behind the pageant, with Annie Kenney, Lady Parsons, Mrs. Mansel, Mrs. Grant and Miss Baker. Crowds of people, sometimes six deep, lined the route, cheering especially the large contingent of nurses.[55]

By six o'clock, about 60,000 people had assembled in front of the platform built in the gardens of the Ministry of Munitions. Emmeline was inside, having led the deputation to Lloyd George. She put her case 'clearly and concisely', reported the *Daily Chronicle*, and there was no mention of the vote. 'We want to make no bargain to serve our country', the astute WSPU leader insisted. A roar of cheering went up when Emmeline, Lloyd George and other members of the deputation came out onto the platform.[56] A jovial and accommodating Minister of Munitions welcomed the deputation, congratulating them on the procession and humorously pointing out that he had been a victim on occasions of the organising capacity of women which was so amply demonstrated that day. He also explained that although the government had agreed to pay the same rate of wage for piece-work to women as to men, Mrs. Pankhurst had asked for more than that, namely the same rate of wages for time-work. A confident Emmeline, determined not to be putty in the hands of the Munitions Minister, immediately interrupted him, expanding on her point that equal pay for time-work was a means to prevent the sweating of women in munitions factories; untrained and unskilled women could not be expected to turn out as much as the skilled men they replaced and were in danger of working longer hours in trying to do so. An amiable Lloyd George regretted that the government could not grant equal pay for time-work but gallantly emphasised that 'Mrs. Pankhurst is perfectly right in insisting that there should be a fixed minimum, which would guarantee that we should not utilise the services of women in order to get cheap labour.'[57]

The cordial relationship between the Minister of Munitions and the WSPU leader was commented upon favourably by the press, including the *New York Journal* which ran the headline 'The Ablest Woman, the Ablest Man in England, Once They Were Enemies, War Has Made Them Friends'.[58] The day after the procession, the press carried an article by Emmeline that expanded further her views about the importance of equal pay, and her vision for the future. 'If at the end of this war there can be ushered in, for the benefit of men and women alike, a reign of liberty, equality, fraternity, to adopt the three watchwords of our allies the French, then we shall find ourselves in the essentials of life not poorer, but infinitely richer than we have ever been before.'[59] Her message struck a resonant chord in the British public. She was hailed as a patriotic heroine, a national asset in the country's hour of need, praise that grated with her pacifist daughters. Sylvia had already written to Lloyd George trying to secure, without success, pledges as to equal pay for both piece-work and time-work. Adela had joined the recently formed Women's Peace Party. While her mother often ended rallies such as that of 17 July by joining in the singing of the National Anthem, Adela's peace meetings usually closed with the singing of the American anti-war ditty, 'I didn't raise my son to be a soldier / I brought him up to be my pride and joy / Who dares to put a musket on his shoulder / To kill some other mother's darling boy?'[60]

Emmeline's estrangement from her two youngest daughters must have brought her sadness and, perhaps, partly accounts for her decision earlier in the year to set up a home for fifty illegitimate female children. But, probably more significantly, her long years of experience as a Poor Law Guardian and Registrar of Births and Deaths in Manchester, when she saw first hand the stigma and sufferings of orphan girls and unmarried mothers, still haunted her. Emmeline's fervent desire to do something practical for the oppressed of her sex was fired during the early months of 1915 by frequent discussions in the press about the alleged problem of 'war babies', that is children born to unmarried mothers who had been made pregnant by soldiers.[61] Early in May she explained her scheme to a sceptical Nancy Astor, stressing that she had no desire to relieve women or men from responsibility for their sexual behaviour but simply wanted to do something 'for illegitimate children. ... There is among them an appalling death rate & of those who survive I should think the majority become criminals & prostitutes. I want these children saved & made useful citizens.'[62]

Emmeline similarly tried to convert Ethel Smyth to her project but Ethel was antagonistic to the idea, feeling it was a mistake in war time to underline the 'delinquencies' of soldiers whose illegitimate children were taken care of in orphanages. 'She did not like her ideas being adversely judged', recollected the musician, 'what autocrat does?' Emmeline sarcastically told Ethel that such a scheme would not appeal to someone who 'preferred dogs to babies' but Ethel was worried that her fifty-seven-year-old friend, without a steady income and no capital, was taking on too much responsibility. 'However, as well as try to hold up an avalanche with a child's spade as persuade Mrs. Pankhurst out of any idea that had once taken root in her mind.'[63]

In the 14 May issue of *The Suffragette* a determined Emmeline outlined her plans and called upon WSPU members for financial support for the scheme.[64] But few were enthusiastic. On the afternoon of 3 June, Emmeline held a public meeting at the London Palladium, during which she deplored the 'lamentable lack of public spirit' for her project and announced that she herself would adopt four little orphan girls if four ladies of means would offer a modest sum to maintain each child, trusting to her to bring up the children and to give them a fair start in life. She favoured the Montessori system of schooling which, she believed, would give a sound preparation for entry into the new world she saw opening up to women.[65]

Emmeline, accompanied by Kitty Marshall, visited a home for unwanted and homeless children and selected four female babies who were eventually brought back to her London address, namely Nurse Pine's nursing home. The birth certificates of the girls were destroyed, and they were given new names – Kathleen King, Flora Mary Gordon, Joan Pembridge and Elizabeth Tudor – and also new birth dates. When someone asked Emmeline why she was taking on such an awesome task, having long since brought up her own family, Emmeline, who adored small children, replied, 'My dear, I wonder I didn't take forty.'[66] Financial support from WSPU members, however, was sparse, the few offers of help soon dwindling to nothing. A group of 'Ex-prisoners and Active Members of the W.S.P.U.', angry about the autocratic way in which Emmeline was attempting to foist on their shoulders what they saw as an ill-conceived venture, printed a leaflet protesting about the way in which she was 'neglecting the Cause of Votes for Women in order to take upon herself, in the name of the Union, without consulting its Members, responsibilities which belong to the State'. Voteless women were asked to 'think twice' before contributing to the upkeep of the war babies and to 'call upon Mrs. Pankhurst to refound the Women's Social and Political Union on a new and democratic basis'.[67]

Emmeline was both hurt and angry at this response; accustomed to being given the money she needed for suffrage work, she never expected to be refused the smaller amount necessary for the babies. The criticisms from some members of the WSPU about her autocratic style of leadership were conveniently ignored as in late July and August, on doctor's advice, she returned to Harrogate to complete an interrupted cure for her still not robust health. 'I hope to be very fit & energetic after all the baths, electric massage etc. that I am having', she explained to Nancy Astor. Emmeline also wrote to WSPU member Elsie Duval, apologising for not being able to attend her wedding. 'I hope that you & your future husband may have all good fortune & spend together a long happy & useful life. Certainly mutual affection & the sharing of high ideal [sic] is the best security for happiness in marriage.'[68] The bride-to-be had written to her some-time earlier saying that she and her fiancé, Hugh Franklin, would feel honoured if Emmeline would be a witness to their wedding and would even fix the date to fit in with the WSPU leader's plans. The wedding eventually took place at the West London Synagogue on 28 September 1915.

Just two days previously, Keir Hardie had died, a broken man. For some time his health had been failing; early in the war, which he strongly opposed, he had had a stroke. Towards the end of May, when the Labour Party decided to join a coalition government, he announced that he would no longer attend parliament but return home to Scotland; here he was nursed by his wife during the final months of his life when he was diagnosed as suffering from a nervous breakdown. Before Hardie left London, he and Sylvia had had a sad, tongue-tied farewell. When Sylvia then discovered that Christabel had reprinted in a July issue of *The Suffragette* a *Punch* cartoon that portrayed the Kaiser giving her old lover a bag of money, she was greatly pained. She wrote to her mother, protesting and pointing out that Hardie was dying and, according to Sylvia, Emmeline did not reply.[69] Perhaps, with Hardie's death, Emmeline reflected on their past friendship when they had stood side by side at socialist and suffrage meetings, but she was prag-matic enough to know that times were different now and that she had a different job to do, especially since too few of the thousands of women who had volun-teered for munitions work had been taken on. She blamed the opposition of the trade unions for the slow pace of change and at a speech at the London Pavilion in the early autumn, even made a threat of a return of militancy:

> Women are exercising far more self-control and self-restraint than perhaps some people give them credit for, but it is extremely trying to

their patience. We hear of strikes and riots amongst men ... what if women lost patience and began to riot – not for money, not in order to have easier conditions, but because they were not allowed to work at the time of their country's need! We hope it won't come to that.[70]

Emmeline temporarily lost her voice when campaigning with Flora Drummond and Norah Dacre Fox in South Wales that late September and October. The work in a strongly 'Red' area was arduous, and she felt obliged to write privately to Lloyd George to warn him that strikes and rumours of strikes filled the air. 'Mrs. Pankhurst ... says there are districts where the people simply don't care whether the Germans are beaten or not', recorded Frances Stevenson, secretary and mistress to Lloyd George, and a supporter of the parliamentary vote for women. 'She says they are sulky and difficult to handle, and will not sing the national anthem.'[71] Such anti-patriotic feeling was alien to Emmeline. She had worked hard to transform the WSPU into an organisation that supported the war effort and brought women into war work, a process that took a further step when *The Suffragette* was renamed *Britannia*, the first issue appearing on 15 October 1915. As Gilbert notes, the 'female intuition' expressed in that renaming, that women were now 'coextensive' with the state, a female state, a Britannia not a Union Jack, was accurate; women would be enfranchised after the war was over, in 1918.[72] Emmeline felt it necessary to explain to the WSPU membership the necessity for the change of name, as in her letter to Mrs. Badley. 'This more comprehensive title ... is adopted in the name of British Women's equality of political right and duty, also as a pledge of devotion to the nation of which we are privileged to be members and through which we as British citizens can do our best work for humanity and human progress.'[73] Edited by Christabel, who lived in Paris, *Britannia*, with the slogan 'For King, for Country, For Freedom', became not only more patriotic but profoundly anti-German, in a way that is offensive to modern ears. Blunt criticisms continued to be made against Prime Minister Asquith's leadership of the government and against the Foreign Secretary, Sir Edward Grey, whose resignation was demanded, as well as 'the disappearance' of Sir Eyre Crowe, the 'principal permanent servant' at the Foreign Office, 'who is connected with Germany both by birth and marriage'. In order to save the country, it was demanded that decisions concerning naval no less than military and diplomatic policy should be made and announced by the Allies jointly, instead of being made and announced by Britain alone.[74]

Emmeline had always held a deep compassion for the poor and the oppressed and her sympathy now moved from the cause of illegitimate children in Britain to the plight of women and children in Serbia, a small Balkan country which the Austrians had been determined to destroy at the outbreak of war and which, she believed, the Asquith government had failed to help. At a meeting at the London Pavilion on 28 October, she loudly condemned Grey's decision not to send British troops to the stricken country, a policy she believed to be dictated by Crowe, 'a man of German birth and German associations'. She asked her audience, 'How can you expect the working people of this country to be loyal to the country when they have grave reason to believe that you have Germans and Pro-Germans directing the foreign policy of the country?' Calling upon Grey and his colleagues to resign, she then pointed out that Britain had entered the war for the sake of small nationalities, for freedom and liberty, and that it should now take the honourable course of sending a sufficient force of troops to Serbia. Further, she insisted that the conduct of the war should be in the hands of a strong war council made up of the representatives of all the Allied nations engaged in the war – and that they should sit in Paris.[75] A copy of *Britannia* in which Emmeline's speech was reported was acquired by the Home Office.

The WSPU arranged for a 'great patriotic meeting' to be held at the Royal Albert Hall, on 18 November, 'to demand the loyal and vigorous conduct of the war', a call that most newspapers, including *The Times*, applauded.[76] However, six days before the scheduled event, Emmeline sent a letter to interested parties making it plain that the meeting would focus on the WSPU's concern about the 'betrayal of Serbia', a firm indication that 'the Prime Minister and Sir Edward Grey are unfit for the great and responsible positions they hold'.[77] The proprietors cancelled the letting. The London Pavilion and other large halls in Central London also refused to let to the WSPU which now had to fall back on small meetings held in its new headquarters in Great Portland Street.[78] Newspapers which had once praised Emmeline now turned against her. A typical response was that of the *Morning Advertiser* that claimed that her attack on Asquith and Grey, was a 'wrong turning' since it would 'foment internecine trouble, a thing to be avoided at all costs at the present juncture'. Arguing for the necessity of a united front, it was pointed out that her letter would create divisions within the British camp, indicating to the enemy that the nerve of the British nation was destroyed. The move was particularly regretted since Mrs. Pankhurst and her fellow-workers of the WSPU had called a truce with the government on the outbreak of war and had done excellent work during the last fifteen months.[79] But these were not the only criticisms being voiced against Emmeline.

Many rank-and-file members of the WSPU were again expressing concerns about her leadership of the WSPU, as the *Daily News and Leader* reported. It was alleged that Emmeline, who was still Honorary Treasurer of the WSPU, was in charge of between £15,000 to £20,000 of Union funds. She had always declared, it was asserted, that women could only be governed by consent, and that her own autocracy was only justified by the consent of the members. 'Now she has used that autocracy to divert the funds of the Union to purposes for which they were never subscribed without making the smallest attempt to discover whether the members have consented or not.' Many of Mrs. Pankhurst's former supporters, the article continued, 'feel for these reasons that her present power over an organisation which she has no moral, or possibly even legal right to control is fraught with danger to the community and should immediately cease'. No name was given of the informant about these matters but on 22 October 1915, WSPU member Rose Lamartine Yates had chaired a meeting of like-minded colleagues who had passed a resolution, later forwarded by registered post to Emmeline and Christabel, protesting against the WSPU's abandonment of the cause of women's suffrage and asking for an audited statement of the accounts. No reply had been received.[80] Six days later, at a Union meeting held at the London Pavilion on 28 October 1915, another incident had occurred that caused anger amongst some members. Mary Leigh attempted to ask a question and was accused by Emmeline of supporting the enemy, Germany. '[T]hat woman is a pro German and should leave the hall. ... I denounce you as a pro German and I wish to forget that such a person ever existed.' Many of those present, as well as ex-Union members, were shocked by Emmeline's public condemnation of an old comrade. Emmeline was asked to retract her statement and to offer an apology at the next meeting at which several women interrupted her speech, repeating the demand. 'I will not apologise', announced a proud Emmeline, to loud applause from different parts of the theatre. The interruptions continued for some time, until the protesters left the theatre.[81] But the criticisms being now so strongly expressed against Emmeline and Christabel would not die down, especially when another 'pro-German' denouncement was made, this time against Annie Bell who had been a hunger striking suffragette. When Annie tried to attend the next Union meeting, she was refused admittance and, since she protested vigorously, was arrested for obstruction and sentenced to a month's imprisonment. She secured a release in five days by going on a hunger strike. The parallel with her suffragette past, 'even down to minor details, is painfully obvious' observed the press.[82]

A group of discontented Union members decided that they should take matters into their own hands. On 25 November 1915, Elinor Penn Gaskell chaired a meeting of the dissidents, at which a manifesto voicing concerns about the control of finances and the formation of WSPU policy was unanimously approved and adopted. It was also stated that 'the time has now come' when Christabel Pankhurst could resign as one of the leaders of the WSPU, 'or else offer a clear explanation to the members of her continued absence from this country, at a time when the services of all women of capacity and goodwill are so sorely needed here'. Emmeline was hurt by the comments, but she was too autocratic to bend to the requests of her critics, too accustomed to having her own way, too old to change her style of leadership, and too confident to question what she was doing. As she explained to a *Weekly Dispatch* interviewer, 'The Women's Social and Political Union is a fighting body and as such it must have autocratic control if it is to wage war successfully. ... When going into battle a general does not take a vote of his soldiers to see whether they approve of his plans. They are there to obey his orders.' She continued: 'That is how the W.S.P.U. has been run and that is how it will continue to be run. Any member who does not approve of our plans must acquiesce or go. There is no time to waste in talk.' She also explained that since the war began the WSPU's work had been diverted into new channels, and the funds contributed for suffrage work had been set aside and not touched for the purposes of the war campaigns. 'If we issue a report and balance-sheet for the year 1914–15 it will mean introducing a record of the suffrage work before the war, and that is most undesirable during the present truce. All our accounts are periodically audited by a firm of accountants.'[83] The statement was not enough to silence her critics in the WSPU, one group of whom left to set up 'The Suffragettes of the WSPU' and another, in March 1916, formed the 'Independent WSPU'; both of the new societies sought to revive the suffrage campaign. Nor did Emmeline's statement quieten unease in government circles about the virulent attacks being made on Asquith and Grey in the 10 December issue of *Britannia*, still being edited by Christabel in Paris. On 15 December, the police seized *Britannia's* printing press which had been installed in a garage in Kensington, an action that was later defended by Herbert Samuel, the Secretary of State for the Home Department, as necessary under the Defence of the Realm Act (DORA) since the paper was printing statements which were 'absolutely untrue' and 'calculated to prejudice our relations with our Allies'. Hereafter *Britannia* appeared in a variety of sizes and types, sometimes just two pages of foolscap produced on a hand-worked duplicating machine. When a second press seizure failed to prevent its publication, Samuel arranged with the post office for issues to be stopped in the mail.[84]

It was a relief to Emmeline when, on 6 January 1916, she sailed from Liverpool on the *St Paul* to New York, to begin a seven-month lecture tour in America and Canada, principally to raise funds for Serbia. This small country, which stood in the way of Germany's push to the East, was fighting back bravely, despite the shortage of munitions and food. Emmeline was to plead especially for the plight of its starving and homeless children, women and elderly folk. On the free days she was not so occupied, she planned to give lectures on social hygiene, the takings from which would be used to help support her second family. Emmeline was accompanied on her visit by Mr. Miyatovich, the former Serbian Secretary of Foreign Affairs, and his attaché, and Joan Wickham, her secretary; Jessie Kenney went in advance to arrange visits. As in 1913, Emmeline was detained when she arrived in New York, on Ellis Island, but this time only for three hours. Although she felt indignant about this treatment, it was soon forgotten as she met – and charmed – the American press. Emmeline Pankhurst looked 'as much as ever like a Watteau shepherdess, with lines of experience in her face and dressed in modern clothes' commented one reporter while another suggested that she looked 'younger than her years' with a face that was 'alert, smiling, sanguine'. 'Mrs. Pankhurst is ideal grandmother' ran another headline as it was pointed out that Emmeline, who had just received from Catherine Pine a photo of the 'war babies', doted on them. For Eleanor Garrison, however, Emmeline looked considerably older, especially with her china front teeth.[85]

In the course of her American tour, Emmeline moved in a variety of settings as in Brooklyn, where she spoke under the auspices of the Imperial Order of

Daughters of the Empire (whose motto was 'One Flag, one Throne, one Empire'), in Philadelphia, where tea was given in her honour by the Equal Franchise Society, and at Bryn Mawr College, where she met the young women students and was the guest of its president, Dr. Carey Thomas.[86] In Canada, where she arrived on 1 March, speaking to large audiences in places such as Montreal, Quebec, Ottawa, Hamilton, London, Sarnia, Toronto and Saskatchewan, her reception was equally enthusiastic. 'Mrs. Pankhurst gave a magnificent address in First Methodist Church' ran a headline for the *Hamilton Daily Times*. She left an impression that 'will never perish. Of course, the militant suffragette was always in evidence, but it was overshadowed by the militant patriot. Her address was full of fire.'[87] Nevertheless, the militant patriot had not forgotten the women's suffrage cause since she often emphasised, as in Saskatchewan, that war service in Britain was bound up with the citizenship of women.[88]

During the course of her tour, as Emmeline pleaded for the starving and homeless of Serbia, she could raise large donations. '[I]t is the women of the invaded countries who have shown to the world the finest example, of the power of womanhood', she told one audience. 'In Belgium and in Serbia to-day are women who have suffered unspeakable torture at the hands of the enemy.'[89] Such views were distinctly at odds with those recently expressed by Adela in her anti-war, anti-British Empire book *Put up the sword* in which she was 'scornful' of accounts of German atrocities, but ready to believe those of the British, and prepared to forgive German soldiers, not those of the Allies, for any incidents of killing and rape.[90] Sylvia too was causing her mother sorrow. The ELFS had recently been renamed the Worker's Suffrage Federation (WSF) and was active in organising anti-war protests. The 20,000 strong demonstration in Trafalgar Square on 8 April 1916, with Sylvia as a key figure on the platform, was organised in opposition to the British government's introduction of conscription, the Munitions Act and DORA. When Emmeline on her tour heard the news of Sylvia's stand, she felt ashamed and angry. Immediately she cabled Christabel, 'Strongly repudiate and condemn Sylvia's foolish and unpatriotic conduct. Regret & cannot prevent use of name. Make this public.' The cable was reprinted in *Britannia* and reported elsewhere in the press.[91]

Emmeline must have hoped that her second family would give her another chance to create the home she longed for. 'I do so long to come home', she wrote to Ethel, 'but how can I till I have earned enough to educate the babes and keep myself in my old age?'[92] Yet her plan to earn enough money during her tour, for the support of the children, fell by the wayside. '[S]omehow when I came to it', she explained to Ethel, 'I couldn't go in for personal money-making in war-time, so I stick to considering the lilies of the field, as usual.'[93] Such a decision was characteristic of Emmeline whose life was to become increasingly burdened by financial difficulties. During the militant struggle for the vote, which had occupied eleven years of her life, she had rarely thought about her future; death for the cause, she believed, was her 'inevitable lot'.[94] But now, at fifty-eight years old, she was forced to think of how to provide for her old age –

and for her second family. When she returned to England in the summer of 1916 she set about making a home for herself, Catherine Pine and the babies by renting and furnishing a house at 50 Clarendon Road, Holland Park, London. Just before she moved in, Emmeline confessed to Ethel, 'All these years I have persuaded myself that I did not want a home of my own. But now that I can have one I am all impatience to get into it.'[95] Her joy, once she moved in, was evident as when she wrote to Una Dugdale, now also a mother, later in the year. '[A]t last I have a settled home ... & I shall be delighted if you will come & see me one day before long. ... Now that you know all about babies I should like to show you ours & have a talk about all the Union is doing in the war.'[96] But the maintenance of 50 Clarendon Road over the next couple of years was always a struggle for Emmeline who had to earn her living by lecturing, a very precarious activity during wartime.

As Grayzel observes, the introduction of conscription by the British government had radically altered the relationship between the franchise and military service. Since parliamentary voting rights were based in property qualifications and length of residence, as well as age, large numbers of men did not possess electoral rights at the beginning of the war; once conscription was introduced, debates about how suffrage, including women's suffrage, should be related to military service and patriotic action resurfaced.[97] Emmeline's efforts in demanding women's war service made an essential contribution to the context of these debates although it would appear that it was others who formally raised the issue of women's and adult suffrage in 1916, including members of the NUWSS, the US, the WSF and the Suffragettes of the WSPU. In May 1916, Millicent Garrett Fawcett had sent a letter on the subject of women's suffrage to Asquith who promptly denied that the government had any intention of introducing a reform bill. However, revision of the franchise was considered urgent since large numbers of men serving abroad in the trenches and men who had changed their residences to take up war work in new locales were inadvertently disenfranchised. On 14 August, Asquith, in a confusing speech, stated that although he had 'no special desire or predisposition to bring women within the pale of the franchise', he had received a great many representations from those authorised to speak for them which presented a 'reasonable' case. '[T]he women of this country', he continued, 'have rendered as effective service in the prosecution of the War as any other class of the community.' Nevertheless, he also warned that 'nothing could be more injurious to the best interests of the country ... than that the floodgates should be opened on all those vast complicated questions of the franchise ... at this stage of the War.'[98]

Emmeline listened in disbelief. She had heard the hated Asquith too many times before ever to trust him again. The women's cause, she insisted, had nothing to do with the case of soldiers and sailors. Before the war, Asquith was an old hand at this kind of reasoning – he used the question of more votes for men to 'dish' the women who wanted votes and now he was reversing the process by using the question of votes for women to 'dish' the men who were heroically sacrificing themselves for the nation.[99] She therefore authorised Commander Bellairs, an MP, to say in the House of Commons that she, on behalf of the WSPU, repudiated the Prime Minister's statement and would not allow the women's case to be used 'to prevent soldiers and sailors from being given the vote'.[100] The government now decided to refer discussion of franchise reform to an all-party committee of thirty-two MPs and peers, chaired by the Speaker of the Commons, which first met in October 1916 and reported early in the New Year. Emmeline, the practical politician, made a strategic decision; she held aloof from these proceedings since she believed that 'a certain detachment' on her part would give 'more effect' to any threat of 'potential, post-war militancy'.[101] Instead of engaging in deliberations about the terms on which women should be given the franchise, she busied herself by continuing her campaigning and voicing her concerns about Asquith's leadership.

On Sunday 10 September Emmeline spoke to large crowds gathered in Hyde Park at a meeting to demand the recall to England of the fiercely pro-British Labour Prime Minister of Australia, Billy Hughes; Hughes was against a compromise peace and argued that victory could be hastened if more men were conscripted and sent to the war front. Emmeline and Christabel wanted Hughes to join the Asquith government, not to prop it up indefinitely, but to bring some 'common sense, foresight, sanity, and determination where those qualities are conspicuously absent'.[102] That autumn, when Hughes announced a referendum on conscription in Australia, Adela vigorously opposed such a move. A sad and angry Emmeline, campaigning throughout England, asking people to sign memorials to support the recall of Hughes as well as for contributions to a victory fund, had no choice but to condemn the views of her daughter. 'I am ashamed of Adela and repudiate her', she cabled the Australian prime minister. 'Wish you all success. Make any use of this.'[103] Adela, reflecting on these events some seventeen years later, cast a light on the disagreement:

> Poor mother was terribly angry at my anti-conscription views and attitudes. I know now that her attitude was ridiculous – but it was the family attitude – Cause First and human relations nowhere. Her new Cause meant as much to her as the old one and she was as impatient of opposition. But after all was that not inevitable? I was young; she was old and our points of view could not be the same. Tolerance was certainly not to be learned in the school in which she had been trained. If she had been tolerant and broadminded, she could not have been the leader of the Suffragettes. She had nearly forgotten me as a daughter – we had never lived together for so many years – and I must confess, I had largely forgotten her as a mother and regarded her as a Leader and a public woman.[104]

Although Emmeline spoke on 1 October at the Queen's Hall, in support of the demand for votes for sailors and soldiers,[105] she was also particularly concerned that autumn about the war situation in Greece and Romania – and about the spread of VD amongst the troops. The issue of venereal diseases, of course, had been raised as a key theme in the later years of the WSPU's militant campaign, and so she had no hesitation in putting her name, alongside other well-known women such as Margaret Mcmillan, Mrs. Lloyd George and Dr. Flora Murray, to a letter published in *The Times* inviting 'all mothers and wives' to join in demanding notification of the disease. 'Soldiers' mothers write that they have given their sons to die for the Empire, but not like this.' It cannot be generally known that the disease is now 'very largely spread by girls of between 15 and 18 years of age. Can we wait while these mere children ... become the mothers of the future generation, and give birth to children more miserable than themselves?'[106]

Christabel in Paris continued in *Britannia* her attacks on Asquith and Grey, claiming they were giving Germany a free hand in the Balkans and threatening to bring ruin to the British Empire. On the 13 December 1916, the offices of the printers were again raided, the police seizing all the printed matter and breaking up the type.[107] In spite of this difficulty, the paper was still printed. It was an important part of Emmeline's and Christabel's strategy that *Britannia* should continue its anti-government attacks, pointing out that the war effort was being mismanaged; it might force the resignation of Asquith and other ministers and it also gave some support to Emmeline's threat that, once peace came again, she could 'reassemble her party' and those troublesome women could 'begin militancy where it had left off'.[108] Emmeline was relieved the December day that Asquith resigned as Prime Minister, to be replaced by Lloyd George, but still concerned about the credentials of some members of the Foreign Office. She went to see the jubilant newspaper proprietor Lord Northcliffe, who claimed that the campaign he had mounted through the right-wing newspapers he owned, had been effective. '[H] was quite like a lunatic, bouncing up and down on the leather seat of his arm-chair, crying out, "I did it!", timing the "I" to the down-bounce.' An embarrassed Emmeline remarked that the worst of the lot, the Foreign Secretary, was still in office, and was some-what startled when Northcliffe leapt up and shouted, 'Don't you worry, my dear girl, I'll get 'em all out!'[109] When, in the New Year of 1917, Christabel returned from Paris to live with Emmeline, at 50 Clarendon Road, she was delighted – and grateful. *Britannia* had been raided again, and life at WSPU headquarters was becoming increasingly difficult. Emmeline, as Honorary Treasurer of the WSPU, was still writing begging letters to members and supporters, asking for donations to carry on 'our Patriotic work',[110] and so was pleased to have her patriotic daughter by her side.

Some welcoming news abroad about women's enfranchisement greeted Emmeline that New Year, namely that Manitoba had granted women the vote, a move soon followed by other Canadian provinces, and also New York. In Britain too, the attitude towards women's suffrage had changed; Emmeline's policy of campaigning for women's right to serve the nation in its time of crisis had paid off as many antis recanted their views. The war effort now offered a 'face-saving reason for owning up to the inevitable'.[111] True to her principle that the WSPU would suspend campaigning for women's suffrage until the war was over, Emmeline refused to join the joint committee of all the suffrage societies, established early in 1917 as a means of presenting a united front on the women's suffrage issue to the Speaker's Conference, due to report at the end of January. On the advice of this Conference, a formula was adopted to require a higher age qualification for women's right to vote than that which applied to men. Thus the report included unanimous recommendations to abolish the property qualification for men, to require only six months' residence in property valued at £10 a year, to enfranchise soldiers and sailors and to confer – by a majority rather than unanimous decision – 'some measure of woman's suffrage', with an age bar of thirty or thirty-five and an implicit property qualification that would enfranchise about 7 million women.[112] Although the restrictions on women's voting caused a lot of dissent amongst suffragists, Emmeline distanced herself from the ensuing discussion so that the WSPU was not initially included in the list of women's suffrage societies which the NUWSS had called upon to form a deputation to Lloyd George on 29 March 1917.

Earlier that month, Emmeline had had other matters on her mind, namely a damage limitation exercise in regard to the WSPU. She was a witness in the trial of Alice Wheeldon and her daughter, Hettie, socialist feminists and one time Union members, who were accused of plotting to assassinate Lloyd George and Arthur Henderson, a member of the Cabinet. Emmeline was anxious that bad publicity about suffragettes could wreck the recent work she had undertaken to promote the WSPU as a patriotic and responsible organisation, whose members could be reintegrated into society. She stood in the dock at the trial, denying a statement made to the witness for the prosecution that the WSPU had spent £500 trying to poison Lloyd George. 'The Women's Social and Political Union regards the Prime Minister's life as of the greatest value in the present grave crisis', she pleaded, 'and its members would if necessary to do so, take great risks themselves to protect it from danger.'[113] Although Alice Wheeldon, but not Hettie, was found guilty and sentenced to 10 years' penal servitude, she was later released, on Lloyd George's orders, after serving nine months.

Once the trial was out of the way, Emmeline decided to write to Millicent Garrett Fawcett, asking if they could meet to discuss the women's suffrage issue. 'Wise & limited action at this moment when change is in the air at home & abroad may win our cause', she stated.[114] Shortly before the 29 March, the day scheduled for the deputation to the Prime Minister, 10 Downing Street rang up Ray Strachey, one of the honorary secretaries of the NUWSS, to say that Lloyd George would receive together all the societies wanting to see him, '& also Mrs. Pankhurst'. Ray confided to her mother, '[O]ne and all objected to Mrs Pankhurst, and I had to go and see her and make an arrangement by which she came in, but was not part of, the deputation.'[115] On the day, Emmeline cast all quibbling aside as she thanked Lloyd George, in the name of the WSPU, for dealing with the question of women's suffrage in a practical way:

> [A]lthough in times of peace we should want to debate every item of a bill ... in war time we want to see this thing done as quickly as possible, with as little dispute and as little difference of opinion as possible. ... And so we ask you, Mr. Lloyd George, to give such a Government measure to the House of Commons to vote upon as you feel to be just and practicable in the war circumstances ... whatever you think can be passed ... we are ready to accept. ... In this room, where so many women have come, one cannot help feeling that there might possibly be amongst us the spirits of those women who have died without seeing the result of their labours and their sacrifices. It will be a wonderful thing if in war time – just as in Canada – just as it will come in Russia – it should come to women at the heart of the British Empire.[116]

Lloyd George explained that that very morning a draft bill had been prepared so there would be no loss of time. 'The attitude of the Government with regard to Women's Suffrage will be this – that they leave the question of voting for women as an open question ... for the House. As far as the Government are concerned, the majority ... will vote for the inclusion of Women's Suffrage – for its retention.' To ripples of laughter, the Prime Minister pointed out that it had not been decided yet which of the two age limits suggested for women would be inserted in the bill.[117] Emmeline, like the majority of suffragists, had come to accept that some compromise would be necessary, if the measure was to receive a majority vote in parliament. Although the proposed bill would not enfranchise women on the same terms as men, the issue on which she had campaigned so determinedly, she was prepared to accept it, with all its limitations, unlike Sylvia, who refused to compromise on equal adult suffrage.[118] To an enthusiastic audience at the Queen's Hall in mid April Emmeline said, 'It will be 50 years on the 17th of May since John Stuart Mill introduced the first Women's Suffrage Bill into the House of Commons. Is it not a remarkable thing that exactly fifty years after ... we should be on the eve of seeing this question settled?'[119] To another audience in Glasgow, she emphasised that women during the war 'had proved their capacity for the rights of citizenship'.[120]

Nevertheless, vestiges of the old mistrust of Asquith, who had moved in March the resolution in favour of the bill, remained. Emmeline was still deeply sceptical about his supposed conversion to the women's cause and fearful lest women should be 'cheated & betrayed' again. 'He wants the support of women at the next election & this is how he gets it.'[121] Further, she was worried that all could be threatened by the level of industrial militancy in Britain, disputes and strikes having now reached threatening proportions. Both she and Christabel believed that industrial unrest was the work of unseen forces, driven by the Germans, the Soviet Bolsheviks and pacifists rather than evidence of class conflict between workers and employers. She warned that all the political work of the WSPU in advancing the cause of women was useless, unless there was industrial peace – 'if we do not calm industrial unrest and restore harmony between the workers and those who direct them, if we do not keep up the supply of munitions at the front, all the other work might just as well never have been done'.[122] Such a message was an important part of the 'industrial campaign', as it was called, that the WSPU had recently launched, with government approval and financial backing of £15,000 from leading capitalists.[123]

Emmeline was now speaking regularly in old London haunts, such as Trafalgar Square or near the Reformer's Tree, in Hyde Park, and, above all else, enjoying living in a home of her own with her 'new' family. Yet, as she wrote on 3 May 1917 to Ethel Smyth, she was living under considerable financial strain:

> I have got to love this home of mine; pray heaven I shall be able to keep it. Sometimes I feel appalled at the responsibility I have undertaken in adopting these four young things at my time of life, especially as I don't find people very keen to share the burden with me! However who knows? I'll go on as long as I can, in the faith that help will come when it's needed. The cost of living increases from week to week. How the poor live God only knows.[124]

However, such worries were soon overshadowed by reports about the war in Russia.

20

WAR EMISSARY TO RUSSIA: EMMELINE VERSUS THE BOLSHEVIKS (JUNE–OCTOBER 1917)

Stories soon came to Emmeline's ears about massive desertions from the army of one of Britain's allies, Russia, and of a growing demand from the Russian people for peace. Such moves were supported by the Bolsheviks, an uncompromising, Marxist revolutionary group who had opposed the war from the beginning; they argued that the war exploited the poorest sections of society and served capitalist interests, thus sharpening rather than abolishing class differences. The call to peace was contrary to the policy of Alexander Kerensky, head of the Provisional Government, who was pledged to continue in the war despite the fact that, since its outbreak, the Russians had suffered five and a half million casualties. Kerensky was a Socialist Revolutionary, a member of a more moderate socialist grouping that grew out of the populist tradition in Russia and was identified mainly with the peasantry.

From her youth, the struggle for freedom under the autocratic rule of the Czar had been of interest to Emmeline. When living in Russell Square, London, many years ago, prominent Russian exiles such as Stepniak and Chaikovsky, had attended gatherings in her house. Then when she moved back to Manchester, two Russian women, a mother and daughter, activists in the workers' revolution, had visited her. Their stories about the hardship of life under such an autocracy had deeply moved her.[1] Emmeline had rejoiced in the overthrow of the Czar in the February 1917 revolution, seeing this as the first step towards parliamentary democracy. But now she feared that the Provisional Government would be pressurised to take Russia out of the war, a move that would have disastrous consequences. A 'premature peace', on German terms, she argued, 'would rob the Russian people of the freedom for which they have had their revolution, and would involve them in a far worse slavery than the old'. Further, it would weaken the Eastern Front, lead also to Britain's withdrawal and the collapse of the Allied war strategy. The war had to go on until 'real freedom' rather than German domination had been secured.[2] To make matters worse in Emmeline's eyes, Sylvia was amongst those campaigning for British and Russian withdrawal while the prominent Labour Party member Ramsay MacDonald, who had opposed Britain's entry into the war and wanted a negotiated peace, was to visit Russia with some pacifists of the Left.

Emmeline acted quickly. She wrote to Lloyd George asking for passports for herself and WSPU colleagues to undertake, as 'patriotic British women, loyal to the national and Allied cause', a visit to Russia.[3] Helen Crawfurd, ex-WSPU member and one of the founders of the Women's Peace crusade, was furious. 'Does Mrs. Pankhurst speak for us? Has her voice ever been raised since this war started on behalf of the workers of this country against the profiteers or exploiters who have taken advantage of this great crisis to rob and plunder the people? ... SHALL WE NOT SPEAK FOR OURSELVES?' The people of Russia, she continued, through their leaders, have appealed to the common people of every country to let their voices be heard, demanding peace.[4] Lloyd George, however, welcomed Emmeline's initiative, and suggested that she travel under government auspices, as a paid lecturer, although funds to finance the trip were raised through appeals in *Britannia*. 'This is not in any sense a class mission', Emmeline explained to the press. 'We shall not appeal especially to the Russian women or to the working classes, but to all Russians irrespective of class or politics. ... We shall work for a closer entente between the Allies, and, especially, between this country and Russia.'[5] She believed that the WSPU could make a special appeal to the Russian people because its members were 'the real revolutionaries' who had suspended their revolution when they realised that their first duty was 'to preserve our country and to be loyal to our Allies in the war'. In particular, she claimed that she could represent the feeling of the mass of the British people much more accurately than the British pacifists travelling to Russia who represented just a very small minority.[6] 'Let me tell you', Emmeline insisted, 'that these minority representatives are going to preach class war and the universal strike. While talking in favour of peace with the German aggressors, they advocate class war. I want to say to the Russian people that those who first taught democratic ideas did not preach the class war.' In particular, Emmeline believed that it was the German socialists who had preached 'discord' amongst those seeking to reform social conditions in Russia; it was they who had 'exploited' every progressive movement in Europe. 'They preach internationalism and have denounced patriotism as a worn-out idea. But they never have lost the idea of Germany over all. ... It is the Allies' duty thus to fulfil the principles and uphold the cause of freedom and liberty of the whole world.'[7] Rather than her views being labelled as a move to the right, the common assumption of most socialist historians,[8] we may interpret them as being opposed to the international Marxists, especially the Bolsheviks. Emmeline was deeply critical of the form of socialism advocated by Marxism; the emphasis in Marxism on a materialist analysis in which political and cultural events are related to the economic mode of production and its historical development, on social class relations, class conflict and class consciousness, held no appeal or relevance for her. The key concern for Emmeline during this time of national crisis was to unite the Allies in one common purpose, the winning of the war, rather than to emphasise class divisions and conflict. Once the war was won, women would be granted the parliamentary vote and be an effective force for social reform.

Accompanied by Jessie Kenney, Emmeline left for Petrograd in early June, due to sail on the same boat as Ramsay MacDonald. She was elated when two leaders of the patriotic Seamen's Union, Captain Tupper and Havelock Wilson, greeted her at the quay with the news that the crew refused to sail until MacDonald disembarked.[9] She not only abhorred his pacifist views but had long held contempt for his class-ridden, dismissive comments on window-breaking expeditions by militant women, as on one occasion when he had said, 'I have the very strongest objection to childishness masquerading as revolution. ... I wish the working women of the country who really care for the vote ... would come to London and tell these pettifogging middle-class damsels who are going out with little hammers in their muffs that if they do not go home they will get their heads broken.'[10]

Arriving on 18 June in Petrograd, where red flags were flying from government offices and most other buildings, Emmeline and Jessie were met by Professor Thomas Masaryk, a friend of Christabel's; he had booked rooms for them in the Hotel Angleterre. Soon to become the first president of Czechoslovakia, Masaryk was in Russia in an attempt to form into independent divisions the many thousands of Czechoslovak troops who had deserted from the Austro-Hungarian army.[11] On the advice of Dr. Anna Shabanova, President of the All Russian Women's Union, the two women soon moved to the Hotel Astoria which was considered safer since many military and naval personnel were staying there. They were told that their balcony, which looked out over the imposing St. Isaac's Square, was the one from which the Kaiser had threatened to address the Russian people when the German army marched into Petrograd.[12]

Emmeline's role as the leader of the British women's militant movement was well known in Russia since her autobiography, My own story, had been widely read in its Russian translation, even in girls' high schools; in particular, the stand she had taken against the British government had been much admired. She soon gathered around her a devoted group of women who helped in any way they could, especially in regard to the food shortage. The helpers waited patiently in queues to buy the white bread Emmeline needed since the black variety had proved indigestible, further exacerbating the gastric problems from which she was still suffering, owing to her imprisonments. When the hotel staff went on strike, the Russian friends came round tidying the rooms, foraging for food, and making tea on a primus stove lent by a soldier. The interpreters assigned to Emmeline visited each day, bringing the Russian papers which they would read and translate.

A steady stream of visitors came to the hotel or left their cards, including a British chaplain, a Commissioner of the British Red Cross, aristocrats and Embassy officials, Lady Egerton, Lady Muriel Paget (who was in charge of an Anglo-Russian hospital and had sailed on the same ship as Emmeline and

Jessie), feminist leaders such as Anna Shabanova, and a flurry of journalists. To the latter, Emmeline clearly stated her mission. 'I came to Petrograd with a prayer from the English nation to the Russian nation, that you may continue the war on which depends the face of civilisation and freedom. ... I believe in the kindness of heart and the soul of Russia.'[13] Such statements sharply divided the press, left-wing journalists condemning her as a hand-maiden of Western capitalism while right-wing commentators sung her praises. One influential writer, wondering whether 'there was anything feminine left in this woman-rebel with a glorious past' concluded that the charming Emmeline Pankhurst was 'both feminine and romantic. She is an ardent patriot in the best sense of the word ... not a chauvinistic Valkyrie, nor a blunt woman-warrior.' Nevertheless he also warned that 'angry Extremists will no doubt raise a good deal of cry and lies about her ... they will no doubt denounce her, too, as a "paid agent of the Anglo-French capitalists".'[14]

The political situation that Emmeline found herself in was far from stable. 'One hears rumours and news all through each day of revolutions, strikes and counter strikes taking place so quickly that we never know what will be happening from hour to hour', recorded Jessie early in her diary. The vulnerable Provisional Government, surrounded by conflicting forces, feared that Emmeline's pro-war stand would alienate their more radical supporters and so refused her permission to address public meetings.[15] Instead, she spoke at gatherings held in private houses and especially at meetings of women's societies, such as the Patriotic Women's Alliance and the All Russian Women's Union, where she entreated women to exert all efforts, either by influencing the men or by their own work, to bring the war to a 'victorious conclusion'. She mentioned, among other things, that she had arrived in Russia at an historic time. On 19 June, the British House of Commons had passed, by a vote of 385 to 55, a clause in the Representation of the People Bill which would confer the parliamentary vote on women over thirty who were householders, wives of householders, occupiers of property of £5 or more annual value, or university graduates. A joyful and relieved Emmeline regarded the news as a 'good omen'.[16] Undoubtedly, the news was also conveyed to other Russian women she met, such as Maria Botchkareva, a strong, unlettered, peasant woman who was the commander of a women's battalion which had been formed by Kerensky, in an attempt to shame the men and restore morale amongst his shattered armies.[17] 'I honour these women who are setting such an example to their comrades', Emmeline said in her stirring speech at a concert held in the Army and Navy Hall, Petrograd, in order to raise funds for another women's battalion:

When I looked at their tender bodies I thought how terrible it was they should have to fight besides bringing children into the world. Men of Russia, must the women fight, and are there men who will stay at home and let them fight alone? One thing women say: Never will we be slaves to Germany! Better that we should die fighting than be outraged and dishonoured like the women in France, in Belgium, in Serbia, in Montenegro and other invaded countries.[18]

On another occasion, when Emmeline took the salute as the Petrograd women's battalion marched by in an impressive ceremony in St. Isaac's Square, she was given a rousing cheer. Although she was now ageing and frail, she stood erect and poised, looking like an elder statesperson in her white linen suit, smart black bonnet and gloves to match, her right hand raised in a firm salute. Botchkareva, who had been wounded and won two St. George's Crosses for her bravery in the trenches, was made a full officer of the Russian army that day. Emmeline spoke of how proud she was of the battalion and explained that although women in England were not in soldiers' uniforms, they were doing soldiers' work in other ways. The beauty of the short religious service, in which priests blessed the colours, especially moved her. 'How Ethel Smyth would love this singing and music', she whispered to Jessie, a comment often made on their frequent visits to the magnificent cathedral in the square where they listened to the worship. Emmeline had been close to death on more than one occasion in the past and perhaps now, as she was getting older, she reflected more on the spiritual meaning of life. When she and Richard had first married, they had attended church regularly,[19] but ceased to do so after Richard became an agnostic. And as their children grew older, they had decided to withdraw them from religious instruction classes at school. But now Emmeline pondered whether that had been a sensible decision. 'Your Mother was a wonderful women', she confided to Jessie one day. 'How wise of her to bring you up to go to Church and Sunday School while you were young, and give you the opportunity when you got older to test all this for yourselves.'[20] As Emmeline reflected on life with her own daughters, she lamented the discontents of Sylvia and Adela, despite the amount of money she had spent on them, and drew a contrast with Jessie's sisters, Caroline and Jane who, with the minimum of expenditure and fuss, had trained in Maria Montessori progressive methods of education and were leading useful and happy lives as teachers. Jessie opined that part of the problem with Sylvia and Adela was the 'little jealousy' they felt towards Christabel, considered 'the one and only' in her mother's eyes. 'I have never had one moment's trouble with Christabel since she was a baby', retorted the proud Emmeline. Jessie also dared to observe that she thought Sylvia was jealous of Annie, of whom Christabel seemed more fond than of her own sisters.[21]

Emmeline had not been long in Petrograd when a private message reached her that the deposed Czar and Czarina, now imprisoned at Tsarskoe Selo, wished to meet her since they had heard much about the British women's suffrage campaign. Regretfully, the invitation had to be turned down since, as a semi-official emissary for Britain, Emmeline had to work with the Provisional Government. However, Emmeline and Jessie did visit Tsarskoe Selo, but as the guest of Plekhanov who had been in exile for a number of years and become a patriot, arguing for support of the war until victory was won by the Western democracies. Here they enjoyed a Russian high tea of fine white bread with plenty of butter and caviar. The samovar sat simmering all the time on the table so that they could partake of fresh cups of hot drinks.

On her return to Petrograd, Emmeline found a quickening pace of events and was warned not to go out when fierce fighting broke out between Cossacks, loyal to Kerensky, and Bolsheviks, who demanded that the Provisional Government must go. She watched from her hotel window as armed Bolshevik soldiers marched by shouting, 'Down with capitalism' and 'Stop the war'. Emmeline was convinced that Germany was financing such peace propaganda and was horrified when she heard that Bolsheviks were trying to terrorise factory workers and to encourage them to go on strike. Despite the political tension, she refused the offer from a group of aristocratic officers to form a body-guard to protect her, pointing out that she was not afraid to move among the people. She also shrugged off the suggestion that she and Jessie should wear proletarian clothes in order not to attract the attention of bourgeois haters. More visitors continued to call, including a friend from suffragette days, the American journalist Rheta Childe Dorr who needed to borrow some money. Emmeline had none to spare.[22] Botchkareva's regiment, known as the 'Battalion of Death' because of its determination to fight Germans long after every man had retreated, was something of a novelty to Americans and the Western world and Rheta wanted to spend two weeks with the battalion, which she soon did, sleeping and living in their spartan barracks. Emmeline related to her American friend the story she had been told about the assassination of Rasputin. The eager journalist swiftly relayed the details back to her home-land.[23]

Emmeline's frustration at the slow pace of her work was made worse by the recurrence of gastric trouble and the chronic shortage of edible food. Nevertheless, she continued to speak at a number of women's meetings, urging her listeners to support the Provisional Government and to prevent anarchy; after all, within a month of taking office, Kerensky had granted women the right to vote. Her main line of argument, however, that Russian women of all social classes should join together, free from affiliation to any political party or creed, was inappropriate in a society where the ending of class privilege was seen as the key priority and where radical Marxism was flowering. Emmeline had little sympathy with the dictates of Marxism. As she explained to a reporter, 'I have always been astonished at the materialistic aspect of Marxian Socialism. I cannot think of Socialism without a spiritual background.'[24]

Her disillusionment, which was later to turn to a hatred of those who upheld the philosophies expounded by communist pioneers, like Karl Marx and Vladimir Ilyich Lenin, was deepened when she eventually met Kerensky in early August in the enormous Winter Palace. It appeared that he had been asking about Emmeline's views before she arrived, and hearing that she was crit-ical of any idea of social reform based on class conflict and class warfare, was slightly antagonistic towards her. The two conversed in French, through an interpreter, but Kerensky vacillated so that it was difficult for Emmeline to follow a line of argument. Nevertheless, he firmly told the leader of the British militant women's suffrage movement that English women could not teach Russian women anything. He also conveyed the impression to Emmeline that he had little time for women's emancipation unless it was for women of the same ideological persuasion as himself. When, during their conversation, he spoke also to the interpreter in Russian, which Emmeline could not understand, she felt uncomfortable. As the two emissaries prepared to leave, Kerensky wrote a note for Emmeline, proudly telling her as he did so, 'This is the pen that the Czar used to sign his documents with.' The two women found his comment chilling and boastful.[25]

It was something of a relief for Emmeline and Jessie when they travelled to Moscow since it seemed further away from the hostilities. They loved the city, especially the Kremlin and the old streets around it; the interior of St. Basil's Cathedral evoked from Emmeline the comment that she thought that William Morris, whose designs she so admired, must have got some of his inspiration from its fine decoration. On a visit to the Moscow women's battalion, they watched the 1,000 women at their drill and felt the weight of their heavy rifles. Emmeline spoke words of comfort to the sick women soldiers, praising them for their sacrifice. Then there were invitations to lunch and dinner and to country houses nearby, and sometimes they met unexpected people, such as Major Raymond Robins, the brother of Elizabeth. Amid such a busy schedule, they managed to do a little sightseeing and even some shopping but money was scarce and so they could only afford a few gramophone records of Russian songs rather than the needlework that Emmeline so admired. Inevitably, with the poor quality of scarce food that was available, both Emmeline and Jessie fell ill. Fearing they had contracted the killer disease of dysentery, a friend obtained some strong drug from a chemist which was administered, with successful results. Emmeline, however, never fully recovered her health.

Later in the month, Emmeline and Jessie attended the great congress to which workers' and soldiers' delegates had been summoned, as well as representatives from most walks of Russian life. They listened to the over-long speeches and nearly fainted through lack of fresh air. Emmeline, who had never had to justify her actions to committees of the WSPU, was unimpressed with Kerensky's highly emotional oratory as he pleaded, threatened and promised at great length, in an attempt to assert his authority. Like the audience, Emmeline was of the view that the Provisional Government could not last and that Kerensky, who had allowed Lenin, the leading spirit of the Bolsheviks, to return to Russia and also released other Bolshevik leaders from prison, including Leon Trotsky, was merely 'a man of straw'.[26]

Travelling on a crowded train back to Petrograd, the two English emissaries considered themselves fortunate not to have lost any luggage or money. But once they arrived at their hotel, a perusal of their room soon revealed that a number of the presents they had been given, which they had left behind in order to travel light, had been stolen. 'We have almost forgotten what we have lost', lamented Jessie. 'I am afraid that the Pankhursts are like Annie and I – bad at holding on to things – lacking in acquisitiveness.'[27] Waiting for them at the British Embassy was some small consolation, another food parcel from England, as well as a copy of *Britannia*. But although these gifts were very welcome, the unexpected quietness of the streets of Petrograd, like a calm before the storm, was disturbing. Professor Masaryk advised Emmeline and Jessie to leave immediately, before the Bolsheviks gained control; the latter seemed well informed about the whereabouts of all English visitors and little sympathy would be shown towards two bourgeois Western women who had been invited by the Czar and Czarina to visit them.

21

LEADER OF THE WOMEN'S PARTY (NOVEMBER 1917–JUNE 1919)

Emmeline arrived back in London in October 1917 ill and exhausted. Her low spirits at the failure of her Russian mission were deepened by a severe attack of pleurisy; in addition she heard that Adela had recently married Tom Walsh, an Irish, working-class, ex-Catholic, radical socialist and trade unionist who was fourteen years older than her daughter. Always prim and proper regarding the formalities of life, Emmeline would hardly have regarded the rough-cut Tom Walsh, a widower with three daughters aged fifteen, twelve and eleven years old, an ideal son-in-law. Yet Adela was happy with her ready-made family, despite the fact that a four-month prison sentence for her anti-war activities was hanging over her head.[1] Two months after her wedding, she wrote to Sylvia, '[T]his is the life, isn't it & I am happy – more than happy in it & hoping that I shall one day have a son or daughter to carry on our father's work.'[2] At this euphoric time for socialists, when Lenin and the Bolsheviks had been swept to power in Russia, it was her dead socialist father to whom Adela felt close rather than her very much alive patriotic mother. Yet Emmeline too had married a man many years her senior. And the Walshes, like Emmeline and Richard Pankhurst, were political comrades, sharing a family life which was always subordinate to their political activities.[3]

Emmeline came back home to find that Christabel had adopted her favourite of the 'war babies', Elizabeth. But more than this, Christabel had been busy in her mother's absence, using WSPU funds to purchase and convert Tower Cressey, a large house in Aubrey Road, Kensington, into a day nursery and adoption home for female orphans. Catherine Pine and a young woman assistant were to take charge of the children while Jane Kenney, trained in the progressive Montessori methods of education, was to be brought over from the USA to administer a non-directive programme with which Miss Pine, 'a stern traditionalist', had little sympathy.[4] When Emmeline visited the home, Ethel Smyth thought her friend seemed 'horrified' by the 'unnecessary luxury, elaborate armchairs, *chaises-longues* and so on' with which it had been refurbished. The blunt Ethel, glancing at the wire-netted windows, sarcastically remarked that it was the best place to commit suicide from that she had ever seen. Always ready to defend Christabel from any criticism, the WSPU leader replied sharply that all the windows were barricaded to prevent the children from falling out.[5]

Emmeline was now nearly sixty years old and beginning to feel her age. The hardships of her imprisonments had played havoc with her body and the desperate food situation in Russia had aggravated her health problems. Although instances of her old fire, power of oratory and iron determination remained, the direction of the WSPU came increasingly under the control of the younger, fitter and more vigorous Christabel. That autumn, Emmeline allowed herself just a short convalescence before she reported to Lloyd George about her Russian trip. With Christabel by her side, she attended a breakfast meeting at 10 Downing Street where she told the Prime Minister in no uncertain terms about the chaotic and desperate situation in Russia, urging him to intervene against the forces of Bolshevism by sending Allied troops to help the Cossacks and other loyal sections regain control. That the Bolsheviks were now in power seemed to Emmeline a tragic consequence of the low standard of education of the Russian masses, 80 per cent of whom were illiterate; 'entirely dependent upon what people told them', they had been deluded by the 'machinations of the German agents'.[6] In press interviews, she bitterly condemned Kerensky, now fallen from power, who had begun his own reign of terror. 'There were wholesale arrests of people whom he feared; no less than forty officers were arrested at the hotel at which I myself was staying. The loyal and patriotic elements in Russia were repressed by methods of outrageous tyranny.' Since the majority of the Russian people were patriotic but lacked armaments, Emmeline now publicly called for armed intervention by the Allies to restore order and to save Russia from the oppression of the armed Bolsheviks who, she believed, were German agents.[7] She was not alone in expressing such views. World-wide, there was a strong condemnation of Bolshevism, as governments and peoples feared it could destabilise the old order.

Emmeline found the situation in England in regard to women's enfranchisement much changed. The House of Commons had passed the clause giving the parliamentary vote to certain categories of women aged thirty years and over and it was now waiting to go through the House of Lords, early in 1918. On the instigation of the Standing Joint Committee of Industrial Women's Organisations, a conference was held in London that October on Women's Civic and Political Responsibilities at which the key issues debated were whether women, once the vote was won, should seek equality with men or the pursuit of goals of specific concern to women, and the forms of political organisation best suited to these differing tasks. The prominent socialist feminist Marion Phillips argued for women to develop 'a strong political organisation embracing both men and women ... not to follow the line of sex division', a stance supported by the majority of the delegates, including Millicent Garrett Fawcett.[8] Emmeline and Christabel were strongly opposed to such a form of organisation and had just relaunched the women-only WSPU as the Women's Party. 'While the Women's Party is in no way based on sex antagonism', it was pointed out, 'it is felt that women can best serve the nation by keeping clear of men's party political machinery and traditions, which, by universal consent, leave so much to be desired.'[9] As Emmeline later explained, women needed a party of their own because 'men had grown so accustomed to managing the world in the past that it had become rather difficult for women in politics to hold their own if they were associated with men'.[10] Whereas the WSPU had campaigned for the parliamentary vote for women, the aim of the Women's Party was to prepare women for their impending citizenship status during wartime and after. With the slogan 'Victory, National Security and Progress', the Women's Party conflated the winning of the war with the women's cause.

An account of the separatist Women's Party manifesto was published in *Britannia*; it was signed by Emmeline (Honorary Treasurer), Christabel (Editor of its official newspaper, *Britannia*), Annie Kenney (Honorary Secretary) and Flora Drummond (Chief Organiser), in that order. The social reform post-war programme, designed to appeal especially to women, was feminist and radical in that it demanded equal pay for equal work, equal marriage laws (including equal conditions of divorce), equality of parental right, the raising of the age of consent, equal opportunity of employment, and equality of rights and responsibilities in regard to the social and the political service of the nation. A system of maternity and infant care was called for, with parents making a financial contribution according to their income, as well as a guarantee that all children would receive an education that would make them worthy citizens. Co-operative housekeeping was also considered necessary, in order to reduce the burden of the married woman, with co-operative housing schemes that had a central heating and hot water supply, central kitchens, a central laundry, medical services, and, if desired, a crèche, nursery school, gymnasium and reading room.

The demands of the Women's Party in regarded to women's war-time duties, on the other hand, were patriotic and imperialist, encompassing both a national and international world-view, but all subservient to the 'national interest'. The war must continue until victory had been secured by the Allies; more radical and vigorous war measures (including food rationing and the reduction or prohibition of all non-essential industry) should be adopted in order to secure a speedy victory; officials in government departments having enemy blood or connections or pacifist and pro-German leanings should be removed from office; the Great War Alliance should be maintained after the war; the British Empire should be strengthened; a solution to the problem of industrial unrest should be sought in the shortening of hours of labour rather than in the direction of control of industry by the workers. Placing faith in the democratic process rather than the dictatorship of the Bolsheviks, it was argued that since 'the interest of the community as a whole transcends that of the employer ... and the employed ... Parliament as the sole representative of the nation, must have the last word in all questions affecting the relations between Capital and Labour and industrial questions generally'.[11] In particular, Emmeline, with her hatred of Marxism, emphasised that the Women's Party stood 'for industrial reform, better wages, and better conditions for women workers, and, indeed, all workers, and believed the result could be attained by class co-operation rather than class division'.[12] In regard to the women's vote, the Women's Party promised to use it 'to make Britain strong for defence against the outside foe, and to strengthen Britain from within by securing more prosperous and more harmonious national development in its educational, industrial, political, and social aspects'.[13]

Such an analysis, which downplayed the crises of capitalism, the existence of social classes, class conflict and economic power, and which argued against workers' control of industry, was contrary to the dominant socialist ideas of the time and their increasing influence; the war was hastening the collapse of the old social order while the new Bolshevik government in Russia indicated that the workers could seize power.[14] In Britain, the expansion of trade unionism with the demand from its membership for at least a share in the control of industry, widespread industrial unrest, and the prospect of mass enfranchisement was creating a climate in which at least one key figure in the Labour Party felt disquiet about 'the potential for a revolutionary situation'.[15] In such an atmosphere, the gulf widened between socialist feminists, such as Sylvia Pankhurst, and feminists who were not allied to socialism, such as her mother and Christabel, a not unexpected development since many feminists who shared the world-wide reaction against Bolshevism were driven to the right.[16] Thus, according to Sylvia, so-called 'advanced women' of the Left tended to distance themselves from the Women's Party, seeing it as an attack upon the entire socialist movement and as a 'phalanx of the Tories'.[17] Unsurprisingly, this view is supported by the majority of present-day socialist historians, such as Rowbotham, Garner and Pugh, who interpret Emmeline Pankhurst's criticisms of socialism as a move to the political right.[18] However, it was not the entire socialist movement of which Emmeline was critical but especially socialism as practised by men in the Labour Party, in which Emmeline had lost faith; in particular, she believed that pacifist socialism had not served the national interest during wartime. As she later explained at a large meeting in Nottingham: 'The organised Labour Party of this country ... had signally failed to take advantage of its opportunities during the great struggle and leaders like Ramsay MacDonald and Philip Snowden had tried to betray their country from the very outset.'[19] Nor did the socialism practised by male trade unionists appeal to her, because male trade unionists did not concern themselves with the needs of women. If 'these autocrats of labour' would come out on strike for 'better conditions for mothers', Emmeline claimed she would like them better.[20] A socialism that would not be distorted by men's interests, promising 'a share of all that is best in life for everyone' was in Emmeline's mind, a socialism that would bring equality to women and greater prosperity to the working classes.[21] She had never forgotten the improvements that she had been able to bring about as a Poor Law Guardian and as a member of an education authority and never lost her cherished dream of using public services to bring about better conditions of living for the poor. 'Poverty, which was removable', she insisted, 'was due to many causes, chiefly bad government'.[22] The problem with the socialism of men, she pointed out, was that it 'had failed to put theory into practice'.[23] The separatist Women's Party, on the other hand, could focus on the interests of the nation and of women.

Emmeline launched the Women's Party at the Queen's Hall on 7 November in an afternoon meeting, since blackouts and possible air raids made evening attendance difficult. She said little to the packed audience about the post-war reform programme but mounted instead a scathing attack on the 'committee mania' that was creating internal chaos in Bolshevik Russia and which was 'an object-lesson' to the democracies of the world. 'In one works where 30,000 men are employed there are 800 committee men, who sit all day deciding how the others are to do their work. Committees manage hospitals; and they decide whether they shall take the pills ordered.' When her audience laughed, Emmeline quickly interjected, 'This is all literally true, ladies and gentlemen', and went on to point out that, even worse, there were committees that discussed and voted whether men should go into the trenches or not. Again she called upon the Allies, especially America and Japan, to intervene in Russia.[24]

The press largely welcomed the advent of the Women's Party. 'We realise that patriotism is the inspiration of Mrs. Pankhurst's new organisation', opined the right-wing *Daily Express*. 'The Labour Party is already angling for the woman vote, and the Labour Party is still liable to fall under the sway of Mr. Ramsay MacDonald. Mrs. Pankhurst intends to use woman suffrage to save the country from MacDonaldism, and for that reason we wish her God-speed.'[25] But for Sylvia, now a revolutionary socialist who had changed the title of the *Women's Dreadnought* to the *Workers' Dreadnought*, it was all too much.[26] She had told the delegates at the Women's Civic and Political Responsibilities conference that 'too much importance should not be attached to the Women's Party, which was using the name "Women's" in a way which none of us could accept'. Similarly, the socialist Susan Lawrence had maintained 'there was an objection to a Party really political calling itself a non-party organisation'.[27] *The Common Cause*, the official newspaper of the NUWSS, warned that the Women's Party 'will of course be an autocracy like the old WSPU'.[28] And it was.

Emmeline summoned all her fathomless reserves of strength and began her patriotic campaign for the Women's Party, gathering about her a formidable team of speakers, including Christabel, Flora Drummond, Annie Kenney, Phyllis Ayrton, Cynthia Maguire and Elsie Bowerman. Since her health was prone to relapses, she was grateful for the continued love and support of Catherine Pine. 'How lucky I am', she wrote to Ethel Smyth, 'to have such a faithful, devoted and useful friend to take care of me and be happy in doing it.'[29] Early in the New Year, on 10 January 1918, the House of Lords passed the women's suffrage clause by a vote of 134 to 71, a majority of 63. Even Lord Curzon, President of the League for Opposing Woman Suffrage and Leader of the House, admitted defeat. In what *The Times* called a remarkable speech, he delivered an onslaught on the principle of women's suffrage and then, in the second half of his speech, offered 'an elaborate apology for the difficulty he felt in translating his words into action'.[30] Emmeline heard the news calmly and quietly, grateful that her trust in the Prime Minister had not been misplaced. Lloyd George invited her to breakfast, to talk over the victory, and she ardently told him of the Women's Party's schemes to help women use their hard-won citizenship effectively. The food problem should be tackled immediately since inflated prices were making the lives of poor women a misery; there must be compulsory food rationing and public cost-price restaurants to lighten the burden of hard-pressed mothers who were working in men's jobs outside the home.[31] But the shadow of the war and the activities of the socialist pacifists who were 'actually talking about and wanting revolution in England'[32] hung heavily over her hopes for the future, as she explained in a letter to Ethel:

> I breakfasted with the P.M. He has worked hard for us and we owe him much. Now we must work harder than ever to keep women out of the clutches of R. MacDonald & Co., who are making bids for them. Construction *versus* destruction is our plan of campaign in home affairs, and I believe we shall carry the best elements in the working class with us when we show them how high production can be reconciled with good pay, short hours, and a share in all that is good in life. We are full of plans and schemes, tackling the food and domestic service problems.[33]

But it was not just politics that occupied Emmeline's thoughts at this time. Helen Archdale had sent her a letter she had recently received from Adela. Grateful to know how her youngest daughter was faring, Emmeline wrote to Helen, thanking her and giving her own news, that Vida Goldstein had written to her saying that Adela's husband 'is worthy & respected'. That is 'something to be thankful for', opined Emmeline. 'Miss Goldstein has been very good to her ... & will keep an eye on her in future. Let us hope her husband will continue the "mothering" without which Adela is helpless.'[34]

But there was no time for Emmeline to be sad and reflective about Adela. Back on the campaign trail, she often received great ovations as she spoke of the critical condition of affairs both on the war and home fronts. '[W]omen ... should take up their responsibilities as citizens and save their country from the enemy abroad and from revolution at home', she told an enthusiastic audience in the Midlands. In particular, she hoped that the women workers in the munitions factories would assert themselves 'and put a stop to the irresponsible behaviour' of those young men, whom she regarded as 'the Bolsheviks of Britain', who organised go-slows at work which led the way to the destruction of industry and national prosperity. What the Women's Party had developed was a policy that would bring 'national safety, national prosperity and national greatness', goals that could be achieved through 'wise legislation' and 'wise arrangements' that would give 'greater prosperity to the people who worked with their hands – more comfort, more leisure, and better pay'.[35] The finer detail of how far Emmeline's vision was to be carried out by state services, elected bodies or private enterprise was not revealed. However, *Britannia* commented that the abolition of poverty and securing of prosperity for all could not be achieved by 'shop stewardism and committee control of industry' but by greater progress in organisation, by more discipline and by a shorter, more productive day with higher remuneration advancing in proportion to increase in output, a view supported by Lord Leverhulme, the industrialist, who also wrote for the newspaper.[36] Such views alienated many socialists, including many male industrial workers, who saw Emmeline Pankhurst as being on the side of the ruling class, conservatism and the Empire. When male munition workers in Manchester complained to Emmeline that she had excluded them from her talk, which was addressed only to their female counterparts, she curtly agreed to give them ten minutes of her time. She appeared when the men were at their tea break. Helped onto a strong table to deliver her message, she was immediately confronted by the banging and breaking of the crockery. Not prepared to tolerate such behaviour, she swiftly stepped down from the table and marched out of the room announcing, 'I'm not going to waste my breath and try my voice for people like you.' A silence fell. Although she was entreated to stay, the leader of the Women's Party refused to do so. She suspected that her reception had been orchestrated by the younger Bolshevik agitators. The women munition workers had been telling her that they were 'disgusted' with some of the men who, not daring because of public feeling to organise a strike openly, were operating, unofficially, a go-slow whereby they restricted production to one-third of a normal day's output. The male workers were trying to get the women out of the factory since they were loyal to the war effort and preventing effective industrial action. They were also refusing to teach the women their work skills, which Emmeline thought vastly overrated; there was nothing, she told Ethel Smyth, that could not be taught to women in three weeks.[37] That the men might be concerned that an influx of lower-paid, unskilled women might bring about a reduction in their wages, or that women's lower remuneration might peg their pay to an unacceptable level, did not hold any weight with Emmeline. What mattered was that women workers were being discriminated against by the men who were diminishing the war effort. Experiences such as these, when she addressed thousands of women in the great munition centres at Birmingham, Coventry, Manchester and the Clyde, where, Emmeline claimed, she met '[n]ot one pacifist', stiffened further her hatred of Bolshevism, the Labour Party and men's socialism.[38] She looked not to the leaders of the Labour Party to fulfil her dreams of a better society and equality for women but to Lloyd George. He was the man who had granted women the parliamentary franchise, the leader promising extensive social reforms, the person who was skilfully leading a coalition government that rose above sectionalism and could usher in the non-party programme that she so desired.[39]

On 6 February 1918, when the Representation of the People Act received the Royal Assent, women who had attained the age of thirty years were entitled to the parliamentary vote if they were householders (and thus on the local government register), the wives of householders, occupiers of property of yearly value of not less than £5, or university graduates. Such restrictions meant that not all women aged thirty and over were included in the Act; about 22 per cent – likely to be working-class or unmarried employed women – were excluded. The eight million enfranchised women were disproportionately middle-class housewives.[40] Since men who had seen active service could vote at nineteen and all other men at the age of twenty-one, women were not granted the franchise on equal terms, the issue on which Emmeline had fought so consistently and so bravely for eleven long years. While the principle of sex discrimination in parliamentary voting had been broken, there were limitations to what had been achieved. Although at long last a government measure for women's enfranchisement had become law, an issue on which the WSPU had campaigned so vigorously, it was a restricted measure. Men had finally allowed women access to the parliamentary vote, but it was on their own terms. And it was painfully obvious that Britain was lagging behind societies such as New Zealand, Australia, Finland, Denmark and Norway where women already had the vote. In 1917, women had been enfranchised too in Canada, apart from Quebec, and in four North American states. While the debate in the Lords was taking place, a woman suffrage amendment was passed by a two-thirds majority in both Houses of Congress in Washington, an amendment that had to be ratified by three-fourths of the states and would not become law for two years.[41]

When Emmeline appeared at the great meeting at the Albert Hall on 16 March to celebrate the suffrage victory, her response was, understandably, somewhat muted. She gave herself no credit for the success but humbly said:

> For those who took part in it, it is a difficult thing to speak of the struggle that is over. I know you will feel with me that we cannot rejoice without thinking of those who are not here to rejoice with us, those pioneers who in the dark and early days undertook the work for the vote without any hope of seeking victory themselves.

Perhaps, as she said these words, Emmeline was thinking of her husband and also the aged Elizabeth Wolstenholme Elmy, who had died just four days before. The emotional reflection over, Emmeline soon got into her stride as she urged the newly enfranchised women not to join the existing political parties but the women of the Women's Party because 'we, from first to last, have been faithful and loyal to women, have worked for them and suffered for them'. Emphasising that women collectively were 'a mighty force', she underlined that in order to serve the nation, women 'must combine and unite', putting aside all class feeling.[42] The meeting, which had begun with the singing of the hymn 'Oh God our help in ages past', ended with a rendering of the national anthem.

To what extent Emmeline's leadership of the WSPU had won the parliamentary vote for women is a matter of debate amongst historians, with a number of influential writers asserting that the more extreme forms of militancy for which she took responsibility were counter-productive.[43] In particular, historians such as Pugh, writing within a masculinist paradigm, wish to deny or diminish her achievements.[44] Disliking her separatist women-only politics, Emmeline is too frequently dismissed as a fanatic who delayed the granting of the vote. Yet, I would argue, without her leadership of the WSPU, partial enfranchisement would not have been granted in 1918. As David Morgan comments, without the 'eruption into politics' of militancy, it is most unlikely that women's suffrage would have been given 'active cabinet consideration, far less cabinet approval'. Similarly, Richard Evans, while attributing the granting of the vote to women to a range of social and political factors, nevertheless asserts that, most important of all, 'perhaps', there was a widespread fear that suffragette violence would break out again if some measure of women's suffrage were not granted. A more recent contributor suggests that fears of a renewed sex war, a war which the WSPU had primarily waged, influenced the male politicians to grant the parliamentary vote to women.[45]

What is frequently overlooked is that Emmeline and her militants changed the way in which women were *perceived* by people generally, including politicians, a process that was further advanced by her strident advocacy of women's war work. There was a new confidence amongst women as well as widespread industrial unrest amongst working men who, many feared, were learning dangerous lessons from revolutionary socialists in Russia. Any resumption of militancy would have been an embarrassment for the government, which would not have wanted to imprison women who were making such a worthy contribution to war work. Emmeline, perhaps, did not reflect long on such matters. Ethel Smyth remarked that the leader of the Women's Party rarely paused 'for one half-second' on what had already been accomplished, moving on to the next point. A friend told her that after the vote was won, Emmeline's mind was so full of thoughts about winning the war and combating communism that she was 'secretly bored to death' when former suffragettes began reminiscing about the brave old days of militancy. Emmeline was looking to the future, keen to help in building the nation and the Empire.[46]

Emmeline, a patriotic feminist, continued her campaign, travelling to big provincial cities, spreading the Women's Party message, advocating the cause of women workers and urging a vigorous prosecution of the war. She condemned the Amalgamated Society of Engineers which admitted 'boot-makers and public-house keepers', but refused to admit women munition workers.[47] The issue was particularly urgent since large numbers of female employees in the armaments factories had been dismissed, including eight thousand from the Woolwich Arsenal. Emmeline felt a particular responsibility for keeping such women, mainly working class, in their jobs since the Women's Party had campaigned hard to get women out of the home and poorly paid traditional feminine work, such as domestic service, into the better paid jobs usually undertaken by men, such as munitions work, transport, banking and public administration. About one million women were now employed in such jobs where they could earn what she termed 'decent wages', and she felt sure, as she told one audience, that the women 'would not consent to go back to their old position of dependence'. Her cry that the women must assert themselves was heeded at large meetings of women munition workers at Birmingham and Coventry where resolutions moved by Emmeline were overwhelmingly carried.[48] At Easter, Emmeline was back in her home town of Manchester, where she spoke in Stevenson Square and at Belle Vue pleasure grounds, as well as in factories, cinemas and music halls.[49] Then she was off to speak in Sheffield and in Glasgow and its surrounding district. It was like the old days of the suffrage campaign although now the pace was a little slower. Since a general election was likely to be held sometime that year, the Women's Party opened a new parliamentary department, with offices, at 5 Victoria Street, in London. Jessie Kenney was in charge.[50] Money flowed into the 'Patriots versus Pacifists' appeal, and there was a general buzz of activity as open-air meetings were held twice daily in London as well as the weekly Monday meetings at the London Pavilion and the weekly Tuesday At Homes.[51] Amid such bustle, Emmeline was overjoyed to be able to visit Alsace in her beloved France, a region that the French had recently taken from the Germans.[52]

In late May 1918 the patriotic Emmeline went further afield, sailing to the USA and Canada. Her mission was to arouse the American public in favour of Japanese intervention in Russia. Russia had withdrawn from the war after peace terms had been agreed with Germany in March 1918, but the cost had been heavy; the Western portion of its former empire was now in German hands. The strengthening of German military power allowed the launch, in the spring, of a Western offensive so that even French and British socialists condemned the Bolsheviks for their withdrawal from the war.[53] Emmeline was horrified. She desperately wanted Germany to be defeated, the war to end and the Bolshevik one-party state to fall. The Bolsheviks had not followed the 'classic process', derived from the French Revolution, of electing an assembly by universal suffrage; instead an undemocratic process had been followed whereby the Bolshevik Party conflated its rule with the notion of the 'dictatorship of the proletariat'.[54] 'It becomes more and more evident that the Russian people, as distinct from their Bolshevik tyrants, look to the Allied forces to come and rescue them from Bolshevik despotism and German conquest', ran Britannia.[55] Thus Emmeline argued for Japanese intervention in Russia, not only as a way of helping the Russian people to bring down their Bolshevik rulers but also as a way to compel Germany to send reinforcements to the Eastern front, thus relieving the Allied fronts on the West.

A number of people were not happy about Emmeline's visit to North America. Questions were asked in parliament about why, when there was a policy of restricting sea travelling of women, a permit had been granted to Mrs. Pankhurst to visit the USA. Was she going as a representative of, or commissioned by, the British government? Were the costs of her journey to be defrayed from public funds? Why had Margaret Bondfield, a delegate from the Parliamentary Committee of the Trade Union Congress to America, been refused a permit? It was pointed out that Mrs. Pankhurst was permitted to travel since it was in the Allied interest she should go and that the cost of her journey was not borne by public money.[56] The *Daily News*, taking up the story, also asked what evidence was there that America desired a visit from Mrs. Pankhurst. The *Daily Chronicle* was more biting. 'It is unfortunate that this egregious person cannot keep her own opinions secret', ran an editorial titled 'Mrs. Pankhurst's indiscretions'. 'No sooner had the slanderer of Lord Grey – who, of all British statesmen, is perhaps the one held in highest esteem in America – landed in New York than she began to make mischief. She attacked the Irish, who are a powerful element in American citizenship, and she gave out a scurrilous interview about Kerensky, who will shortly be acclaimed with enthusiasm by the American democracy.'[57]

Emmeline arrived in New York amid controversy on both sides of the Atlantic about her mission. As on her three previous visits, she was soon sought by the press, giving long interviews to the *New York Times*, the *New York Sun* and the *New York Tribune*, as well as other leading newspapers. Although Emmeline found great enthusiasm amongst the American people for the war effort, her tour was not all plain sailing. At one address on 'How to save Russia', delivered to over a thousand people, she found strong opposition to her views. After telling her audience that Bolshevik internationalists, who declared that patriotism was worn out, and love of country old-fashioned, must be 'curbed', she asked, 'Who are our friends in Russia, those who want real democracy or the Bolsheviki internationalists?' The reply shouted from many parts of the auditorium was 'The Bolsheviki'. The *New York Evening Telegraph* reported that three policemen had to be called in, although they had nothing to do since the meeting proceeded in an orderly manner. 'We are fighting to preserve the great and small from autocratic domination', cried the undaunted Emmeline, as she skilfully handled her audience. 'We are fighting for one class alone. I am against a dominant autocratic class as much as I am against a dominant working class.'[58] Her closing remarks reiterated her view that Russia could only be saved by military aid; Americans were asked to join in the call upon Japan to enter Siberia.

Not all American suffragists were enthusiastic either about Emmeline's plans or mode of operation. An indignant Anna Howard Shaw, Chair of the Woman's Committee, the Council of Nation Defense, in Washington, confessed her disillusionment to the sympathetic ear of ex-WSPU member Helen Fraser, telling her that when Emmeline Pankhurst first arrived, 'without consulting Mrs. Catt or any of our suffrage leaders, she gave out an interview saying we should drop all suffrage work and work only to win the war. This was just a day or two before our vote was to come up in the Senate.' Shaw disliked Emmeline's tone, saying that the leader of the British Women's Party 'should at least consider that suffragists here know what they ought to do under our conditions better than she'. Nor did she think that socialists would welcome Emmeline's visit. 'I learn that the Labor people resent her coming and assumption that they are not able to manage their own problems without the interference and leadership of a foreigner.'[59] And to her pacifist, socialist daughter, Sylvia, Emmeline's call for armed intervention in Russia was a betrayal of all the fine ideals she had once upheld, especially her support for the development of a people 'with whose long struggle for liberty she had sympathized from youth upward'. Sharing her views with her sister, Adela, Sylvia wrote, 'Mother is in America. It is strange she takes the opposite view on everything. The most extreme jingoism is scarcely extreme enough for her. I only look in wonder and ask myself, "Can those two [her mother and her sister, Christabel] really be sane?"'[60]

But the patriotic Emmeline was sane and had lost none of her power of oratory. She felt honoured to participate in a special tribute to the bravery and heroism of the French who had stayed Germany's progress at the Marne. The mass meeting, attended by nearly 4,000 people, was held on Bastille Day, 14 July, in Rochester, New York. 'Mrs. Emmeline Pankhurst, Famous Englishwoman, Surprises Audience in Beautiful Eulogy of French Soldiers, and Pictures Touching Scene in Alsace.' ran the headlines of the *Rochester Herald*. With emotion in her voice, Emmeline spoke of how France, in the fight for liberty, had borne the heat and burden of war 'for all of us', and how the time had come to share that burden. 'To-day we are all one in soul and aspiration, fighting for that great cause, as we pay tribute to that mother of freedom. Say with me: "Vive la France".'[61] The lessons that the nine-year-old Emmeline had learnt from Carlyle's *The French revolution* had never left her but remained, as noted earlier, 'a source of inspiration' all her life.[62]

While Emmeline was in the USA, some Canadian women contacted her, pleading with her to visit them and so she spent the last ten days of her tour in Canada. When she spoke to the Canadian Club in Toronto, in mid September, the themes were familiar. Emmeline expressed her grave disappointment that after its revolution, Russia had not moved on and taken her place with the democratic nations of the world. Instead all the talk was of the revolution 'being one step nearer' the day when the working classes would rule the world. 'Class rule is an evil thing, whether the authority is that of an aristocracy or a mobocracy, and whether it is exercised by a single tyrant or by a whole class.' A Bolshevik, pro-German element could be found in Britain, the USA and Canada, preaching, she scornfully noted, that 'the war was an imperialist war and not a people's war, a war of capitalists and not of workers. The very people whose sons and brothers were dying in the trenches were being invited to take a class advantage out of it.'[63]

On returning to England in mid October, a welcome meeting was arranged for Emmeline at the Queen's Hall on 30 October at which she gave an account of her five-month tour. A patriotic feminist, she called not only upon the rhetoric of imperial ideologies to vigorously reaffirm her faith in the British Empire, but also to advocate a particular role for the new women citizens within such discourses as reformers who could aid its progress:

It is the fashion nowadays to attack Imperialism. Some talk about the Empire and Imperialism as if it were something to decry and something to be ashamed of. It seems to me that it is a great thing to be the inheritors of an Empire like ours ... [which is] great in territory, great in potential wealth. ... If we can only realise and use that potential wealth we can destroy thereby poverty, we can remove and destroy ignorance, and we can create a people worthy to inherit this worthy and magnificent Empire.

Such an ideal could not be attained, Emmeline insisted, if class domination – 'an enemy to real democracy' – prevailed. 'Some people have said that we may see a Labour Government in this country. Well, we are not going to have that or any other kind of class Government in the future.' She continued, 'Now that we women have got the vote, we are going to have ... Governments formed, without distinctions of class, without favour to any class, of the best citizens, best in their instincts, best in their training, best in their experience to control the affairs and destinies of this Empire of the future.' She closed her speech by calling upon the women in the audience to help the Women's Party to achieve these aims and to get rid of 'this horrible, fanatical Bolshevism, which is seeking to destroy the moral [sic] of the British people'.[64] Her hatred of Bolshevism, of class consciousness, of class conflict, of the Labour Party had reached its apogee. Never again would Emmeline turn her face to the socialism of men.

Emmeline was greatly relieved that the war was drawing to an end, an armistice being called on 11 November. The carnage, especially amongst young men in the trenches, had been horrendous. Ten million people had died and a further twenty million had been mutilated.[65] There was scarcely a woman she knew who had not lost a son, husband, relative or friend in a war that she, like so many others, hoped would end all wars. The birth of Adela's baby, a boy, as the armistice was being agreed, was probably a bitter-sweet experience for Emmeline; her renegade daughter, whom she had denounced on more than one occasion, had named the child Richard, after her father.[66] The approaching general election, however, barely gave Emmeline time to pause and think about such matters since the Women's Party sought to mobilise the new eight million women voters.[67] Then suddenly Emmeline heard that Ethel Smyth, who was back in England after service in Europe as a radiographer, was one of the thousands stricken down by the influenza epidemic which was stretching the medical services to the limit. Despite her hectic schedule, the loyal friend arrived on Ethel's doorstep with a nursing volunteer. When Ethel's own doctor pronounced her case as 'very serious', Emmeline promptly took command of the situation and summoned Dr. Chetham Strode who devotedly attended, unpaid, her own adopted children. It was to Dr. Strode 'directly, and indirectly to Mrs. Pankhurst', that Ethel later claimed she owed her life.[68]

Emmeline was now caught up in a flurry of excitement; parliament had passed a bill which made women eligible to stand for election to the Commons, a demand for which none of the pre-war suffragists had dared to campaign. Although some of her friends urged Emmeline to stand, she had no wish to do so; she wanted that honour for Christabel. At a Women's Party meeting on 19 November, Emmeline proudly introduced her eldest daughter as the Women's Party candidate. 'I am her most ardent disciple', she announced. '[S]he was the strategist who drew up the plan of campaign which had the result of taking the question of the citizenship of women out of the region of fads into practical politics in this country.'[69] Lloyd George, as leader of the Coalition government. had decided to issue 'coupons' of approval to all Coalition candidates and the determined Emmeline demanded this recognition for her daughter. Had not she and Christabel supported him through the dreadful war years? When Christabel contacted him about her possible candidacy in the Westbury Division of Wiltshire, Lloyd George responded positively. Immediately he wrote to Bonar Law, the Unionist leader and one of his Coalition allies (the Labour Party had left the Coalition before the election and was campaigning on its own behalf), pointing out that he was not sure whether they had any women candidates, but thought it 'highly desirable' that there should be some. The Women's Party, he continued, 'has been extraordinarily useful, as you know, to the Government – especially in the industrial districts where there has been trouble during the last two very trying years. They have fought the Bolshevist and Pacifist element with great skill, tenacity, and courage.'[70] By late November, Christabel had switched her candidacy to the new industrial, working-class constituency of Smethwick and soon after Lloyd George and Bonar Law prevailed upon the already approved Coalition candidate, a Major Thompson, to stand down.[71] Her campaign was financed by donations from sympathetic women and by a £1,000 cheque given by the British Commonwealth Union.[72]

While Emmeline was relishing the thought of fighting a parliamentary election on Christabel's behalf, Sylvia regarded the whole election process with disdain. She had already refused an invitation to stand as a Labour Party candidate for Sheffield Hallam, and developed a strong, left-wing repudiation of parliamentary procedures. The Labour Party, she believed, would only bring 'a wishy-washy Reformist Government' which, when the big issues that really mattered came to be decided, would be swept away 'in the wake of a capitalist policy'.[73] Christabel, on the other hand, stood in the parliamentary election, facing just one opponent, the Labour Party candidate, J. E. Davison, an experienced trade union official and national organiser for the Ironfounders' Society. In her election leaflet for the Women's Party, she was described as 'Patriotic Candidate for Smethwick and Supporter of the Coalition'. She pledged to work for two main aims – a victorious peace based on material guarantees against German aggression as well as compensation, paid by Germany, to war victims, and for social reform. Her desire to abolish poverty and democratise prosperity was a theme that she often emphasised when scoring points against her Labour rival whose manifesto claimed that the Labour Party was the party for the woman voter. It was the Women's Party, Christabel insisted, that was 'the true

Labour Party. We aim at the abolition of poverty by the increased production of wealth so that there may be enough wealth for all.' She promised, if elected, to demand for the workers 'not cottages but better houses, fitted throughout with hot water as well as bathrooms and labour-saving devices, which the Government should help to finance'.[74] When Christabel called Davison and his supporters 'Bolsheviks' and told the voters that they had to choose between the Red Flag or the Union Jack, charges that were commonly made by Conservative candidates during the 1918 election, the exchange of views became more fiery.[75] Davison angrily retorted that the Labour Party worked for social reform on constitutional lines 'without breaking a single window, firing a single pillar box or burning down a single church'. Contemptuously, he called Christabel and her supporters 'Christabelligerents' who were famous for 'all things by turn and nothing long'. Sharply, he reminded the Women's Party candidate that it was 'from a haven of safety in Paris' that she had incited her followers to violence.[76]

Such insults did nothing to daunt Emmeline's spirits. 'Mother ... is absolutely bent upon my getting elected', Christabel told Lloyd George.[77] Since Christabel was the only one of the sixteen women candidates standing for election who had received the Coalition 'coupon', Emmeline felt sure her daughter would be successful. Although lesser known Women Party workers such as Elsie Bowerman, Christabel's agent, Flora MacDonald, Phyllis Ayrton and the crippled May Billinghurst worked hard on her daughter's behalf, it was the celebrity Emmeline Pankhurst who was the star of the show, feverishly sparing herself no rest. On one occasion, she climbed in the rain onto a table in front of a beerless public house and gave an impassioned speech 'of mingled patriotism and zeal for reform' to a small group of working men, soldiers and boys who came out of the mist to listen.[78] At other times, she proudly emphasised that her daughter was not only the best candidate to represent the women and men voters but that Christabel's international status would make Smethwick 'known to the whole of the British Empire and the whole of the world'.[79] Emmeline's hopes were bolstered by the fact that an ardent supporter of the Women's Party, Lord Northcliffe, the influential press baron, made sure that positive coverage to the campaign was given in his newspapers, including *The Times*.

One week after the country had gone to the polls on 14 December, Emmeline heard the devastating news that Christabel had lost the election by a narrow margin. A recount was demanded but Christabel had to concede defeat by 775 votes. It was the bitterest disappointment of Emmeline's life and no consolation to know that the only successful woman candidate was Countess Markievicz in Dublin, a Sinn Feiner who had pledged not to take her seat.[80] Christabel, who had been tired and depressed throughout the campaign, a complication following from a recent attack of the lethal flu, seemed to accept her failure better than her mother, probably because by this time, she had converted to Second Adventism. As Larsen explains, Christabel identified with the Church of England and its North American sister churches and was an

'Adventist' in the sense that she expected the return of Christ, an important message that needed to be proclaimed, especially since His return was considered imminent.[81] In the 1918 December election, Christabel appears not to have spoken of Adventism to the electors. An outsider to the constituency, she had had just three weeks to campaign and according to Elsie Bowerman seemed somewhat aloof from the voters, unable to establish 'the homely human contacts' which win votes.[82] Further, her anti-socialist jibes in an industrial, working-class area had aroused some hostility. However, Emmeline would tolerate no talk about Christabel's defeat bringing an end to her daughter's possible career in politics; she would have none of it. Ever optimistic, she wrote to Ethel Smyth that she pinned her hopes on Christabel's success at some by-election.[83]

Tired and deflated after the hopes of the election campaign, Emmeline travelled with Catherine Pine to Paris for the New Year of 1919 for a much needed change of scene. She met up with old friends, including Alice Morgan Wright and Eleanor Garrison. When they all dined at Alice's studio, 'Mrs. P. was geniality itself', commented Eleanor, '& there was no end of talk of militant experiences. She can talk books & pictures & social life as well & is just as charming as one could wish.' Catherine Pine appeared 'a most amusing person & she makes Mrs. Pankhurst laugh & laugh'. Emmeline, in her turn, invited some of her friends to a meal at an excellent restaurant, La Maisonette.[84] But all was not play. Emmeline wanted to keep an eye on the Peace Conference which began on 18 January and would involve negotiations, over six months, with thirty-seven nations; although peace had returned to the Western fronts, fighting was continuing elsewhere, particularly in Russia where a civil war raged. Neither the old Russia nor the Soviet Union sent delegates to the talks but the threat of a 'Bolshevik tide'[85] cast a long shadow over the proceedings which made her extremely anxious. She did not want Germany nor Bolshevism to be influential in the post-war situation and feared that too much would be given away to the defeated enemy at the possible cost of weakening the alliance between Britain and France. She lost no opportunity while in Paris to discuss the situation with influential persons who would listen, including the French Foreign Minister, Monsieur Briand whom she met at a social gathering at the home of one of Ethel Smyth's friends.[86]

Despite her worries about the peace process, Emmeline arrived back home in March in joyful mood since she had heard that a parliamentary seat was likely to become vacant in April; the MP for the Westminster Abbey division had stated that he thought he should retire from parliament, owing to poor health. Immediately Emmeline penned a letter asking members of the Women's Party for donations to fund a campaign to support Christabel's candidature. 'We look upon Westminster as an ideal constituency for us to contest. When John Stuart Mill introduced the question of Women's Suffrage in the House of Commons he was its member.' The Abbey Division of Westminster was the premier constituency of the country since it contained 'Westminster Abbey, the Houses of Parliament and Downing Street and is the very heart of our great Empire. This is to me a most inspiring thought and I feel that it will make us all work with might and main to win the seat for women.'[87] But Emmeline's enthusiasm was not echoed elsewhere. Many of the devoted followers who had surrounded her in the suffrage struggle had drifted away while her patriotic and vigorous support for the war effort was regarded now, in peace time, with something like revulsion as demobilisation revealed the extent of the slaughter and mutilation in the trenches. Membership of the Women's Party was dwindling and the General Secretary of the British Commonwealth Union was threatening to discontinue any further financial support since no information had been supplied about how the previous donations had been spent.[88]

This falling away of support was keenly felt by the ageing Emmeline. Many years later, Christabel reflected that after the war she and her mother were 'two *virtually exiled leaders*' so that loyalty to Emmeline and herself was 'a very costly ... & a risky thing' to those who had to grapple with a world which did not want any of their followers 'who were "too loyal"'.[89] Emmeline's participation in the Victory Loan Rally, in Trafalgar Square, on 28 June, was her last major appearance for the Women's Party which faded away shortly after; nothing more was heard of Christabel's candidature.

Martin Pugh claims that what seems striking at this time is that neither Emmeline nor Christabel envisaged playing any further part in the women's movement in Britain.[90] Such a statement reveals a considerable lack of under-standing of not only the women's movement but of Christabel's and Emmeline's interests. As noted earlier, Christabel had a new interest in life, namely Second Adventism, while Emmeline's feminism and interests were out of tune for the times. Although a long struggle lay ahead to end the inequalities that women faced in enfranchisement, pay, employment opportunities, divorce and marriage laws, Emmeline's message about the evils of Bolshevism and socialism were seen as old-fashioned by many feminists and as overshadowing her concern for a range of other feminist issues, including co-operative housing to lessen the drudgery of housewives. But, primarily, Emmeline's insistence upon the primacy of gender rather than class, plus her autocratic style of leadership, were consid-ered more appropriate to the old social order than the new. The *Daily News* had opined late in 1918 that 'the Pankhurst coterie has for some time been a spent force in Feminist circles' and this was indeed the case. The feminist movement that had once focused on the struggle for the vote was beginning to fracture into a range of causes, including pleasurable sex within marriage, birth control, socialism and pacifism. In March 1918, Dr. Marie Stopes, one-time member of the WSPU, had published *Married love*, a book that taught men and women the techniques of love-making, the importance of foreplay and the desirability of female sexual pleasure. Although the text was condemned as immoral, two thousand copies were sold within a fortnight and it reached its seventh edition by summer 1919. *Wise parenthood, the treatise on birth control for married people*, published in November 1918, had a similar success.[91] A pull towards socialism, communism and pacifism was evident among other feminists, including Emmeline's own daughters, Sylvia and Adela; some of these women were speaking of marriage under capitalism as 'legal prostitution', advocating early sex education and scorning the 'spinsterly ideals' of the older generation of feminists.[92] Many years later, one member of this younger generation of feminists analysed the change in post-war feminism as a move from the political to the economic. Thus for Vera Brittain, pre-war feminist leaders like Emmeline Pankhurst and Millicent Garrett Fawcett were 'leisured' women who spent endless hours in unpaid political work on public platforms and committees while the post-war feminists wanted professional work that would give them economic independence.[93]

Had Emmeline been alive when Vera Brittain's essay was published, she would have understood the argument about the importance of economic independence for women and, undoubtedly, questioned the assertion that she was 'leisured'. Ever since her widowhood, she had had to earn a living and had often faced financial hardship. The salary she had been paid as a key speaker for the WSPU and then the Women's Party had never been enough to cover any personal needs and now that the Women's Party had faded away, she found herself saddled with its liabilities, especially Tower Cressey, and, yet again, hard pressed for money for the upkeep of her own home and the support of her adopted children. A decision was made to present Tower Cressey to Princess Alice as a War Memorial Adoption Home while another lucrative lecture tour of North America was planned for the autumn. Optimistic as ever, Emmeline wrote to Ethel Smyth on 21 June 1919 saying that now that she had only her own interests to consider, she was sure she could earn enough to support herself and the children for the rest of her days. She hoped, on her return, to find a small house in the country not too far from London or Woking.[94]

Before Emmeline left Britain that autumn, she spent the summer resting with the children at a cottage in Peaslake, Surrey. When Ethel visited one day, she was shocked to see the airs and graces which the children had been taught – they 'flitted about like fairies, offered you scones with a curtsey, and kissed their hands to you when they left the room'. Having been a tomboy as a child, Ethel bluntly told Emmeline that she preferred to see children brought up 'naturally'. An annoyed Emmeline hastily muttered something about 'old maids' always thinking they know best how the young should be brought up. The incidence did not sour the close friendship between the two women, however, so Emmeline also made a short visit to Ethel at *Coign*. On 23 July, Emmeline and Christabel each signed their wills which stated that, subject to the payment of funeral expenses and debts, the estate of each was bequeathed to the other who was also appointed the executrix.[95] In September, Emmeline sailed with Catherine Pine for the United States and Canada. Although she often longed to return home, she was obliged to stay away and earn her living for six years.

22

LECTURER IN NORTH AMERICA
AND DEFENDER OF THE
BRITISH EMPIRE (SEPTEMBER
1919–DECEMBER 1925)

On 13 September 1919, Emmeline arrived in New York on the White Star liner *Adriatic*. 'The great work confronting the women now is the suppression of Bolshevism', she told the press, 'and this is one of the principal reasons for my tour of Canada and the United States.' For the preservation of the peace of the world, she urged an immediate alliance be formed openly by the three democracies of England, France and the United States.[1] 'Parlour Bolshevism', she suggested, 'seems to be quite prevalent here. Men and women during the war were awakened as never before to an interest in labor conditions and received many false ideas. They fell victims to the Bolshevist propaganda ... [and] were reached through their best side – their sympathy with the workers.' But the Bolsheviks were undemocratic and did not represent the working class as a whole but only those members who agreed with their doctrines. Through a form of class domination, they sought to impose their views on society. '[I]t is incumbent on us all', insisted Emmeline, 'to defend Christian civilization.'[2] As Mitchell notes, Emmeline was ploughing no lone furrow since America was at the height of an hysterical red scare, whipped up by industrialists and financiers who were determined to undermine militant unionism. But Emmeline's message of social service to the community, of the importance of reconstruction after the war, of the critical role of democracy, was intended just as much for the wealthy as for the poorer and unionised sections of society.[3] With such words, reminiscent of the defunct Women's Party, Emmeline began her tour in earnest.

As she travelled south, she met many old suffrage friends rejoicing in the fact that, just two weeks before her arrival, all American women had finally been given voting rights on equal terms with men. Mary Kilbreth, the disgruntled President of the American National Association to Oppose Woman Suffrage, used the occasion to question whether Emmeline Pankhurst, who had lead a 'reign of terror' that involved 'bombs, kerosene and vitriol throwing' was an appropriate person to preach to American women about their patriotic duty. Emmeline's friend, the journalist Rheta Childe Dorr, immediately leapt to the defence. In a much discussed letter in the *New York Times* headed 'The Militant Suffragist in the Role of World Reconstructor', she pointed that if the anti-suffragists were counting 'on that long past fight between the suffragettes and

Mr. Asquith's Government to prevent Mrs. Pankhurst from doing a 100 per cent efficient piece of reconstruction work, both here and in Europe, they were making another mistake'.[4] No stranger to controversy, Emmeline was unruffled by the incident as she prepared to travel north, to Halifax, Nova Scotia, in order to begin a long winter journey to Victoria and then Vancouver, Canada, where she was to speak under the auspices of the Women's Canadian Club.

Arriving in Vancouver in late November, Emmeline received a warm welcome from the club women who held a reception in honour of 'one to whom thanks is due for woman suffrage, in the British Empire, at least'.[5] Representatives were there not only from the Women's Canadian Club but also from the Women's New Era League, Woman's Forum, Women's Conservative Association, Women's Liberal Association, and the Widows, Wives and Mothers of Great Britain's Heroes' Association. The themes of her talks in the city were similar to those she had been delivering for the last few years. Thus on 27 November, she spoke to a packed theatre of 1,200 on 'Class co-operation versus class war'. It was an 'inspiring address', interrupted with 'frequent outbursts of applause', claimed the *Victoria Daily Times*. 'Mrs. Pankhurst brought all the oratorial fire and enthusiasm with which she gained the admiration of both supporter and opponent during her long and strenuous campaign for women's suffrage ... the gospel of Imperialism could have no better disciple than this clever woman.'

Emmeline opened her address by stating her belief in the greatness of the British Empire 'and in its duty and responsibility to the rest of the world'. She then went on to decry the class war which was evident in all corners of the globe and, in particular, expounded how the cult of Karl Marx had inspired Bolshevism, which was 'the absolute negation of everything we have been taught to look upon as right in our civilization – patriotism, religion, family life and the relationship between father and child, husband and wife'. The proletariat, as the lower classes call themselves, she continued, say they cannot hope to rise to the level of the middle class or bourgeoisie and so must drag the bourgeoisie down so that both 'wallow in a common misery'. 'I take issue at once with that theory', cried Emmeline, amid applause. 'I say it is possible to level up the masses to the place of the middle class.' In conclusion, she appealed for co-operation by the people of the British Empire against the monster of Bolshevism, outlining her plan for an improvement in social conditions in a society based on Christian ideals.[6]

This was Emmeline's fourth tour of Canada and her warnings about Bolshevism and class conflict had a particular edge. As Mitchell notes, despite the many parades during the spring and summer to welcome back Canadian troops who had fought bravely, especially at Ypres, in the Battle of the Somme, and in the offensive of 1918 that finally broke German resistance, there was a profound discontent amongst the people, partly inspired by the socialist revolution in Russia. The civic authorities had reacted with alarm to a spate of strikes, and brought in federal police and troops to crush them. Between 1896 and

1911, over three and a half million immigrants had entered the country, including Germans, Scandinavians and Ukrainians, with small minorities of Russians, Poles, Austrians and Italians, all with their own cultures. Even the normally conservative farmers of the prairies were in revolt, not because of any sympathy with the ideas of Karl Marx but because they wished to preserve their livelihood in a society increasingly dominated by industry and capitalist finance. Such a diversity of peoples and interests created particular problems for the federal government which felt it had to shape the economic future of Canada and take bold and decisive steps to forge a sense of a common identity and unity, in which justice was for all rather than the privileged few.[7]

It was while Emmeline was in Vancouver that she heard the bitter-sweet news that Nancy Astor, with whom she had occasionally corresponded, had been elected by a huge majority in the Sutton constituency of Plymouth as their Coalition MP in the British House of Commons. Emmeline rose to the occasion, commenting to the press, '[O]ur hope as women will be that the first woman elected to this body will measure up to the enormous responsibilities she has undertaken.'[8] It was a bitter blow to know that the first woman MP had not been active in the women's suffrage campaigns nor known for her feminist achievements but an outsider, an American, born in Virginia. Nancy Astor, an ardent Christian Scientist, actively involved in old-style community and national service, including the gift of nursery schools and maternity centres, had stood in the shoes of her husband when, on the death of his father, he had to take his seat in the House of Lords.[9]

Emmeline returned to the United States after her short stay in Canada, but was back in that country by early May 1920 when she addressed the Women's Canadian Club in Toronto. Her commitment to the British Empire and imperialism had not wavered, and her advocacy of a particular role for women within this work continued to be frequent themes in her talks as she mingled amongst a network of like-minded women. Thus, in early May, she paid a warm tribute to the Canadians for the welcome they had given the English war-brides and expressed the hope that 'we British women – whether born in Canada or the Mother Country – have the power as well as the opportunity to develop this wonderful country and make it one of the biggest and best in our wonderful Empire'. Emmeline's representation of the Empire as a family, with Britain as the mother of colonial daughters, was not unusual and enabled women to participate in the ideological work of empire, shaping what was considered their womanly role and duty.[10] In particular, while she emphasised that both sons and daughters should be trained for service to the nation, women of a high social standing had a particular feminine role to play in imperial work. 'The daughters of the rich should be taught nursing, so that in time there might be developed a vast national organization which would ensure that every woman, in no matter how remote a district, would receive proper care and attention in time of childbirth or illness.'[11]

The warm receptions that Emmeline received seemed to revitalise her. But despite her fame, she was forever conscious of the financial pressures upon her.

'Now that I have to earn an independence for my old age and also to provide for the infants', she wrote to Ethel Smyth, 'I'm only too thankful I can do it, and in doing it help a little to keep the Empire together and defeat the Bolshevists and *defaitists* who are hard at work here trying to destroy the victory our armies won in the war.' The incentive to avoid living on the breadline was strong. 'This much is certain', she continued. 'I cannot reduce my standard of comfort to one of constant pinch and save, and I intend to carry out my plans for the children.' Some of the bitter-sweet news about the election of Nancy Astor was now seen in a different light. 'I and Christabel intend to return to the plough like Cincinnatus and see what other women will do with the power we won for them. We kept our noses to the grindstone for a long time because some one had to do it, not because, as people (even you) think sometimes, we are women of one idea, obsessed by it.' Reflecting on her life, Emmeline wistfully commented, 'Speaking for myself, there are many things I would have liked to be and to do, but I had to stick to my job.' Such a comment was undoubtedly tempered by her disillusionment with having so little money and being 'forced to work summer and winter' to support the children. Nevertheless, despite these moments almost of regret, Emmeline expressed a great enthusiasm for the Canadians and for Canada.[12]

This enthusiasm did not wane so that, after completing a lucrative Chautauqua tour of the West, where she addressed crowds of 70,000, she decided to make Victoria, a small city of about 38,000 inhabitants on Vancouver Island, her headquarters, at least for the summer holiday. Victoria, with its English-looking homes set close to the sea, complete with tennis courts and neatly tended gardens, was considered the most British of all Canadian cities. It had been founded as a fort by the Hudson Bay Company in 1843 and then developed in the 1860s as a naval base. Its garrison atmosphere had been further enhanced by the presence of Royal Engineers who, in its days as a crown colony, had built roads and policed the area, many later staying to settle there.[13] Emmeline was enchanted with the place and, at long last, had accumulated enough money to bring her adopted children from England. Kathleen was nearly six years old, and Mary and Joan about six months younger. In great excitement, Emmeline and Catherine Pine travelled to New York to meet the children and the French governess (she spoke little English) who had travelled with them on the ship. The little group stayed together in New York for a few days before Emmeline departed to give a talk, and Catherine and the French governess took the children on the long train journey across the Rockies, to British Columbia. It was a great adventure for the girls who felt very grown up when they had their meals in the dining car, although the evening meal – usually the boiled eggs they liked so much – was brought to their cabin. They took little notice of Emmeline's much loved Pomeranian dog, Tiny, who travelled with them, and was placed in quarantine once they crossed the mainland to Vancouver Island.[14]

On 19 August 1920, the *Victoria Daily Colonist* reported that the girls had finally reached Victoria and were staying with their adoptive mother at the St.

James Bay Hotel, by the sea. 'This is a lovely spot and very cheap', wrote a contented Emmeline to Ethel, so happy to have her small children around her again. She also confessed that she had been dabbling in a little spiritualism, buying a Ouija board which she now used as a travelling tea-tray since she did not want to believe in it. Thinking she might earn some extra money by writing, she had tried her hand at this, without success. 'I am really very reluctant to do anything except potter about, sewing for myself and the children, and reading. Also I found I was getting fatter than I have ever been, and am having massage and "rolling" exercise to reduce my weight.'[15] Before her breakfast each morning, Emmeline now began to drink a cup of hot water, claiming that it helped to keep her slim.[16] As the summer was beginning to fade away, she had to prepare herself for more addresses and lecture tours, the means whereby she earned her living.

In early October 1920, Emmeline spoke on 'Citizenship' at the Metropolitan Methodist Church on behalf of the Women's Canadian Club fund for the Jubilee Hospital. The main theme of her talk involved defining the responsibilities which their recently granted citizenship had imposed on woman. 'One of the greatest objections to women having the vote had been that they did not understand Imperial politics', Emmeline pointed out, as she spoke forcibly against those who advised that Canada should cut its ties from Britain.[17] Later in the month, when she addressed the Municipal Chapter, the Imperial Order Daughters of the Empire which had been working hard for the cause of the Empire, especially through its educational schemes for the children of permanently disabled soldiers, she stressed again that 'loyal support to the Empire is most needed today', especially when there were constant attacks on it. Women should advance through their influence and through their newly won citizenship 'the feeling of loyalty and faithfulness to the Mother Country', something that could be realised through the work that was most needed at present, that of helping in the stabilisation, construction and reconstruction of war-torn societies. In the old days, she concluded, her complaint had been that women were not asked to do enough. '[N]ow the time has come for women to make sacrifices and work for the salvation of the Empire, and save this great Empire of ours from all the dangers that threaten.'[18]

Emmeline's speech was enthusiastically received and she was presented with a bouquet of roses and violets. Such occasions were often complemented by invitations to dinner by local residents or influential British visitors. That autumn, she received such an invitation from a Mrs. Neville Rolphe, secretary of Britain's Social Hygiene Council, formed mainly to campaign against venereal disease which was spreading at an alarming rate, primarily due to the return home of infected soldiers.[19] Mrs. Rolphe was in Victoria as part of a world tour to collect more information about the problem, and included also on her dinner list was a recently demobilised doctor from the Canadian Army Medical Corps, Dr. Gordon Bates. Dr. Bates was a pioneer in the public health field and had founded the Canadian National Council for Combating Venereal Diseases

(CNCCVD) as part of a much wider campaign to help the various educational and curative programmes developed by the Canadian Social Hygiene Council. Special clinics, partly supported by federal grants, had been opened, a team of medical lecturers recruited, and various forms of educational leaflets and films prepared. What was missing was a lecturer with the common touch, who could communicate easily with the people, and lead a moral crusade. Dr. Bates had no doubt that Emmeline Pankhurst was the ideal person for the job. The problem would be to persuade the Executive Committee of the National Council that the well-known militant, with her forthright views, was the right person.

By mid December, when Emmeline had left Victoria and was in Raleigh, North Carolina, the United States, she was writing to Dr. Bates asking him to send the necessary literature to an address in Chicago, promising to make of it what she could in her present speaking tour. Emmeline enclosed with her letter a cutting from the *Raleigh News and Observer* about a recent court case where a Mecklenburg jury had awarded a woman damages against her husband for infecting her 'with a foul and loathsome disease'. For Emmeline this was an encouraging sign that the double sexual standard, which she had condemned so forcibly in the past, was no longer being accepted. 'It shows that even in the backward Southern States a far better public opinion is growing', she informed Dr. Bates. 'I want to do more to mould that opinion than I am doing. My difficulty is that as yet the ordinary lecture agencies are not ready to take up the question and no single individual can arrange speaking engagements without an agency of some kind.' Angling for a lecturing post with the CNCCVD, Emmeline expressed the hope that, after the end of this season, she would be speaking under 'other auspices & have more freedom. In any case I shall not be tied down so closely to the Anti-Bolshevist work because now many other people are doing the work I started in 1917 & I can turn my attention to other subjects.'[20] Emmeline did not want to miss the opportunity of crusading against venereal diseases, a subject dear to her heart and about which Christabel had written so effectively in *The great scourge*. She had never forgotten her time as a Registrar of Births and Deaths when sometimes the mother registering the death of a baby did not know that the doctor's certificate in the sealed envelope listed venereal disease as the cause.

With Emmeline being away so much from home, the children were brought up by Catherine Pine who, recollected Mary, was 'terribly strict, really like an old-fashioned nanny'. Emmeline, revelling in having the small girls by her side, always made sure that they were dressed alike, in pretty Kate Greenaway-type clothes which she usually made herself. The girls spent most of their time in the nursery but, in typically Victorian manner, were always dressed up in their best clothes for tea, hair fully brushed, and had a rather formal relationship with 'Mother', as they called Emmeline. Kathleen remembered that, in the mornings, on the infrequent occasions when Mother was at home, they would knock on her bedroom door and she would say, 'Come in'. Then they would enter the room very quietly, kiss Emmeline on the cheek, and go out again.

Late afternoon, if Mother was still in the house, the smartly dressed girls would be brought down about four or four thirty to see her, just before tea time. 'If we weren't good, we didn't get to see Mother', Mary later told one historian. 'That was the greatest punishment you could have given us. ... She was our God; she was everything to us.' But, despite the somewhat formal relationship that Emmeline had with her adopted daughters, when she returned from a trip the girls would be bursting with joy to see her again and she was delighted to see them. 'And yet I can't remember her ever cuddling or kissing us', Mary said, who was regarded as Emmeline's favourite. 'She never took us on her knee or cuddled us.'[21]

Kathleen remembered too that Miss Pine 'never cuddled us and was always careful never to show favouritism to anyone of us. I did not realise it at the time, but Miss Pine was always on my side – because I was always being spanked for the others she told me.' Kathleen had been told that she was the eldest, and so if anything went wrong, she always said she did it.[22] Such an apparent lack of demonstrative affection by both Emmeline and Catherine Pine, a typically Victorian trait, does not indicate that the girls were not loved or cared for. In particular, Kathleen remembered how Auntie Kate would tuck them up in bed at night, giving each a kiss, hear them say their prayers and, in winter, wrap their feet in warm cloths. Early in the New Year of 1921, when Emmeline and Catherine Pine were in New York, Miss Pine sent Kathleen a postcard of the Statue of Liberty in New York Harbour. 'My darling Kathleen', the warm greeting read. 'We send lots of kisses & hope you are well. This statue at night has a bright light in the torch to show the ships out at sea where they are, like your lighthouse. Your loving Auntie Kate.'[23] In Kathleen's view, although Auntie Kate appeared to be strict, she was 'in fact very lenient' with her charges. She remembered her with affection as the person who taught the girls to read and write, introducing them to the Peter Rabbit series of books by Beatrix Potter.[24]

By early 1921, when Emmeline was on another tour, accompanied this time by Catherine Pine, the little girls, who rarely stayed in one place more than three months, were living with a Mrs. Goodman on a farm in Esquimalt, near Victoria. Their French governess was also with them. When the girls had first arrived at the farm, in November 1920, Emmeline had given Kathleen a doll for her birthday, and Auntie Kate a doll's pram. Kathleen thought the pram was 'wonderful because I was wheeled around in it and let the others be wheeled'. However, she hated the doll which was broken, the very same day, much to Emmeline's anger, when it was dropped on the stairs. Emmeline, who had never been in favour of formal schooling for her own daughters when they were young, fearing that it would crush originality, was of much the same view now and was paying Mrs. Goodman, a widow with a small son, to teach the three girls. 'I'm afraid we were not very good scholars', recollected Kathleen. 'We used to go and hide in the hayloft and have one of us down below saying she could not find us – and that ended our lessons.' Emmeline had hoped that the French mademoiselle would teach the girls to converse in the French language but it was not very successful. The children did not like her because if they were naughty she would lock them in a dark cupboard, a particular ordeal for Mary and Joan who, unlike Kathleen, were frightened of the dark. The dislike of their governess intensified when, one day, she squashed a mouse behind the very same cupboard.[25]

Emmeline, on a lecture tour in the USA, arrived in Pittsburgh in late January 1921. It was here she heard the unexpected, delayed news that her brother, Herbert, had died one month previously. Weeping in sorrow, she wrote on 28 January to Ethel Smyth:

> My heart yearns for the few I love to-day, for I have just heard that my dear brother Herbert, whom you met, died on 28th December, and was laid on New Year's Day beside my sister Mary. ... It is a dreadful blow that he, so much younger than I am, should go first. There was never any one like him, so unselfish, so always ready to help, never claiming anything for himself. ... To-day I feel life and its burden almost intolerable and yet one must go on to the end. Thank God dear old Lady Pine is with me. ... If only I had been better to him, more with him, made him feel how much I loved him, my heart would not be so sore ... Oh the unavailing tears![26]

Emmeline now had few relatives for whom she cared deeply. There were the adopted children and, of course, her eldest daughter, Christabel, but her two other daughters, Sylvia and Adela, were supporting the communism she so hated. Sylvia, according to her biographer, had now become 'a political pariah' to her mother while Adela, who had recently given birth to a baby girl, rarely kept in contact.[27] With a heavy heart, Emmeline threw herself into her lecturing. On 7 March she wrote to Ethel Smyth from the Hotel Pennsylvania, New York, where she was staying for about one month, full of hope that she could earn enough to purchase 'one of these dear little houses in Victoria with 1 to 3 acres of garden and orchard, where I could live happily and comfortably with the babes, ekeing [sic] out my income with a few weeks lecturing and a little writing.'[28] Emmeline cherished the dream that Christabel and little Elizabeth would come and live with her. Then suddenly, in an abrupt way, Emmeline ended her close friendship with Ethel Smyth.

The blunt Ethel Smyth, not known for her tact, had written to Emmeline, telling her about a testimonial fund that had been set up in England, in tribute to the work that she and Christabel had done for the women's cause. A number of Emmeline's old friends, such as Lady Constance Lytton, Dr. Flora Murray, Sybil Rhondda, Kitty Marshall, May Billinghurst, Ada Wright, Barbara Wylie and Elsie Bowerman had been involved in the fund raising which reached only £3,000 rather than the hoped for £10,000. Although the intention was to spend the money on purchasing a country house which could be presented to

Emmeline on her return from America, the fund organisers and Ethel felt that Emmeline's plans depended on Christabel who was now a Second Adventist. In plain language and without any varnishing, Ethel tried to explain to Emmeline the dilemma in which the fund organisers found themselves. Emmeline was deeply offended by the tone and sentiments that were expressed and on 10 March 1921 returned Ethel's letter, attaching to it a brief note. 'My dear Ethel, I return your letter. You may wish to destroy it. I would if I were you. Em.' Emmeline wrote once more to Ethel, pointing out that the efforts of her old suffrage comrades in trying to ease her financial situation were wounding to her pride. Reflecting on the days when she had been an impoverished widow, Emmeline could not bear this new humiliation. How could they treat her like a pauper? Ethel, however, surmised that the 'real sting' was that 'certain persons, including myself, should venture to question the propriety of any mortal thing her daughter thought, said, or did'.[29] When, sometime later, half of the money raised was spent on buying and furnishing a country house in England, Westward Ho in Devon, Emmeline could not afford to maintain it; the property had to be let and it was, finally, sold.[30]

After the break with Ethel, a bruised yet proud Emmeline, still in New York, ploughed herself into her lecturing and was very persistent in chasing Dr. Bates for talks she might undertake, since she needed the money. She had already written to him in early March and wrote again, on the 13th, explaining that she had met some of the officials of the American Society for Combating Venereal Disease and also watched some of their films. She advised him that if he wanted to interest the masses in the movement, then it was wise to take advantage of real-life tragedies that had attracted public attention. 'In England we got legislation for better care of Infant life through bad cases of "Baby Farming"; for the mother's right to a share in guardianship of Infants because of a lawsuit that revealed a father's abuse of his legal power; the married women's property Act came for the same reason.' Again she pressed her point that she was free after the 25 April and could go to Montreal the following day, give interviews to the press and meet representative people as a way of working up interest for the CNCCVD meeting on 1 May. 'Would it not be well to secure some prominent local man or woman as Chairman of the meeting?' Perhaps mindful that she might be seen as too eager and forceful, Emmeline added tactfully, 'I am making these suggestions because when we met you invited me to make them not because I am interfering.'[31]

When the Edmonton Women's Institute wrote to Emmeline saying they would be very pleased to have her speak for them, for a fee of $100 plus hotel expenses, Emmeline asked Catherine Pine to write to Dr. Bates, on her behalf, as her 'secretary', enquiring again as to whether this talk and others in her proposed tour, could be conducted under the auspices of the CNCCVD. Dr. Bates replied that there was now no opposition to the scheme since eleven of the nineteen members of the Executive of the Council were in favour of it, six were doubtful and only two opposed. He also asked Emmeline for a summary of the address she usually gave on Social Hygiene as well as details about the fees she charged.[32] Emmeline told him that the lecture bureaux charged $250 to $500 for her services, but she only asked for $100 from the women's clubs since she took a special interest in their work. 'I am very keen to help your move-ment', she continued, 'so keen that if I were a rich woman I would give you a whole year for nothing and pay my own expenses.' Her reply in regard to the question about the line in her addresses is revealing for the way she presented herself in order to be engaged as a CNCCVD lecturer:

> I appeal for a higher standard of public health & public morals and I illustrate the need for both from my experience in England as a member for some years of two elective bodies the School Board and the Board of Poor Law Guardians and later as a Registrar of Births & Deaths under the Local Government Board.
>
> A great many people think of me as a worker for women's suffrage only. As a matter of fact I have had a good deal of practical experience in Poor Law Hospitals, workhouses, schools etc. I prefer leaving medical details to medical men although of course if no expert is present I can speak generally as to venereal disease. My conclusion is that physical health & moral health must go together. I have no manuscript address for I am an extempore speaker. Your Council must trust me to say the right & the tactful things in the right way if I speak under their auspices.[33]

Emmeline's lecture tour of the United States, on the evils of Bolshevism, was drawing to an end, and once an agreement had been reached with Dr. Bates about her fees and the payment of her travelling expenses, she was ready to begin her new career as lecturer on social hygiene for the CNCCVD.

On 21 April Emmeline arrived in Toronto brimming with confidence, ready to speak at Massey Hall the following day. True to her suggestion that in order to have successful meetings one had to rouse the public and work up an interest, she held a number of press interviews before the meeting where she revealed that she had lost none of her dramatic flair for catching attention. Sexual diseases, she announced to an eager reporter for the *Toronto Evening Telegram*, which come from sex promiscuity, are closely related to Bolshevism which was like an infectious mental disease. 'If you get a healthy race ... mental and moral diseases will disappear.' The *Toronto Daily Star* had no doubt that Mrs. Pankhurst, who had come to plead the cause of 'moral sanity', was 'one of the great women of this or any other age'. When the suffrage for which she fought did not come, she did not sulk but devoted her considerable talents to the war effort. 'She is one of the great agitators who have learned that in quietness and confidence, as the Scripture saith, there is unconquerable strength.'[34]

Crowds flocked to hear Emmeline's Massey Hall address on 'Social hygiene and the world's unrest'. Mr. Justice Riddell, President of the CNCCVD, opened proceedings by pointing out that the main reason why the venereal diseases that afflicted 40,000 people in Toronto and half a million in the Dominion were not spoken about was due to the false idea that they were invariably the 'wages of sin'. Nothing could be further from the truth. The vast majority of surgical operations performed on women were due to such diseases. After Dr. Fred Marlow had addressed the audience, emphasising that venereal diseases were preventable, only if their spread was fought with a sensible strategy, it was Emmeline's turn to speak. She lifted the tone, claimed the *Toronto Globe*, 'from that of the purely medical to that of the spiritual'. In a speech reminiscent of her suffrage days, she emphasised that people's health was the cause of women and that women's viewpoint must be adopted when fighting the evil of venereal diseases. She drew upon her life experiences as member of a School Board and as a Registrar of Births and Deaths, emphasising that venereal diseases had contributed to the high death rates she recorded in congested areas. Although it might come as 'a surprise' to many in the audience, her belief that such things must not continue had been a key impetus for the militant campaign that she and her daughter Christabel began. While it would be a big struggle, Emmeline insisted, to stamp out venereal diseases in crowded Britain, in 'a young country like Canada', with its small population, results could be achieved more quickly, especially through educational programmes. 'As a practical woman', she concluded, to much applause, 'and it is the women who are practical; you men are the romancers – I ask you to send cheques as large as the importance of the work to the Council under whose auspices I am speaking to-night.'[35]

Further successful meetings were soon held in Windsor, Ontario, at Winnipeg and Brandon in Manitoba, and at Regina, Saskatchewan. Writing to Dr. Bates from Medicine Hat, Emmeline ventured to make a few suggestions for improvement. 'It seems necessary to find some way of interesting the large mass of people who will not go to "lectures". In order to do this I suggest that the meetings might be called "public health demonstrations" or "Mass Meetings to support a Campaign against Social Disease".' Part of the halls should be free with a charge for reserved seats and collections taken to defray expenses and for educational work. Educational literature should not be free, but on sale at every meeting. '*This I think very important*', Emmeline emphasised. One had also to be prepared for invitations to speak outside the advertised programme, particularly by institutions such as churches and clubs.[36]

By 21 May, Emmeline and Catherine Pine were back in Victoria and living with the children at 1610 Hollywood Crescent, in a select, residential area with magnificent views over the bay. But although she was tired after her exhausting tour, Emmeline had little time to settle into domesticity; her talks on venereal diseases had to continue and she was also in demand as a speaker on 'The ideals of empire' and 'Rights of women', to the International Order of the Daughters of the Empire and the Women's Canadian Club, respectively.[37] In early August, again under the auspices of the CNCCVD, she began a twelve-day tour of Vancouver Island, happy in the knowledge that Christabel, Elizabeth and Grace

Roe were coming to stay for a holiday. Arriving in Montreal on 7 August, en route to Victoria, Christabel explained that she had no plans to address meetings although she did hope to gather material about the possibilities for British women in Canada. All the objections that anti-suffragists raised about women's suffrage had been disproved, she insisted, and in Quebec, where women still did not have the provincial vote, the situation would right itself in time. Militant women in an intensely conservative England had broken open the door, she explained, making it unnecessary for other women to do what they had to do, but now was not the time to recall fights of the past. 'Men and women now have votes and that is all that is necessary. What they have to do is to forget old grievances and work together in a spirit of co-operation for the new future that lies in front of them.'[38]

There was great excitement in the Pankhurst household with the arrival of Aunts Christabel and Grace, and little Elizabeth. Yet the happy but ever restless Emmeline could not afford to be idle. 'I am wondering how your plans for an autumn campaign are working out and how soon work is likely to begin', she asked Gordon Bates on 14 August. She suggested that in the early autumn, while the weather was good, they should tour the more scattered districts, asking local organisations, such as the women's institutes, to arrange meetings. Her second suggestion was the holding in the larger cities of a week's mission to which local clergy and doctors would be invited to give their services. 'I should greatly like to undertake that kind of work', Emmeline enthused. 'In the cities I would visit the "prominent citizens" & try to get their financial support & would speak at the meeting making a different speech every time. I find with practice how possible this is for the question is many sided!'[39]

A reply to Emmeline's letter was some time coming and during the intervening period she moved to nearby 1428 Beach Drive, Oak Bay. The rented, one-storey house was close to a large hotel which, Kathleen remembered, 'had Chinamen as servants. It frightened the life out of Joan but it never bothered the rest of us.' Emmeline dismissed the unpopular French mademoiselle and decided, probably on grounds of finance, to send the children to the local school where a bully pushed Joan into a prickly hedge. 'Later, the school was moved to another place and, yes, our little bully came along too', continued Kathleen. 'One day I saw him sitting on a low wall near the school so I made one big rush at him and pushed him over! He never bullied Joan again.'[40]

Such experiences undoubtedly confirmed for Emmeline the view that formal schooling should be supplemented with parental lessons. When she was at home, she used to encourage the children to express themselves by dancing to music, such as Mendelssohn's flight of the bumble bee. As Mary recollected, 'We all used to dance, to gramophone records ... and she used to say, "Now do what you think ... flowery attitudes", and we did it.' Emmeline also insisted on speaking to the children equally in French and English so that they became bilingual. When one of the children asked about something, Emmeline would say ' "read it for yourself" and ... "find a book". She was very grim like that'.

Once when the children were given a copy of Charles Lamb's *Tales from Shakespeare* Emmeline took the book away and gave them Shakespeare to read instead. As the children struggled with the text, they would ask Mother about words and descriptions. Classics, such as Dickens and Thackeray were read too, as well as the Bible which was treated as history rather than religion. 'And another thing', continued Mary, 'if we ever said, "I'm bored", or "I don't know what to do", she'd say, "*Never* say that". She'd get *very* angry with that. Mother wouldn't *allow* anybody to be bored. She'd say, "Don't be bored. You've got a brain, think for yourself".'[41]

An apologetic Dr. Bates, who was soon to be married, eventually replied in mid September to Emmeline's letter, suggesting that she might work with the CNCCVD at its headquarters in Toronto, giving addresses to attract funds for the Toronto Branch. If that campaign was successful, then they might mount a campaign similar to that arranged last spring only this time they would cover the eastern provinces and the remainder of Ontario.[42] At the time, Emmeline was busy helping in the general election campaign, hoping that the Union government under Prime Minister Arthur Meighen, a Liberal-Conservative, would be returned and so suggested 17 October as a provisional date for starting the Toronto work. Because she depended upon the lecturing for her livelihood, she had to face the embarrassment of discussing the financial aspects of her employment:

> I don't know what to suggest as to renumeration. What are your ideas on the question. I have never before been paid for that kind of work. I should like to leave the matter in your hands just pointing out that the work will be done during the very short lecture season, that my household expenses will go on in my absence & that the work if done with enthusiasm is rather exhausting to me.[43]

Now sixty-three years old, the constant strain of travelling and speaking was beginning to tell on Emmeline. Nothing in her life had been easy and there were further hiccups before she could begin work in Toronto. On receipt of Emmeline's letter, a worried Gordon Bates immediately sent her a telegram, advising that no prominent speaker for the CNCCVD should be allied to any political party at the present time, especially since that body depended on the government for financial support. Reluctantly, Emmeline conceded the point only to find in early October that another potential embarrassment arose. Dr. Bates wrote an anxious letter asking for a clear statement, for publicity purposes, regarding her activities before and during the war. 'One difficulty of a particularly insidious character with which we have to deal has been the suggestion that instead of opposing Bolshevism you were a protaganist [sic] of Bolshevism during the period of the War. If you will forgive the suggestion I believe this to be due to a mis-reporting of some of the work which Miss Sylvia Pankhurst has undertaken of recent years.'[44] That her own name had been confused with that of 'Red' Sylvia, recently expelled under a blaze of publicity from the Communist Party, must have deeply upset Emmeline who was applying for Canadian citizenship. The necessary statement was drafted quickly, and by mid October she was lecturing in Toronto.

Emmeline's standing was so high in Canadian society that she was the subject of a feature article in *Maclean's Magazine*, early in the New Year of 1922. She stated that she wanted to live in Canada because she believed the country offered a future for her adopted children. '[T]here seems to be more equality between men and women [here] than in any other country I know ... there are such unlimited opportunities.' The journalist marvelled at the versatility of Mrs. Pankhurst who, 'always beautifully and becomingly gowned', had shown a remarkable gift for adapting her address to suit her audience. Emmeline Pankhurst had been working 'like a slave' during her first six weeks in Toronto and been well received by groups as diverse as the Masonic Lodge, the Canadian Manufacturers' Association, the Imperial Order of Daughters of the Empire, the Women's Institutes, the Women's Law Association, the Women's Press Club, Mothers' Meetings in Settlements, women in factories, men in factories, several men's luncheon clubs, men and women students in universities, college women's alumni associations, theological students, church congregations, men's and women's and young people's organisations in connection with churches, women in reformatories, printers on strike, and a number of drawing-room gatherings in the homes of social leaders and other women of influence in the city.[45] But such work was exhausting, and living in hotels a lonely experience. Emmeline decided to rent a house in Toronto, at 78 Charles Street West, and hoped to settle there as soon as the house in Victoria could be let. 'It has been a bit lonely without my babies', she told the *Toronto Globe*, 'and I shall be glad to have them and my own little house and my dear Miss Pyne [*sic*], with her mending basket, and all the rest of it.'[46]

Kathleen, Mary and Joan were very excited during the train trip to Toronto, finding the bunk beds in their cabin great fun. Auntie Kate had decided that she did not want Tiny to be put in quarantine again, as they travelled from Vancouver Island onto the Canadian mainland, and so smuggled the small dog out by keeping her in a covered birdcage. Although Catherine Pine worried a lot about coping with Tiny during the journey, the porter on the train was very helpful, recollected Kathleen. 'But at about twelve o'clock one night the train broke down and we had to get out and wait for another. The next train that came was not a sleeper like we had been on before.'[47]

Emmeline was overjoyed to see the children again but had little time to spend with them since she was often away, speaking on the moral uplifting of the imperial race. 'I am an imperialist, and I have even been called a reactionary because I am an imperialist', she told one reporter. Although it was fashionable to talk of empires as oppressive, she continued, she believed that they had accomplished a great deal so that it would be cowardice to break up the British Empire into separate parts. 'If, in our modern idea of empire, we eliminate the oppressive and work for the noble, we will be much better off. The great battles which have been won, our institutions and our great reforms which have been fought for, will be largely in vain unless we build up an imperial race worthy of the heritage.'[48]

With such messages of hope to the people of the Dominion, Emmeline's popularity soared so that thousands wore the pin she invented for the CNCCVD, a shield in the WSPU colours of purple, white and green. On her spring tour of Ontario and the eastern provinces, local and provincial dignitaries were proud to speak on the same platform with her, occasionally wincing under the directness of her feminist tongue. The Mayor of Bathurst, New Brunswick, took Emmeline on a tour of the city, pointing out that an impressive new building was a Home for Fallen Women. 'Ah', Emmeline replied, 'where is your Home for Fallen Men?'[49]

Emmeline's eminence was such that she was invited to be one of Canada's main representatives at a meeting of the Pan American Conference of Women which began in Baltimore on 20 April and adjourned to Washington later in the month. Although Nancy Astor was the key speaker, it was the internationally renowned Emmeline Pankhurst who, despite being restricted to just a five-minute address on the Canadian government's work for social hygiene, stole the limelight. The 3,000 women delegates stood on their seats, cheering her and waving their handkerchiefs. Privately, Emmeline discussed with Nancy an issue she could not raise on the National Council platform, prohibition. She had heard too much about the evils of bootlegging to support legislation that forbade the making and sale of alcohol and believed that reform should not come from without but from within.[50] Released from National Council lecturing for the summer, so that she speak on the Chautauqua circuit as a lecturer on social hygiene, Emmeline visited sixty-three different towns between mid May and the end of August, attracting large and sympathetic audiences. She had already written to Christabel, who had not returned to England but was speaking in California, asking her to join her – which she did, leaving Elizabeth with Catherine Pine in Toronto. Christabel ended her talks with a message about the Second Coming of Christ. Although Emmeline was not particularly enthusiastic about this new direction in Christabel's life, it was like old times to have her eldest daughter by her side as they travelled by car on the Chautauqua circuit.[51]

That autumn, Emmeline swung back into her CNCCVD lecturing and also addressed a number of women's organisations on social reform, including the Woman's Christian Temperance Union in Toronto which she urged, once they had won the prohibition battle, to take up the fight against sexual immorality.[52] Christabel was seeking her own independent life and was not drawn into her mother's campaign against venereal diseases. In November 1922 she preached to a huge congregation in the John Knox Presbyterian Church in Toronto and continued her religious speaking throughout the following summer, touring on the Protestant circuit.[53] As the chilly autumn and winter of 1922 settled in,

Emmeline had a reminder of her 'unbroken bond' with suffragettes in the past when, before Christmas, the Testimonial Fund Committee sent the balance left over after the purchase of Westward Ho; the message accompanying the gift was carefully worded, to avoid wounding her pride.[54]

As usual, a big Christmas tree was bought for the children who were very excited since it was only at Christmas and birthdays they received gifts. Kathleen remembered that the girls were given presents of big dolls by the gardener of a nearby park, that Christmas of 1922, a toy she especially hated since they were regarded as suitable to play with on Sundays. 'Most of the time we stayed in the nursery but it was the occupation always on a Sunday morning that we had to go down to the drawing room and play with the dolls. ... If I could sneak out and go into the kitchen where Auntie Kate was, I did.' That winter, the children sat fascinated when Mother took them to the theatre to see the famous Russian ballerina Anna Pavlova dance. Trips to the pantomine were great fun especially when, between the acts, two clowns played games with an umbrella and sausages. A visit to the circus with Mother was another vivid memory since the girls came home proudly carrying gas-filled balloons. Auntie Kate got fed up with standing on a chair, trying to retrieve the balloons from the ceiling, and eventually suggested that they were taken into the garden. Within five minutes, the girls were back in the house, crying to her that their balloons had flown away, high into the sky. 'I am very sorry', she told the children, 'but I cannot go that high.' Catherine Pine's care for the children was now complemented by the services of a daily governess, Mrs. Cookson. 'We were told we must be very good to her because she only had one arm. We tried but it did not last long.'[55]

It was probably early in the New Year of 1923 that Emmeline, Christabel, Catherine Pine and the children moved house again, to 76 St. Mary's Street. Emmeline continued the hectic pace of her work with the CNCCVD, which was later renamed the Canadian Social Hygiene Council, coming home on infrequent occasions. Tired after travelling, she was often strict with her adopted daughters who gave their idolised Mother little peace. In the new house there was a safety gate at the top of the stairs, as a precautionary measure against accidents. On one occasion, when Kathleen and Joan were rushing to get to the bathroom, Joan fell through the gate, tumbling to the landing below. 'Mrs. Pankhurst was home at that time', recollected Kathleen, 'and said I had done it deliberately. I got spanked for that.' On another occasion, Mother made Kathleen a dress. 'It was a red dress with white spots and blue trimming. She made me stand on the table while she put up the hem. I didn't like the dress and tore it not long after, which got me into trouble again.' Emmeline was especially upset that her handiwork had been spoiled since, on the rare days when visitors called, she liked the children to appear in their best clothes and hand around plates of cakes. When she was at home, Emmeline sometimes found too that she had also to deal with the usual childhood ailments. Thus, on one such occasion, she had to arrange for the tonsils of Kathleen and Joan to be taken out by a local doctor, the operation being performed on the dining-room table. 'Auntie Kate was a trained nurse and so we did alright after that, with lots of ice cream and jellies.'[56] Perhaps during these busy times as a mother with her second family, Emmeline reflected on her own daughters, especially Adela who had given birth to another girl, Christian, early in 1923, and now had a family of six (seven with the birth of Nancy Ursula the following year). That Adela had become disillusioned with the Communist Party and left it, and rejoined the Victorian Socialist Party, as an Honorary Organiser, was a small crumb of comfort to her mother.[57]

In June 1923, Emmeline – now a Canadian citizen – was elected as a Vice President of the Public Health Association. This new responsibility, together with her lecturing duties, left little opportunity to slacken the pace of her life. That summer she undertook an arduous but successful tour amongst the scattered population of northern Ontario. Together with Mrs. R. A. Kennedy, president of the Ottawa Women's Club, and Estelle Hewson, secretary of the Ontario Social Hygiene Council, who acted as chauffeur and general manager, Emmeline spoke in some thirty towns and travelled nearly three thousand miles.[58] She had already taken Mary, her favourite adopted daughter, on one of her speaking tours and now it was Kathleen's turn, with Auntie Kate by her side, to accompany Mother to St. Catherines, Ontario. On the back of a postcard of St. Thomas's Church, St. Catherines, Kathleen wrote, 'Sept. 16 1923 I went to this Church to-day with Mother.' Mother, Auntie Kate and Kathleen also spent a few days at Niagara Falls.[59] But none of the children ever understood Mother's work, nor why she was considered so important. At home, Kathleen had found a photograph album with pictures in it of Mother and Christabel in prison clothing. 'Auntie Kate quickly took the book from us and we never heard anymore about it.' Emmeline did tell the children, however, that their mothers had died just after they were born and that their fathers had been killed in the war. She also had the girls christened and promised that later they could have the surname of Pankhurst.[60]

During September, Emmeline spoke frequently at the Toronto Exhibition and throughout the autumn continued to spread the message of social hygiene to a wide range of groups, including delegates from the women's institutes who assembled in October at the Eastern Ontario Convention in Ottawa. Paying tribute to the institutes – whose motto was 'For Home and Country' – as 'the greatest and finest women's organizations in Canada', she begged for the support of the farm women in her cause. 'Help us to educate the people of the Dominion to the necessity of a single standard of morals – that of the highest. Teach your children reverence for the marriage vow of men and women – instil into their minds the belief in purity of body, mind and soul.'[61] The Canadian people and the press adored her. James Pond, the well-known Lecture Bureau Manager, claimed that Mrs. Pankhurst was one of the 'most womanly women' he had ever known, while Dr. Hastings, Toronto's medical health officer, described Emmeline as 'a motherly soul, whom to know was to love'.[62]

Emmeline had succeeded in wooing the Canadian public and proving herself worthy of her Canadian citizenship, but all was not well.

Ever since the arrival of Christabel and Elizabeth into her home, Emmeline was aware of the tension between her eldest daughter and Catherine Pine. Catherine Pine, with impish good humour, was apt to joke privately to Emmeline that if Christabel's gloomy prediction for the Second Coming of Christ was so imminent, it hardly seemed worthwhile to cook the dinner.[63] But worse than such comments were the differing approaches each adopted to the upbringing of the children. Catherine Pine was an old-fashioned disciplinarian, with sanctions such as no jam, nor reading of a favourite book or other treats for a week if Kathleen, Mary or Joan were naughty. Christabel, on the other hand, was much more lax with Elizabeth. 'Elizabeth wasn't punished at all', remembered Mary. 'Auntie Christabel would say to her "Why did you do it, darling?" and we were furious in our little baby minds. We used to stand on the sidelines all bereft of whatever treat it was, and there was Elizabeth eating her strawberries and cream.'[64] Matters came to a head and Emmeline was deeply upset when Catherine Pine decided to leave and sail back home to England. She never saw her again although they kept up a regular correspondence until a few weeks before Emmeline's death.[65] The news that Auntie Kate was soon to leave was kept carefully from the children. 'I woke up one morning and she was not there', Kathleen remembered. 'She left me her Bible, a hymn book and a Japanese letter box in which was a little chain necklace with a lucky charm spider. The spider was in gold and its web and the chain in silver.' A few days before, Auntie Kate had taken Kathleen to the shops – which the children never visited – and asked her what she would like in the way of toys. Finding herself in such an unfamiliar situation, Kathleen did not know what to say. She chose a toy which she did not care for afterwards.[66]

With the departure of Catherine Pine, Emmeline lost not only a devoted friend but also the children's nurse. A succession of nurses and governesses were subsequently employed, but the strain of organising it all on top of the fact that for four and a half years Emmeline had had no respite from her arduous work to support her household was too much; her health broke down. The Canadian government granted their popular speaker six months' leave of absence. At the Toronto Exhibition, Emmeline had noticed the Bermuda stall and fallen in love with the place; a British colony with a warm, balmy climate, it seemed an ideal hideaway to recuperate. In the spring of 1924 she travelled there, together with Christabel, the girls and Mrs. Cookson.[67]

Emmeline stayed in Bermuda for about one year, enjoying the more leisurely pace of life. Initially the family stayed at Glencoe, a guesthouse in Paget (Salt Kettle) but by March 1925 they were renting Roche Terre, a large house on a slight hill overlooking the Sound near Buena Vista. The house had two floors. Emmeline lived on the second floor where a spacious lounge, dining room and library were located while the children stayed in the bottom floor, with Mrs. Cookson whose husband soon joined them from Alaska. 'We could not forget him', said Kathleen, 'because we woke at five o'clock in the morning full of spirits, and woke them up'. Emmeline responded to Mr. Cookson's complaints by spanking the girls, with a slipper. Soon he and his wife left, and then another governess was employed.[68]

Emmeline decided that the children must learn to swim and accepted the offer of an old Bermudan to undertake this task. However, she was horrified when he threw the children overboard from a boat, and then rowed away so that they could swim after him. Such hard lessons were complemented by the safer methods of the new governess. Emmeline, dressed in a knee length, blue serge swimming costume with red braiding, complete with bloomers and mob cap, enjoyed playing and swimming with the girls in the sea. It was during this summer of 1924 that she wrote again to Ethel Smyth, in an attempt to resume their friendship. But her efforts were thwarted since Ethel found the tone of the letter cool and haughty, as though she were being 'forgiven' for having 'failed' her friend; she also suspected that Emmeline was lonely and bored.[69]

Christabel, by now a successful author of religious books, was often away from home, preaching on the mainland. Even when she was at Roche Terre she frequently withdrew from family life in order to write, even leaving the table during the middle of a meal, something the children were forbidden to do.[70] Emmeline missed the company of her eldest daughter and, now that her health was restored, was finding domesticity tedious. However, her presence in the colony was a great encouragement to the leaders of the women's suffrage struggle there and she eagerly accepted their invitation the following spring to speak in support of a women's suffrage bill. Crowds flocked to hear her at the Mechanics Hall, Queen Street, Hamilton, and were pleasantly surprised when they saw a petite, fragile woman who spoke softly, with humour and sparkle. Emmeline expressed astonishment that the old question of the parliamentary vote for women, which belonged to the pre-war days, was still unsettled in Bermuda. 'Really, gentlemen', she chided, amid laughter, 'I could not have believed that your women had not yet got the vote – even Spain is thinking of giving it! ... Bermuda claims not only to be the oldest colony but the oldest Parliament amongst the colonies – I wonder that you haven't more courage!' But even the support of a world-famous suffrage leader failed to break down the conservatism of the Island legislators. The bill was defeated by a heavy majority, women in Bermuda not being granted the vote until 1944.[71]

Financial matters now became pressing for Emmeline; she had no regular income and was living on her rapidly dwindling savings. Reflecting on her future, she decided she did not want to return to her lecturing job in Canada; the very thought of the severe winters made her shudder. But how else could she earn a living? She hit upon the idea of opening a family business with Christabel and perhaps a close woman friend in a warm climate closer to England, possibly on the Mediterranean coast. Christabel could continue with her writing while Emmeline and the friend ran the business; that way they could earn enough to support themselves and also have a home. Although

Christabel was not keen on the idea, Emmeline persevered with her plan, writing to Mabel Tuke, one-time WSPU Honorary Secretary, who was not only enthusiastic but also suggested that they open a tea-shop on the French Riviera where tourists and expatriates would be plentiful. Mabel's enthusiasm, which was backed up by an offer to put up most of the capital, seems to have won over the reluctant Christabel. Before Emmeline's scant savings could be invested in such an enterprise, however, she had to reappraise her situation and, in particular, the cost of running her large household. She could no longer afford to employ a nurse and a governess, nor support three children. Reluctantly, she decided that Kathleen and Joan would have to be sent back to England, and arranged, through friends, for the girls to be adopted by well-to-do people (this was a time when adoption procedures were very lax) who could give them the chances in life she could not. It was a difficult decision to make, but Emmeline made it, reasoning that it was kinder to make the break with the girls now than to wait until they were older. However, she did not part with the fiery, red-headed Mary who was not only her favourite child but had also been left a small legacy, in trust, by a Mrs. Home, possibly her mother. Elizabeth, of course, stayed with Christabel.

It must have been hard for the children to part, especially so for Mary and Kathleen who were close friends, and for Emmeline to part with the children. Emmeline was unsure how to convey the news and eventually decided to tell the ten-year-old Kathleen, the eldest, who was given the responsibility of looking after Joan during the journey. 'Mrs. Pankhurst told me one day', recollected Kathleen, 'that we were going to see an aunt in England. So I was scrubbed well as I had a sunburnt neck. I nearly took all the skin off myself trying to get the sunburn out. We sailed on a ship in a first class cabin. That was great. I was in charge of Joan.' When they arrived in England, the two girls were met by Emmeline's sister, Ada Goulden Bach. After staying with her for a couple of days, they went to the Tower Cressy orphanage and were eventually adopted, Kathleen by John Coleridge Taylor, an *Evening Standard* journalist, and Joan by a wealthy couple in Scotland.

Shortly after the departure of the two girls, Emmeline, Christabel, Mary and Elizabeth left for London and met up with Mabel Tuke. In the late summer of 1925, the group travelled to Paris where they stayed in Christabel's flat. Mary and Elizabeth in their smart Kate Greenaway clothes, with kid boots and floppy hats, were greatly admired by the Parisians. Emmeline bought the children roller skates and since she was frequently out, the ten-year-olds had a lot of freedom, skating 'all round the boulevards alone for hours and hours', recollected Mary. If she had known, Emmeline would have been horrified so the girls were careful not to spill the beans. '[W]hen we came into Mother's presence again, we were like little angels.'[72] Emmeline did, however, enrol the girls in the local libraries where they devoured the English classics. By mid August, the household had moved to Nice since Emmeline wanted to find suitable premises, possibly in Antibes, before the winter set in; the Paris apartment was sublet.

Juan-les-Pins was finally chosen for the English Tea-Shop of Good Hope which looked very elegant with its tangerine-clothed tables, big window-seat and pretty window box with flowers. Christabel continued with her writing while Mabel Tuke cooked the cakes and scones. But few customers called. Only a few elderly British women of straitened means wanted to drink tea and eat Mabel Tuke's cakes.[73] Emmeline was in despair. She had little money left and the winter was much harsher than she imagined.

Former suffragettes in England, hearing of her plight, wanted to help. Lady Rhondda wrote to Emmeline saying that if she came back to England and worked with the Six Point Group, a feminist pressure group that worked for equality for women, including an equal franchise for women under thirty, she would be guaranteed an income of £400 for a minimum of three years. The proud Emmeline politely refused anything that hinted of 'charity'. But she was also of the view that the time was not opportune to raise the women's franchise issue again. 'The situation, both international and national, is exceedingly and increasingly serious and alarming', she replied. 'It seems to me undesirable to reopen the franchise agitation in such a world-crisis as this, especially as women have already enough voting power, if effectively employed, to secure the various ends to which the vote is a means.' Emmeline did, however, express her enthusiasm for an effort to make wise and constructive use of the voting power that women already possessed.[74] Emmeline must have had misgivings about working in the women's movement in England with its left-wing, pacifist leanings. Her feminism was now a maternal, imperial feminism that gave high priority to women's role in raising the moral tone of the nation and Empire. She was not likely to have much sympathy with those left-wing, 'progressive' feminists, like her socialist daughter, Sylvia, who advocated class war, an end to imperialism and free love. Soon after she had replied to Lady Rhondda, Emmeline developed bronchial symptoms, induced by the bleak French winter. Ill and nearly penniless, she had no choice but to return with Mary to England, arriving just before Christmas 1925.

23

LAST YEARS: CONSERVATIVE PARLIAMENTARY CANDIDATE (1926–JUNE 1928)

Emmeline went to live with her sister Ada Goulden Bach, at 2 Elsham Road, Kensington and for the first few weeks over Christmas and the New Year of 1926, while she was recovering her health, all press enquiries were handled by her old suffrage friend, Flora Drummond. She was deeply shocked when she heard that Sylvia was living with an Italian socialist and anarchist, Silvio Erasmus Corio, whom she refused to marry. For Emmeline who had been crusading for the moral uplifting of society, Sylvia's behaviour emulated the sexual irresponsibility of men and did not bring emancipation for women. She had once told Rheta Childe Dorr, 'I think it might be a good thing if Sylvia found a husband, an artist preferably, for Sylvia began by being a painter.'[1] But a socialist and anarchist, who already had two children from previous liaisons, without a marriage licence, was not regarded as a suitable partner for a Pankhurst daughter.

As soon as she knew her mother was in London, Sylvia hastened to visit her and, according to her account, 'the old affection overwhelmed us. Then, as the first rush of joy and sadness passed, a gulf remained.' Mary, however, who was sitting down to tea with Mother and Aunt Ada when Sylvia called, had a different recollection of the meeting. When the door opened and Sylvia came in 'Mother put her cup down, and I can remember this – I must have been about 11 – put her cup down with quite a crack, and she got up and she walked out. She walked straight past this lady, went upstairs and shut her bedroom door, and nothing would make her come down.' Sylvia was extremely upset and wept, uncontrollably. 'Aunt Ada was giving her tea and trying to comfort her and everything else, and she cried and cried and cried, because she couldn't get Mother to speak to her.'[2]

By the end of January 1926, the press was buzzing with the news of Emmeline's return after eight years' absence. The *Manchester Guardian* reported that although her hair was white, she had the same erect bearing, the same bright, watchful eyes, and the old skill in answering or turning difficult questions. Emmeline explained that although a new campaign was beginning to win an equal franchise for women, her next fight would not be for this cause but for industrial peace, improved housing, new electricity schemes for homes and cities – which would take some of the drudgery out of housework and clean up the smoky, dirty atmosphere – and the Empire. 'It was always a great grief to me', she told a *Daily News* reporter, 'to have to put aside all my wider interests for the sake of a single object – to break down the sex barrier. Now I think I deserve to be allowed to work for the general questions affecting women and the country generally.'[3] On 2 March, she attended the dinner organised by the Six Point Group in her honour at the Hyde Park Hotel where Nancy Astor, in a eulogy to the distinguished guest, offered to resign her seat as an MP in favour of the one-time militant suffragette leader. Gracefully, Emmeline declined the offer but expressed her willingness to contest a seat that might fall vacant; she denied a rumour that she had accepted an invitation to become a Conservative candidate.[4]

While the rumours continued, Emmeline was facing a still more pressing issue – how to earn some money. She initiated a discussion with the McClure Syndicate in New York about publication of a series of articles but the essays never materialised. Emmeline was not a writer but a skilled orator who thought best through the spoken word; the immediate response of an audience was what she thrived on. Nevertheless, she published short articles in the English press about women's improved status in British society. 'Sixty years ago in England every girl, with one exception – the Queen upon the throne – could be described as a compulsory feminine Peter Pan – a human being who politically, and to a great extent legally, never grew up but was all her life an infant', she wrote in the *Evening News*. Although women had not yet secured equal political rights with men, the 'barrier of sex' had been broken; women were now voters and, with the passing of the 1919 Sex Disqualification Act, could now enter the professions and become magistrates, lawyers, police women and top civil servants. 'What a change from the time when to be healthy and active, to be intelligent and intellectual, to be ambitious to take part in the world's work, was to be unladylike and unwomanly and unsexed!'[5] However, despite such reminiscences, it was the approaching General Strike of May 1926 that now preoccupied Emmeline.

She had returned to an England in which class conflict and industrial disputes were endemic. For a few months, Emmeline had been corresponding with Esther Greg, a wealthy Conservative whose husband, John, was a Major in the Special Reserve. Esther had put up the money for the Women's Guild of Empire (WGE), founded by Flora Drummond and Elsie Bowerman in 1920, and which had grown to more than thirty branches with a membership of about forty thousand women, most of them the wives of working men.[6] The WGE, which strongly disapproved of fascism, promoted co-operation between employers and workers and campaigned against communism and trade union tyranny; strikes and lockouts, it was argued, only caused misery and unemployment, and it was working wives, who were never consulted about stoppages at work, who bore the brunt of the poverty as they scrimped and scraped to feed their hungry children and pay the rent. As the industrial situation became increasingly serious early in 1926, Flora Drummond, the Guild's Controller-in-Chief, called on wives to go on strike and to join a women's demonstration against strikes and lockouts to be held on 17 April through the streets of London to the Royal Albert Hall. Emmeline watched the enormous demonstration and then sat, at Esther Greg's invitation, in her box at the Albert Hall.[7] During the following weeks, the situation worsened when coal miners, who refused to accept wage cuts or to work longer hours for the same pay, were locked out. The government drew up plans for a state of emergency and a General Strike was declared on 1 May, some 2,500,000 workers eventually being involved. Although the strike only lasted just over a week, its presence and the events surrounding it made Emmeline declare her political allegiance.

Emmeline had never been a member of the WGE and it was not to this organisation but to the Women's Auxiliary Service, headed by Commandant Mary Allen, another ex-suffragette, that she turned. Mary Allen, best remembered for her pioneering work with women police during the war, refused to disband her Women Police once the war was over; instead, she formed her own unofficial Women's Police Reserve, later named the Women's Auxiliary Service. On 1 May, the day the General Strike was declared, Emmeline phoned Mary Allen, putting her services at the Commandant's disposal. During the following days, Emmeline went into slum areas organising meetings and concerts for women, with the aim of keeping them off the streets and away from agitators' meetings.[8] On 3 May 1926, she also offered her services to Nancy Astor. 'How I wish that I could do what I did at the outbreak of war', she wrote, 'that is set a whole organization to work. ... Do use me if you can.'[9]

Although the strike soon ended, Emmeline's admiration for the way Stanley Baldwin, the Conservative Prime Minister, had handled the crisis, undoubtedly influenced her decision to stand as a Conservative parliamentary candidate. She thought long and hard before making such a commitment. She had always argued against party political allegiance but now the 'constructive use' of the women's vote was her main concern. 'To strengthen the British Empire and draw closer together its lands and people' was a cause dear to her heart.[10] She needed employment, and her oratorical skills could be effectively utilised in such important work. Emmeline had no inclination to stand as a parliamentary candidate for either the Liberal or Labour parties; her bitter conflict with the Liberals during her suffrage years made such an alliance impossible while the Labour Party, with its pacifist and anti-Empire leanings, its concern with state socialism, and its allegiance to the male-oriented trade unions, had marginalised women's issues. She had nowhere else to turn for the hope of a parliamentary career where she might bring women's issues to the forefront than to the Conservatives.

In early June, newspapers in England, the USA and Canada were humming with the news of the 'conversion' of the former ILP member and militant suffrage leader to the Conservative Party. The North American press, always fascinated by the petite, dignified Englishwoman who had once been an agitator, were delighted to interview her later in the year. If elected to parliament, Emmeline told one interviewer, 'reforms concerning women and children will, of course, be one of my chief concerns'. She would work for equal adult suffrage for women as well as for legislation to bring 'absolutely equal rights with men' in other walks of life. 'How absurd to think a youth of twenty-one ... knows better how to vote than a girl of twenty-one. Why, everybody admits that a girl of twenty-one is usually years older in common sense than a boy of the same age.' Prison reform, for both women and men, would be another task. 'I was put into solitary confinement because in the exercise yard I spoke to my daughter. ... My daughter was also penalised because she waited for me to catch up with her as we marched round the yard. This seems a bit harsh.' The reporter noted that although a few years ago Emmeline's views were considered 'advanced', today in any crowd of fashionable women she appeared not to be so – her hair was not bobbed, her clear complexion had no make-up and her dress, although by no means dowdy, was hopelessly behind in dress length. 'The other day in the drawing-room of her sister's London home she wore a black frock which was very smart without being at all extreme. It came a trifle more than midway to her ankles. Her grey hair, beautifully waved and coiffed, was crowned with a Spanish comb of conservative design.'

Had it not been for Mrs. Pankhurst and the struggle of women led by her for greater freedom, the article continued, it was doubtful whether emancipated dress would have reached its present lengths. 'Aren't they ridiculous?' remarked Emmeline, referring to the short skirts that younger women now wore. Emmeline explained that although she did not like short skirts nor heavily rouged faces, it was not that she was narrow-minded, but old-fashioned enough to consider that there was a difference between style and good taste. Tactfully she added that she did not expect young girls, like her nieces Enid and Sybil Goulden Bach, to dress like her and that 'while the post-war girl may do and wear things that shock her grandmother, she is still just as sweet and moral and fine as the average girl has always been. I believe in women, you know. Completely.' The article ended on a high note, praising Emmeline's integrity of character and common sense.[11]

The British press, on the other hand, greeted the news of Emmeline's 'conversion' in a sour manner. The *Evening Standard* commented that the announcement was hardly surprising since Mrs. Pankhurst had not run the WSPU democratically, but like an autocracy.[12] When an interviewer for the *Morning Post* asked Emmeline why, in view of her previous association with more 'advanced' political causes, she had decided to stand as a Conservative, she replied that she no longer believed, as she once did, that the state could do everything. 'Certainly in my younger days I believed in State Socialism of the kind advocated by Mr. Sidney Webb', Emmeline said, but now:

> I can no longer support the view that State ownership of the means of distribution, production, and exchange would be of any benefit to the

community. My war experience and my experience on the other side of the Atlantic, particularly in Canada, where I have spent a considerable time, have changed my views profoundly. Then came the general strike, and I saw that there were only two issues before the country, and that anyone who had the real interests of women at heart would stand firmly behind Mr. Baldwin and the Government. I am now an Imperialist.[13]

Emmeline had turned to the Conservative Party as the key political force that would uphold the British Constitution and Empire, support democracy, advance the cause of women and resist communism. As she later emphasised at a talk at the Ladies' Carlton Club, at which Mrs. Baldwin was the guest of honour, she thought there were only two parties in British politics – the Constitutional Party, represented by Stanley Baldwin and the Conservatives, and the Revolutionary Party which would destroy the material and spiritual aspects of Christian civilisation. 'The women in this country number eight million voters', she told her audience. 'If we can get these eight million voters on our side then we can save the situation. If you can only convince the ordinary woman that her home is threatened, her religion is threatened, and even her security in marriage is threatened, then we shall have her support.'[14] Although Emmeline had no particular constituency in mind for her candidature, she hoped to stand for a London division. Meanwhile she took part in the great Equal Franchise Demonstration, held on 3 July, to demand votes for women on the same terms as men. Emmeline was a Vice President of the demonstration's council, as were Charlotte Despard and Emmeline Pethick Lawrence, but the higher posts of Honorary President and President were held by Millicent Garrett Fawcett, now a Dame, and Eleanor Rathbone, respectively.[15] Emmeline's participation in the demonstration was merely a gesture since she had played her part in securing a promise from Baldwin to implement an equal franchise, a theme of his address in the Albert Hall some two months previously.[16]

Emmeline now began campaigning on behalf of the Conservative Party, touring rural Norfolk that August. In mid July she had written to Esther Greg, 'I have not yet succeeded in getting a car but am trying more people today. It is so many years since the old campaigning days when one could always get them easily.' Esther had taken the hint and offered her own vehicle, which was gratefully received. In mid August, Emmeline wrote again, from The Feathers Inn, Holt, expressing the hope that Esther could join her in a forthcoming by-election campaign but warning, 'I will go if they pay my expenses although one is always out of pocket at the end! I shall be when the Norfolk tour is finished I know. However I have had a small unexpected windfall that will meet that. So all is well.' Back home in early September, Emmeline pessimistically reported to Esther that, 'Something will have to be done if the agricultural counties are to be kept for the Con. Party.'[17] Communist Party members were making house-to-house calls amongst the agricultural workers and their wives, as well as organising large public meetings and talks in the more intimate atmosphere of the pub. Emmeline was told too that there were several communist or proletarian Sunday schools in the area, where religion was described as superstition, and materialism and class hatred taught to the children who attended. Such information fired her to work even harder to beat the communist menace and so she was delighted when, soon after her return, she was asked to propose the vote of thanks to Stanley Baldwin at a large Conservative Party meeting in the Albert Hall.

Sylvia, on the other hand, was advocating the communism her mother so detested while Christabel undertook, that autumn, a campaign tour in Britain for the Advent Testimony. The ideological separation between the Pankhurst women, and the various causes each independently supported, did not go unnoticed in the press, even in North America. 'Trio of Pankhursts Far Apart in Ideals' ran a headline in the *Toronto Daily Star*. 'Mrs. Pankhurst Against Communism, Sylvia Teaches It, Christabel Very Religious'.[18] Once a declared atheist, Emmeline had mellowed in her opinions about religion; her experiences in Russia and her hatred of the communist attack on Christian civilisation had made her more tolerant of and receptive towards Christianity, especially since Christabel's religious conversion. Although Emmeline appears not to have expressed herself publicly on Christabel's religious crusade, she continued to take great pride in her eldest daughter's achievements. On 4 November she wrote to Esther, 'The last meetings of Christabel's present tour were in the Queen's Hall on Tuesday last. I feared she would be worn out especially as she had just come from Dublin (a tiresome journey) but she was wonderful at both meetings. I wish you had been there to hear her.'[19] In early December, shortly after she had published an article in the *Evening News* titled 'Women Can Defeat The "Reds"!', Emmeline wrote to Esther telling her that she expected to be formally adopted, early in the New Year, as the Conservative candidate for the working-class constituency of Whitechapel and St. George's, in London's East End. Since this was a poor, socialist constituency that she had no hope of winning in the 1929 general election, Martin Pugh claims that Emmeline's willingness to accept nomination was made 'in order to spite Sylvia' while for Brian Harrison, Emmeline's concern for the British Empire, her distaste for socialism, and her support for Baldwin had 'displaced feminism from her list of priorities'.[20] What both fail to acknowledge is that Emmeline wanted a working-class constituency since she believed it was the working classes, especially the women, who were being most exploited by communism. Furthermore, since she was poor herself, she had to rely on the financial backing and patronage of others. As she explained to Esther, 'A lady who wants me to stand there has subscribed enough money for a good start and it has been put into an election fund. Miss [Barbara] Wylie is going to take charge of speakers & speaking I am glad to say and another good suffrage friend is taking charge of the social side of the work.' Emmeline confided that at present nothing would appear publicly for although Conservative Headquarters approved the local people had not formally invited her yet.[21]

Rejoicing in the good news, Esther invited Emmeline and Christabel to come for dinner on Christmas Day. 'I shall love to dine with you', replied a chirpy Emmeline, 'How kind of you to ask me.' Christabel was now leading her own independent life and her mother explained that she thought it highly likely that her eldest daughter would spend Christmas in Bournemouth, which she did. On New Year's Day, 1927, Emmeline wrote a note of thanks to Esther. 'I did so enjoy your Christmas Day party and have been telling my young relations how without any children or young people we wore our paper caps and pulled our crackers.'[22]

When Sylvia heard the news that her mother was standing as a Conservative candidate, she wept. Although she was passionately loyal to her father, and his socialist beliefs, she still wanted her mother's love and acceptance, despite their political differences. Emmeline's years in Canada had come as a relief to Sylvia since her mother was no longer present to embarrass her with her attacks on Bolshevism. That Christabel, whom she persisted in seeing as the 'prime family traitor and the corrupter of her mother's better instincts', had been in North America too, had dulled the pain that Emmeline preferred her eldest daughter.[23] But now that both were back in England, Sylvia had to face the humiliation her mother was inflicting on her. She wrote to the socialist journal *Forward* denouncing her mother:

> Permit me, through your columns, to express my profound grief that my mother should have deserted the cause of progress. ... For my part I rejoice in having enlisted for life in the socialist movement, in which the work of Owen, Marx, Kropotkin, William Morris and Keir Hardie, and such pioneering efforts as those of my father, Richard Marsden Pankhurst, both before and during the rise of the movement in this country, are an enduring memoir. It is naturally most painful to me to write this, but I feel it incumbent upon me, in view of this defection, to reaffirm my faith in the cause of social and international fraternity, and to utter a word of sorrow that one who in the past has rendered such service should now, with that sad pessimism which sometimes comes with advancing years, and may result from too strenuous effort, join the reaction ... [24]

Since the letter was summarised in most of the daily newspapers, there was no escape for Emmeline from what was now a very public family feud.

Emmeline responded to the situation by immersing herself in her election campaign, posing for the official election photograph. She wrote to friends, such as Margaret Bates in Toronto, with all her news. 'Tell Dr. Bates that I hope I may be able to do something for S.H. [Social Hygiene] if I am elected.' Everyone in the Conservative Party was very friendly, she stated, and old suffrage friends were rallying around her as she planned to take her election message especially to the women of the constituency:

> We begin our work of preparation next week by forming a woman's Social Club which will meet weekly to hear short speeches and be entertained by the very best music vocal & instrumental. We shall also have community singing of good old English songs. We are making plans for the children later on. Our idea is to make friends with everybody and replace class hatred & suspicion by Friendliness and Cooperation.[25]

Soon Emmeline was to attend the first public function at which she would appear as the prospective adopted candidate for Whitechapel and St. George's, and so she wrote again to Esther Greg, on 7 February, two weeks before the important event, inviting her and Major Greg to attend. 'It is to be a smoking concert (men & women). Sir William Bull Chairman of the London members is to speak with me. We shall have a good concert to enliven the proceedings.' The people of the East End, liking a fighter, were warming to Emmeline's presence. 'Already I am invited to speak at Mothers' Meetings, mission halls etc. and altogether things look encouraging.'[26] Just over a week later, Emmeline was writing with more good news. 'We had our first women's meeting yesterday', she cheerfully told Esther, 'and formed our Women's Club with about 60 members. Not bad for a beginning.' In addition to the help of Barbara Wylie, as chair of meetings, and Kitty Marshall, of social activities, a committee had been formed of four women who, continued Emmeline 'know artistes of all sorts to keep up a regular supply of entertainers. We have still to find the right head of a supply of cars for transport purposes. I expect she will materialise in due time.'[27] Emmeline's adoption as a Conservative candidate offered no relief, however, from the necessity of raising money for political and social work, something that was specially necessary since she had heard rumours that she might have to fight Wedgwood Benn in a by-election. With her usual optimism, Emmeline told Esther, that if the by-election came about they would need 'good money getters but I am not worrying about this for I am sure that good work will bring the funds'.[28] Inviting Esther to one of the women's meetings, Emmeline reassured her that her car would be quite safe since it was 'a quiet respectable well kept square inhabited by evidently well to do people who live in early Georgian houses & have lace curtains to the windows'.[29] But the pressure to find financial backers for the buying or renting of suitable premises for her East End work was relentless.

In high spirits, the indefatigable Emmeline was drawing upon her extensive knowledge of campaigning to fight her corner. She threw herself into the work, visiting every shop, every tenement, every public house, and even held open-air meetings.[30] But she was now sixty-eight years old and it was all too much; by Easter her health had broken down. Emmeline's old friends, Alfred and Kitty

Marshall, with whom she often stayed at their home in Chipping Ongar, took her away on a cruise to Gibraltar. When she returned, apparently fit, the arduous life began again. There were more clubs for women ('Fuchsia Clubs') to establish and more trips to be arranged to entertain the women. 'Next month', Emmeline wrote to Esther on 20 September 1927, 'the club members are having an outing to the Shredded Wheat Factory at Welwyn Garden City. We have chartered two buses. ... The factory owners supply tea.' In addition, Emmeline had to trail behind Commander Venn, the Conservative candidate for a possible London County Council election, making up for his deficiencies as speaker. Since she knew, too, that she could not defeat the local socialist candidate in her own constituency, Emmeline succumbed to the pressure to accept invitations from far and wide to speak for the Conservative Party. As she explained to Esther, since the party provided her agent and paid for the expenses of a canvass, she, in return, was doing 'a certain amount of "outside" speaking. I go for three meetings to Lancashire (our county) next week.'[31] Travelling hither and thither, at short notice, Emmeline worked too hard. Friends told Ethel Smyth that when Emmeline arrived at their home, due to speak at some meeting or the other, she was usually so worn out that she sank into an armchair, 'motionless and almost speechless', until it was time to start. But once on the platform, her whole being became transfigured. 'Radiant, inspired, she was as magnificent in attack, as irresistible in persuasion, as deadly in her methods with rowdies and hecklers as ever. Opposition had always called forth her full powers.'[32]

By the autumn, Nellie Hall-Humpherson had accepted Emmeline's invitation to be her secretary and Emmeline was living with Ada at a new address. 'I succeeded in persuading my sister to leave that dreadful Elsham Rd & come here where it is so much more convenient for me', she wrote to Esther in November, from the new home at 35 Gloucester Street, SW1. 'We are close to Eccleston & Warwick Square in what is called Pimlico or if one is snobbish South Belgravia. I get down to Whitechapel in half the time & Westminster in a few minutes.'[33] Emmeline was increasingly popular amongst her constituents. 'The East Enders adored her', recollected Nellie. 'She was a lovely person to them ... she never talked down to them and she was interested in them rather than expecting them to be interested in her. She was a compassionate woman in all her dealings with people, but particularly women.'[34] But Emmeline's relationship with both the central and branch offices of the Conservative Party was far from ideal. Used to running matters autocratically, staff in the Central Office found her difficult to deal with. Without money, property, landed family connections or even a motor car, she was not true blue. Nellie remembered sadly that Emmeline was 'so badly treated by the Conservative Central Office ... like a poor and unwanted step-relation' that she often wondered how the party survived 'if they treat other people so cavalierly'.[35] Emmeline's election themes of the importance of a democratic society based on class co-operation where women would work for the moral uplifting of both Britain and the British

Empire seemed out of touch with the recession of the late 1920s, especially the rapidly rising rate of unemployment, and were not particularly welcome. Emmeline did not fit 'into' the Conservative Party any more than some of its sexist, patronising propaganda suited her taste. 'When you put on your very best pair of artificial silk stockings with extra-strong toes and double cotton tops', ran one pamphlet, 'does it ever occur to you that not only are you clothing your shapely legs in beautiful silk stockings, but that you have also found one of the many things for which you should say thank you to the Conservative Government?'[36] The strained and uneasy relationship between Central Office and the once militant suffragette extended to the local branch office. 'The staff may have been devoted Conservatives', continued Nellie, 'but they were not devoted to Mrs. Pankhurst, her candidacy or me. ... In the end, we only dealt with them when it was necessary, officially.'[37]

The pea soup fog of that December did not make Emmeline's work any easier nor improve her health; since she was so tired most of the time, she worried about whether she was eating sensibly. Dr. May Williams, an ex-suffragette, advised both Emmeline and Nellie that they must eat 'proper meals'.[38] The Christmas break offered little chance of rest. Nellie, who telephoned Emmeline every morning, heard her in tears one day. Dashing around to Gloucester Road, she found Emmeline fretting; the Pomeranian dog that Christabel had given her as a Christmas present was ill and Emmeline was afraid her daughter would think she had neglected the highly bred animal. The dog died and Nellie, instead of enjoying the Christmas festivities, wandered around Hammersmith, carrying the little body to where it could be decently interred, while her husband waited for her in a West End restaurant, wondering why she had not turned up for dinner.[39]

Such devotion to the increasingly frail Emmeline, and the desire to look after and protect her, was not unusual. And there was some family news that was being kept from her – and most of the public – in order to shield Emmeline from what her friends feared could be fatal consequences. The unmarried Sylvia, cohabiting with Corio, had become pregnant earlier in the year and on 3 December 1927, a son had been born. Ada took careful steps to keep the news secret, fearful of its effect upon Emmeline's health. Usually Nellie would arrive at 35 Gloucester Road at nine o'clock each morning, and while Emmeline sat in her dressing gown by the fire, eating her breakfast, the two would go through the post. Now, while Emmeline was away campaigning, Ada vetted her post, looking for a envelope addressed in Sylvia's hand; when it arrived she hastily took it away. Nellie, who was not taken into Ada's confidence and could not understand what all the cloak and dagger mystery was about, was told that it was all for the best.[40] The secret was kept for some time longer, until April 1928. Meanwhile, on 29 March, when the second reading of the Representation of the People (Equal Franchise) Act was passed, Emmeline was sitting in the Ladies' Gallery. Her presence evoked much nostalgic comment in the press, which published pictures of her on the front page together with that of the

Home Secretary, Sir William Joynson-Hicks. Emmeline, watching Nancy Astor in action in the Lords, admired the way she dealt with opponents of the Act. She must have hoped that she would soon would be in parliament, displaying her oratory. But even allowing for the difficulty of being elected for an unpromising seat, Emmeline's prospects of becoming an MP looked increasingly remote. 'She looked very frail and old', commented one reporter, 'not even the shadow of an Amazon.'[41]

Despite the odds stacked against her, Emmeline's optimism prevailed. She decided that life would be easier if she lived in her constituency; the travelling was making her tired and she had a deep dread of using the London underground trains, refusing even to use the District Line when it ran above ground.[42] But, as she later explained to Esther, it was really necessary to live in the constituency 'if Whitechapel is to be won at the next election.'[43] Kitty Marshall found for her furnished rooms at 9 High Street, Wapping, and Emmeline took delight in making the place more comfortable. She bought a black carpet for the sitting room, mainly to quieten down the pseudo Chinese wallpaper of bright royal blue and gold; her desk and a few other things were moved from Gloucester Road.[44] But before Emmeline took up residence, the family secret erupted, in a most cruel way. Commander Venn heard that at a meeting of his to be held that evening, chaired by Emmeline, questions would be asked about whether one of Mrs. Pankhurst's daughters had had a baby, out of wedlock. At a time when unmarried mothers were stigmatised as wanton, sexually promiscuous women, Venn warned Emmeline what to expect. Shell-shocked by the rumour, Emmeline had time to prepare herself. When a working-class woman abrasively raised the question, she curtly replied that it was not her custom to discuss private matters in public and, trembling inside, went on with her speech. This was the last time Emmeline spoke on a public platform. When the Marshalls took her down to Ongar on Maundy Thursday, 5 April 1928, for the Easter break, Emmeline looked desperately ill.[45]

On Easter Sunday she went to church with the Marshalls, the very day that the news of Sylvia's baby became public. On the front page of the *News of the World*, not considered a respectable newspaper, was an article titled '"Eugenic" Baby Sensation. Sylvia Pankhurst's Amazing Confession.' Drawing upon an interview that Sylvia had given to the American Press the day before, the article told how the forty-six-year-old 'Miss Pankhurst' advocated 'marriage without a legal union', that her 'husband' was a foreigner, fifty-three years old, and that she considered her son a 'eugenic' baby since both his parents were intelligent and healthy people. The baby had been named Richard Keir Pethick Pankhurst, the first name being after the child's grandfather, Keir being after the famous Labour leader, the late Keir Hardie, who was a great friend of the Pankhurst family, while the name Pethick was given after Mrs. Pethick Lawrence, the wife of Mr. Frederick Pethick Lawrence, the MP. Sylvia had given the baby her own surname, not that of his father, and professed that she could not understand why the Pankhurst family, particularly her mother, ignored her. She had written to her mother about the birth of the child, 'but there was no reply'.[46] When Emmeline read the news she sunk into a deep depression, weeping all day long. That one of her daughters should disgrace the Pankhurst name, in such a vulgar way, and flout the moral standards that she had advocated, was too much to bear. The dread of taunts from communist interrupters when she spoke from the platform sent shivers down her spine.[47] 'I shall never be able to speak in public again', she kept saying, between the sobs.[48] The sensational story was repeated around the world, especially in the tabloid press. Worse, many members of the public thought that the newspaper posters headlining 'Miss Pankhurst' referred to Christabel. Twenty-three years later, Christabel still remembered the pain of the scandal. 'That was the biggest blow I ever received and the repercussions have not really ceased', she told Grace Roe. 'The whole publicity was skilfully engineered to harm me.'[49] As Ada, several other members of the family, friends and former WSPU supporters had feared, Sylvia's blaze of vulgar publicity, plus the insinuation that the baby was Christabel's, broke the heart of her already weakened mother and hastened her death. It also ended abruptly any hope of Emmeline's political career.

On Easter Monday, a more composed Emmeline wrote a consoling letter to Esther Greg whose son had injured his leg. 'A buoyant spirit can surmount all sorts of difficulties', she said, pensively, also expressing the hope that Esther might visit her in her new home at 9 High Street. 'You will be amused at my quarters over a hairdressers shop. His wife is my landlady & their name is Chipperfield. It sounds like Dickens. They are a nice couple & are good Conservatives.'[50] But such a cheerful attitude soon wilted under the strain of all the troubles that were gnawing at Emmeline's heart. In addition to the disgrace about Sylvia, Emmeline was living on a pittance without the adopted daughter she loved. She wanted the twelve-year-old Mary to have a good education and good prospects in life and knew she was unable to provide these things. Reluctantly, she had given up Mary, who first stayed with ex-suffragette, Marion Wallace Dunlop, and then moved in with the Coleridge Taylors who had adopted Kathleen. Alone and burdened with sorrows, Emmeline fell ill and took to her bed. Scheduled meetings that Nellie, Barbara Wylie or Edith Fitzgerald could not undertake were cancelled. Dr. May Williams, and Dr. Abrahams of the Westminster Hospital, looked after her, but although she was in pain, with no appetite and constant sickness, an X-ray did not reveal the cause. 'What can it be?' Emmeline asked. The doctors suggested it might be blood poisoning. 'If only I could get back my strength', she kept repeating, 'I know I've got five years of good work in me yet!'[51] On 16 April she explained to Esther that her doctor had stopped attending, now 'that the attack of gastric flu or whatever it is' was over:

I am having a masseuse daily for a time. She seems very capable & is going to give me douches or cavages or whatever one ought to call the treatment. I told her about your wonderful improvement under treatment and she wanted to know the ingredients. ... If you will let me know it will be most kind of you.[52]

Old and new friends came to call, including Lady Katherine Japp, a Canadian actress who had married Sir Henry Japp, a well-known engineer; she brought the pillow that Emmeline had asked for, some fruits and other things.[53] Christabel came occasionally and also wrote her mother weekly long letters about the current political situation. Emmeline took comfort in asking Nellie to sit on the end of her bed reading them out loud. But of most joy to Emmeline was the letter she received from Adela saying that she and Tom had come round to her viewpoint about the destructiveness of class conflict; they were now promoting the idea of employers and workers acting together, for the common good. Emmeline immediately replied to her youngest daughter, 'full of regret for the long rift'.[54] But Sylvia's requests to visit her mother were firmly refused. Emmeline would never forgive her for the disgrace she had brought to the name of Pankhurst and the vindictive way in which she had implicated Christabel.

As she failed to get well quickly, Emmeline worried about how she could support herself, especially since Dr. Williams had insisted that she had a nurse. Some well-meaning friends, such as Harriet Kerr, the former WSPU office manager, knowing of her financial plight started a collection with the aim of buying an annuity or some form of investment; Nancy Astor and Stanley Baldwin were said to be sympathetic.[55] Emmeline rallied for a little. But the small airless room in which she was nursed, with the constant noise of traffic and the smells and clatter of the shop below, did little to help. The plan to travel, with her nurse, to the Marshalls on 31 May had to be discarded when she had a relapse a few days beforehand.

Christabel and Ada hastily had Emmeline transferred to a nursing home in Hampstead. On 22 May, her thirteenth birthday, Mary came up to London to visit Mother. 'She was marvellous. It was the only time I can remember her kind of hugging and kissing and kind of weeping over me. She was delighted to see me again.' It was a great comfort to Emmeline to hear that Mary had had an offer of readoption, from a Miss Beves, and she seemed to pick up a little. One week later, Christabel wrote to Esther saying that she hoped her mother 'will show a definite improvement tomorrow & if not further advice will have to be taken. I gave her messages from you.'[56] But as Emmeline failed to improve, she begged to be attended by Dr. Chetham Strode; in the past he had treated her after her many hunger strikes by pumping her stomach. Dr. Williams and Nellie were strongly opposed to such a form of treatment, fearing the shock would weaken the patient, but Christabel felt she had no choice but to comply with her mother's wishes, as she explained to Esther:

> After a very anxious week I have put Mother under the treatment of the doctor who 14 years ago, after 13 hunger strikes had wrecked her health, restored her to health & enabled her to do fourteen years

strenuous service in the war & after. He is of course her own doctor & understands as no one else can, her constitution. She so greatly wished to have him, that I must have put the case in his hands even had my own judgment not also dictated that course.[57]

Emmeline was moved to a nursing home in 43 Wimpole Street quite near to where Strode lived 'so that at any hour of the day or night he is on the spot in case of need'.[58] Four days later, 5 June, Christabel informed Esther that the patient was showing some improvement.[59] But no amount of medical care, even if stomach pumping had been used, could save the broken spirit and broken body of Emmeline.

Emmeline was so weak that only Christabel was allowed to see her. When Nellie phoned the nursing home on 12 June, the matron told her that they had been trying to get in touch with her for days. Hastening to the nursing home, Emmeline burst into tears when a breathless Nellie entered her room, saying she had been asking for her ever since her move to Wimpole Street. She wanted Nellie to send Barbara Wylie to her since there was some urgent business to discuss. When Barbara arrived the following day Emmeline was past speaking although she indicated that she understood Barbara's message from Conservative head office that she was not to worry about money.[60] 'She can *just* show her pleasure', Christabel told Esther, thanking her for the bunch of sweet peas that she had sent to the nursing home, 'but she is very, *very* weak & in a very critical condition.'[61] On the morning of Thursday, 14 June, just one month before her seventieth birthday, Emmeline died peacefully. 'My greatest comfort is the look of joy on her face that I saw when I went back into the room where we had watched beside her to the end', Christabel later wrote to Esther. 'It seemed to fade afterwards & just peace & contentment & beauty were left – as I have never seen them on any other. But that first look of great joy I shall always have before me.'[62] Septicaemia due to influenza was listed as the cause of Emmeline's death on her death certificate.

News vendors in Britain soon had the headline, 'Mrs. Pankhurst dead' on their billboards, but the coverage of her passing was not just extensive in Britain but also abroad, especially in Canada and the USA.[63] On Sunday, Emmeline's body lay in state on the purple catafalque, surrounded by roses, lilies and carnations, in the little chapelle ardente in Cambridge Place in the West End. A soft light was shed on her from a reading lamp which stood beside the little gold cross above her head. Her calm features, framed by her soft, silvery hair, looked very beautiful. All day long women famous and obscure came to pay homage, including Ada and Christabel. Christabel returned several times, as though she was unable to believe that her mother who had so humbly claimed that she was her daughter's follower in the old suffrage days, was no longer by her side. Later that day, the coffin was conveyed to St. John's Church, Smith Square, Westminster, chosen for its nearness to the Houses of Parliament to which Emmeline had led so many suffrage demonstrations. Four ex-suffragettes kept vigil that night.[64]

The following day, 18 June, an impressive funeral took place as Emmeline went to her last resting place 'like a dead general in the midst of a mourning army'.[65] Long before the service began at 11 a.m. the church was packed to capacity with a congregation chiefly of women, old and young, rich and poor, many of them wearing their WSPU insignia – sashes, ribbons and rosettes in purple, white and green, medals and broad-arrow prison badges. Before the clergy arrived, Nellie Hall-Humpherson and a woman Conservative worker Elfreda Acklom, carrying respectively the flag of the WSPU and a Union Jack draped with black, marched up the nave, 'dipped' their colours, and then stood as a guard of honour at the foot of the catafalque. After the singing of the chief hymn, Emmeline's favourite, 'Sun of my soul, Thou Saviour dear', the Rev. W. F. Geikie Cobb, an old friend of the women's movement, gave an address in which he said that Emmeline Pankhurst had fought her fight consistently and coura-geously. 'We salute her to-day as an heroic leader and staunch friend.' As the organist played Chopin's Funeral March, former members of the WSPU – Barbara Wylie, Marion Wallace Dunlop, Harriet Kerr, Ada Wright, Georgina and Marie Brackenbury, Rosamund Massy, Kitty Marshall, Marie Naylor and Mildred Mansel – acted as pall bearers to attend the coffin to the door.

It had been intended that the thirteen-year-old Mary, who had been in the church, should not go to the service at Brompton Cemetery but when one of the women in the funeral cortège saw her crying in the vast reverent crowds that lined the streets, she leapt out of her car and gave up her seat to the distressed child. More than a thousand women wearing the Union colours followed the cortège to the graveyard where, under Flora Drummond's order 'Rally! For the last time', they marched eight abreast through the cemetery. The chief mourners included Ada and her four children, Robert Goulden (Emmeline's brother), Annie Kenney, Flora Drummond and especially Emmeline's two warring daughters. By the open grave stood a red-eyed and tearful Christabel, supported by one of her friends. Sylvia stood a little distance apart. Defiant to the last, she had brought her young son to the funeral. He was not in Sylvia's arms at that moment but was being looked after by women friends who stood nearby.[66] Adela, in faraway Australia, grieved for her dead mother who had become a public figure.

When Christabel went through her mother's papers at Ada's house, she found the letters her father had written to Emmeline, when he was courting her. Although, as noted earlier, many years ago Emmeline had given to Sylvia most of her father's papers, so that she could write his biography, these letters she had kept back; they were too precious to part with. She had little else to leave. Her estate amounted to just £86 5s. 6d. Probate was granted to Christabel.

24

NICHE IN HISTORY

After Emmeline's death, many tributes were paid to her; although she had spent her life campaigning for a number of varied social causes, it was for her leadership of the militant wing of the women's suffrage movement that she was remembered, at home and abroad. 'Emmeline Goulden Pankhurst', proclaimed the *New York Herald Tribune*, was 'the most remarkable political and social agitator of the early part of the twentieth century and the supreme protagonist of the campaign for the electoral enfranchisement of women', a view echoed in the British press, even by the left-wing *Daily Herald*.[1] Mrs. Pankhurst belonged to that class of famous women like Joan of Arc and Florence Nightingale claimed the *Evening Standard*; she was the very edge 'of that weapon of will-power by which British women freed themselves from being classed with children and idiots in the matter of exercising the franchise'.[2] Even Emmeline Pethick Lawrence, now president of the WFL, spoke generously of the 'gentle' autocrat who had ended her connection with the WSPU. 'Not only all women in Britain, but all women in the world, owe a deep debt of gratitude and honour to Mrs. Pankhurst. Without her genius and courage they could not have attained for many, many years the position they hold to-day.'[3] But perhaps it was Beatrice Harraden, writer and ex-WSPU member, who encapsulated most of what Emmeline Pankhurst had represented. 'She was a born leader', Beatrice wrote, 'one had only to hear her even for a short time to be caught by her eloquence, and to be convinced that she had greatness of spirit – and vision.' She continued:

> Christabel Pankhurst may have supplied the youthful vivacity of the new suffrage organization [WSPU], but it was her mother's character which formed its bedrock. It was at Mrs. Pankhurst's bidding that women of all conditions of life, young and old alike, sprang up to join in the militant campaign for votes for women, justice for women, equal chances for women, the open road, a free pass for women – demands so long and patiently toiled for through long years of discouragement, by the older constitutional societies. Her selfishness, her courage, and her endurance will remain implanted in our memories as an abiding source

of inspiration. We are mourning for her to-day, but with a grief which has in it the balm of pride and triumph: for we are consoled by the certain belief that time will give to her the honoured niche in history which is her due.[4]

Kitty Marshall was determined that the great militant leader should be commemorated in some way and together with Rosamund Massy as joint honorary secretary and Lady Rhondda as honorary treasurer, set up a Memorial Fund. The plan was to raise £2,500 which would pay for a headstone for Emmeline's grave in Brompton Cemetery, the purchase of a portrait that had been painted by Georgina Brackenbury for presentation to the National Portrait Gallery, and a statue to be erected in Victoria Tower Gardens, adjacent to the House of Commons. '[M]en commemorate their heroes and liberators by erecting statues', it was claimed. 'Shall not women claim equal honour for her who led them to victory?'[5] Rachel Barrett, knowing of Emmeline's 'devotion to Canada', wrote to Margaret Bates in Toronto, asking her to help organise a collection in that city and also invited Mrs. Kennedy in Ottawa and Mrs. Murphy in Edmonton to do the same in their part of the world.[6] Similar requests were also sent to the USA.[7]

Meanwhile, Emmeline's daughters were remembering their mother, each in her own way. Adela was telling her children stories about how their grandmother had won the vote for women while Christabel announced that she was going to write a memoir of her mother.[8] Sylvia had a book contract too, for *The suffragette movement*, but was finding that the constant demands of a small baby interrupted the time she tried to put aside for writing. In desperation, she wrote to Norah Walshe, a former suffrage colleague, seeking her help.[9] Although Norah was unable to look after Richard, other old friends offered their services. Aware that she was despised by those close to her mother, who blamed her for Emmeline's death, Sylvia was determined to record her own version of events. It would be very different from Christabel's and also from Ray Strachey's history of the women's movement in Britain, '*The cause*', published in the autumn of 1928. Strachey, a former member of the NUWSS and a great admirer of Millicent Garrett Fawcett's liberal reformist approach to the suffrage issue, was very critical of the WSPU leaders and their militant tactics. Emmeline and Christabel Pankhurst, she claims, brushed aside 'the ordinary niceties of procedure' and did not care whom they 'shocked and antagonised ... nor was democracy much to their taste'. They laughed at all talk of persuasion since they believed in 'moral violence'. By this force, and the driving power of their own determination, they hoped to 'coerce' the government into granting their demand. With such an 'aggressive and headlong' approach, they 'deliberately put themselves in the position of outlaws dogged by the police'. The organisation of the WSPU was inadequate too, since no thorough membership or financial records were kept.[10] As Kathryn Dodd persuasively argued many years later, Strachey uses the political vocabulary of liberalism to position Millicent

Garrett Fawcett and the NUWSS as the 'rational' wing of the women's movement that was responsible for the partial enfranchisement of women in 1918
and their full enfranchisement, on equal terms with men, in 1928. Emmeline
Pankhurst and her militants, on the other hand, are cast out 'of the making of
women's history because of their reckless activity, their passion for change, their
angry propaganda and their autocratic organisation'.[11]

When Sylvia reviewed '*The cause*', early in 1929, however, what she strongly
objected to was not Strachey's representation of her mother but her omission of
any reference to the East London campaign and to her claim that the WSPU
had kept no audited balance sheets.[12] Sylvia discussed the issue in correspondence with Emmeline Pethick Lawrence, who had helped her financially and
emotionally during her pregnancy, and was now a close friend. Both women had
been ousted by Emmeline Pankhurst from the WSPU, a bitter experience that
cast a long shadow on their assessment of the militant leader. Somewhat incred-
ulously, Emmeline Pethick Lawrence wrote to Sylvia on 17 December 1929, 'I
regard your Mother dispassionately (as you do) as a most interesting human
problem.' While conceding that the militant leader had been 'a *great force*'
affecting the current of human history, like Napoleon, it was also suggested that
Emmeline Pankhurst's enthusiasm for the suffrage cause, which began in a spirit
of 'generous enthusiasm' in the end:

> obsessed her like a passion & she completely identified her own career
> with it – & in order to obtain it she threw scruple, affection, human
> loyalty & her own principles to the winds. ... The Movement devel-
> oped her powers – *all* her powers for good & for evil. Cruelty,
> ruthlessness – as you say – I should add *betrayal* – courage, resourceful-
> ness & diplomacy. She was capable of beautiful tenderness & [a]
> magnificent sense of justice in self-sacrifice. These things in the course
> of the struggle became changed. We all sacrificed many things – she
> sacrificed her very soul.[13]

Sylvia concurred with such views; her mother and Christabel had treated her
in a most cruel way, putting the women's cause before family loyalty. Even now,
Christabel was attempting to tell her what to do; she had recently visited
Sylvia, asking that Richard should not bear the surname Pankhurst since people
thought the boy was her son. The row that broke out between the sisters ended
with the younger telling the elder that her private life was none of her
business.[14]

The New Year of 1930 brought a different recognition of Emmeline
Pankhurst's niche in history. Kitty Marshall's persistence had paid off so that on
6 March 1930 thousands gathered in Victoria Tower Gardens, close to the
Houses of Parliament, for the unveiling of the statue of the militant leader.
Ironically, of Emmeline's three daughters, it was Sylvia, from whom she became
estranged, who was present amongst the crowds with baby Richard in her arms;

Christabel was lecturing in America while Adela was too poor to afford the fare from Australia. For an hour before the unveiling, the metropolitan police band played music in honour of the woman the metropolitan police had arrested and rearrested under the Cat and Mouse Act, and then Ethel Smyth, in her academic robes, conducted the band in a rendering of 'The March of the Women'. At 12 noon, Flora Drummond opened the proceedings by paying tribute to Emmeline's human qualities as well as to her leadership. She then read a telegram from the absent Christabel. No reference was made to Sylvia; Kitty Marshall had purposely excluded her from the planning and notification of the day's events, much to Sylvia's anger. To a fanfare of trumpets, no less a person than the ex-Prime Minister, Stanley Baldwin, unveiled the statue proclaiming, 'I say with no fear of contradiction, that whatever view posterity may take, Mrs. Pankhurst has won for herself a niche in the Temple of Fame which will last for all time.' After prayers had been said by the Reverend Canon Woodward and a hymn sung, speeches were made by Viscountess Rhondda and Fred Pethick Lawrence. Fred, now a Labour MP, stressed that the statue was fashioned in the likeness of the woman 'who typifies for all time the revolt of womanhood' against the old false conception that women should remain outside the mainstream of life, and be 'ministers to the happiness, the comforts, or the vices of man'.[15] Once the speeches had ended, friends of Emmeline and especially veterans of her old army of militants decked with prison brooches and other WSPU insignia, placed wreaths at the base of the statue. The ceremony was broadcast so that millions could listen at home.

The shunned Sylvia was determined to have her say, in print. The day before the unveiling ceremony, she had published in *The Star* an article titled 'My Mother. Rebel to Reactionary' which, as expected, 'mixed vinegar with honey'.[16] The essay began, 'My Mother, in an indefinable way, had the dynamic quality which gets things done, though she herself did not possess any great organising or executive ability.' The suffrage cause 'gave full scope to her dramatic power, without demanding from her the difficult task of discovering precise solutions'. After reminding her readers that it was her father who had been prominent in the advanced causes of his day, including women's suffrage, and that her mother had 'adopted him as her guide', Sylvia praised the contribution of the Pethick Lawrences to the movement since they 'supplied the very qualities' her mother lacked. In particular, 'Mrs. Lawrence had ... the gift of making the most of her co-workers; she took the lead in weaving an atmosphere of ardour and romance about the personality of Mrs. Pankhurst and other heroines of the Suffragette movement'. Her mother's breach with the Lawrences was 'always a matter for deep regret'. Turning back for a final assessment of her mother, Sylvia wrote:

> She could do the outrageous thing without appearing outrageous, or losing her charm. A detective confided in after years to an ex-militant: 'Mrs. Pankhurst was my idea of a queen'. ... Her interest in dress and

shopping, her desultory reading, mainly confined to novels, were surprising in one whose life was so largely given to public causes. Her greatness was in her courage and devotion, indomitable and unflinching, deaf to all criticism, prepared to meet all hardships. ... That she lost the reformer's quality in her declining years and grew as intolerant in her reaction as she had been stubborn in her pioneering, will not be recorded against her. That failing has been a common one amongst reformers.[17]

Such articles, including another by Sylvia with the title 'Mrs. Pankhurst. A Daughter's Memories', helped to fashion a particular representation of the militant leader, a portrayal written by a daughter who was earning a reputation as a left-wing writer on social issues, such as the need for a free maternity service.[18] By Christmas 1930, Emmeline Pethick Lawrence was writing to Sylvia:

> I wish *you* could have written your Mother's Life, because I feel that you would have made of it – a work of art. Her life & character present rare materials for a deeply human story. There are great heights & depths, marvelous [sic] light, & sombre darkness. Even in her villainies she is intensely dramatic ... as when she repudiated you & Adela & again when she expressed extreme horror & reprobation of you in following the example of Mary Woolstonecraft [sic], Elizabeth Elmy & many other pioneers of the Woman's Movement [in becoming pregnant while single] ... Her arc of flight, through Liberalism, Socialism, extreme revolution, to Conservatism is full of interest. If Christabel ever writes her life, it will be the unutterably dull, 'Me & Mother' stuff, which has fallen absolutely flat, outside the ever diminishing numbers of devoted followers – nobody is interested in a paragon of wisdom & conduct. Christabel's idea of Mother – & also of Herself – is that of the ultimate triumph of a vindicated Christ returning to rule the world as a benevolent despot![19]

As noted in the Introduction, Sylvia did later publish a life of her mother, in 1935, at about the same time that Christabel completed her manuscript. But Sylvia's biography of Emmeline was not widely read. It was her autobiographical account of the women's suffrage campaign, *The suffragette movement, an intimate account of persons and ideals*, published in 1931, that was her most influential literary achievement. As observed in the Introduction, in this book Sylvia presents Emmeline as a failed mother and a failed leader, easily swayed by the hated Christabel, a view that was not lost on contemporary reviewers who pointed out that Mrs. Pankhurst is presented as 'almost a tool' in Christabel's hands, 'driven by her elder daughter as a ship before the wind'.[20] Christabel, the separatist feminist who marginalises class and socialism by recruiting middle-class women into the movement, is damned as the sister who led their mother astray from the goal of building a broadly based movement. Further, Emmeline is also portrayed as a rather vain woman, so fastidious about being well dressed that she could leave a socialist meeting because she found a bug on her glove. She deliberately sought the limelight, not just for the women's cause but for her own personal reasons. 'You have balked me – both of you!', Emmeline is alleged to have said of Keir Hardie and Sylvia when they deterred her from creating a disturbance in the House of Commons. 'I thought there would have been one little nitch [sic] in the temple of fame for me!'[21]

Although, unsurprisingly, Emmeline Pethick Lawrence praised *The suffragette movement* as a story told 'with a faithfulness to the facts' in a spirit of 'impersonal passion', Ray Strachey was condemnatory. 'There is much bitterness and misrepresentation in its pages, much inaccuracy and misstatement, and an evident and undisguised animus against Mrs. Pankhurst and Christabel which is almost tragic in its intensity.'[22] When Adela, in Australia, finally read the book she was filled with sorrow and indignation. In an unpublished comment, she noted that Sylvia:

> makes out that my father was faultless, my mother full of faults. Readers should understand that in Sylvia's eyes to cease to be a socialist, if one had ever been one, is a moral crime. ... I am convinced that had my mother remained in the I.L.P. or become a pacifist or communist, her conduct in relation to Harry and myself would not have received any censure from Sylvia and the bitter feelings she writes about her childhood would never have been penned.[23]

But perhaps it was especially Christabel and the ageing, loyal ex-WSPU members who were horrified and hurt by the contents of Sylvia's *The suffragette movement*.

Many of the old militants were members of the Suffragette Fellowship, founded in 1926 by former WSPU and WFL members to perpetuate the memory of the pioneers and outstanding events connected with women's emancipation, especially with the militant suffrage campaign. The Suffragette Fellowship wrote to Christabel asking her to publish her own account of events. Politely but firmly Christabel replied that she would not disagree with a member of her family in public, a position from which she would not budge during her lifetime.[24] 'It is a pity that Sylvia has not emulated her elder sister's loyalty and greatheartedness and kept a fine book free from a personal bitterness that had nothing to do with the Movement', opined Geraldine Lennox, a comment that provoked an angry reply from a socialist loyal to Sylvia. 'Except when it came to the hunger-strike', wrote an acerbic Charlotte Drake, ' I am afraid the lot of even the most hard-worked of the Suffrage leaders was lighter than that of the working-class mother of a large family.'[25]

As noted in the Introduction, it was Sylvia's *The suffragette movement* that became the authoritative reading of events, especially after George Dangerfield adopted and adapted this script in *The strange death of Liberal England*, first published in 1935 and reprinted at least up to 1972. Whether Annie Kenney read Dangerfield's account we do not know, but by the early 1940s she was still worried about the influence of *The suffragette movement* and wrote to Christabel:

> I do so hope that you have written the real true history of our move-
> ment. … Is Sylvia's book of your family and early life to be the only
> family book to which film writers, historians, etc., have to go for the
> history of your family and the history of the work that absolutely
> changed the position of women?[26]

But Christabel remained adamant that the manuscript she had written should not be published during her lifetime, especially during wartime when the record of the brutality of the Liberal government towards the suffragettes could be embarrassing and damaging. The manuscript was found in a trunk after her death in 1958 and prepared for posthumous publication by Fred Pethick Lawrence.[27] The general account of the WSPU campaign in *Unshackled*, in which Emmeline figures prominently and is represented sympathetically, was no match for Sylvia's richly detailed autobiographical narrative. In contrast to *The suffragette movement*, *Unshackled* has a rather flat, matter-of-fact tone. Significantly, it omits any reference to the split with Sylvia, in 1914. Yet Fred Pethick Lawrence claimed it was written with a 'remorseless objectivity' while for Adela it was 'accurate as far as it goes & very fair to all concerned'.[28]

Annie Kenney's fears had been well founded. Sylvia's representation of Emmeline Pankhurst in *The suffragette movement* is still the dominant represen-tation within history, and has only recently been subjected to critical scrutiny. This biography has continued that interrogation, pointing out that it is a pitfall for any researcher to accept blindly the story told in that text. As this biography has illustrated, it is time to reclaim Emmeline Pankhurst from the denigration of Sylvia and of historians who have marginalised her as a middle-class oppor-tunist, ruthless, patriotic and right wing, a woman driven by her eldest daughter, Christabel, the autocratic leader of a militant movement that was bourgeois, reactionary and narrow in its aims, a movement that failed to mobilise the working classes and address their economic, social and political needs. It is time to represent Emmeline Pankhurst as she was seen in her time, a 'Champion of Womanhood',[29] to give to her that 'honoured niche' in history of which Beatrice Harraden spoke.

Emmeline Pankhurst's feminism was born out of a sense of the burning injus-tice of the wrongs done to her sex in a male-dominated society where women were regarded as subordinate and inferior beings, a secondary status epitomised by the denial to them of the citizenship right that was granted to certain cate-gories of men, the right to the parliamentary vote. It was a feminism that embraced all women, stressing gender not class issues, recognising that divisions between women perpetuated male power, even within socialism. It was also a feminism that was above party politics and involved putting women first.

Consequently, Emmeline shed her membership of the Liberal Party and then the ILP when she became disillusioned with their male-centred agendas. In the last year of her life, when women finally won the vote on equal terms with men under a Conservative government, she became a member of the Conservative Party, hoping that it might help women use their new voting powers constructively. She died before that dream could be shattered.

Emmeline Pankhurst had the vision to realise that it was women themselves who had to be roused to demand their own political rights and founded the WSPU as a women-only organisation although men could, and did, become supporters of the women's cause. A charismatic leader and powerful orator, she inspired her followers by her resolute determination not to be deflected from the cause she espoused; her courage and her flair for the dramatic even won grudging admiration from many of those who disagreed with her policies. Charlotte Despard, a one-time rival, commented that Emmeline Pankhurst's great service to women was that she discovered, stimulated and, through her personal initiative, harnessed for action, a spirit of revolt. Ethel Smyth, one-time close friend of the WSPU leader, similarly claimed that the supreme achievement of Mrs. Pankhurst was in creating in women 'a new sense of power and responsibility, together with a determination to work out their destiny on other lines than those laid down for them since time immemorial by men'.[30] As these comments and countless others illustrate, Emmeline Pankhurst's desire to arouse the women of Britain to claim their citizenship birthright succeeded.

Women from a wide variety of backgrounds were recruited into the WSPU to form a movement that was unparalleled in British history. Engaging in militant action that was never to endanger human life, WSPU members developed a new confidence and a new awareness of their political disabilities in a male-dominated society that excluded women from the parliamentary vote, because of their sex. This consciousness-raising about the wrongs of women presented a formidable challenge to the prevailing gender ideology that formed the bedrock of Edwardian society. Emmeline's campaign during the war years for women's right to war work and to equal pay continued the challenge, while the threat of a post-war return to militancy, with the prospect of pre-war brutalities being inflicted on women who had proved their worth, would not have been tolerated by a disillusioned and demoralised population. Militant tactics shook the complacency of the British government, making it most unlikely, as Morgan suggests, that without it women's suffrage would have been granted. Militancy was a necessary step for winning the vote as Harold Laski and Fred Pethick Lawrence amongst others have argued.[31] Constance Rover expressed the view that 'While one would like to say that law and order should always be maintained, it is almost impossible to find a legal means of protest, open to those outside the constitution, which is effective.' Without subscribing to the doctrine that 'the end justifies the means', she continues, 'it is possible to hold the opinion that the end was a worthy one and that as suffragette methods stopped short of endangering human life, they were justifiable.'[32] It can be argued that the non-militants exploited the opening that the suffragettes had forced through the wall of resistance to women's suffrage.

Under Emmeline's leadership the struggle for the vote became a spiritual struggle, a holy war that would bring about not only enfranchisement for women but also a just society where the sexual subjection of women was no more. Contrary to the impression given by most historians, she upheld not only the ending of women's oppression but a wide programme of social change that included the abolition of the exploitation of the working classes, and of the sexual and economic exploitation of children. Even as a Conservative candidate, Emmeline still held to these dreams, hoping that the standard of living of the working classes would be brought up to that of the bourgeoisie. But she did not believe that such wide-ranging reforms could be achieved by state ownership of the means of production and state socialism alone, but by some mix of public and private enterprise which emphasised class co-operation rather than class hatred. Her feminism therefore complicates the categories of feminism with which we have commonly worked in the late twentieth and twenty-first centuries and requires us to rethink those categories.

During the course of her leadership of the militant campaign for the right of women to exercise the parliamentary vote, Emmeline Pankhurst could be autocratic, defending the undemocratic structure of the WSPU. But such strong leadership also attracted recruits to the cause, and won support. Further, her autocracy contained a contradiction in that her followers were encouraged to exercise their own independent judgment as to which militant acts they should engage in, especially in local branches which were run more democratically. Emmeline was not simply a tool in the hands of her eldest daughter, Christabel, but an active participant in their joint decision-making. During the course of the militant campaign, her leadership role changed so that from 1912, when Christabel was in exile in Paris, she became the more powerful figure.

Emmeline Pankhurst's part performing on the international stage has largely been ignored. Yet she pioneered links with like-minded women overseas, especially in America and Canada, which helped her to develop a world-view of women's suffrage and women's issues. Her feminism changed over time. As she grew older and faced a world of social, economic and political changes, she became an outspoken critic of the emerging communism, with its totalitarian, non-democratic structures and advocacy of 'free love' which, she upheld, did not bring dignity and equality for women. In particular, she believed that working-class women would be exploited and made poorer by communism, which, amongst other things, advocated the ending of marriage and increased the double burden of home and employment responsibilities. These views, together with her patriotic stand during the First World War and her later enthusiasm for the British Empire, have made her unfashionable amongst present-day feminists who, through the lens of the late twentieth century, associate feminism with socialism, with peace movements, and with de-colonisation. But for Emmeline Pankhurst, as for many other feminists of her time, militarism and imperialism were 'as intuitive' as anti-militarism and anti-imperialism have been to feminists in recent times.[33]

Although her extraordinary life may seem far removed from the lot of the majority of women, in other ways her life was ordinary. Like so many widowed women in history she was left with heavy debts when her husband died. Untrained for any vocation, she had to make her living as best she could as she struggled financially to bring up her own family of four children and then, in later life, her adopted daughters. Although her vision of a society in which women were free from sexual subjection has not materialised, it is a vision that casts its light into the present as women, ordinary and extraordinary, still struggle for equality and emancipation.

NOTES

INTRODUCTION

1 I am defining as 'feminist' a woman who believes that her sex are discriminated against and oppressed by men, and who devotes much of her time to fighting or rebelling against this. 'Feminism' is thus a political movement that seeks to eradicate the injustices that women experience and to end women's subordination to men. Although the terms 'feminist' and 'feminism' appear not to have been used in Britain until the late nineteenth century, their application to an earlier period may be justified. As B. Taylor, *Eve and the new Jerusalem: socialism and feminism in the nineteenth century* (London, Virago, 1983), p. x points out, 'at least a century prior to the entry of the actual word into popular political discourse there existed the ideology which it described – a distinct and identifiable body of ideas and aspiration commonly known as "the rights of women", the "condition of women" question, the "emancipation of women" and so on.'

2 R. Pankhurst, Introduction to the 1987 reprint of Dame C. Pankhurst, *Unshackled: the story of how we won the vote* (London, Cresset Library).

3 M. Mackenzie, *Shoulder to shoulder: a documentary* (London, Penguin, 1975).

4 Women of the century, *The Observer*, 29 June 1997; *Daily Mirror*, 12 October 1999.

5 As far as I am aware, Claudia Fitzherbert is writing a biography of Emmeline Pankhurst while Paula Bartley's *Emmeline Pankhurst* will be published in 2002 as part of Routledge's Historical Biographies Series.

6 Dame C. Pankhurst, *Unshackled: the story of how we won the vote* (London, Hutchinson, 1959).

7 E.S. Pankhurst, *The life of Emmeline Pankhurst: the suffragette struggle for women's citizenship* (London, T. Werner Laurie Ltd, 1935).

8 Socialist feminism stresses that the subordinate position of women in society may be attributed to both the nature of capitalism and to the control that men exercise over women; importance is attached to men and women working together, as comrades, in the building of a socialist society, although socialist feminists may also form women-only groupings as a means of raising feminist consciousness.

9 E. S. Pankhurst, *Emmeline Pankhurst*, p. 71.

10 Ibid., pp. 46–7.

11 Ibid., p. 165.

12 E. S. Pankhurst, *The suffragette movement: an intimate account of persons and ideals* (London, Longmans, 1931), hereafter *TSM*.

13 K. Dodd, Introduction, to her edited *A Sylvia Pankhurst reader* (Manchester, Manchester University Press, 1993), pp. 21–2.

14 J. Marcus, Introduction, re-reading the Pankhurst and women's suffrage, in her edited *Suffrage and the Pankhursts* (London and New York, Routledge & Kegan Paul, 1987), pp. 5–6.

15 Dodd, Introduction, p. 24.

16 E. S. Pankhurst, *TSM*, p. 221.

17 H. Kean, Searching for the past in present defeat: the construction of historical and polit-
    ical identity in British feminism in the 1920s and 1930s, *Women's History Review*, 3, 1994,
    p. 73; J. Purvis, A 'pair of ... infernal queens'? A reassessment of the dominant representa-
    tions of Emmeline and Christabel Pankhurst, First Wave feminists in Edwardian Britain,
    Women's History Review, 5, 1996, p. 266.

18 E. S. Pankhurst, *TSM*, p. 320 and her *Emmeline Pankhurst*, p. 93.

19 J. Craigie to David Mitchell, 2 September 1996, Author's Collection.

20 Marcus, Introduction, p. 3. For discussion of 'masculinist' approaches to suffrage history
    see S. S. Holton, The making of suffrage history, in *Votes for women*, ed. J. Purvis and S. S.
    Holton (London, Routledge, 2000), pp. 13–33. Holton, p. 29, draws on a 1986 paper by
    M. Lake in which Lake 'categorises as "masculinist" certain responses to the women's
    movement in Australia, where "Feminists were mocked, abused and insulted" by the press
    of the day, and argues that such responses were culturally reproduced in the accounts of
    the building of the nation by subsequent generations of male historians.'

21 G. Dangerfield, *The strange death of Liberal England* (London, MacGibbon & Kee, 1966,
    first published 1935), pp. 132, 165, 130, 155–6.

22 Ibid., pp. 122, 125, 128.

23 Holton, The making of suffrage history, pp. 22, 24.

24 D. Mitchell, *The fighting Pankhursts: a study in tenacity* (London, Jonathan Cape, 1967), p.
    339.

25 M. Pugh, *The Pankhursts* (Harmondsworth, Allen Lane, Penguin Press, 2001), p. 15.

26 Ibid., pp. 60, 105, 155, 161, 163, 206, 208, 404.

27 Ibid., pp. 213–14.

28 V. Thorpe and A. Marsh, Diary reveals lesbian love trysts of suffragette leaders, *The
    Observer*, 11 June 2000.

29 Pugh, *The Pankhursts*, pp. 220–1; B. Winslow, *Sylvia Pankhurst: sexual politics and political
    activism* (London, UCL Press, 1996), p. 34.

30 Three categories of thought were usually identified in 'Second Wave Feminism' from the
    late 1960s in Western Europe and the USA – liberal feminism, socialist feminism and
    radical feminism. Liberal feminism emphasises gradual, piecemeal reform as a way to gain
    equal rights for women and stresses the importance of women and men working together
    to attain such rights. For socialist feminism, see note 8, where I stress that socialist femi-
    nism emphasises that the subordinate position of women may be attributed to both the
    nature of capitalism and to the control that men exercise over women. For radical femi-
    nism, on the other hand, male control over women has primacy over all other oppressions
    and cannot be reduced to anything else, such as the power of capital over labour. The
    distinguishing feature of women's oppression is their oppression as women and not as
    members of other social groupings, such as social class groupings. The idea of the shared
    oppression that links all women leads to a strong emphasis upon sisterhood and a focus on
    the similarities between women rather than their differences. Radical feminism encour-
    ages a degree of separation from men, usually involving the formation of women-only
    organisations or women-only communities. It is argued that the way to change sexual
    oppression in a social order dominated by men is by focusing on women and putting
    women first.

31 See S. Rowbotham, *Hidden from history: 300 years of women's oppression and the fight against
    it* (London, Pluto Press, 1973), pp. 78–82; J. Liddington and J. Norris, *One hand tied behind
    us: the rise of the women's suffrage movement* (London, Virago, 1978), pp. 167–9, 204–5,
    252, 258; G. Lewis, *Eva Gore Booth and Esther Roper: a biography* (London, Pandora Press,
    1988), pp. 9, 165; M. Davis, *Sylvia Pankhurst: a life in radical politics* (London, Pluto Press,
    1999), pp. 1, 20–32.

32 B. Harrison, Two models of feminist leadership, Millicent Garrett Fawcett and Emmeline Pankhurst, in his *Prudent revolutionaries: portraits of British feminists between the wars* (Oxford, Oxford University Press, 1987), pp. 17–43. See also D. Barker, Mrs Emmeline Pankhurst, in his *Prominent Edwardians* (London, Allen & Unwin, 1969), pp. 174–245; P. Brendon, Mrs Pankhurst, in his *Eminent Edwardians* (London, Secker and Warburg, 1979), pp. 131–94; M. Pugh, *The march of the women: a revisionist analysis of the campaign for women's suffrage, 1866–1914* (Oxford, Oxford University Press, 2000), pp. 252–83.

I am following conventional usage in applying the terms 'militant' and 'constitutional' to the tactics of the WSPU and the NUWSS respectively, while recognising that a hard-and-fast distinction between these terms has been questioned in recent years. S. S. Holton, *Feminism and democracy: women's suffrage and reform politics in Britain 1900–1918* (Cambridge, Cambridge University Press, 1986), p. 4, notes that if 'militancy' involved a preparedness to resort to extreme forms of violence, few 'militants' were 'militant' and then only from 1912. If, on the other hand, 'militancy' involved a willingness to take the issue onto the streets, then many 'constitutionalists' were also 'militant'. A. Morley with L. Stanley, *The life and death of Emily Wilding Davison* (London, The Women's Press, 1988), p. 152, point out that at the local level of political activity, there is 'no convincing evidence' of a divide between NUWSS and WSPU members; many women from different organisations worked closely together over various issues. This theme is further developed in S. S. Holton, *Suffrage days: stories from the women's suffrage movement* (London, Routledge, 1996) where the stress is upon the fluidity of membership between different groups. It is useful if we broaden the term 'militancy', as K. Cowman suggests in *Engendering citizenship: the political involvement of women in Merseyside, 1890–1920*, unpublished Ph.D. thesis, University of York, 1994, p. 238, to include a 'breadth of actions' which were about challenging views of feminine behaviour rather than just law-breaking; women sold newspapers on the street, chalked pavements to advertise meetings, made protests at places of entertainment and in churches, we well as set fire to empty buildings. While utilising such a broad definition of 'militancy', as I do in this book, it is nevertheless also important to acknowledge that there were differences in policies and tactics between the WSPU and NUWSS which cannot be ignored and that it was the WSPU, in particular, that embraced law-breaking militancy. See also L. E. N. Mayhall, Defining militancy: radical protest, the constitutional idiom, and women's suffrage in Britain, 1908–1909, *Journal of British Studies*, 39, 1994, pp. 340–71.

33 See Dangerfield, *The strange death of Liberal England*, pp. 121–77; R. Fulford, *Votes for women: the story of a struggle* (London, Faber & Faber, 1957), pp. 298–307; A. Rosen, *Rise up women! The militant campaign of the Women's Social and Political Union 1903–1914* (London, Routledge & Kegan Paul, 1974), pp. 243–5; B. Harrison, *Separate spheres: the opposition to women's suffrage in Britain* (London, Croom Helm, 1978), pp. 196–7; Brendon, *Eminent Edwardians*, pp. 133–94; B. Harrison, The act of militancy, violence and the suffragettes, 1904–1914, in his *Peaceable kingdom: stability and change in modern Britain* (Oxford, Oxford University Press, 1982), pp. 48 and 75; L. Garner, *Stepping stones to women's liberty: feminist ideas in the women's suffrage movement 1900–1918* (London, Heinemann, 1984), pp. 44–60; Harrison, Two models of feminist leadership, pp. 17–43; H. L. Smith, *The British women's suffrage campaign 1866–1928* (Harlow, Longman, 1998), pp. 82–4; Pugh, *The march of the women*, pp. 252–83.

34 See, for example, C. Rover, *Women's suffrage and party politics in Britain 1866–1914* (London, Routledge & Kegan Paul, 1967); A. Raeburn, *The militant suffragettes* (London, Michael Joseph, 1973); D. Atkinson, *Suffragettes* (Museum of London, 1988); M. Vicinus, Male space and women's bodies: the suffragette movement in her *Independent women: work and community for single women 1860–1920* (London, Virago, 1985), pp. 247–80; S. K. Kent, *Sex and suffrage in Britain 1860–1914* (New Jersey, Princeton University Press, 1987); D. Atkinson, *The suffragettes in pictures* (Stroud, Sutton Publishing, 1996); C. R.

Jorgensen-Earp, 'The transfiguring sword': the just war of the Women's Social and Political Union (Tuscaloosa, University of Alabama Press, 1997).

35 J. Kamm, The story of Mrs. Pankhurst (London, Methuen, 1961); H. Champion, The true book about Emmeline Pankhurst (London, Frederick Muller, 1963); R. Butler, As they saw her ... Emmeline Pankhurst: portrait of a wife, mother and suffragette (London, Harrap & Co., 1970); L. Hoy, Emmeline Pankhurst (London, Hamish Hamilton. 1985); M. Pollard, Tell me about Emmeline Pankhurst (London, Evans Brothers, 1996); M. Hudson, Emmeline Pankhurst (Oxford, Heineman, 1997).

36 D. Spender, Women of ideas and what men have done to them: from Aphra Behn to Adrienne Rich (London, Routledge & Kegan Paul, 1982), pp. 394–434; Marcus, Introduction, pp. 1–17; S. S. Holton, 'In sorrowful wrath': suffrage militancy and the romantic feminism of Emmeline Pankhurst, in British feminism in the twentieth century, ed. H. L. Smith (Aldershot, Edward Elgar, 1990), pp. 7–24; Purvis, 'Infernal queens', pp. 259–80; J. Purvis, Emmeline Pankhurst (1858–1928) and votes for women, in Votes for women, eds Purvis and Holton, pp. 109–34; J. Purvis, Emmeline Pankhurst: suffragette, militant feminist and champion of womanhood, in Representing lives: women and auto/biography, eds A. Donnell and P. Polkey (Basingstoke, Macmillan, 2000), pp. 218–27.

37 See, for example, I. B. Nagel, Biography: fact, fiction and form (London, Macmillan, 1984); E. Homberger and J. Charmley (eds), The troubled face of biography (London, Macmillan, 1988); C. Heilbrun, Writing a woman's life (London, The Women's Press, 1988); U. O'Connor, Biographers and the art of biography (London, Quartet Books, 1993); T. Iles (ed.), All sides of the subject: women and biography (New York and London, Teachers College, Columbia University, 1992); C. Steedman, Past tenses: essays on writing, autobiography and history (London, Rivers Oram, 1992); L. Stanley, The auto/biographical I: the theory and practice of feminist auto/biography (Manchester, Manchester University Press, 1992); B. Caine, Feminist biography and feminist history, Women's History Review, 3, 1994, pp. 247–61; M. Evans, Missing persons: the impossibility of auto/biography (London, Routledge, 1999); R. Holmes, Sidetracks: explorations of a romantic biographer (London, Harper Collins, 2000); J. Burr Margadant (ed.), The new biography: performing femininity in nineteenth-century France (Berkeley and Los Angeles, University of California Press, 2000).

38 S. Grogan, Flora Trisan: life stories (London, Routledge, 1998), p. 10.

39 O. Banks, The biographical dictionary of British feminists, Vol I 1800–1930 (Brighton, Wheatsheaf Books, 1985), pp. 146–52; E. Sarah, Christabel Pankhurst: reclaiming her power, in Feminist theorists: three centuries of women's intellectual traditions, ed. D. Spender (London, Women's Press, 1983), pp. 256–84. For further elaboration of my views here see Purvis, 'Infernal queens'.

40 E. Bowerman and G. Roe, The ideals of the Women's Social and Political Union, Calling All Women (News Letter of the Suffragette Fellowship), 1975, pp. 18–22. For further elaboration of this point and of the construction of suffragette narratives, see L. N. M. Mayhall, Creating the 'suffragette spirit': British feminism and the historical imagination, Women's History Review, 4, 1995, pp. 319–44.

41 Examples that adopt a chronological, narrative form and the thematic, shifting identities approach include P. W. Romero, E. Sylvia Pankhurst: portrait of a radical (New Haven and London, Yale University Press, 1987) and A. V. John, Elizabeth Robins: staging a life, 1862–1952 (London and New York, Routledge, 1995), respectively. For the web of friendships focus see especially Morley with Stanley, Emily Wilding Davison.

42 Stanley, The auto/biographical I, p. 158.

43 E. Pankhurst, My own story (London, Eveleigh Nash, 1914).

44 Rosen, Rise up women!, p. 167; B. Harrison, review of M. Mackenzie Shoulder to shoulder, Times Literary Supplement, 13 February 1976; M. Pugh, Women's suffrage in Britain 1867–1928 (London, The Historical Association, 1980), p. 40.

45 Pugh, The Pankhursts, pp. xiv, 129.

46 J. Purvis, Using primary sources when researching women's history from a feminist perspective, *Women's History Review*, 1, 1992, pp. 273–306, suggests that we may identify three main categories of primary sources which, while not offering a neat but somewhat arbitrary classification, nonetheless distinguish groups of texts that share characteristics in common. 'Official texts' includes state, bureaucratic, institutional and legal texts, official reports of societies and institutions, memoranda and official letters. 'Published commentary and reporting' covers accounts of events that might be written or constructed without the direct help of the participants and includes novels, films, photographs, advertisements, the writings of key political, social and literary figures, and newspapers. The approach in 'personal texts' is in terms of a person's subjective experience, and such texts include letters, diaries, autobiographies and life histories.

1 CHILDHOOD AND YOUNG WOMANHOOD
(1858–1879)

1 See E. S. Pankhurst, *Emmeline Pankhurst*, p. 7 and C. Pankhurst, *Unshackled*, p. 16. After her death, the Suffragette Fellowship regularly celebrated her birthday on the 14 July. Ray Strachey in her entry on Emmeline in *The dictionary of national biography 1922–1930*, ed. J. R. H. Weaver (Oxford, Oxford University Press, 1937), pp. 652–4, gives 4 July 1858 as the date of birth, presumably a printing error, and the same error is repeated in the entry by A. Rosen, *Biographical dictionary of modern British radicals, Vol. 3: 1870–1914, L–Z*, eds J. O. Baylen and N. J. Gossman (New York and London, Harvester Wheatsheaf, 1988), pp. 631–5. Butler, *As they saw her*, p. 10, is one of the few biographies to state the date of birth as 15 July. Emmeline's name is spelt 'Emiline' on her birth certificate. Whether this was an error made by the registrar, or whether her name was originally spelt this way, I have been unable to ascertain.

2 *Votes for Women* (hereafter *VfW*), 31 December 1908, p. 230.

3 E. S. Pankhurst, *TSM*, pp. 53–4; E. S Pankhurst, *Emmeline Pankhurst*, p. 7; E. Pankhurst, *My own story*, p. 3.

4 E. S. Pankhurst, *Emmeline Pankhurst*, p. 9.

5 E. Pankhurst, *My own story*, p. 1.

6 Ibid., p. 3.

7 Holton, In sorrowful wrath, pp. 13–14.

8 C. Pankhurst, *Unshackled*, p. 16; E. S. Pankhurst, *Emmeline Pankhurst*, p. 9.

9 C. Dyhouse, *Girls growing up in late Victorian and Edwardian England* (London, Routledge & Kegan Paul, 1981), p. 11.

10 E. Pankhurst, *My own story*, p. 5.

11 For the claim that by the middle of the nineteenth century there had emerged in Britain a particular family form amongst the middle classes that stressed separate spheres for men and women – men to be placed in the public world of business, commerce and politics, women in the private sphere of the home, as wives and mothers, financially dependent upon their husbands, see L. Davidoff and C. Hall, *Family fortunes: men and women of the English middle class 1780–1850* (London, Hutchinson, 1987). For a critique of this claim see A. Vickery, Golden age to separate spheres? A review of the categories and chronology of English women's history, *Historical Journal*, 36, 1993, pp. 383–414.

12 E. S. Pankhurst, *Emmeline Pankhurst*, p. 7.

13 Dyhouse, *Girls growing up*, Chapter 2; J. Purvis, *A history of women's education in England* (Milton Keynes, Open University Press, 1991), Chapter 4.

14 E. Pankhurst, *My own story*, p. 6.

15 Ibid., p. 8. Emmeline does not state the name of the sister but I have assumed that it was Mary since she was the closest to Emmeline in age, being born on 12 December 1861, and therefore most likely to be dressed in the same style as the eldest girl.

16 C. Pankhurst, *Unshackled*, p. 16.

17 See H. Blackburn, *Women's suffrage: a record of the women's suffrage movement in the British Isles with biographical sketches of Miss Becker* (London, Williams & Norgate, 1902) and entry in E. Crawford, *The women's suffrage movement: a reference guide 1866–1928* (London, UCL Press, 1999), pp. 42–7.

18 E. Pankhurst, *My own story*, p. 9. O. Banks, *Becoming a feminist: the social origins of 'First Wave' feminism* (Brighton, Wheatsheaf Books, 1986), p. 30, emphasises the importance of childhood socialisation in aiding the development of feminist consciousness. Similarly P. Levine, *Feminist lives in Victorian England: private roles and public commitment* (Oxford, Basil Blackwell, 1990), pp. 15–16, while recognising that we are unable to rescue the full quota of those 'multiple historical strands which create and mould human action' acknowledges the importance of radical family histories amongst Victorian feminist women, a point also made in her earlier book, *Victorian feminism 1850–1900* (London, Hutchinson, 1987), p. 21.

19 See Holton, *Suffrage days*, Chapter 1.

20 Interview with Mrs. Pankhurst, *The Woman's Herald*, 7 February 1891, p. 241.

21 E. S. Pankhurst, *Emmeline Pankhurst*, p. 12; E. S. Pankhurst, *TSM*, p. 54.

22 Interview with Mrs. Pankhurst, 1891, p. 241.

23 E. S. Pankhurst, *Emmeline Pankhurst*, p. 13.

24 C. Pankhurst, *Unshackled*, p. 17; E. S. Pankhurst, *Emmeline Pankhurst*, p. 13.

25 C. Pankhurst, *Unshackled*, p. 17.

26 E. S. Pankhurst, *Emmeline Pankhurst*, p. 14.

27 R. West, Mrs. Pankhurst, in *The post Victorians*, with an introduction by The Very Rev. W. R. Inge (London, Ivor Nicholson, 1933), p. 482. In contrast, Adela Pankhurst, The philosophy of the suffragette movement, 1934, p. 6, suggests that Grandmother Goulden was 'a handsome, imperious woman, whose word was law to her husband and her sons', Adela Pankhurst Walsh Papers, National Library of Australia, Canberra.

28 C. Pankhurst, *Unshackled*, pp. 18–19.

29 For discussion of the issue of actresses and respectability in the Victorian theatre, see K. Powell, *Women and Victorian theatre* (Cambridge, Cambridge University Press, 1997), Chapter 3. John, *Elizabeth Robins*, p. 76, notes, ' the actress … was set apart yet presumed to be available, a woman in a public position who became off stage another private individual, crossing from fantasy to reality'.

30 E. S. Pankhurst, *Emmeline Pankhurst*, p. 15. In contrast, Adela Pankhurst Walsh, The philosophy of the suffragette movement, p. 6, claimed that her mother's brothers were 'the most sweet-natured men it is possible to imagine, and in their households the women certainly struck the dominant note', Pankhurst Walsh Papers.

31 Interview with Mrs. Pankhurst, 1891, p. 241.

32 E. S. Pankhurst, *TSM*, p. 55.

33 Dr. Pankhurst, *Manchester faces and places*, IV, 1893, p. 33; E. S. Pankhurst, *TSM*, p. 6.

34 E. S. Pankhurst, *Emmeline Pankhurst*, pp. 17–18; D. Mitchell, *Queen Christabel: a biography of Christabel Pankhurst* (London, MacDonald and Jane's, 1977), p. 18. See also the entry in Crawford, *The women's suffrage movement*, pp. 514–15.

35 C. Pankhurst, *Unshackled*, p. 21

36 West, Mrs. Pankhurst, p. 482.

37 See T. W. G., In Bohemia, citizen Pankhurst, *Manchester City News*, 12 April 1913.

38 E. S. Pankhurst, *TSM*, pp. 42–5, 49–51; L. Holcombe, *Wives and property: reform of the married women's property law in nineteenth-century England* (Oxford, Martin Robertson, 1983), p. 128.

39 E. S. Pankhurst, *TSM*, p. 56.

40 C. Pankhurst, *Unshackled*, pp. 21–2.

41 Ibid., p. 18.

42 M. Lyndon Shanley, *Feminism, marriage and the law in England, 1850–1895* (New Jersey, Princeton University Press, 1989), Chapter 2; Holcombe, *Wives and property*, Chapter 9.

43 C. Pankhurst, *Unshackled*, p. 21.
44 E. S. Pankhurst, *TSM*, p. 31. See S. S. Holton, Free love and Victorian feminism: the divers matrimonials of Elizabeth Wolstenholme and Ben Elmy, *Victorian Studies*, Winter, 1994, pp. 199–222.
45 Millicent Garrett Fawcett to Mrs. Elmy, 10 December [1875], copy in the Women's Library (hereafter WL), formerly the Fawcett Library, London Guildhall University.
46 C. Pankhurst, *Unshackled*, p. 22.
47 Ibid., p. 21.
48 E. S. Pankhurst, *TSM*, p. 57.
49 Ibid., p. 57.

2 MARRIAGE AND ENTRY INTO POLITICAL LIFE (1880–MARCH 1887)

1 E. S. Pankhurst, *TSM*, p. 57; E. S. Pankhurst, *Emmeline Pankhurst*, p. 18.
2 *Women's Suffrage Journal*, 1 March 1880, p. 50.
3 E. S. Pankhurst, *TSM*, p. 97; Holton, *Suffrage days*, p. 35.
4 E. S. Pankhurst, *TSM*, p. 57.
5 C. Pankhurst, *Unshackled*, p. 21.
6 Ibid., p. 23.
7 E. S. Pankhurst, *TSM*, p. 57.
8 J. Lewis, *Women in England 1870–1950: sexual divisions and social change* (Brighton and Bloomington, Wheatsheaf Books, 1984), p. 117; K. Gleadle, *British women in the nineteenth century* (Basingstoke, Palgrave, 2001), p. 180.
9 E. S. Pankhurst, *TSM*, p. 58.
10 E. Pankhurst, *My own story*, p. 13.
11 E. S. Pankhurst, *TSM*, p. 60.
12 Ibid., pp. 60–1.
13 Ibid., p. 64.
14 See Holton, *Suffrage days*, p. 39; S. A. van Wingerden, *The women's suffrage movement in Britain, 1866–1928* (Basingstoke, Macmillan, 1999), pp. 35–7.
15 Some of the letters preserved in *Lydia Becker's Letter Book* (letters sent in a personal capacity, as Honorary Treasurer of the Manchester Committee for the Married Women's Property Bill, but mostly as Secretary of the Manchester National Society for Women's Suffrage, Manchester Central Library, Manchester, UK, M50/1/3), from Lydia Becker to Richard Pankhurst sound almost flirtatious. The letter 20 June 1868 to 'My dear Dr. Pankhurst', for example, states: 'I think you are quite right. It is an important crisis, and I am prepared to do and dare everything!' The letter 7 June [1868] to Sarah Jackson, speaks of Dr. Pankhurst as 'a very clever little man – with some most extraordinary sentiments about life in general – and women in particular – and so much to say on them, that it is really dangerous to venture into his den – I called at his chambers on Friday to give him a paper & intended to stay five minutes, & found it impossible to escape under two hours!'
16 *Women's Suffrage Journal*, 1 October 1883, p. 179; E. S. Pankhurst, *TSM*, p. 64.
17 C. Pankhurst, *Unshackled*, p. 27.
18 E. S. Pankhurst, *TSM*, pp. 65–6.
19 E. S. Pankhurst, *Emmeline Pankhurst*, pp. 18–19.
20 E. S. Pankhurst, *TSM*, p. 68.
21 Ibid., p. 67.
22 E. S. Pankhurst, *Emmeline Pankhurst*, p. 19.
23 E. S. Pankhurst, *TSM*, p. 68.
24 Ibid., p. 71.

25 Emmeline Pankhurst (hereafter EP) to Miss Biggs, August 1885, E. Sylvia Pankhurst Archive (hereafter ESPA), Institute of Social History, Amsterdam; EP to Florence Balgarnie, 17 August 1885, ESPA.

26 A. Pankhurst Walsh, My mother: an explanation & vindication, p. 7, Pankhurst Walsh Papers.

27 E. S. Pankhurst, TSM, p. 75.

28 E. Pankhurst, My own story, p. 18.

29 E. S. Pankhurst, TSM, p. 77.

30 E. S. Pankhurst, Emmeline Pankhurst, p. 22.

31 E. S. Pankhurst, TSM, p. 77.

32 Christabel Pankhurst (hereafter CP) to Lord Pethick-Lawrence, 22 April 1957, Pethick-Lawrence Papers (hereafter P-L Papers), Trinity College, University of Cambridge.

33 C. Pankhurst, Unshackled, p. 25.

34 A. Pankhurst Walsh, My mother, p. 5. Sylvia did not hold this view. In a letter postmarked 25 June 1957 to Lord Pethick-Lawrence she notes that her mother 'had the foolish dream that she might get rich so he [Richard] would be able to abandon law for politics. That my father could never have done. I have often heard him say his legal profession was "a fine profession" and he was interested and keen on his work and able to help many people by it', P-L Papers.

3 POLITICAL HOSTESS
(JUNE 1887–1892)

1 E. S. Pankhurst, Emmeline Pankhurst, p. 26.

2 C. Pankhurst, Unshackled, p. 26.

3 E. S. Pankhurst, TSM, pp. 82–4.

4 C. Pankhurst, Unshackled, p. 27.

5 E. Pankhurst, My own story, p. 19.

6 A. Taylor, Annie Besant: a biography (Oxford, Oxford University Press, 1992), pp. 193–6.

7 Ibid., pp. 206–8.

8 E. Pankhurst, My own story, p. 19; S. Lewenhak, Women and trade unions: an outline history of women in the British trade union movement (London, Ernest Benn, 1977), pp. 79–80.

9 E. S. Pankhurst, TSM, pp. 87–8.

10 Walter Richard Craine Goulden, the eldest child in the Goulden family, was born on 21 August 1856 and therefore was two years older than Emmeline.

11 C. Pankhurst, Unshackled, p. 27.

12 E. S. Pankhurst, TSM, p. 88.

13 E. S. Pankhurst, Emmeline Pankhurst, p. 23. J. F. C. Harrison, Late Victorian Britain 1875–1901 (Glasgow, Fontana, 1990), p. 59, makes the point that the two main groups that made up the bulk of the lower middle class were first, shopkeepers and small businessmen and, secondly, white-collar employees such as teachers and, especially, clerks.

14 [A. Mearns] The bitter cry of outcast London (New York, A. M. Kelly reprint, 1970, first pub. 1883). G. R. Sims, How the poor live was also published in 1883 – see Selections from How the poor live reprinted in Into unknown England 1866–1913: selections from the social explorers, ed. P. Keating (London, Fontana, 1976), pp. 65–90.

15 E. S. Pankhurst, TSM, p. 89.

16 Ibid., p. 89; Sylvia Pankhurst in Myself when young by famous women of to-day, ed. M. Oxford (London, Frederick Muller, 1938), p. 263.

17 E. S. Pankhurst, TSM, p. 90.

18 Ibid., pp. 71, 90; Banks, Biographical dictionary: Vol. 1, p. 129.

19 E. S. Pankhurst, TSM, p. 90.

20 West, Mrs. Pankhurst, p. 483.

21 C. Pankhurst, Unshackled, p. 30.

22 E. S. Pankhurst, *TSM*, pp. 90–1; C. Pankhurst, *Unshackled*, pp. 28–9.

23 E. S. Pankhurst, *TSM*, p. 91.

24 van Wingerden, *The women's suffrage movement*, pp. 58–9.

25 Crawford, *The women's suffrage movement*, p. 500.

26 *Women's Suffrage Journal*, 1 January 1889, p. 8; Strachey, '*The cause*', pp. 281–2.

27 *Women's Suffrage Journal*, 1 January 1889, p. 2; E. S. Pankhurst, *TSM*, p. 94; Holton, *Suffrage days*, pp. 75–6.

28 *Women's Suffrage Journal*, 1 April 1889, p. 48.

29 Holton, *Suffrage days*, p. 75.

30 E. S. Pankhurst, *TSM*, p. 103.

31 C. Pankhurst, *Unshackled*, p. 28.

32 The literature here is extensive, but see Rubinstein, *Before the suffragettes*, pp. 12–20; J. Gardiner (ed.), *The new women, women's voices 1880–1918* (London, Collins & Brown, 1993); E. Showalter (ed.), *Daughters of decadence, women writers of the fin de siècle* (London, Virago, 1993); S. Ledger, *The new woman, fictions and feminism at the fin de siècle* (Manchester, Manchester University Press, 1997); Caine, *English feminism*, Chapter 4.

33 S. Stanley Holton, Now you see it, now you don't: the Women's Franchise League and its place in contending narratives of the women's suffrage movement, in *The women's suffrage movement*, eds Joannou and Purvis, p. 19. I draw heavily upon Holton's chapter in the following discussion. See also Rubinstein, *Before the suffragettes*, pp. 143–5. The only Minute Book I have been able to locate is the Women's Franchise League, Minute Book of the Executive Committee, 1890–6, in the Special Collections, Northwestern University Library, Illinois, USA (hereafter WFLMB), and I am grateful to R. Russell Maylone, the Curator, for arranging for a microfilm version to be sent to me.

34 Holton, The Women's Franchise League, p. 19.

35 Interview with Mrs. Pankhurst, *The Woman's Herald*, 7 February 1891, p. 241.

36 H. Stanton Blatch and A. Lutz, *Challenging years: the memoirs of Harriot Stanton Blatch* (New York, G.P. Putnam's Sons, 1940), p. 73; E. S. Pankhurst, *TSM*, pp. 111–12.

37 Holton, The Women's Franchise League, pp. 23–4. On the importance of these transatlantic links see also S. S. Holton, 'To educate women into rebellion': Elizabeth Cady Stanton and the creation of a transatlantic network of radical suffragists, *American Historical Review*, 99, 4, October 1994, pp. 1,112–36; S. S. Holton, From anti-slavery to suffrage militancy: the Bright circle, Elizabeth Cady Stanton and the British women's movement, in *Suffrage & beyond: international feminist perspectives*, eds C. Daley and M. Nolan (Auckland, Auckland University Press, 1994), pp. 213–33.

38 Holton, The Women's Franchise League, p. 25; Rosen, *Rise up women!*, p. 17.

39 Holton, The Women's Franchise League, p. 25.

40 Ibid., pp. 24–5.

41 Ibid., p. 21.

42 C. Pankhurst, *Unshackled*, p. 29.

43 E. Pankhurst, *My own story*, p. 16.

44 Women's Franchise League Leaflet, dated 1891, Appendix 2, Scott Papers, *Manchester Guardian* Archive, John Rylands University Library, University of Manchester.

45 Holton, *Suffrage days*, p. 76. Holton states that Elmy drafted this 1889 bill.

46 E. S. Pankhurst, *TSM*, p. 97; E. S. Pankhurst, *Emmeline Pankhurst*, p. 30.

47 Rosen, *Rise up women!*, p. 17.

48 Alice Scatcherd to Harriet McIlquham, 28 October 1890, WL.

49 For the circumstances surrounding her resignation see Holton, The Women's Franchise League, p. 21.

50 EP to Mrs. Wood, 11 July 1890, WL.

51 Minutes of the Executive Committee, 25 July 1890, WFLMB.

52 Interview with Emmeline Pankhurst, 1891, p. 241.

53 Minutes of the Executive Committee, 25 July 1890, WFLMB, for example, state that Mrs. Pankhurst moves, Mrs. Burrows seconds 'that no formal receipts be given except by or through the Treasurer' while those for 15 September 1890, record that Mrs. Scatcherd moves and Mrs. Pankhurst seconds 'that the Hon Secs be empowered to engage such secretarial help as they think necessary'. The Minutes for 24 November 1890 note that 'Mrs. Pankhurst suggested that *The Gentlewoman*, the *Pall Mall Gazette* and *The Star* should be asked if they would give every week a column or ½ a column to the objects of the League.' The meetings that Emmeline chaired include those held on 24 November 1890, 5 January and 14 July 1891 and 5 August 1892.

54 E. S. Pankhurst, *TSM*, p. 97.

55 Ursula Bright to EP, 28 November 1893, ESPA.

56 Interview with Mrs. Pankhurst, 1891, pp. 241–2 for all the following quotes.

57 C. Pankhurst, *Unshackled*, p. 34.

58 Interview with Mrs. Pankhurst, 1891, p. 242.

59 Minutes of the Executive Committee, 2 October and 30 November 1891, WFLMB; A. Bott (ed.), *Our mothers* (London, Victor Gollancz, 1932), p. 165.

60 Coleman, *Adela Pankhurst*, p. 14.

61 A. Pankhurst Walsh, My mother, p. 4.

62 E. S. Pankhurst, *TSM*, p. 101.

63 Ibid., p. 101.

64 Ibid., p. 108; A. Pankhurst Walsh, My mother, pp. 8–9.

65 West, Mrs. Pankhurst, p. 483.

66 E. S. Pankhurst, *TSM*, p. 98; C. Pankhurst, *Unshackled*, pp. 28–9.

67 A. Pankhurst Walsh, My mother, pp. 9–10.

68 Ibid., p. 3.

69 Coleman, *Adela Pankhurst*, pp. 14–15.

70 Holton, *Suffrage days*, p. 85; *The Times*, 27 April 1892.

71 Minutes of the Executive Committee, 2 May 1892, WFLMB.

72 *The Times*, 27 April 1892.

73 Ibid.; Rubinstein, *Before the suffragettes*, p. 144.

74 Ursula Bright to EP, 28 November 1893, ESPA.

75 Crawford, *The women's suffrage movement*, p. 501.

76 Minutes of the Executive Committee, 2 May 1892, WFLMB.

77 EP to J. H. Nodal Esq., 28 April 1892, Author's Collection.

78 E. S. Pankhurst, *TSM*, p. 112.

79 E. S. Pankhurst, *Emmeline Pankhurst*, p. 30.

80 See *Women's Penny Paper*, 15 November 1890.

4 SOCIALIST AND PUBLIC REPRESENTATIVE
(1893–1897)

1 C. Pankhurst, *Unshackled*, p. 31.

2 See Dyhouse, *Girls growing up*, pp. 55–78; Purvis, *A history of women's education*, pp. 75–84.

3 E. S. Pankhurst, *TSM*, p. 113; Coleman, *Adela Pankhurst*, p. 17.

4 E. S. Pankhurst, *Emmeline Pankhurst*, p. 30.

5 E. S. Pankhurst, *TSM*, p. 114.

6 Minutes of the Executive Committee, 17 November 1893, WFLMB.

7 Ursula Bright to EP, 27 and 28 November 1893, ESPA.

8 Report of the Executive Committee of the Manchester National Society for Women's Suffrage (hereafter MNSWS), presented at the Annual General Meeting, 29 November 1893 (Manchester, Aston & Redfern), Manchester Central Library, UK, M50/1/4/24.

9 Crawford, *The women's suffrage movement*, p. 648.

10 Report of the Executive Committee of the MNSWS, presented at the Annual General Meeting, 20 November 1894 (Manchester, 'Guardian' General Printing Works, 1894), p. 8. Liddington and Norris, *One hand tied behind us*, p. 167, assert that this was 'an isolated event' for Emmeline Pankhurst, who had taken 'little interest in women's suffrage' in the 1890s, a claim that cannot be substantiated.
11 Ursula Bright to EP, 30 May 1894, ESPA.
12 Ursula Bright to EP, 1 and 15 June 1894, ESPA.
13 C. Benn, *Keir Hardie* (London, Hutchinson, 1992), p. 65; see also K. O. Morgan, *Keir Hardie: radical and socialist* (London, Weidenfeld and Nicholson, 1975).
14 *Labour Leader* (*LL*), 7 July 1894.
15 Ursula Bright to EP, 10 July 1894, ESPA.
16 C. Pankhurst, *Unshackled*, p. 32.
17 Ibid., p. 32; E. Pankhurst, *My own story*, p. 35.
18 Ursula Bright to EP, 10 July 1894, ESPA.
19 R. Anderson to Dear Comrade, 20 July 1894, ESPA; *Manchester Guardian*, 25 July 1894.
20 H. S. B. [Harriot Stanton Blatch] to EP, 25 July [1894], ESPA.
21 *LL*, 24 November 1894.
22 Mrs. Newton of the Lancashire and Cheshire Union to EP, 19 September 1894, ESPA.
23 E. Pankhurst, *My own story*, p. 15.
24 Sylvia Pankhurst in *TSM*, p. 119, plays down this fact – 'On July 20th Mrs. Pankhurst was unanimously adopted as I.L.P. candidate for the Manchester School Board, though it was not until September that Dr. Pankhurst's letter declaring his decision to join the Independent Labour Party appeared in the Press.'
25 C. Pankhurst, *Unshackled*, p. 32.
26 *LL*, 15 September 1894.
27 E. S. Pankhurst, *TSM*, p. 120.
28 Ibid., pp. 120–1.
29 Mrs. Pankhurst, *LL*, 4 July 1896.
30 E. S. Pankhurst, *TSM*, pp. 124–5.
31 *LL*, 8 December 1894.
32 E. S. Pankhurst, *Emmeline Pankhurst*, pp. 34–5; E. S. Pankhurst, *TSM*, pp. 129–30.
33 *LL*, 22 December 1894.
34 E. S. Pankhurst, *Emmeline Pankhurst*, p. 35.
35 E. S. Pankhurst, *My own story*, p. 24.
36 Ibid., p. 24.
37 Ibid., p. 27.
38 E. S. Pankhurst, *Emmeline Pankhurst*, p. 36. Hollis, *Ladies elect*, p. ix, notes, 'On the whole, elected local government women were less authoritarian, less censorious, and more respectful of the views of the poor than their male colleagues, both elected members and officers alike.'
39 E. S. Pankhurst, *TSM*, p. 132.
40 E. Pankhurst, *My own story*, p. 24; *LL*, 1 June 1895.
41 E. Pankhurst, *My own story*, p. 25.
42 Ibid., p. 28.
43 E. S. Pankhurst, *Emmeline Pankhurst*, p. 37.
44 Ibid., pp. 37–8; E. S. Pankhurst, *TSM*, pp. 133–4.
45 E. S. Pankhurst, *TSM*, p. 133; Morgan, *Keir Hardie*, Chapter 4.
46 E. S. Pankhurst, *TSM*, p. 134.
47 Ibid., p. 135.
48 See Benn, *Keir Hardie*, Chapter 6.
49 E. S. Pankhurst, *TSM*, pp. 135–6.
50 Ibid., p. 136.

51 Benn, *Keir Hardie*, p. 127, notes that Hardie and all the twenty-seven other ILP candidates were not elected in 1895.
52 E. S. Pankhurst, *TSM*, p, 136; E. S. Pankhurst, *Emmeline Pankhurst*, p. 38.
53 E. S. Pankhurst, *TSM*, p. 137.
54 *Manchester Evening News*, 12 June 1896.
55 E. S. Pankhurst, *TSM*, p. 137.
56 Entry for 21 June 1896, Bruce Glasier Diaries, Sydney Jones Library, University of Liverpool; *LL*, 27 June 1896.
57 See Rosen, *Rise up women!*, p. 21.
58 Mrs. Pankhurst, *LL*, 4 July 1896.
59 Boggart Ho' Clough, *LL*, 11 July 1896.
60 Rosen, *Rise up women!*, p. 22.
61 E. S. Pankhurst, *TSM*, p. 139.
62 C. Pankhurst, *Unshackled*, p. 34.
63 E. S. Pankhurst, *TSM*, pp. 101 and 147; A. Pankhurst Walsh, My mother, p. 17.
64 Coleman, *Adela Pankhurst*, p. 21.
65 Entry for 24 October 1896, Bruce Glasier Diaries. See also Steedman, *Margaret McMillan*, pp. 103–4.
66 E. S. Pankhurst, *TSM*, p. 141.
67 Nell Hall Humpherson to David Mitchell, 12 June 1964, David Mitchell Collection (hereafter DMC), Museum of London.
68 *LL*, 20 and 27 March 1897.
69 E. S. Pankhurst, *TSM*, p. 146.
70 *LL*, 29 May 1897.
71 E. S. Pankhurst, *TSM*, p. 132.
72 Ibid., p. 145.
73 Ibid., p. 144.
74 C. Pankhurst, *Unshackled*, p. 35.

5 WIDOWHOOD AND EMPLOYMENT
(1898–FEBRUARY 1903)

1 *LL*, 16 April 1898.
2 E. S. Pankhurst, *TSM*, p. 124. Sylvia tells another story on the same page about which I am dubious and to which, therefore, I have made no reference. 'One Sunday morning when Christabel was about sixteen, the Doctor spoke of her future. "Christabel has a good head", he ejaculated, "I'll have her coached; she shall matriculate!" Mrs. Pankhurst burst into tears, protesting that she would not have her daughters brought up to be High School teachers.' I have omitted this story since, as Sylvia herself later acknowledges on p. 164, Christabel did matriculate, and this was at a time when Emmeline was a widow and encouraging her daughter in academic pursuits. Furthermore, the letters written by Emmeline to Mr. Nodal, to which I refer towards the end of this chapter, make it quite clear that, despite her straitened financial circumstances, Emmeline was keen for her daughters to be educated and was using money of her own and from a fund set up after Richard's death for this purpose.
3 E. S. Pankhurst, *TSM*, p. 147; C. Pankhurst, *Unshackled*, p. 35.
4 E. S. Pankhurst, *Emmeline Pankhurst*, pp. 40–1; E. S. Pankhurst, *TSM*, p. 147.
5 C. Pankhurst, *Unshackled*, p. 35.
6 CP to Sylvia Pankhurst, 1 July 1898, ESPA.
7 E. S. Pankhurst, *TSM*, p. 140. Sylvia, when trying to keep up with Christabel on one cycling trip, had been thrown over the handle-bars.
8 C. Pankhurst, *Unshackled*, p. 35.

9 E. S. Pankhurst, *TSM*, p. 150, where Sylvia states that her father dictated the words on Monday [4 July 1898], the telegram being sent by someone else. C. Pankhurst, *Unshackled*, p. 35, offers another version – ' "Father ill. Come" said the telegram', which implies that Sylvia sent it although Christabel does not explicitly say so. See *Manchester Evening News* Tuesday, 5 July 1898, 'Death of Dr. Pankhurst' which notes that Dr. Pankhurst was well on the Saturday but that on the Monday 'his condition was regarded as hopeless'.

10 E. S. Pankhurst, *TSM*, p. 151.

11 Ibid., p. 151; C. Pankhurst, *Unshackled*, p. 36.

12 C. Pankhurst, *Unshackled*, p. 38.

13 *LL*, 9 July 1898.

14 *Manchester Guardian*, 11 July 1898; *LL*, 16 July 1898; Entry for 9 July 1898, Bruce Glasier Diaries.

15 Benn, *Keir Hardie*, p. 147.

16 E. S. Pankhurst, *TSM*, p. 152.

17 See *Manchester Evening News*, 16 July 1898.

18 EP to Mrs. Glasier, 12 July 1898, Bruce Glasier Papers, Sydney Jones Library, University of Liverpool.

19 Entries for 21 and 23 July 1898, Bruce Glasier Diaries.

20 C. Pankhurst, *Unshackled*, p. 36.

21 A. Pankhurst Walsh, *My mother*, p. 25.

22 Ibid., p. 25; E. S. Pankhurst, *TSM*, p. 152.

23 Dr. Pankhurst Deceased, List of shares, ESPA.

24 C. Pankhurst, *Unshackled*, p. 37.

25 E.S. Pankhurst, *TSM*, p. 153.

26 Letter from J. F. B. *Manchester Guardian*, 13 July 1898; letter from W. H. Dixon and John J. Graham, *Manchester Evening News*, 23 July 1898.

27 Dr. Pankhurst Fund, List of subscriptions, Author's Collection. The Dr. Pankhurst Fund, the Hon. Treasurer's account of receipts and payments to 31 December 1899, lists the receipts as just over £1,153, Author's Collection.

28 Clerk to the Guardians of the Manchester Union to Sylvia Pankhurst, 4 February 1929, ESPA.

29 C. Pankhurst, *Unshackled*, p. 37.

30 A. Pankhurst Walsh, *My mother*, p. 25; The Dr. Pankhurst Fund, the Hon. Treasurer's account of receipts and payments to December 31st, 1899, notes that on 1 September 1899 a payment of £317 16s. 2d. was made for 'Furniture purchased for use of Mrs. Pankhurst and Children', Author's Collection.

31 C. Pankhurst, *Unshackled*, p. 38.

32 E. S. Pankhurst, *TSM*, p. 155.

33 A. Pankhurst Walsh, *My mother*, p. 25.

34 Entry for 29 November 1898, Bruce Glasier Diaries; E. S. Pankhurst, *TSM*, p. 154.

35 E. S. Pankhurst, *TSM*, p. 154; C. Pankhurst, *Unshackled*, p. 38; A. Pankhurst Walsh, *My mother*, p. 28.

36 E. S. Pankhurst, *TSM*, p. 157, notes that at the end of 1901, Sylvia won the Lady Whitworth Scholarship of £30 plus fees, as the best woman student of her year, which enabled her to attend full time again.

37 A. Pankhurst Walsh, *My mother*, p. 28.

38 Ibid., pp. 25–7.

39 E. S. Pankhurst, *TSM*, p. 156.

40 E. Pankhurst, *My own story*, p. 32.

41 E. S. Pankhurst, *TSM*, p. 156. L. E. N. Mayhall, The South African War and the origins of suffrage militancy in Britain, 1899–1902, in *Women's suffrage in the British Empire*, eds I. C. Fletcher, L. E. N. Mayhall and P. Levine (London and New York, Routledge, 2000),

pp. 3–17, argues that pro-Boer activists such as Emmeline, Christabel and Sylvia Pankhurst 'developed an analysis of the war that critically engaged with every argument made in defense of the war, eventually putting that analysis to use on behalf of British women's franchise rights'. While highlighting the ways in which imperial and franchise questions were intertwined, Mayhall does not present a particularly convincing case in regard to Emmeline's train of thought, nor does she consider a range of other issues and experiences that were influential in her life at this time.

42 E. S. Pankhurst, *TSM*, p. 157.

43 Entry for 27 October 1900, Bruce Glasier Diaries.

44 E. Pankhurst, *My own story*, p. 33.

45 Ibid., pp. 34–5.

46 Ibid., p. 35.

47 *Manchester Guardian*, 2 April 1902. Liddington and Norris, *One hand tied behind us*, p. 169, in an 'anti' Emmeline and Christabel chapter erroneously claim that at this time 'Mrs. Pankhurst put all her energies into routine ILP business rather than combining it with suffrage.'

48 Rosen, *Rise up women!*, p. 27 notes that in June 1902 Emmeline had become a member of the newly formed central committee of the Manchester ILP while Liddington and Norris, *One hand tied behind us*, p. 169, claim that Emmeline was a founder member of a new local ILP branch, Manchester Central, formed in August 1902.

49 EP to Mr. Nodal, 18 July 1902, Author's Collection.

50 EP to Mr. Nodal, 20 July 1902, Author's Collection.

51 C. Pankhurst, *Unshackled*, p. 40.

52 Report of the Executive Committee of the North of England Society for Women's Suffrage, Presented at the annual meeting, 29 November 1901 (Manchester, Taylor, Garnett & Co), p. 18, lists Emmeline's and Christabel's subscription at 5 shillings and 10 shillings, respectively; Report of the Executive Committee of the North of England Society for Women's Suffrage, Presented at the annual meeting, 24 November 1902 (Manchester, 'Guardian' General Printing Works), p. 10.

53 *Manchester Guardian*, 2 August 1902; Rosen, *Rise up women!*, p. 26.

54 E. S. Pankhurst, *TSM*, p. 158.

55 Ibid., p. 159.

56 Ibid., pp. 160–2.

57 EP to Mr. Nodal, 27 November 1902, Author's Collection.

58 Mr. Nodal to EP, 29 November 1902, ESPA.

59 EP to Mr. Nodal, 29 November [1902], Author's Collection.

60 EP to Mr. Nodal, 29 November 1902, Author's Collection.

61 EP to Mr. Nodal, 1 December 1902, Author's Collection.

62 EP to Mr. Nodal, 28 December 1902, Author's Collection. Sylvia Pankhurst in *TSM*, p. 164, does not mention that Adela had to be isolated and describes the incident in terms that portray Christabel in a harsh light. 'Christabel adored her [Eva Gore-Booth], and when Eva suffered from neuralgia, as often happened, she would sit with her for hours, massaging her head. To all of us at home, this seemed remarkable indeed, for Christabel had never been willing to act the nurse to any other human being. She detested sickness, and had even left home when Adela had scarlet fever and Harry had chicken-pox, on the first occasion going into hired lodgings, on the second to stay with friends.' Sylvia was still in Italy when Adela fell ill.

63 EP to Sir William Bailey, 7 January 1903, Author's Collection.

64 Sir William Bailey to Mr. Nodal, 8 January 1902, Author's Collection.

65 EP to Mr. Nodal, 26 January 1903, Author's Collection.

66 Ibid.

67 EP to Mr. Nodal, 31 January 1903, Author's Collection.

68 EP Mr. Nodal, 17 February 1903, Author's Collection.

6 FOUNDATION AND EARLY YEARS OF THE WSPU (MARCH 1903–JANUARY 1906)

1 C. Pankhurst, *Unshackled*, pp. 42–3; E. S. Pankhurst, *TSM*, pp. 163–4; A. Pankhurst Walsh, My mother, p. 29.
2 *LL*, 13 March 1903.
3 E. S. Pankhurst, *TSM*, p. 167.
4 EP to Mrs. Glasier, 10 June 1903, Glasier Papers.
5 E. S. Pankhurst, *TSM*, p. 167; *I.L.P. News*, August, 1903.
6 Smith, *The British women's suffrage campaign*, p. 16.
7 Ibid., Chapter 2. See Introduction, note 32 for a discussion of the terms 'constitutional' and 'militant'.
8 E. Pankhurst, *My own story*, p. 37.
9 Ibid., p. 36.
10 See Fulford, *Votes for women*, p. 114. Holton, *Suffrage days*, p. 108, states that the WSPU was a 'ginger group within the ILP'. I suspect that the source of this claim is Sylvia's *TSM*, p. 168, and yet a careful reading reveals that Sylvia does not state that the WSPU was affiliated to the ILP, although it is implied. Sylvia notes that originally Emmeline intended the new organisation to be called the Women's Labour Representation Committee but changed the name to 'The Women's Social and Political Union' when Christabel pointed out that the former name had already been chosen by Esther Roper and Eva Gore-Booth for an organisation they were forming amongst women textile workers. Sylvia claims that it was her mother's intention to conduct 'social as well as political work' for the members of the new organisation, which at that time 'she intended should be mainly composed of working women, and politically a women's parallel to the I.L.P., though with primary emphasis on the vote'. The following evidence in this chapter illustrates how the new organisation was initially centred in the local labour movement since the early WSPU members were also members of the ILP. Neither Emmeline in *My own story* nor Christabel in *Unshackled* repeats Sylvia's claim that it was the intention that the WSPU should be mainly composed of working women. Both women, of course, writing retrospectively, would have no wish to state otherwise since during the active years of campaigning they constantly emphasised that the WSPU aimed to attract women of all social groupings. However, see also Sylvia's 1911 book *The suffragette*, p. 7, where it is claimed that the WSPU was founded to be 'entirely independent of Class and Party'. Thanks to Sandra Holton and Elizabeth Crawford for discussion of these issues.
11 C. Pankhurst, *Unshackled*, p. 43.
12 E. Pankhurst, *My own story*, p. 38.
13 Ibid., p. 38.
14 E. S. Pankhurst, *Emmeline Pankhurst*, p. 49.
15 C. Pankhurst, *Unshackled*, p. 44.
16 Teresa Billington-Greig (hereafter TBG) Papers, Emmeline Pankhurst. The home, WL.
17 Rosen, *Rise up women!*, p. 31; TBG Papers, WL, Box 397, Folder A6.
18 TBG Papers, Early days. 1903–4–5: militancy in plan, in C. McPhee and A. Fitzgerald (eds), *The non-violent militant, selected writings of Teresa Billington-Greig* (London and New York, Routledge, 1987), p. 95; C. Pankhurst, *Unshackled*, p. 44.
19 TBG Papers, Emmeline Pankhurst. The home.
20 TBG Papers, Teacher Conscience Period 1902–4.
21 TBG Papers, Early WSPU, the Gore-Booth & Roper connection.
22 *Clarion*, 1 January 1904.
23 E. Pankhurst, *My own story*, p. 40.
24 Ibid., p. 40.
25 Ibid., p. 40.
26 *LL*, 9 April 1904.
27 Entry for 5 April 1904, Bruce Glasier Diaries.

28 *LL*, 16 April 1904. For further discussion of these issues see Holton, *Feminism and democracy*, Chapter 3 and K. Hunt, *Equivocal feminists, the Social Democratic Federation and the woman question 1884–1911* (Cambridge, Cambridge University Press, 1996), Chapter 6.

29 *LL*, 23 April 1904.

30 *LL*, 16 April 1904.

31 *LL*, 18 November 1904.

32 E. Pankhurst, The political betrayal of women, *LL*, 27 January 1905.

33 *LL*, 3 February 1905.

34 EP to Mrs. Cooper, 2 February 1905, Papers of Selina Jane Cooper (1865–1946), Lancashire Record Office, Preston. See also Liddington and Norris, *One hand tied behind us*, pp. 184–7.

35 Crawford, *The women's suffrage movement*, p. 503.

36 E. S. Pankhurst, *TSM*, p. 181.

37 EP to Mrs. Montefiore, 19 February 1905, in D. B. Montefiore, *From a Victorian to a modern* (London, E. Archer, 1927), pp. 117–18.

38 E. S. Pankhurst, *Emmeline Pankhurst*, pp. 50–1.

39 E. Pankhurst, *My own story*, p. 42.

40 Early accounts by participants in both the constitutional and militant wings suggest that the movement was in the doldrums. Strachey '*The cause*', p. 284, stated: 'The agitation had been going on so long that the Press and the public were tired of hearing of it … the winning of the vote seemed in the early nineties to be farther away than ever before in the history of the agitation.' For the militant side, E.S. Pankhurst, *Emmeline Pankhurst*, p. 50, claimed that the movement 'had sunk into an almost moribund coma of hopelessness'. These assessments have recently been questioned by Rubinstein in *Before the suffragettes* and especially by Holton in *Suffrage days* and in her chapter on The Women's Franchise League, where her discussion of the tactics of the League indicates that the movement was far from being at a standstill. See Smith, *The British women's suffrage campaign*, p. 14, for an excellent summary of these points.

41 E. S. Pankhurst, *TSM*, p. 182.

42 See the letters in the *Clarion* and *LL*, 21 April 1905.

43 *LL*, 28 April 1905.

44 E. S. Pankhurst, *The suffragette*, p. 14.

45 West, *Mrs. Pankhurst*, p. 490.

46 Mrs. Pankhurst, The defeat of the Women's Bill, *LL*, 19 May 1905.

47 E. Pankhurst, *My own story*, p. 43.

48 Ibid., p. 43; Emmeline Pethick Lawrence to Sylvia Pankhurst, 26 December 1903, ESPA.

49 See Introduction, note 32 where I state that I shall follow Cowman's approach, in her thesis Engendering citizenship, where she broadens the definition of militancy to include a breadth of actions that were about challenging views of conventional feminine behaviour rather than just law-breaking.

50 E. Pethick-Lawrence, *My part in a changing world* (London, Victor Gollancz, 1938), p. 151. Emmeline and Frederick Pethick Lawrence did not hyphenate their surname during their time in the suffrage movement but afterwards, and I follow that pattern here.

51 Elizabeth Wolstenholme Elmy (hereafter EWEP) to Harriet McIlquham, 21 June 1905, Letters of Mrs. E. C Wolstenholme Elmy, British Library, Add MS 47,454 Vol. VI.

52 A. Kenney, *Memories of a militant* (London, Edward Arnold & Co., 1924), p. 29. Annie, born on 13 September 1879, in the village of Springhead in Lancashire, was one year older than Christabel; E. S. Pankhurst, *TSM*, p. 185.

53 E. S. Pankhurst, *TSM*, pp. 186–7; T. J. Berry, The female suffrage movement in South Lancashire with particular reference to Oldham 1890–1914, MA dissertation, Huddersfield Polytechnic, May 1968, pp. 49–50; G. Mitchell (ed.), *The hard way up: the autobiography of Hannah Mitchell suffragette and rebel* (London, Faber, 1968), p. 128.

54 *LL*, 7 July 1905. Sylvia in her *TSM*, pp. 184–5, makes no mention of her mother's work here, indeed, on p. 182 she states, 'Keir Hardie's lone fight for the unemployed received a measure of encouragement that session; the King's speech contained a promise of legislation. In earlier years this would have delighted Mrs. Pankhurst. She dismissed it now with the observation that when women had won the vote such matters would be dealt with as a matter of course.'

55 Mrs. Pankhurst, The defeat of the Women's Bill.

56 Bessie Hatton, A chat with Christabel Pankhurst, LL.B. *Sunday Times*, 8 March 1908.

57 See K. Hardie, Women and politics, in *The case for women's suffrage*, ed. B. Villers (London, T. Fisher Unwin, 1907), p. 79, and, more recently, Holton, From anti-slavery to suffrage militancy; Mayhall, Defining militancy; J. Lawrence, Contesting the male polity: the suffragettes and the politics of disruption in Edwardian Britain, in *Women, privilege and power: British politics, 1750 to the present*, ed. A. Vickery (Stanford, California, Stanford University Press, 2001).

58 TBG Papers, Plan period of study & teaching record.

59 C. Pankhurst, *Unshackled*, p. 50.

60 E. Pankhurst, *My own story*, p. 49.

61 E. Sharp, Emmeline Pankhurst and militant suffrage, *Nineteenth Century*, April 1930, pp. 518–19.

62 *Manchester Evening News*, 16 October 1905.

63 Kenney, *Memories*, p. 41.

64 *LL*, 27 October 1905; Kenney, *Memories*, p. 42.

65 Marcus, Introduction, p. 9; Rosen, *Rise up women!*, p. 55.

66 E. Pankhurst, *My own story*, p. 50.

67 E. S. Pankhurst, *Emmeline Pankhurst*, p. 47.

68 E. S. Pankhurst, *TSM*, p. 192.

69 Interview with Grace Roe, 22 September 1975, DMC; letter from CP to Helen Lady Pethick-Lawrence, 19 April 1957, Craigie Collection.

70 C. Pankhurst, *Unshackled*, pp. 228–9.

71 Ibid., p. 239.

72 Ibid., p. 262.

73 Harrison, Two models of feminist leadership, pp. 32–3, claims that 'Mother ... deferred to daughter on short-term strategy, crediting her with political genius and tolerating no criticism of her; daughter deferred to mother on long-term objectives, while ruthlessly exploiting her mother's talents for the cause.'

74 C. Pankhurst, *Unshackled*, speaks of decision-making as being shared between her and her mother, frequently referring to 'Mother and I' – see, for example, pp. 43, 229.

75 Smyth, *Female pipings*, p. 202.

76 Kenney, *Memories*, p. 56.

77 *LL*, 3 and 17 November 1905.

78 *LL*, 22 December 1905.

79 *LL*, 15 December 1907; M. Gawthorpe, *Up hill to Holloway* (Penobscot, Maine, Traversity Press, 1962), p. 207.

80 Fulford, *Votes for women*, p. 132; Benn, *Keir Hardie*, p. 208.

81 C. Pankhurst, *Unshackled*, p. 61.

82 Ibid., p. 61.

83 Kenney, *Memories*, pp. 58–61.

7 TO LONDON
(FEBRUARY 1906–JUNE 1907)

1 Kenney, *Memories*, p. 59; E. S. Pankhurst, *TSM*, p. 197. Montefiore, *From a Victorian to a modern*, pp. 50–1 questioned this version of events, first printed in an article by Sylvia in

VfW, 5 November 1908. She claimed that when Annie first arrived in London she came to her house in Hammersmith and that she took Annie to Minnie Baldock, where she lodged for the first weeks of her stay in London. Years afterwards, when Dora asked Sylvia why she had 'so wilfully distorted facts', Sylvia replied 'that she was very young at the time and entirely under the influence of her mother, who wished my name to be suppressed … I did not consider Sylvia's excuse satisfactory and I told her so.'

2   E. Sylvia Pankhurst, The inheritance, a typed synopsis, ESPA, pp. 13–14.

3   Kenney, *Memories*, p. 67.

4   *Daily Mirror*, 20 February 1906.

5   E. Pankhurst, *My own story*, p. 56.

6   E. S. Pankhurst, *Emmeline Pankhurst*, p. 57.

7   E. Pethick-Lawrence, *My part in a changing world*, p. 146.

8   Ibid., p. 147; Kenney, *Memories of a militant*, pp. 71–2.

9   E. Pethick-Lawrence, *My part in a changing world*, Preface.

10 See J. Balshaw, Sharing the burden: the Pethick Lawrences and women's suffrage, in *The men's share? Masculinities, male support and women's suffrage in Britain, 1890–1920* (London and New York, Routledge, 1997), pp. 135–7, and the entries on Emmeline and Fred Pethick Lawrence in Crawford, *The women's suffrage movement*, pp. 534–43.

11 Women's Social & Political Union, *Manifesto*, leaflet, nd, reprinted in *Labour Record*, March 1906.

12 *Daily Mirror*, 10 March 1906; CP to Dora Montefiore, 22 March 1906, in Montefiore, *From a Victorian to a modern*, p. 116.

13 Crawford, *The women's suffrage movement*, p. 504.

14 *LL*, 6 April 1906.

15 *LL*, 4 May 1906; Rosen, *Rise up women!*, pp. 65–6.

16 Hannam, *Isabella Ford*, p. 116.

17 E. Pankhurst, *My own story*, p. 62.

18 Ibid., p. 64.

19 E. S. Pankhurst, *TSM*, p. 211.

20 Helen Moyes, *A woman in a man's world* (Sydney, Alpha Books, 1971), p. 301.

21 A. Pankhurst Walsh, *My mother*, p. 32.

22 E. S. Pankhurst, *Emmeline Pankhurst*, p. 60.

23 *Manchester Guardian*, 21 May 1906.

24 *LL*, 18 May 1906; Rosen, *Rise up women!*, p. 67.

25 E. Pankhurst, *My own story*, p. 65.

26 Ibid., pp. 68–9.

27 E. S. Pankhurst, *Emmeline Pankhurst*, p. 61.

28 *Daily Graphic*, 28 June 1906.

29 *LL*, 29 June 1906; Mitchell, *The hard way up*, p. 142; Coleman, *Adela Pankhurst*, p. 36.

30 A. Pankhurst Walsh, *My mother*, p. 33; Coleman, *Adela Pankhurst*, p. 37.

31 *LL*, 13 and 27 July 1906; *Labour Record*, August, 1906.

32 Entry 21 July 1906, Bruce Glasier Diaries.

33 E. S. Pankhurst, *TSM*, p. 215; Sylvia Pankhurst to CP, 10 July 1957, Craigie Collection.

34 E. S. Pankhurst, *TSM*, p. 216.

35 C. Pankhurst, *Unshackled*, p. 66; *Manchester Guardian*, 2 July 1906.

36 E. S. Pankhurst, *TSM*, pp. 215–16.

37 See Holton, *Suffrage days*, p. 123. I am grateful to Sandra Holton for discussion of this point.

38 Letter from Marion Coates Hansen, *LL*, 10 August 1906.

39 C. Pankhurst, *Unshackled*, p. 69.

40 Gawthorpe, *Up hill to Holloway*, pp. 222–5.

41 Letter from EP, *LL*, 24 August 1906.

42 Minutes of Manchester ILP Central Branch Meeting, 4 September 1906, Manchester Central Library, Archives Department.

43 John, *Elizabeth Robins*, p. 144.

44 EP to Miss Robins, 6 October 1906, Elizabeth Robins Papers, Fales Library at the Elmer Holmes Bobst Library of New York University.

45 *Forward* (Glasgow), 20 October 1906.

46 E. S. Pankhurst, *The suffragette*, p. 96, and *TSM*, p. 221.

47 See Garner, *Stepping stones*, pp. 44–7 and Liddington and Norris, *One hand tied behind us*, p. 207.

48 *Daily Mirror*, 25 and 26 October 1906.

49 Letter from Millicent Garrett Fawcett, *The Times*, 27 October 1906.

50 *The Times*, 29 October 1906.

51 *Daily Mirror*, 1 November 1906.

52 F. Pethick-Lawrence, *Fate has been kind* (London, Hutchinson & Co. n.d. [1943]), p. 73.

53 Interview with Jessie Kenney, 2 July 1965, DMC.

54 EP to Miss Robins, 19 November 1906, Elizabeth Robins Papers, Harry Ransom Humanities Research Center (herafter HRHRC), University of Texas at Austin.

55 E. Pankhurst, *My own story*, p. 77.

56 *LL*, 1 February 1907.

57 E. S. Pankhurst, *Emmeline Pankhurst*, pp. 64–5.

58 L. Moore, The woman's suffrage campaign in the 1907 Aberdeen by-election, *Northern Scotland*, 5, 1983, p. 160.

59 E. S. Pankhurst, *TSM*, p. 249. My interpretation here differs but does not exclude that offered by Holton, *Suffrage days*, p. 124, who suggests that Emmeline may have argued as she did primarily as a way of distinguishing her society clearly from the Aberdeen branch of the NUWSS which, after 'years of bowing to the anti-suffrage view of the Liberal MP there' had at last 'agreed to take a slightly less supine position. It had persuaded the new local Liberal candidate to support the parliamentary vote for women municipal voters – something short both of sexual equality, and of adult suffrage – in return for its support during his election campaign.'

60 E. Pankhurst, *My own story*, p. 81.

61 *The Times* and *Daily Chronicle*, 14 February 1907.

62 *Daily News*, 14 February 1907.

63 EP to Mr. Robinson, 2 March 1907, Hannah Mitchell Papers, Manchester Central Library.

64 *Daily Telegraph*, 18 February 1907.

65 *The Times*, 22 March 1907.

66 E. Pankhurst, *My own story*, p. 86.

67 C. Pankhurst, *Unshackled*, p. 79.

68 WSPU, *First annual report, including balance sheet and subscription list for the year ending February 28th, 1907* (London, Clement's Inn, WSPU [1907]).

69 Mrs. Pankhurst's post, *Daily Chronicle*, 23 March 1907; Resistrar General to EP, 4 March 1907, Craigie Collection.

70 *Labour Record*, April 1907; CP to Sylvia, 3 August [1957], Richard Pankhurst Suffrage Collection, reprinted in R. Pankhurst, Suffragette sisters in old age: unpublished correspondence between Christabel and Sylvia Pankhurst, 1953–57, *Women's History Review*, 10, 2001, p. 498; Sylvia Pankhurst to Fred Pethick Lawrence, 24 June 1957, P-L Papers. The issue of a pension for Emmeline Pankhurst was discussed by Emmeline Pethick Lawrence in a letter to Maud Sennett, 27 March 1907 – 'I bless you for your generous thought about the Pankhurst Pension. I have that idea in reserve to discuss with the Committee. I know how intensely independent our dear leader woman is and how very delicately such an idea would have to be handled, but it is an idea that has my entire

approval and sympathy and I hope will develop into a scheme worthy of the woman', Maud Arncliffe Sennett Collection (hereafter MASC), British Library, c121g1, Vol. 1.

71 EP to Mr. Robinson, 2 March and 28 February 1907, Hannah Mitchell Papers.

72 Independent Labour Party, *Report of the fifteenth annual conference, Temperance Hall, Derby, April 1st and 2nd 1907* (London, Independent Labour Party, May 1907), p. 48; *LL,* 5 April 1907.

73 EP to Helen Fraser [Moyes], 3 April 1907, SFC.

74 CP to Miss Robins, Robins Papers, Fales Library.

75 EP to Miss Phillips, 19 April 1907, Watt Collection, Aberdeen Art Gallery and Museum.

76 Sylvia Pankhurst to Lord Pethick Lawrence [early July 1959], P-L Papers. Emmeline's papers were kept by her sister, Ada.

77 Ramsay MacDonald to Bruce Glasier, 3 May 1907, Bruce Glasier Papers; Frank Smith to MacDonald, 30 April 1907, J. Ramsay MacDonald Papers, Public Record Office.

78 Entry for 26 November 1913, Bruce Glasier Diaries. This is misquoted in both Morgan, *Keir Hardie,* p. 164, and Benn, *Keir Hardie,* pp. 225–6.

79 B. K. Scott (ed.), *Selected letters of Rebecca West* (New Haven and London, Yale University Press, 2000), p. 461.

80 Romero, *E. S. Pankhurst,* p. 37, although on p. 50 it is claimed that the love affair began in 1908!

81 Ibid., p. 37.

82 Benn, *Keir Hardie,* p. 226, favours this explanation; Morgan, *Keir Hardie,* p. 164, suggests that there was no substance to the rumours of an affair.

83 E. Pankhurst, The present position of the women's suffrage movement, in *The case for women's suffrage,* ed. Villiers, p. 49.

8 AUTOCRAT OF THE WSPU?
(JULY 1907–SEPTEMBER 1908)

1 Lily Bell, The woman's movement and democracy, and Mary Phillips, Woman's point of view, *Forward,* 2 November 1907; T. Billington-Greig, The difference in the women's movement, *Forward,* 23 November 1907; Rosen, *Rise up women!,* pp. 88–9; Holton, *Feminism and democracy,* pp. 41–2; P. Bartley, *Votes for women 1860–1928* (London, Hodder & Stoughton, 1998), p. 35.

2 EP to Mr. Robinson, 22 June 1907, Hannah Mitchell Papers; EP to Sylvia, 22 June 1907, ESPA.

3 EP to Mr. Robinson, 15 August 1907, Hannah Mitchell Papers.

4 C. Pankhurst, *Unshackled,* p. 82; CP to Lord Pethick-Lawrence, 25 May 1957, P-L Papers; Sylvia Pankhurst to CP, 10 July 1957, Craigie Collection.

5 Edith How Martyn, undated, New members who are unacquainted with the history and development of the 'militant' movement for Women's Suffrage, Maude Arncliffe Sennett Collection, C121g1 Vol. 7; undated paper beginning 'The Women's Social and Political Union', SFC, Z6070 (27); *Morning Post,* 13 September 1907; E. S. Pankhurst, *Emmeline Pankhurst,* p. 70. See E. Pethick-Lawrence, *My part in a changing world,* p. 176, for a different account where she does not mention that she urged Emmeline Pankhurst to take such steps but suggests, instead, that the WSPU leader made these decisions on her own. My interpretation of these events also differs from the account given by Harrison, Two models of feminist leadership, pp. 40–1, where he relies solely upon this source. In 1912, Emmeline and Christabel Pankhurst expelled the Pethick Lawrences from the WSPU and these events undoubtedly helped to shape the content of *My part in a changing world.*

6 For accounts of the Women's Freedom League see C. Eustance, 'Daring to be free': the evolution of women's political identities in the Women's Freedom League 1907–1930, D.Phil. thesis, University of York, 1993; H. Francis, ' … Our job is to free women … ', the sexual politics of four Edwardian feminists from c.1910 to c.1935, D.Phil. thesis,

University of York, 1996; C. Eustance, Meanings of militancy: the ideas and practice of political resistance in the Women's Freedom League, 1907–14, in *The women's suffrage movement*, eds Joannou and Purvis, pp. 51–64, and H. Francis, 'Dare to be free!': the Women's Freedom League and its legacy, in *Votes for women*, eds Purvis and Holton, pp. 181–202.

7 EP to Miss Robins, 13 September 1907, Robins Papers, HRHRC.

8 Ibid., 19 September 1907.

9 Mitchell, *The hard way up*, p. 170.

10 Elizabeth W. Elmy to Dearest Friend, 11 and 15 September 1907, EWEP, British Library, Add Ms 47,455, Vol. VII.

11 Billington-Greig, The difference in the women's movement.

12 T. Billington-Greig, *The militant suffrage movement emancipation in a hurry* (London, Frank Palmer, 1911), pp. 83–6.

13 E. Pankhurst, *My own story*, p. 59.

14 West, Mrs. Pankhurst, p. 500.

15 E. S. Pankhurst, *TSM*, pp. 264–5. This view is also upheld in Sylvia's *Emmeline Pankhurst*, p. 70, 'having accepted the role of dictator, she [EP] played it resolutely. ... The W.S.P.U. was now disciplined like an army; unquestioning obedience was demanded.'

16 E. S. Pankhurst, *TSM*, p. 266; Fulford, *Votes for women*, p. 167; Brendon, Mrs. Pankhurst, p. 162; Liddington and Norris, *One hand tied behind us*, p. 208; Pugh, *The march of the women*, pp. 176–80.

17 Pethick-Lawrence, *Fate has been kind*, pp. 75–6.

18 Jessie Kenney, Notes on Ethel Smyth, Mrs. Pankhurst and Christabel, Kenney Papers, University of East Anglia, KP/5.

19 Interview with Jessie Kenney, 3 March 1964, DMC.

20 West, Mrs. Pankhurst, p. 479.

21 Cicely Hamilton, *Life errant* (London, Dent & Sons, 1935), p. 77.

22 West, Mrs. Pankhurst, p. 480.

23 Smyth, *Female pipings*, pp. 194–5.

24 Mary Stocks, *My commonplace book* (London, Peter Davies, 1970), p. 70.

25 E. S. Pankhurst, *Emmeline Pankhurst*, p. 72.

26 Smyth, *Female pipings*, p. 221.

27 EP to Mrs. Baines, 29 January 1907, Jennie Baines Papers, Fryer Library, University of Queensland.

28 EP to Miss Phillips, 10 December 1907, Watt Collection.

29 E. S. Pankhurst, *TSM*, p. 272; Romero, *E. Sylvia Pankhurst*, p. 50; Benn, *Keir Hardie*, p. 234.

30 Ethel Smyth to My darling Em, 9 December 1913, Ethel Mary Smyth Letters, Walter Clinton Jackson Library (hereafter WCJL), University of North Carolina Library, Green Boro, North Carolina, USA.

31 E. S. Pankhurst, *TSM*, p. 272.

32 Interview with Grace Roe, 22 September 1965, DMC.

33 E. Pankhurst, *My own story*, pp. 92–3.

34 E. S. Pankhurst, *TSM*, p. 273.

35 *VfW Supplement*, 20 February 1908, p. lxviii.

36 E. Pankhurst, *My own story*, p. 96. Barker, Mrs. Pankhurst, p. 209, refers to this meeting in the following condemnatory terms, 'She [Mrs. Pankhurst] had become a daemoniac, and the frenzy flowed out of her into others.'

37 Frances Rowe to Mrs. McIlquham, 5 January 1908, WL.

38 *VfW Supplement*, 20 February 1908, p. lxxviii.

39 *Evening Standard & St. James's Gazette*, 12 February 1908; *VfW Supplement*, 20 February 1908, p. lxxvii.

40 E. Pankhurst, *My own story*, p. 98.

41 *VfW Supplement*, 20 February 1908, p. lxxviii.

42 E. Pankhurst, *My own story*, p. 99.

43 Entry 14 February 1908, Mary Blathwayt Diaries, Dryham Park, South Gloucestershire.

44 By an old militant, Notes on Mrs Pankhurst, August 1943, Craigie Collection.

45 E. Pankhurst, *My own story*, pp. 100–1.

46 Ibid., p. 102.

47 Ibid., pp. 102–3.

48 E. S. Pankhurst, *TSM*, p. 278.

49 E. Pankhurst, *My own story*, p. 104. Emmeline Pethick-Lawrence in *My part in a changing world*, p. 151, claimed that Emmeline Pankhurst could have been 'a queen on the Stage or in the Salon. Circumstances had baulked her in the fulfilment of her destiny.'

50 *VfW*, April 1908, p. 112.

51 Ibid., p. 98.

52 *VfW*, April, 1908, p. 113.

53 Mrs. Pankhurst, *The importance of the vote* (London, The Woman's Press, n.d. [1908]), p. 8.

54 Ibid., p. 12.

55 See D. Riley, *'Am I that name?' Feminism and the category of 'women' in history* (Basingstoke, Macmillan, 1998), Chapter 3.

56 See Vicinus, *Independent women*, pp. 263–4 and Mary Jean Corbett, *Representing femininity: middle-class subjectivity in Victorian and Edwardian women's autobiographies* (New York, Oxford University Press, 1992), p. 154, for discussion of these points, especially in regard to the stylish, feminine dress of the suffragettes.

57 *VfW Supplement*, 26 March 1908, ciii; C. Pankhurst, *Unshackled*, p. 90.

58 *Glasgow Herald*, 28 March 1908. Fulford, *Votes for women*, p. 160, claims that WSPU by-election policy had no 'real effect' on election results.

59 E. Pankhurst, *My own story*, p. 108.

60 E. S. Pankhurst, *TSM*, p. 282; E. Pankhurst, *My own story*, p. 110.

61 *The Times*, 22 June 1908; *Daily Chronicle*, 22 June 1908, gives a figure of 300,000. The following account is drawn from these sources and also the *Daily News*.

62 E. Pankhurst, *My own story*, p. 113.

63 *Daily Chronicle* and *The Times*, 22 June 1908.

64 *The Times*, 24 June 1908.

65 E. Pankhurst, *My own story*, p. 116.

66 *VfW*, 4 June 1908, p. 217.

67 Morley and Stanley, *Emily Wilding Davison*, p. 153.

68 Holton, *Suffrage days*, p. 134.

69 Pankhurst, *My own story*, p. 118; *Daily Mirror*, 1 July 1908.

70 *Daily Chronicle* and *The Times*, 2 July 1908.

71 E. Pankhurst, *My own story*, pp. 118–19. Leneman, *A guid cause*, p. 64.

72 *The Times*, 2 July 1908.

73 Pankhurst, *My own story*, p. 119.

74 Vicinus, *Independent women*, p. 262; Morley and Stanley, *Emily Wilding Davison*, pp. xiii and 153.

75 L. Leneman, A truly national movement: the view from outside London, in *The women's suffrage movement*, eds Joannou and Purvis, pp. 37–30; Hannam, 'I had not been to London', pp. 226–45.

76 *VfW*, 9 July 1908, p. 290; 23 July 1908, p. 322; 30 July 1908, p. 347.

77 *VfW*, 25 June and 9 July 1908, pp. 266 and 293, respectively.

78 Entries for 6 and 7 July 1908, Mary Blathwayt Diaries.

79 EP to Professor Ayrton, 4 July 1908, WL.

80 Entry for 6 July 1908, Mary Blathwayt Diaries.

81 *VfW*, 30 July 1908, p. 349.

82 Ibid., 23 July 1908, pp. 331–2.

83 Ibid., 27 August 1908, p. 404. Even while on 'holiday', Emmeline gave a number of talks – see VfW, 10 September 1908, pp. 445–6.

84 C. Collette, For labour and for women, the Women's Labour League, 1906–18 (Manchester, Manchester University Press, 1989), p. 73; D. Neville, To make their mark: the women's suffrage movement in the North East of England 1900–1914 (Newcastle upon Tyne, North East Labour History Society, 1997), p. 22.

85 Woman Worker, 25 September 1908.

86 Garner, Stepping stones to women's liberty, p. 29; Pugh, The march of the women, p. 221; E. S. Pankhurst, TSM, Chapter 7; E. S. Pankhurst, Emmeline Pankhurst, pp. 46–7.

87 See Holton, Suffrage days, especially Chapter 5; J. Hannam and K. Hunt, Socialist women: Britain, 1880s to 1920s (London and New York, Routledge, 2001); K. Cowman, 'Incipient Toryism'? The Women's Social and Political Union and the Independent Labour Party, 1903–14, History Workshop Journal, 53, 2002.

88 Leneman, A guid cause, p. 52.

89 K. Cowman, 'The stone-throwing has been forced upon us': the functions of militancy within the Liverpool W.S.P.U., 1906–14, Transactions of the Historic Society of Lancashire and Cheshire, 145, 1996, p. 177, and her 'Crossing the great divide', p. 44. See also Hannam, 'I had not been to London', pp. 233–6.

90 VfW, October 1907, p. 6.

91 Ibid., 10 September 1908, p. 440.

92 Ibid., 24 September 1908.

9 EMMELINE AND CHRISTABEL (OCTOBER 1908–JANUARY 1909)

1 VfW, 8 October 1908, p. 24.

2 E. Pankhurst, My own story, p. 120.

3 VfW, 15 October 1908, p. 36.

4 Ibid., p. 36.

5 C. Lytton and J. Warton, Spinster, Prisons and prisoners, some personal experiences (London, William Heinemann, 1914), pp. 20–7.

6 Ibid., pp. 27–8; C. Pankhurst, Unshackled, p. 105.

7 E. Pankhurst, My own story, p. 122.

8 C. Pankhurst, Unshackled, pp. 106–7.

9 VfW, 29 October 1908, p. 69.

10 Evening News, 14 October 1908; Daily News, 26 October 1908; Weekly Dispatch, 25 October 1908; Purvis, Christabel Pankhurst and the Women's Social and Political Union, p. 161.

11 Pethick-Lawrence, My part in a changing world, p. 205. See Daily Mirror, 22 October 1908; Weekly Dispatch Photographic Supplement, 25 October 1908.

12 EP to Miss Robins, 23 October 1908, HRHRC.

13 The speeches from the dock, VfW, 29 October 1908, pp. 77–8. See I. C. Fletcher, 'A star chamber of the twentieth century': suffragettes, Liberals, and the 1908 'Rush the Commons' case, Journal of British Studies 35, 1996, pp. 504–30, for an analysis of the behind-the-scenes management of public order by the state.

14 Pethick-Lawrence, My part in a changing world, p. 204.

15 See E. A. Accampo, Private life, public image: motherhood and militancy in the self-construction of Nelly Roussel, 1900–1922, in The new biography, ed. Burr Margadant, pp. 218–61.

16 The speeches from the dock, pp. 81–2.

17 Ibid., p. 82.

18 E. S. Pankhurst, Emmeline Pankhurst, p. 81.

19 S. Pankhurst, Women's fight for the vote, *Weekly Dispatch*, 1 November 1908.

20 'General' Drummond, The story of my third imprisonment, *VfW*, 12 November 1908, p. 108.

21 E. Pankhurst, *My own story*, pp. 132–3.

22 Ibid., p. 133.

23 *VfW*, 12 November 1908, pp. 107 and 109.

24 Keir Hardie to Dear Friend [EP], 7 November 1908, Viscount Gladstone Papers, BL Add 46066; Lady Frances Balfour to Mrs. Fawcett, 11 November 1908, WL; *The Times*, 14 November 1908.

25 *VfW*, 26 November 1908, p. 155.

26 Ibid., p. 148. The letter was also reproduced in some of the newspapers, e.g. *Daily Chronicle*, 24 November 1908.

27 Kathleen Brown to Una Dugdale, 6 January 1909, Author's Collection.

28 Sylvia Pankhurst to Mr. Scott, Editor of the *Manchester Guardian*, 11 December 1908, Scott Papers, *Manchester Guardian* Archive, John Rylands University Library, University of Manchester. I have found no evidence to support Sylvia's later claim in her *TSM*, p. 292, that through her efforts, C. P. Scott, the powerful Liberal editor of the *Manchester Guardian*, said to have the ear of the Liberal Party leadership, visited Emmeline in Holloway – see EP to Scott, 7 January 1909, Scott Papers. Further, on p. 292, Sylvia claims that it was Scott who procured the concession in regard to newspapers, thus contradicting her earlier statement in her letter of 11 December that it was Keir Hardie.

29 Sylvia Pankhurst to Mr. Scott, 11 December 1908, *Scott Papers*; Sylvia Pankhurst to Miss Robins, 26 November 1908, HRHRC.

30 Holton, *Suffrage days*, p. 169.

31 Constance Lytton to Mr. Gladstone, 21 December 1908, Viscount Gladstone Papers.

32 *VfW*, 24 December 1908, p. 217.

33 *Daily News*, 23 December 1908.

34 *VfW*, 31 December 1908, p. 230.

35 Ibid., p. 230.

36 E. Pankhurst, March on! *VfW*, 31 December 1908, p. 232.

37 Ibid., p. 232.

38 *VfW*, 21 January 1908, p. 276.

39 Ibid., pp. 276–8.

40 EP to Miss Robins, 16 January 1909, HRHRC.

41 Z. Procter, *Life and yesterday* (Kensington, Favil Press, 1960), p. 95.

42 *Forward*, 2 January 1909.

10 'A NEW AND MORE HEROIC PLANE' (JANUARY–SEPTEMBER 1909)

1 The phrase is used in E. Pankhurst, *My own story*, p. 149, to refer to the hunger strike adopted by the imprisoned suffragettes, and the forcible feeding inflicted on them by the government.

2 Ibid., p. 136.

3 E. S. Pankhurst, *The suffragette*, p. 360.

4 *VfW* 4 February 1909, pp. 305 and 311.

5 Ibid., 28 January and 4 February 1909, pp. 289 and 306, respectively.

6 EP to Mr. Scott, 7 February 1909, Scott Papers.

7 H. Gladstone to Scott, 9 February 1909, Scott Papers.

8 EP to Mr. Scott, 12 February 1909, Scott Papers.

9 *VfW*, 18 February 1909, p. 358.

10 Ibid., p. 359. Sylvia had travelled to Aberdeen in January, with instructions to put the local WSPU in order ready for the arrival of its organiser, Ada Flatman.

11 Moyes, *A woman in a man's world*, p. 30.
12 EP to Mr. Scott, 17 February 1909, Scott Papers.
13 H. Gladstone to Scott, 19 February 1909, Scott Papers.
14 Helen Watts to Mother & Father & all, 24 February 1909, photocopies of Helen Watts Papers, Nottinghamshire County Record Office.
15 *VfW*, 5 March 1909, pp. 406–7.
16 Ibid., 12 March 1909, pp. 434 and 436.
17 Ibid., 19 March 1909, pp. 445, 448, 452, 454.
18 EP to Mr. Scott, 8 and 11 March 1909, Scott Papers.
19 *VfW*, 26 March 1909, p. 476.
20 Ibid., 2 April 1909, pp. 506–7
21 E. Pankhurst, *My own story*, p. 137.
22 E. S. Pankhurst, *TSM*, p. 306.
23 EP to Dr. Mills, 1 April 1909, WL.
24 Untitled paper about Sylvia Pankhurst, Teresa Billington-Greig Papers, Box 3987, THG2/B4/1.
25 EP to Dr. Mills, 7 May 1909, WL.
26 Quoted p. 147 of C. Pankhurst, *Unshackled*.
27 *VfW*, 9 April 1909, p. 533.
28 Ibid., 23 April 1909, pp. 567 and 574.
29 Quoted in Tickner, *The spectacle of women*, p. 211.
30 See EP to Miss Carwin, 24 September 1909, SFC, 'Women have reason to be grateful that you & others have the courage to play a soldier's part in the war we are waging for the political freedom of women.'
31 *VfW*, 29 April 1909, p. 565. This newspaper had been formally handed over to the WSPU by the Pethick Lawrences in January 1909. For further discussion of some international aspects of the women's movement see Evans, *The feminists*, especially Chapter 4; L. J. Rupp, *Worlds of women, the making of an international women's movement* (New Jersey, Princeton University Press, 1997); I. C. Fletcher, L. E. N. Mayhall and P. Levine (eds), *Women's suffrage in the British Empire: citizenship, nation, and race* (London and New York, Routledge, 2000).
32 M. Bosch with A. Kloosterman (eds), *Politics and friendship, letters from the International Woman Suffrage Alliance 1902–1942* (Columbus, Ohio State University, 1990), p. 45.
33 Rupp, *Worlds of women*, p. 137.
34 *VfW*, 7 May 1909, pp. 633–4.
35 Bosch and Kloosterman (eds), *Politics and friendship*, pp. 83–4.
36 *VfW*, 7 May 1909, p. 633.
37 E. S. Pankhurst, *TSM*, p. 304.
38 *VfW*, 14 May 1909, pp. 659 and 667.
39 National Women's Social & Political Union, *The women's exhibition 1909 programme* (London, The Woman's Press, n.d.); *VfW*, 21 May 1909, pp. 689–90.
40 Crawford, *The women's suffrage movement*, p. 506.
41 Interview with Teresa Billington-Greig, 12 September 1964, DMC.
42 E. S. Pankhurst, *TSM*, p. 306.
43 M. Richardson, *Laugh a defiance* (London, Weidenfeld and Nicholson, 1953), p. 1.
44 *VfW*, 4 June 1909, p. 757.
45 Sylvia's claim in her *TSM*, p. 306, that Emmeline brushed aside Dr. Mills' advice that Harry should not return to the farm, on the grounds that he was too delicate to endure the exposure and hard toil of farm life, must be questioned. As we have seen, Emmeline, in her letter of 1 April 1909, sought the advice of Dr. Mills and was unlikely to have acted against it. Sylvia presents Emmeline as a neglectful mother, implying that her lack of concern for her son eventually led to his death.
46 *VfW*, 18 and 25 June 1909, pp. 810 and 843, respectively

47 EP to Elizabeth Robins, 23 June 1909, Robins Papers, HRHRC.

48 *VfW*, 25 June 1909, p. 844.

49 Ibid., 2 July 1909, p. 872.

50 E. Pankhurst, *My own story*, pp. 138–9; *VfW*, 2 July 1909, p. 887; F. A. Bather, Men's Committee for Justice to Women, to Keir Hardie, 2 July 1909, Author's Collection.

51 *Daily News*, 30 June 1909.

52 E. Pankhurst, *My own story*, p. 141.

53 *Daily Chronicle*, 30 June 1909.

54 *Letters of Constance Lytton, Selected and arranged by Betty Balfour* (London, William Heinemann, 1925), p. 168.

55 *VfW*, 16 July 1909, p. 948

56 *VfW*, 9 July 1909, p. 920.

57 Ibid., 2 and 16 July 1909, pp. 876–9 and 935–42, respectively, and 3 December 1909, pp. 145, 147–9.

58 Ibid., 3 December 1909, p. 145.

59 E. Pankhurst, *My own story*, p. 148.

60 Ibid., p. 149.

61 *VfW*, 16 July 1909, p. 934.

62 Ibid., 23 July 1909, pp. 971–2.

63 EP to Mr. Scott, 17 and 21 July 1909, Scott Papers.

64 Entry for 21 July 1909, Bruce Glasier Diaries.

65 *VfW*, 30 July 1909, pp. 1,004–5.

66 See *VfW*, 20 August 1909, p. 1,085, from where the majority of these quotes are taken in relation to the Prime Minister's meeting at Bletchley on 13 August.

67 Ibid., 27 August 1909, p. 1,110.

68 Ibid., 27 August and 3 September 1909, pp. 1,109–20 and 1123, respectively.

69 EP to Elizabeth Robins, 28 August 1909, Robins Papers, HRHRC.

70 *VfW*, 24 September 1909, pp. 1,206–10; *Dundee Advertiser*, 20 September 1909; *The Times*, 23 September 1909.

71 *Daily News*, 25 September 1909.

72 *The Times*, 21 September 1909; *VfW*, 24 September 1909, p. 1,205.

73 See J. Purvis, The prison experiences of the suffragettes in Edwardian Britain, *Women's History Review*, 4, 3, 1995, pp. 103–33; C. J. Howlett, Writing on the body? Representation and resistance in British suffragette accounts of forcible feeding, *Genders*, 23, 1996, pp. 3–41.

74 Tickner, *The spectacle of women*, p. 107.

75 Letter in *The Times*, 29 September 1909.

76 *VfW*, 1 October 1909, p. 4.

11 PERSONAL SORROW AND FORTITUDE (SEPTEMBER 1909–EARLY JANUARY 1911)

1 *VfW*, 1 October 1909, pp. 1 and 4; E. Pankhurst, *My own story*, pp. 156–7.

2 E. Pankhurst, The fiery cross, *VfW*, 1 October 1909, p. 8.

3 *VfW*, 8 October 1909, p. 19; *The Times*, 5 October 1909.

4 EP to Mr. Nevinson, 4 October 1909, Evelyn Sharp Nevinson Papers, Bodleian Library, Oxford.

5 Rosen, *Rise up women!*, p. 124; Myall, 'No surrender!', p. 178.

6 C. Pankhurst, *Unshackled*, pp. 146–7.

7 Dubois, *Harriot Stanton Blatch*, p. 94. Dubois notes that the focus of the Equality League on working women distinguished it from the many other suffrage societies at that time in New York City.

8 Ibid., p. 95.

9 *VfW*, 27 August 1909, p. 1,115.

10 EP to Miss Robins, 11 and 17 August 1909, Robins Papers, HRHRC.

11 EP to Miss Birnstingl, 30 July 1909, Craigie Collection.

12 *VfW*, 15 October 1909, p. 43.

13 EP to Miss Birnstingl, 30 July 1909, Craigie Collection.

14 A. Pankhurst Walsh, My mother, p. 48.

15 C. Pankhurst, *Unshackled*, p. 147.

16 E. S. Pankhurst, *TSM*, p. 320.

17 A. Pankhurst Walsh, My mother, pp. 47–8.

18 E. S. Pankhurst, *Emmeline Pankhurst*, p. 93.

19 CP to Miss Robins, 22 August 1909, Robins Papers, HRHRC.

20 *New York Times*, 20 October 1909.

21 Leaflet, Mrs. Pankhurst (New York, J. B. Pond Lyceum Bureau, n.d.), National American Woman Suffrage Association (hereafter NAWSA) Papers, Library of Congress, Washington DC.

22 Dubois, *Harriot Stanton Blatch*, p. 113.

23 E. Pankhurst, *My own story*, p. 160. For a discussion of the suffrage movements in the USA and Britain see C. Bolt, *The women's movements in the United States and Britain from the 1790s to the 1920s* (Hemel Hempstead, Harvester Wheatsheaf, 1993), Chapter 5; C. Bolt, America and the Pankhursts, in *Votes for Women: the sstruggle for suffrage revisited* ed. J. H. Baker (Oxford, Oxford University Press, 2002).

24 *New York Times*, 21 October 1909.

25 Ibid.

26 Leaflet advertising Mrs. Pankhurst's meeting, Mary Hutcheson Page Papers, Schlesinger Library, Radcliffe College, MA; *VfW*, 8 November 1909, p. 85.

27 *The Woman's Journal* (Boston), 30 October 1909.

28 *New York Times*, 26 October 1909; Dubois, *Harriot Stanton Blatch*, p. 114.

29 H. Stanton Blatch and A. Lutz, *Challenging years, the memoirs of Harriot Stanton Blatch* (New York, G. P. Putnam's Sons, 1940), p. 114.

30 E. Pankhurst, *My own story*, p. 160.

31 Stocks, *My commonplace book*, p. 70.

32 F. L. Bullard, Mrs. Pankhurst at close range – a talk with a remarkable personality, *Sunday Herald Boston*, 31 October 1909, magazine section.

33 *VfW*, 12 November 1909, p. 101.

34 A. Ruhl, Mrs. Pankhurst – practical politician, undated cutting, Sophia Smith Collection (hereafter SSC), Smith College, Northampton, Massachusetts.

35 EP to Miss Robins, 27 October 1909, Robins Papers, HRHRC.

36 *VfW*, 19 November and 10 December 1909, pp. 122 and 170, respectively; Blatch and Lutz, *Challenging years*, p. 115.

37 *The Woman's Journal* (Boston), 11 December 1909, p. 199.

38 Ibid., pp. 199–202.

39 Dubois, *Harriot Stanton Blatch*, p. 115.

40 Alice Morgan Wright to Edith Shephard, 10 December [1909], SSC.

41 *VfW*, 10 December 1909, p. 161.

42 CP to Dr. Mills, 4 October 1909, WL.

43 E. S. Pankhurst, *Emmeline Pankhurst*, p. 94.

44 *VfW*, 17 December 1909, p. 181.

45 Ibid.

46 E. S. Pankhurst, *TSM*, p. 321.

47 E. S. Pankhurst, *Emmeline Pankhurst*, p. 94.

48 *VfW*, 31 and 24 December 1909, pp. 210 and 200, respectively.

49 E. S. Pankhurst, *TSM*, p. 323.

50 Jill Craigie interview with Grace Roe [1975?], Craigie Collection.

51 E. S. Pankhurst, *TSM*, p. 323.
52 EP to Miss Robins, 31 December 1909, Robins Papers, HRHRC.
53 E. S. Pankhurst, *TSM*, p. 324.
54 Quoted in Crawford, *The women's suffrage movement*, p. 506.
55 Romero, *E. Sylvia Pankhurst*, p. 51.
56 E. S. Pankhurst, *Emmeline Pankhurst*, p. 94; E. S. Pankhurst, *TSM*, p. 324.
57 Sharp, Emmeline Pankhurst, p. 516.
58 U. Dugdale, Memories of Mrs. Pankhurst, n.d., Author's Collection.
59 Rosen, *Rise up women!*, p. 130.
60 C. Pankhurst, *Unshackled*, p. 153.
61 *VfW*, 7 January 1910, p. 225.
62 Lytton and Warton, *Prisons and prisoners*, p. 235; *VfW*, 28 January 1910, p. 276; *The Times* and *Daily Telegraph*, 26 January 1910.
63 EP to Miss Robins, 3 February 1910, Robins Papers, HRHRC.
64 Ibid., 6 February 1910.
65 *VfW*, 11 February 1909, p. 314.
66 Rosen, *Rise up women!*, p. 134.
67 Entry for 14 April 1910, Nevinson Diaries.
68 *VfW*, 30 December 1910, p. 207; Sylvia Pankhurst to Mrs. Norah Walshe, 18 October 1928, DMC.
69 Coleman, *Adela Pankhurst*, p. 47.
70 Dobbie, *A nest of suffragettes*, pp. 40–1 and 62.
71 Thorpe and Marsh, Diary reveals lesbian love trysts.
72 The difficulties of defining 'lesbianism' are highlighted in the following. The Lesbian History Group, *Not a passing phase: reclaiming lesbians in history 1840–1985* (London, The Women's Press, 1989), p. 15, asks, 'Do we define "lesbian" as only applying to women who had genital connection with each other? Or only to women who prioritised their love for women and made it central to their existence, refusing to organise their lives around men as society demanded?' Writers in this important book answer these questions differently. E. Hamer, *Britannia's glory: a history of twentieth-century lesbians* (London and New York, Cassell, 1996), p. 3, suggests, 'If a relationship looks like that of lovers, it usually is that of lovers. Lesbians are women who love women and this love of women is visible in how they have chosen to live their lives.' Hammer includes (p. 23) amongst what she sees as 'the large number of lesbians' in the militant suffrage movement Mary Allen, Rachel Barrett, Eva Gore-Booth, Vera Holme, Evelina Haverfield and Christopher St. John.
73 A. Oram and A. Turnbull, *The lesbian history sourcebook: love and sex between women in Britain from 1780 to 1970* (London and New York, Routledge, 2001), p. 1. They continue, pp. 1–2, 'Our own working definition of "lesbian-like" cultures and behaviour … ideally includes some evidence of eroticism, or sexual feeling in love relationships between women, as important in the past.'
74 Pugh, *The Pankhursts*, p. 212.
75 Ibid., p. 213.
76 Ibid., p. 212.
77 *VfW*, 3 June 1910, p. 574.
78 Ibid., p. 574.
79 *Morning Leader*, 20 June 1910; see also the reports in *The Times*, *Daily News*, *Daily Chronicle* for that day and *VfW*, 24 June 1910, pp. 628–30.
80 *VfW*, 24 June 1910, p. 635.
81 *VfW*, 1 July 1910, p. 645.
82 EP to Miss Robins, 6 July 1910, Robins Papers, HRHRC.
83 E. Pankhurst, *My own story*, p. 176; *VfW*, 15 July 1910, p. 699.
84 *VfW*, 22 July 1910, pp. 711–14.

85 Millicent Garrett Fawcett to Societies affiliated to the NUWSS (marked confidential), 16 July 1910, WL; Tickner, *The spectacle of women*, p. 116.

86 *VfW*, 29 July 1910, pp. 724–5.

87 *Daily News, Daily Mirror* and *Manchester Guardian*, 25 July 1910.

88 *VfW*, 29 July 1910, p. 724.

89 Ibid., p. 725; *Clarion*, 29 July 1910.

90 Rosen, *Rise up women!*, p. 137.

91 Kenney, *Memories*, p. 163.

92 *VfW*, 5 August 1910, p. 745.

93 EP to Mr. Scott, 16 August 1910, Scott Papers.

94 Ibid., 22 August 1910.

95 *VfW*, 19 August and 2 September 1910, pp. 769 and 786, respectively.

96 EP to Una Dugdale, 8 August 1910, Author's Collection.

97 M. Ward, *Hanna Sheehy Skeffington: a life* (Cork, Attic Press, 1997), p. 71; C. Murphy, *The women's suffrage movement and Irish society in the early twentieth century* (Hemel Hempstead, Wheatsheaf Harvester Press, 1989), pp. 63–4.

98 Form letter from EP to Dear Friend, 27 October 1910, SFC.

99 EP to Miss Sharp, 31 October 1910, Sharp Nevinson Papers.

100 Entry for 9 November 1910, Nevinson Diaries. See especially John and Eustance (eds), *The men's share?* for discussion of men's role in the women's suffrage campaigns.

101 *VfW*, 18 November 1910, p. 102.

102 E. Pankhurst, *My own story*, p. 180.

103 *The treatment of the women's deputations by the Metropolitan Police, Copy of evidence collected by Dr. Jessie Murray and Mr. H. N. Brailsford, and forwarded to the Home Office by the Conciliation Committee for Women's Suffrage, in support of its demand for a public enquiry* (London, The Woman's Press, 1911), p. 9. It would appear that many of the police on duty on the 18th were drafted in from other areas of London, including East End districts; C. R. Jorgensen-Earp, *Speeches and trials of the militant suffragettes, the Women's Social and Political Union 1903–1918* (Cranbury, New Jersey and London, Associated University Presses, 1999), p. 122.

The way the sexual nature of the assaults has been commented on by some male historians is offensively sexist and gendered. Rosen's, *Rise up women!*, p. 142, notes, 'By attempting to rush through or past police lines, these women were bringing themselves repeatedly into abrupt physical contact with the police. That the police found in the youthful femininity of many of their assailants an invitation to licence, does not seem, all in all, completely surprising.' Mitchell, *Queen Christabel*, p. 160, writes, 'Clothes were ripped, hands thrust into upper and middle-class bosoms and up expensive skirts. Hooligans, and occasionally policemen, fell gleefully upon prostrate forms from sheltered backgrounds. Wasn't this, they argued, what these women *really* wanted?

Perhaps in some cases, and in a deeply unconscious way, it was.'

104 E. Pankhurst, *My own story*, p. 182.

105 *Daily News*, 19 November 1910; *VfW*, 25 November 1910, pp. 120–3; Morgan, *Suffragists and liberals*, p. 71.

106 *VfW*, 25 November 1910, p. 127.

107 E. Pankhurst, *My own story*, p. 183.

108 *VfW*, 25 November 1910, p. 127.

109 C. Pankhurst, *Unshackled*, pp. 167–8.

110 *VfW*, 25 November and 2 December 1910, pp. 128 and 142, respectively.

111 Ibid., 25 November 1910, p. 129.

112 Ibid., 24 May 1912, p. 534; WSPU leaflet, *Plain facts about the suffragette deputations* (London, The Woman's Press, n.d. [c.1910]), p. 4.

113 *VfW*, 2 December 1910, p. 148.

114 Ibid., p. 148.

115 Holton, In sorrowful wrath, p. 20.

116 *VfW*, 2 December 1910, p. 148.

117 Entry for 29 November 1910, Nevinson diaries.

118 *VfW*, 9 December 1910, p. 160; Jill Craigie interview with Grace Roe [1975?], Craigie Collection.

119 E. Pankhurst, *My own story*, p. 186.

120 E. S. Pankhurst, *TSM*, p. 346.

121 EP to Mr. Scott, 27 December 1910, Scott Papers.

122 EP to Una Dugdale, 1 January 1911, Author's Collection.

123 EP to Miss Robins, 5 January 1911, Robins Papers, HRHRC.

124 E. S. Pankhurst, *Emmeline Pankhurst*, p. 98.

12 THE TRUCE RENEWED
(JANUARY–NOVEMBER 1911)

1 Coleman, *Adela Pankhurst*, p. 48

2 E. S. Pankhurst, *TSM*, p. 367.

3 A. Pankhurst Walsh to Helen Moyes, 11 February 1961, SFC.

4 Ibid.

5 H. W. Nevinson *Fire of life* (London, James Nisbet & Co. Ltd, 1935), p. 252.

6 Quoted in Moyes, *A woman in a man's world*, p. 32; Coleman, *Adela Pankhurst*, p. 50.

7 EP to Mr. Scott, 9 January 1911, Scott Papers.

8 *Anti-suffrage Review*, February 1911, p. 29; *Daily Express*, 17 January 1911.

9 *Daily Express*, 18 January 1911.

10 T. Billington-Greig, *The militant suffrage movement: emancipation in a hurry* (London, Frank Palmer, n.d. [1911]).

11 Entry for 17 January 1911, Nevinson Diaries.

12 Mitchell, *Queen Christabel*, pp. 163–4; Holton, *Suffrage days*, p. 154.

13 Ethel Smyth to EP, 15 September 1910, Ethel Mary Smyth Letters, WCJL.

14 *VfW*, 27 January 1911, p. 272.

15 Pugh, *The march of the women*, p. 140, makes the point that the £10 qualification was dropped because of fears that it would encourage 'faggot voting', that is the endowment of pieces of property on women with the aim of manufacturing extra votes.

16 Quoted in Raeburn, *The militant suffragettes*, pp. 162–3; L. Collis, *Impetuous heart: the story of Ethel Smyth* (London, William Kimber, 1984), p. 90.

17 Raeburn, *The militant suffragettes*, p. 163.

18 Ibid.

19 EP to Miss Flatman, 16 February 1911, SFC.

20 *VfW*, 17 and 24 February 1911, pp. 320 and 343, respectively.

21 *VfW*, 3 and 17 March 1911, pp. 358 and 391, respectively.

22 CP to Constance Lytton, 1 March 1911, SFC.

23 Smyth, *Female pipings*, p. 211; *VfW*, 31 March 1911, p. 420.

24 E. Pankhurst, *My own story*, p. 191.

25 *The Times*, 20 March 1911.

26 E. Pankhurst, *My own story*, p. 193.

27 Ibid., p. 194.

28 Smyth, *Female pipings*, p. 194. Pugh, *The Pankhursts*, p. 214, fails to mention what Ethel specifies, that 'sometimes' she would occupy 'the second bed' in Emmeline's room, and claims, in a subtle change of words, that Ethel 'often shared Emmeline's room'.

29 M. Vicinus, Fin-de-siècle theatrics: male impersonation and lesbian desire, in *Borderlines: genders and identities in war and peace 1870–1930*, ed. B. Melman (London and New York, Routledge, 1998), p. 182.

30 E. S. Pankhurst, *TSM*, p. 377.

31 Vicinus, Fin-de-siècle theatrics, p. 183.

32 Marcus, Introduction, p. 8.

33 Ibid., pp. 8, 11.

34 S. Raitt, The singers of Sargent: Mabel Batten, Elsie Swinton, Ethel Smyth, *Women: A Cultural Review*, 3, 1, 1992, p. 27, states that Mrs. Pankhurst was a lover of Ethel Symth's; Winslow, *Sylvia Pankhurst*, p. 7, proposes 'In all probability both Christabel and Emmeline were involved in lesbian relationships, although there is little documentation on the subject. ... Their mother's relationship with Smythe [sic] was something that both [Sylvia] Pankhurst and Christabel wanted to play down, and they urged Smythe [sic] not to write about it. Yet, in her book, *Female pipings in Eden*, she not only hints at her own and Emmeline's homosexuality but also indicates that [Sylvia] Pankhurst's heterosexuality might have been a reason for her estrangement from mother and sister.' Hamer, *Britannia's glory*, p. 23, points out 'It has been suggested that Ethel Smyth had an affair with Emmeline Pankhurst; they certainly had a very intimate relationship. If this is true it would put lesbianism at the heart of the suffrage movement.' J. Trautmann Banks in her edited volume *Congenial spirits: the selected letters of Virginia Woolf* (London, The Hogarth Press, 1989), offers a more cautious note. On page 339, a letter dated December 3 [1933] from Virginia Woolf to Quentin Bell, is reprinted where Woolf states, 'I have Ethel Smyth and Rebecca West to tea [next week] to discuss the life of Mrs Pankhurst. In strict confidence, Ethel used to love Emmeline – they shared a bed.' In a footnote on p. 339, Banks notes that Ethel Smyth was an ardent supporter of both the women's suffrage movement and its redoubtable leader, Emmeline Pankhurst, but the 'bed bit is less certain', despite the fact that Ethel herself wrote (in *Female Pipings in Eden*) about 'some intense emotional intimacy in a two-bedded room'.

L. Collis, in *Impetuous heart: the story of Ethel Smyth* (London, William Kimber, 1984), pp. 72–3, also offers a cautionary statement. 'What she [Ethel] really sought in her continual romances was highly charged friendship supplemented by the preliminaries of sex: kisses, hugs, being arm in arm, or hand in hand. For all her talk of love, her constant pursuit of new objects, it could be said that she was a chaste woman and also emotionally immature. This is not to say she never consummated an affair with a woman, but it was rare in proportion to the number of times she declared herself, and indeed was, head over heels, hopelessly, helplessly, in love.' Pugh, *The Pankhursts*, pp. 214–15, falls short of calling the 'loving and intense relationship' between Ethel and Emmeline 'lesbian', but implies that there was something sexual happening.

35 Smyth, *Female pipings*, p.188. Pugh, *The Pankhursts*, pp. 214–15, conveniently ignores this point.

36 C. St John, *Ethel Smyth: a biography* (London, Longmans, Green and Co., 1959), p. 185.

37 Vicinus, Fin-de-siècle theatrics, p. 181.

38 *VfW*, 14 April 1911, p. 463; Murphy, *The women's suffrage movement*, p. 64.

39 EP to Miss Flatman, n.d., Carnarvon, Tuesday, SFC.

40 EP to Miss Flatman, 13 April 1911, SFC.

41 E. Sylvia Pankhurst to Hardie, 26 Feburary [1911], as quoted in Romero, *E. Sylvia Pankhurst*, p. 59.

42 K. Hardie to Sylvia [Pankhurst], 10 March 1911, ESPA.

43 R. Childe Dorr, *A woman of fifty* (New York and London, Funk and Wagnalls Co., 1924), p. 265.

44 *VfW*, 28 April 1911, p. 491.

45 A. E. Metcalfe, *Woman's effort: a chronicle of British women's fifty years' struggle for citizenship (1865–1914)* (Oxford, B. H. Blackwell, 1917), pp. 171–2; *VfW*, 5 May 1911, p. 514.

46 *VfW*, 12 May 1911, p. 532.

47 EP to Miss Robins, 26 May 1911, Robins Papers, Fales Library.

48 Smyth, *Female pipings*, p. 191.

49 Quoted in Raeburn, *The militant suffragettes*, p. 163.

50 The following information is taken from Smyth, *Female pipings*, pp. 197–8.

51 E. Pankhurst, *My own story*, p. 195.

52 Rosen, *Rise up women!*, p. 148.

53 *VfW*, 2 June 1911, p. 581.

54 Ibid., 16 June 1911, p. 609.

55 EP to Miss Robins, 9 June 1911, Robins Papers, HRHRC.

56 Rosen, *Rise up women!*, p. 149.

57 E. Pankhurst, *My own story*, p. 197.

58 Tickner, *The spectacle of women*, p. 122.

59 *VfW*, 23 June 1911, p. 625; *Daily News*, 19 June 1911.

60 Tickner, *The spectacle of women*, p. 122.

61 M. G. Fawcett to Mrs. Sennett, 26 June 1911, MASC.

62 *VfW*, 23 June 1911, p. 630.

63 Tickner, *The spectacle of women*, p. 122.

64 EP to Alice Morgan Wright, 26 June 1911, SSC.

65 *VfW*, 7 July 1911, p. 662.

66 EP to Miss Robins, 27 June 1911, Robins Papers, Fales Library.

67 Ibid., EP to Miss Robins, 4 July 1911.

68 Quoted in John, *Elizabeth Robins*, p. 156.

69 *VfW*, 7 July 1911, pp. 654 and 656.

70 EP to Miss Flatman, 8 July 1911, SFC; EP to Mrs. Archdale, 8 July 1911, Craigie Collection.

71 *VfW*, 21 July 1911, p. 689.

72 EP to Miss Birnstingl, 31 July 1911, Craigie Collection.

73 *VfW*, 4 August 1911, p. 726.

74 Ibid., 18 August 1911, p. 742.

75 E. Pankhurst, *My own story*, p. 198.

76 *VfW*, 25 August 1911, p. 754.

77 Lloyd George to the Master of Elibank, 5 September 1911, Elibank Papers, National Library of Scotland.

78 EP to Una Dugdale, 18 August 1911, Author's Collection.

79 *VfW*, 15 September 1911, p. 791.

80 EP to Miss Birnstingl, 25 August 1911, Craigie Collection.

81 EP to Mrs Archdale, n.d. [August 1911?], Craigie Collection.

82 EP to Mrs Archdale, n.d. [late August 1911?], Craigie Collection.

83 C. Pankhurst, *Unshackled*, p. 186.

84 EP to Miss Wright, 18 September 1911, SSC.

85 *VfW*, 6 October 1911, pp. 5 and 10.

86 *The Standard*, 5 October 1911; *VfW*, 6 October 1911, p. 5; E. S. Pankhurst, *TSM*, p. 377.

87 J. B. Pond Lyceum Leaflet, *Second American-Canadian Lecture Tour October to January 1911–12 Mrs. Pankhurst, the world famous leader of the English suffragettes* (New York, n.d.), NAWSA Records, Box 69, Reel 49, Library of Congress, Washington DC, USA.

88 EP to Mrs. Page, 13 October 1911, Mary Hutcheson Page Papers.

89 *VfW*, 3 November 1911, p. 67.

90 E. Pankhurst, *My own story*, p. 200.

91 *VfW*, 3 November 1911, p. 67.

92 Eleanor Garrison to her mother, 22 October 1911, SSC; *VfW*, 3 and 17 November 1911, pp. 67 and 106, respectively.

93 Eleanor Garrison to her mother, 25 October 1911, SSC.

94 *VfW*, 3 November 1911, p. 67.

95 E. Pankhurst, *My own story*, p. 201; E. S. Pankhurst, *Emmeline Pankhurst*, p. 101.

96 *VfW*, 1 December 1911, p. 150.

97 *The Times*, 8 November 1911.
98 E. Pankhurst, *My own story*, p. 202.

13 THE WOMEN'S REVOLUTION
(NOVEMBER 1911–JUNE 1912)

1 EP to Alice Morgan Wright, 11 November 1911, SSC.
2 *VfW*, 24 November 1911, p. 119.
3 Quoted in Rosen, *Rise up women!*, p. 154.
4 *Daily Express*, 22 November 1911.
5 *The Standard*, 24 November 1911.
6 Jorgensen-Earp, 'The transfiguring sword', p. 27.
7 EP to Alice Morgan Wright, 23 November 1911, SSC.
8 Extract from Lloyd George's speech, Bath, 24 November 1911, John Johnson Collection, Women's Suffrage, Box 1, Bodleian Library, Oxford.
9 *VfW*, 8 December 1911, pp. 160–1.
10 T. Wilson (ed.), *The political diaries of C. P. Scott 1911–1928* (London, Collins, 1970), p. 58, entry for 2 December 1911.
11 Canadienne, Mrs. Pankhurst in Toronto, *The Canadian Courier*, 23 December 1911, p. 15.
12 EP to Alice Morgan Wright, 13 December 1911, SSC.
13 EP to Miss Robins, 28 December 1911, Robins Papers, HRHRC.
14 *The Standard*, 15 December 1911; *VfW*, 22 December 1911, p. 196.
15 *VfW*, 29 December 1911, p. 212.
16 Morley and Stanley, *Emily Wilding Davison*, pp. 156–7.
17 E. Pankhurst, *My own story*, p. 210.
18 Morley and Stanley, *Emily Wilding Davison*, pp. 93 and 156–7.
19 C. Pankhurst, Broken windows, *VfW*, 1 December 1911, p. 142.
20 E. S. Pankhurst, *Emmeline Pankhurst*, p. 103.
21 *VfW*, 26 January 1912, p. 262.
22 *The Times*, 23 January 1912.
23 Quoted Rosen, *Rise up women!*, pp. 156–7.
24 EP to Alice Morgan Wright, 11 February 1912, SSC.
25 Quoted in C. Pankhurst, *Unshackled*, p. 196.
26 Mrs. Pankhurst, The argument of the broken pane *VfW*, 23 February 1912, p. 319.
27 E. S. Pankhurst, *TSM*, p. 373.
28 Mrs. Pethick Lawrence, Inciting to violence, *VfW*, 23 February 1912, p. 325. Syliva in her *TSM*, p. 373, misquotes a part of Emmeline Pethick Lawrence's speech and states that she said, 'We can win the victory of Votes for Women by far less dramatic methods of protest than those indicated by Mr. Hobhouse' – thus implying that the stone-throwing policy was upheld by only her mother and Christabel, which was untrue. Emmeline Pethick Lawrence wrote, 'Nevertheless we realise that without causing serious results of this nature, we can embarrass the Government, and oblige them to concede our just and reasonable demand, if when we adopt far less drastic methods of protest than those indicated by Mr. Hobhouse, we act in large numbers and act together.'
29 Lady Constance Lytton to Dr. Alice Ker, 27 February 1912, WL.
30 Smyth, *Female pipings*, pp. 208–9.
31 Quoted in the prosecution evidence presented, 20 March 1912, *VfW*, 22 March 1912, p. 389.
32 *The Times*, *Pall Mall Gazette* and *Daily Telegraph*, 2 March 1912.
33 *VfW*, 8 March 1912, p. 360.
34 *The Times*, 5 March 1912.
35 *VfW*, 8 March 1912, p. 359.
36 C. Pankhurst, *Unshackled*, pp. 202–3; Sharp, *Hertha Ayrton*, pp. 234–5.

37 E. Pankhurst, *My own story*, p. 222.

38 Ibid., p. 222.

39 *The Times*, 2 March 1912; Liberty letter quoted in E. D. Rappaport, *Shopping for pleasure: women in the making of London's West End* (Princeton, Princeton University Press, 2000), p. 215.

40 *The Times*, 6 March 1912.

41 Elizabeth Garrett Anderson to Millicent Garrett Fawcett, 9 and 12 March 1912, WL.

42 *VfW*, 8 March 1912, p. 359.

43 *VfW*, 15 March 1912, pp. 378 and 370.

44 Purvis, The prison experiences of the suffragettes, p. 120, under Rule 243a the Secretary of State approved 'ameliorations ... in respect of the wearing of prison clothing, bathing, hair-curling, cleaning of cells, employment, exercise, books, and otherwise'; Crawford, *The women's suffrage movement*, p. 507; *VfW*, 29 March 1912, p. 412; letter to the editor from Ethel Smyth, *The Times*, 19 April 1912.

45 Smyth, *Female pipings*, p. 209.

46 Ibid., pp. 210–11.

47 *The Times*, 28 March 1912.

48 *VfW*, 5 April 1912, p. 424; Rosen, *Rise up women!*, pp. 160–3.

49 *VfW*, 29 March 1912, p. 404.

50 EP to Lady Constance Lytton, 12 April 1912, WL.

51 EP to Mrs. Billinghurst, 18 April 1912, ESPA.

52 *VfW*, 26 April 1912, p. 469.

53 E. S. Pankhurst, *Emmeline Pankhurst*, p. 106.

54 E. S. Pankhurst, TSM, pp. 382–3.

55 Ibid., p. 316.

56 See Holton, *Suffrage days*, pp. 176–7

57 E. S. Pankhurst, TSM, p. 383.

58 Romero, *E. Sylvia Pankhurst*, p. 62.

59 E. S. Pankhurst, TSM, p. 384.

60 Kenney, *Memories*, p. 175.

61 *VfW*, 26 April 1912, p. 477.

62 EP to Miss Robins, n.d., Robins Papers, HRHRC.

63 EP to Una Dugdale, 25 April 1912, Author's Collection.

64 E. Pankhurst, *Emmeline Pankhurst*, p. 107.

65 *VfW*, 24 May 1912, pp. 531–4; Housman quoted in Holton, *Suffrage days*, p. 185.

66 Entry for 21 May 1912, Nevinson Diaries.

67 *The Standard*, 23 May 1912.

68 Thompson and Thompson, *They couldn't stop us!*, pp. 46–50.

69 A. Pankhurst Walsh, My mother, p. 39; Crawford, *The women's movement*, p. 507.

70 *VfW*, 31 May 1912, p. 567; Rosen, *Rise up women!*, p. 166.

71 E. Pankhurst, *My own story*, p. 251.

72 Crawford, *The women's movement*, p. 507. I have found no evidence to support Sylvia's claim in her TSM, p. 406, about her mother's attitude towards Adela – 'The idea of becoming a gardener ... was a reaction from the knowledge that ... she was often regarded with more disapproval than approbation by Mrs. Pankhurst and Christabel, and was the subject of a sharper criticism than the other organizers had to face.' As noted earlier, the extant letters from Emmeline to Adela, and from Emmeline to Helen Archdale about her daughter, express motherly concern and affection for Adela.

73 Public Record Office (herafter, PRO), PCOM 8/175, report dated 21 June 1912.

74 E. Pankhurst, *My own story*, pp. 251–2.

75 Ibid., pp. 254–5.

76 *VfW*, 5 July 1912, p. 648.

77 *VfW*, 28 June 1912, p. 633.

14 BREAK WITH THE PETHICK LAWRENCES
(JULY–OCTOBER 1912)

1 EP to Alice Morgan Wright, 6 and 11 July 1912, SSC.
2 *VfW*, 2 August 1912, pp. 712–13.
3 *The Standard*, 22 October 1912.
4 E. Pankhurst, *My own story*, p. 256.
5 Pethick-Lawrence, *Fate has been kind*, pp. 98–9.
6 EP to Mrs. Archdale, 14 July 1912, Craigie Collection.
7 *Official programme of the great suffragette demonstration in Hyde Park, Sunday, July 14th, 1912, in honour of the Leader's birthday* (London, E. Marks & Sons, Clerkenwell, n.d.), Author's Collection.
8 *VfW*, 19 July 1912, p. 686.
9 Ibid., 26 July 1912, pp. 696–7; Rosen, *Rise up women!*, p. 170 notes that after prolonged hunger strikes, Mary Leigh was released on 21 September and Gladys Evans on 3 October on licences that restricted their activities and movements. Substantial legal complications led to the cases being eventually allowed to drop, the two women serving only sixteen weeks of their five-year sentences.
10 C. Pankhurst, *Unshackled*, p. 222.
11 Crawford, *The women's movement*, p. 507. The expense account for Emmeline for July included £2 7s. for railway fares to Paris, fares and cabs Paris to London and back £5 10s., and £2 10s. for her hotel in London, Rex v. Kerr & Others File, SL.
12 EP to Miss Robins, n.d., and EP to Miss Robins, 30 July 1912, Robins Papers, HRHRC.
13 *VfW*, 16 August 1912, p. 749.
14 *Manchester Guardian*, 22 August 1912.
15 Quoted in Coleman, *Adela Pankhurst*, p. 50.
16 Ibid., p. 50.
17 EP to Mrs. Lawrence, 8 September 1912, typed copy, P-L Papers.
18 E. Pethick Lawrence to EP, 22 September 1912, typed copy, P-L Papers.
19 *The Standard*, 21 September 1912.
20 EP to Alice Morgan Wright, 2 October 1912, SSC.
21 Pethick-Lawrence, *My part in a changing world*, p. 280.
22 Pethick-Lawrence, *Fate has been kind*, p. 99.
23 Ibid., p. 99.
24 Ibid., p. 100.
25 Memo, n.d. but signed by C. Pankhurst, E. Pankhurst, F. W. Pethick Lawrence and E. Pethick Lawrence, written in Fred Pethick Lawrence's hand, Craigie Collection.
26 Quoted in John, *Elizabeth Robins*, p. 169, from which the information about this meeting is taken.
27 Form letter, EP to Dear Friend, 16 October 1912, SFC.
28 EP to Mr. Lawrence, 17 October 1912, P-L Papers.
29 Pethick-Lawrence, *My part in a changing world*, p. 285.
30 Entry for 23 December 1913, Nevinson Diaries.
31 Pethick-Lawrence, *My part in a changing world*, pp. 278, 283.
32 E. S. Pankhurst, *Emmeline Pankhurst*, p. 114; E. S Pankhurst, *TSM*, p. 412.
33 Kenney, *Memories*, pp. 192–3.
34 Miscellaneous notes by Jessie Kenney, n.d., 'Jessie – notes on Ethel Smyth, Mrs. Pankhurst and Christabel', Kenney Papers, KP/5. I have tidied up this quote in regard to punctuation and typing errors.
35 David Mitchell interview with Jessie Kenney, 31 July 1964, DMC.
36 Ibid.
37 Ibid.

15 HONORARY TREASURER OF THE WSPU AND AGITATOR (OCTOBER 1912–APRIL 1913)

1 *The Suffragette*, 25 October 1912, pp. 16–17.
2 Pethick-Lawrence, *My part in a changing world*, p. 283.
3 *The Suffragette*, 25 October 1912, p. 18.
4 Ibid., 18 October 1912, p. 7.
5 *Daily Herald*, 19 October 1912.
6 *VfW*, 25 October 1912, p. 18.
7 Kenney, *Memories*, p. 195; Anonymous [E. Robins], *Ancilla's share: an indictment of sex antagonism* (London, Hutchinson & Co., 1914), p. 244.
8 E. S. Pankhurst, *TSM*, p. 415.
9 *Punch*, 30 October 1912; David Mitchell interview with Jessie Kenney, 24 March 1964, DMC; Barrett quoted in entry for 28 January 1913, Nevinson Diaries.
10 E. S Pankhurst, *Emmeline Pankhurst*, pp. 115–16.
11 Entry for 7 November 1912, quoted in Dobbie, *A nest of suffragettes*, p. 53.
12 *The Suffragette*, 25 October 1912, p. 24; E. S. Pankhurst, *TSM*, pp. 416–17.
13 E. S. Pankhurst, *TSM*, p. 419.
14 E. S. Pankhurst, *Emmeline Pankhurst*, p. 120. Pugh, *The Pankhursts*, p. 254, suggests that 'the Pankhursts took advantage of Lansbury's good nature by encouraging him to maintain his criticism of his own party leadership'! This is not suggested by G. Lansbury in his autobiography, *My life* (Constable and Co., 1928), p. 121.
15 Rosen, *Rise up women!*, pp. 180–1.
16 *The Suffragette*, 15 November 1912, p. 64.
17 See Winslow, *Sylvia Pankhurst*, p. 36, who takes Sylvia's part in this.
18 Ibid., p. 25; Romero, *E. Sylvia Pankhurst*, pp. 65 and 79.
19 E. S. Pankhurst, *TSM*, p. 425.
20 Winslow, *Sylvia Pankhurst*, p. 25.
21 *The Suffragette*, 29 November 1912, p. 100.
22 Quoted in Schneer, *George Lansbury*, p. 112.
23 Rosen, *Rise up women!*, p. 182.
24 *Daily Herald*, 28 November 1912.
25 Neville, *To make their mark*, p. 40.
26 E. S. Pankhurst, *TSM*, p. 427.
27 PRO HO 45/10695/231366/2, copy of Metropolitan Police account of WSPU meeting, London Opera House, 3 December 1912.
28 Entry for 2 December 1912, Nevinson Diaries.
29 *The Suffragette*, 6 December 1912, p. 124.
30 Ibid., 6 December 1912, p. 114; *Daily Herald*, 10 December 1912.
31 S. Jeffreys, *The spinster and her enemies: feminism and sexuality 1880–1930* (London, Pandora Press, 1985); M. Jackson, *The 'real' facts of life: feminism and the politics of sexuality c1850–1940* (London, Taylor & Francis, 1994); L. Bland, *Banishing the beast: English feminism and sexual morality 1885–1914* (Harmondsworth, Penguin, 1995).
32 EP to Alice Morgan Wright, 10 December 1912, SSC.
33 EP to Henry Harben, 20 December 1912, Henry Harben Papers, British Library, Add Ms 58226.
34 *The Times*, 17 December 1912.
35 Form letter, EP to Dear Friend, 10 January 1913, Craigie Collection.
36 PRO, HO 45/10695/231366/10, copy of Metropolitan Police account of WSPU meeting Pavilion Theatre, 13 January 1913.
37 *Westminster Gazette*, 23 January 1913; *The Suffragette*, 31 January 1913, p. 230.
38 *The Suffragette*, 31 January 1913, p. 230.
39 Ibid., p. 240.

40 *Pall Mall Gazette*, 29 January 1913. Sylvia and Flora Drummond were both later released since the WSPU paid their fines. Crawford, *The women's suffrage movement*, p. 522, comments, 'Presumably the WSPU wanted, if possible, to keep its personnel out of prison, relying on the arson campaign and the hunger striking of those who had received terms of imprisonment not redeemable by the paying of a fine, to keep the campaign in the front of the public and Parliament.'

41 Entry for 28 January 1913, Nevinson Diaries.

42 PRO, HO45/10695/231366/16, copy of Metropolitan Police account of WSPU meeting Essex Hall, Strand, 30 January 1913.

43 EP to Mrs. Harben, 30 January 1913, Goode Collection.

44 Entry for 31 January 1913, Nevinson Diaries.

45 *The Times*, 1 February 1913; *Morning Post*, 14 April 1913.

46 PRO, HO45/10695/231366/23, copy of Metropolitan Police account of WSPU meeting, London Pavilion, 10 February 1913.

47 EP to Miss Robins, 11 February 1913, Robins Papers, Fales Library.

48 PRO, HO45/10695/231366/27, copy of Metropolitan Police account of Putney Branch of WSPU meeting, 18 February 1913.

49 PRO, HO45/10695/231366/27 transcript by Edward James of WSPU meeting, Cory Hall, Cardiff, 19 February 1913.

50 Crawford, *The women's suffrage movement*, p. 508.

51 *The Times*, 25 February 1913; *Pall Mall Gazette*, 24 February 1913; *The Standard*, 25 February 1913.

52 *The Suffragette*, 28 February 1913, p. 311. See also *The Times* and *Western Mail*, 26 February 1913.

53 I shall follow here Winslow, *Sylvia Pankhurst*, p. 202, note 1, where she states that to December 1913, when the East London Federation of the Suffragettes was a part of the WSPU, she uses the letters ELFS/WSPU, and ELFS after its expulsion from the WSPU.

54 CP to Elizabeth Robins, 7 March 1913, Robins Papers, HRHRC.

55 EP to Elizabeth Robins, 10 March 1913 and n.d., Robins Papers, HRHRC.

56 PRO, HO45/10695/231366/42, speech by Mrs. Pankhurst at the London Pavilion, 17 March 1913.

57 Quoted in E. Pankhurst, *My own story*, p. 334.

58 Sylvia Pankhurst to EP, 18 March 1913, SFC.

59 EP to Miss Robins, n.d. [c. 22 March 1913?], Robins Papers, HRHRC.

60 E. S. Pankhurst, *TSM*, p. 450.

61 Letter to the editor, *Everyman*, 5 March 1931.

62 EP to Miss Robins, n.d. [c. 25 March 1913?], Robins Papers, HRHRC.

63 E. S. Pankhurst, *TSM*, p. 447.

64 EP to Helen Archdale, n.d. [c. 25 March 1913], Craigie Collection.

65 EP to Adela, n.d. [c. 25 March 1913], Craigie Collection.

66 Crawford, *The women's suffrage movement*, p. 486.

67 EP to Miss Robins, 1 April 1913, Robins Papers, HRHRC.

68 *The Suffragette*, 11 April 1913, p. 422.

69 Ibid., p. 423.

70 Ibid., 11 April 1913, p. 423.

71 PRO, HO45/10695/231366/45, A. Kenney speech at Essex Hall, 3 April 1913.

72 *The Times* and *The Standard*, 5 April 1913.

73 J. Gale, 50 years later the suffragettes remember, *The Observer Colour Magazine*, 7 February 1965, p. 9.

74 E. Pankhurst, Address at Hartford, 13 November 1913, reprinted in Jorgensen-Earp (ed.), *Speeches and trials of the militant suffragettes*, p. 341.

75 *The Standard*, 5 April 1913.

16 PRISONER OF THE CAT AND MOUSE ACT
(APRIL–AUGUST 1913)

1 Cited in Crawford, *The women's suffrage movement*, p. 508.
2 Smyth, *Female pipings*, p. 213.
3 *The Times*, 10 April 1913.
4 E. Pankhurst, *My own story*, pp. 307–8.
5 Smyth, *Female pipings*, pp. 213–14.
6 Jill Craigie interview with Grace Roe [1975?], Craigie Collection.
7 EP to Mrs. Harben, n.d. [c. 23 April 1913], Goode Collection.
8 Sharp, *Hertha Ayrton*, p. 239.
9 *The Times*, 29 April 1913.
10 Crawford, *The women's suffrage movement*, p. 508; *The Suffragette*, 2 May 1913, p. 493.
11 Quoted in *The Suffragette*, 18 April 1913, p. 455.
12 See *Daily Mirror* and *Daily Sketch*, 1 May 1913.
13 *Daily Mail*, 1 May 1913.
14 *The Times*, 3 May 1913.
15 See *The Suffragette*, 23 May 1913, p. 524; *London Budget*, 11 May 1913.
16 *The Times*, 3 May 1913.
17 *Daily Express*, 3 May 1913.
18 Entry for 4 May 1913, Nevinson Diaries; *VfW*, 9 May 1913, p. 456; *Daily Herald*, 5 May 1913.
19 Smyth, *Female pipings*, p. 214.
20 See By one of the rank and file, An impression of Mrs. Pankhurst, *VfW*, 14 June 1912, p. 602.
21 *The Suffragette*, 9 May 1913, p. 495.
22 *VfW*, 9 May 1913, p. 461.
23 See *Daily Sketch*, *Daily Telegraph* and *The Times*, 7 May 1913; *Daily Mirror*, 8 May 1913.
24 J. Hannam, 'Suffragettes are splendid for any work': the Blathwayt diaries as a source for women's suffrage, in *A suffrage reader: charting new directions in British suffrage history* (London, Leicester University Press, 2000), p. 63.
25 Kenney, *Memories*, p. 218.
26 Smyth, *Female pipings*, p. 214.
27 *The Standard*, 27 May 1913.
28 See ibid., for example, and *Daily Sketch* for same date.
29 *The Standard*, 31 May 1913.
30 PRO, HO 144/1254/234646/58a, Report dated 31 May 1913 of Inspector George Riley; Ada Wright to Maude Arncliffe Sennett, 15 June 1913, MASC.
31 E. S. Pankhurst, *Emmeline Pankhurst*, p. 132.
32 EP to Mr. Harben, 2 June 1914, Harben Papers; PRO HO 144/1254/234646/62, note dated 6 June 1913.
33 David Mitchell interview with Ruth Gollancz, 22 March 1965, DMC.
34 See Morley and Stanley, *Emily Wilding Davison*, pp. 163–6.
35 Ibid., p. 93.
36 *Daily Herald*, 10 June 1913.
37 EP to Mr. Thompson, 13 June 1913, WL.
38 *Daily Telegraph*, *The Times*, *Daily Herald*, *Daily Sketch*, *Newcastle Daily Chronicle* and *Illustrated Chronicle*, 16 June 1913; *VfW*, 20 June 1913.
39 Morley and Stanley, *Emily Wilding Davison*, p. 173.
40 R. Strachey, 'The cause': a short history of the women's movement in Great Britain (London, G. Bell and Sons, 1928), p. 332; L. Housman, *The unexpected years* (London, Jonathan Cape, 1937), pp. 295–6.
41 PRO HO 144/1254/234646/72, Report on Emmeline Pankhurst in Holloway Prison, 15 June 1913.

42 *North Mail*, 18 June 1913; *The Times*, 19 June 1913; *Clarion*, 20 June 1913.

43 *The New Freewoman*, 15 June 1913, p. 3.

44 E. S. Pankhurst, *TSM*, p. 215; Smyth, *Female pipings*, p. 202.

45 Letter to the editor, *Everyman*, 5 March 1931.

46 Quoted in D. Mitchell, Pankhursts in Paris, unpublished manuscript, DMC.

47 Mitchell, *Queen Christabel*, p. 218.

48 EP to Miss Robins, 24 June 1913, Robins Papers, Fales Library.

49 EP to Miss Lake, n.d. [c. 25 June 1913?], Women's Suffrage Papers, Girton College, Cambridge.

50 EP to Miss Robins, n.d. [c. 30 June 1913?], Robins Papers, Fales Library.

51 A. Pankhurst Walsh, My mother, pp. 40–1.

52 Ibid., pp. 40–1; Coleman, *Adela Pankhurst*, p. 53.

53 E. S. Pankhurst, *TSM*, pp. 473–80; *VfW* and *The Suffragette*, 11 July 1913, pp. 602 and 658, respectively.

54 E. S. Pankhurst, *Emmeline Pankhurst*, p. 134.

55 *The Suffragette*, 18 July 1913, p. 677.

56 Ibid., 18 July 1913, p. 678; *The Times*, 15 and 16 July 1913.

57 *The Standard*, 21 July 1913; *The Suffragette*, 25 July 1913, pp. 694, 699–701.

58 Ibid., 1 August 1913, p. 722.

59 Quoted in Crawford, *The women's suffrage movement*, p. 509.

60 E. Pankhurst, My own story, p. 320; *The Suffragette*, 1 August 1913, p. 723.

61 *The Suffragette*, 1 August 1913, p. 718.

62 *The Times*, 17 July 1913; Crawford, *The women's suffrage movement*, p. 509.

63 Entry for 28 July 1913, Nevinson Diaries; *The Suffragette*, 1 August 1913, p. 722.

64 C. P. Scott to Lloyd George, 28 July 1913, Lloyd George Papers.

65 *VfW*, 6 and 15 August 1913, pp. 652 and 662, respectively.

66 *Globe and Traveller*, 4 August 1913.

67 Metcalfe, *Woman's effort*, p. 301.

68 *The Suffragette*, 8 August 1913, p. 738.

69 See, for example, *The Suffragette*, 4 July 1913, p. 633.

70 E. S. Pankhurst, *TSM*, p. 491.

71 *The Suffragette*, 15 August 1913, p. 768.

72 Ibid., 15 August 1913, p. 758; *The Scotsman*, 12 August 1913.

73 *The Suffragette*, 5 December 1913, p. 177

74 Raeburn, *The militant suffragettes*, pp. 212–13.

17 OUSTING OF SYLVIA AND A FRESH START FOR ADELA (AUGUST 1913–JANUARY 1914)

1 *Daily Sketch*, 22 August 1913.

2 Jill Craigie in telephone conversation with the author, 17 July 1998.

3 EP to Helen Archdale, 2 September 1913, Craigie Collection.

4 C. Pankhurst, *Unshackled*, p. 258.

5 *The Suffragette*, 12 September 1913, p. 834; *New York Times*, 14 September 1913.

6 Dorr, A woman of fifty, pp. 246–50; PRO HO 144/1254/234646/105a, note dated 9 October 1913.

7 Smyth, *Female pipings*, pp. 215–16.

8 *The Suffragette*, 17 October 1913, pp. 4 and 15.

9 Dorr, A woman of fifty, p. 250.

10 *VfW*, 24 October 1913, p. 52; *New York Times*, 19 October 1913.

11 *The Suffragette*, 24 October 1913, p. 28.

12 [Mrs. Pankhurst], *Why we are militant, a speech delivered in New York, October 21st, 1913* (London, The Woman's Press, pamphlet, n.d.), pp. 2–3.

13 *New York Times*, 22 October 1913; Eleanor Garrison to Dear Mother, 22 November 1913, SSC.

14 Kay Sloan, Sexual warfare in the silent cinema: comedies and melodramas of woman suffragism, *American Quarterly*, 33, Fall, 1981, p. 430, claims that the film was released on 10 November, Crawford, *The women's suffrage movement*, p. 510, on the 29th.

15 *The Suffragette*, 21 November 1913, p. 124.

16 See Morley and Stanley, *Emily Wilding Davison*, p. 83; A. Burton, *Burdens of history: British feminists, Indian women, and imperial culture* (Chapel Hill, University of North Carolina Press, 1994).

17 Quoted in Jorgensen-Earp, 'The transfiguring sword', pp. 117 and 115.

18 C. Pankhurst, *Plain facts about a great evil* (New York, The Medical Review of Reviews, 1913). C. Pankhurst, *The great scourge and how to end it* (London, E. Pankhurst, Lincoln's Inn, 1913).

19 EP to Mrs. Belmont, 8 November 1913, National Woman's Party Papers 1913–1974 (hereafter NWPP), Smithsonian Institutions Libraries, National Museum of American History, Washington DC.

20 *The Suffragette*, 14 November 1913, p. 98.

21 EP to Mrs. Archdale, 11 December 1913, Craigie Collection.

22 *New York Times*, 25 November 1913.

23 *The Suffragette*, 28 November 1913, p. 146.

24 C. Pankhurst, *Unshackled*, p. 259; Pankhurst, *My own story*, p. 326; *The Suffragette*, 7 November 1913, p. 77 and 21 November 1913, p. 125; PRO HO 45/10695/ 236973/143, Metropolitan Police note dated 2 December 1913.

25 *Daily Herald*, 3 November 1913.

26 CP to Sylvia Pankhurst, 7 November 1913, ESPA.

27 *The Suffragette*, 14 November 1913, p. 95.

28 See E. S. Pankhurst, *TSM*, p. 384.

29 Morley and Stanley, *Emily Wilding Davison*, p. 176.

30 Sylvia Pankhurst to Dear Friend, 19 November 1913, ESPA.

31 *The Suffragette*, 21 November 1913, p. 134

32 Entry for 28 November 1913, Nevinson Diaries.

33 Annie Kenney to Dear Friend, 25 November 1913, ESPA.

34 Theodora Bonwick to Miss Pankhurst, 29 November 1913, ESPA.

35 CP to Sylvia Pankhurst, 27 November 1913, ESPA.

36 Ethel Smyth to EP, 9 December 1913, Smyth Letters.

37 EP to Mrs. Belmont, 3 December 1913, NWPP.

38 E. Pankhurst, *My own story*, p. 327.

39 See, for example, Fulford, *Votes for women*, Chapter 32 and Rosen, *Rise up women!*, Chapter 18.

40 *VfW*, 12 December 1913, p. 166.

41 Rheta Childe Dorr to Sylvia Pankhurst, 5 December 1913, ESPA.

42 PRO HO 45/10695/236973/143 Transcript of shorthand notes taken at the Empress Theatre, Earl's Court, at a meeting held on 7 December 1913, under the auspices of the Women's Social and Political Union.

43 EP to Ethel Smyth, 10 December 1913, quoted in Smyth, *Female pipings*, pp. 216–17.

44 PRO HO 144/1254/234646/119, Metropolitan Police Reports dated 13 and 15 December 1913.

45 *The Suffragette*, 19 December 1913, p. 218; E. Pankhurst, *My own story*, pp. 328–9.

46 *Morning Post*, 13 July 1914.

47 Ethel Smyth to EP, 16 December 1913, Smyth Letters.

48 EP to Ethel Smyth, 19 December 1913, quoted in Smyth, *Female pipings*, pp. 217–18.

49 *The Suffragette*, 26 December 1913, p. 252.

50 Ibid., 19 December 1913, p. 219; Ethel Smyth to EP, 19 December 1913, Smyth Letters.

51 EP to Ethel Smyth, 22 December 1913, quoted in Smyth, *Female pipings*, pp. 218–19.

52 Jessie Kenney, Miscellaneous notes titled, Condemn the thirst strike, With Christabel in Paris, and Christabel and I in Paris, Kenney Papers, KP/5.

53 EP to Ethel Smyth, 26 December 1913, quoted in Smyth, *Female pipings*, p. 219.

54 Ethel Smyth to EP, 26 December 1913, Smyth Letters.

55 EP to Ethel Smyth, 29 December 1913, quoted in Smyth, *Female pipings*, pp. 219–20; Ethel Smyth to EP, 29 December 1913, Smyth Letters.

56 Ethel Smyth to EP, 31 December 1913 and 1 January 1914, Smyth Letters.

57 EP to Helen Archdale, 26 December 1913, Craigie Collection.

58 E. S. Pankhurst, *TSM*, pp. 517–18.

59 Ibid., p. 521.

60 See *Daily Sketch* and *New York Times*, 7 February 1914.

61 *The Suffragette*, 13 February 1914, p. 387.

62 West, Mrs. Pankhurst, p. 495.

63 Ethel Smyth to EP, 15 January 1914, Smyth Letters.

64 See Elsa Daglish to Sylvia Pankhurst, 17 Feburary 1914, ESPA.

65 EP to Sylvia Pankhurst, 29 January 1914, ESPA.

66 EP to Sylvia Pankhurst, n.d. [1 February 1914?], ESPA.

67 A. Pankhurst Walsh, My mother, pp. 41–2.

68 Ibid., p.42.

69 Coleman, *Adela Pankhurst*, p. 54, 'Strategist Christabel shrewdly assessed Adela's unpredictability, independence and originality as dangerous to her policy.'

70 EP to Helen Archdale, 27 January 1914, Craigie Collection.

71 A. Pankhurst Walsh, My mother, p. 44.

72 Quoted in Smyth, *Female pipings*, p. 221.

73 A. Pankhurst Walsh, My mother, p. 44.

18 FUGITIVE
(JANUARY–AUGUST 1914)

1 Copies of correspondence Beatrice Harraden [BH] to CP, 13 January 1914; CP to BH, 16 January 1914; BH to CP, 20 January 1914; CP to BH, 26 January 1914, Janie Allen Papers, Acc. 4498, National Library of Scotland (hereafter, Allen Papers)

2 *VfW*, 6 February 1914, p. 281; K. Cowman, 'A party between revolution and peaceful persuasion': a fresh look at the United Suffragists in, *The women's suffrage movement*, eds Joannou and Purvis.

3 Emmeline Pethick Lawrence to Sylvia Pankhurst, 17 December 1929, ESPA; Holton, 'In sorrowful wrath', p. 22.

4 *The Suffragette*, 13 February 1914, p. 397.

5 Quoted in Smyth, *Female pipings*, pp. 221–2.

6 EP to Ethel Smyth, 21 February 1914, quoted in ibid., p. 223.

7 EP to Ethel Smyth, 29 February 1914, quoted in ibid., p. 224; *The Suffragette*, 27 February 1914, pp. 444–5.

8 *The Suffragette*, 13 March 1914, p. 486.

9 Ibid., 20 March and 3 April 1914, pp. 520 and 563, respectively.

10 Ibid., 27 March 1914, p. 535.

11 EP to Ethel Smyth, 8 March 1914, quoted in Smyth, *Female pipings*, p. 226.

12 Quoted in Leneman, *A guid cause*, p. 184.

13 *The Suffragette*, 13 March 1914, p. 492.

14 *Daily Telegraph* and *Glasgow Herald*, 10 March 1914; *The Suffragette*, 13 and 20 March 1914, pp. 493 and 511, respectively; PRO HO 144/1254/234646/131, Metropolitan Police Report dated 11 March 1914.

15 *The Times*, 11 March 1914.

16 *The Suffragette*, 20 March 1914, pp. 518–19.
17 PRO HO 144/1254/234646/136, Holloway Prison reports on Mrs. Pankhurst, dated 12 and 14 March 1914.
18 Ethel Smyth to EP, 14 March 1914, Smyth Letters.
19 EP to Ethel Smyth, 13 [14] March 1914, quoted in Smyth, *Female pipings*, p. 227.
20 EP to Ethel Smyth, 17 March 1914, quoted in ibid., pp. 227–8.
21 Ethel Smyth to EP, 18 March 1914, Smyth Letters.
22 EP to Ethel Smyth, 8 April 1914, quoted in Smyth, *Female pipings*, pp. 229–30.
23 Ethel Smyth to EP, 3 April 1914, Smyth Letters.
24 Ethel Smyth to EP, 9 April 1914, Smyth Letters.
25 EP to Helen Archdale, Good Friday [1914], Craigie Collection.
26 E. Pankhurst, *My own story*, p. 334.
27 EP to Ethel Smyth, 21 April 1914, quoted in Smyth, *Female pipings*, p. 230.
28 Ethel Smyth to EP, 22 April 1914, Smyth Letters.
29 Quoted in Smyth, *Female pipings*, p. 231.
30 EP to Ethel Smyth, 4 May 1914, quoted in ibid., pp. 231–2.
31 Ethel Smyth to EP, 6 May 1914, Smyth Letters.
32 Crawford, *The women's suffrage movement*, p. 511.
33 *Evening News*, 21 May 1914; *Daily Mirror*, 22 May 1914.
34 *The Suffragette*, 29 May 1914, p. 120.
35 EP to Ethel Smyth, 29 May 1914, quoted in Smyth, *Female pipings*, pp. 233–4.
36 *The Suffragette*, 12 June 1914, front page; The drugging case, 30 June 1914, Nancy Astor Collection (hereafter Astor Collection), University of Reading, 1416/1/2/18.
37 I. A. R. Wylie, *My life with George: an unconventional autobiography* (New York, Random House, 1940), p. 180.
38 EP to Mrs. Badley, 8 June 1914, WL.
39 *Evening Standard*, 9 June 1914.
40 *Daily Mail*, 12 June 1914; *The Suffragette*, 19 June 1914, pp. 168–9.
41 EP to Ethel Smyth, 13 June 1914, quoted in Smyth, *Female pipings*, p. 234.
42 E. S. Pankhurst, *TSM*, pp. 564–8.
43 Ibid., p. 570.
44 EP to Ethel Smyth, quoted in Smyth, *Female pipings*, p. 235.
45 Morgan, *Suffragists and liberals*, p. 131; E. S. Pankhurst, *TSM*, p. 576.
46 Romero, *E. Sylvia Pankhurst*, p. 84.
47 Marcus, Introduction, p. 6.
48 G. Lansbury, *My life* (London, Constable, 1928), p. 127; E. S. Pankhurst, *TSM*, p. 582.
49 Romero, *E. Sylvia Pankhurst*, p. 85.
50 E. S. Pankhurst, *TSM*, pp. 582–3.
51 Ibid., p. 583; *The Suffragette*, 17 and 24 July 1914, pp. 240 and 260, respectively.
52 EP to Eleanor Garrison, 18 June 1914, SSC.
53 *The Suffragette*, 17 July 1914, p. 239; Leneman, *A guid cause*, p. 200.
54 *The Times*, 8 July 1914.
55 Crawford, *The women's suffrage movement*, p. 511.
56 PRO HO 144/1254/234646/149, Holloway Prison report on Mrs. Pankhurst and report of proceedings of the Visiting Committee, on 10th July 1914; *The Suffragette*, 24 July 1914, p. 257.
57 *The Suffragette*, 17 July 1914, p. 238.
58 *Morning Post* and *Daily Herald*, 17 July 1914.
59 *The Suffragette*, 24 July 1914, p. 262.
60 Ibid., p. 262.
61 Ibid., p. 258.
62 Coleman, *Adela Pankhurst*, p. 61.
63 *The Suffragette*, 31 July 1914, p. 279; *VfW*, 31 July 1914, p. 668.

64 E. Smyth, *Beecham and pharaoh* (London, Chapman and Hall, 1935), p. 180; Smyth, *Female pipings*, p. 235.

65 Smyth, *Female pipings*, p. 235; E. Pankhurst, *My own story*, foreword.

66 E. S. Pankhurst, *Emmeline Pankhurst*, p. 150.

67 Dobbie, *A nest of suffragettes*, p. 58; K. Marion typescript quoted in Rosen, *Rise up women!*, p. 247.

68 E. Pankhurst, *My own story*, foreword; *Evening News and Evening Mail*, 10 August 1914.

69 Form letter, EP to Dear Friend, 12 August 1914, Goode Collection.

19 WAR WORK AND A SECOND FAMILY
(SEPTEMBER 1914–JUNE 1917)

1 E. Pankhurst, *My own story*, pp. 363–4.

2 Caine, *English feminism*, p. 133.

3 C. Pankhurst, *Unshackled*, p. 288.

4 Tickner, *The spectacle of women*, pp. 321 and 230.

5 Quoted in Rosen, *Rise up women!*, p. 252.

6 See, for example, ibid.; Harrison, *Prudent revolutionaries*; Pugh, *The march of the women*.

7 J. Beaumont, Whatever happened to patriotic women, 1914–1918? *Australian Historical Studies*, 115, 2000, pp. 273–86; see also Evans, *Comrades and sisters*, p. 151.

8 *The Suffragette*, 23 April 1915, p. 26.

9 J. de Vries, Gendering patriotism: Emmeline and Christabel Pankhurst and World War One, in *This working-day world: women's lives and culture(s) in Britain 1914–1945*, ed. S. Oldfield (London, Taylor & Francis, 1994), pp. 75–88.

10 J. Kenney, Russian Diary, 6 September 1917, Kenney Papers.

11 A. Burton, The feminist quest for identity: British imperial suffragism and 'global sisterhood', 1900–1915, *Journal of Women's History*, 3, 2, 1991, p. 69.

12 Tickner, *The spectacle of women*, p. 230; S. Kingsley Kent, *Making peace: the reconstruction of gender in interwar Britain* (Princeton, Princeton University Press, 1993), Chapter 4.

13 *Britannia*, 2 June 1916, p. 193; *The Sketch*, 23 March 1915.

14 *Daily Mail* and *Manchester Guardian*, 9 September 1914.

15 C. Pankhurst, *The war: a speech delivered at the London Opera House on September 8th, 1914* (London, The Women's Social and Political Union, n.d.), pp. 6, 12 and 16.

16 E. S. Pankhurst, *The home front: a mirror to life in England during the World War* (London, Hutchinson & Co., 1932), p. 66.

17 Ibid., pp. 66–7.

18 Coleman, *Adela Pankhurst*, p. 63.

19 See Pugh, *The march of the women*, p. 221; Pugh, *The Pankhursts*, Chapter 13.

20 *Britannia*, 6 June 1917, p. 7.

21 This claim is made in B. Castle, *Sylvia and Christabel Pankhurst*, p. 140, and is probably based on statements made in Sylvia's *TSM* p. 594. However, in the latter, Sylvia claims that it was Emmeline's 'supporters', and not Emmeline herself, who handed out white feathers. See N. F. Gullace, White feathers and wounded men: female patriotism and the memory of the Great War, *Journal of British Studies*, April 1997, pp. 178–206.

22 *Sussex Herald*, 22 September 1914.

23 *Ladies' Field Supplement*, 21 November 1914, p. 12.

24 *Western Daily Mercury*, 17 November 1914.

25 Romero, *E. Sylvia Pankhurst*, pp. 98–101.

26 E. S. Pankhurst, *The home front*, p. 124.

27 *Jus Suffragii*, 1 January 1915, p. 228.

28 *Daily Sketch*, 27 January 1915.

29 Butler, *Emmeline Pankhurst*, pp. 105–6.

30 Ethel Smyth to EP, Xmas Day 1914, Smyth Letters.

31 Butler, *Emmeline Pankhurst*, p. 105.
32 *Minneapolis Daily News*, 30 March 1915.
33 *VfW*, 26 March 1915, p. 211.
34 EP to Nancy Astor, 26 March 1915, Astor Papers.
35 *The Suffragette*, 23 April 1915, p. 26.
36 *Minneapolis Daily News*, 30 March 1915.
37 *Sunday Pictorial*, 11 April 1915.
38 E. S. Pankhurst, *The home front*, pp. 149–51; Romero, *E. Sylvia Pankhurst*, pp. 113–14.
39 *The Suffragette*, 7 May 1915, p. 63.
40 Smyth, *Female pipings*, p. 242.
41 *The Suffragette*, 23 April 1915, p. 26; *The Sketch*, 23 March 1915.
42 F. Thebaud, The Great War and the triumph of sexual division, in *A history of women: towards a cultural identity in the twentieth century*, ed. F. Thebaud (Massachusetts, Harvard University Press, 1994), p. 63.
43 *The Suffragette*, 2 July 1915, p. 184.
44 G. Roe, Mrs. Pankhurst and the 1914–1918 crisis, *Calling All Women (News Letter of the Suffragette Fellowship)*, February 1969, p. 7.
45 *The Suffragette*, 2 July 1915, pp. 184–5.
46 Buckingham Palace to Lloyd George, 28 June 1915, LG Papers.
47 C. Pankhurst, *Unshackled*, p. 290.
48 EP to Mrs. Astor, 4 July 1915, Astor Papers.
49 Tickner, *The spectacle of women*, p. 231.
50 Mrs. Humphry Ward to Lord Cromer, 9 July 1915, PRO Foreign Office (FO), 633/24.
51 Tickner, *The spectacle of women*, p. 231.
52 EP to Dear Madam, 9 July 1915, Hugh Franklin–Elsie Duval Papers, WL.
53 *The Suffragette*, 9 and 16 July 1915, pp. 197 and 213, respectively.
54 Butler, *Emmeline Pankhurst*, p. 108.
55 *The Observer*, 18 July 1915; *Daily Telegraph*, 19 July 1915.
56 *Daily Chronicle*, 19 July 1915.
57 *The Suffragette*, 23 July 1915, p. 236.
58 *New York Journal*, 12 November 1915.
59 *Daily Express*, 19 July 1915.
60 E. S. Pankhurst, *TSM*, p. 597; Coleman, *Adela Pankhurst*, pp. 66–7.
61 See S. R. Grayzel, 'The mothers of our soldiers' children': motherhood, immorality, and the war baby scandal, 1914–18, in *Maternal instincts: visions of motherhood and sexuality in Britain, 1875–1925*, eds C. Nelson and A. Sumner Holmes (Basingstoke, Macmillan, 1997), pp. 122–40.
62 EP to Nancy Astor, 10 May 1915, Astor Collection.
63 Smyth, *Female pipings*, pp. 237–8.
64 *The Suffragette*, 14 May 1915, p. 69.
65 Smyth, *Female pipings*, p. 237.
66 E. Katherine Willoughby Marshall, Suffragettes during the war, SFC.
67 The Women's Social and Political Union leaflet, n.d. [c. 1915], photocopy in DMC.
68 EP to Elsie Duval, 14 July 1915, WL.
69 Benn, *Keir Hardie*, pp. 344–51; E. S. Pankhurst, *The home front*, pp. 228–9.
70 *Britannia*, 15 October 1915, p. 9.
71 EP to Lloyd George, 14 October 1915, LG Papers; F. Stevenson, *Lloyd George: a diary* (London, Hutchinson, 1971), p. 64.
72 S. M. Gilbert, Soldier's heart: literary men, literary women, and the Great War, in *Behind the lines: gender and the two world wars*, eds M. R. Higonnet, J. Jenson, S. Michel and M. C. Weitz (New Haven and London, Yale University Press, 1987), p. 223.
73 EP to Mrs. Badley, 4 October 1915, WL.
74 Pankhurst, *The home front*, p. 270; *Britannia*, 15 October 1915, p. 5.

75 *Britannia*, 5 November 1915, p. 44.

76 *The Suffragette*, 5 November 1915, p. 46; *The Times*, 6 November 1915.

77 EP to Dear Sir, 12 November 1915, Hugh Franklin–Elsie Duval Papers.

78 E. S. Pankhurst, *The home front*, p. 270. The old headquarters in Lincoln's Inn House, Kingsway, had been given up in September.

79 *Morning Advertiser*, 17 November 1915; see also *Evening Standard & St. James's Gazette* and *Daily Chronicle*, 16 November 1915.

80 *Daily News and Leader*, 17 and 18 November 1915.

81 Particulars of slander on Mary Leigh uttered by Mrs. Pankhurst at The Pavilion on October 28th 1915, MAS Collection, Vol. 26; *Morning Advertiser*, 5 November 1915.

82 *Daily News and Leader*, 27 November 1915.

83 *Weekly Dispatch*, 5 December 1915.

84 B. Wasserstein, *Herbert Samuel: a political life* (Oxford, Oxford University Press, 1992), p. 190.

85 *New York Sun*, 16 January 1916; *New York World*, 17 January and 10 February 1916; Eleanor Garrison to her mother, 17 February 1916, SSC.

86 *Brooklyn Daily Eagle*, 15 February 1916; *Philadelphia Public Ledger*, 24 and 26 February 1916.

87 *Hamilton Daily Times*, 8 March 1916.

88 *Britannia*, 4 August 1916, p. 228.

89 Ibid., 2 June 1916, p. 193.

90 A. Pankhurst, *Put up the sword* (Melbourne, Cecilia John, 1917, third edition, first pub. 1915); Coleman, *Adela Pankhurst*, p. 67.

91 *Britannia*, 28 April 1916, p. 174; Winslow, *Sylvia Pankhurst*, p. 85.

92 Smyth, *Female pipings*, p. 239.

93 Ibid., p. 240.

94 E. S. Pankhurst, *Emmeline Pankhurst*, p. 155.

95 Smyth, *Female pipings*, p. 241.

96 EP to Una Dugdale, 11 October 1916, Author's Collection.

97 S. R. Grayzel, *Women's identities at war: gender, motherhood, and politics in Britain and France during the First World War* (University of North Carolina Press, 1999), p. 191.

98 Pugh, *The march of the women*, p. 287; Rosen, *Rise up women!*, pp. 258–9.

99 *Britannia*, 18 August 1916, p. 235.

100 Ibid., p. 236.

101 C. Pankhurst, *Unshackled*, p. 293.

102 *Britannia*, 25 August 1916, p. 240.

103 Undated cutting Rose Scott Papers, Mitchell Library, Australia, 38/62, 3/13.

104 A. Pankhurst Walsh, My mother, p. 45.

105 *Britannia*, 6 October 1916, p. 265.

106 *The Times*, 23 October 1916.

107 *Daily Express*, 14 December 1916.

108 West, Mrs. Pankhurst, p. 497.

109 St. John, *Ethel Smyth*, p. 121. In an undated letter [10 December 1916?] to Lloyd George, Emmeline asked to meet him to discuss the composition of his Cabinet, especially in regard to the Foreign Office, 'before irrevocable decisions are made', LG Papers. She argued, 'Women unfortunately cannot be directly represented in it [the Cabinet] but I am sure you will be the first to acknowledge that they have a right to be consulted in a matter so vital to them & to the country as a whole at a time when our very existence is at stake.' There is no evidence to suggest that a meeting took place or that the two discussed the matter.

110 *Daily Express*, 16 January 1917; EP to Hugh Franklin, 23 January 1917, WL.

111 van Wingerden, *Women's suffrage movement*, p. 169.

112 Tickner, *The spectacle of women*, p. 235; van Wingerden, *Women's suffrage movement*, p. 167; Holton, *Feminism and democracy*, pp. 148–50.

113 *Britannia*, 12 and 19 March 1917, p. 345; see S. Rowbotham *Friends of Alice Wheeldon* (London, Pluto Press, 1986); *The Guardian*, 28 November 1997, M15 behind suffragette plot to kill PM, reveals that the charge was the result of a set-up by undercover agents, especially Alex Gordon who won Alice Wheeldon's friendship by masquerading as a conscientious objector.

114 EP to Mrs. Fawcett, 23 March 1917, WL.

115 Ray Strachey to her Mother, 1 April 1917, Hannah Whitall Smith Papers, Lilly Library, Indiana University, Bloomington, Indiana; Harrison, *Prudent revolutionaries*, p. 35.

116 Women's suffrage deputation to the Right Hon. David Lloyd George (Prime Minister), At no. 10 Downing Street, S.W. On Saturday, March 29th, 1917 (London, National Press Agency, n.d.), p. 19.

117 Ibid., pp. 22–3.

118 Holton, *Suffrage days*, p. 226.

119 *Britannia*, 23 April 1917, p. 364.

120 Ibid., 6 June 1917, p. 6.

121 EP to Constance Lytton, 30 April 1917, Constance Lytton Papers, Knebworth House.

122 *Britannia*, 6 June 1917, p. 7.

123 Mitchell, *Queen Christabel*, p. 265; Garner, *Stepping stones*, pp. 56–7

124 EP to Ethel Smyth, 3 May 1917, quoted in Smyth, *Female pipings*, p. 242.

20 WAR EMISSARY TO RUSSIA: EMMELINE VERSUS THE BOLSHEVIKS (JUNE–OCTOBER 1917)

1 E. S. Pankhurst, *Emmeline Pankhurst*, p. 160. I am grateful to my colleague, Paul Flenley, for comments on this chapter, but any errors remain my own.

2 *Manchester Guardian*, 8 June 1917.

3 *Britannia*, 6 June 1917, p. 3.

4 *Forward*, 16 June 1917.

5 *Manchester Guardian*, 8 June 1917.

6 *Daily Graphic*, 8 June 1917; Romero, *E. Sylvia Pankhurst*, pp. 120–3.

7 *Britannia*, 6 June 1917, p. 8.

8 See, for example, Garner, *Stepping stones*, pp. 56–7 and Pugh, *The march of the women*, p. 221; Pugh, *The Pankhursts*, p. xv and Chapter 14.

9 E. S. Pankhurst, *Emmeline Pankhurst*, p. 161. I also draw in this section on D. Mitchell, *Women on the warpath: the story of the women of the First World War* (London, Jonathan Cape, 1966), Chapter 4.

10 D. Marquand, *Ramsay MacDonald* (London, Jonathan Cape, 1977), p. 148.

11 Mitchell, *Women on the warpath*, p. 66.

12 Jessie Kenney, Russian diary typed notes, Kenney Papers, KP5. Most of the following account is taken from this source, unless indicated otherwise. Since Jessie is often unsure as to exact dates of events, I cannot always give these for some quotes, but do so, when possible.

13 *Britannia*, 13 July 1917, p. 44.

14 Ibid., 10 August 1917, p. 78.

15 J. McDermid and A. Hillyar, *Midwives of the revolution: female Bolsheviks and women workers in 1917* (London, UCL Press, 1999), p. 180.

16 *Britannia*, 20 July 1917, p. 55.

17 Childe Dorr, *A woman of fifty*, p. 360, describes Botchkareva as 'a big peasant woman, strong as a horse, rough of manner, eating with her fingers by choice, unlettered, but of much native intelligence'.

18 *Britannia*, 10 August 1917, p. 77.
19 T. Larsen, *Christabel Pankhurst: fundamentalism and feminism in coalition* (Woodbridge, Suffolk, Boydell Press, 2002).
20 Entry for 22 July [1917], Kenney, Russian diary.
21 J. Kenney, Miscellaneous notes, Kenney Papers, KP/5.
22 Dorr, *A woman of fifty*, p. 362.
23 Ibid., p. 359.
24 *Britannia*, 13 July 1917, p. 44.
25 Entry for 3 August 1917, Kenney, Russian diary, although elsewhere Jessie gives 1 August as the date they met Kerensky.
26 Mitchell, *Women on the warpath*, p. 69.
27 Entry for 3 September 1917, Kenney, Russian diary.

21 LEADER OF THE WOMEN'S PARTY
(NOVEMBER 1917–JUNE 1919)

1 Coleman, *Adela Pankhurst*, pp. 79–81.
2 Adela Pankhurst to Sylvia Pankhurst, 23 November 1917, ESPA.
3 Coleman, *Adela Pankhurst*, pp. 80–1.
4 Jessie Kenney Papers, DMC; Mitchell, *Queen Christabel*, p. 263.
5 Smyth, *Female pipings*, p. 243.
6 *Britannia*, 21 December 1917, p. 227.
7 *Sunday Chronicle* and *Sunday Herald*, 11 November 1917.
8 Quoted in C. Law, *Suffrage and power: the women's movement, 1918–1928* (London, Tauris, 1997), pp. 44–5.
9 *The Women's Party* (London, The Women's Party, n.d.), p. 1.
10 *Britannia*, 23 November 1917, p. 196.
11 Ibid., 2 November 1917, pp. 171–2.
12 Ibid., 25 January 1918, p. 260.
13 Ibid., 11 January 1918, front page.
14 Garner, *Stepping stones*, p. 58; B. Campbell, *The iron ladies: why do women vote Tory?* (London, Virago, 1987), p. 56.
15 Pugh, *Women and the women's movement*, p. 44; E. S. Pankhurst, *Emmeline Pankhurst*, p. 163.
16 E. C. Dubois, Woman suffrage and the left: an international socialist-feminist perspective, in her *Woman suffrage and women's rights* (New York, New York University Press, 1998), pp. 272–3. A version of this chapter was originally published in *New Left Review*, 186, 1991.
17 E. S. Pankhurst, *Emmeline Pankhurst*, p. 163.
18 Rowbotham, *Hidden from history*, p. 117; Garner, *Stepping stones*, pp. 56–9; Pugh, *Women and the women's movement*, pp. 44–5; Pugh, *The march of the women*, p. 221; Pugh, *The Pankhursts*, p. 540. Pugh, *The Pankhursts*, p. 342, even makes the outrageous statement that by 1917, Christabel, through her work for the Women's Party, 'was on the high road that leads to fascism'.
19 *Britannia*, 1 March 1918, p. 341.
20 Dangers on the home front, Mrs. Pankhurst's tilt with the pacifists, *Liverpool Post*, 7 February 1918.
21 E. S. Pankhurst, *Emmeline Pankhurst*, pp. 164–5; *Liverpool Post*, 7 February 1918; *Britannia*, 8 February 1918, pp. 291, 302.
22 *Britannia*, 25 January 1918, p. 260.
23 War till victory, Mrs. Pankhurst on the danger at home, *Liverpool Courier*, 7 February 1918.
24 *Britannia*, 16 November 1917, pp. 187 and 192.

25 Quoted in *The Women's Party* (London, The Women's Party, leaflet, n.d.), p. 6.

26 Romero, E. *Sylvia Pankhurst*, pp. 124–5; Winslow, *Sylvia Pankhurst*, p. 104.

27 *The Labour Woman*, November 1918, p. 76.

28 Quoted in Garner, *Stepping stones*, p. 58; *The Common Cause*, 9 November 1917, p. 361.

29 Quoted in Smyth, *Female pipings*, p. 244.

30 *The Times*, 11 January 1918.

31 E. S. Pankhurst, *Emmeline Pankhurst*, p. 162.

32 Dangers on the home front, Mrs. Pankhurst's tilt with the pacifists.

33 EP to Ethel Smyth, 11 January 1918, quoted in Smyth, *Female pipings*, p. 244.

34 EP to Helen Archdale, 12 January 1918, Craigie Collection.

35 *Britannia*, 8 February 1918, pp. 291 and 302.

36 Ibid., 8 February and 15 March 1918, pp. 301 and 374.

37 Smyth, *Female pipings*, p. 245.

38 *Britannia*, 5 April 1918, p. 405.

39 E. S. Pankhurst, *Emmeline Pankhurst*, p. 165.

40 Smith, *The British women's suffrage campaign*, p. 69.

41 Bartley, *Votes for women*, p. 98; Pugh, *The march of the women*, pp. 84–101.

42 *Britannia*, 22 March 1918, p. 389.

43 See, for example, Harrison, *Separate spheres*, pp. 196–7; Harrison, Two models, pp. 42–3; Hume, *NUWSS*, p. 227; Pugh, *The march of the women*, pp. 252–83; Smith, *The British women's suffrage campaign*, p. 83

44 Pugh, *The march of the women*, pp. 252–83; Pugh, *The Pankhursts*, pp. 329–31.

45 Morgan, *Suffragists and liberals*, p. 159; Evans, *The feminists*, p. 223; S. K. Kent, The politics of sexual difference: World War I and the demise of British feminism, *Journal of British Studies*, July 1988, pp. 232–53; Kent, *Making peace*, pp. 31–50.

46 Smyth, *Female pipings*, p. 288.

47 *Britannia*, 15 March 1918, p. 373.

48 Ibid.; *Britannia*, 5 April 1918, pp. 405 and 407.

49 Ibid., p. 407.

50 Ibid., 19 April 1918, p. 429.

51 Ibid., 19 April and 26 April 1918, pp. 431 and 438, respectively.

52 Ibid., 14 June 1918, p. 491.

53 J. Horne, Socialism, peace, and revolution, 1917–1918, in *The Oxford illustrated history of the First World War*, ed. H. Strachan (Oxford, Oxford University Press, 1998), pp. 235–6.

54 Ibid., p. 235.

55 *Britannia*, 28 June 1918, p. 15.

56 Ibid., 21 June 1918, p. 3.

57 Ibid., p. 8; *Daily News*, 14 June 1918; *Daily Chronicle*, 10 July 1918.

58 *Britannia*, 26 July 1918, p. 66.

59 Anna Howard Shaw to Helen Fraser, 5 and 10 July 1918, Helen Fraser Papers.

60 E. S. Pankhurst, *Emmeline Pankhurst*, p. 166; Sylvia Pankhurst to Adela, 11 July 1918, Pankhurst Walsh Papers.

61 *Britannia*, 4 October 1918, pp. 147 and 151.

62 E. Pankhurst, *My own story*, p. 3.

63 *Britannia*, 11 October 1918, p. 157.

64 Ibid., 8 November 1918, pp. 187–8.

65 M. Eksteins, Memory and the Great War, in *The Oxford illustrated history of the First World War*, ed. Strachan, p. 307.

66 Coleman, *Adela Pankhurst*, p. 86.

67 A. Kenney to Dear Fellow Member, 1 November 1918, on headed notepaper of the Women's Party, Hugh Franklin-Elsie Duval Papers.

68 Smyth, *Female pipings*, p. 246.

69 *Britannia*, 22 November 1918, p. 203.

70 Lloyd George to Bonar Law, 21 November 1918, LG Papers.
71 *Daily Sketch*, 4 December 1918.
72 *Smethwick Telephone*, 14 December 1918; J. Hannon to Jessie Kenney, 29 November 1918, Patrick Hannon Papers, HLRO.
73 E. Sylvia Pankhurst to Adela Pankhurst, 11 July 1918, Pankhurst Walsh Papers; *Workers' Dreadnought*, 14 December 1918.
74 Miss Pankhurst's Election Address, General Election December 14th, 1918 (E. Bowerman, Smethwick, n.d.); *Britannia*, 6 December 1918, p. 222.
75 M. Hilson, Women voters and the rhetoric of patriotism in the British general election of 1918, *Women's History Review*, 10, 2, 2001, p. 334.
76 *The Times*, 14 December 1918.
77 CP to Lloyd George, 21 November 1918, LG Papers.
78 *Britannia*, 29 November 1918, p. 212.
79 *Smethwick Telephone*, 14 December and 30 November 1918.
80 Smyth, *Female pipings*, p. 246.
81 Larsen, *Christabel Pankhurst*. Larsen notes that no precise date can be given for her conversion, but suggests that it was between Easter 1918 and Armistice day of that year, 11 November.
82 E. Bowerman, Note dated 11 October 1964, DMC.
83 Smyth, *Female pipings*, p. 246.
84 Eleanor Garrison to her Mother, 2 and 7 January 1919, SSC.
85 Z. Steiner, The peace settlement, in *The Oxford illustrated history of the First World War*, ed. Strachan, p. 291.
86 Smyth, *Female pipings*, p. 247.
87 Form letter from EP to Dear Friend, The Women's Party, n.d., Author's Collection.
88 P. J. Hannon to E. Manville, MP, 21 March 1919, Hannon Papers.
89 Christabel Pankhurst to Esther Greg, 12 March 1938, Author's Collection.
90 Pugh, *The Pankhursts*, p. 355.
91 *Daily News*, 9 December 1918; M. Carmichael Stopes, *Married love: a new contribution to the solution of sexual difficulties* (London, Putnam's Sons, 1918) and *Wise parenthood: the treatise on birth control for married people* (London, Putnam's Sons, 1918).
92 J. Alberti, *Beyond suffrage: feminists in war and peace, 1914–28* (Basingstoke, Macmillan, 1989), p. 94; Mitchell, *Queen Christabel*, pp. 278–9; J. Alberti, 'A symbol and a key': the suffrage movement in Britain, 1918–1928, in *Votes for women*, eds Purvis and Holton, p. 268. On feminism in the 1920s see also Harrison, *Prudent revolutionaries* and H. Smith (ed.), *British feminism in the twentieth century* (Aldershot, Edward Elgar, 1990), esp. Part II.
93 V. Brittain, Committees versus professions, in *Testament of a generation: the journalism of Vera Brittain and Winifred Holtby*, eds P. Berry and A. Bishop (London, Virago, 1985), pp. 106–7, previously unpublished, 1929.
94 EP to Ethel Smyth, 21 June 1919, quoted in Smyth, *Female Pipings*, p. 247.
95 Wills of Emmeline and Christabel Pankhurst, 23 July 1919, former in Principal Probate Registry, London, the latter, Author's Collection.

22 LECTURER IN NORTH AMERICA AND DEFENDER OF THE BRITISH EMPIRE (SEPTEMBER 1919–DECEMBER 1925)

1 *New York Tribune*, 14 September and 2 October 1919.
2 *New York Evening Post*, 14 September 1919.
3 D. Mitchell, *The fighting Pankhursts* (London, Jonathan Cape, 1967), p. 130. I draw heavily on this book in this chapter.
4 Ibid., p. 133; *New York Times*, 26 October 1919.
5 *Vancouver Daily Sun*, 28 November 1919.

6 *Victoria Daily Times*, 28 November 1919.

7 Mitchell, *The fighting Pankhursts*, pp. 135–6.

8 *Vancouver Daily Sun*, 29 November 1919.

9 C. Sykes, *Nancy: the life of Lady Astor* (London, Collins, 1972), pp. 190–1.

10 See Burton, *Burdens of history* and J. Bush, *Edwardian ladies and imperial power* (London, Leicester University Press, 2000), especially Chapter 10 for further discussion of such themes.

11 *Victoria Daily Times*, 5 May 1920.

12 Quoted in Smyth, *Female pipings*, pp. 250–1.

13 Mitchell, *The fighting Pankhursts*, p. 137.

14 Information about the children is obtained from a variety of sources, including telephone conversations with Kathleen King but especially tape recorded interviews with her, 30 May 1992 and 1 July 2000 (hereafter referred to as Kathleen King interviews), at author's home in Portsmouth. Kathleen King now has a different name, but since she does not wish to be identified, she has asked me if I would not use this name but the name Emmeline Pankhurst gave her.

15 EP to Ethel Smyth, 30 August and 26 September 1920, quoted in Smyth, *Female pipings*, p. 252

16 Kathleen King interviews.

17 *Victoria Daily Colonist*, 6 October 1920.

18 Ibid., 15 October 1920.

19 I am indebted to Mitchell, *The fighting Pankhursts*, pp. 137–8 for most of the information in this paragraph.

20 EP to Dr. Bates, 12 December 1920, photocopy in DMC.

21 Brian Harrison interview with Mary Hodgson, at her home at 60, Glenholt Road, Crownhill, Plymouth, 2 July 1976, copy in DMC; Kathleen King interviews.

22 Kathleen King interviews.

23 Postcard postmarked 6 January 1921 from Catherine Pine to Kathleen King, in possession of Kathleen King.

24 Kathleen King interviews.

25 Ibid.

26 EP to Ethel Smyth, 28 January 1921, quoted in Smyth, *Female pipings*, p. 253.

27 Romero, *E. Sylvia Pankhurst*, p. 152; Coleman, *Adela Pankhurst*, p. 89.

28 EP to Ethel Smyth, 7 March 1921, quoted in Smyth, *Female pipings*, p. 253.

29 Ibid., pp. 254–5.

30 E. S. Pankhurst, *Emmeline Pankhurst*, p. 169.

31 EP to Dr. Bates, 3 and 13 March 1921, photocopies in DMC.

32 Catherine Pine to Dr. Bates and Dr. Bates to EP, 23 March 1921, Dr. Bates to Miss Pine, 24 March 1921, photocopies in DMC.

33 EP to Dr. Bates, 25 March 1921, photocopy in DMC.

34 *Toronto Evening Telegram* and *Toronto Daily Star*, 22 April 1921.

35 *Toronto Globe* and *Toronto Mail and Empire*, 23 April 1921.

36 EP to Dr. Bates, 18 May 1921, photocopy in DMC.

37 *Victoria Colonist*, 28 May, 29 June, 17 and 27 July 1921.

38 *Montreal Star*, 8 August 1921.

39 EP to Dr. Bates, 14 August 1921, photocopy in DMC.

40 Kathleen King interviews.

41 Harrison interview with Mary Hodgson.

42 Dr. Bates to EP, 12 September 1921, photocopy in DMC.

43 EP to Dr. Bates, 23 September 1921, photocopy in DMC.

44 Dr. Bates to EP, 10 October 1921, photocopy in DMC.

45 E. Chapman, Mrs. Pankhurst – Canadian, *MacLean's Magazine*, 15 January 1922.

46 *Toronto Globe*, 17 January 1922.

47 Kathleen King interviews.
48 *Toronto Daily Star*, 11 February 1922.
49 Gordon Bates to David Mitchell, 29 April 1965, DMC.
50 Mitchell, *The fighting Pankhursts*, p. 146.
51 *Victoria Daily Times*, 31 August 1922.
52 Quoted by the librarian of the *Montreal Star* Library to David Mitchell, 29 October 1964, DMC.
53 *Toronto Mail and Empire*, 14 November 1922; Mitchell, *The fighting Pankhursts*, p. 148.
54 C. Pankhurst, *Unshackled*, p. 196.
55 Kathleen King interviews.
56 Ibid.
57 Coleman, *Adela Pankhurst*, pp. 92–5.
58 *Victoria Daily Times*, 16 July and 14 September 1923.
59 David Mitchell interview with Mary Hodgson, 19 April 1975, DMC; postcard in possession of Kathleen King.
60 Kathleen King interviews; Mary Hodgson to David Mitchell [18 November 1974], DMC.
61 Quoted by the librarian of the *Montreal Star* to David Mitchell, 29 October 1964, DMC.
62 *Toronto Star Weekly*, 8 December 1923 and 23 February 1924.
63 Smyth, *Female pipings*, p. 257.
64 Harrison interview with Mary Hodgson.
65 Smyth, *Female pipings*, p. 256.
66 Kathleen King interviews.
67 C. Pankhurst, *Unshackled*, pp. 296–7.
68 Kathleen King interviews.
69 Ibid.; Harrison interview with Mary Hodgson; Smyth, *Female pipings*, p. 256.
70 Harrison interview with Mary Hodgson.
71 Terry Tucker to David Mitchell, 10 February 1965, DMC; *New York Times*, 19 April 1925.
72 Harrison interview with Mary Hodgson.
73 Mitchell, *The fighting Pankhursts*, pp. 155–6.
74 Quoted in Smyth, *Female pipings*, p. 259.

23 LAST YEARS: CONSERVATIVE PARLIAMENTARY CANDIDATE (1926–JUNE 1928)

1 Dorr, *A woman of fifty*, p. 265.
2 Harrison interview with Mary Hodgson, 2 July 1976, DMC.
3 *Manchester Guardian* and *Daily News*, 28 and 26 January 1926, respectively.
4 *Toronto Daily Star*, 4 March 1926.
5 General Secretary of McClure's to EP, 13 April 1926, DMC; *Evening News*, 20 April 1926.
6 Mitchell, *The fighting Pankhursts*, p. 163.
7 *Sunday Express*, 31 January 1926; EP to Esther Greg, 18 March 1926, Author's Collection.
8 *New York Herald Tribune*, 11 May 1926; M. S. Allen, *Lady in blue* (London, Stanley Paul & Co., 1936), p. 94; J. V. Gottlieb, *Feminine fascism: women in Britain's fascist movement 1923–1945* (London, I. B. Tauris, 2000), p. 157.
9 Cited in Harrison, Two models of feminist leadership, p. 35.
10 C. Pankhurst, *Unshackled*, p. 297.
11 *Toronto Star Weekly*, 16 October 1926.
12 Quoted in Mitchell, *The fighting Pankhursts*, p. 174.
13 *Morning Post*, 3 June 1926
14 Ibid., 16 November 1926.

15 *United Franchise Demonstration*, arranged by the National Union of Societies for Equal Citizenship, programme for Queen's Hall meeting, 8 March 1928 (London, Hodgsons, n.d.), Author's Collection.

16 *Votes for women at twenty-one: extracts from a speech by the Prime Minister at the Albert Hall, London, May 27, 1927* (London, McCorquodale and Co., 1927).

17 EP to Esther Greg, 26 July, 20 August and 4 September 1926, Author's Collection.

18 *Toronto Daily Star*, 2 October 1926.

19 EP to Esther Greg, 4 November 1926, Author's Collection.

20 Pugh, *Women and the women's movement*, p. 46; Harrison, Two models of feminist leadership, p. 35.

21 *Evening News*, 6 December 1926; EP to Esther Greg, 9 December 1926, Author's Collection.

22 EP to Esther Greg, 12 December 1926 and 1 January 1927, Author's Collection.

23 Mitchell, *The fighting Pankhursts*, p. 177.

24 Quoted in Mitchell, *The fighting Pankhursts*, p. 177.

25 EP to Margaret Bates, 5 February 1927, Author's Collection.

26 EP to Esther Greg, 7 February 1927, Author's Collection.

27 EP to Esther Greg, 15 February 1927, Author's Collection.

28 Ibid.

29 EP to Esther Greg, 4 March 1927, Author's Collection.

30 Smyth, *Female pipings*, pp. 263–4, from which the information in the following paragraph is taken.

31 EP to Esther Greg, 20 September 1927, Author's Collection.

32 Smyth, *Female pipings*, p. 264

33 EP to Esther Greg, 21 November 1927, Author's Collection.

34 Statement by Nellie Hall-Humpherson, DMC, 73.83/36 (c).

35 N. Hall-Humpherson to David Mitchell, 12 June 1984, DMC

36 Quoted in Mitchell, *The fighting Pankhursts*, p. 195.

37 Statement by Nellie Hall-Humpherson.

38 Ibid.

39 Ibid.

40 Ibid.

41 Quoted in Mitchell, *The fighting Pankhursts*, p. 196.

42 David Mitchell interview with Commander Lindsay Venn, 13 July 1965, DMC.

43 EP to Esther Greg, 9 April 1928, Author's Collection

44 Statement by Nellie Hall-Humpherson.

45 Smyth, *Female pipings*, p. 268.

46 *News of the World*, 8 April 1928.

47 Arthur Marshall to Ethel Smyth, 4 July 1928, Nancy Astor Papers.

48 Smyth, *Female pipings*, p. 269.

49 CP to Grace Roe, 2 April 1950, Craigie Collection.

50 EP to Esther Greg, 9 April 1928, Author's Collection.

51 Smyth, *Female pipings*, p. 270.

52 EP to Esther Greg, 16 April 1928, Author's Collection.

53 David Mitchell telephone conversation with Lady Japp, 24 June 1965, DMC.

54 Statement by Nellie Hall-Humpherson; Coleman, *Adela Pankhurst*, p. 108.

55 Smyth, *Female pipings*, p. 270.

56 Harrison interview with Mary Hodgson; CP to Esther Greg, 29 May 1928, Author's Collection.

57 CP to Esther Greg, 1 June 1928, Author's Collection.

58 Ibid.

59 CP to Esther Greg, 5 June 1928, Author's Collection.

60 Smyth, *Female pipings*, p. 271.

61 CP to Esther Greg, 13 June 1928, Author's Collection.
62 CP to Esther Greg, 20 June 1928, Author's Collection.
63 See, for example, *The Times, Daily Telegraph, Daily Herald, Manchester Guardian* and *New York Herald Tribune*, 15 June 1928.
64 *Daily News*, 18 June 1928.
65 *Daily Mail*, 19 June 1928.
66 *Daily Telegraph*, 19 June 1928; *The Vote*, 22 June 1928, p. 194; Mary Hodgson to David Mitchell [18 November 1974], DMC; *Daily Express*, 19 June 1928.

24 NICHE IN HISTORY

1 *New York Herald Tribune, Daily Herald, Manchester Guardian* and *The Times*, 15 June 1928. In contrast, the *Daily Telegraph* for this date states that Emmeline Pankhurst was a 'sincere, but sadly misguided, believer in herself and the cause of which she had made herself the champion'.
2 *Evening Standard*, 14 June 1928.
3 *Daily News*, 14 June 1928.
4 *The Times*, 16 June 1928.
5 *The Mrs. Pankhurst Memorial*, leaflet, Author's Collection.
6 R. Barrett to Mrs. Gordon Bates, 3 January 1929, Author's Collection.
7 The National Woman's Party held a memorial meeting for Emmeline in early December 1929, see *New York Herald Tribune*, 9 December 1929.
8 Coleman, *Adela Pankhurst*, p. 122; letter from CP to *The Times*, 22 June 1928.
9 Sylvia Pankhurst to Norah Walshe, n.d., transcript in DMC.
10 R. Strachey, *'The cause': a short history of the women's movement in Great Britain* (London, G. Ball & Sons, 1928), pp. 307–8.
11 K. Dodd, Cultural politics and women's history writing: the case of Ray Strachey's *'The cause', Women's Studies International Forum*, 13, 1/2, 1990, p. 131, *Special Issue, British feminist histories*, ed. L. Stanley.
12 *Everyman*, 31 January 1929, p. 14.
13 Emmeline Pethick Lawrence to Sylvia Pankhurst, 17 December 1929, ESPA.
14 David Mitchell interview with Charlotte Drake, 2 September 1965, DMC.
15 *Daily Sketch, Daily Mirror* and *The Times*, 7 March 1930; *The Ceremonial Unveiling of the Statue of Emmeline Pankhurst*, leaflet, Author's Collection; Statue of Mrs. Pankhurst, Mr. Pethick Lawrence. M.P. at the Unveiling 6th March, 1930, Author's Collection.
16 Romero, *E. Sylvia Pankhurst*, p. 175.
17 *The Star*, 5 March 1930.
18 *Manchester Guardian*, 6 March 1930; E. Sylvia Pankhurst, *Save the mothers* (London, Alfred Knopf, 1930).
19 Emmeline Pethick Lawrence to Sylvia Pankhurst, 26 December 1930, ESPA.
20 Reviews of *The suffragette movement* by R. Ensor in *Everyman* and anonymously in *The Times Literary Supplement*, 19 February 1931.
21 E. S. Pankhurst, TSM, p. 209.
22 Reviews by Emmeline Pethick Lawrence and R. Strachey, *New Leader* and *The Woman's Leader* 20 February 1931, respectively.
23 A. Pankhurst Walsh, My mother, p. 2.
24 Crawford, *The women's suffrage movement*, p. 663, notes that the Suffragette Fellowship was originally founded as the 'Suffragette Club'; information given to the author by Jill Craigie in a telephone conversation 18 September 1998.
25 Letters to the editor by G. Lennox and C. Drake, *Everyman*, 5 and 19 March 1931, pp. 186 and 249, respectively.
26 Annie Kenney to CP, n.d. c. 1942, DMC.
27 F. Pethick-Lawrence, Preface to *Unshackled*, by Dame C. Pankhurst.

28 Ibid.; Adela Pankhurst Walsh to Helen (Moyes) Fraser, 22 January 1960, Helen Fraser Papers.
29 E. Hill and O. Fenton Shafer, *Great suffragists – and why: modern makers of history* (London, H. J. Drane, 1909), p. 280.
30 Mrs. Despard, A valiant leader of women, *The Vote*, 22 June 1928; Smyth, *Female pipings*, p. 280.
31 H. Laski, *The militant temper in politics*, typescript of a lecture given on 18 November 1932 to the Suffragette Fellowship, SFC; F. Pethick-Lawrence to Professor G. M. Trevelyan, 3 October 1949, reprinted in V. Brittain, *Pethick-Lawrence: a portrait* (London, Allen & Unwin, 1963), pp. 215–18.
32 Rover, *Women's suffrage and party politics*, p. 99.
33 Beaumont, Whatever happened to patriotic women?, p. 283.

SELECT BIBLIOGRAPHY

Collections of papers

Janie Allan Papers, National Library of Scotland, Edinburgh
Nancy Astor Papers, University of Reading
Jennie Baines Papers, photocopies held in the Fryer Library, University of Queensland
A. J. Balfour Papers, British Library, London
Teresa Billington-Greig Papers, Women's Library, London Guildhall University
Mary Blathwayt Diaries, Dryham Park, South Gloucestershire
Jill Craigie Private Suffrage Collection
Master of Elibank Papers, National Library of Scotland, Edinburgh
Elizabeth Wolstenholme Elmy Papers, British Library, London
Hugh Franklin and Elsie Duval Papers, Women's Library, London Guildhall University
Helen Fraser Papers, Museum of London
Viscount Gladstone Papers, British Library, London
Bruce Glasier Papers, Sydney Jones Library, University of Liverpool
Philip and Nyra Goode Private Suffrage Collection
Patrick Hannon Papers, House of Lords Record Office
Henry Harben Papers, British Library, London
Home Office Papers, Public Record Office, Kew, Surrey
John Johnson Collection, Women's Suffrage, Bodleian Library, Oxford
Jessie and Annie Kenney Papers, Archive Collections, The Library, University of East Anglia
Rex v. Kerr and Others File, Schlesinger Library, Radcliffe College, Massachusetts
David Lloyd George Papers, House of Lords Record Office, London
Constance Lytton Papers, Archives of Knebworth House
Manchester ILP Central Branch Minutes, Manchester Central Library
Manchester National Society for Women's Suffrage Papers, Manchester Central Library
Dora Marsden Papers, Princeton University Libraries
David Mitchell Collection, Museum of London
Hannah Mitchell Papers, Manchester Central Library
National American Woman Suffrage Association Papers, Library of Congress, Washington DC
National Woman's Party Papers, Smithsonian Libraries, National Museum of American History, Washington DC
Evelyn Sharp Nevinson Papers, Bodleian Library, Oxford
Henry Woodd Nevinson Diaries, Bodleian Library, Oxford
Mary Hutcheson Page Papers, Schlesinger Library, Radcliffe College, Massachusetts
E. Sylvia Pankhurst Papers, the Institute of Social History, Amsterdam
Pethick-Lawrence Papers, Trinity College, University of Cambridge
Caroline Phillips Papers, Watt Collection, Aberdeen Art Gallery and Museum
June Purvis Private Suffrage Collection

Elizabeth Robins Papers, Harry Ransom Humanities Research Center, University of Texas at Austin

Elizabeth Robins Papers, Fales Library at the Elmer Holmes Bobst Library of New York University

C. P. Scott Papers, *Manchester Guardian* Archive, John Rylands University Library, University of Manchester

Rose Scott Papers, Mitchell Library, State Library of New South Wales

Maud Arncliffe Sennett Collection, British Library, London

Hanna Sheehy Skeffington Papers, National Library of Ireland, Dublin

Sophia Smith Collection, Smith College, Northampton, Massachusetts

Hannah Whitall Smith Papers, Lilly Library, Indiana University, Bloomington

Ethel Mary Smyth Letters, Walter Clinton Jackson Library, University of North California Library, Green Boro, North Carolina

Suffragette Fellowship Collection, Museum of London

Adela Pankhurst Walsh Papers, National Library of Australia, Canberra

Helen Watts Papers, photocopies, Nottinghamshire County Record Office, Nottingham

Women's Franchise League, Minute Book of the Executive Committee, microfilm from the Special Collections, Northwestern University, Illinois

Women's Social and Political Union, various booklets, leaflets etc., Women's Library, London Guildhall· University

Women's Suffrage Collection, including Autograph Letter Collection, Women's Library, London Guildhall University

Women's Suffrage Papers, Girton Library, University of Cambridge

Journals and newspapers

Anti-Suffrage Review
Britannia
Brooklyn Daily Eagle
Clarion
Daily Chronicle
Daily Express
Daily Graphic
Daily Herald
Daily Mail
Daily Mirror
Daily News
Daily News and Leader
Daily Sketch
Daily Telegraph
Dundee Advertiser
Evening News
Evening Standard
Evening Standard & St. James's Gazette
Everyman
Forward (Glasgow)
Glasgow Herald
Globe and Traveller
Hamilton Daily Times
Jus Suffragii
Labour Leader
Labour Record

Labour Woman
Ladies' Field Supplement
Liverpool Post
London Budget
Manchester Evening News
Manchester Guardian
Minneapolis Daily News
Montreal Star
Morning Advertiser
Morning Leader
Morning Post
New York Evening Post
New York Herald Tribune
New York Journal
New York Times
New York Tribune
New York World
News of the World
Pall Mall Gazette
Philadelphia Public Ledger
Smethwick Telephone
Sunday Chronicle
Sunday Express
Sunday Herald
Sunday Pictorial
Sussex Herald

The Canadian Courier
The Common Cause
The Guardian
The New Freewoman
The Observer
The Scotsman
The Standard
The Star
The Suffragette
The Sunday Times
The Vote
The Woman's Journal (Boston)
Toronto Daily Star
Toronto Daily Telegram

Toronto Globe
Toronto Mail and Empire
Toronto Star Weekly
Vancouver Daily Colonist
Vancouver Daily Sun
Victoria Colonist
Victoria Daily Times
Votes for Women
Weekly Dispatch
Western Daily Mercury
Western Mail
Westminster Gazette
Women's Penny Paper
Women's Suffrage Journal

Books and articles

Published up to and including 1928

Place of publication is London unless otherwise stated

Balfour, B., Letters of Constance Lytton, selected and arranged by Betty Balfour (William Heinemann, 1925).

Bell, L., The woman's movement and democracy, Forward, 23 November 1907.

Billington-Greig, T., The difference in the women's movement, Forward, 23 November 1907.

—— The militant suffrage movement: emancipation in a hurry (Frank Palmer, n.d. [1911]).

Blackburn, H., Women's suffrage: a record of the women's suffrage movement in the British Isles with biographical sketches of Miss Becker (Williams & Norgate, 1902).

Bullard, F. L., Mrs Pankhurst at close range – a talk with a remarkable personality, Sunday Herald Boston, 31 October 1909, magazine section.

By one of the rank and file, An impression of Mrs. Pankhurst, Votes for Women, 14 June 1912.

Chapman, C., Mrs. Pankhurst – Canadian, MacLean's Magazine, 15 January 1922.

Dangers on the home front, Mrs. Pankhurst's tilt with the pacifists, Liverpool Post, 7 February 1918.

Despard, Mrs., A valiant leader, The Vote, 22 June 1928.

Dorr, R. Childe, A woman of fifty (New York and London, Funk & Wagnalls, 1924).

Drummond, 'General', The story of my third imprisonment, Votes for Women, 12 November 1908.

Glasgow, N. A. John, Holloway jingles: written in Holloway Prison during March and April, 1912 (Glasgow, Glasgow Branch of the WSPU, n.d.).

Hardie, K., Women and politics, in The case for women's suffrage, ed. B. Villiers (T. Fisher Unwin, 1907).

Hill, E. and Shafer, O. Fenton, Great suffragists – and why: modern makers of history (H. J. Drane, 1909).

Independent Labour Party, Report of the fifteenth annual conference, Temperance Hall, Derby, April 1st and 2nd 1907 (Independent Labour Party, May 1907).

Interview with Mrs Pankhurst, The Woman's Herald, 7 February 1891.

Kenney, A., Memories of a militant (Edward Arnold & Co., 1924).

Lansbury, G., My life (Constable, 1928).

Lytton, C. and Warton, J., Spinster, Prisons and prisoners: some personal experiences (William Heinemann, 1914).

Manchester Faces and Places, IV, 1893, Dr. Pankhurst.

Metcalfe, A. E., Woman's effort: a chronicle of British women's fifty years' of struggle for citizenship (1865–1914) (Oxford, B. H. Blackwell, 1917).

Montefiore, D. B., *From a Victorian to a modern* (E. Archer, 1927).

Pankhurst, A., *Put up the sword* (Melbourne, Cecilia John, 1917, third edition).

Pankhurst, C., Broken windows, *Votes for Women*, 1 December 1911.

—— *The great scourge and how to end it* (E. Pankhurst, Lincoln's Inn, 1913).

—— *Plain facts about a great evil* (New York, The Medical Review of Reviews, 1913).

—— *The war: a speech delivered at the London Opera House on September 8th, 1914* (The Women's Social and Political Union, n.d.).

Pankhurst, E., The present position of the women's suffrage movement, in *The case for women's suffrage*, ed. B. Villiers (T. Fisher Unwin, 1907).

—— March on! *Votes for Women*, 31 December 1908.

—— *The importance of the vote* (The Woman's Press, n.d., 1908).

—— The fiery cross, *Votes for Women*, 1 October 1909.

—— March, breast forward! *Votes for Women*, 2 July 1909.

—— The argument of the broken pane, *Votes for Women*, 23 February 1912.

—— *Why we are militant, a speech delivered in New York, October 21st, 1913* (The Woman's Press, pamphlet, n.d.).

—— *My own story* (Eveleigh Nash, 1914).

—— The defeat of the Women's Bill, *Labour Leader*, 19 May 1905.

Pankhurst, E. Sylvia, *The suffragette: the history of the women's militant suffrage movement 1905–1910* (New York, Sturgis & Walton Co., 1911).

—— Women's fight for the vote, *Weekly Dispatch*, 1 November 1908.

Pethick Lawrence, Mrs., Inciting to violence, *Votes for Women*, 23 February 1912.

Phillips, M., Woman's point of view, *Forward*, 23 November 1907.

[Robins, E.], Anonymous, *Ancilla's share: an indictment of sex antagonism* (Hutchinson & Co., 1914).

Sharp, E., *Hertha Ayrton 1854–1923* (Edward Arnold & Co., 1926).

Speeches from the dock, *Votes for Women*, 29 October 1908.

Stopes, M. Carmichael, *Wise parenthood: the treatise on birth control for married people* (Putnam's Sons, 1918).

—— *Married Love: a new contribution to the solution of sexual difficulties* (Putnam's Sons, 1918).

Strachey, R., *'The cause': a short history of the women's movement in Great Britain* (G. Bell and Sons, 1928).

T. W. G., In Bohemia, citizen Pankhurst, *Manchester City News*, 12 April 1913.

The treatment of the women's deputation by the Metropolitan Police. Copy of evidence collected by Dr. Jessie Murray and Mr. H. N. Brailsford and forwarded to the Home Office by the Conciliation Committee for Women Suffrage, in support of its demand for a public enquiry (The Woman's Press, 1911).

Votes for women at twenty-one: extracts from a speech by the Prime Minister at the Albert Hall, London, May 27, 1927 (McCorquodale & Co., 1927).

War till victory, Mrs. Pankhurst on the danger at home, *Liverpool Courier*, 7 February 1918.

Published after 1928

Place of publication is London unless otherwise stated

Accampo, E. A., Private life, public image: motherhood and militancy in the self-construction of Nelly Roussel, 1900–1922, in *The new biography: performing femininity in nineteenth-century France*, ed. M. Burr Margadant (Berkeley and Los Angeles, University of California Press, 2000).

Alberti, A., *Beyond suffrage: feminists in war and peace, 1914–28* (Basingstoke, Macmillan, 1989).

Alberti, J., 'A symbol and a key': the suffrage movement in Britain, 1918–1928, in *Votes for women*, eds J. Purvis and S. S. Holton (London and New York, Routledge, 2000).

Allen, M. S., *Lady in blue* (Stanley Paul & Co., 1936).

Atkinson, D., *Suffragettes* (Museum of London, 1988).

—— *The suffragettes in pictures* (Stroud, Sutton Publishing, 1996).

Balshaw, J., Sharing the burden: the Pethick Lawrences and women's suffrage, in *The men's share? Masculinities, male support and women's suffrage in Britain, 1890–1920* (London and New York, Routledge, 1997).

Banks, J. Trautmann, *Congenial spirits: the selected letters of Virginia Woolf* (The Hogarth Press, 1989).

Banks, O., *Becoming a feminist: the social origins of 'First Wave' feminism* (Brighton, Wheatsheaf Books, 1986).

—— *The biographical dictionary of British feminists Vol. 1: 1800–1930* (Brighton, Wheatsheaf Books, 1985).

Barker, D., Mrs. Pankhurst, in his *Prominent Edwardians* (Allen & Unwin, 1969).

Bartley, P., *Votes for women 1860–1928* (Hodder & Stoughton, 1998).

—— *Emmeline Pankhurst* (Routledge, 2002).

Beaumont, J., Whatever happened to patriotic women, 1914–1918? *Australian Historical Studies*, 115, 2000.

Benn, C., *Keir Hardie* (Hutchinson, 1992).

Bland, L., *Banishing the beast: English feminism and sexual morality 1885–1914* (Harmondsworth, Penguin, 1995).

Blatch, H. Stanton and Lutz, A., *Challenging years: the memoirs of Harriot Stanton Blatch* (New York, G. P. Putnam's Sons, 1940).

Bolt, C. *The women's movements in the United States and Britain from the 1790s to the 1920s* (Hemel Hempstead, Harvester Wheatsheaf, 1993).

—— America and the Pankhursts, in *Votes for Women: the struggle for suffrage revisited* ed. J. H. Baker (Oxford: Oxford University Press, 2002).

Bosch, M. with Kloosterman, A. (eds), *Politics and friendship, letters from the International Woman Suffrage Alliance 1902–1942* (Columbus, Ohio State University, 1990).

Bott, A. (ed.), *Our mothers* (Victor Gollancz, 1932).

Bowerman, E. and Roe, G., The ideals of the Women's Social and Political Union, *Calling All Women (News Letter of the Suffragette Fellowship)*, 1975.

Brendon, P., Mrs. Pankhurst, in his *Eminent Edwardians* (Secker & Warburg, 1980).

Brittain, V., Committees versus professions, in *Testament of a generation: the journalism of Vera Brittain and Winifred Holtby*, eds P. Berry and A. Bishop (Virago, 1985), previously unpublished, 1929.

—— *Pethick-Lawrence: a portrait* (Allen & Unwin, 1963).

Burton, A., The feminist quest for identity: British imperial suffragism and 'global sisterhood', 1900–1915, *Journal of Women's History*, 3, 2, 1991.

—— *Burdens of history: British feminists, Indian women, and imperial culture* (Chapel Hill, University of North Carolina Press, 1994).

Bush, J., *Edwardian ladies and imperial power* (Leicester University Press, 2000).

Butler, R., *As they saw her … Emmeline Pankhurst: portrait of a wife, mother and suffragette* (Harrap & Co., 1970).

Caine, B., Feminist biography and feminist history, *Women's History Review*, 3, 1994.

—— *English feminism 1780–1980* (Oxford, Oxford University Press, 1997).

Campbell, B., *The iron ladies: why do women vote Tory?* (Virago, 1987).

Castle, B., *Sylvia and Christabel Pankhurst* (Harmondsworth, Penguin Books, 1987).

Champion, H., *The true book about Emmeline Pankhurst* (Frederick Muller, 1963).

Coleman, V., *Adela Pankhurst: the wayward suffragette 1885–1961* (Melbourne, Melbourne University Press, 1996).

Collette, C., *For labour and for women, the Women's Labour League, 1906–18* (Manchester, Manchester University Press, 1989).

Collis, L., *Impetuous heart: the story of Ethel Smyth* (William Kimber, 1984).

Corbett, M. J., *Representing femininity: middle-class subjectivity in Victorian and Edwardian women's autobiographies* (New York, Oxford University Press, 1992).

Cousins, J. H. and M. E., *We two together* (Madras, Ganesh & Co., 1950).

Cowman, K., 'The stone-throwing has been forced upon us': the functions of militancy within the Liverpool W.S.P.U., 1906–14, *Transactions of the Historical Society of Lancashire and Cheshire*, 145, 1996.

—— 'A party between revolution and peaceful persuasion': a fresh look at the United Suffragists, in *The women's suffrage movement: new feminist perspectives*, eds M. Joannou and J. Purvis (Manchester, Manchester University Press, 1998).

—— 'Crossing the great divide': inter-organizational suffrage relationships in Merseyside, 1895–1914, in *A suffrage reader: charting directions in British suffrage history*, eds C. Eustance, J. Ryan and L. Ugolini (London and New York, Leicester University Press, 2000).

—— 'Incipient Toryism'? The women's social and political union and the Independent Labour Party, 1903–14, *History Workshop Journal*, 53, 2002.

Craigie, J., Introduction to *My own story, the autobiography of Emmeline Pankhurst* (Virago reprint, 1979).

Crawford, E., *The women's suffrage movement: a reference guide 1866–1928* (UCL Press, 1999).

Dangerfield, G., *The strange death of Liberal England* (MacGibbon & Kee, 1966, first pub. 1935).

Davidoff, L. and Hall, C., *Family fortunes: men and women of the English middle class 1780–1850* (Hutchinson, 1987).

Davis, M., *Sylvia Pankhurst: a life in radical politics* (London, Pluto Press, 1999), pp. 1, 20–32.

Dobbie, B. M. Willmott, *A nest of suffragettes in Somerset* (Batheaston, The Batheaston Society, 1979).

Dodd, K., Cultural politics and women's historical writing: the case of Ray Strachey's *The cause, Women's Studies International Forum*, 13, 1/2, 1990, *Special Issue; British feminist histories*, ed. L. Stanley.

—— Introduction, to her edited *A Sylvia Pankhurst reader* (Manchester, Manchester University Press, 1993).

Dubois, E. C., *Harriot Stanton Blatch and the winning of woman suffrage* (New Haven and London, Yale University Press, 1997).

—— Woman suffrage and the left: an international socialist-feminist perspective, in her *Woman suffrage and women's rights* (New York, New York University Press, 1998). A version of this chapter was originally published in *New Left Review*, 186, 1991.

Dyhouse, C., *Girls growing up in late Victorian and Edwardian England* (London and New York, Routledge & Kegan Paul, 1981).

Eksteins, M., Memory and the Great War, in *The Oxford illustrated history of the First World War*, ed. H. Strachan (Oxford, Oxford University Press, 1998).

Ensor, R., Review of *The suffragette movement, Everyman*, 19 February 1931.

Eustance, C., Meanings of militancy: the ideas and practice of political resistance in the Women's Freedom League, 1907–14, in *The women's suffrage movement: new feminist perspectives*, eds M. Joannou and J. Purvis (Manchester, Manchester University Press, 1998).

Eustance, C., Ryan, J. and Ugolini, L. (eds), *A suffrage reader: charting new directions in British suffrage history* (London and New York, Leicester University Press, 2000).

Evans, M., *Missing persons: the impossibility of auto/biography* (London and New York, Routledge, 1999).

Evans, R. J., *The feminists: women's emancipation movements in Europe, America and Australasia 1840–1920* (Croom Helm, 1977).

Fletcher, I. C., 'A star chamber of the twentieth century': suffragettes, Liberals, and the 1908 'Rush the Commons' case, *Journal of British Studies*, 35, 1996.

Fletcher, I. C., Mayhall, L. E. N. and Levine, P. (eds) *Women's suffrage in the British Empire: citizenship, nation and race* (London and New York, Routledge, 2000).

Francis, H., 'Dare to be free!': the Women's Freedom League and its legacy, in *Votes for women*, eds J. Purvis and S. S. Holton (London and New York, Routledge, 2000).

Fulford, R., *Votes for women: the story of a struggle* (Faber & Faber, 1957).

Gale, J., 50 years later the suffragettes remember, *Observer Colour Magazine*, 7 February 1965.

Gardiner, J. (ed.), *The new women: women's voices 1880–1918* (Collins & Brown, 1993).

Garner, L., *Stepping stones to women's liberty: feminist ideas in the women's suffrage movement 1900–1918* (Heinemann, 1984).

Gawthorpe, M., *Up hill to Holloway* (Penobscot, Maine, Traversity Press, 1962).

Gilbert, S. M., Soldier's heart: literary men, literary women, and the Great War, in *Behind the lines: gender and the two world wars*, eds M. R. Higonnet, J. Jenson, S. Michel and M. C. Weitz (New Haven and London, Yale University Press, 1987).

Gleadle, K., *British women in the nineteenth century* (Basingstoke, Palgrave, 2001).

Gottlieb, J. V., *Feminine fascism: women in Britain's fascist movement 1923–1945* (I. B. Tauris, 2000).

Grayzel, S. R., 'The mothers of our soldiers' children: motherhood, immorality, and the war baby scandal, 1914–18, in *Maternal instincts: visions of motherhood and sexuality in Britain, 1875–1925*, eds C. Nelson and A. Sumner Holmes (Basingstoke, Macmillan, 1997).

—— *Women's identities at war: gender, motherhood, and politics in Britain and France during the First World War* (University of North Carolina Press, 1999).

Green, B., *Spectacular confessions: autobiography, performative activism, and the sites of suffrage 1905–1938* (Basingstoke, Macmillan, 1997).

Grogan, S., *Flora Tristan: life stories* (London and New York, Routledge, 1998).

Gullace, N. F., White feathers and wounded men: female patriotism and the memory of the Great War, *Journal of British Studies*, April 1997.

Hamer, E., *Britannia's glory: a history of twentieth-century lesbians* (Cassell, 1996).

Hamilton, C., *Life errant* (Dent & Sons, 1935).

Hannam, J., *Isabella Ford* (Oxford, Basil Blackwell, 1989).

—— 'I had not been to London': women's suffrage – a view from the regions, in *Votes for women*, eds J. Purvis and S. S. Holton (London and New York, Routledge, 2000).

—— 'Suffragettes are splendid for any work': the Blathwayt diaries as a source for suffrage history, in *A suffrage reader: charting directions in British suffrage history*, eds Eustance, C., Ryan, J. and Ugolini, L. (Leicester University Press, 2000).

Hannam, J. and Hunt, K., *Socialist women: Britain, 1880s to 1920s* (London and New York, Routledge, 2001).

Harrison, B., Review of M. Mackenzie, *Shoulder to shoulder*, *The Times Literary Supplement*, 13 February 1976.

—— *Separate spheres the opposition to women's suffrage in Britain* (Croom Helm, 1978).

—— The act of militancy, violence and the suffragettes, 1904–1914, in his *Peaceable kingdom: stability and change in modern Britain* (Oxford, Oxford University Press, 1982).

—— Two models of feminist leaders, Millicent Garrett Fawcett and Emmeline Pankhurst, in his *Prudent revolutionaries: portraits of British feminists between the wars* (Oxford, Oxford University Press, 1987).

Harrison, J. F. C., *Late Victorian Britain 1875–1901* (Glasgow, Fontana, 1990).

Heilbrun, C., *Writing a woman's life* (The Women's Press, 1988).

Hilson, M., Women voters and the rhetoric of patriotism in the British general election of 1918, *Women's History Review*, 10, 2, 2001.

Holcombe, L., *Wives and property: reform of the married women's property law in nineteenth-century England* (Oxford, Martin Robertson, 1983).

Hollis, P., *Ladies elect: women in English local government 1865–1914* (Oxford, Oxford University Press, 1987).

Holmes, R., *Sidetracks: explorations of a romantic biographer* (Harper Collins, 2000).

Holton, S. S., *Feminism and democracy: women's suffrage and reform politics in Britain 1900–1914* (Cambridge, Cambridge University Press, 1986).

—— 'In sorrowful wrath': suffrage militancy and the romantic feminism of Emmeline Pankhurst, in *British feminism in the twentieth century*, ed. H. L. Smith (Aldershot, Edward Elgar, 1990).

—— 'To educate women into rebellion': Elizabeth Cady Stanton and the creation of a transatlantic network of radical suffragists, *American Historical Review*, 99, 4, October 1994.

—— From anti-slavery to suffrage militancy: the Bright circle, Elizabeth Cady Stanton and the British women's movement, in *Suffrage and beyond: international feminist perspectives*, eds C. Daley and M. Nolan (Auckland, Auckland University Press, 1994).

—— Free love and Victorian feminism: the divers matrimonials of Elizabeth Wolstenholme Elmy and Ben Elmy, *Victorian Studies*, Winter, 1994.

—— *Suffrage days: stories from the women's suffrage movement* (London and New York, Routledge, 1996).

—— Now you see it, now you don't: the Women's Franchise League and its place in contending narratives of the women's suffrage movement, in *The women's suffrage movement: new feminist perspectives*, eds M. Joannou and J. Purvis (Manchester, Manchester University Press, 1998).

—— The making of suffrage history, in *Votes for women*, eds J. Purvis and S. S. Holton (London and New York, Routledge, 2000).

Homberger, E. and Charmley, J. (eds), *The troubled face of biography* (Macmillan, 1988).

Horne, J., Socialism, peace and revolution, 1917–1918, in *The Oxford illustrated history of the First World War*, ed. H. Strachen (Oxford, Oxford University Press, 1998).

Housman, L., *The unexpected years* (Jonathan Cape, 1937).

Howlett, C. J., Writing on the body? Representation and resistance in British suffragette accounts of forcible feeding, *Genders*, 23, 1996.

Hoy, L., *Emmeline Pankhurst* (Hamish Hamilton, 1985).

Hudson, M., *Emmeline Pankhurst* (Oxford, Heinemann, 1997).

Hunt, K., *Equivocal feminists, the Social Democratic Federation and the woman question 1884–1911* (Cambridge, Cambridge University Press, 1996).

Iles, T. (ed.), *All sides of the subject: women and tenses, essays on writing, autobiography and history* (Rivers Oram, 1992).

Israel, K., *Names and stories Emilia Dilke and Victorian culture* (Oxford, Oxford University Press, 1999).

Jackson, M., *The 'real' facts of life: feminism and the politics of sexuality c1850–1940* (Taylor & Francis, 1994).

Jeffreys, S., *The spinster and her enemies: feminism and sexuality 1880–1930* (Pandora Press, 1985).

Joannou, M. and Purvis, J. (eds), *The women's suffrage movement: new feminist perspectives* (Manchester, Manchester University Press, 1998).

John, A. V., *Elizabeth Robins: staging a life, 1862–1952* (London and New York, Routledge, 1995).

John, A. and Eustance, C. (eds), *The men's share? Masculinities, male support and women's suffrage in Britain, 1890–1920* (London and New York, Routledge, 1997).

Jorgensen-Earp, C. R., *'The transfiguring sword': the just war of the Women's Social and Political Union* (Tuscaloosa and London, University of Alabama Press, 1997).

—— (ed.), *Speeches and trails of the militant suffragettes, the Women's Social and Political Union 1903–1918* (Cranbury, New Jersey and London, Associated University Presses, 1999).

Kamm, J., *The story of Mrs. Pankhurst* (Methuen, 1961).

Kean, H., Searching for the past in present defeat: the construction of historical and political identity in British feminism in the 1920s and 1930s, *Women's History Review*, 3, 1994.

Keating, P. (ed.), *Into unknown England 1866–1913* (Fontana, 1976).

Kent, S. Kingsley, The politics of sexual difference: World War I and the demise of British feminism, *Journal of British Studies*, July 1998.

—— *Sex and suffrage in Britain 1860–1914* (New Jersey, Princeton University Press, 1987).

—— *Making peace: the reconstruction of gender in interwar Britain* (Princeton, Princeton University Press, 1993).

Larsen, T., *Christabel Pankhurst: fundamentalism and feminism in coalition* (Woodbridge, Suffolk, Boydell Press, 2002).

Law, C., *Suffrage and power: the women's movement, 1918–1928* (Tauris, 1997).

Ledger, S., *The new woman, factions and feminism at the fin de siècle* (Manchester, Manchester University Press, 1997).

Leneman, L., *A guid cause: the women's suffrage movement in Scotland* (Aberdeen, Aberdeen University Press, 1991).

—— *A truly national movement: the view from outside London*, in *The women's suffrage movement: new feminist perspectives*, eds M. Joannou and J. Purvis (Manchester, Manchester University Press, 1998).

Lesbian History Group, *Not a passing phase: reclaiming lesbians in history 1840–1985* (The Women's Press, 1989).

Levine, P., *Victorian feminism 1850–1900* (Hutchinson, 1987).

—— *Feminist lives in Victorian England: private roles and public commitment* (Oxford, Basil Blackwell, 1990).

Lewenhak, S., *Women and trade unions: an outline history of women in the British trade union movement* (Ernest Benn, 1977).

Lewis, G., *Eva Gore Booth and Esther Roper: a biography* (Pandora Press, 1988).

Lewis, J., *Women in England 1870–1950: sexual divisions and social change* (Brighton and Bloomington, Wheatsheaf Books, 1984).

Liddington, J. and Norris, J., *One hand tied behind us: the rise of the women's suffrage movement* (Virago, 1978).

Mackenzie, M., *Shoulder to shoulder: a documentary* (Penguin, 1975).

Marcus, J., Introduction, re-reading the Pankhursts and women's suffrage, in her edited *Suffrage and the Pankhursts* (London and New York, Routledge & Kegan Paaul, 1987).

Margadant, J. Burr (ed.), *The new biography: performing femininity in nineteenth-century France* (Berkeley and Los Angeles, University of California Press, 2000).

Marquand, D., *Ramsay MacDonald* (Jonathan Cape, 1977).

Mayhall, L. E. N., Creating the 'suffragette spirit': British feminism and the historical imagination, *Women's History Review*, 4, 1995.

—— Defining militancy: radical protest, the constitutional idiom, and women's suffrage in Britain, 1908–1909, *Journal of British Studies*, 39, 2000.

—— The South African War and the origins of suffrage militancy in Britain, 1899–1902, in *Women's suffrage in the British Empire*, eds I. C. Fletcher, L. E. N. Mayhall and P. Levine (London and New York, Routledge, 2000).

McDermid, J. and Hillyar, A., *Midwives of the revolution: female Bolsheviks and women workers in 1917* (UCL Press, 1999).

McPhee, C. and Fitzgerald, A. (eds), *The non-violent militant, selected writings of Teresa Billington-Greig* (London and New York, Routledge, 1987).

[Mearns, A.], *The bitter cry of outcast London* (New York, A. M. Kelly reprint, 1970, first pub. 1883).

Mitchell, D., *Women on the warpath: the story of the women of the First World War* (Jonathan Cape, 1966).

—— *The fighting Pankhursts: a study in tenacity* (Jonathan Cape, 1976).

—— *Queen Christabel: a biography of Christabel Pankhurst* (MacDonald and Jane's, 1977).

Mitchell, G. (ed.), *The hard way up: the autobiography of Hannah Mitchell suffragette and rebel* (Faber & Faber, 1968).

Morgan, D., *Suffragists and Liberals: the politics of woman suffrage in Britain* (Oxford, Basil Blackwell, 1975).

Morgan, K. O., *Keir Hardie: radical and socialist* (Weidenfeld & Nicholson, 1975).

Morley, A. and Stanley, L., *The life and death of Emily Wilding Davison* (The Women's Press, 1988).

Moyes, H., *A woman in a man's world* (Sydney, Alpha Books, 1971).

Murphy, C., *The women's suffrage movement and Irish society in the early twentieth century* (Hemel Hempstead, Harvester Wheatsheaf, 1989).

Myall, M., 'No surrender!': the militancy of Mary Leigh, a working-class suffragette, in *The women's suffrage movement: new feminist perspectives*, eds M. Joannou and J. Purvis (Manchester, Manchester University Press, 1998).

Nagel, I. B., *Biography: fact, fiction and form* (Macmillan, 1984).

Neville, D., *To make their mark: the women's suffrage movement in the North East of England 1900–1914* (Newcastle upon Tyne, North East Labour History Society, 1997).

Nevinson, H. W., *Fire of life* (James Nisbet & Co., 1935).

O'Connor, U., *Biographers and the art of biography* (Quartet Books, 1993).

Owen, R. Cullen, *Smashing times: a history of the Irish women's suffrage movement 1889–1922* (Dublin, Attic Press, 1984).

Oxford, M. (ed.), *Myself when young by famous women of to-day* (Frederick Muller, 1938).

Pankhurst, Dame C., *Unshackled: the story of how we won the vote* (Hutchinson, 1959).

Pankhurst, E. Sylvia, *Save the mothers* (Alfred Knopf, 1930).

—— *The suffragette movement: an intimate account of persons and ideals* (Longmans, 1931).

—— *The home front: a mirror to life in England during the World War* (Hutchinson & Co., 1932).

—— *The life of Emmeline Pankhurst: the suffragette struggle for women's citizenship* (T. Werner Laurie Ltd., 1935).

Pankhurst, Richard, Suffragette sisters in old age: unpublished correspondence between Christabel and Sylvia Pankhurst, 1953–57, *Women's History Review*, 10, 3, 2001.

Pankhurst, Rita, Introduction, to reprint of Dame C. Pankhurst, *Unshackled: the story of how we won the vote* (Cresset Library, 1987).

Pethick Lawrence, Review of *The suffragette movement*, *New Leader*, 20 February 1931.

Pethick-Lawrence, E., *My part in a changing world* (Victor Gollancz, 1938).

Pethick-Lawrence, F., *Fate has been kind* (Hutchinson & Co., n.d., 1943).

—— Preface to *Unshackled: the story of how we won the vote* by Dame Christabel Pankhurst (Hutchinson, 1959).

Pollard, M., *Tell me about Emmeline Pankhurst* (Evans Brothers, 1996).

Powell, K., *Women and Victorian theatre* (Cambridge, Cambridge University Press, 1997).

Procter, Z., *Life and yesterday* (Kensington, Favil Press, 1960).

Pugh, M., *Women's suffrage in Britain 1867–1928* (The Historical Association, 1980).

—— *The march of the women: a revisionist analysis of the campaign for women's suffrage, 1866–1914* (Oxford, Oxford University Press, 2000).

—— *The Pankhursts* (Allen Lane, Penguin Press, 2001).

Purvis, J., *A history of women's education in England* (Milton Keynes, Open University Press, 1991).

—— Using primary sources when researching women's history from a feminist perspective, *Women's History Review*, 1, 1992.

—— The prison experiences of the suffragettes in Edwardian Britain, *Women's History Review*, 4, 1, 1995.

—— A 'Pair of … infernal queens'? A reassessment of the dominant representations of Emmeline and Christabel Pankhurst, first wave feminists in Edwardian Britain, *Women's History Review*, 5, 2, 1996.

—— Christabel Pankhurst and the Women's Social and Political Union, in *The women's suffrage movement: new feminist perspectives*, eds M. Joannou and J. Purvis (Manchester, Manchester University Press, 1998).

—— Emmeline Pankhurst: suffragette, militant feminist and champion of womanhood, in *Representing lives: women and auto/biography*, eds A. Donnell and P. Polkey (Basingstoke, Macmillan, 2000).

427

—— Emmeline Pankhurst (1858–1928) and votes for women, in *Votes for women*, eds J. Purvis and S. S. Holton (London and New York, Routledge, 2000).

Raeburn, A. *The militant suffragettes* (Michael Joseph, 1973).

Raitt, S., The singers of Sargent: Mabel Batten, Elsie Swinton, Ethel Symth, *Women: A Cultural Review*, 3, 1, 1992.

Rappaport, E. D., *Shopping for pleasure: women in the making of London's West End* (Princeton, Princeton University Press, 2000).

Richardson, M., *Laugh a defiance* (Weidenfeld & Nicolson, 1953).

Riley, D., 'Am I that name?' Feminism and the category of 'women' in history (Basingstoke, Macmillan, 1998).

Roe, G., Mrs. Pankhurst and the 1914–1918 crisis, *Calling All Women (News Letter of the Suffragette Fellowship)*, February 1969.

Romero, P. W., *E. Sylvia Pankhurst: portrait of a radical* (New Haven and London, Yale University Press, 1987).

Rosen, A., *Rise up women! The militant campaign of the Women's Social and Political Union 1903–1914* (London and Boston, Routledge & Kegan Paul, 1974).

—— Entry on Emmeline Pankhurst, in *Biographical dictionary of modern British radicals, Vol. 3: 1870–1914, L-Z*, eds J. O. Baylem and N. J. Gossman (New York and London, Harvester Wheatsheaf, 1988).

Rover, C., *Women's suffrage and party politics in Britain 1866–1914* (Routledge & Kegan Paul, 1967).

Rowbotham, S., *Friends of Alice Wheeldon* (Pluto Press, 1986).

—— *Hidden from history: 300 years of women's oppression and the fight against it* (Pluto Press, 1973).

Rubinstein, D. W., *Before the suffragettes: women's emancipation in the 1890s* (Brighton, Harvester Press, 1986).

Rupp, L. J., *Worlds of women: the making of an international women's movement* (Princeton, Princeton University Press, 1997).

Sarah, E., Christabel Pankhurst: reclaiming her power, in *Feminist theorists: three centuries of women's intellectual traditions*, ed. D. Spender (The Women's Press, 1983).

Schneer, J., *George Lansbury* (Manchester, Manchester University Press, 1990).

Scott, B. K., (ed.), *Selected letters of Rebecca West* (New Haven & London, Yale University Press, 2000).

Shanley, M. Lyndon, *Feminism, marriage and the law in England, 1850–1895* (New Jersey, Princeton University Press, 1989).

Sharp, E., Emmeline Pankhurst and militant suffrage, *Nineteenth Century*, April 1930.

Showalter, E. (ed.), *Daughers of decadence, women writers of the fin de siècle* (Virago, 1993).

Sloan, K., Sexual warfare in the silent cinema: comedies and melodramas of woman suffragism, *American Quarterly*, 33, Fall, 1981.

Smith, H. (ed.), *British feminism in the twentieth century* (Aldershot, Edward Elgar, 1990).

—— *The British women's suffrage campaign 1866–1928* (Harlow, Longman, 1998).

Smyth, E., *Female pipings in Eden* (Edinburgh, Peter Davies, 1933).

—— *Beecham and pharaoh* (Chapman and Hall, 1935).

Spender, D., *Women of ideas and what men have done to them: from Aphra Behn to Adrienne Rich* (London and New York, Routledge & Kegan Paul, 1982).

St. John, C., *Ethel Smyth: a biography* (Longmans, Green & Co., 1959).

Stanley, L., *The auto/biographical I: the theory and practice of feminist auto/biography* (Manchester, Manchester University Press, 1992).

Steedman, C., *Childhood, culture and class in Britain: Margaret McMillan 1860–1931* (Virago, 1990).

Steiner, Z., The peace settlement, in *The Oxford illustrated history of the First World War*, ed. H. Strachan (Oxford, Oxford University Press, 1998).

Stevenson, F., *Lloyd George: a diary* (Hutchinson, 1971).

Stocks, M., *My commonplace book* (Peter Davies, 1970).

Strachey, R., Review of *The suffragette movement*, *The Woman's Leader*, 20 February 1931.

—— Entry on Emmeline Pankhurst, *The dictionary of national biography 1922–1930*, ed. J. R. H. Weaver (Oxford, Oxford University Press, 1937).

Sykes, C., *Nancy: the life of Lady Astor* (Collins, 1972).

Taylor, A., *Annie Besant: a biography* (Oxford, Oxford University Press, 1992).

Taylor, B., *Eve and the new Jerusalem: socialism and feminism in the nineteenth century* (Virago, 1983).

Thebaud, F., The Great War and the triumph of sexual division, in her edited *A history of women: towards a cultural identity in the twentieth century* (Massachusetts, Harvard University Press, 1994).

Thompson, M. E. and Thompson, M. D., *They couldn't stop us! Two (usually law-abiding) women in the years 1909–1913* (Ipswich, W. E. Harrison & Sons, Ancient House Press, 1957).

Thorpe, V. and Marsh, A., Diary reveals lesbian love trysts of suffragette leaders, *The Observer*, 11 June 2000.

Tickner, L., *The spectacle of women: imagery of the suffrage campaign 1907–14* (Chatto & Windus, 1987).

Times Literary Supplement, Review of *The suffragette movement*, 19 February 1931.

van Wingerden, S. A., *The women's suffrage movement in Britain 1866–1928* (Basingstoke, Macmillan, 1999).

Vicinus, M., Male space and women's bodies: the suffragette movement, Chapter 7 in her *Independent women: work and community for single women 1850–1920* (London, Virago, 1985).

—— Fin-de-siècle theatrics: male impersonation and lesbian desire, in *Borderlines: genders and identities in war and peace 1870–1930*, ed. B. Melman (London and New York, Routledge, 1998).

Vickery, A., Golden age to separate spheres? A review of the categories and chronology of English women's history, *Historical Journal*, 36, 1993.

Vries, J. de, Gendering patriotism: Emmeline and Christabel Pankhurst and World War One, in *This working-day world: women's lives and culture(s) in Britain 1914–1945*, ed. S. Oldfield (Taylor & Francis, 1994).

Ward, M., *Hanna Sheehy Skeffington: a life* (Cork, Attic Press, 1997).

Wasserstein, B., *Herbert Samuel: a political life* (Oxford, Oxford University Press, 1992).

West, R., Mrs Pankhurst, in *The post Victorians*, with an Introduction by The Very Rev. W. R. Inge (Ivor Nicholson, 1933).

Wilson, T., (ed.), *The political diaries of C. P. Scott 1911–1928* (Collins, 1970).

Winslow, B., *Sylvia Pankhurst: sexual politics and political activism* (London, UCL Press, 1996).

Wylie, I. A. R., *My life with George: an unconventional autobiography* (New York, Random House, 1940).

Unpublished dissertations and theses

Berry, T. J., The female suffrage movement in South Lancashire with particular reference to Oldham 1890–191hil.4, M.A. Dissertation, Huddersfield Polytechnic, 1968.

Cowman, K., Engendering citizenship: the political involvement of women in Merseyside, 1890–1920, D.Phil. thesis, University of York, 1994.

Eustance, C., 'Daring to be free': the evolution of women's political identities in the Women's Freedom League 1907–1930, D.P thesis, University of York, 1993.

Francis, H., ' … Our job is to free women … ', the sexual politics of four Edwardian feminists from c. 1910 to c.1935, D.Phil. thesis, University of York, 1996.

INDEX

Aberdeen 84, 90, 94, 124
abolitionism 10, 28, 31
Abrahams, Dr. 350
Acklom, Elfreda 353
Actresses' Franchise League 128, 147, 158, 192–3
Addams, Jane 171
adopted children *plate*, 279–80, 321, 323–5, 329–30
adult suffrage: *see* suffrage
Adventism 314–15, 344
Albert Hall meetings: Conciliation Bill 149; Second Conciliation Bill 159, 183; socialism and trade unions rally 237–8; suffrage victory 307; WSPU 200–3, 217
Aldwych Skating Rink 159
Aldwych Theatre 126–7
Alice, Princess 317
All Russian Women's Union 295
Allan, Janie 111, 254
Allen, Mary 341
Allies, World War I 292, 293–4
Amalgamated Society of Engineers 308
America: *see* USA
American National Association to Oppose Woman Suffrage 318
American Society for Combating Venereal Disease 326
Anderson, Elizabeth Garrett 128, 150, 181
Anderson, Louisa Garrett 179, 180, 251
anti-government policy 206
Anti-Suffrage Review 156
anti-suffragists 107, 178, 276–7, 318–19
Antrim, Lady 166
Archdale, Helen: imprisonment 177; Pankhurst, Adela 167, 169, 191–2, 213, 225–6, 232–3, 248, 257, 305
arson attempts 190, 193, 194, 209, 216

arson campaign 220–1, 242, 253
Asquith, H. H.: Birmingham speech 133; Cat and Mouse Act 227; Conciliation Bill 148, 151; Conciliation Committee for Women's Suffrage 167, 168; criticisms 189, 275, 281–2; deputations 3, 122, 130, 131, 150–1, 173, 227, 262, 263; dissolution of parliament 150; Fawcett 286; Hardie 150–1; Lansbury 189; Leigh 133–4; Lytton 164; Manhood Suffrage Bill 172, 173–4, 207, 208; Pankhurst, Emmeline 83–4, 272, 286–7; Pankhurst, Sylvia 262, 263; Prime Minister 107, 157; Reform Bill 107; resignation 288; Second Conciliation Bill 176; suffrage 286–7; Ulster 252–3; War Minister 256; Women's Enfranchisement Bill 113, 146–7; women's suffrage 162, 164, 166–7, 273, 286–7; WSPU 108, 193
assassination plot 289
Astor, Nancy 320, 321; House of Lords 349; Pan American Conference of Women 332; Pankhurst, Emmeline 280, 340, 351; war babies 279; women's wartime work 274, 276
Australia: conscription 287; Goldstein 159; Hughes 287; Hyde Park demonstration 147; Pankhurst, Adela 248–9, 257, 266; Women's Political Association 270; women's suffrage 72, 307
Ayrton, Hertha 124, 150, 180, 218, 227, 251
Ayrton, Phyllis 304, 314

Bach, Ada Goulden 337, 339–40, 347, 353
Badley, Mrs. 261
Bailey, Sir William 63
Baines, Jenny 100–1

Baker, Miss 277–8
Baker, Winnie 206
Baldock, Minnie 79, 88, 103, 380n1
Baldwin, Mrs. 343
Baldwin, Stanley 341, 344, 351, 357
Balfour, Arthur 72
Balfour, Lady Betty 124, 130, 166, 168
Balfour, Lady Frances 130
Balgarnie, Florence 22, 29
Bancroft, Elias 51
Banks, Olive 6
Barclay, Lady 266
Barrett, Rachel 102, 203, 219, 355
Bartels, Olive 254, 261
Bastille Day 9, 120, 192–3, 311
Bates, Dr. Gordon 322–3, 326–7, 330
Bates, Margaret 345, 355
Beaumont, Joan 268–9
Becker, Lydia 12, 18, 20, 29, 40, 370n15
Beecher, Henry Ward 10
Belgium 49, 60, 271, 285
Bell, Annie 283
Bellairs, Commander 287
Belmont, Mrs. 232, 233, 235, 236, 239
Bennett, Sarah 177
Bermuda 335–6
Bernhardt, Sarah 196
Besant, Annie 26, 28
Best, Nellie 110, 111
Bigelow, William F. 234
Biggs, Caroline 22
Bill of Rights (1689) 129, 130
Billinghurst, May 208, 314, 325–6
Billington, Teresa (later Billington-Greig)
    156; arrested 88; Pankhurst, Emmeline
    67–8, 265; Pankhurst, Harry 128; WSPU
    72, 74–6, 83, 86, 96–7
Birmingham 133
Birnstingl, Miss 137, 167, 169
birth control 26, 316
Black, Mrs. 84
Black Friday 150, 152
Bland, L. 206
Blatch, Harriot Stanton: education 41;
    Equality League 136, 138; letter to
    Emmeline 126; political corruption film
    235; social equality 138–9; Women's
    Franchise League 31, 37; Women's
    Political Union 171, 234
Blatchford, Robert 49, 54
Blathwayt, Emily 145, 203
Blathwayt, Mary 103, 110, 145, 221

Bloody Sunday 26
Bodkin, Mr. 219
Boer War 57, 270, 376n41
Boggart Hole Clough 46–8, 84–5, 261
Bolsheviks 309, 327; class struggle 318;
    industrial unrest 290–1; internationalism
    310; Lenin 298, 300; Marxism 292, 319;
    Pankhurst, Sylvia 330–1; in Russia 292,
    297, 299, 300, 301, 303, 304; USA 318
bombing 210, 214–15, 216
Bondfield, Margaret 310
Bonwick, Theodora 239
Boston 138
Boston Herald 138
Botchkareva, Maria *plate*, 295–6, 297,
    409n17
Bouvier, Mrs. 130
Bowerman, Elsie 304, 314, 325–6, 340
Brackenbury, Georgina 147, 251, 353, 355
Brackenbury, Marie 147, 353
Bradford 49, 142
Bradlaugh, Charles 26
Brailsford, H. N. 135, 143–4, 149–50, 152–3,
    177
Brailsford, Jane 251
Brannan, Mrs. and Dr. John 171
Briand, Aristide 315
Brierley, Charles 47
Bright, Jacob 12, 16, 20, 28, 31–2, 54, 119
Bright, Ursula 12, 20, 119; Dr. Pankhurst
    Fund 54; Local Government Bill 40;
    Pankhurst, Emmeline 31, 41; Rollit's bill
    36; Women's Franchise League 31–2,
    33–4, 37
Bristol 178
Britannia: Asquith and Grey 284, 288;
    Bolsheviks 309; Pankhurst, Sylvia 285;
    poverty 306; press seized 284, 288;
    Russian visit 293; Women's Party 302; *see
    also The Suffragette* journal
British Commonwealth Union 313, 316
Brittain, Vera 317
Brocklehurst, Fred 48, 53
Brooklyn 284–5
Brooklyn Academy of Music 170–1
Brown, Kathleen 119
Bryant and May factories 26
Bryce, James 28
Bryce, Marjorie Annan 164–5
Bryn Mawr College for Women 171, 285
Buckingham Palace 266
Buffalo 139

Bull, Sir William 346
Bullard, F. L. 139
Burns, John 26, 106
Burns, Lucy 133
Burns, Robert 265
Burrows, Herbert 26, 36, 37
Burton, Antoinette 269
Busk, Edward 228
Butler, George 31
Butler, Josephine 31
Butler, R. 6, 273
by-election campaigning 99, 143, 194; Bow
    and Bromley 207; Cheltenham 161;
    Colne Valley 96; Hexham 92;
    Huddersfield 89; Jarrow 96; Newcastle
    110; Newton Abbot 101–2; Peckham Rye
    105, 107; Pudsey 110; Scotland 123–4;
    South Shields 149; Wales 110;
    Walthamstow 149; Wellington 167;
    Westbury 158; Wiltshire 158

Caine, B. 268
California 332
Campbell-Bannerman, Sir Henry 77, 81, 83,
    107
Canada 309, 331–2, 334, 335;
    commemoration 355; immigrants 320;
    Imperial Suffrage Movement 195;
    industrial unrest 319–20; lecture tours
    139, 169, 285, 311, 319, 326–7, 328–9;
    press 175, 237; Public Health Association
    334; Votes for Women 174; women's
    suffrage 288–9, 307; WSPU 177
Canadian National Council for Combating
    Venereal Diseases 322–3, 326–7, 330,
    332–3
Canadian Social Hygiene Council 333
capitalism 303, 313
Cardiff meeting 210
Carlyle, Thomas 10
Carnegie Hall 237
Carson, Sir Edward 226, 252–3, 265, 275
Castlereagh, Lord 151
Cat and Mouse Act 217–18, 262; Asquith
    227; clergymen 229; Hardie 228;
    International Medical Congress 229–30;
    Kenney, Annie 226, 257; Pankhurst,
    Emmeline 215, 221, 222–3, 240, 242–3,
    251–2, 259–60, 266, 357; Pankhurst,
    Sylvia 226, 228, 246
Catt, Carrie Chapman 138
Caxton Hall meetings 79, 88, 90–1, 151

Cecil, Lord Robert 131
Census boycott 159
Central National Society for Women's
    Suffrage 29
Champion, Harold 6
Chapman, Rev. Hugh 183
charity 45, 55
Chaykovsky, Nikolay Vasilyevich 292
checkweighing bill 80
Cheltenham by-election 161
Chicago 236, 237
child prostitution 201, 215
children, socialisation 369n18
Chorlton Board of Guardians 42–3, 49
Chorlton Workhouse 44–5, 53
Christabel Pankhurst's Day 120
Christmas 101, 243, 244
Christmas Presents Sale 206
Church League for Women Suffrage 192–3
Churchill, Winston 84, 150, 152
Cincinnati 174
citizenship rights 322, 379n49; Glasgow 290;
    Liberal Party 135; Ulster Unionists 226;
    women 102, 106, 268, 311–12; Women's
    Party 305; see also women's suffrage
The Clarion 49, 54, 148, 223, 226
Clarke, Mary (née Goulden): arrested 109,
    122–3, 151; death 153–4; Gladstone 124;
    Pankhurst, Adela 155; Pankhurst, Harry
    137; Registrar 82–3, 92; WSPU 81, 92
class: co-operation 303, 319; gender divisions
    368–9n11; legislation 36–7; politics 69;
    prison treatment 140, 176; solidarity 310,
    311, 312; women's movements 98,
    110–11
class struggle 140, 291, 318, 340
Clayton, Edwy 219
clergymen's protests 229, 240
Cleveland 236
coal miners 130, 341
Coalition 275, 313
Cobb, Rev. W. F. Geikie 353
Cobden, Richard 88
Cobden-Sanderson, Annie 88, 89, 93, 94,
    150, 155
Cobden-Sanderson, Mr. 88
Cobden-Unwin, Mrs. 88
Cockermouth campaign 86, 87, 93
Coign cottage 158, 162–3, 178–9, 183, 207,
    211, 220
Coleman, V. 48
Coleridge, Judge 187

Coleridge Taylor family 337, 350
Collegiate Equal Suffrage League, USA 139
Colne Valley by-election 96
Committee for the Relief of the Unemployed 43
Committee on Local Government 40
The Common Cause 304
communism 325, 331, 334, 343–4, 362
Comstock, Anthony 237
Conciliation Bill 148, 149, 151
Conciliation Committee for Women's Suffrage 168–9; Asquith 167, 168; Brailsford 143, 144; Pankhurst, Christabel 152–3; police brutality 392n103; private members' ballot 157; Women's Enranchisement Bill 144, 146
Connolly, James 237
Conolan, Gertrude 124
conscription 268, 270, 286, 287
Conservative candidacy 2, 340, 341–2
Conservative Party 144, 343, 346, 347–8, 361
Cook, Lady 88, 89
Cookson, Mrs. 335–6
Cooper, Selina Jane 70, 83
Corbett, Mrs. 266
Corio, Silvio Erasmus 339, 348
Corn Laws 9, 88
Coronation Procession 165
Council of Nation Defense 310
Cousins, Gretta 149
coverture doctrine 32
Cowman, K. 111, 366n32, 379n49
Craggs, Helen 142, 190
Craigie, Jill 3
Crane, Walter 57
Crawford, E. 70, 259, 265, 378n10
Crawfurd, Helen 111, 293
Crocker, Nellie 124
Cromer, Lord 276
Crowe, Sir Eyre 281
Crystal Palace 164
Cunard, Lady 273
Curtis Bennett, Henry 113–14, 117
Curzon, Lord 304–5
Cymric Suffrage Society 192–3
Czar of Russia 296, 299

Daily Chronicle 108, 310
Daily Express 156, 304
Daily Herald 202, 205, 212, 237, 238, 246, 354

Daily Herald League 230, 238
Daily Mail 79
Daily Mirror 1, 88
Daily News 134, 135, 310, 316, 340
Daily News and Leader 282
Daily Telegraph 277
Dangerfield, George 3–4, 359
Davison, Emily Wilding 170, 175–6, 222–3
Davison, J. E. 313–14
Dayton, Ohio 236
Defence of the Realm Act 284
Denmark 307
deputations: Asquith 3, 122, 130, 131, 150–1, 173, 227, 262, 263; Lloyd George 289–90; Pankhurst, Christabel 172; petition rights 129–30; Tumultuous Petitions Act 102–3; women's suffrage 124, 208–9, 257–8, 289–90; WSPU 87–8, 108–9
Derby Day 222
Despard, Charlotte: Albert Hall rally 237; arrested 91; Equal Franchise Demonstration 343; Free Speech Defence Committee 230; Pankhurst, Emmeline 361; Women's Freedom League 97, 125; WSPU 85, 93, 96, 97
Dickinson, W. H. 91, 92
Dilke, Lady 31
Dilke, Sir Charles 31, 32, 40, 55
Disley 39
divorce 32, 106
Dixon, W. H. 54, 61
Dodd, Kathryn 2, 355–6
Dodge, Mary 157–8
Dorr, Rheta Childe 7, 234, 237, 240, 297, 318, 339, 409n17
Dove-Willcox, Lillian 254
Dr. Pankhurst Fund 54, 58–9, 60–4
Drake, Charlotte 359
Drew, Sidney 219
drum and fife band 128, 129, 147
Drummond, Flora 103, 107, 117, 147, 164–5, 218; arrested 81, 113–14, 219; Empress Theatre 240; Pankhurst, Emmeline 256, 353; press enquiries 339; Scotland 110, 124; statue 357; Women's Guild of Empire 340, 341; Women's Party 304; WSPU 81, 112, 208–9, 254, 271, 281
Dublin 193
Dubois, E. C. 138, 140
Dufaux, Frederic 14, 83
Dufaux, Noémie 14, 29, 59–60, 193

Dugdale, Una *plate*, 119, 143, 148–9, 154, 168, 186, 286
Dunlop, Marion Wallace 129, 131, 350, 353
Duval, Elsie 280
Duval, Victor 170
Dyhouse, Carol 10–11

East London Federation of the Suffragettes: see ELFS
Ede, Dr. Frances 240, 241
Edinburgh 137
Edmonton 355
Edmonton Women's Institute 326
education: adopted children 324–5, 329–30; Blatch 41; gender differences 11, 15–16, 64; Imperial Order 322; Pankhurst children 36
Edward III 226
Edward VII 146
Egerton, Lady 294
ELFS/WSPU: Pankhurst, Christabel 246–8; Pankhurst, Sylvia 2, 211, 262, 270; People's Army 238; renamed Workers' Suffrage Federation 285
Elmy, Ben 17, 37
Elmy, Elizabeth Wolstenholme 12, 17, 18, 20, 70, 307; Boggart Hole Clough 84–5; Pankhurst, Emmeline 98; processions 107, 164–5; public testimonial 148; Rollit's bill 37; Women's Emancipation Union 36; Women's Enfranchisement Bill 72, 73; Women's Franchise League 31, 33
Emerson, Zelie 5, 204, 212
Emerson's shop: see shop (Emerson's)
Empire: see imperialism
Empress Theatre 237, 240
enfranchisement: see suffrage
Equal Franchise Demonstration 343
Equal Franchise Society 285
Equality League 136, 138
Evans, Dorothy 253
Evans, Gladys 193, 398n9
Evans, Richard 308
Evans, Samuel 82
Evening News 340
Evening Standard 342

Fabian Society 33, 57, 147
Fawcett, Millicent Garrett 72; Asquith 286; Lady Balfour 130; Brailsford 177; Elmy 17; Equal Franchise Demonstration 343;

International Woman Suffrage Alliance 127; Manhood Suffrage Bill 207; men co-workers 5, 301; National Society for Women's Suffrage 29; Pankhurst, Emmeline 289–90; peaceful protest 66, 181, 274, 356; on suffragettes 88, 194; *see also* National Union of Women's Suffrage Societies
femininity 10–11, 107, 116, 139, 269, 271
feminisms 360–1, 362–3, 364n1; imperial 338; liberal 365n30; militarism 268; nationalism 268; pacifism 316–17; patriotic 268–9, 271, 308, 311–12, 406n21; radical 6, 365n30; Second Wave Feminism 5, 7, 365n30; Six Point Group 338; socialism 2, 5, 140, 203, 205, 303, 316–17, 364n8, 365n30; working class 203–4, 211
Fenton, W. Hugh 135
Fenwick Miller, Florence 88
Fenwick Miller, Irene 81
Festival of Empire 164
Field, Frank 77
Fife, East 256
Finland 307
fire alarms 203
Fitzgerald, Hon. Edith 266
Flatman, Ada 124, 147, 158, 161, 167
forcible feeding 134, 135, 136, 140, 229–30, 240, 264–5; *see also* hunger strikers
Ford, Isabella 65, 69, 70, 72, 79, 82, 93
Forsyth, William 20
Forward 345
Fox, Norah Dacre 271, 281
France 12–13, 28–9, 193, 309, 311
franchise reform 221, 286, 287, 289; *see also* suffrage; women's suffrage
Franklin, Hugh 280
Fraser, Helen 93, 109, 124, 194, 310
Fraserburgh 168
free speech 26, 48, 230
Free Speech Defence Committee 230
Free Trade Hall, Manchester 143–4

Garibaldi, Giuseppe 76
Garner, L. 111, 303
Garrison, Eleanor 171–2, 235, 264, 284, 315
Garrison, William Lloyd 28, 31
Garrud, Edith 128
Gaskell, Elinor Penn 283
Gawthorpe, Mary *plate*, 100, 101; Independent Labour Party 77; Women's

Labour League 86; WSPU 97, 102, 110, 156
Gay, Louisa 208
gender differences 6; class 368n11; education 11, 15–16, 58, 64; militancy 191, 235, 254, 266; politics 69; suffrage 11–12, 69–70, 290; wage levels 57–8, 273–4, 278, 306, 308–9; *see also* sex solidarity
general elections 57, 74, 77
General Strike 340, 341
Geneva 51–2, 54, 59–60
George V 257–8
Germany 13, 60; socialism 293; women's status 271, 275; World War I 267, 269
Gibraltar cruise 347
Gibson, Robert 55
Gilbert, S. M. 281
Gladstone, Herbert: Clarke 124; hunger strikers 132; petition 117; political prisoner status 88; Scott 123; subpoenaed 114–15; women's suffrage 104
Gladstone, William Ewart 22, 42, 115
Glasgow 87, 124, 132, 253–4, 290
Glasgow Forward 226
Glasier, Bruce 42, 47, 53, 54, 57, 66, 132
Glasier, Katherine 42, 53, 66
Gloucestershire WSPU 158
Goldstein, Vida 159, 164, 248, 249, 305
golf courses 209
Gollancz, Ruth 222
Good Housekeeping 234
Gordon, Flora Mary *plate*; Pankhurst, Emmeline 279, 324, 330, 334, 337; Pankhurst, Sylvia 339; Pine 323, 335; re-adopted 350, 351
Gordon, Frances 264
Gore-Booth, Eva 59, 74, 83, 377n62
Gorton United Trades and Labour Council 74
Goulden, Emmeline 10–14; *see also* Pankhurst, Emmeline
Goulden, Herbert: death 325; Pankhurst, Emmeline 56, 188, 219; Pankhurst, Harry 56, 142; Pankhurst, Sylvia 246; Paris 243; sister Mary 153
Goulden, Mary 11, 14, 21, 26, 47, 52, 56; *see also* Clarke, Mary (née Goulden)
Goulden, Robert (brother) 353
Goulden, Robert (father) 9, 12, 14–15; abolitionism 10; death 37–8; property

settlement 18–19, 22; suffrage campaign 11–12
Goulden, Sophie Jane 9, 14–15, 16, 144–5
Graham, John J. 54, 61–2
Grant, Mrs. 277–8
Grantham, Justice 23
Grayzel, S. R. 286
Great College Street Society 29
Greece 288
Greg, Esther 340, 343, 345, 346, 350
Greg, John 340
Grenfell, Mrs. J. G. 70
Grey, Sir Edward 74–5, 163–4, 166, 208, 281–2
Grogan, Susan 6
Guthrie, Mrs. Baillie 128
Gye, Elsa 124

Haberton, Lady 92
The Hague 274
Haig, Florence 111–12
Haldane, R. B. 28, 32
Hall, Emmeline 261
Hall, Leonard 43, 46, 47, 48, 49, 53, 261
Hall, Marion 261
Hall, Nellie 261
Hall-Humpherson, Nellie 347, 348, 351–2, 353
Hallett, Lilias Ashworth 29
Hamilton 285, 336
Hamilton, Cecily 157
Hamilton, Colonel 22
Hamilton Daily Times 285
Hampstead Road shop 25
Hannam, J. 221
Harben, Agnes 209, 218, 251
Harben, Henry 207, 222, 239, 251, 264
Harcourt, Lewis 190
Hardie, Keir: Asquith 150–1; Cat and Mouse Act 228; death 280; elected to parliament 41, 57; Free Speech Defence Committee 230; ill health 94; Labour leader 79–80; *The Labour Leader* 47, 53; Men's Committee for Justice to Women 129; Merthyr Tydfil 77; Pankhurst, Emmeline 119, 135, 188, 217; Pankhurst, Sylvia 2, 3, 5, 94, 101, 161, 185, 204–5, 212–13; socialism 40–1, 345; as speaker 42, 48, 49, 83; unemployment 43, 74, 380n54; Women's Enfranchisement Bill 70, 71; women's suffrage 66, 68, 82, 85, 90; WSPU 88, 108, 192–3

Harding, Gertrude 231
Harker, J. 41, 46, 47
Harraden, Beatrice 205, 250, 251, 354–5, 360
Harrison, Brian 5
Hartford 236
Hastings, Dr. 334–5
Haverfield, Evelina 130, 141, 147, 150, 158, 251
Hawkins, Mrs. 152
Headlam, Mr. 47
Healy, T. H. 186
Heaton Park, Manchester 74, 110
Helensburgh 168
Hempshall, John 47
Henderson, Arthur 289
Henry, E. R. 219
Hewson, Estelle 334
Hexham by-election 92
Heywood, Abel 19
Hobhouse, Charles 178, 179
Hobhouse, Emily 274
Hodgson, Caroline 97
Holland Park Hall meeting 265–6
Holloway brooches 127–8
Holloway Jail 84, 111, 117–18, 254–5
Holme, Vera 132, 147
Holton, S. S. 4, 10, 29–30, 30–1, 251, 366n32, 378n10
Home Office petitions 228
Home Rule 183, 204, 226, 252
Hood, Rev. Paxton 19
Horne, Rev. T. 53
Horsley, Victor 135, 228
Houldsworth, Mr. 20
House of Commons 79–80, 82
House of Lords 16, 33, 304–5, 349
Housman, Laurence 187, 223, 251
Howey, Elsie 111–12, 127, 144
Huddersfield by-election 89
Hughes, Billy 287
hunger strikers: Craggs 190; Pankhurst, Emmeline 211, 217, 218, 223, 240, 242–3, 255, 265; Pankhurst, Sylvia 3, 211, 212–13, 226, 235; protests 131, 135–6, 188; see also forcible feeding
Hunslet Moor 102
Husband, Agnes 111
Hyde Park: Bastille Day 192–3; Hughes meeting 287; processions 107, 126–7, 147; railings 178, 179; WSPU 84, 105
Hyland, Rose 54, 57
Hyndman, H. M. 36

illegitimacy 321; Pankhurst, Sylvia's son 348, 349–50; Poor Law Guardian 279; see also adopted children; war babies
I.L.P. News 66
immigrants 320
Imperial Order Daughters of the Empire 285, 322
Imperial Suffrage Movement 195
imperialism 311–12, 322, 331–2, 338, 343, 363
imprisonment 74–5, 176, 177, 397n44; see also hunger strikers
incendiarism 176, 178, 221
incest 56–7
incitement to bombing charge 214–15
Independent Labour Party: Bastille Day demonstration 192–3; expulsions threatened 86–7; Gawthorpe 77; Hardie 41; Heaton Park 74; Manchester 46–7, 93; National Administrative Council 51, 55–6, 57, 65, 69, 72; Pankhurst, Emmeline 82, 95, 361; Pankhurst, Sylvia 101; Stockton-on-Tees conference 82; suffrage 69–70; women's franchise bill 68–9; women's suffrage 86, 87; WSPU 73–4, 378n10
Independent Women's Social and Political Union 284
industrial unrest: Bolsheviks 290–1; Canada 319–20; General Strike 340, 341; Pankhurst, Emmeline 25–6, 271; poverty 340–1; trade unions 303; Wales 281; women 340–1
Industrial Women's Organisations 301
infantile mortality 106
inheritance rights 32
International Congress of Women 274
International Labour Conference 41
International Medical Congress 229–30
International Woman Suffrage Alliance 127
International Women's Franchise Club 147
internationalism 268, 269, 270, 310
Ireland 149, 160–1; Home Rule 183, 204, 226, 252; Nationalism 22, 23, 183; Suffragists 147
Irish League for Women Suffrage 192–3
Irish Women's Franchise League 149

Jackson, M. 206
James, Edward 210
Japan 309, 310
Japp, Lady Katherine 351

Japp, Sir Henry 351
Jarrow by-election 96
Jeffreys, S. 206
Joachim, Maud 111–12, 147, 225
Joan of Arc symbol 127, 164
Jones, Leif 167
Jorgensen-Earp, C. R. 150, 174, 236
Joynson-Hicks, Sir William 349
Jus Suffragii 272

Kamm, Josephine 5–6
Keevil, Gladice 103
Kemp, Sir George 157
Kennedy, Mrs. R. A. 334, 355
Kenney, Annie *plate*, 145; arrested 75, 81, 88,
    218, 219; Cat and Mouse Act 226, 257;
    flat raided 219; militancy 216; munitions
    276; Pankhurst, Adela 248; Pankhurst,
    Christabel 180, 184, 186; Pankhurst,
    Emmeline 148, 229, 353; Pankhurst,
    Sylvia 239, 296, 380–1n1; Pembrokeshire
    110; Pethick Lawrences 80, 194, 199;
    rearrested 227; speaker 73–4, 77, 147,
    202, 215–16; on *The suffragette movement*
    360; USA tour 170; war effort 271; War
    Service Procession 277–8; Women's Party
    304; working women 92; WSPU 78, 79,
    80, 83, 103, 144, 203
Kenney, Caroline 296
Kenney, Jane 296, 300
Kenney, Jessie 124; arrested 109; militancy
    203; Pankhurst, Christabel 180, 199, 224,
    243–4; Pankhurst, Emmeline 89, 99, 100,
    224, 284; Russia 294, 298, 409n12;
    Women's Party 309
Kerensky, Alexander 292, 297–8, 301, 310
Kerr, Harriet 219, 351, 353
Kerr, Thomas 133
Kew Gardens 209
Kilbreth, Mary 318
King, Kathleen *plate*, 413n14; Pankhurst,
    Emmeline 279, 323–4, 333–4, 336; Pine
    335; re-adopted 337; USA 321, 323–4,
    333–6
Knight, Adelaide 84
Kropotkin, Pyotr 28, 345

Labouchere, Mr. 72
The Labour Leader 47, 51, 53, 65, 69, 72, 81
Labour Party: distrust of 271; election wins
    77–8; and Liberals 230; MacDonald 303,
    304; male control 303; social conditions
314; suffrage 90; WSPU 89–90, 202, 205;
    see also Independent Labour Party
Labour Representation Committee 65
Ladies' Carlton Club 343
Lake, Agnes 219, 225
Lamb, Charles 330
Lancashire and Cheshire Union 41–2
Lancashire campaigns 125
Lansbury, George 204, 399n14; Asquith 189;
    Daily Herald 246; imprisoned 230;
    Pankhurst, Sylvia 3, 263–4; political
    prisoner status 188; speaker 193, 202,
    226, 237; summons 218; United
    Suffragists 251; Women's Franchise
    League 36; WSPU support 204, 205
Larkin, Delia 237
Larkin, Jim 237
Laski, Harold 361
Law, (Andrew) Bonar 260, 313
Lawrence, Susan 304
leadership: Women's Party 304; WSPU 96–7,
    250, 280, 282–3, 307–8, 362
League for Opposing Woman Suffrage 304
lecture tours: Canada 139, 169, 285, 311,
    319, 326–7, 328–9; USA 126, 136,
    137–41, 169, 175, 236–7, 272, 284–5,
    317
Leeds 110
Leigh, Mary *plate*; Asquith 133–4; forcible
    feeding 140; Pankhurst, Christabel 224;
    prison 110, 119, 176, 398n9; window-
    breaking 109; WSPU 120, 124, 147, 283
Leneman, L. 111
Lenin, Vladimir Ilyich 297, 298, 300
Lennox, Geraldine 219, 224, 359
lesbianism: alleged 4–5, 145, 146, 394n34;
    defined 391n72, 391n73; Smyth 160
letter box attacks 175–6, 203
Leverhulme, Lord 306
Lewis, Lady 166
Liberal Party: anti-women's suffrage 107;
    citizenship rights 135; electoral success
    77, 157; Labour Party 230; Pankhurst,
    Emmeline 12, 361; petition rights 122;
    pro-war 19; repression 34–5; women
    excluded from public meetings 132;
    WSPU 77, 167
Liberty, Lasenby 180–1
Lighting of Vehicles Bill 71, 72
Linnell, Alfred 26
Liverpool 111, 137, 274

living conditions 27, 44, 362; Poor Law 187, 201, 303–4; poverty 27, 303–4
Lloyd George, David 114–15, 148; Asquith's leadership 275; assassination plot 289; Coalition 313; deputation 289–90; heckled 84; house bombed 210, 214–15; Minister of Munitions 276–8; mistress 281; NUWSS 289; Pankhurst, Emmeline 148, 276–8, 301, 305; Pankhurst, Sylvia 263–4; prime minister 288; Scott 175, 229; Second Conciliation Bill 163, 167, 168–9, 174; subpoenaed 114–15; suffrage 183; women's suffrage 148, 157, 289–90; Women's Suffrage Bill 147; WSPU 175
Lloyd George, Mrs. 288
Local Government Bill 40
London, Canada 285
London, East End 203–4, 205, 346, 347–8
London, homes: Cheyne Walk 85–6; Clarendon Road 286; Elsham Road 339, 347; Gloucester Street 347; High Street, Wapping 349; Knightsbridge 209; Park Walk 70, 79; Russell Square 27–8
London Graduates' Union for Women's Suffrage 228
London Opera House 269–70
London Palladium meeting 279
London Pavilion 176, 227–8, 228–9, 280–1
London Symphony Orchestra 166
Louisville Courier 171
Lush, Justice 215
Lytton, Lady Constance: arrested 124; Highlands 133; imprisonment 140, 143, 176; letter to Gladstone 119; Pankhurst, Emmeline 114, 170; speaker 147, 158, 178; testimonial fund 325–6
Lytton, Lord 144, 146, 152–3, 164, 168

McCulloch, Catharine Waugh 128
MacDonald, Flora 314
MacDonald, Mrs. J. R. 71
MacDonald, Ramsay 57, 94, 292, 294, 303, 304
McIlquham, Harriet 31, 33, 70, 73, 98, 102
McKenna, Reginald 255, 260, 261–2, 267, 274–5
Mackenzie, Midge 1
McLaren, Sir Charles 68
McLaren, Walter 40
Maclean's Magazine 331
McMillan, Margaret 49, 93, 288
Madison Square meeting 235

Maguire, Cynthia 304
Malicious Injuries to Property Act (1861) 210
Man, Isle of 10
Manchester: Boggart Hole Clough 46–8, 84–5, 261; dissenters 9–10; Free Trade Hall 143–4; Heaton Park 110; Independent Labour Party 46–7, 93; suffrage campaign 12; unemployment 43–4
Manchester, homes: Buckingham Crescent 39, 42; Drayton Terrace 18; High Street, Oxford Road 40; Nelson Street 55, 66, 81, 85; Sloan Street 9; Upper Brook Street 85, 93–4
Manchester, Salford and District Women's Trades and Labour Council 74
Manchester and Salford Trades and Labour Council 74
Manchester City Council 50
Manchester Guardian 123, 131–2, 148, 339
Manchester Liberal Association 19, 20
Manchester Married Women's Property Committee 16–17, 18
Manchester National Society for Women's Suffrage 12, 18, 22, 40
Manchester School Board 41, 57–8, 374n24
Manchester Technical College 58
Manchester Women's Suffrage Society 20
Manchester Women's Trade Council 59
Manhood Suffrage Bill 172, 173–4, 207, 208
Mann, Tom 28, 41, 46
Mansel, Mildred 277–8, 353
Manus, Rosa 128
Marchef-Girard, Mlle 13
Marcus, Jane 2–3, 76, 160, 263
Margesson, Lady Isabel Hampden 266
Marion, Kitty 268
Markievicz, Countess 314
Marlow, Dr. Fred 328
married women: coverture doctrine 32; employment 106; Poor Law Guardians 31; property rights 16–17, 326; women's suffrage 20, 29, 40
Marsden, Dora 125, 147, 156, 223–4
Marsh, Charlotte 119, 133–4, 141, 147, 164–5
Marshall, Alfred 170, 182, 219, 261, 346–7
Marshall, Kitty 170, 279, 346–7, 349; commemoration 355; Pankhurst, Emmeline's funeral 353; statue 356–7;

testimonial fund 325–6; window-breaking 179

Martel, Nellie Alma *plate*, 72, 81, 97–8, 101–2, 108

Martin, Dr. 43

Martin, Selina 143, 144

Martyn, Edith How 85, 96, 97

Marx, Karl 297, 319, 345

Marxism 292, 293–4, 297, 302–3, 319

Marxist Social Democratic Federation 36

Masaryk, Thomas 294, 299

Massy, Rosamund 102, 353, 355

Match-Makers Union 26

maternity care 302

maternity insurance 161–2

Mather, Sir William 45

Mayo, Isabella 90

Mearns, Andrew 27

Medical Review of Reviews 236

Medical Women's Society 139

Meighen, Arthur 330

members of parliament 68, 70, 312–13

Memorial Fund 355

men: militancy 191, 235, 254, 266; munition work 276, 306; violence 202, 235; women's suffrage 5, 132, 152–3, 301; *see also* suffrage, adult

Men's Committee for Justice to Women 129, 147

Men's Federation 192–3

Men's League for Women's Suffrage 147, 192–3, 205

Men's Political Union 147, 238–9

Merthyr Pioneer 226

Merthyr Tydfil 77

Midlands campaigns 125

militancy 4, 5, 209, 366n32; effectiveness 191, 235, 266, 308; gender differences 191, 235, 254, 266; Kenney, Annie 216; Nevinson 206; Pankhurst, Emmeline 139–40, 200–1, 207–8, 226–7, 235; public opinion 194, 236; return threatened 280–1; truce 143–4; WSPU 5, 73, 76–7, 81, 82, 92, 108, 125, 190–1, 203

militarism 268, 363

military service 286, 287–8

Mill, John Stuart 28, 290, 315

Miller, Florence Fenwick 28, 31

Mills, Dr. 125–6, 137, 141

Minneapolis 236, 237

Minneapolis Daily News 273

Mitchell, D. 4, 318, 319–20

Mitchell, Hannah 98

Miyatovich, Mr. 284

Mond, Sir Alfred 151

Montefiore, Dora 71, 72, 79, 83, 84

Montessori education 279, 296, 300

Montreal 285

Moorhead, Ethel 265

morality, double standards 200, 206, 236–7, 253, 265, 323

Morgan, David 308

Morissey, Mrs. 111

Morley, A. 109, 176, 222, 238, 366n32

Morning Advertiser 282

Morning Leader 146

Morning Post 342

Morris, William 26, 28, 298, 345

Moss, Charles 47

Moullin, C. Mansell 135, 149

Moxon, Dr. Frank 261

munition workers: female 276, 280–1, 306, 308–9; male 276, 306

Munitions Bill 276

Munro, Anna 111

Murphy, C. 160–1

Murphy, Mrs. 355

Murray, Dr. Flora 218, 221, 226, 255, 261, 288, 325–6

Murray, Dr. Jessie 150

Murray, James 41, 114, 210, 276

Muskett, Mr. 103

Nashville 236

National American Woman Suffrage Association 128, 139, 171

National Political League 226

National Society for Women's Suffrage 29, 234

National Union of Teachers 256

National Union of Women Workers 58

National Union of Women's Suffrage Societies (NUWSS): *The Common Cause* 304; Davison 223; International Woman Suffrage Alliance 127; Lloyd George 289; Pankhurst, Sylvia 72; peaceful protest 181, 274; private members' bills 74; Roper 59; suffragists 68; women's suffrage 74, 286; WSPU 73, 88, 147, 165; *see also* Fawcett, Millicent Garrett

national unity 275, 282

National Women's Social & Political Union *plate*, 97; *see also* Women's Social & Political Union

nationalisation 16
nationalism 268, 269
Naylor, Marie 353
Neal, Mary 81, 97, 197
Needham, Mr. 46, 47
Neligan, Dorinda 130, 150
Nevinson, Henry W.: Hyde Park procession
    148; Men's Political Union 238–9;
    militancy 206; Pankhurst, Emmeline
    129–30, 135, 144, 149, 151, 156, 187,
    209, 229; Pankhurst, Sylvia 3; Pethick
    Lawrences 198; resignation 135; United
    Suffragists 251, 262
New, Edith 109, 110
New Age 156
New Constitutional Society of Women
    Suffrage 192–3
New Constitutional Suffrage Society 147
New Forest 154
The New Freewoman 223–4
New Union for Men and Women 147
new woman stereotype 30, 35
New York 138–9, 170–1, 237, 311
New York Evening Telegraph 310
New York Herald Tribune 354
New York Journal 233, 278
New York Post 139
New York Sun 310
New York Times 138, 233, 235, 247, 310, 318
New York Tribune 310
New Zealand 147, 307
Newcastle by-election 110
News of the World 210, 348, 349
Newton Abbot by-election 101–2
Nodal, Mr. 58–9, 60–4
North Mail 223
North of England Society for Women's
    Suffrage 59
Northcliffe, Lord 277, 288, 314
Northwood, Eric 148
Norway 307
Nottingham 110
Nottingham Castle 178, 179
nurses 277–8

The Observer 1, 276, 277
O'Connor, T. P. 45
Ontario tour 332, 334
Oram, Alison 145
Ottawa 285
Owen, Robert 345

pacifism: feminism 316–17; Pankhurst,
    Adela 270, 274; Pankhurst, Richard 15,
    19, 270; Pankhurst, Sylvia 270, 272, 285;
    socialist 303, 305; World War I 268,
    316–17
Paget, Lady Muriel 294
paintings damaged 216, 255, 266
Pall Mall Gazette 23, 27, 107, 209, 210
Pan American Conference of Women 332
Pankhurst, Adela Constantia Mary plate, 4,
    21; Archdales 167, 169, 191–2, 213,
    225–6, 232–3, 248, 257, 305; arrested 88,
    132; Australia 248–9, 257, 266; Boggart
    Hole Clough 84–5; Britannia 288;
    communism 325, 334; conscription 287;
    education 39, 42, 55, 56, 169;
    employment 83, 214, 245–6, 397n72; ill
    health 48, 63, 64, 71, 167; imprisoned 84;
    Kenney, Annie 248; marriage and
    children 300, 312, 325, 334; Mary
    (Aunt) 155; pacifism 270, 274;
    Pankhurst, Christabel 155; Pankhurst,
    Emmeline 35–6, 57, 133, 155, 188, 237,
    248–9, 278–9, 351; Pankhurst, Richard
    24, 52, 300; Pankhurst, Sylvia 225;
    Pethick Lawrence 155; Put up the sword
    285; Scotland 124, 137; socialism 155,
    194; on The suffragette movement 359;
    Women's Peace Party 278; WSPU 92,
    118, 147, 155, 169, 194
Pankhurst, Christabel Harriette plate, 4–5,
    19, 114–17; adopted child 300; arrested
    75, 91, 113–14; Britannia 284;
    Conciliation Committee 152–3; Davison
    222; demonstrations 74, 108; deputation
    172; education 39, 42, 49, 59, 62, 65, 85,
    375n2; Geneva 51–2, 54; Gore-Booth
    377n62; The great scourge 236–7, 245,
    323; Independent Labour Party 93, 95;
    Kenney, Annie 180, 184, 186; Kenney,
    Jessie 180, 199, 224, 243–4; leadership
    96–7, 99, 250, 362; Leigh 224; NUWSS
    66; The Observer 276; Pankhurst, Adela
    155; Pankhurst, Emmeline 76–7, 190,
    224, 240–1, 243, 244, 266–7, 314–15,
    351, 353, 355; Pankhurst, Harry 141;
    Pankhurst, Richard 24; Pankhurst, Sylvia
    2, 3, 56, 85–6, 185–6, 237–9, 246–9, 350;
    Paris 180, 190, 243–4; Pethick Lawrences
    194, 199; Pine 335; Plain facts about a
    great evil 236–7; prison 119, plate; religion
    314–15, 336, 344; return to England 268,

288; Robins 211; Scotland 124; Smyth 258–9; statue 357; *The Suffragette* journal 198, 238; on *The suffragette movement* 359; tactics 75–6, 90–1; *The Times* 134; *Unshackled: the story of how we won the vote* 1, 76, 360; USA lecture tour 272, 332; Victoria 328–9; *Votes for Women* 174, 184; Women's Party 304, 313–15; WSPU 1–3, 74–5, 85–6, 110, 147, 152–3, 164–5, 269–70, 283, 301

Pankhurst, Emmeline *plates*, 7, 354; arrested *plate*, 103, 113–14, 130, 151, 179, 210, 259–60; Asquith 83–4, 272, 286–7; autobiography 7–8, 234, 294; biographies 1–2, 4, 5–6; Canadian citizenship 331, 334, 335; Cat and Mouse Act 215, 221, 222–3, 240, 242–3, 251–2, 259–60, 266, 357; death 352; family background 9, 10–11; Fawcett 289–90; femininity 116, 139; financial problems 285–6, 291, 320–1, 325–6, 336–7, 340; Francophile 269, 275; funeral 353; Honorary Secretary of WSPU 97; Honorary Treasurer of WSPU 203, 233, 261, 282, 288; hunger strike *plate*, 211, 217, 218, 223, 240, 242–3, 255, 265; ill health 55–6, 117, 118, 178, 181, 188, 228, 298, 300, 338, 346–7, 348, 350–2; imprisonment *plate*, 104, 118–19, 181–2, 187–8; leadership 96–7, 99, 283–4; Manchester School Board 41, 57–8, 374n24; marriage 17, 25; militancy 139–40, 200–1, 207–8, 226–7, 235; motherhood 19, 35, 48; political allegiance 2, 41–2, 82, 340, 341–3; Poor Law Guardian 42–4, 50, 51, 55; Registrar of Births and Deaths 55–7, 78, 116, 279, 323, 328

Pankhurst, Frank (Henry Francis Robert) 21, 26, 27

Pankhurst, Harry *plate*, 3, 388n45; apprenticeship 92; childhood 30, 36, 48, 57; death 142; education 61–2, 83, 92; ill health 56, 63–4, 125–6, 128, 137, 141–2; Pankhurst, Emmeline 103; Pankhurst, Richard 52; politics 102; WSPU Exhibition 128–9

Pankhurst, Richard Marsden *plate*, 15; children 21–2, 27; correspondence 94; death 2, 52–3; ill health 49, 51–2; Independent Labour Party 41–2; letters to Emmeline 353; libel 22–3; pacifism 15,

19, 270; parliamentary candidacy 19–21, 22–3, 45–6; political beliefs 16, 19–20, 40–1, 345; religious education 296; Rollit's bill 36; solicitor's practice 21, 42, 49; suffrage campaign 12, 16; Women's Disabilities Removal Bill 32

Pankhurst, (Estelle) Sylvia *plate*, 2–3, 4, 5, 19; arrested 88, 91, 230; art 51, 55, 66–7, 70, 126, 128; Asquith 262, 263; Bolsheviks 330–1; capitalism 313; Cat and Mouse Act 226, 228, 246; communism 325, 331, 344; Corio 339; disgrace 351; education 39, 42, 59, 85; ELFS 2, 211, 262, 272; Free Speech Defence Committee 230; Geneva 59–60; Hardie 2, 5, 94, 101, 161, 185, 204–5, 212–13; hunger strike 3, 211, 212–13, 226, 235; ill health 56, 212–13; illegitimate child 348, 349–50; Independent Labour Party 101; Kenney, Annie 239, 296, 380–1n1; Lansbury 3, 263–4; *The life of Emmeline Pankhurst* 1; Lloyd George 263–4; NUWSS 72; pacifism 270, 272, 285; Pankhurst, Adela 225; Pankhurst, Christabel 2, 3, 56, 85–6, 185–6, 237–9, 247–9; Pankhurst, Emmeline 27, 54, 111, 219, 222, 262–3, 311, 339, 345, 353, 356–7; Pankhurst, Harry 137, 141, 142; Pankhurst, Richard 46, 52, 94; Paris 246; passport refused 274–5; Pethick Lawrences 356, 357–8; released from prison 232; return from Venice 65; Robins 119; Smyth 160; social welfare 272; socialism 3, 184–5, 270, 304, 313; *The suffragette* 87, 154; *The suffragette movement* 2, 3, 5, 29, 70, 87, 99, 137, 184–5, 199, 224, 246, 263–4, 355, 358–9; summons 226; Women's Franchise League 33–4; working class feminists 203–4; WSPU 2, 80–1, 85, 137, 147, 208–9, 226

Pankhurst Hall 66–7

Paris 13, 180, 190, 243–4, 246, 272–3, 315

Paris International Socialist Congress 41

Parker, Frances 265

Parker, Inspector Edward 255

Parliament Street Society 29

Parnell, Charles 22, 23

Parsons, Lady 277–8

passports 274–5

patriotic feminism 268–9, 271, 308, 311–12, 406n21

Patriotic Women's Alliance 295
Patriots *versus* Pacifists appeal, Women's Party 309
Paul, Alice 133
pauperism 45
Pavlova, Anna 333
Payne, Mr. and Mrs. 226
Peace Conference 274, 315
Pearson, Karl 228
Peckham Rye by-election 105, 107
Pembridge, Joan *plate*, 279, 329, 333–4, 335, 337
Pembrokeshire 110
Penal Servitude Acts 217
People's Army 238, 263
Percy, Lady Maude 158
Personal Rights Journal 37
Peterloo franchise demonstration 9
Pethick, Dorothy 136, 141, 147, 169–70
Pethick Lawrence, Emmeline *plate*; anti-militancy 191; arrested 88, 174, 183; Boggart Hole Clough 84–5; Equal Franchise Demonstration 343; Hague peace conference 275; imprisonment 125, 187–8; Kenney, Annie 80, 194, 199; New Forest 154; ousted 194–5, 196, 198; Pankhurst, Adela 155; Pankhurst, Emmeline 114, 178, 251, 354; Pankhurst, Sylvia 356, 357–8; on *The suffragette movement* 359; United Suffragists 251; *Votes for Women* 125, 197, 396n28; WSPU 80–1, 83, 92, 96–7, 99, 126, 142, 147, 149, 164–5, 174
Pethick Lawrence, Frederick 88, 89; Albert Hall rally 237–8; bailing prisoners out 91; committed for trial 183; imprisonment 187; militancy 191, 361; ousted 194–5, 196, 198; Pankhurst, Christabel 199; statue 357; WSPU 80, 83, 96–7, 99
petition rights 122, 125, 129–30, 131, 141
Philadelphia 285
Phillips, Caroline 94, 101
Phillips, Marion 301
Phillips, Mary 107, 111, 142
Pine, Catherine *plate*; adopted children 279–80, 286, 323–4, 333, 335; departure 335; Pankhurst, Christabel 335; Pankhurst, Emmeline 218, 220, 241, 255, 260, 265, 304; Pankhurst, Harry 125, 137; Paris visit 240, 243, 272, 315; Tower Cressey 300; USA stay 317, 323–4, 333
Pittsburg 139

Plekhanov, G. V. 296–7
Plural Voting Bill 84
Plymouth 271–2, 276
police brutality 109, 130, 150, 152, 254, 255, 259, 392n103
police intimidation 91, 92, 113
police raids 180, 219–20, 261
police surveillance 206, 218
police women 341
political corruption film 235
Political Equality Association 233
political prisoner status: denied 117, 140, 181; hunger strike 131, 181; Lytton 114; protests 132; WSPU 88, 188
Pond, James 334
J. P. Pond Lyceum Bureau 138, 169, 170, 334
Pooll, Mrs. Batten 214
Poor Law Guardians: illegitimacy 279; living conditions 187, 201, 303–4; married women 31; Pankhurst, Emmeline 42–4, 50, 51, 55
Poplar Labour Representation Committee 205
Portman Rooms, London 158
portrait 355
Pott, Rosina Mary 210
poverty: *Britannia* 306; food problem 305; industrial unrest 340–1; living conditions 27, 303–4; Serbia 281–2; stigma 45; women's suffrage 139
Pratt, Hodgson 28
press 175, 237; *see also* individual newspapers
Preston, Aileen 157–8
prison sentence volunteers 120–1
Prisoners' Pageant 146, 164
Prisoners Temporary Discharge for Ill-Health Bill: *see* Cat and Mouse Act
private members' bills 74, 80, 146, 157, 220
processions 91–2, 102, 107, 126–7, 146–7, 164–5
prohibition 332
property acts 326
prostitution 201, 230
Protest Fund 266
Public Health Association, Canada 334
public health demonstrations 328
public opinion 88, 113, 191, 216, 236, 259
Pugh, Martin: lesbianism 145, 146; militancy 308; Pankhurst, Emmeline 8, 111, 303, 344; *The Pankhursts* 4–5; women's movement 316
Putney Branch meeting 210

Quebec 285
Queen's Hall: concert 159, 166; meetings 152–3, 311–12; votes for sailors and soldiers speech 287–8; Women's Party 304–5

race course death 222
race factors 236
radicalism 23–4, 29–30, 31, 33
Raleigh, North Carolina 323
Raleigh News and Observer 323
Rathbone, Eleanor 343
rational dress 28
Redmond, John 193
Reform Act (1867) 11–12, 28, 187
Reform Bill 107, 177, 178
Register of Women for War Service 274
Registrar of Births and Deaths 55, 78; illegitimacy 279; incest stories 56–7; Mary acting as 82–3, 92; resignation 116; venereal disease 323, 328
religious education 296
Representation of the People Act 306–7
Representation of the People Bill 295
Representation of the People (Equal Franchise) Act 348–9
Rhondda, Sybil 325–6, 338, 355, 357
Richardson, Mary 212, 255
Riddell, Justice 327–8
Riddell, Sir George 210
Riviera tea-shop 337, 338
Robins, Elizabeth 87; ill health 225; Pankhurst, Christabel's letters 211; Pankhurst, Emmeline's letters 115, 121, 129, 133, 136, 139, 142, 144, 147, 154, 162, 164, 166, 175, 186, 209–10, 211, 212, 214; Pankhurst, Sylvia 119; Pethick Lawrences 197–8, 203; writings 89, 93–4, 97–8; WSPU 97
Robins, Margaret Drier 139
Robins, Raymond 298
Robinson, Frederic H. 236–7
Robinson, Sam 75–6, 91, 93, 96
Rochefort, Henri de 28
Rochefort, Noémie 13, 51; *see also* Dufaux, Noémie
Rochester, USA 139
Rochester Herald 311
Roe, Grace 145; arrested 261; Craggs 142; Davison 222; imprisoned 265; Pankhurst, Sylvia 350; Victoria 328–9; WSPU 153, 204, 220, 231, 271, 277

Roe, Lucy 81
roller skating 159, 337
Rollit, Sir Albert 36–7
Rolphe, Mrs. Neville 322
Romania 288
Romero, P. W. E. 94, 205, 263, 264
Roper, Esther 40, 59, 65
Rotherhithe Liberal and Radical Association 22
Rover, Constance 361
Rowbotham, S. 303
Rowe, Frances 98, 102, 177
Rowley, Charles 55
Ruhl, Arthur 139
Rupp, L. J. 127
Russia: Czar 296, 299; desertions from army 292; fighting 297; food shortages 297; Japan 309, 310; Kenney, Jessie 294, 298, 409n12; Peace Conference 315; visit 293–9; war with Turkey 15; withdrawal 309; women's battalion 295–6, 297, 298; women's suffrage 297; workers' revolution 292; *see also* Bolsheviks
Rutzen, Sir Albert de 131

sacrifice 82–3, 127–8, 269
St. Andrew's Hall, Glasgow 253–4
St. Malo 266–7
St. Paul 236, 237
St. Paul's Cathedral protest 229
Sale, Mrs. 50
Salford 10, 19, 21
Samuel, Herbert 284
Sanders, Beatrice 219
sanitation 27
Sarah, Elizabeth 6
Sarnia 285
Saskatchewan 285
Savill, Dr. Agnes 188
Sayers, Alfred 81
Scantlebury, Chief Inspector 130
Scatcherd, Alice Cliff 18, 28, 53; Dr. Pankhurst Fund 54; Rollit's bill 36; Women's Franchise League 30–1, 33
Schack, Countess 33
Schütze, Dr. and Gladys 252
Scotland: by-elections 123–4; Edinburgh 137; holiday 110; Pankhurst, Adela 137; socialism 111; tours 133, 148–9, 168; Women's Freedom League 111; WSPU 93, 111; *see also* Glasgow
Scott, C. P.: Lloyd George 175, 229;

Manchester Guardian 123, 131–2, 148; Pankhurst, Emmeline 125, 154, 155–6, 387n28
Scott, Rachel 67
Scurr, John 230
Seamen's Union 294
Seattle 175
Second Conciliation Bill 157, 162, 165; Albert Hall meeting 159, 183; Asquith 176; Grey 163–4; Lloyd George 163, 167, 168–9, 174
Second Wave Feminism 5, 7, 365n30
Seedley Cottage 10, 19, 21
Self-Denial Week 105
separatism 308, 368n11
Serbia 281–2, 284–5
Sex Disqualificatiion Act 340
sex solidarity 112, 140, 236
Sexton, James 49
sexuality 145–6; *see also* lesbianism
Seymour, Isabel 124
Shabanova, Dr. Anna 294, 295
Shackleton, D. J. 59, 146
Shackleton, Edith 272
Sharp, Evelyn 75, 149, 180, 208, 251, 262
Shaw, Dr. Anna Howard 171, 234, 310
Shaw, George Bernard 37, 223
Sheffield 126, 155
Shipman, Dr. 71
shop (Emerson's) 25, 38, 55, 65, 85
Shrewsbury 178
Simms, Lisbeth 110, 111
Singh, Princess Sophia Dhuleep 150, 170
Six Point Group 338
Slack, Bamford 71, 72
slate-throwing 133
sleep strike 212, 242–3
Smalley, Samuel 47, 219, 241
Smethwick constituency 313, 314
Smillie, Robert 86, 87
Smith, Florence Evelyn 251
Smith, Frank 41, 94, 230
Smith, Lady Sybil 166, 170
Smith, Margaret 132
Smith, Mrs. Douglas 110
Smyth, Ethel 4, 160; arrest 179; on Asquith 273; chairing meeting 170; *Coign* cottage 158, 162–3, 178–9, 183, 207, 211, 220; Egypt 160; Emmeline's letters 217, 237, 244–5, 255–6, 291, 305, 315, 321, 336; France 266–7; imprisonment 181, 182; influenza 312; lesbianism 160, 394n34;

letters to Emmeline 244, 245; London Symphony Orchestra 166; 'The march of the women' 157, 159, 192, 357; Pankhurst, Christabel 239, 258–9; Pankhurst, Emmeline 100, 159–60, 186, 218, 242–3, 308, 325–6, 361; Pankhurst, Sylvia 101, 239; war babies 279, 300, 317
Smyth, Nora 246, 262, 264, 272
Snowden, Ethel 82, 93
Snowden, Philip 66, 69, 85, 135, 303
social conditions 10, 111, 176, 272, 314, 339–40; *see also* living conditions
Social Democratic Federation 74
social hygiene 284, 334, 345
Social Hygiene Council 322–3, 327–8
social reform 272, 362
socialisation of children 369n18
socialism 6, 69; Germany 293; pacificism 303, 305; Pankhurst, Adela 155, 194; Pankhurst, Emmeline 40–1, 342–3; Pankhurst, Richard 40–1, 345; Pankhurst, Sylvia 3, 184–5, 270, 304, 313; Scotland 111; USA 310–11; WSPU 72, 81–2, 86, 202
socialism and trade unions rally 237
socialist feminism 2, 5, 140, 203, 205, 303, 316–17, 364n8, 365n30
solidarity: class 310, 311, 312; sex 112, 140, 236
Solomon, Daisy 124
Solomon, Georgiana 125, 130, 150
South Shields by-election 149
Southport 38, 39
Sparboro, Jane 84
Spencer, Anna Garlin 138
spiritualism 322
Stacey, Enid 41
The Standard 170, 195, 216, 221
Stanger, Mr. 102, 104, 107, 113
Stanley, L. 7, 109, 176, 222, 238, 366n32
Stanton, Elizabeth Cady 28, 31
The Star 357
statue 355, 356–7
Stead, William 23, 79, 81
Stephen, Jessie 111
Stepniak 28, 292
Stevenson, Frances 281
Stevenson Square rally 85
Stewart, Bessie 111
Stewart, J. 41
Stocks, Mary 100
Stockton-on-Tees conference 82

stone-throwing 130, 139–40, 178–9, 211
Stopes, Marie 316
Stowe, Harriet Beecher 10
Strachey, Ray 223, 289, 355–6, 359, 379n40
strip-search 265
Strode, Dr. Chetham 312, 351–2
Stroud 178
suffrage, adult: Asquith 286–7; gender equality 11–12, 69–70, 290; Labour Party 90; Lloyd George 183; masculinist history 365n20; military services 286, 287–8; Reform Bill 177; working men 147; *see also* Manhood Suffrage Bill; women's suffrage
suffrage movements, USA 138, 233, 235–6, 318
Suffragette Fellowship 359
The Suffragette journal: arrests 219; illegitimate children's home 279; Labour/Liberal Parties 202, 230, 264; national unity 275; Pankhurst, Christabel 198, 238; Pankhurst, Emmeline to Switzerland 243; Pankhurst, Sylvia 238; presses 220; publication ceased 268; *Punch* cartoon of Hardie 280; relaunch 274, 275; renamed *Britannia* 281; split in WSPU 200–1; Ulster Unionists 260; USA sales 237; violence 253; War Service Procession 277–8; White Slave Traffic 206; *see also Britannia*
'Suffragette Week' 258
suffragettes 5, 88, 194; arsenal 260–1; Boggart Hole Clough 84–5; Caxton Hall meeting 79; doctors 230; Hyde Park 84; imprisonment 397n44; martyr's death 222; police brutality 150, 152; prejudice against 183; sacrifice 127–8; sexuality 145–6; USA 171
The Suffragettes of the Women's Social and Political Union 284, 286
suffragists 28, 68, 150, 310–11
Sunday Pictorial 274
Sunday World 237
Susannah, servant 19, 22, 26, 39, 52
Swansea Socialist Society 77

Taylor, Helen 28, 36
Taylor, Mona 205
Taylor, Tom 41
tea-shop 337, 338
teachers 57–8
testimonial fund 325–6, 333

Thebaud, F. 275
thirst strike 212, 226, 242–3, 255, 265
Thomas, Carey 171, 285
Thompson, Katie 181
Tickner, L. 164, 268, 276
Tillett, Ben 49, 230
The Times 314; Census protest 159; Curzon 304; forcible feeding 264–5; letters to 182–3, 223; Pankhurst, Christabel 134; Pankhurst, Emmeline 135–6, 179, 180; Reform Bill 177; suffragists 108; venereal disease 288; WSPU 282
Toronto 139, 237, 285, 311, 327–8, 331–2, 332
Toronto Daily Star 327–8, 344
Toronto Evening Telegram 327–8
Toronto Exhibition 334
Toronto Globe 328, 331
Tower Cressey 300, 317, 337
Townend, Gertrude 125, 137
Trade Union Bill 204
trade unions 271, 273–4, 303, 308
Trafalgar Square demonstrations 83, 113, 220, 230, 316
transport strike 168
Trotsky, Leon 298
Tudor, Elizabeth *plate*, 279, 300, 328–9, 335
Tuke, Mabel: acquitted 183; Festival of Empire 164; Normandy tour 193; Pankhurst, Emmeline 154, 170; Pethick Lawrences 194; prison visits 124; tea-shop 337, 338; warrant for arrest 180; window-breaking 179; WSPU 97, 147, 164–5, 195–6, 202
Tumultuous Petitions Act 102–3, 130
Turkish–Russian war 15
Turnbull, Annmarie 145
Tweedale, William 47

Ulster Unionists 226, 252–3, 254, 260, 265
Unemployed Workmen Relief Bill 74
unemployment 43–4, 74, 348, 380n54
United Suffragists 250–1, 262, 286
USA: adopted children 321, 323–5; Bolsheviks 318; Carnegie Hall 237; lecture tours 126, 136, 137–41, 169, 175, 236–7, 272, 284–5, 317; socialism 310–11; suffrage movements 138, 233, 235–6, 318; suffragettes 171; suffragists 28, 310–11; visit 309–10, 323–4, 333; Women's Political Union 170–1;

women's suffrage 138, 233, 235–6, 318; WSPU 177

Vale Wood Farm 49
Vancouver 319
Vancouver Island 321–2, 328–9
venereal disease 201, 230, 288, 322–3, 328
Venn, Commander 347, 349
Vicinus, M. 109, 160
Victoria 321–2, 328
Victoria Daily Colonist 321–2
Victoria Daily Times 319
Victoria House Press 219
Victorian Socialist Party 334
Victory Loan Rally 316
Villard, Helen Garrison 139
violence 178, 201, 202, 235, 253; *see also* police brutality
Virago Press 5
Vomers, George 47
Votes for Women 111; Canada 174; Conciliation Bill 167; Leigh and Evans 193; Pankhurst, Christabel 174, 184; Pankhurst, Emmeline 118–19, 135, 182; Pethick Lawrence 125, 197–8, 396n28; printer terrorised 180; race 236; split in WSPU 200–1
Vries, J. de 269

wage levels 57–8, 273–4, 278, 306, 308–9
Wales 148, 161, 167, 176, 210, 281
Walsh, Tom 300
Walshe, Norah 355
Walthamstow by-election 149
Walton Heath house 214–15
war babies 279–80, 284, 317; *see also* Tower Cressey
war effort campaigning 271
War Memorial Adoption Home 317
War Service Procession 277–8
Ward, Margaret 149
Ward, Mrs. Humphry 276
Warner, Marina 127
wartime: women in employment 269–76, 308–9; Women's Party 302; WSPU 276–7
Washington state 175
Watts, Helen 124
Webb, Sidney 228, 342
Wedgwood, Joseph 3
Weekly Dispatch 283–4
Wellington by-election 167

Wentworth, Vera 111–12, 177
West, Rebecca 16, 28, 72, 99, 100, 223
Westbury by-election 158
Western Mail 210
Westminster Abbey constituency 315–16
Wharry, Olive 177
Wheeldon, Alice 289
Wheeldon, Hettie 289
White Slave Traffic 200–1, 206, 215, 237
Whitechapel campaigning *plate*, 346
Wickham, Joan 233, 284
Widows, Wives and Mothers of Great Britain Heroes' Association 319
William Lloyd Garrison League 139
Williams, Dr. May 350, 351
Williams, Mrs. 254
Wills, Lucy 171
Wilson, T. Woodrow 235
Wiltshire 158
Winchester riots 130
window-breaking: arrests 151, 177, 179–80; police brutality 130; public opinion 191; WSPU 108, 132, 133, 174, 177–8, 179–80
Winslow, Barbara 5, 205
Winson Green Gaol 134, 135
Wisbech 153
Wolstenholme, Elizabeth Elmy: *see* Elmy, Elizabeth Wolstenholme
Woman's Christian Temperance Union 332
The Woman's Dreadnought 246–7
Woman's Forum 319
The Woman's Herald 34
women: Belgium 285; citizenship rights 102, 106, 268, 311–12; confidence 308; economic independence 317; education 11, 15–16, 58, 64; graduates 146; industrial unrest 340–1; members of parliament 312–13; munition work 280–1, 306, 308–9; Serbia 285; socialism 69; trade union members 308; voters 312; wartime employment 269–76, 308–9; workers 2, 40, 69, 92; *see also* married women; women's suffrage
Women Writers Suffrage Society 192–3
Women's Auxiliary Service 341
women's battalion 295–6, 297, 298
Women's Canadian Club 319, 320, 322
Women's Civic and Political Responsibilities conference 301, 304
Women's Conservative Association 319
Women's Co-operative Guild 72

Women's Coronation Procession 164
Women's Disabilities Removal Bill 32
Women's Dreadnought 304
Women's Emancipation Union 36, 70
women's enfranchisement: *see* women's
    suffrage
Women's Enfranchisement Bill 71–3, 89–90,
    144, 146; Asquith 113, 146–7; Hardie 70,
    71; Independent Labour Party 68–9;
    Stanger 104, 107, 113
Women's Franchise League 31–4, 36, 37, 40,
    372n33, 379n40
Women's Freedom League 97, 98, 111, 125,
    147, 192–3
Women's Guild of Empire 340, 341
women's history 368n46
Women's Labour League 86, 110
Women's Liberal Association 41–2, 83–4,
    319
Women's Liberal Federation 32, 42
Women's Liberation 6–7, 316–17
Women's Local Government Society 58
'Women's Marseillaise' 157
women's missions 144
Women's New Era League 319
Women's Parliament 90–1, 91–2, 102, 108,
    124, 125
Women's Party 301–2; citizenship rights 305;
    Kenney, Annie 304; Kenney, Jessie 309;
    leadership 304; Marxism 302–3; national
    prosperity 305–6; officials 302;
    Pankhurst, Emmeline 309; parliamentary
    candidate 313–16; Patriots *versus* Pacifists
    appeal 309; Queen's Hall launch 304–5;
    war-time duties 302; women voters 307,
    312
Women's Peace Party 278
Women's Political Association, Australia 270
Women's Political Union, USA 170–1, 234
Women's Progression Suffrage Union, USA
    139
Women's Social and Political Union
    (WSPU) 1, 5, 6–7, 67, 81, 128–9;
    Aberdeen 94; Asquith 108, 193; 'At
    Homes' 110–11, 276; bands 48, 128, 129;
    bodyguard 231, 254; breakfast parties
    110, 111–12, 119, 126, 129; campaign
    fund 165; Campbell-Bannerman 81;
    Canada 177; constitution 96–7, 98–9;
    criticism 181; demonstrations 75, 105,
    108; deputation to parliament 87–8,
    108–9; dissidents 283–4; exhibition

128–9; fine-paying 400n40; funds 89,
    121, 180, 266; Hardie 88, 108, 192–3;
    Independent Labour Party 73–4, 378n10;
    International Woman Suffrage Alliance
    127; Labour Party 89–90, 202, 205;
    leadership 96–7, 250, 280, 282–3, 307–8,
    362; Liberal Party 77, 167; Lloyd George
    175; militancy 5, 73, 76–7, 81, 82, 92,
    108, 125, 190–1, 203, 245; militarism
    268; NUWSS 73, 88, 147, 165;
    Pankhurst, Christabel 1–2, 3, 74–5, 85–6,
    110, 147, 152–3, 164–5, 269–70, 283,
    301; Pankhurst, Sylvia 2, 80–1, 85, 137,
    147, 208–9, 226; Pethick Lawrence 80–1,
    83, 92, 96–7, 99, 126, 142, 147, 149,
    164–5, 174; police intimidation 91, 92,
    113; police raid 180, 219–20, 261;
    processions 91–2, 164–5; public meetings
    73, 83, 88, 200–3, 217, 220; public
    sympathy 88, 113; regional branches 109;
    Scotland 93, 111; Self-Denial Week 105;
    socialism 72, 81–2, 86, 202; speakers
    67–8, 147; sponsorship 79; symbolic
    colours 107–8, 119–20; tensions 96–7,
    156–7, 203; USA 177; war babies
    279–80; wartime 276–7; window-
    breaking 108, 132, 133, 174, 177–8,
    179–80; Women's Party 301–2; *see also*
    by-election campaigning
women's suffrage 1, 342; Asquith 162, 164,
    166–7, 273, 286–7; Australia 72, 307;
    Campbell-Bannerman 83; Canada 288–9,
    307; Carson 252–3; class 139; deputation
    124, 208–9, 257–8, 289–90; Gladstone
    104; Glasier 132; Hardie 66, 68, 82, 85,
    90; House of Lords 304–5; imprisonment
    74–5; Independent Labour Party 65, 86,
    87; Lloyd George 148, 157, 289–90;
    married women 20, 29, 40; men 152–3;
    militancy 208–9; moral force 201–2, 206;
    Northcliffe 277; NUWSS 74, 286;
    Pankhurst, Richard 16; Plural Voting Bill
    84; poverty 139; private members' bill
    220; qualification 144, 157, 295, 307,
    393n15; qualifications 307; radicalism
    29–31; Representation of the People Bill
    295; Rollit 36–7; Russia 297; self-
    representation 106–7; sex solidarity 94–5;
    spiritual struggle 362; USA 138, 233,
    235–6, 318; WSPU 284
Women's Suffrage Bill 146–7
Women's Suffrage Journal 12

Women's Tax Resistance League 147, 192–3
Women's Trade Union League 26, 139
Women's War Service 277
Woodlock, Patricia 125, 129
Woodward, Rev. Canon 357
Woolwich Arsenal 308
workers: control of industry 303; Russian
    revolution 292; suffrage 147; women 2,
    40, 69, 92, 269–76, 308–9
The Workers' Dreadnought 247, 304
Workers' Suffrage Federation 285, 286
workhouse 43, 44–5
working class feminists 203–4, 211
World War I: Allies 292, 293–4; armistice
    312; declaration of 267; France 311;
    pacifism 271; patriotic feminism 268–9

Wright, Ada Cecile 222, 325–6, 353
Wright, Alice Morgan: militancy 196;
    Pankhurst, Emmeline 141, 165–6;
    Pankhurst, Emmeline's letters 169–70,
    173, 174, 175, 177, 190, 206; Paris 315
Wright, Sir Almroth 182
Wylie, Barbara 195, 325–6, 344, 346, 352,
    353
Wylie, Ida and Barbara 261

Yates, Rose Lamartine 283
Yorkshire Miners' Association 41
Yorkshire WSPU 118

Zangwill, Israel 149
Zangwill, Mrs. Israel 251